STRATEGIC
MANAGEMENT

CASES

FOURTH EDITION

STRATEGIC MANAGEMENT

CASES

Peter Wright

The University of Memphis

Mark J. Kroll

University of Texas at Tyler

John A. Parnell

Texas A & M University-Commerce

 Prentice Hall, Upper Saddle River, NJ 07458

Acquisitions Editor: David Shafer
Associate Editor: Lisamarie Brassini
Editorial Assistant: Chris Stogdill
Editor-in-Chief: Natalie E. Anderson
Marketing Manager: Tammy Wederbrand
Senior Production Editor: Cynthia Regan
Production Coordinator: Carol Samet
Managing Editor: Dee Josephson
Manufacturing Supervisor: Arnold Vila
Manufacturing Manager: Vincent Scelta
Senior Designer: Ann France
Design Director: Patricia Smythe
Interior Design: Suzanne Behnke
Cover Design: Amanda Kavanaugh
Illustrator (Interior): TSI Graphics
Composition: TSI Graphics
Cover Art/Photo: Letraset Phototone

Copyright © 1998, 1996 by Prentice Hall, Inc.
A Simon and Schuster Company
Upper Saddle River, New Jersey 07458

The Library of Congress has cataloged the Combined Volume as follows:
Wright, Peter.
    Strategic management : concepts and cases / Peter Wright, Mark J.
Kroll, John A. Parnell. — 4th ed.
        p.   cm.
    Includes bibliographical references and index.
    ISBN 0-13-681750-5
    1. Strategic planning.   2. Strategic planning—Case studies.
I. Kroll, Mark J.   II. Parnell, John A. (John Alan)
III. Title.
HD30.28.W75   1998
658.4′012—dc21   97-36699
                                                        CIP

Printed in the United States of America
10   9   8   7   6   5   4   3   2   1

ISBN: 0-13-631623-9 (Concepts)
ISBN: 0-13-628801-4 (Cases)

Prentice-Hall International (UK) Limited, *London*
Prentice-Hall of Australia Pty. Limited, *Sydney*
Prentice-Hall Canada Inc., *Toronto*
Prentice-Hall Hispanoamericana, S. A., *Mexico*
Prentice-Hall of India Private Limited, *New Delhi*
Prentice-Hall of Japan, Inc., *Tokyo*
Simon & Schuster Asia Pte. Ltd., *Singapore*
Editoria Prentice-Hall do Brazil, Ltda., *Rio de Janeiro*

Contents

GOODS PRODUCERS

NOT-FOR-PROFIT ORGANIZATIONS

ETHICS AND SOCIAL RESPONSIBILITY

Preface

This fourth edition reflects the truth of one of our book's basic tenets: environmental change is inevitable. In fact, changes in the business environment and developments in the academic field of strategic management drove us to begin revising *Strategic Management Cases* less than a year after the third edition first appeared on the market. This new edition not only contains those changes, but it also benefits significantly from the perceptive feedback of our reviewers and the adopters of the first, second, and third editions.

The text portion synthesizes and builds upon the most recent strategy-related literature from numerous fields. And virtually every concept, theory, or idea is illustrated with examples from real organizations. The cases represent the works of knowledgeable and discerning authors who have provided highly readable information on enterprises ranging from small, local businesses to huge, global corporations.

CASES

As with every revision of our text, all of the cases are new to this edition.

A special introductory section preceding the cases, "Strategic Management Case Analysis," is designed to help students prepare written and oral case analysis by offering specific guidelines and methodologies. Concluding this section are several suggestions for enhancing student performance in the strategic management course and for working within a group.

We have selected cases that students and instructors should find interesting and thought-provoking to read. Our case selection includes some of the largest, best-known businesses in the world as well as small, developing organizations. The companies examined include huge multi-divisional corporations, mid-size firms competing in only one or two markets, and small sole-proprietorships.

We have sought out cases which provide students an opportunity to be exposed to great diversity, both in terms of the industries covered as well as location. A vast array of industries are represented in the case selection. The global breadth of the cases is also extensive with cases covering firms in such locations as Poland, France, and Mexico. However, we have also included cases that involve organizations as familiar as the nearest fast-food restaurant or department store. The case selection also reflects a conscious effort to expose students not only to a diversity of enterprises but also to the diversity of the individuals who manage those enterprises. The following are key features of our case selection:

- In keeping with the increasing globalization of business and AACSB's concern for the internationalization of the business curriculum, we have selected cases that provide a more global perspective of business. These cases include enterprises based outside the United States and U.S. based firms with multinational operations.
- A concerted effort was made to include cases that not only detail the history and present condition of organizations, but also present the future issues that managers must face if the enterprises are to survive and prosper. Whether the issues involve exploiting new opportunities in the environment or taking steps to avoid threats, the student analyzing the case must make critical decisions regarding the future of the organizations examined.
- The extensive case selection gives students an opportunity to make strategic management decisions at the corporate level, the business unit level, and the functional level.
- Several small business cases are included, addressing such issues as confronting competition from much larger organizations, making a small business acquisition decision, and managing the growth of a successful small business.
- Not-for-profit cases range from Presque Isle State Park to The University of Texas Health Center at Tyler.

As in the earlier editions of this text, our primary criterion for our case selection was the overall quality of the cases. Special attention was also given to finding cases that were not only well written and interesting but also contained ample information for analysis.

SUPPLEMENTS

Internet Support Site—StratPlus—a Web site that supports all of Prentice Hall's publications in Strategic Management—contains additional information on Value Chains, Industrial Chains, Porter's Five Factors, SWOT Analysis, Industrial Organization, and Environmental Analysis. In addition, there is an on-line annotated "How To Do a Case" section along with Internet resources and bimonthly new updates.

Instructor's Resource Manual—includes test items and extensive case notes containing a synopsis, a mini-S.W.O.T. analysis, and transparency masters for each case.
Computerized Instructor's Resource Manual—offers all the features of the IRM on a 3.5" disk.
Overhead Transparencies—covering the major concepts for the first 12 chapters.
PowerPoint Transparencies—Electronic version of the Overhead Transparency program available on 3.5" disk.

ACKNOWLEDGMENTS

We are deeply indebted to our colleagues who have so generously permitted us to use their high quality cases in this text. The selection process was lengthy and rigorous, and we take considerable pride in presenting these cases. The author(s) of each case is identified on the first page of the case. A list of case contributors appears below:

Claire J. Anderson, *Old Dominion University*
Chi Anyansi-Archibong, *North Carolina A&T State University*
Joann Babiak, *University of Tulsa*
Ida Robinson-Backmon, *North Carolina A&T State University*
Betty L. Brewer, *North Carolina A&T State University*
Gary Bridges, *University of Southern Colorado*
Julius S. Brown, *Loyola Marymount University*
William D. Chandler, *University of Southern Colorado*
Maclyn L. Clouse, *University of Denver*
Carol J. Cumber, *South Dakota State University*
Otto P. Dobnick, *SouthEastern Wisconsin Regional Planning Commission*
Dorothy Dologite, *CUNY-Baruch College*
Casey Donoho, *Northern Arizona University*
Julie Driscoll, *Bentley College*
W. Jack Duncan, *University of Alabama at Birmingham*
John S. Dunkelberg, *Wake Forest University*
Andrew D. Dyer, *Georgetown University*
Herbert B. Epstein, *University of Texas at Tyler*
Patricia Feltes, *Southwest Missouri State University*
Caroline M. Fisher, *Loyola University*
Marshall Foote, *University of North Dakota*

David R. Frew, *Gannon University*
Cynthia V. Fukami, *University of Denver*
Ronald P. Garrett, *United States Air Force*
Peter M. Ginter, *University of Alabama at Birmingham*
Troy Gleason, *University of North Dakota*
Thomas S. Goho, *Wake Forest University*
Walter Greene, *University of Texas Pan American*
Phillip Hall, *St. Ambrose University*
Jean M. Hanebury, *Texas A&M University at Corpus Christi*
W. Harvey Hegarty, *Indiana University*
Todd E. Himstead, *Georgetown University*
Alan N. Hoffman, *Bentley College*
John Holm, *The University of Texas at Tyler*
C. Thomas Howard, *University of Denver*
Horace O. Kelly, Jr., *Wake Forest University*
Mark Kroll, *University of Texas at Tyler*
Jeffrey A. Krug, *The University of Memphis*
Sharon Ungar Lane, *Bentley College*
Angela R. Lanning, *University of Guelph*
Donald L. Lester, *Union University*
Robert C. Lewis, *University of Guelph*
Daniel O. Lybrook, *Purdue University*
Zbigniew Malara, *Technical University of Wroclaw, Poland*
Aaron Martin, *University of North Dakota*
Michael D. Martin, *HealthSouth Corporation*
Robert P. McGowan, *University of Denver*
Robert N. McGrath, *Embry-Riddle Aeronautical University*
Michael L. Menefee, *Purdue University*
Albert J. Milhomme, *Southwest Texas State University*
Robert J. Mockler, *St. John's University*
Mary Mulligan, *Loyola Marymount University*
John Noland, *University of Alabama at Birmingham*
Brent Olson, *University of North Dakota*
Godwin Osuagwa, *Jarvis Christian College*
Jon Ozmun, *Northern Arizona University*
John A. Parnell, *North Carolina Central University*
Charles A. Rarick, *Transylvania University*
Paul Reed, *Sam Houston State University*
Dr. Woodrow D. Richardson, *University of Alabama at Birmingham*

Patrick Asubonteng Rivers, *University of Alabama at Birmingham*
George C. Rubenson, *Salisbury State University*
Alison Rude, *Bentley College*
Carol Rugg, *Bentley College*
C. Louise Sellaro, *Youngstown State University*
Frank M. Shipper, *Salisbury State University*
William S. Silver, *University of Denver*
Bonnie Silveria, *Bentley College*
Douglas L. Smith, *University of Alabama at Birmingham*
N. Craig Smith, *Georgetown University*
Kellie F. Snell, *HealthSouth Corporation*
Leslie Toombs, *The University of Texas at Tyler*
Isaiah O. Ugboro, *North Carolina A&T State University*
Jennifer Videtto, *The University of Texas at Tyler*
John J. Vitton, *University of North Dakota*
Donna M. Watkins, *University of Southern Colorado*
Brian Wavra, *University of North Dakota*
Joan Winn, *University of Denver*
Joseph Wolfe, *University of Tulsa*
Jan Zahrly, *University of North Dakota*

Special thanks are due to our editor, David Shafer, and our production editor, Cynthia Regan, for overseeing this project from inception to completion. We are deeply indebted to Professor Charles "Hemingway" Pringle for the quality he imputed to the development of the first two editions of this text. His brilliance will live on and carry us through the subsequent revisions.

Administrators at each of our universities have been most supportive of our work. We particularly wish to thank Dean Donna Randall and Management Chairman Robert Taylor, University of Memphis; and President George F. Hamm, Vice President of Academic Affairs Bill Baker, and Dean Jim Tarter of the University of Texas at Tyler.

Finally, but certainly not least, the support, patience, and understanding of special family members—William, Mahin, and Teresa Wright; Nghi Kroll; and Denise Parnell—were not only helpful but essential in making this book a reality.

About the Authors

Peter Wright is a Professor of Management who holds the University of Memphis Endowed Chair of Excellence in Free Enterprise Management. He received his M.B.A. and his Ph.D. in management from Louisiana State University. He has acted as a consultant to many business organizations and was president/owner of an international industrial trading firm. Professor Wright is widely published in journals such as the *Harvard Business Review, Strategic Management Journal, Academy of Management Journal, Journal of Management, Journal of Business Research, Journal of Banking and Finance, Long Range Planning, British Journal of Management, Journal of the Academy of Marketing Science, Business Horizons, Planning Review, Managerial Planning,* among others. Some of his academic publications have been reported in the media such as *The CBS Television Evening News, The Washington Post, Business Week, The Economist,* the *Wall Street Journal,* and *Smart Money.*

Mark J. Kroll is Professor Chair of the Management and Marketing Department at the University of Texas at Tyler. He received his M.B.A. from Sam Houston State University and his D.B.A. in management from Mississippi State University. His articles on strategic management topics have appeared in many journals including the *Academy of Management Executive, Academy of Management Journal, Academy of Management Review, Journal of Business Research, Journal of the Academy of Marketing Science,* and *Strategic Management Journal.* He has also authored a number of cases, which have appeared in various strategic management textbooks and in the *Case Research Journal.* Professor Kroll consults for a wide variety of business organizations and teaches the capstone strategic management course at both the undergraduate and graduate levels.

John A. Parnell is Professor and Head of the Marketing and Management Department at Texas A & M University-Commerce. He received his M.B.A. from East Carolina University, his Ed.D. from Campbell University, and his Ph.D. from The University of Memphis. He served three years as president/owner of a direct-mail firm and is the author of over 100 journal articles, published cases, and conference proceedings. His works appear in such leading journals as *Administration and Society, British Journal of Management, Human Resource Management Review, International Journal of Organizational Analysis,* and *International Journal of Value-Based Management.* Professor Parnell teaches the capstone strategic management course at the undergraduate and graduate levels.

STRATEGIC MANAGEMENT

CASES

II CASES IN STRATEGIC MANAGEMENT

Strategic Management Case Analysis

Most of you are majoring in some aspect of business administration and are already familiar with case analysis. A case portrays a real organizational situation and requires you to analyze that situation and then develop recommendations for future action. The difference between the cases in strategic management and those in previous courses is that the cases here assume a broader perspective. Cases in finance have a financial orientation, and those in organizational behavior usually focus on individual or group behavior, but the cases in this book reflect a broad, companywide perspective. Each case presents a real organization, and organizations in a wide variety of industries and operating situations are represented.

You have probably already taken a series of courses that specialize in various functional areas, such as marketing, accounting, finance, and production/operations management. This knowledge can prove very useful to you when you begin working as a functional specialist (e.g., accountant, financial analyst, or sales representative). However, most successful business executives need strategic skills, particularly as they move up into general management positions. As this upward movement occurs, they typically encounter a very different set of problems from those that they dealt with as functional specialists. Unfortunately, their functional expertise is of limited assistance to them in either diagnosing or resolving these general management problems. Success in such activities requires the integration of knowledge in a wide variety of areas, both theoretical and functional. Hence, the goal of this textbook—and the course it accompanies—is to help you develop a general management capability by exposing you to a number of situations that require the integration of knowledge from different areas. The contents of this book provide the fundamental framework needed to bring together and integrate what you have learned in other courses so that you will be able to analyze these cases from a companywide perspective.

This introduction should help you to analyze the cases contained in this textbook and assist you in organizing and presenting your thoughts in written (or oral) form.

READING THE CASE

Case analysis requires you to read the case carefully and to read it more than once. Some students read the case quickly to get an overview of the situation presented and then reread it slowly, taking notes on the important issues and problems. Subsequently, they begin to organize and analyze the case information. However, each person must develop his or her own approach to case analysis. No single technique works well for everyone.

Since cases reflect reality, it should not be surprising that some of the information is not well organized, that irrelevant information is presented, and that relevant information may be dispersed throughout the case. Information rarely comes to us in neatly tied packages. One of your first tasks, therefore, is to organize the information in the case. An outline that can help you organize the material is discussed in the following section, or your professor may provide you with his or her own guidelines for organizing the issues in the case.

Students often have questions about the time frame of a particular case. We have found it most efficient to assume that you are analyzing the case in the year(s) that the case covers. For instance, if the last year covered in the case is 1994, then you should not ordinarily analyze the case with information gathered since that date. In some instances, however, your professor may ask you to update the case, particularly if, at the case's end, significant pending problems and issues are still unresolved.[1]

WRITING THE CASE ANALYSIS

The guidelines presented in the following subsections for the written analysis of cases are offered to help you organize and present your thoughts. (If your professor gives you a set of guidelines, by all means, use those.) As you read the case carefully, you may organize and analyze the information in the case under each of the headings used for the following subsections.

■ Macroenvironment

The macroenvironment, the broadest of all the sections in your analysis, is intended to help you decipher the macroenvironmental information you extract from the case and organize it selectively under such headings as "Political-Legal," "Economic," "Technological," and "Social," as shown in chapter 2. You should read the case for both explicit and implicit information in these categories. Outside research may be necessary to increase the information available in one or more of these areas. Then within each category, your task is to determine what opportunities and threats are presented to the firm featured in the case by the macroenvironmental force.

One way of accomplishing this end is to use headings and, under each heading, discuss how the external forces may act as opportunities or threats to management. Another way is to use brief, descriptive sentences for each heading's topic. For example, if the case is on General Motors (GM), the following "Economic" heading may be used with a brief sentence:

Economic (Opportunity) The relatively low recent value of the dollar (compared with its value in the early 1980s) versus foreign currencies has helped GM become more price competitive.

A threat or constraint may be noted as follows:

Political-Legal (Threat)   The U.S. government is demanding higher and higher fuel efficiency standards from U.S. automakers.

A number of different factors may be listed under each of the macroenvironmental headings, depending upon the range of information provided in the case and the extent of your research outside what's given in the case. Some cases may have many relevant factors under, for instance, the heading "Political-Legal" but few under "Technological."

■ Industry Environment

The industry environment section requires you to extract information from the case and from any other available source through your own research and then organize and analyze it under the five industry forces discussed in chapter 2: "Threat of Entry," "Intensity of Rivalry Among Existing Competitors," "Pressure from Substitute Products," "Bargaining Power of Buyers," and "Bargaining Power of Suppliers." You should use these headings to help you organize your analysis.

For example, assume that the case you are analyzing is on GM's automobile business units. Under the heading "Threat of Entry," you might mention that economies of scale act as a barrier to domestic companies that may seek to enter the U.S. automobile industry. However, more and more vehicle producers from abroad have entered the American market over the years. Thus, although the threat of new entry from U.S. sources is limited, the threat of foreign automakers' exporting their products to America and even building manufacturing facilities in the United States is certainly present.

Under "Bargaining Power of Suppliers," you might mention that most suppliers of automobile parts do not have strong positions relative to GM. For instance, the major U.S. steel companies are not working at full capacity and, hence, would be anxious to sell to GM.

This is not to say that suppliers generally have weak bargaining power. In certain industries, some suppliers possess relatively strong bargaining power relative to buyers. For instance, Monsanto's NutraSweet unit had a strong bargaining position as a supplier to the soft-drink producers until its patent for aspartame expired in 1992.

The point of analyzing the macroenvironment and industry environment, of course, is to relate the opportunities and threats in these two areas to the firm featured in the case. A review of chapter 2 should help you in this analysis.

■ The Firm's Resources, Mission, Goals, Objectives, Social Responsibility, and Ethics

Parts or all of the heading "The Firm's Resources, Mission, Goals, Objectives, Social Responsibility, and Ethics" may be used for your analysis. Sometimes, information is explicitly provided on these topics; other times, it is implicit, forcing you to read between the lines. One question that you might consider posing and analyzing is the following:

1. What are the firm's strengths and weaknesses?

As discussed in chapter 3, a firm's strengths and weaknesses reside in its resources. Consequently, you may wish to use the questions posed in chapter 3 regarding the firm's human, organizational, and physical resources to determine the corporation's particular strengths and weaknesses.

You might also pose the following:

2. Is there an explicit or an implicit statement of the firm's mission? Does it accurately portray the direction in which the firm is going, or are the firm's operations incompatible with its mission?

You may recall that in chapter 3, the mission of GM (to continue our example) is stated in the following way:

> The fundamental purpose of General Motors is to provide products and services of such quality that our customers will receive superior value, our employees and business partners will share in our success, and our stockholders will receive a sustained, superior return on their investment.

Unfortunately for GM, there has been a gap between its mission and its actual operating results. Surveys of car owners indicate that GM is not perceived as offering superior value to its customers.[2] In fact, a car produced by Toyota and sold under the GM brand (Geo Prism) has sales far below those of its "twin" product, Corolla, which is produced and marketed by Toyota.[3] Furthermore, GM has laid off large numbers of employees, and its stock has not been a top performer.

Another question you might consider:

3. Are the expressed or implied goals and objectives of the firm consistent with one another? Is there evidence that these goals and objectives are being attained?

In Chapter 3, we indicated that the goals of various stakeholders often differ. And Chapter 9 pointed out that compromise may be important in helping resolve these differences. Sometimes, however, compromise is not attainable, and the effectiveness of the firm suffers as a result. For example, in the middle to late 1980s, H. Ross Perot—head of Electronic Data Systems, a subsidiary of GM; a member of the GM board of directors; and a major stockholder in GM— desired a course of action for GM that differed significantly from the course favored by GM's top management. Because compromise was unattainable, GM's management purchased Perot's stock holdings for about $750 million, at a time when GM had just incurred a large quarterly loss.

Here is another question you might consider for your analysis.

4. Is the firm operating in a socially responsible manner? Are the decisions and actions of its managers ethical?

As we emphasized in chapter 3, analysis in the areas of social responsibility and ethics can be difficult because the guidelines are not always clear-cut. If the case contains these issues, you may have to formulate your own answer to dilemmas such as whether it is socially responsible to lay off employees to enhance a firm's competitiveness or whether social responsibility can be better served by keeping the employees on the payroll, even at the expense of the firm's profits and, perhaps, survival.

■ Corporate-Level Strategies

As we pointed out in chapter 4, a basic question facing top management at the corporate level is, In what particular businesses or industries should we be operating? The answer to this question depends upon the firm's particular resource strengths and weaknesses and the opportunities and threats in the external environment.

The next step is to answer the following questions: Which specific strategies has the firm adopted—growth, stability, or retrenchment? How effective have these strategies been? Some corporations have effectively adopted growth strategies, but others have been less successful. Some companies have grown by developing or acquiring businesses with a common core. General Electric, for example, has attained success through involvement in businesses that share a common technological core. As another instance, Philip Morris has been one of the world's largest consumer product firms, particularly with its tobacco and food businesses. However, Philip Morris was unable to transfer its expertise in consumer products to its marketing of 7-Up, which it eventually divested.

Some corporations or business units have effectively adopted the stability strategy. This strategy enables the corporation to focus managerial efforts on the existing businesses with the goal of enhancing their competitive postures. Top executives may also adopt this strategy if they perceive that the cost of adding new businesses is more than the potential benefits. At the business unit level, the stability strategy may be chosen for other reasons. For instance, some enterprises have decided not to expand because of concern that growth may reduce the quality of their products and services. In a number of industries, some large businesses may elect stability to avoid being prosecuted for engaging in monopolistic practices.

A strategy of retrenchment may be appropriate in certain situations. For instance, Tambrands diversified in the 1980s from a single-product company into such unrelated businesses as home diagnostics and cosmetics. These acquisitions, however, provided "little more than a stream of operating losses and management distraction that has hurt its basic tampon business."[4] In its retrenchment strategy, Tambrands sold both the diagnostics and cosmetics businesses at a loss. However, since pruning those operations, it has performed well by concentrating solely on its tampon business.

Your answer to the question—In what businesses or industries should we be operating?—may be made more specifically by examining the discussion in the next section.

■ Corporate Portfolio Management and Related Issues

Many firms operate multiple business units in various industries, as we saw in chapter 5. At the corporate level of such enterprises, the task is to use S.W.O.T. analysis to evaluate each business unit within a portfolio framework context. For example, a weak business unit that faces external threats would be placed in compartment H or I of our proposed S.W.O.T. framework. (Alternatively, this same business would be classified as a "dog" in the original BCG framework, would be placed in the "divest" compartment of the revised BCG frame-work, and would be considered an "unsuccessful business unit" in the GE framework.) Once the business unit is placed in the appropriate category in the portfolio framework, then the guidelines associated with its placement may be used to recommend corporate growth, stability, or retrenchment strategies. In the example we are using, the guideline in our S.W.O.T. framework is to turn-around, divest, or liquidate the business. (The original BCG, revised BCG, and GE frameworks recommend either liquidating or divesting the business.)

You may also wish to determine how involved corporate-level top manage-ment should get in formulating and implementing business unit strategies. Recall from chapter 5 that relatively centralized decision making may be appropriate for corporations with related businesses, while relatively more decentralization may be better for firms operating unrelated businesses. Finally, you may wish to explore such issues in the case as corporate returns and top management's motives for engaging in acquisitions.

■ Business Unit Strategies and Functional Strategies

If the case is about a corporation with individual business units, then the units may have adopted different generic business unit strategies. If the firm is in a single business, such as McDonald's or Tambrands, then its business unit and corporate-level strategies are the same. In either case, your task is to identify which business unit strategy the firm has adopted and to evaluate how appro-priate that strategy is. Is it compatible with the firm's corporate strategies and with its objectives for market share? Does it enable the company to compete effectively? Here you will wish to refer to chapter 6 and review the seven generic strategies available to business units.

As discussed in chapter 7, business unit strategies influence functional strat-egies; conversely, the extent to which functional strategies are effectively for-mulated helps determine the success of the business strategies. In this section of your analysis, you will want to explore the consistency of the business unit strategies and the supporting functional strategies.

For example, if the corporation emphasizes scope economies and if the busi-ness unit has adopted a low-cost strategy, then it would be inconsistent for the business unit to formulate a marketing strategy with costly advertising and pro-motion. However, expensive promotional campaigns would be consistent with corporate scope innovations and the adoption of the differentiation strategy.

Your analysis may extend to other considerations as well. For instance, a firm that produces a high-priced luxury product with the niche-differentiation strategy should not pursue a goal of substantially increasing its production/operations capacity and market share. Consumers who purchase luxury prod-ucts or services do so only as long as the items are perceived as exclusive.

■ Strategy Implementation

The actual implementation of corporate, business unit, and functional strate-gies is considered in this part of your analysis. Reference to chapter 8 will help you in evaluating the relationship of the firm's organizational structure to its strategies. Is this structure suitable for a firm with these strategies? Or has the firm outgrown the need for this structure?

Chapter 9 should assist you in determining whether the CEO's leadership style and use of power are appropriate for the firm's strategies. Also consider whether the organization's culture is supportive of the strategies that it is attempting to implement.

Note that some cases will give you considerable information on strategy implementation, organizational charts, organizational culture, and the CEO. Others will provide little data on these matters. If your professor encourages outside research, you can usually collect at least some information on these issues if the firm is a large, publicly held corporation.

■ Strategic Control

Although strategic control was discussed in chapter 10, the actual process involves every aspect of strategic management. That is, strategic control is a process that must occur in the analysis of the following aspects of the firm:

- Macroenvironment
- Industry environment
- Firm resources, mission, goals, objectives, social responsibility, and ethics
- Strategy formulation
- Strategy implementation

In this section of your analysis, you will want to determine which aspects of the case are in particular need of strategic control scrutiny and, if possible, attempt to bring them together to draw overall conclusions. It is helpful, as chapter 10 points out, to compare this year's results with those of the firm in previous years. Alternatively, strategic control may be examined by comparing the firm's qualitative and quantitative results with those of its rivals or other firms. If you have access to the Profit Impact of Market Strategies (PIMS) program, you may wish to use it for these comparisons.

Besides PIMS, there are other sources of data available for assessing strategic control. They include Dun & Bradstreet's *Industry Norms and Key Business Ratios* and various publications by Value Line, Standard and Poor's, Moody's, and Robert Morris Associates. Additional information can be gleaned from annual reports and 10-K reports of the firm's chief competitors. Recall that strategic control involves not only quantitative data but also qualitative information. Annual reports and industry analyses, such as those by Standard and Poor's and Moody's, are particularly rich in qualitative information.

You may also wish to analyze the financial aspects of the case. Financial information can be revealing. For instance, a top manager stated to one of the authors that his firm not only was "recession-proof," but also continuously faced an increase in market demand. Yet, the inventories of the firm had jumped dramatically during the previous three years.

Financial ratios may be used in your quantitative analysis. The idea is to discern trends by calculating certain key ratios and then comparing them with (a) the median ratios in the industry, (b) the ratios of the firm's major competitors, and (c) the firm's ratios in prior years. Exhibit 1 lists many of the most important ratios, shows how to calculate them, and indicates what they mean.

Although a firm's financial ratios are normally analyzed in relation to industry ratios, you may wish to allow for some flexibility in your analysis. For

Exhibit 1   **Financial Ratios**

Ratios	Formula	What Ratios Represent
Liquidity		
Current ratio	$\dfrac{\text{Current assets}}{\text{Current liabilities}}$	This ratio is an indication of a firm's ability to meet current obligations. Ordinarily a ratio of 2 to 1 or better is desirable.
Quick ratio	$\dfrac{\text{Current assets} - \text{inventory}}{\text{Current liabilities}}$	This ratio indicates how much of the current liabilities the current assets can immediately cover, excluding the inventory (since inventories may not be subject to immediate sale or may have a lower market value than book value).
Sales-to-receivables ratio	$\dfrac{\text{Net sales}}{\text{Trade receivables} - \text{net}}$	This ratio measures the times trade receivables turn over during a year, indicating how frequently they are converted to cash.
Days in receivables ratio	$\dfrac{365}{\text{Sales/receivables ratio}}$	This figure expresses the average time in days that receivables are outstanding.
Inventory turnover ratio	$\dfrac{\text{Cost of sales}}{\text{Average Inventory}}$	This ratio measures the times the firm's inventory turns over during a year, indicating how efficiently inventory is being managed.
Days in inventory ratio	$\dfrac{365}{\text{Sales/inventory ratio}}$	Dividing the inventory turnover ratio into 365 days yields the average length of time units are in inventory. Normally, the smaller this number is, the more efficiently inventories are being managed.
Cost of sales-to-payables ratio	$\dfrac{\text{Cost of sale}}{\text{Trade payables}}$	This ratio measures the number of times trade payables turn over during the year, or how quickly the firm pays them.
Days in payables ratio	$\dfrac{365}{\text{Sales/payable ratio}}$	Division of the payable turnover ratio into 365 days yields the average length of time trade debt is outstanding. Typically, a small number of days suggests the firm is paying its bills in a timely fashion.
Sales-to-working capital ratio	$\dfrac{\text{Net sales}}{\text{Net working capital}}$	This is a measure of the firm's ratio of sales to working capital. The greater the number, the less adequate is the firm's working capital base relative to its sales.
Coverage		
Times interest earned ratio	$\dfrac{\text{EBIT}}{\text{Annual interest expense}}$	Measures the capability of the firm to make good on its yearly interest costs.
Leverage		
Net fixed assets-to-tangible net worth ratio	$\dfrac{\text{Net fixed assets}}{\text{Tangible net worth}}$	This ratio measures the extent to which the owner's equity has been invested in plant and equipment.
Debt-to-net worth ratio	$\dfrac{\text{Total liabilities}}{\text{Net worth}}$	This ratio expresses the relationship between the capital contributed by creditors and that contributed by shareholders.
Operating		
Percent of profits before taxes-to-net worth ratio	$\dfrac{\text{Profits before taxes}}{\text{Tangible net worth} \times 100}$	This ratio expresses the rate of return on tangible capital employed by the firm. Normally, the larger this number is, the better the firm's performance.
Percent of profits before taxes-to-total assets	$\dfrac{\text{Profits before taxes}}{\text{Total assets} \times 100}$	This ratio expresses the pre-tax return on total assets and measures the effectiveness of management in employing the resources available to the firm.

Exhibit 1 (continued)   **Financial Ratios**

Ratios	Formula	What Ratios Represent
Operating		
Sales/net fixed assets ratio	$\dfrac{\text{Total sales}}{\text{Net fixed assets}}$	This ratio measures the productivity of a firm's fixed assets by determining the number of times fixed assets turned over in the last year.
Sales/total assets ratio	$\dfrac{\text{Total sales}}{\text{Total assets}}$	This ratio is a measure of a firm's ability to generate sales in relation to total assets. Normally, the larger the number, the more productive the firm is thought to be.
Percent of depreciation, amortization, depletion expenses-to-sales	$\dfrac{\text{Depreciation amortization depletion expenses}}{\text{Total sales x 100}}$	This is the measure of the amount of total sales absorbed by non-cash expenses.
Market-to-book ratio	$\dfrac{\text{Market price of firm's stock}}{\text{Book value per share}}$	This ratio measures the securities market's expectations concerning the firm's future earnings. Any value greater than 1 suggests the securities market expects future return on equity to be greater than the firm's cost of equity capital.
Return on equity ratio	$\dfrac{\text{Net profit after taxes}}{\text{Stockholder's equity}}$	This measures the rate of return on the book value of total stockholder's equity.

example, a lower current ratio for some businesses may be less of a concern. As a case in point, Avon sells its cosmetics to consumers door-to-door for cash. Many of its rivals, however, sell cosmetics via retailers. Select retailers not only have the right to return unsold products, but also make payments over a period of weeks or even months (which is not as attractive as cash on delivery).

A less common ratio, market-to-book value, should also be calculated. Simply divide the firm's latest stock price by its book value per share; the result helps indicate whether investors view the firm's future positively. If the ratio is greater than 1, then investors forecast that the company's return on equity is expected to be greater than its required rate of return. If it is less than 1, then the firm's forecasted return on equity is less than its required rate of return. This ratio allows you to assess how favorably the stock market views the strategic direction of the firm.

■ Your Recommendations for Future Action

In the preceding sections of your analysis, you have probably identified issues, problems, and inconsistencies that need to be addressed. You may have made more specific suggestions in response to them—that is, in some cases, you may have stated that modifications be made in the firm's corporate-level or business unit strategies; in others, you may have suggested that one or several of the functional strategies be improved. Alternatively, you may have recommended that changes be made in the way that strategies are implemented. At this point, you might make broader recommendations, involving the overall firm.

Exhibit 2	Cross-Reference Information for Case Analyses

Section of Analysis	Textbook Chapter
Macroenvironment	Chapter 2, "External Environmental Opportunities and Threats"
Industry environment	Chapter 2, "External Environmental Opportunities and Threats"
The firm's resource, mission, goals, objectives, social responsibility, and ethics	Chapter 3, "The Internal Environment: The Firm's Resources, Organizational Mission, and Goals"
Corporate-level strategies	Chapter 4, "Corporate-Level Strategies"
Corporate portfolio management and corporate-level strategy related issues	Chapter 5, "Corporate Portfolio Management and Related Corporate-Level Strategy Issues"
Business unit strategies and functional strategies	Chapter 6, "Business Unit Strategies"; Chapter 7, "Functional Strategies"
Strategy implementation	Chapter 8, "Strategy Implementation: Organizational Structure"; Chapter 9, "Strategy Implementation: Leadership, Power, and Organizational Culture"
Strategic control	Chapter 10, "Strategic Control Process and Performance"

Remember that a change that you recommend in one aspect of the organization's strategies or operations may affect several other parts of the company.

The recommendations should be addressed to the firm's top management and should be well organized and thought through. They also should be feasible in terms of human, organizational, and physical resources. Here, your ability to convince your instructor and classmates of the accuracy of your analysis and the power of your recommendations is of utmost importance.

We must emphasize that not all cases provide comprehensive information on all of the topics discussed in the previous pages. Some may focus only on specific areas, such as ethics or new product development. The framework presented here encompasses the total organization within its external environment. Consequently, you may or may not be able to use this entire set of topics in analyzing any particular case. However, in any case analysis, you may find the information in Exhibit 2 useful. This exhibit relates each section of your analysis to the corresponding chapter in this textbook. Before beginning your analysis, it may help to reread the discussion in the text regarding a particular issue.

COURSEWORK SUGGESTIONS

We would like to conclude by offering you some suggestions on how to perform well in the strategic management course.

1. Be actively involved in the course. At a minimum, you should attend all classes and participate fully in the class discussions. Participation involves asking questions, expressing your views, providing relevant examples from your own experience or outside reading, and helping extend the discussion to other related issues. Of course, case discussions can be exciting only when you have prepared for each class by knowing the facts and understanding the issues in the case. Thorough preparation will enable you to convey your knowledge and understanding to others clearly and persuasively. These skills are of considerable importance to a practicing manager.

2. As you participate, remember that this is a broad-based course in strategic management. Regardless of your particular academic major, attempt to view the issues in the case more broadly than you ordinarily might from the more limited perspective of a marketing major or a finance major, for instance. Remember that the goal is an integrated set of recommendations to top management.

3. Do not approach class discussions with a closed mind. A good discussion can bring out many different facets in a case—probably more than you can generate through an individual analysis. Listen to the other members of the class and evaluate their contributions carefully.

4. Do not let yourself be intimidated by a bad experience. Eventually, everyone in class may make an inane comment, may panic and lose the train of thought in midsentence, or may realize as he or she is speaking that what is being said is incorrect. Do not let these experiences affect your willingness to participate in the future. Participation in case analysis is an excellent training ground for future business presentations and committee meetings.

5. Do not suggest the use of a consultant. You are the consultant and should have specific, detailed recommendations for top management.

6. Learn to work well within a group. Many professors form teams of students in the strategic management course. Teamwork adds realism to the study of cases since, in reality, groups of key executives deal with strategic planning in business organizations. Working in a group, however, presents a particular set of challenges. Hence, we offer these suggestions.

   - If you are allowed to select your group members, ensure that they have similar objectives for their grade in the course (if you are aiming for an A, do not join a group of students who wish to just squeak by, even if they are your best friends) and that you all have compatible schedules that permit you to meet outside of class.

   - Try to form a group of individuals with different academic majors. Synergy is more likely to occur when the group has students who are majoring in different fields, such as finance, accounting, information systems, human resource management, and production/operations management.

   - Do not divide the case into parts and assign an individual to each part. This technique will result in a fragmented, piecemeal, and disjointed analysis. Even if the primary responsibility for various parts of the case is assigned to specific individuals, every member of the group should be involved in all parts of the case analysis.

   - Cooperate closely with one another. Through cooperation and a free exchange of ideas, the team should be able to devise innovative solutions to case problems. But the only way to accomplish this is for every member to participate fully during the team meetings. Ideally, only one person should talk at a time, while the others listen. One member should record all of the ideas expressed. If one person is particularly shy, others should encourage that person to talk by using such techniques as asking "What is your opinion on that issue?"

- Divide the work equitably. If one member is not doing his or her fair share, you must diplomatically, but quickly, inform that person that more is expected.

- Prepare thoroughly for the oral presentation. It is essential that you rehearse, as a group, several times. Ensure that each member knows his or her cue for speaking. Do not bring extensive notes and read from them. On the other hand, do not memorize your part word for word. Rather, prepare an outline of your part, and then let the key points on the outline guide your presentation.

- Be sure that your oral presentation fits neatly into the time allotted by your professor. It is not uncommon to see case presentations that either do not fully utilize the time allotted or run out of time before alternatives and recommendations can be thoroughly addressed. It is your responsibility to know the time allotment, to provide detailed analysis, and to set priorities so that key issues can be covered without rushing at the end.

- Get accustomed to speaking before people. Such presentations are routine in most aspects of the business world, so this course gives you an excellent opportunity to overcome your hesitancy to talk before a large group. If you have prepared well and have rehearsed several times, your presentation will be well received by your audience, even though you personally may feel a bit uncomfortable.

SUMMARY

The remainder of this book contains cases. A case portrays a real organizational situation and requires you to analyze that situation and then develop recommendations for future action. To accomplish these ends, you will need to take a broad, companywide perspective.

After reading the case carefully several times, you will want to take notes to organize your analysis and presentation. We suggest that you analyze the case by using the following outline:

- Macroenvironment
- Industry environment
- The firm's resources, mission, goals, objectives, social responsibility, and ethics
- Corporate-level strategies
- Corporate portfolio management and related issues
- Business unit strategies and functional strategies
- Strategy implementation
- Strategic control
- Your recommendations for future action

Finally, we offer several suggestions for enhancing your performance in the strategic management course and for working within a group.

NOTES

1. M.M. Helms and W.W. Prince, "Focused Library Instruction for Business Strategy Students and Strategy Practitioners," *Journal of Management Education* 17 (1993): 390–398.

2. R.L. Simon, D. Lavin, and J. Mitchell, "Tooling Along," *The Wall Street Journal*, 4 May 1994, pp. A1, A16; K. Kerwin, J.B. Treece, T. Peterson, L. Armstrong, and K.L. Miller, "Detroit's Big Chance," *Business Week*, 29 June 1992, pp. 82–90.

3. J.B. Treece, "Will Detroit Cut Itself Loose from Captive Imports?" *Business Week*, 4 September 1989, p. 34.

4. A. Dunkin, "They're More Single-Minded at Tambrands," *Business Week*, 28 August 1989, p. 28.

Saturn Corporation: American Automobile Manufacturing in Transition

John A. Parnell, Texas A & M University Commerce
Michael L. Menefee, Purdue University

Internet sites of interest: **www.gm.com**
www.saturncars.com

THE BIRTH OF SATURN

"In 1985 when I joined the Saturn team, the auto industry in this country was undergoing some significant challenges. Today it is no different. We are being attacked from all sides. The competition is unrelenting in their pursuit of market dominance, if not subjugation. . . .These are challenging times for the heartiest of times, the most well established businesses. . . .These are not times for sissies or whiners in the closet. Rather, these are times when boldness is required from people who can see beyond today into the world of the future."

ALAN G. PERRITON, VICE
PRESIDENT, MATERIALS
MANAGEMENT, SATURN
CORPORATION

By the early 1980s, Asian imported vehicles had made significant inroads into the American automobile market. General Motors' response—the "J-Car" design introduced in 1982 as the Chevrolet Cavalier, Pontiac 2000, Oldsmobile Firenza, Buick Skylark, and Cadillac Cimarron—did nothing to slow its continued erosion in the small car market. Then CEO Roger Smith decided to start from scratch, considering the best production technology and labor-management techniques from around the world in pursuit of lost market share. In 1982, Smith initiated a project to innovatively design and manufacture small cars in the United States that were competitive with imported vehicles.

In 1984, 99 United Auto Workers (UAW) members, GM managers, and staff personnel from 55 plants joined to form the "Group of 99" to plan for the pursuit of this goal. Together, this group was charged "to identify and recommend the best approaches to integrate people and technology to competitively manufacture a small car in the United States."

Shortly thereafter, GM unveiled its first demonstration vehicle. In 1985, Saturn Corporation was formed as an independent, wholly owned subsidiary of

This case is intended for classroom discussion only, not to depict effective or ineffective handling of administrative situations. All rights reserved to the author(s).
When ordering this case from the Prentice Hall Custom Case Program, please use ISBN 0-13-079933-5.

GM to continue the project under the direction of newly appointed president Joseph Sanchez. Sanchez served only 19 days until his death, succeeded for one year by William Hoglund, and then by current president Richard "Skip" LeFauve. Whereas most new organizations attempt to fight employee organization efforts, Saturn was created and organized with union involvement from the beginning.

In 1987, construction began on Saturn's manufacturing, assembly, and training and development operations facility, now covering 4 million square feet located on 2400 acres in Spring Hill, Tennessee, a small community 45 miles south of Nashville. By early 1988, Saturn began recruiting the first of 3000 workers for its Spring Hill plant from 136 GM/UAW facilities in the United States. Roger Smith and UAW President Owen Bieber drove the first Saturn vehicle off the final assembly line on July 30, 1990.

Today, Saturn's Spring Hill facility employs 8,200 people and is currently producing over 300,000 vehicles annually. Vehicle quality and satisfaction rates rival or exceed those of many of Saturn's Asian competitors. Saturn is seeking expansion, selling more cars, and contributing to GM's financial turnaround. Saturn has embarked on a distinctively different course for automotive success.

■ The Automobile Industry

The genesis of the automobile can be traced back to the development of steam engines, gasoline engines, and electric motors in the 1890s. By 1910, 187,000 automobiles were sold annually at approximately $750 each. Henry Ford's application of standardization, specialization, and mass production concepts contributed to Ford's emergence as industry leader. However, in the 1920s, Buick, Cadillac, Chevrolet, Oldsmobile, Delco, and Fisher Body came together to form General Motors. Unlike Ford, GM focused not on efficiency, but on product choice, offering a wide range of products updated annually to reflect engineering and styling innovations. GM secured industry leadership in 1931.

Imports began to challenge the domestic oligopoly in the late 1950s with smaller, more economical vehicles. However, weak dealer networks, parts availability, and service problems spelled failure for the imports. GM responded by producing larger, more expensive cars loaded with options. GM abhorred the slim margins of small cars and believed that the potential for such imports would remain insignificant. Meanwhile, Japanese automakers were back at the drawing board.

In the early 1970s, imported vehicles—particularly Japanese manufacturers—made a second surge into the domestic market. With cars more in tune to American preferences, improved quality, and a stronger dealer network, Japanese manufacturers carved out a sizable niche in the American market. By 1975, imports had secured one-fourth of the domestic automobile market.

Today, Japanese manufacturers account for approximately thirty percent of U.S. car sales. The Big Three auto makers consistently account for about 65%, with European manufacturers holding most of the remaining five percent of the market. Saturn's production increased from 280,002 cars in 1994 to 301,613 in 1995, improving its percentage of total U.S. production from 3.2 percent to 3.6 percent (see Exhibit 1).

Today, domestic production of automobiles is heavily concentrated among three firms: GM, Ford, and Chrysler. However, distinction between "domestic" and "import" can become blurred. In the 1980s, many Japanese manufacturers

Exhibit 1   **North American Car Production**

Make	Car Sales 1995	Car Sales 1994	1995 Share	1994 Share
General Motors	3,066,627	3,046,755	36.7	35.2
Chevrolet/GEO	1,013,897	833,150	12.1	9.6
Pontiac	622,851	653,936	7.4	7.6
Buick	509,821	572,212	6.1	6.6
Oldsmobile	390,964	481,326	4.7	5.6
Cadillac	187,481	226,129	2.2	2.6
Saturn	301,613	280,002	3.6	3.2
Ford	1,802,654	2,048,112	21.6	23.7
Chrysler	840,669	968,634	10.1	11.2
Toyota	733,568	618,970	8.8	7.1
Honda	657,896	607,018	7.9	7.0
Nissan	571,043	638,199	6.8	7.4
All Others	691,928	729,293	8.3	8.4
TOTAL	8,364,385	8,656,981	100.0	100.0

Based on data obtained from *Automotive News*, January 9, 1996.

Note: See the current issue of *Automotive News* for the most recent figures. Above figures do not include trucks or vehicles produced outside of the U.S.

constructed production facilities in the United States, including Honda (Marysville, Ohio), Nissan (Smyrna, Tennessee), Mazda (Flat Rock, Michigan), and Toyota (Georgetown, Kentucky). Joint ventures between "big three" firms and Japanese companies were also prevalent. The New United Motors Manufacturing, Inc. (NUMMI) project began producing vehicles in Fremont, California, in 1984 under a 50/50 GM-Toyota agreement. Diamond-Star Motors Corporation began production in Bloomington, Indiana, in 1988 under a 50/50 Chrysler-Mitsubishi agreement. Domestic auto manufacturers also hold significant ownership in Japanese manufacturers: GM owns 39% of Isuzu, Ford owns 30% of Mazda, and Chrysler owns 25% of Mitsubishi.

General Motors experienced moderate declines in the production of both cars and trucks as well as revenues in the late 1980s and early 1990s. Since GM's recorded loss in 1992, the company has posted modest and growing profits through 1995 (see Exhibits 2 & 3).

SATURN CORPORATION: MISSION, PHILOSOPHY, & VALUES

As an independent, wholly-owned subsidiary of General Motors, Saturn drafted the following mission:

Market vehicles developed and manufactured in the United States that are world leaders in quality, cost, and customer satisfaction through the integration of

Exhibit 2   **Consolidated Income Statements for General Motors**

	1995	1994	1993	1992
Total Net Sales & Revenues	$168,826.6	$154,951.2	$138,219.5	$132,429.4
Cost of Goods Sold	126,535.3	117,220.5	106,421.9	105,063.9
Gross Margin	42,291.3	37,730.7	31,797.6	27,365.5
Expenses				
Selling, General, and Admin.	13,514.7	12,233.7	11,531.9	11,621.8
Interest Expense	5,302.2	5,431.9	5,673.7	7,305.4
Depreciation Expense	8,554.4	7,124.4	6,576.3	6,144.8
Amortization of Special Tools	3,212.0	2,900.7	2,535.3	2,504.0
Amortization of Intangible Assets	255.3	226.2	330.4	310.2
Other Deductions	1,678.4	1,460.5	1,624.7	1,575.4
Special Provision for Scheduled Plant Closings and Other Restructurings	—	—	950.0	1,237.0
Total Expenses	32,517.0	29,377.4	29,222.3	30,698.6
Net Income (Loss) Before Taxes	9,776.3	8,353.3	2,575.3	($3,333.1)
Adjustments for credits and accounting changes	(51.8)	(758.1)	—	(20,165.2)
Net Income (Loss)	$9,724.5	$7,595.2	$2,575.3	($23,498.3)

Dollars in millions
Source: *General Motors Annual Report, 1995.*

people, technology, and business systems and to transfer knowledge and experience throughout General Motors.

The Saturn team has also articulated the "Saturn Philosophy" to fulfill the mission:

We, the Saturn Team, in concert with the UAW and General Motors, believe that meeting the needs of Customers, Saturn Members, Suppliers, Dealers, and Neighbors is fundamental to fulfilling our mission.
To meet our customer needs:

• Our products and services must be world leaders in value and satisfaction.

To meet our members' needs:

• We will create a sense of belonging in an environment of mutual trust, respect, and dignity.
• We believe that all people want to be involved in decisions that affect them, care about their jobs and each other, take pride in themselves and in their contributions, and want to share in the success of their efforts.
• We will develop the tools, training, and education for each member, recognizing individual skills and knowledge.
• We believe that creative, motivated, responsible team members who understand that change is critical to success are Saturn's most important asset.

Exhibit 3   **Consolidated Balance Sheet for General Motors**

	1995	1994
Assets		
Cash and Cash Equivalents	$ 11,044.3	$ 10,939.0
Other Marketable securities	5,598.6	5,136.6
Total Cash and Marketable Securities	16,642.9	16,075.6
Finance receivables	58,732.0	54,077.3
Accounts and Notes receivables	9,988.4	8,977.8
Inventories (less allowances)	11,529.5	10,127.8
Contracts in process	2,469.2	2,265.4
Net Equipment on operating leases (less accum. depreciation)	27,702.3	20,061.6
Deferred income taxes	19,028.3	19,693.3
Property	37,739.8	34,780.6
Intangible assets	11,898.9	11,913.8
Other assets	21,392.1	20,625.5
Total Assets	$217,123.4	$198,598.7
Liabilities		
Accounts Payable	$ 11,898.8	$ 11,635.0
Notes and loans payable	83,323.5	73,730.2
U.S., foreign, and other income taxes—deferred and payable	3,231.6	2,721.0
Postretirement benefits other than pensions	41,595.1	40,018.2
Pensions	6,842.3	14,353.2
Other liabilities and deferred credits	46,886.6	42,867.3
Total Liabilities	193,777.9	185,324.9
Stocks Subject to Repurchase	—	450.0
Preference stocks	1.2	2.4
Common stock—$1-2/3 par value	1,255.0	1,257.2
Common stock—Class E	44.3	26.8
Common stock—Class H	9.7	7.9
Capital surplus	18,870.9	13,149.4
Net income retained for use in the business	7,185.4	1,785.8
Subtotal	27,366.5	16,229.5
Minimum pensions liability adjustment	(4,736.3)	(3,548.4)
Accumulated foreign currency translation adjustments	222.5	100.4
Net unrealized gains on investments in certain debt and equity securities	492.8	243.1
Total Stockholder's Equity	23,345.5	12,823.8
Total Liabilities and Stockholder's Equity	$217,123.4	$198.598.7

Dollars in millions

Source: *General Motors Annual Report, 1995.*

To meet our suppliers' and dealers' needs:

- We will strive to create real partnerships with them.
- We will be open and fair in our dealings, reflecting trust, respect, and their importance to Saturn.
- We want dealers and suppliers to feel ownership in Saturn's mission and philosophy as their own.

To meet the needs of our neighbors, the communities in which we live and operate:

- We will be good citizens, protect the environment, and conserve natural resources.
- We will seek to cooperate with government at all levels and strive to be sensitive, open, and candid in all our public statements.

The Saturn philosophy is founded on a unique approach to decision making and management of the organization known as "the partnership." Saturn is attempting to overcome many of the traditional management-labor problems that have for so long become synonymous with the United States automobile industry. The Saturn approach brings together leaders of Saturn management and the UAW to improve trust and efficiency in decision making. The memorandum of agreement is quite short in comparison to UAW agreements with other auto manufacturers. The model has worked well in practice. For instance, when GM and its suppliers laid off 20,000 workers in early 1996 in response to the strike at the Delphi Chassis Systems in Dayton, Ohio, Saturn kept its 8,200 workers on the payroll at a daily cost of $1.6 million. In return, the UAW agreed to work Easter, Memorial Day, and several additional Sundays to make up for lost production during the strike.

As in other organizations, management is responsible for securing resources, legal and regulatory matters, employee selection and promotion, and the formal dispersion of expenditures. Likewise, the UAW is primarily concerned with fulfilling its duty of fair representation (DFR). However, there exists a partnership arena where management and the UAW work together and share responsibilities. Activities in this arena include the mission, philosophy and values, memorandum of agreement, strategic and tactical planning, operational planning, and operational performance. The partnership does not eliminate conflict, but instead attempts to promote a less adversarial, more advocative means of problem resolution.

Within the management-UAW partnership, Saturn has also adopted five corporate values to support the commitment to be one of the world's most successful car companies:

- *Commitment to Customer Enthusiasm*: We continually exceed the expectations of internal and external customers for products and services that are world leaders in cost, quality, and customer satisfaction. Our customers know that we really care about them.
- *Commitment to Excel*: There is no place for mediocrity and half-hearted efforts at SATURN. We accept responsibility, accountability, and authority for overcoming obstacles and reaching beyond the best. We choose to excel in every aspect of our business, including return on investment.
- *Teamwork*: We are dedicated to singleness of purpose through the effective involvement of members, suppliers, dealers, neighbors, and all other stakeholders. A fundamental tenet of our philosophy is the belief that effective teams engage the talents of individual members while encouraging team growth.
- *Trust and Respect for the Individual*: We have nothing of greater value than our people! We believe that demonstrating respect for the uniqueness of every

individual builds a team of confident, creative members possessing a high degree of initiative, self-respect, and self-discipline.
- *Continuous Improvement*: We know that sustained success depends on our ability to continually improve the quality, cost, and timeliness of our products and services. We are providing opportunity for personal, professional, and organizational growth and innovation for all SATURN stakeholders.

HUMAN RESOURCE STRATEGIES

The Saturn-UAW agreement necessitates that all Saturn team members be selected from a pool of employees from other GM plants for as long as laid-off UAW workers are available. In other words, Saturn is not free to hire local Tennesseans as long as there exist reasonably qualified unemployed UAW workers from other GM facilities. UAW officials praise this provision of the Saturn agreement, arguing that no GM facility should hire outside workers when other GM workers have been laid off and are jobless. Interestingly, this policy leads to a 100 percent geographically transplanted work force for the Spring Hill, Tennessee, plant.

Saturn promotes the utilization of self-directed, integrated teams of between six and fifteen members that manage their own work and are involved in decisions that affect them. Each team is led by a work unit counselor (WUC), who initiates group activities and represents the group. Decisions are not made by voting, but instead by consensus. The Saturn model does not require 100 percent agreement. Instead, teams seek at least 70 percent agreement and demand 100 percent support from all members.

Saturn applicants for team members must complete a detailed 12-page assessment that asks for specific information on skills, attitudes, and behaviors. For those who are selected, there are no time clocks, no privileged parking spots, and no private dining rooms at Saturn. Dress is casual, and all employees are on salary. Words such as "manager" and "executive" are not frequently used.

Training is an integral part of the Saturn human resource strategy. In 1992, 5% of a worker's salary is tied to the successful completion of 92 hours of approved training, on Saturn time.

PRODUCTION & TECHNOLOGY STRATEGIES

The Saturn facility is a unique, vertically integrated manufacturing and assembly complex that boasts approximately 95% U.S. product content. The design and engineering processes are tackled by multidisciplinary teams that include product engineers, materials managers, financial managers, marketers, and representatives of the UAW. All of Saturn's in-house product design is done electronically using computer-aided design (CAD), computer-aided manufacturing (CAM), and computer-aided engineering (CAE) techniques.

Saturn's simultaneous engineering approach integrates people and automation to form a more efficient workplace. Saturn does not follow the conventional practice of dividing product development into separate tasks to be done sequentially. For example, the car frame and other components that are to be added meet at each work station. One goal of simultaneous engineering is to reduce in-process inventory between the engine component machining operations, engine assembly, the concurrent transmission assembly, and the final car assembly process. This creates an enormous potential for cost avoidance.

A key tenet of Saturn's strategic approach to vehicle production is the flexible assembly system. Flexible assembly plays its most important role in assembly of the engine and transmission, where heavy components can be readily rotated and repositioned for a variety of assembly operations. Flexible assembly systems are helping manufacturers cut production costs, improve quality, increase factory output, and build different versions of a product while on the same production line. Specifically, flexible assembly can save more than 40 percent of floor space.

Perhaps the most compelling example of how Saturn has utilized team member involvement in its operations design is the skillet system method of assembly. Under the traditional chain-and-drive system, workers move along the line to complete production tasks. A group of Saturn engineers and team members sought a more effective system, given four primary parameters: ergonomics, quality, member utilization, and cost-effectiveness. After two years of research, the skillet system was recommended. The skillet system can be described as a moving sidewalk; workers step on the skillet, perform their necessary operations, and step off when done. The vehicle continues to travel on the skillet to other workers. The result, according to Saturn officials, is a more user-friendly system that requires fewer team members and is consistent with Saturn's world-class quality mission.

Another waste-reduction technique employed by Saturn is lost foam casting. When using this form of casting the engine block, head, and other internal parts are formed from styrofoam. The foam is covered with ceramic and sand and placed into steel casts. The aluminum is then poured into the cast and is formed into the shape of the foam. The foam is then melted by the hot aluminum, eliminating substantial waste and much of the machine work involved in the normal casting process.

Thermoplastic body panels lower manufacturing costs while scrap materials can be reprocessed. These panels also make the car lighter, allowing for better gas mileage and higher performance with a smaller engine. This also allows Saturn to produce cars at a lower cost.

Saturn also seeks just-in-time (JIT) partnerships with suppliers to improve efficiency and reduce storage costs associated with excess inventories. JIT principles are also employed in the production facility, where the inventory created at any stage of production may supply the next stage for two hours or less. Hence, this approach creates a unique challenge for Saturn. Problems on the production line or with suppliers stop the entire production line throughout the complex.

MARKETING STRATEGIES

The Saturn-retailer relationship is a focal point of Saturn's comprehensive approach to marketing its vehicles. Saturn's preference for the word "retailer" to "dealer" signifies its belief that retailers and customers should establish relationships, not make deals. Retailers sell only Saturns but get wide territories, so they compete with rival auto makers and not each other. In 1991, more cars were sold per dealer at Saturn retailers than those associated with any other manufacturer.

Saturn strongly encourages a bottom-line pricing approach to increase retailer-consumer trust. Customers entering a Saturn showroom are told exactly what each vehicle will cost up front. Saturn customers appear to appreciate the elimination of pressure, haggling, and negotiating at the retailers. And if a customer is not satisfied with the vehicle, he or she is free to return it within 30 days or 1500 miles for a full refund.

The automaker recently introduced a certification program for used vehicles, and Saturn retailers make a special effort to repurchase used Saturns for resale on their lots. Vehicles are "certified" if they meet quality standards for maintenance and performance. In early 1996, Saturn became the first automobile manufacturer in decades to use network media to promote used vehicles. Dealers began selling the certified used vehicles at no-haggle prices. Analysts see the move as an attempt to bolster the confidence in resale values of the vehicles as well as secure sales from an increasing market for used automobiles.

Saturn's marketing strategy also appears to be integrated with its approach to customer service and satisfaction. For example, upon discovering that faulty Texaco coolant had been placed in some of its vehicles, Saturn offered new cars, free rentals until they were delivered, and extra options at no extra charge to the 1836 affected customers. While some analysts noted the positive publicity received by Saturn as a result, Saturn officials maintain that the move was designed to take care of its owners.

Saturn aggressively targets the typical Asian vehicle purchaser: young to middle-aged, educated, family-oriented consumers with median incomes of around $50,000. Today, the average Saturn owner is 38 years old; 50% of owners have college degrees, compared to 38% for other domestic manufacturers. Seventy percent of Saturn customers named a non-GM vehicle as their second choice, and 45% said they would have purchased an Asian car if their Saturn choice were not available. Saturn is particularly interested in treating female consumers with the respect and integrity often perceived to be lacking at competitive dealerships.

Saturn marketing success depends on its ability to sway buyers who are already predisposed to a belief that facets such as dependability, durability, quality, and high resale value are paramount in Japanese vehicles. Indeed, Saturn's advertising efforts have been aimed at such persuasion. Marketing analysts have suggested that this feat depends on Saturn's ability to distance itself from General Motors. To date, Saturn has enjoyed some success in this arena. In one survey, only 26% of Saturn customers associated Saturn with GM. Saturn has also shunned traditional domestic car makers' approaches to advertising that primarily rely on themes of sex appeal, prestige, and excitement. Instead, advertising more resembles its Japanese counterparts, emphasizing "a different kind of car, a different kind of car company."

Saturn likes to view its customers as family. The company hosted the "Saturn Homecoming" in June 1994, mailing invitations to more than 600,000 Saturn owners. Festivities included plant tours, car shows, arts and crafts events, concerts, and a fireworks display. Approximately 40,000 people attended the event in Spring Hill, while another 100,000 owners attended Saturn retailer-sponsored events nationwide.

Saturn's sales account for approximately three percent of the U.S. car market. Further, J.D. Powers & Associates reported that Saturn customer satisfaction (score of 160) trailed only Lexus (179) and Infinity (167), while scoring ahead of industry leaders Acura (148), Mercedes-Benz (145), Toyota (144), Audi (139), Cadillac (138), and Jaguar (137), as well as the industry average (129).

FUTURE CHALLENGES AT SATURN

Regardless of GM's estimated $3 billion investment, including $1.9 for the Spring Hill facility, Saturn's profit status is difficult to analyze because of the allocation of start-up expenses to the corporation at large. Saturn is believed to have lost $800 million in 1991, and GM reports that Saturn's first profit was generated in May 1993. Several analysts have charged that high profits will be difficult to sustain, saddled by labor charges in excess of $30 per hour and the huge Spring Hill investment.

There is a considerable amount of financial confusion surrounding Saturn. Mounting evidence suggests Saturn executives believe that greater volume is necessary to cover the high administrative and marketing expenses associated with the division. Critics charge that GM's investment in Saturn well exceeds $5 billion and the division has not yet achieved a profit. However, outsiders can only speculate since financial documents at the business level are not available.

The increase in profit pressure on Saturn has been accompanied by an increase in control exercised at the corporate level. As a result, Saturn is buying more GM-made parts, considering production of its vehicles at other GM facilities, and preparing to launch GM's electric vehicles in the coming decade. In effect, Saturn is becoming "General Motorized," and may fear the mystique or the "different kind of car company" is beginning to evaporate as the division becomes just another business unit within the GM bureaucracy.

Saturn produced its one-millionth car on June 1, 1995. Although there has been talk of a plant expansion in Spring Hill, Saturn has been hesitant to do so without assurances that quality will not decline. Production beyond 500,000 can only be accomplished with a major expansion at Spring Hill or the development of a second Saturn facility. If it chose to do so, Saturn could retool an older GM plant or build a new one from scratch.

Saturn officials have also expressed an interest in developing a larger Saturn model for the late 1990s. There are rumors that the carmaker will add a larger sedan based on the 1996 Adam Opel AG Vectra and build 200,000 annually by 1999 at a Wilmington, Delaware, plant scheduled to be idled. However, although larger cars typically bring heftier margins, an additional $1 billion would likely be required to develop the vehicle. In a recent survey, 94% of Saturn owners said they would likely repurchase a Saturn even if a larger option were not available. Further, the interest in smaller Saturns may continue to grow if gasoline prices rise substantially.

However, much of the impetus for a larger vehicle has come from the corporate level. Not only has GM decided that any larger vehicles will likely be remakes of existing cars, it has also suggested that the Spring Hill labor agreement would not be in force in the other plants that produce them. UAW officials have voiced opposition to the production of the Opel-clone.

The integration of Saturn's business level strategy with GM's corporate strategy remains a key concern. In some respects, Saturn is an extension of

General Motors, a model for other divisions to follow. Some analysts predict that Saturn will look more like other divisions in the future and less like the experiment which created it. However, many others also believe that the ultimate success of Saturn depends on its ability to disassociate itself from General Motors and remove the negative perceptions concerning inferior quality and poorly motivated workers. Even GM officials and dealers associated with other divisions—typically GM's largest division, Chevrolet—have begun to express some dissatisfaction with the high amount of perceived support given to Saturn. As Skip LeFauve put it, "We've got to earn our capital just like anyone else at GM. That's the way it should be." While Saturn's sales climb, Chevrolet's market share continues to decline from 20% two decades ago to 12% today. Competition with GM divisions for capital appears inevitable.

REFERENCES

Bemowski, K. (1995). To boldly go where so many have gone before. *Quality Progress, 28*(2), 29-33.

Bennett, M.E. (1992). The Saturn Corporation: New management-union partnership at the factory of the future. *Looking Ahead, 8*(4), 15-23.

Carey, R. (1995). Five top coporate training programs. *Successful Meetings, 44*(2), 56-62.

Economist (1992). General Motor's Saturn: Success at a price. *Economist, 323*(7765), 80-81.

Dessler, G. (September 1995). Enriching and empowering employees—the Saturn way. *Personnel Journal*, p. 32.

Direct Marketing (November 1995). Saturn Corp. homecoming sparks interest. pp. 24-25.

Garfield, B. (1992). Old imagery powers old perceptions of Detroit cars. *Advertising Age, 63*(13), S20.

Geber, B. (1992). Saturn's grand experiment. *Training, 29*(6), 27-35.

Gelsi, S. (1995). Saturn slots upwards of $20M to bring used cars into marketing mix. *Brandweek, 36*(38), 4.

General Motors Corporation (1991). *Annual Report*. Detroit, MI: General Motors Corporation.

Holzwarth, F. (1992). Ten theses in pursuit of lean production. *Looking ahead, 8*(4), 10-13.

J.D. Power and Associates (1992). *The Saturn Way*. New York: J.D. Power and Associates.

Kilburn, D., & Halliday, J. (1995). Saturn chooses Japan shop. *Adweek, 36*(50), 2.

LeFauve, R.C. (1992). The Saturn Corporation: A Balance of people, technology, and business systems. *Looking Ahead, 8*(4), 14.

LeFauve, R.C., & Hax, A.C. (Spring 1992). Managerial and technological innovations at Saturn Corporation. *MIT Management*, pp. 8-19.

Manji, J.F. (1990). Saturn: GM fights back. *Automation, 37*(10), 28-30.

Morris, K. (1992). Sales: Saturn-GM. *Financial World, 161*(8), 48.

Moskal, B.S. (1989). Hybrid incubator hatches workers. *Industry Week, 238*(15), 27, 30.

O'Connor, L. (November 1991). Flexible assembly: Saturn's road to success. *Mechanical Engineering*, pp. 30-34.

O'Toole, J., & Lewandowski, J. (1990). Forming the future: The Marriage of people and technology at Saturn. *Stanford University Industrial Engineering & Engineering Management*, March 29, 1990.

Overman, S. (March 1995). Saturn teams working and profiting. *HRMagazine*, pp. 72-74.

Perriton, A.G. (March 18, 1992). A different kind of car—A different kind of company: A different materials management. *A.I.A.G. Presentation*.

Rickard, L. (1996). Saturn. Unpublished manuscript.

Saturn Corporation (1992). Saturn fact sheet and other company literature. Spring Hill, TN: Saturn Corporation.

Schlossberg, H. (1991). It's lift-off for Saturn. *Marketing News, 25*(8), 1, 29.

Serafin, R. (1990). GM's Saturn enters crucial period. *Advertising Age, 61*(10), 16.

Serafin, R., & Horton, C. (1992). Automakers focus on service. *Advertising Age, 63*(27), 3, 33.

Solomon, C.M. (1991). Behind the wheel at Saturn. *Personnel Journal, 70*(6), 72-74.

Taylor, A., III (1988). Back to the future at Saturn. *Fortune, 118*(3), 63-72.

Templin, N. (June 16, 1993). GM's Saturn subsidiary is fighting for its future. *Wall Street Journal*, B4.

Treece, J.B. (1990). Here comes GM's Saturn. *Business Week, 3153*, 56-62.

———— (1991). The planets may be perfectly aligned for Saturn's lift-off. *Business Week, 3184*, 40.

———— (1991). Getting mileage from a recall. *Business Week, 3215*, 38-39.

Vasilash, G.S. (1989). Business strategies: Nearing Saturn. *Production, 101*(6), 42-43.

Ward's Auto World (1995). Saturn is meeting 'financial targets.' Vol. 31, No. 12, p. 35.

Wetzel, J.J. (1991). Managing the interfaces for the success of the product, the customer, the company. University of Michigan 1991 Management Briefing Seminar, Traverse City, Michigan, August 8.

Winter, D. (1995). Saturn turns 10. *Ward's Auto World, 31*(7), 67-71.

Womack, J.P. (1992). The lean difference: An international productivity comparison and the implications for U.S. industry. *Looking Ahead, 8*(4), 3-9.

Woodruff, D. (1991). At Saturn, what workers want is . . . fewer defects. *Business Week, 3242*, 117-118.

———— (1992). Saturn. *Business Week, 3279*, 86-91.

———— (1992). What's this—Car dealers with souls? *Business Week, 3260*, 66-67.

The Allen Organ Company

Herbert B. Epstein, University of Texas at Tyler

Mark Kroll, University of Texas at Tyler

John Holm, University of Texas at Tyler

After only fifty years of business, the Allen Organ Company has come to dominate the church organ industry, which has existed for over eight hundred years. With a market share of over 50% of the world market, and with its products in use in churches all around the world, the company has secured its position as the industry leader. However, as church attendance has flattened out and as the competition has managed to bring its technology closer to Allen's, the Allen Organ Company finds itself in a very mature industry with few apparent opportunities for significant growth. Company president Steven Markowitz, who inherited the position from his father, the company founder, must decide how to position his firm so it may achieve the growth objectives he envisions. He conceptualizes his central challenge as determining whether to grow the business in the musical products area, or diversify into other fields.

ALLEN ORGAN COMPANY HISTORY

■ Early Lessons

Jerome Markowitz, founder of the Allen Organ Company, had a fascination with radios and electronics at an early age. He grew up in New York (Jamaica, Long Island) during the depression of the 1930's. His early education was in the New York public schools, prep school, and Muhlenberg College in Pennsylvania. He never did graduate, as he was too preoccupied with his dream of an electronic organ.

Some of his early radio projects in the 1930's led him to an interest in electronics and to electronic oscillators. An oscillator is a device that changes an electrical current to a signal of a desired frequency that can produce sounds. He ultimately used this knowledge to develop the first commercially successful electronic organ.

Markowitz became fascinated by pipe organs through his early exposure to them in movie theaters, radio, and in college. This interest caused him to become curious about how the sounds of a pipe organ are generated, and if those sounds could be duplicated. (See the appendix for a brief description of how a pipe organ works.) One early experiment grew out of his application for an amateur radio operator's license, which required him to learn Morse Code. Markowitz practiced with a key-switch connected to a tone generator. He later recalled, "As I tapped out the code pattern on the key, the tone generator would beep back at me, faithfully generating an on/off pattern in synchronism with whatever patterns I chose to 'key in.' That's when the idea hit me. If I built a group of oscillators similar to those I built for the radio equipment but tuned to various musical frequencies, I could connect these oscillators to the keys of an organ keyboard—the whole thing flashed through my mind. I could build an organ using electronic oscillators!" (Markowitz 1989, p. 8)

At the time Markowitz began his work in 1936, there were two electrically powered organ-like instruments on the market—the Rangertone and the Hammond Organ. Both instruments were based on a complex arrangement of rotating electro-mechanical disks. The Hammond Organ, though pleasing in sound, sounded quite different from a pipe organ.

■ Evolution of the Organ: Pipe Organs to Electronic Organs

Organs had been in use in U.S. churches and synagogues since at least the 1600's. The history of the church organ in the U.S. involves the pipe organ almost exclusively until the middle of this century (Ochse 1975). However, primitive electronic organs made an appearance in the 1930's. In 1935 the Hammond Company made claims to the effect that its instruments could serve a church as well as a pipe organ that cost much more. Hammond's use of the term "organ" in describing its new electrical instrument unnerved both the traditional pipe organ builders and the organists. There was considerable anxiety within the church organ community concerning the new technology.

In 1937 the Federal Trade Commission held hearings to address the representations made by Hammond that its device was an "organ." A lively series of debates ensued between professors of physics using tone analyzers to compare the Hammond instrument with pipe organs. "Disinterested musicians" evaluated the relative musical qualities of the Aeolian-Skinner pipe organ (a leading pipe organ brand) compared with the Hammond Organ. Final hearings took place in April 1938, at which time Hammond's attorney predicted that pipe organ building would soon be as lively a business as making kerosene lamps. On July 12, 1938, the Federal Trade Commission ordered the Hammond Company to cease its claims that its instrument could equal a pipe organ in its range of harmonics, that it could produce the tone colors necessary for proper rendition of the great works of organ literature, or that it was comparable to a $10,000 pipe organ.

In 1937 Jerome Markowitz, in Allentown, Pennsylvania, began his experiments with hopes of developing a tone generator that could simulate the sounds of the pipe organ with great fidelity. He was aware of the Hammond controversy but he felt that the Hammond sound was not a pipe organ sound (Markowitz 1989, p. 8). His immediate goal was to develop and build a practical electronic organ based on vacuum tube oscillators which could emulate the sound of the pipe organ. It was not until Markowitz set out to simulate pipe organ sound with an instrument without pipes, and made that goal the mission of the Allen Organ Company, that electronic organs truly came close to imitating pipe organ sounds.

■ The Basement Workshop

In 1937 Markowitz set up a basement workshop to develop the organ. He rented considerable time on the pipe organ at the Masonic Temple in Allentown to hear organ sounds and learn how they worked. With the help of a fellow ham radio enthusiast, George Ehrig, he found enough used parts and unfinished pipe organ consoles to get started. He was able to obtain parts for his organ in New York City from people anxious to do any kind of work during the Depression, but lack of resources resulted only in "an inventor experimenting in a basement workshop" (Ibid, p. 13). In an attempt perhaps to develop a joint venture with an existing organ company, he visited three major pipe organ builders—M.P. Moeller, Aeolian Skinner, and Kilgen Organ Company—but to no avail; nor were the piano companies interested. He proceeded on his own.

In 1939, with Norman Koons, a factory maintenance man, Markowitz built the Allen Organ Company Organ No. 1, which had electronic oscillators. He formed a company and named it after Allentown. From 1939 until December 7, 1941, the Allen Organ Company sold organs to a Catholic church in Allentown, to a restaurant in Quakertown, Pennsylvania, and to Temple Kenneth Israel in Allentown. The company was then closed down due to World War II and Markowitz's taking a job as an electronics engineer with a company in the defense industry.

■ Starting Again

In mid-1945 Markowitz took the business out of mothballs. He invested in incomplete organs and organ parts inventories from other organ experimenters, and in 1945 the Allen Organ Company was incorporated. The corporation had enough capital to lease factory space, buy some equipment, and hire people. At the end of 1945, the Allen Organ Company had 15 employees, a cabinet shop to build consoles and pedal boards, an electronics area, and a small testing area.

From 1946 to the early 1950's, the company fought for survival. In 1946 some of the employees were laid off. It was so traumatic for Markowitz that he vowed never to fire people again. The company's no-layoff commitment is now a fundamental Allen Organ policy (Ibid, p. 24).

■ Building a Company

The period from 1953 to 1962 was a stable, generally profitable one, but Allen was a minor player against the church pipe organ competition. Even so, Allen organs sounded and acted more like pipe organs than any other non-pipe instrument on the market (Ibid, p. 32).

Markowitz had decided early in his company's history to concentrate on the church organ market. It appeared more permanent, stable, and predictable. Therefore, the Allen organ would not be "off-the-shelf" like the competition, but rather each organ would be custom designed to meet the unique needs of each church. Custom features included both three- and four-manual organs, as contrasted with the competitors' smaller two-manual organs. (In traditional pipe organ terminology, a keyboard is usually referred to as a "manual.")

In 1959, the Allen Organ Company went "Solid-State," replacing vacuum tube generators with transistorized tone generators. This represented a significant technical edge over the competition. In 1961, another innovation was introduced: the "random motion" noise generator to simulate pipe sounds more faithfully. Also in 1961, the first public offering of Allen Organ Company stock was made.

In 1960, a survey of church music of that period documented the well recognized popularity of electronic instruments, or organs, in small churches. It was reported that in a survey of nineteen churches with memberships of 40 to 297 people, fourteen of those churches used electronic instruments. Also, seven of nine churches with memberships of 300 to 600 used electronic instruments. Only two used pipe organs (Ibid, p 74). It appeared that small church congregations could not afford pipe organs and the pipe organ companies were limited in their ability to build a small, quality pipe organ at a competitive price for the low end of the market.

By the late 1960's organ sales were flattening and other builders of electronic organs were closing in technologically. Nevertheless, by 1970, Allen organs were found on six of seven continents and installed in such prominent facilities as Lincoln Center. More and more noted organists played recitals on Allen organs, including David Craighead of the Eastman School of Music; Pierre Cochereau, organist of the Cathedral of Notre Dame, Paris, France; and Virgil Fox, internationally recognized organist of the Riverside Church of New York City. Fox would later purchase an Allen Digital Computer Organ. Noted concert organist and composer Dr. Robert Elmore played Allen's four-manual, 132-stop organ at the largest Presbyterian church in Philadelphia.

■ The Development of Microelectronics for Musical Instruments

In the 1960's, the Autonetics Division of North American-Rockwell Corporation had developed metal-oxide semiconductor/large-scale integrated (MOS/LSI) circuit technology for their military and space programs. Rockwell wanted to capitalize on this technology in commercial applications, so in October of 1968 Ralph Deutsch of Rockwell contacted Markowitz. Deutsch and Rockwell were developing a new musical system based on these new technologies, all completely foreign to Jerome Markowitz. They invited Markowitz to Anaheim, California, for a visit and demonstration of its electronically modified Lowery spinet. (Lowery was another electronic organ builder in the 1960's.) Rockwell stated that "The whole organ tone generator with total harmonic control could be shrunk to the size of a magazine" (Ibid, p. 73).

Harold Downes, a vice president of Rockwell, outlined a joint-venture plan. "Allen would fund the project and provide organ/musical know-how. Rockwell would do the engineering design, manufacture the resulting MOS/LSI circuit devices, and provide technical support. Allen would have exclusive rights to the new digital organ technology, would buy the MOS/LSI circuit devices from Rockwell, and sell organs based on the new technology." (Ibid, pp. 73–74)

Rockwell had approached other organ manufacturers before Allen but all had turned Rockwell down. Allen was last on their list, though Markowitz did not know this at the time. However, in May 1969, a joint agreement between Rockwell and Allen was signed with the following conditions: first, Allen would pay $1.5 million to Rockwell plus royalties; second, patents would be licensed exclusively to Allen; and third, Allen's license to produce organs would be exclusive.

During Stage 1 development, Rockwell developed an engineering model to prove-out the hardware and concept. The engineering model was to use standard digital parts. Allen provided two stripped-down consoles, keys, stops, and audio systems for this model. During Stage 2 development Rockwell designed and built the actual production prototype of the digital organ.

In September 1969, during the engineering model development, various technical problems arose that were resolved early with the cooperation of both the Rockwell and Allen companies. Likewise, problems developed with the production prototype that required resolution by the organ specialists (Allen) and the electronic specialists (Rockwell).

At the end of 1970 the final MOS board containing 22 LSI devices mounted on a single printed circuit board was delivered, which gave Allen control over harmonics and other aspects of sound. The equivalent of about 48,000 transistors were on that single tone-generator board, approximately the size of a magazine. In January 1971, Markowitz accepted the two production prototypes and remitted the agreed-upon money to Rockwell. On May 20, 1971, Allen introduced its "Allen Digital Computer Organ." In June 1971, the organ was placed on display at the National Association of Music Merchants Show (NAMM) in Chicago. Exhibit 1 lists the evolution of Allen's electronic organ models since the inception of Allen Digital Computer Organ in 1971.

After Allen's payment to Rockwell upon acceptance of the production prototype, Rockwell turned to Yamaha, a noted Japanese company, to exploit further the use of the Rockwell-developed circuitry and devices. This led to several lawsuits for patent infringement filed by Allen.

■ The Japanese Connection

Allen's problems with Ralph Deutsch, Rockwell, and Yamaha began with an incident at the NAMM show in June 1971. Deutsch requested a demonstration for the president of Yamaha. Markowitz agreed reluctantly. Genichi Kawakami, president of Yamaha, and 25 other Japanese associates showed up. Markowitz later discovered that Deutsch had given the detailed workings of the computer organ to Yamaha's engineering management without Allen's knowledge and/or approval.

Deutsch contacted Allen after the NAMM show to indicate the interest of Yamaha in the new technology for small organs. On July 19, 1971, Deutsch and Japanese representatives visited Allen but were unable to come to terms. Markowitz learned that despite Deutsch's employment with Rockwell, he was now collaborating with the Japanese and providing information that accelerated Japanese entrance into the new digital technology. In January 1972,

Exhibit 1   **Evolution of Allen Digital Organs**

Date	Technology
1971	The Allen Digital Computer Organ MOS-I (metal-oxide semiconductor) was introduced. This was the first digital musical instrument in the world. It used 7-bit technology. The hardware was mainly custom integrated circuits developed in conjunction with Rockwell International.
1981	MOS-II organs were introduced. With this technology, Allen redesigned the Rockwell system to take advantage of more standard integrated circuits that became available. This enabled Allen to offer options by changing circuitry. Also, with the advent of EPROM (Erasable Program Read Only Memory) technology, Allen could change some of the voices on an organ-by-organ basis. This remained a 7-bit system.
1984	ADC (Allen Digital Computer) technology was introduced. This system helped Allen to meet the newly defined EMI (Electro-magnetic interference) emission standards relating to electronic computers of all types. It was the first system to utilize a card cage which also gave Allen flexibility in the design of different instruments. All of the sounds were now on EPROM memory. This system was 8-bit.
1989	MDS (Master Design Series) organs were introduced. This system, the first 16-bit system used in digital organs, enabled Allen to offer even more sophisticated sounds.
1993	The MDS system was upgraded further by including 32 megabits ROM, the largest memory devices used in the organ industry.

Source: *Allen Organ Company*

Deutsch left Rockwell and signed a three-year agreement with Yamaha as a digital musical consultant. On February 14, 1972, less than six weeks after leaving Rockwell, he applied for a new digital organ patent. "Deutsch swore under oath that the new invention had no connection to his employment at Rockwell and Allen, which he had left six weeks before applying for the patent. The final patent ran 15 pages in fine print including the explanation of the system with diagrams, parts listing, etc. According to Markowitz, anyone familiar with high-tech patents would doubt Deutsch's explanation" (Ibid, p. 124). Markowitz felt betrayed. He once commented, "If these were national secrets, it would be treason. On the other hand, in the commercial world most people are unconcerned" (Ibid, p. 120).

By the late 1980's, Japan was the preeminent force in the electronics industry, including electronic musical instruments (Ibid, p. 118). In the 1960's, only Rockwell and Allen were developing, behind closed doors, the digital instrument concept. However, because of Rockwell's liaison with Yamaha, Yamaha was able to gain a major competitive advantage quickly in the popular or home organ field. Markowitz sued both Rockwell and Yamaha for contract violation and pirating of intellectual property, and won over $1 million in damage awards from the courts. However, the damage was already done. Yamaha was able to learn from the trials and errors of Rockwell and Allen, and apply those lessons to the consumer market.

THE NATURE OF THE ORGAN INDUSTRY

■ Forces Influencing the Organ's Destiny

In his memoirs, Jerome Markowitz talked about the evolution of pipe organs from early history, through the Baroque period, the 1800's, and through 1989. His observation: "The fact that the pipe organ still plays a role in today's music world (against the piano, violin, symphony orchestras) is a tribute to the tenacity of organ enthusiasts of the last century" (Ibid, p. 158). This is in spite of the fact that costs of pipe organs have skyrocketed and that the performance of pipe organs in terms of meeting engineering specifications remains a "shot in the dark due to the variables of temperature, tuning, mechanical failures, and other inherent quirks" (Ibid, p. 158).

Electronic organ builders also confronted the problem of the influence of "elitists" vs. "the regular people" in controlling the purchase decisions and uses of organs in churches as well as the direction of development and the role of the organ. Allen defined "elitists" as "those favoring only traditional pipe organs." Markowitz complained that the "elitists" were more concerned with the form of the organ rather than its overall utility. Elitists regarded the Allen Digital Computer Organ as a threat to the pipe organ, which they still considered the only true organ. Markowitz once observed, "Sometimes the tactics of the elitists take on the vehemence of a holy war" (Ibid, p. 165). Steven Markowitz, current president of Allen, said, "There is an emotional side to the business where some customers believe that only pipe organs are 'real.'" In spite of the difference in cost between pipe and electronic organs, some people believe that nothing can compete with the pipe organ despite no objective proof (Markowitz 1995).

The Allen Organ Company believed its research on electronic simulation of pipe sounds had improved fidelity dramatically. According to Steve Markowitz, digital technology research received a big boost in 1985 with the construction of a million-dollar technology center adjacent to the Macungie, Pennsylvania, plant. This very sophisticated R & D center contained computer-aided design systems, and also had anechoic and echoic chambers for analyzing various organ sounds that digital engineering specialists need to continuously refine and advance digital technology. The 1995 Allen organs reflected these developments. It was difficult for even sophisticated and knowledgeable organists to tell the difference between a custom Allen organ and a pipe organ (Marta 1995). Both types of organ were able to play the widest range of music, from Bach to the most contemporary composers.

One of the leading American pipe organ builders said: "Unfortunately, we are one of those labor-intensive industries which find it difficult to survive in an era of increasing technology. I feel there will always be those who wish to have the "Real Thing" rather than imitations; however, perhaps few people will be able or willing to spend the money it takes to build real organs" (Redman 1995).

■ The Organ Industry Today

After 58 years of business, the Allen Organ Company dominates the church organ market worldwide. This church organ builder successfully parlayed

Exhibit 2   **Electronic and Pipe Organ Builders**

Electronic Organ Builders

Company	1995 Sales
Allen Organ Company	$ 30 Million
Rodgers Instrument Company	$ 17 Million
Baldwin Piano and Organ	$122 Million
Lowrey	$ 6 Million

Pipe Organ Builders

Company	1995 Sales
Schantz	$ 6 Million
Wicks	$ 4 Million
Austin	$ 3 Million
Reuter	$ 2 Million
Home Organ Sales	$ 84.2 Million
Institutional Organ Sales	$ 57.6 Million

Sources: *Music Trades, April 1996.*
         Ward's Business Directory, 1996

digital electronics technology in the form of church organs into the most revered of venues, music in houses of worship.

The worldwide church organ market in 1995 had sales of $57.8 million, up slightly from 1994 sales of $56.1 million. The home organ market saw its sales decline from $85.9 million in 1994 to $84.2 million in 1995. In 1995 14,111 home organs were sold, down 9% from 1994 and down 13.8% from 1991. Sales of institutional organs, primarily those sold to churches, have been fairly steady. In 1995, 3,375 units were sold, 25 units more than in 1994 but a 6.5% decrease from 1991. The Allen Organ Company's sales in 1995 were $30 million, representing a 52% market share and a 4% increase over 1994 sales. The total sales of all the pipe organ companies in the United States was less than $20 million (*Music Trades* 1996, April). Exhibit 2 lists 1995 sales for selected electronic and pipe organ builders.

MARKETING THE ALLEN ORGANS

Early in the history of the Allen Organ Company, Jerome Markowitz had an important marketing decision to make. The Hammond Organ was so well established in 1945 that it essentially became the non-pipe organ standard by which other non-pipe organs were measured. From the outset, Markowitz had to decide whether to "clone" the Hammond or go an entirely different direction using new technology. He chose new technology. As a result, he felt that the early Allen organ was much more like a pipe organ than the Hammond. He deliberately chose to distance himself from Hammond "by making the Allen sound so much like a pipe organ as to be indistinguishable from it" (Markowitz 1989, p. 180).

Since the church organ purchase decision is so heavily influenced by the musicians who will actually play the organ, it became necessary to seek endorsements from organists, writers of religious music, church music ministers, and professional organ teachers. In addition, the electronic organ is a complex instrument made up of many components requiring virtually 100 percent reliability. The majority of sub-assemblies in every Allen organ are manufactured and assembled in-house to ensure optimal quality control. Allen's original approach to design, manufacturing, quality control, and service sought to incorporate the best practices of the leading companies in the electronics and aerospace industries. This approach to design, manufacture, and service was to continue. Markowitz firmly believed potential customers must be convinced that the musical sounds of the traditional church organ were preserved and the instrument was reliable and Allen could and would service it promptly.

■ Position in the Market

Management felt that Allen had achieved dominance in the church organ market through its technical, musical, and business acumen. Its sales were twice that of its nearest electronic organ competitor in the church market and five times that of its nearest pipe organ competitor. The company had developed an electronic church organ line that apparently satisfied the small, low end, and moderate size church market, and the company enjoyed some success in selling Allen organs to large churches that had previously purchased only pipe organs.

■ Pricing

The prices of the Allen electronic organs were competitive with those of their electronic organ competitors and much less expensive than comparable pipe organs. The lowest priced small pipe organ started at about $100,000, while the electronic "equivalent" in sound and versatility was priced at about $25,000. Normally, the size of an organ was delineated by the number of ranks, or rows of pipes, an organ had. A small pipe organ costing about $100,000 normally had between ten and fourteen ranks. For $25,000 a church could purchase an electronic organ that was the musical equivalent of a 25-rank pipe organ.

In the category of large pipe organs, pipe organ executives reluctantly quoted prices ranging from $10,000 to $18,000 per rank as a simplistic measure of price. They caution that the size and shape of churches, their acoustic quality, and other quality requirements all directly affected the ultimate cost of any church organ installation. Likewise, executives like Markowitz expressed the same cautions about price influences on custom-designed electronic organ installations. Markowitz noted as a rough rule of thumb that a custom Allen organ would cost between $2,000 and $4,000 per voice, which, in Allen's parlance, was roughly equivalent to a rank.

■ Service

The Allen Organ Company is committed to servicing over 70,000 installations worldwide. Its network of retail outlets included musical and organ specialists who can service its instruments. Spare parts were furnished by a combination of factory and retail outlets which were required to maintain a minimum inventory of designated spare parts related to the Allen organ that was sold. As part of the Allen Organ design philosophy, component parts were interchangeable from model to model to minimize the number of different parts required. The sub-assemblies of Allen organs were modular in design, which meant that if an assembly needed to be replaced, it was just unplugged from the unit and a spare part was inserted (Allen Home Page).

Since Allen organs are sold worldwide, it developed a service plan for its organs that were not in an area with a local dealer. In such cases, sales and service were handled directly from the factory. An organ sold to a customer who was not near a dealer came with a service kit that included spare parts and a service manual such that any local electronic technician could repair the organ. Of course, factory assistance was also availabe. Allen also provided seminars and workshops for organists to help them keep up with changes in the music industry (Ibid).

In a recent interview, Steven Markowitz noted, "The customer expectations have gotten higher and higher. Not only do they expect specific types of styles of pipe organ sounds, but they also expect our instruments to be long lasting and serviceable. We are proud to say that throughout our fifty plus year history, there has never been an Allen taken out of service for lack of a replaceable part" (Markowitz 1995).

According to organists who play both pipe organs and electronic ones, the pipe organ must be tuned at least annually, and with severe temperature variations, possibly twice or more annually (Marta 1995). Having a pipe organ tuned typically costs about $1,000. Digital electronic organs do not require regular tuning.

■ Sales Distribution

The Allen Organ Company sold its standard organs through its dealer network, usually independent retail music stores that had both sales and service responsibilities. These dealers were located both domestically and internationally. A close relationship between the factory and the dealers was maintained via regular marketing meetings, certified factory training programs, and routine headquarters audits. The dealers administered the Allen 10-year limited warranty program and were responsible for all direct customer relations. Allen was represented by dealers in all fifty states, and in Canada, Europe, Africa, South America, and Asia (Allen Home Page).

Allen allowed its customers the option of ordering custom-designed organs. Options such as voices (the types of pipes used), console design, and other features could be chosen. The custom organs could be as small as twenty stops or as large as 200 stops and five manuals (Ibid).

Another Allen innovation was its SmartMIDI system. This allowed an organist to record specific settings on a computer disk and transfer those sounds to any other Allen organ. Allen's Smart Recorder system used a SmartMIDI sequencer and could control the playback of any sound recorded from an Allen organ (Ibid).

■ Advertising and Promotion

Allen organ products are exhibited each year to both dealers and customers at the National Association of Music Merchants Conventions. In 1995, Allen organs were exhibited at international fairs, such as the one in Frankfurt, Germany. Domestic and international participation in such events is part of the Allen marketing program. Domestic and international advertising is normally initiated by Allen's marketing department which takes a national orientation. The local dealer is responsible for local advertising and promotion.

OTHER POTENTIAL MARKETS FOR ALLEN

Another domestic market that Allen has considered and that seems to fit its technical expertise is the home organ market, which had sales of $85.9 million in 1994 and $84.2 million in 1995. Other possible markets include the digital piano market which had sales of $124.2 million in 1994 and $129.4 million in 1995, a 4% increase; and the portable keyboard market, with 1994 sales of $151.4 million and 1995 sales of $136.5 million, a 9.8% decrease (*Music Trades* 1996).

Allen diversified in a limited way with its Smart Musical Instrument Digital Interface (MIDI) equipment and its digital sequencers described above, and the introduction of its lower-cost digital electronic organs for the home market. Allen also competed in the electronic church organ market in Europe, the Far East, and Canada, which represented approximately 18% of Allen's total sales (Allen 10-K). Though their products have been in these markets for years, Allen management still did not have a good feel for the potential size of these markets.

An infusion of new digital engineering talent in the last ten years has resulted in digital organ technology with patents that have kept Allen ahead of the competition technologically. Allen has also recently entered into two new industry segments: data communications and electronic assemblies.

Allen Integrated Assemblies was formed as Allen's subsidiary in the electronic assemblies market. It manufactured assemblies for outside customers and accounted for 10% of Allen's revenues in 1995 (Allen 10-K). It used the same technology developed by Allen for use in its organs.

Allen began competing in the data communications industry in 1995 with the acquisition of VIR, Inc., and two other firms. VIR produced patch and testing equipment used to connect, test, and troubleshoot data lines in large computer installations (Ibid). The other two acquisitions, Eastern Research Inc. and Linear Switch Corporation, manufactured data communications hardware and software, and a high speed matrix switch, respectively. Both companies' products were used in local and wide-area network environments. The management of Allen Organ believed that its state-of-the-art manufacturing facilities and capital structure complemented these diverse high technology companies (*Music Trades* 1995, September). Though small contributors to sales and profits, Allen had hopes of growing these units in the future.

Allen had many challenges to face as it entered new markets. Not the least among them was Yamaha and Roland, the two Japanese electronic music firms with sales of $600 million and $110 million, respectively. They already had extensive name recognition and distribution networks in the U.S. and abroad. According to Allen, American companies seriously committed to entering foreign markets with different political, economic, legal, and cultural environments faced management changes in their home offices. These differences in the world's various music markets can have a profound impact on the culture and management strategy of the parent firm (Hill 1994).

Exhibit 3   **Allen Organ Company and Subsidiaries—Consolidated Financial Summaries—Five Year Summary**

	1995*	1994	1993	1992	1991
			Years Ended December 31,		
Net Sales	$30,024,761.00	$28,842,789.00	$26,477,983.00	$26,238,092.00	$25,276,374.00
Net Income	4,015,105.00	4,449,703.00	3,456,154.00	3,397,045.00	3,689,207.00
Earnings per share	2.94	3.25	2.48	2.41	2.55
Cash dividends per share	.55	.55	.50	.50	.48
At Year End					
Total Assets	$65,299,426.00	$58,464,695.00	$55,752,570.00	$53,581,050.00	$51,115,657.00
Long-Term Debt, net of curr. portion	$1,388,000.00	0	0	0	0

*The 1995 results of operations include the data communications segment acquired August 1, 1995.

ALLEN FINANCIALS

Exhibits 3, 4, and 5 contain financial summaries of the Allen Organ Company and its subsidiaries for different periods from 1991 to 1995.

The Allen financial results were highlighted in an article in CFO magazine in April 1991, which profiled companies with good management and strong financial positions. In the CFO research, the authors were looking for companies which excelled at balancing profits and risk over the past decade. The companies they identified were not necessarily the largest, the fastest growing, or the most innovative in a given industry. Rather, as the article noted, the companies selected managed to grow and prosper over the long haul without reducing liquidity to a dangerous level or taking on more debt than they could handle in a slump. "Today these companies have a competitive edge with secure cash flows and no or low debt" (Driscoll and Hullman 1991, p. 17). According to the CFO analysts, the Allen Organ Company was considered the seventh financially strongest company among the firms examined with sales of less than $275 million over a 10-year period.

FUTURE OUTLOOK

Allen's market share was about 50% of the world church organ market. Any company so dominant was a threat for every other church organ builder. However, history is replete with dominant companies whose sales levels have flattened and whose competitors have closed the technology gap. So Allen's management feared it could be with them.

Since the 1930's, electronic organs have dominated the small church organ market (Ochse 1975). Progressively the electronic digital organs have moved

Exhibit 4

Allen Organ Company and Subsidiaries
Consolidated Statements of Income and Retained Earnings

	Years Ended December 31,		
	1995	1994	1993
Net Sales	$30,024,761	$28,842,789	$26,477,983
Costs and Expenses			
Cost of sales	20,109,427	18,910,136	17,540,539
Selling, administrative & other exp.	4,695,956	4,058,058	3,774,830
Research and development	1,307,691	625,190	612,631
Total Costs and Expenses	26,113,074	23,593,384	21,928,000
Income from operations	3,911,687	5,249,405	4,549,983
Other income (expense)			
Investment income	2,115,551	1,436,182	1,108,957
Other, net	26,810	265,116	(6,786)
Interest expense	(42,856)	—	—
Minority interests in consolidated subsidiaries	23,913	—	—
Total Other Income (Expense)	2,123,418	1,701,298	1,102,171
Income before Taxes on Income	6,035,105	6,950,703	5,652,154
Taxes on Income			
Current	1,559,000	2,525,000	2,228,000
Deferred	461,000	(24,000)	(32,000)
Total Taxes on Income	2,020,000	2,501,000	2,196,000
Net Income	4,015,105	4,449,703	3,456,154
Retained Earnings			
Balance, January 1	46,524,142	42,828,013	40,067,860
Deduct cash dividends (1995 - $.55, 1994 - $.55, 1993 - $.50)	(753,084)	(753,574)	(696,001)
Balance, December 31	$49,786,163	$46,524,142	$42,828,013
Earnings per Share	$ 2.94	$ 3.25	$ 2.48

into larger and larger churches all over the world (Markowitz 1995). One central question was at what point does the perception that "real church music" can be played only on a pipe organ limit market entry of the electronic organ? Was it according to size of the cathedral and existing pipe organ installations? Was it limited by donors who wanted only a pipe organ in their church? Were both electronic and pipe organ new installations limited by some contemporary trends in church music that utilize other instruments and rely less on an organ? These were critical questions confronting the company.

Electronic organ companies such as Allen, Rodgers, and Baldwin were competitive in the standard electronic church organ field. The newest market niche gradually being explored by Allen and others, as evidenced by sales to large

Exhibit 5

Allen Organ Company and Subsidiaries—Consolidated Balance Sheets

	December 31, 1995	1994
Assets		
Current Assets		
Cash	$196,100	$105,067
Investments, including accrued interest	30,766,266	36,783,908
Accounts receivable	4,431,499	3,052,683
Inventories	13,428,585	8,794,765
Prepaid income taxes	856,630	276,580
Prepaid expenses	103,420	98,903
Deferred income tax benefits	—	67,420
Total Current Assets	49,782,500	49,179,326
Property, Plant and Equipment, at Cost, Less Accumulated Depreciation	7,778,498	7,163,476
Other Assets		
Prepaid pension costs	1,021,517	—
Intangible pension asset	—	443,273
Inventory held for future service	1,219,872	1,145,511
Deferred income tax benefits	—	43,116
Goodwill, net	4,227,600	—
Cash value of life insurance	629,481	408,138
Note receivable	122,586	81,855
Intangible and other assets, net	517,372	—
Total Other Assets	7,738,428	2,121,893
Total Assets	$65,299,426	$58,464,695
Liabilities and Shareholders' Equity		
Current Liabilities		
Current portion of long-term debt	$347,000	—
Accounts payable	535,276	171,791
Deferred income taxes	64,322	—
Other accrued expenses	1,691,328	623,100
Customer deposits	463,019	446,657
Total Current Liabilities	3,100,945	1,241,548
Noncurrent Liabilities		
Deferred liabilities	841,687	77,917
Accrued pension cost	—	1,374,007
Long-term debt, net of current portion	1,388,000	—
Total Noncurrent Liabilities	2,229,687	1,451,924
Total Liabilities	5,330,632	2,693,472
Commitments and Contingencies		
Shareholders' Equity		
Common stock, par value $1 per share	1,537,993	1,537,993

Exhibit 5 (continued) **Allen Organ Company and Subsidiaries—Consolidated Balance Sheets**

| | December 31, | |
	1995	1994
Liabilities and Shareholder's Equity		
Capital in excess of par value	$12,758,610	$12,610,377
Retained earnings	49,786,163	46,524,142
Unrealized gain (loss) on investments	94,136	(98,399)
Pension liability adjustment	—	(489,823)
Minority interest	313,941	—
Sub-total	64,490,843	60,084,290
Less cost of common shares in treasury	4,522,049	4,313,067
Total Shareholders' Equity	59,968,794	55,771,223
Total Liabilities and Shareholders' Equity	$65,299,426	$58,464,695

prestigious churches, was the upper end of the pipe organ market that was slowly succumbing to electronic organs. It was this market which represented a crucial last stand for the pipe organ companies competing with custom-built electronic organs whose pipe sounds were becoming more and more like the best of the pipe organs. It was probable that the "elitists," who previously did not accept electronic organs as replacements for pipe organs, would gradually accept the best of the electronic organs as a reasonable alternative for many pipe organ installations. Recent interviews with professors of organ music at leading U.S. universities tend to support this contention (Minor 1991, Marta 1995).

Also, since electronic organ design includes computer electronics, semi-conductors, and microprocessing technology, all of which were changing radically based on recent developments, it was possible that the electronic organ industry worldwide could undergo joint-venturing in several directions. Some examples of industries that could combine were electronic organ manufacturers with pipe organ companies; U.S. electronic organ companies with other foreign electronic organ companies, with the competitive edge going to the company that could best market its musical expertise; and electronic organ companies with other electronic companies in such complementary fields as communications and commercial applications of electronic assemblies.

What about the church environment of the future? Recent studies have shown Western culture becoming focused on individual work and leisure time activities as opposed to group activities. For example, the use of personal computers and video games is an individual rather than a group activity. This trend appears to be growing. Attendance in traditional churches has been declining. At the same time there has been an increase in new churches with contemporary church services emphasizing individual participation and the use of solo instruments. Similarly, some traditional churches are following this approach. These changes tend to reduce the size of the church organ market. This is a concern for all church organ builders.

The Allen Organ Company has proven to be a resourceful company producing church organs that its founder, Jerome Markowitz, had predicted would one day produce electronic organ music indistinguishable from that of the pipe organ. In the face of a declining market, how important is it to continue to emphasize that goal? Steven Markowitz and Allen management have apparently decided that pipe organ fidelity is not their only goal. Their acquisitions of other diverse high technology companies to supplement Allen's state-of-the-art manufacturing capabilities and capital structure is already underway (*Music Trades* 1995, September). Can the old-fashioned family business remain competitive in the new global environment?

Appendix: The Basic Mechanism of the Pipe Organ

Sound on the organ is produced when wind passes through the pipe. The process of getting the wind to that pipe follows this path: first, a motor blows air into a reservoir. Weights on top of the reservoir keep the air under pressure so that the sound does not waver. From the reservoir, the air moves into the wind chest, which is a box with rows of holes on the top. The pipes stand on top of the wind chest, one pipe to a hole. To make the pipe speak, the wind must move from the wind chest to the pipe. If the holes connecting the pipes to the wind chest remained open all the time, all the pipes would speak at once whenever the organ was turned on. There are two mechanisms that control two separate barriers to the flow of air from the wind chest to the pipe: stop action and key action. Exhibit 6 presents an illustration of how air flows through a pipe.

The holes in the top of the wind chest have a movable barrier that is controlled by the drawknobs or tabs on the console. When a stop is turned off, the barrier blocks the holes. By pulling the stop out, or the "on" position, the barrier between the air supply and the holes moves so that the wind can get to the pipes. The organ has a separate stop action for each stop in the organ. The organist could remove the barrier to several sounds by turning their corresponding stops on. This would allow several pipes to speak at once when only one note is played.

Of course, the organist needs control over each note individually. The stop action removes the barrier to all the pipes of one stop. These pipes cannot be allowed to speak all at once or there would be no music. The key action works with the stop action. After a stop is turned on, and the barrier to the holes is removed, the key action can control the wind flow to the pipe. When the key is depressed, it opens a valve beneath the pipe so that the wind can finally get through the hole in the wind chest. However, a stop must be on, removing one barrier to the pipe. If no stops are on, there will be no sound, even though the valve is opening when the key is pressed. Different styles of building over the last 400 years have resulted in two kinds of key action: mechanical and electro-pneumatic. In mechanical action, depressing a key physically opens the valve to the wind chest. In electro-pneumatic action, a circuit causes an electro-magnet to open and close the valve.

A keyboard, playable with the hands, is called a "manual." A keyboard for the feet is called a "pedal." Manuals usually encompass 4 to 5 octaves, and the pedal usually encompasses 2 to $2^1/_2$ octaves. Each rank of pipes begins in front with the large, low-pitched pipes and ends with the small, high-pitched ones on the far side of the chest. Each set of pipes produces a specific tone color and is called a "stop." Ordinarily, a stop has one pipe for each key.

The number of keys and stops varies depending on the size of the organ. Small organs may have 20 to 40 stops while large organs can have up to 200

Exhibit 6   **Pipe Sounds Are Determined by Pipe Dimensions and Air Flow**

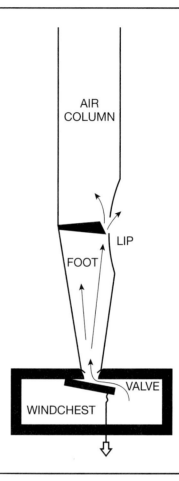

stops. "Stop knobs" facilitate the drawing or canceling of stops at the organist's discretion. The stop knobs are located close to the keyboards. As a rule the stops belonging to a given keyboard are mounted on one wind chest. Thus, a three-manual organ has at least four wind chests, one for each manual and one for the pedal (Klotz 1969, Fancey 1996).

REFERENCES

Allen Organ Company (1996). Form 10-K.

Allen Organ Company (1996). Internet Home Page: http://www.allenorgan.com.

Driscoll, M., and Hulihan, H. (1991 April). America's Strongest Companies. *CFO* pp. 17-23.

Fancey, Marya J. (1996). The Pipe Organ Education Project. Internet: http://www.music.sc.edu/Virtual_Classrooms/index.htm

Hill, Charles W. L. (1994). *International Business: Competing in the Global Marketplace*. Burr Ridge, Illinois: Irwin.

Johnson, Dale (1995). Interview between organ distributor/businessman and Dr. H. B. Epstein, August 3, 1995.

Klotz, Hans (1969). *The Organ Handbook: Structure, Design, Maintenance, History, and Function of the Organ*. St. Louis, Missouri: Concordia Publishing House.

Markowitz, Jerome (1989). *Triumphs and Trials of an Organ Builder*. Macungie, PA: Allen Organ Company Publisher.

Markowitz, Steven (1995). Letter to Dr. H.B. Epstein, August 14, 1995.

Marta, Larry (1995). Interview between organists/teacher and Dr. H.B. Epstein, August 15, 1995.

Minor, Theodore (1991). *Management of Church Music Programs*. Michigan: Tad Minor Keyboard Services.

Music Trades (1996 April). The Music Products Industry Census. 144(3) 84-96.

Music Trades (1996 April). The Top 100: The Leading Suppliers of the Music Products Industry. 144(3) 114-120.

Music Trades (1995 September). Allen Organ Expands With Hi-Tech Acquisitions. 143(8) 40.

The NPM/APOBA Guide (1994). Buying a Pipe Organ For Less Than $100,000. Publishers of The National Association of Pastoral Musicians and Associated Pipe Organ Builders of America.

Ochse, Orpha (1975). *The History of the Organ in the United States*. Bloomington and London: Indiana University Press.

Redman, Roy (1995). Letter to Dr. H.B. Epstein, July 30, 1995.

Ward's Business Directory of U.S. Private and Public Companies (1996). Musical Instruments SIC 3931.

Perdue Farms, Inc.

George C. Rubenson, Salisbury State University

Frank M. Shipper, Salisbury State University

Jean M. Hanebury, Texas A&M University (Corpus Christi)

Internet site of interest: **www.skipjack.net/le_shore/home.html**

"I have a theory that you can tell the difference between those who have inherited a fortune and those who have made a fortune. Those who have made their own fortune forget not where they came from and are less likely to lose touch with the common man."

(BILL STERLING, 'JUST BROWSIN' COLUMN IN EAST-ERN SHORE NEWS, MARCH 2, 1988)

I n 1917, Arthur W. Perdue, a Railway Express agent and descendant of a French Huguenot family named Perdeaux, bought 50 leghorn chickens for a total of $5 and began selling table eggs near the small town of Salisbury, Maryland. A region immortalized in James Michener's *Chesapeake*, it is alternately known as "the Eastern Shore" or the "Delmarva Peninsula" and includes parts of *DEL*aware, *MAR*yland, and *Virgini*A.

Initially, the business amounted to little more than a farm wife's chore for "pin money," raising a few "biddies" in a cardboard box behind the wood stove in the kitchen until they were old enough to fend for themselves in the barnyard. But, in 1920, when Railway Express asked "Mr. Arthur" to move to a station away from the Eastern Shore, at age 36 he quit his job as Salisbury's Railway Express agent and entered the egg business full-time. His only child, Franklin Parsons Perdue, was born that same year.

"Mr. Arthur" soon expanded his egg market and began shipments to New York. Practicing small economies such as mixing his own chicken feed and using leather from his old shoes to make hinges for his chicken coops, he stayed out of debt and prospered. He tried to add a new chicken coop every year. By the time young Frank was 10, he had fifty chickens or so of his own to look after, earning money from their eggs. He worked along with his parents, not always enthusiastically, to feed the chickens, clean the coops, dig the cesspools, and gather and grade eggs. A shy, introverted country boy, he went for five years to a one-room school, eventually graduated from Wicomico High School, and attended the State Teachers College in Salisbury for two years before returning to the farm in 1939 to work full-time with his father.

By 1940, it was obvious to father and son that the future lay in selling chickens, not eggs. But, the Perdues made the shift to selling broilers only after careful attention to every detail—a standard Perdue procedure in the years to come. In 1944, "Mr. Arthur" made his son Frank a full partner in what was then A. W. Perdue and Son, Inc., a firm already known for quality products and fair dealing in a toughly competitive business. In 1950, Frank took over leadership of Perdue Farms, a company with 40 employees. By 1952, revenues were $6,000,000 from the sale of 2,600,000 broilers.

By 1967, annual sales had increased to about $35,000,000 but it was becoming increasingly clear that additional profits lay in processing chickens. Frank recalled in an interview for *Business Week* (September 15, 1972) " . . . processors were paying us 10 cents a live pound for what cost us 14 cents to produce. Suddenly, processors were making as much as 7 cents a pound."

A cautious, conservative planner, Arthur Perdue had not been eager for expansion and Frank Perdue himself was reluctant to enter poultry processing. But, economic forces dictated the move and, in 1968, Perdue Farms became a vertically integrated operation, hatching eggs, delivering the chicks to contract growers, buying grain, supplying the feed and litter, and, finally, processing the broilers and shipping them to market.

The company bought its first plant in 1968, a Swift and Company operation in Salisbury, renovated it, and equipped it with machines capable of processing 14,000 broilers per hour. Computers were soon employed to devise feeding formulas for each stage of growth so birds reached their growth potential sooner. Geneticists were hired to breed larger-breasted chickens and veterinarians were put on staff to keep the flocks healthy, while nutritionists handled the feed formulations to achieve the best feed conversion.

From the beginning, Frank Perdue refused to permit his broilers to be frozen for shipping, a process that resulted in unappetizing black bones and loss of flavor and moistness when cooked. Instead, Perdue chickens were (and some still are) shipped to market packed in ice, justifying the company's advertisements at that time that it sold only "fresh, young broilers." However, this policy also limited the company's market to those locations that could be serviced overnight from the Eastern Shore of Maryland. Thus, Perdue chose for its primary markets the densely populated towns and cities of the East Coast, particularly New York City, which consumes more Perdue chicken than all other brands combined.

During the 1970s, the firm entered the Baltimore, Philadelphia, Boston, and Providence markets. Facilities were expanded rapidly to include a new broiler processing plant and protein conversion plant in Accomac, Virginia; a processing plant in Lewiston, North Carolina; a hatchery in Murfreesboro, North Carolina; and several Swift and Company facilities including a processing plant in Georgetown, Delaware; a feed mill in Bridgeville, Delaware; and a feed mill in Elkin, North Carolina.

In 1977, "Mr. Arthur" died at the age of 91, leaving behind a company with annual sales of nearly $200,000,000, an average annual growth rate of 17 percent compared to an industry average of 1% a year, the potential for processing 78,000 broilers per hour, and annual production of nearly 350,000,000 pounds of poultry. Frank Perdue—who says without a hint of self-deprecation that "I am a B-minus student. I know how smart I am. I know a B-minus is not as good as an A"—said of his father simply, "I learned everything from him."

Stew Leonard, owner of a huge supermarket in Norwalk, Connecticut, and one of Perdue's top customers, describes Frank Perdue as "What you see is what you get. If you ask him a question you will get an answer." Perdue disapproves the presence of a union between himself and his associates and adds, "The absence of unions makes for a better relationship with our associates. If we treat our associates right, I don't think we will have a union." On conglomerates, he states, "Diversification is the most dangerous word in the English language." His business philosophy is, "I'm interested in being the best rather than the biggest. Expansion is OK if it has a positive effect on product quality. I'll do nothing that detracts from product quality."

Frank Perdue is known for having a temper. He is as hard on himself, however, as he is on others, readily admitting his shortcomings and even his mistakes. For example, in the '70s, he apparently briefly discussed using the influence of some unsavory characters to help alleviate union pressure. When an investigative reporter in the late 1980s asked him about this instance, he admitted that it was a mistake, saying " . . . it was probably the dumbest thing I ever did."

In 1981, Frank Perdue was in Massachusetts for his induction into the Babson College Academy of Distinguished Entrepreneurs, an award established in 1978 to recognize the spirit of free enterprise and business leadership. Babson College President Ralph Z. Sorenson inducted Perdue into the academy which, at that time, numbered 18 men and women from four continents. Perdue had the following to say to the college students:

> There are no, nor will there ever be, easy steps for the entrepreneur. Nothing, absolutely nothing, replaces the willingness to work earnestly, intelligently towards a goal. You have to be willing to pay the price. You have to have an insatiable appetite for detail, have to be willing to accept constructive criticism, to ask questions, to be fiscally responsible, to surround yourself with good people, and most of all, to listen. (Frank Perdue, speech at Babson College, April 28, 1981)

The early 1980s proved to be a period of further growth as Perdue diversified and broadened its market. New marketing areas included Washington, D.C.; Richmond, Virginia; and Norfolk, Virginia. Additional facilities were opened in Cofield, Kenly, Halifax, Robbins, and Robersonville, North Carolina. The firm broadened its line to include value-added products such as "Oven Stuffer" roasters and "Perdue Done It!" a new brand of fresh, prepared chicken products featuring cooked chicken breast nuggets, cutlets, and tenders. James A. (Jim) Perdue, Frank's only son, joined the company as a management trainee in 1983.

The latter 1980s also tested the mettle of the firm. Following a period of considerable expansion and concentric diversification, a consulting firm was brought in to recommend ways to cope with the new complexity. Believing that the span of control was too broad, the consulting firm recommended that strategic business units, responsible for their own operations, be formed. In other words, the firm should decentralize.

Soon after, the chicken market leveled off and eventually began to decline. At one point the firm was losing as much as one million dollars a week and, in 1988, Perdue Farms experienced its first year in the red. Unfortunately, the decentralization had created duplication of duties and enormous administrative costs. MIS costs, for example, had tripled. The firm's rapid plunge into turkeys and other food processing, where it had little experience, contributed to the losses. Waste and inefficiency had permeated the company. Characteristically, Frank Perdue took the firm back to basics, concentrating on efficiency of operations, improving communications throughout the company, and paying close attention to detail.

On June 2, 1989, Frank celebrated 50 years with Perdue Farms, Inc. At a morning reception in downtown Salisbury, the Governor of Maryland proclaimed it "Frank Perdue Day." The Governors of Delaware and Virginia did the same.

The 1990s have been dominated by market expansion to North Carolina; Atlanta, Georgia; Pittsburgh, Pennsylvania; Cleveland, Ohio; Chicago, Illinois; and Florida. New product lines have included fresh ground chicken, fresh ground turkey, sweet Italian turkey sausage, turkey breakfast sausage, fun-shaped chicken breast nuggets in star and drumstick shapes, and barbecue- and oven-roasted chicken parts in the "Perdue Done It!" line. A new "Fit 'n Easy" label was introduced as part of a nutrition campaign using skinless, boneless chicken and turkey products. By 1994, revenues had increased to about $1.5 billion, Frank Perdue was Chairman of the Executive Committee, and Jim Perdue was Chairman of the Board.

In January 1995, Perdue Farms became the 3rd largest producer in the broiler industry when it bought Showell Farms, Inc., of Showell, Maryland, the twelfth largest producer in the U.S. with about 8,000 employees and revenues of approximately $550,000,000. Thus, Perdue Farms estimates total revenue for FY 1996 at more than $2.0 billion.

Sitting in the small, unpretentious office that had been his dad's for 40 years, Jim looked out the window at the house where he had grown up, the broiler houses Frank built in the 1940s, his grandfather's homestead across the road where Frank was born, and a modern hatchery. "Dad would come home for dinner, then come back here and work into the early hours of the morning. There's a fold-out cot behind that credenza. He got by on three or four hours of sleep a night."

MISSION STATEMENT AND STATEMENT OF VALUES

From the beginning, "Mr. Arthur's" motto had been to " . . . create a quality product, be aware of your customers, deal fairly with people, and work hard, work hard, work hard. . . ." In a speech in September 1991 to the firm's lenders, accountants, and Perdue associates, Frank reiterated these values, saying:

> If you were to ask me what was the biggest factor in whatever success we have enjoyed, I would answer that it was not technology, or economic resources, or organizational structure. It . . . has been our conscious decision that, in order to be successful, we must have a sound set of beliefs on which we premise all our policies and actions. . . . Central to these beliefs is our emphasis on quality. . . . Quality is no accident. It is the one absolutely necessary ingredient of all the most successful companies in the world.

The centrality of quality to the firm is featured in its Mission Statement and its Statement of Values. To ensure that all associates know what the company's mission, quality policy, values, and annual goals are, managers receive a fold-up, wallet-size card with those items imprinted on it (see Exhibit 1).

Exhibit 1   **Perdue—Fiscal Year 1994**

Mission Statement

Our mission is to provide the highest quality poultry and poultry-related products to retail and food service customers.

We want to be the recognized industry leader in quality and service, providing more than expected for our customers, associates, and owners.

We will accomplish this by maintaining a tradition of pride in our products, growth through innovation, integrity in the management of our business, and commitment to Team Management and the Quality Improvement Process.

Quality Policy

We shall produce products and provide services at all times which meet or exceed the expectations of our customers.

We shall not be content to be of equal quality to our competitors.

Our commitment is to be increasingly superior.

Contribution to quality is a responsibility shared by everyone in the Perdue organization.

Statement of Values

Our success as a company, and as individuals working at Perdue, depends upon:

- Meeting customer needs with the best quality, innovative food and food-related products and services.
- Associates being team members in the business and having opportunities to influence, make contributions, and reach their full potential.
- Working together as business partners by implementing the principles of the QIP so that mutual respect, trust, and a commitment to being the best are shared among associates, customers, producers, and suppliers.
- Achieving the long-term goals of the company and providing economic stability and a rewarding future for all associates through well-planned, market-driven growth.
- Being the best in our industry in profitability as a low-cost producer, realizing that our customers won't pay for our inefficiencies.
- Staying ahead of the competition by investing our profits to provide a safe work environment; to pay competitive wages; to maintain up-to-date facilities, equipment, and processes; and to create challenging opportunities for associates.
- Serving the communities in which we do business with resources, time, and the creative energies of our associates.

Fiscal Year 1994 Company Goals

1. PEOPLE—Provide a safe, secure, and productive work environment.
   - Reduce OSHA recordable incidents by 12%.
   - Reduce per capita workers' compensation by 28%.
   - Implement an associates' satisfaction survey process.
   - Provide an annual performance evaluation for all associates.
2. PRODUCTS—Provide the highest quality products and services at competitive costs.
   - Develop an improved measurement of consumer satisfaction.
   - Improve the "Customer Service Satisfaction Index."
   - Improve our quality spread over competition.
   - Consistently achieve a plant weighted ranking score for product quality of 212 points.
   - Increase sales from new products.
3. PROFITABILITY—Lead the industry in profitability.
   - Achieve a 10% ROAE.
   - Broiler Agrimetrics Index to be equal to the Southeast Best Eight Average.
   - Turkey Agrimetrics Index to be equal to the Best Eight National Average.
   - Increase market share by growing at a rate which exceeds the industry.

SOCIAL RESPONSIBILITY

To realize its corporate statement of values, Perdue Farms works hard to be a good corporate citizen. Two areas in which this is especially clear are its code of ethics and its efforts to minimize the environmental damage it causes.

■ Code of Ethics

Perdue Farms has taken the somewhat unusual step of setting forth explicitly the ethical standards it expects all associates to follow. Specifically, the Code of Ethics calls upon associates to conduct every aspect of business in the full spirit of honest and lawful behavior. Further, all salaried associates and certain hourly associates are required to sign a statement acknowledging that they understand the code and are prepared to comply with it. Associates are expected to report to their supervisor dishonest or illegal activities as well as possible violations of the code. If the supervisor does not provide a satisfactory response, the employee is expected to contact either the vice president for Human Resources or the vice president of their division. The code notes that any Perdue manager who initiates or encourages reprisal against any person who reports a violation commits a serious violation of the code.

■ Minimizing Environmental Damage

Historically, chicken processing has been the focus of special interest groups whose interests range from animal rights to repetitive-motion disorders to environmental causes. Perdue Farms has accepted the challenge of striving to maintain an environmentally friendly work place as a goal which requires the commitment of all of its associates, from Frank Perdue down. Frank Perdue states it best: "We know that we must be good neighbors environmentally. We have an obligation not to pollute, to police ourselves, and to be better than EPA requires us to be."

For example, over the years, the industry had explored many alternative ways of disposing of dead birds. Perdue research provided the solution—small composters on each farm. Using this approach, dead birds are reduced to an end product that resembles soil in a matter of a few days. This has become a major environmental activity. Another environmental challenge is the disposal of hatchery wastes. Historically, manure and unhatched eggs that make up these wastes were shipped to a landfill. Perdue produces about 10 tons of this waste per day! However, Perdue has reduced the waste by 50% by selling the liquid fraction to a pet food processor who cooks it for protein. The other 50% is recycled through a rendering process. In 1990, Perdue spent $4.2 million to construct a state-of-the-art waste water treatment facility at its Accomac, Virginia, plant. This facility uses forced hot air heated to 120 degrees to cause the microbes to digest all traces of ammonia, even during the cold winter months. In April 1993, the company took a major step with the creation of the Environmental Steering Committee. Its mission is ". . . to provide all Perdue Farms work sites with vision, direction, and leadership so that they can be good corporate citizens from an environmental perspective today and in the future." The committee oversees how the company is doing in such environmentally sensitive areas as waste water, storm water, hazardous waste, solid waste, recycling, biosolids, and human health and safety.

Jim Perdue sums it up as follows: " . . . we must not only comply with environmental laws as they exist today, but look to the future to make sure we don't have any surprises. We must make sure our policy statement is real, and that there's something behind it, and that we do what we say we're going to do."

MARKETING

In the early days, chicken was sold to groceries as a commodity, i.e., producers sold it in bulk and butchers cut and wrapped it. The consumer had no idea what company grew the chicken. Frank Perdue was convinced that higher profits could be made if Perdue's products were premium quality so they could be sold at a premium price. But, the only way the premium quality concept would work was if consumers asked for it by name—and that meant the product must be differentiated and "branded" to identify what the premium qualities are. Hence, the emphasis over the years on superior quality, a higher meat-to-bone ratio, and a yellow skin (the result of mixing marigold petals in the feed), which is an indicator of bird health.

In 1968, Perdue spent $40,000 on radio advertising. In 1969, the company spent $80,000 on radio, and in 1970, $160,000, split 50-50 between radio and television. The advertising agency had recommended against television advertising, but the combination worked. TV ads increased sales and Frank Perdue decided the old agency he was dealing with did not match one of the basic Perdue tenets: "The people you deal with should be as good at what they do as you are at what you do."

That decision set off a storm of activity on Frank's part. In order to select a new ad agency, Frank studied intensively and personally learned more about advertising than any poultry man before him. He began a ten-week immersion on the theory and practice of advertising. He read books and papers on advertising. He talked to sales managers of every newspaper and radio and television station in the New York City area, consulted experts, and interviewed 48 ad agencies. On April 2, 1971, Perdue Farms selected Scali, McCabe, Sloves as their new advertising agency. As the agency tried to figure out how to successfully "brand" a chicken—something that had never been done—they realized that Frank Perdue was their greatest ally. "He looked a little like a chicken himself, and he sounded a little like one, and he squawked a lot!" Ed McCabe, partner and chief copywriter of the firm, decided that Frank Perdue should be the firm's spokesperson. Initially Frank resisted. But, in the end, he accepted the role and the campaign based on "It takes a tough man to make a tender chicken" was born. Frank set Perdue Farms apart by educating consumers about chicken quality. The process catapulted Perdue Farms into the ranks of the top poultry producers in the country.

The firm's very first television commercial showed Frank on a picnic in the Salisbury City Park saying:

> A chicken is what it eats . . . And my chickens eat better than people do . . . I store my own grain and mix my own feed . . . And give my Perdue chickens nothing but pure well water to drink . . . That's why my chickens always have that healthy golden yellow color . . . If you want to eat as good as my chickens, you'll just have to eat my chickens . . . Mmmm, that's really good!

Additional ads, touting superior quality and more breast meat, read as follows:

> Government standards would allow me to call this a grade A chicken . . . but my standards wouldn't. This chicken is skinny . . . It has scrapes and hairs . . . The fact is, my graders reject 30% of the chickens government inspectors accept as grade A . . . That's why it pays to insist on a chicken with my name on it . . . If you're not completely satisfied, write me and I'll give you your money back.

> . . . Who do you write in Washington? . . . What do they know about chickens?

> Never go into a store and just ask for a pound of chicken breasts . . . Because you could be cheating yourself out of some meat . . . Here's an ordinary one-pound chicken breast, and here's a one-pound breast of mine . . . They weigh the same. But as you can see, mine has more meat, and theirs have more bone. I breed the broadest breasted, meatiest chicken you can buy . . . So don't buy a chicken breast by the pound . . . Buy them by the name . . . and get an extra bite in every breast.

The ads paid off. In 1968, Perdue Farms held about three percent of the New York market. By 1972, one out of every six chickens eaten in New York was a Perdue chicken. Fifty-one percent of New Yorkers recognized the label. Scali, McCabe, Sloves credited Frank Perdue's "believability" for the success of the program. "This was advertising in which Perdue had a personality that lent credibility to the product." Today, 50 percent of the chickens consumed in New York are Perdue.

Frank had his own view. As he told a Rotary audience in Charlotte, North Carolina, in March 1989, " . . . the product met the promise of the advertising and was far superior to the competition. Two great sayings tell it all: `nothing will destroy a poor product as quickly as good advertising' and `a gifted product is mightier than a gifted pen!'"

Today, the Perdue marketing function is unusually sophisticated. Its responsibilities include deciding (1) how many chickens and turkeys to grow; (2) what the advertising and promotion pieces should look like, where they should run, and how much the company can afford; and (3) which new products the company will pursue. The marketing plan is derived from the company's five-year business plan and includes goals concerning volume, return on sales, market share, and profitability. The internal Marketing Department is helped by various service agencies including:

- Lowe & Partners/SMS—advertising campaigns, media buys
- R. C. Auletta & Co.—public relations, company image
- Gertsman & Meyers—packaging design
- Group Williams—consumer promotional programs
- Various research companies for focus groups, telephone surveys, and in-home-use tests.

OPERATIONS

Two words sum up the Perdue approach to operations—quality and efficiency —with emphasis on quality over efficiency. Perdue more than most companies represents the Total Quality Management (TQM) slogan, "Quality, a journey without end." Some of the key events are listed in Exhibit 2. The pursuit of

Exhibit 2   **Milestones in the Quality Improvement Process at Perdue Farms**

1924	Arthur Perdue buys leghorn roosters for $25
1950	Adopts the company logo of a chick under a magnifying glass
1984	Frank Perdue attends Philip Crosby's Quality College
1985	Perdue recognized for its pursuit of quality in *A Passion for Excellence* 200 Perdue Managers attend Quality College Adopted the Quality Improvement Process (QIP)
1986	Established Corrective Action Teams (CAT's)
1987	Established Quality Training for all associates Implemented Error Cause Removal Process (ECR)
1988	Steering Committee formed
1989	First Annual Quality Conference held Implemented Team Management
1990	Second Annual Quality Conference held Codified Values and Corporate Mission
1991	Third Annual Quality Conference held Customer Satisfaction defined
1992	Fourth Annual Quality Conference held "How to" implement Customer Satisfaction explained for team leaders and QIT's

quality began with Arthur Perdue in 1924 when he purchased breeding roosters from Texas for the princely sum of $25 each. For comparison, typical wages in 1925 were $1.00 for a 10-hour workday. Frank Perdue's own pursuit of quality is legendary. One story about his pursuit of quality was told in 1968 by Ellis Wainwright, the State of Maryland grading inspector, during start-up operations at Perdue's first processing plant. Frank had told Ellis that the standards that he wanted were higher than the Government Grade A standard. The first two days had been pretty much disastrous. On the third day, as Wainwright recalls,

> We graded all morning, and I found only five boxes that passed what I took to be Frank's standards. The rest had the yellow skin color knocked off by the picking machines. I was afraid Frank was going to raise cain that I had accepted so few. Then Frank came through and rejected half of those.

To ensure that Perdue continues to lead the industry in quality, it buys about 2000 pounds of competitors' products a week. Inspection associates grade these products and the information is shared with the highest levels of management. In addition, the company's Quality Policy is displayed at all locations and taught to all associates in quality training (Exhibit 1).

Perdue insists that nothing artificial be fed or injected into its birds. The company will not take any shortcuts in pursuit of the perfect chicken. A chemical- and steroid-free diet is fed to the chickens. Young chickens are vaccinated against disease. Selective breeding is used to improve the quality of the chickens sold. Chickens are bred to yield more breast meat because that is what the consumer wants.

Efficiency is improved through management of details. As a vertically integrated producer of chickens, Perdue manages every detail including breeding and hatching its own eggs, selecting growers, building Perdue-engineered chicken houses, formulating and manufacturing its own feed, overseeing the care and feeding, operating its own processing plants, distributing via its own trucking fleet, and marketing. Improvements are measured in fractional cents per pound. Nothing goes to waste. The feet that used to be thrown away are now processed and sold in the Orient as a bar room delicacy.

Frank's knowledge of details is also legendary. He not only impresses people in the poultry industry, but those in others as well. At the end of one day the managers and engineers of a new Grumman plant in Salisbury, Maryland, were reviewing their progress. Through the door unannounced came Frank Perdue. The Grumman managers proceeded to give Frank a tour of the plant. One machine was an ink-jet printer that labeled parts as they passed. Frank said he believed he had some of those in his plants. He paused for a minute and then he asked them if it clogged often. They responded yes. Frank exclaimed excitedly, "I am sure that I got some of those!" To ensure that this attention to detail pays off, eight measurable items—hatchability, turnover, feed conversion, livability, yield, birds per man-hour, utilization, and grade—are tracked.

Frank Perdue credits much of his success to listening to others. He agrees with Tom Peters that "Nobody knows a person's 20 square feet better than the person who works there." To facilitate the transmission of ideas through the organization, it is undergoing a cultural transformation beginning with Frank (Exhibit 3). He describes the transition from the old to the new culture and himself as follows:

> . . . we also learned that *loud and noisy* were worth a lot more than mugs and pens. What I mean by this is, we used to spend a lot of time calling companies to get trinkets as gifts. Gradually, we learned that money and trinkets weren't what really motivated people. We learned that when a man or woman on the line is going all out to do a good job, that he or she doesn't care that much about a trinket of some sort; what they really want is for the manager to get up from behind his desk, walk over to them and, in front of their peers, give them a hearty and sincere "thank you."

> When we give recognition now, we do it when there's an audience and lots of peers can see. This is, I can tell you, a lot more motivating than the "kick in the butt" that was part of the old culture—*and I was the most guilty!*

Changing the behavioral pattern from writing up people who have done something wrong to recognizing people for doing their job well has not been without some setbacks. For example, the company started what it calls the "Good Egg Award" which is good for a free lunch. Managers in the Salisbury plant were all trained and asked to distribute the awards by "catching" someone doing a good job. When the program manager checked with the cafeteria the following week to see how many had been claimed, the answer was none. A meeting of the managers was called to see how many had been handed out. The answer was none. When the managers were asked what they had done with their award certificates, the majority replied they were in their shirt pocket. A goal was set for all managers to hand out five a week.

The following week, the program manager still found that very few were being turned in for a free lunch. When employees were asked what they had done with their awards, they replied that they had framed them and hung them up on walls at home or put them in trophy cases. The program was changed again. Now the "Good Egg Award" consists of both a certificate and a ticket for a free lunch.

Exhibit 3   **Perdue Farms, Inc., Cultural Transformation**

Old Culture

1. Top-down management
2. Poor communication
3. Short-term planning
4. Commitment to quality
5. Profitability focus
6. Limited employee recognition
7. Limited associate training
8. Short-term cost reduction
9. Annual goals as end target
10. Satisfied customers

New Culture

1. Team management
2. Focused message from senior management
3. Long-range planning
4. Expanded commitment to quality
5. Focus on People, Product, and Profitability
6. Recognition is a way of life
7. Commitment to training
8. Long-term productivity improvements
9. Continuous improvement
10. Delighted customers

Perdue also has a beneficial suggestion program that it calls "Error Cause Removal." It averages better than one submission per year per three employees. Although that is much less than the 22 per employee per year in Japan, it is significantly better than the national average in the United States of one per year per five employees. As Frank has said, "We're `one up'. . . because with the help of the Quality Improvement Process and the help of our associates, we have *thousands* of `better minds' helping us."

MANAGEMENT INFORMATION SYSTEMS (MIS)

In 1989, Perdue Farms employed 118 IS people who spent 146 hours per week on IS maintenance—"fix it"—jobs. Today, the entire department has been reduced to 50 associates who spend only 52 hours per week in "fix it," and 94 percent of their time building new systems or reengineering old ones. Even better, a six-year backlog of projects has been eliminated and the average "build-it" cost for a project has dropped from $1950 to $568—an overall 300 percent increase in efficiency.

According to Don Taylor, Director of MIS, this is the payoff from a significant management reorientation. A key philosophy is that a "fix-it" mentality is counterproductive. The goal is to determine the root cause of the problem and reengineer the program to eliminate future problems.

Developer-user partnerships—including a monthly payback system—were developed with five functional groups: sales and marketing, finance and human resources, logistics, quality assurance, and fresh-poultry and plant systems. Each has an assigned number of IS hours per month and defines its own priorities, permitting it to function as a customer.

In addition, a set of critical success factors (CSFs) were developed. These include (1) automation is never the first step in a project—it occurs only after superfluous business processes are eliminated and necessary ones simplified; (2) senior management sponsorship—the vice-president for the business unit—must sponsor major projects in their area; (3) limited size, duration, and scope—IS has found that small projects have more success and a cumulative bigger payoff than big ones. All major projects are broken into 3-6 month segments with separate deliverables and benefits; (4) precise definition of requirements—the team must determine up front exactly what the project will accomplish; and (5) commitment of both the IS staff and the customer to work as a team.

Perdue considers IS key to the operation of its business. For example, IS developed a customer ordering system for the centralized sales office (CSO). This system automated key business processes that link Perdue with its customers. The CSO includes 13 applications including order entry, product transfers, sales allocations, production scheduling, and credit management.

When ordering, the Perdue salesperson negotiates the specifics of the sale directly with the buyer in the grocery chain. Next, the salesperson sends the request to a dispatcher who determines where the various products are located and designates a specific truck to make the required pickups and delivery, all within the designated one-hour delivery window that has been granted by the grocery chain. Each truck is even equipped with a small satellite dish that is connected to the LAN so that a trucker on the New Jersey Turnpike headed for New York can call for a replacement tractor if his rig breaks down.

Obviously, a computer malfunction is a possible disaster. Four hours of downtime is equivalent to $6.2 million in lost sales. Thus, Perdue has separate systems and processes in place to avoid such problems. In addition to maximizing on-time delivery, this system gives the salespeople more time to discuss wants and needs with customers, handle customer relations, and observe key marketing issues such as Perdue shelf space and location.

On the other hand, Perdue does not believe that automation solves all problems. For example, it was decided that electronic monitoring in the poultry houses is counterproductive and not cost effective. While it would be possible to develop systems to monitor and control almost every facet of the chicken house environment, Perdue is concerned that doing so would weaken the invaluable link between the farmer and the livestock, i.e., Perdue believes that poultry producers need to be personally involved with conditions in the chicken house in order to maximize quality and spot problems or health challenges as soon as possible.

RESEARCH AND DEVELOPMENT

Perdue is an acknowledged industry leader in the use of technology to provide quality products and service to its customers. A list of some of its technological accomplishments is given in Exhibit 4. As with everything else he does, Frank

---

Exhibit 4   **Perdue Farms, Inc., Technological Accomplishments**

- Breed chickens with 20% more breast meat
- First to use digital scales to guarantee weights to customers
- First to package fully-cooked chicken products on microwaveable trays
- First to have a box lab to define quality of boxes from different suppliers
- First to test both its chickens and competitors' chickens on 52 quality factors every week
- Improved on-time deliveries 20% between 1987 and 1993

Perdue tries to leave nothing to chance. Perdue employs 25 people full-time in the industry's largest research and development effort, including five with graduate degrees. It has specialists in avian science, microbiology, genetics, nutrition, and veterinary science. Because of its research and development capabilities, Perdue is often involved in U.S.D.A. field tests with pharmaceutical suppliers. Knowledge and experience gained from these tests can lead to a competitive advantage. For example, Perdue has the most extensive and expensive vaccination program among its breeders in the industry. As a result, Perdue growers have more disease-resistant chickens and one of the lowest mortality rates in the industry.

Perdue is not complacent. According to Dr. Mac Terzich, Doctor of Veterinary Medicine and laboratory manager, Perdue really pushes for creativity and innovation. Currently, they are working with and studying some European producers who use a completely different process.

HUMAN RESOURCE MANAGEMENT

When entering the Human Resource Department at Perdue Farms, the first thing one sees is a prominently displayed set of human resource corporate strategic goals (see Exhibit 5). Besides these human resource corporate strategic goals, Perdue sets annual company goals that deal with "people." FY 1995's strategic "people" goals center on providing a safe, secure, and productive work environment. The specific goals are included on the wallet-size, fold-up card mentioned earlier (Exhibit 1).

Strategic Human Resource planning is still developing at Perdue Farms. According to Tom Moyers, Vice President for Human Resource Management, "Every department in the company has a mission statement or policy which has been developed within the past 18 months . . . Department heads are free to update their goals as they see fit. . . . Initial strategic human resource plans are developed by teams of three or four associates. . . . These teams meet once or twice a year company-wide to review where we stand in terms of meeting our objectives."

To keep associates informed about company plans, Perdue Farms holds "state of the business meetings" for all interested associates twice a year. For example, during May 1994, five separate meetings were held near various plants in Delmarva, the Carolinas, Virginia, and Indiana. Typically, a local auditorium is rented, overhead slides are prepared, and the company's progress toward its goals and its financial status is shared with its associates.

Exhibit 5   **Human Resource Corporate Strategic Goals**

Provide leadership to the corporation in all aspects of human resources including safety, recruitment and retention of associates, training and development, employee relations, compensation, benefits, communication, security, medical, housekeeping, and food services.

Provide leadership and assistance to management at all levels in communicating and implementing company policy to ensure consistency and compliance with federal, state, and local regulations.

Provide leadership and assistance to management in maintaining a socially responsible community image in all our Perdue communities by maintaining positive community relations and encouraging Perdue associates to be active in their community.

Provide leadership and assistance to management in creating an environment wherein all associates can contribute to the overall success of the company.

Be innovative and cost efficient in developing, implementing, and providing to all associates systems which will reward performance, encourage individual growth, and recognize contribution to the corporation.

Discussion revolves around what is wrong and what is right about the company. New product lines are introduced to those attending and opportunities for improvement are discussed.

Upon joining Perdue Farms, each new associate attends an extensive orientation that begins with a thorough review of the "Perdue Associate Handbook." The handbook details Perdue's philosophy on quality, employee relations, drugs and alcohol, and its code of ethics. The orientation also includes a thorough discussion of the Perdue benefit plans. Fully paid benefits for all associates include (1) paid vacation, (2) eight official paid holidays, (3) health, accident, disability, and life insurance, (4) savings and pension plans, (5) funeral leave, and (6) jury duty leave. The company also offers a scholarship program for children of Perdue associates.

Special arrangements can be made with the individual's immediate supervisor for a leave of absence of up to 12 months in case of extended non-job related illness or injury, birth or adoption of a child, care of a spouse or other close relative, or other personal situations. Regarding the Family and Medical Leave Act of 1993, although opposed by many companies because its requirements are far more than their current policies, the Act will have little impact on Perdue Farms since existing leave of absence policies are already broader than the new Federal law.

Perdue Farms is a non-union employer. The firm has had a longstanding open door policy and managers are expected to be easily accessible to other associates, whatever the person's concern. The open door has been supplemented by a formal peer review process. While associates are expected to discuss problems with their supervisors first, they are urged to use peer review if they are still dissatisfied.

Wages and salaries, which are reviewed at least once a year, are determined by patterns in the poultry industry and the particular geographic location of the plant. Changes in the general economy and the state of the business are also considered.

Informal comparisons of turnover statistics with others in the poultry industry suggest that Perdue's turnover numbers are among the lowest in the industry. Perdue also shares workers' compensation claims data with their competitors and incidence rates (for accidents) are also among the lowest in the industry. Supervisors initially train and coach all new associates about the proper way to do their jobs. Once trained, the philosophy is that all associates are professionals and, as such, should make suggestions about how to make their jobs even more efficient and effective. After a 60-day introductory period, the associate has seniority based on the starting date of employment. Seniority is the determining factor in promotions where qualifications (skill, proficiency, dependability, work record) are equal. Also, should the work force need to be reduced, this date is used as the determining factor in layoffs.

A form of Management by Objectives (MBO) is used for annual performance appraisal and planning review. The format includes a four-step process:

1. Establish accountability, goals, standards of performance, and their relative weights for the review period.
2. Conduct coaching sessions throughout the review period and document these discussions.
3. Evaluate performance at the end of the review period and conduct appraisal interview.
4. Undertake next review period planning.

The foundation of human resources development includes extensive training and management development plus intensive succession planning and career pathing. The essence of the company's approach to human resource management is captured in Frank Perdue's statement:

> We have gotten where we are because we have believed in hiring our own people and training them in our own way. We believe in promotion from within, going outside only when we feel it is absolutely necessary—for expertise and sometimes because our company was simply growing faster than our people development program. The number one item in our success has been the quality of our people.

FINANCE

Perdue Farms, Inc., is a privately held firm and considers financial information to be proprietary. Hence, available data is limited. Its stock is primarily held by the family and a limited amount is held by Perdue management. *Forbes* (December 5, 1994) estimates Perdue Farms revenues for 1994 at about $1.5 billion, net profits at $50 million, and the number of associates at 13,800. The January 1995 purchase of Showell Farms, Inc., should boost revenues to more than $2 billion and the number of associates to about 20,000.

The firm's compound sales growth rate has been slowly decreasing during the past twenty years, mirroring the industry which has been experiencing market saturation and overproduction. However, Perdue has compensated by wringing more efficiency from its associates; e.g., 20 years ago, a 1% increase in associates resulted in a 1.3% increase in revenue. Today, a 1% increase in associates results in a 2.5% increase in revenues (see Exhibit 6).

Perdue Farms has three operating divisions: Retail Chicken (62% of sales–growth rate 5%), Foodservice Chicken and Turkey (20% of sales–growth rate

Exhibit 6	**Annual Compound Growth Rate—Revenues and Associates**	
	Revenue Growth	*Associate Growth*
past 20 years	13%	10%
past 15 years	11%	8%
past 10 years	9%	5%
past 5 years	5%	2%

12%), and Grain and Oilseed (18% of sales–growth rate 10%). Thus, the bulk of sales comes from the sector—retail chicken—with the slowest growth rate. Part of the reason for the slow sales growth in retail chicken may stem from Perdue Farm's policy of selling only fresh—never frozen—chicken.

This has limited its traditional markets to cities that can be serviced overnight by truck from production facility locations, i.e., New York, Boston, Philadelphia, Baltimore, and Washington—which are pretty well saturated. (Developing markets include Chicago, Cleveland, Atlanta, Pittsburgh, and Miami.) On the other hand, foodservice and grain and oilseed customers are nationwide and include export customers in eastern Europe, China, Japan, and South America. Perdue Farms has been profitable every year since its founding with the exception of 1988. Company officials believe the loss in 1988 was caused by a decentralization effort begun during the early eighties. At that time, there was a concerted effort to push decisions down through the corporate ranks to provide more autonomy. When the new strategy resulted in higher costs, Frank Perdue responded quickly by returning to the basics, reconsolidating and downsizing. Now the goal is to streamline constantly in order to provide cost-effective business solutions.

Perdue Farms uses a conservative approach to financial management, using retained earnings and cash flow to finance asset replacement projects and normal growth. When planning expansion projects or acquisitions, long-term debt is used. The target debt limit is 55% of equity. Such debt is normally provided by domestic and international banks and insurance companies. The debt strategy is to match asset lives with liability maturities, and have a mix of fixed rate and variable rate debt. Growth plans require about two dollars in projected incremental sales growth for each one dollar in invested capital.

THE U.S. POULTRY INDUSTRY

U.S. annual per capita consumption of poultry has risen dramatically during the past 40 years, from 26.3 pounds in 1950 to almost 80 pounds in 1990. Consumption continued to grow through 1994 according to a broiler industry survey of the largest integrated broiler companies. Output of ready-to-cook product increased 5.8 percent in 1991, 5.3 percent in 1992, 6.0 percent in 1993, and 7.9 percent in 1994 to 508 million pounds per week.

PERDUE FARMS, INC.

Recent growth is largely the result of consumers moving away from red meat due to health concerns and the industry's continued development of increased value products such as pre-cooked or roasted chicken and chicken parts. Unfortunately, this growth has not been very profitable due to chronic overcapacity throughout the industry which has pushed down wholesale prices. The industry has experienced cyclical troughs before and experts expect future improvement in both sales and profits. Still, razor-thin margins demand absolute efficiency.

Fifty-three integrated broiler companies account for approximately 99 percent of ready-to-cook production in the United States. While slow consolidation of the industry appears to be taking place, it is still necessary to include about 20 companies to get to 80% of production. Concentration has been fastest among the top four producers. For example, since 1986 market share of the top four has grown from 35 percent to 42 percent (see Exhibit 7).

Although the Delmarva Peninsula (home to Perdue Farms, Inc.) has long been considered the birthplace of the commercial broiler industry, recent production gains have been most rapid in the southeast. Arkansas, Georgia, and Alabama are now the largest poultry producing states—a result of abundant space and inexpensive labor. The southeast accounts for approximately 50% of the $20 billion U.S. chicken industry, employing 125,000 across the region. Still,

Exhibit 7	Nation's Top Four Broiler Companies, 1995*		
		Million Head	Million Pounds
	1. Tyson Foods, Inc.	26.70	88.25
	2. Gold Kist, Inc.	13.40	44.01
	3. Perdue Farms, Inc.	10.97**	42.64**
	4. ConAgra, Inc.	10.50	37.91

*Based on average weekly slaughter; Broiler Industry Survey, 1995

**Includes figures for Showell Farms, Inc., which Perdue acquired in January 1995.

Exhibit 8	Integrated Broiler Producers Operating on Delmarva Peninsula*	
		National Rank
	Tyson Foods, Inc.	1
	Perdue Farms, Inc. (includes Showell Farms, Inc., which Perdue acquired in January 1995)	3
	ConAgra, Inc.	4
	Hudson Foods, Inc.	7
	Townsend, Inc. (Hq in Millsboro, DE)	10
	Allen Family Foods, Inc. (Hq in Seaford, DE)	14
	Mountaire Farms of Delmarva, Inc. (Hq in Selbyville, DE)	26

*Delmarva Poultry Industry, Inc.; May 1995 fact sheet

Delmarva chicken producers provide about 10 percent of all broilers grown in the United States. This is due largely to the region's proximity to Washington, Baltimore, Philadelphia, New York, and Boston. Each weekday, more than 200 tractor-trailers loaded with fresh dressed poultry leave Delmarva headed for these metropolitan markets.

Seven integrated companies operate 10 feed mills, 15 hatcheries, and 13 processing plants on the Delmarva Peninsula, employing approximately 22,000 people and producing approximately 10 million broilers each week (see Exhibit 8).

THE FUTURE

Considering Americans' average annual consumption of chicken (almost 80 pounds per person in 1990), many in the industry wonder how much growth is left. For example, after wholesale prices climbed from 14 cents per pound in 1960 to about 37 cents per pound in 1989, the recession and a general glut in the market caused prices to fall back (see Exhibit 9). Although prices have rebounded somewhat in 1993 and 1994, in real terms the price of chicken remains at an all-time low. A pound of chicken is down from 30 minutes of an average worker's wage in 1940 to only 4.5 minutes in 1990.

While much of this reduction can be justified by improved production efficiencies, prices are clearly depressed due to what some consider overcapacity in the industry. For example, in 1992, ConAgra, Inc., temporarily stopped sending chicks to 30 Delmarva growers to prevent an oversupply of chickens and several chicken companies have started to experiment with producing other kinds of meats—from pork to striped bass—to soften the impact (Kim Clark, *The Sun*, July 4, 1993).

The trend is away from whole chickens to skinless, boneless parts. Perdue has responded with its line of "Fit 'n Easy" products with detailed nutrition labeling. It is also developing exports of dark meat to Puerto Rico and chicken feet to China. Fresh young turkey and turkey parts have become an important product and the "Perdue Done It!" line has been expanded to include fully cooked roasted broilers, Cornish hens, and parts. Recently the company has expanded its lines to include ground chicken and turkey sausage.

Frank Perdue reflected recently that " . . . we have a very high share of the available supermarket business in the Middle Atlantic and Northeastern United States, and if we were to follow that course which we know best—selling to the consumer through the retailer—we'd have to consider the Upper Midwest—Pittsburgh, Chicago, Detroit, with 25 to 30 million people."

REFERENCES

Barmash, Isadore. "Handing Off to the Next Generation." *The New York Times*, July 26, 1992, Business, p. 1.

Bates, Eric, and Bob Hall. "Ruling the Roost." *Southern Exposure*, Summer 1989, p. 11.

Broiler Industry, January 1995, "Nation's Broiler Industry."

Clark, Kim. "Tender Times: Is Sky Falling on the Chicken Boom?" *The Sun*, July 4, 1993, p. 4F/Business.

"Facts About the DelMarVa Broiler Industry—1973." Industry Bulletin, Feb. 25, 1974.

Exhibit 9   **Wholesale Price/Pound of Live Broilers as Received by Farmers**

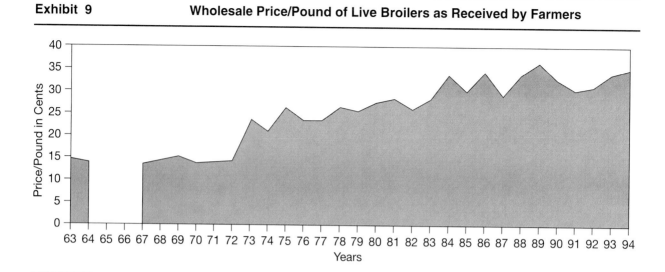

"Facts About the DelMarVa Poultry Industry," DelMarVa Poultry Industry, Inc., May 1995.

Fahy, Joe. "All Pain, No Gain." *Southern Exposure*, Summer 1989, pp. 35-39.

Flynn, Ramsey. "Strange Bird." *The Washingtonian*, December 1989, p. 165.

Forbes, December 5, 1994, "The 400 Largest Private Companies in the U.S."

Gale, Bradley T. "Quality Comes First When Hatching Power Brands." *Planning Review*, July/August 1992, pp. 4-48.

Goldoftas, Barbara. "Inside the Slaughterhouse." *Southern Exposure*, Summer 1989, pp. 25-29.

Hall, Bob. "Chicken Empires." *Southern Exposure*, Summer 1989, pp. 12-19.

"Golden Jubilee! Company Honors Frank Perdue for His 50 Years of Service." *Perdue Courier (Special Edition)*, July 1989.

"In the Money: Downhome Retailer is Nation's Richest, Forbes says." *The Washington Post*, Oct. 14, 1986.

MacPherson, Myra. "Chicken Big." *The Washington Post, Potomac Magazine*, May 11, 1975, p. 15.

"Perdue Chicken Spreads Its Wings." *Business Week*, Sept. 16, 1972, p. 113.

Perdue Farms Incorporated–Historical Highlights. Perdue Farms publication, September 1992.

Perdue, Frank. Speech at Babson College, April 28, 1981.

Perdue, Frank. Speech to firm's lenders, accountants, and Perdue Associates, September 1991.

Poultry Industry file–miscellaneous newspaper clippings from 1950 to 1994. The Maryland Room, Blackwell Library, Salisbury State University.

Santosus, Megan. "Perdue's New Pecking Orders." *CIO*, March 1993, pp. 60-68.

Scarupa, Henry. "When is a Chicken Not a Football?" *The (Baltimore) Sun Magazine*, March 4, 1973, pp. 5-12.

"Silent Millionaires in America." *Economist*, V270, #7072, March 17, 1979.

Sterling, Bill. "Just Browsin'" *Eastern Shore News*, March 2, 1988.

"The Perdue Story. And the Five Reasons Why Our Consumers Tell It Best." Perdue Farms, Inc. publication, October 1991.

Thornton, Gary. "Data from BROILER INDUSTRY." Elanco Poultry Team, Partner with the Poultry Industry, December 1993.

Yeoman, Barry. "Don't Count Your Chickens." *Southern Exposure*, Summer 1989, pp. 21-24.

XEL Communications, Inc. (A)

Robert P. McGowan, University of Denver
Cynthia V. Fukami, University of Denver

As he was turning into the parkway that curves around his company's plant, Bill Sanko, President of XEL Communications, glanced at a nearby vacant facility that once housed a now-defunct computer manufacturer. Over the next few months, in May 1995, XEL would be moving into this building. While this move was a sign of how far XEL had come in the last ten years, Bill considered that they might have met the same fate as the previous tenant. He also wondered whether they would be able to sustain the same culture that enabled the company to succeed in a rapidly changing, highly competitive industry. At the same time, he realized that change could also create opportunities.

After parking and completing the short walk to his office, Bill grabbed a copy of that day's *Wall Street Journal*. One article which caught his attention was entitled, "Baby Bells Lobby Congress for Regulatory Freedom." As one of many suppliers of telecommunications equipment to the Regional Bell Operating Companies (RBOCs), this development posed some interesting issues for XEL Communications. If the RBOCs were allowed to pursue their own manufacturing (which they are currently prohibited from doing), how would this affect XEL's existing contracts? As telephone and cable companies develop more strategic alliances and partnerships, would this provide an opportunity for XEL? At the same time, it appeared that the telecommunications industry was now becoming a global industry in which developing countries allow outside companies to establish and maintain telecommunications services. What role could XEL play in this rapidly growing market?

THE TELECOMMUNICATIONS INDUSTRY

A decade after the breakup of the telephone monopoly, the prospect of intense competition driving the telecommunications industry was creating some interesting scenarios.[1] The AT&T of old was the model for the telecommunications company of the future. "You're going to see the re-creation of five or six former AT&Ts—call them 'full-service networks'—over the next five years or more," said Michael Elling, first vice president at Prudential Securities. Marketing and capital-equipment dollars are invested more efficiently if distribution is centralized, he continued. "It could be that U S WEST, Time Warner, and Sprint get together. It could be that Bell Atlantic, Nynex, and MCI get together. It could be that GTE, AT&T, and a few other independents (local providers not affiliated with a regional Bell) get together."

The inevitability of such combinations was matched by the uncertainty over what form they would take. A business known for its predictability had suddenly found itself unpredictable. "I think you can't rule anything out in this industry anymore," says Simon Flannery, a vice president at J.P. Morgan Securities. "All the rules of the game are up for review."

In most cases, telecommunications systems transmitted information by wire, radio, or space satellite. Wire transmission involved sending electrical signals over various types of wire lines such as open wire, multipair cable, and coaxial cable. These lines could be used to transmit voice frequencies, telegraph messages, computer-processed data, and television programs. Another somewhat related transmission medium that had come into increasingly wider use, especially in telephone communications, was a type of cable composed of optical fibers. Here, electrical signals converted to light signals by a laser-driven transmitter carried both speech and data over bundles of thin glass or plastic filaments.

Radio communication systems transmitted electronic signals in relatively narrow frequency bands through the air. They included radio navigation and both amateur and commercial broadcasting. Commercial broadcasting consisted of AM, FM, and TV broadcasting for general public use.

Satellite communications allowed the exchange of television or telephone signals between widely separated locations by means of microwaves—that is, very short radio waves with wavelengths of 4 to 0.4 inches, which corresponded to a frequency range of 3 to 30 gigahertz (GHz), or 3 to 30 billion cycles per second. Since satellite systems did not require the construction of intermediate relay or repeater stations as did ground-based microwave systems, they could be put into service much more rapidly.

Not only had the mode of delivery changed, but also the content. Modern telecommunications networks not only sent the traditional voice communications of telephones and the printed messages of telegraphs and telexes, they also carried images—the still images of facsimile machines or the moving images of video in video conferences in which the participants could see as well as hear each other. Additionally, they carried encoded data ranging from the business accounts of a multinational corporation to medical data relayed by physicians thousands of miles from a patient.

The U.S. telecommunications services industry was expected to continue to expand in 1994.[2] Revenues were expected to rise about 7.7 percent, compared with a 6 percent increase in 1993. In 1994, revenues generated by international services increased about 20 percent, and local exchange telephone service was expected to rise by 3 percent. Sales of domestic long distance services were expected to grow more than 6 percent in 1994, depending on overall growth in the economy. Value-added network and information services were to climb an estimated 15 percent in 1994. Revenues from cellular mobile telephone services were to increase 39 percent in 1994; satellite service revenues in 1994 were to grow nearly 25 percent.

Local telephone services were provided by about 1,325 local telephone companies (telcos), including 7 Regional Bell Operating Companies (RBOCs), telcos owned by GTE, Sprint (United Telecom and Centel franchises), and independent local telephone companies. Many of these small, local companies operated as rural telephone cooperatives. Long distance service was provided by AT&T, MCI, Sprint, WilTel, Metromedia Communications, Litel Telecommunications, Allnet, and more than 475 smaller companies.

In 1993, the local exchange telephone companies were confronted with increasing competitive pressures in certain local services they had monopolized for decades. In response to these pressures, and to possible future competition from cable TV companies and others for local exchange telephone service itself, the RBOCs stepped up their campaign to obtain authority to enter the long distance and telecommunications equipment manufacturing businesses, and to offer video programming services.

The major long distance carriers, meanwhile, focused their attention on wireless technologies and made plans to work with or acquire companies in the wireless market. This would enable them to provide long distance services to cellular users and possibly to develop a more economical local access network to reach their own subscribers. Internationally, the large service providers continued to make alliances and seek out partners in efforts to put together global telecommunications networks and offer the international equivalent of the advanced telecommunications services available in the U.S. domestic market.

In terms of policy developments that affect the telecommunications industry, the Clinton Administration had focused its attention on the national telecommunications infrastructure, or the "information superhighway." Bills were introduced in both houses of Congress that addressed this and other key telecommunications policy issues. There was broad consensus that the Federal Government should not finance the construction of a national network. Rather, the Government was being urged to help promote competition in network access, advance interconnection and interoperability standards, see that customers would have access to new services provided over the digital infrastructure at reasonable rates, and support pilot projects for applications in education and health care. Under proposed legislation, the digital infrastructure would be extended to tap information resources at libraries, research centers, and government facilities. Congress was to consider major telecommunications legislation in the future and would then face how it would resolve the contentious issues involved that concerned so many large and powerful interests. There were also signs that some states would also open up their exchange and local service markets to competition.

Cable TV companies were likely to become another group of competitors the local telephone companies would face in the near future. Cable companies already had connections with 60 percent of U.S. households, and cable facilities extended into areas where another 30 percent of the households were located.

New digital and fiber optic technologies would allow them to provide telephone services over their networks, something cable companies already were doing in Britain.

XEL COMMUNICATIONS: THE BEGINNING

XEL Communications was born not only with an opportunity but with a challenge as well. Bill Sanko started with General Telephone and Electronics (GTE) as a product manager after spending six years in the U.S. Army.[3] He was chosen in 1972 to help establish the GTE Satellite Corporation. After he was successful with this enterprise, GTE then selected Bill for another startup business called Special Service Products in 1980.

The Special Service Products division was established to manufacture certain telecommunications products to compete with small companies who were making inroads into GTE's market. These products ranged from voice and data transmission products to switches customized to specific business needs. After two previous failures, it was GTE's third (and perhaps final) try at starting such a division. Company officials granted Sanko almost full autonomy to build the division, including recruiting all key executives, establishing a location in Aurora, Colorado, a rapidly growing region east of Denver, and in designing the division's overall operating philosophy.

By 1984, the division realized its first year of break-even operations, but it wasn't enough to win over GTE executives. Despite its initial success and the prospect of a fast-growing market, SSPD found itself heading toward orphan status in GTE's long-range plans.[4] After divestiture in telecommunications, GTE opted to concentrate primarily on providing telephone service rather than hardware. (GTE has subsequently divested all of its manufacturing divisions.) "Even though we were doing the job expected of us in building the business," Sanko said, "GTE's and SSPD's strategic plans were taking different directions." They opted to close the division. Sanko lobbied and ultimately persuaded GTE to sell the division.

The result was an action as unlikely as it was logical. On July 3, 1984, appropriately one day before Independence Day, Sanko and fellow managers from SSPD signed a letter of intent to buy the division from GTE. Two months later, the bill of sale was signed and XEL Communications, Inc. became an independent company. Sanko gathered a group of managers and raised the money—some through second mortgages on homes. GTE loaned Sanko and his colleagues money, and the rest was supplied by venture capitalists. In fact, just before the new company was scheduled to begin operations, one of the banks backed out of the arrangement. According to Julie Rich, one of the co-founders and Vice President for Human Resources, "we didn't have any money lined up from September to December of 1984. Making the first payroll for a company of 180 employees was one of the major challenges. Christmas that first year was particularly lean."

The financing was eventually arranged, and XEL was underway. Sanko reflected on the perils and rewards of leaving the corporate nest to seek one's fortune: "In the end, it was the right thing to do, but it wasn't an easy decision to make. After 17 years with GTE, I had achieved vice president status; and I was more than a little nervous about leaving the corporation."[5]

EARLY YEARS

One of the more interesting exercises in starting any new company is what to name it. John Puckett, Vice President for Manufacturing and also one of the original founders, recalled: "We did a lot of brainstorming about what to call this new company—including taking initials from the original founders' names and seeing what combinations we could come up with. Usually, they didn't make a whole lot of sense. We finally decided on XEL, which is a shortened version of excellence."

More than simply naming the company, one of the key concerns for XEL Communications was whether their customers would stay with them once they were no longer part of GTE—not that XEL has ever exactly been an abandoned child. GTE may have kicked XEL out the door in 1984, but it remains XEL's biggest customer, with GTE Telephone Operations accounting for about 35 percent of the company's total business. In fact, the relationship between the two companies continues to be close and mutually beneficial: Ever the proud parent, GTE recognized XEL as its Quality Vendor of the Year in both 1987 and 1988, and as a Vendor of Excellence in subsequent years.

At first, all XEL produced was a handful of products for GTE. Even so, the company showed a profit in its first year of independent operation. "We were off to a better start than you might expect, just because we had always had a certain independence," says Sanko. "We had our own engineers, we were a non-union shop (unlike most of the other divisions of GTE at the time), we had installed our own computer systems, and we were out here in Colorado, on our own. We were doing things differently from the start, and so we just continued."

Weaning itself from GTE was a corporate goal entirely dependent on new product development, and XEL spent over 10 percent of its revenues on R&D. That focus on development would not likely change: The XEL product line is custom manufactured and therefore constantly evolved and changed as customers' needs changed. "Running a small company has a lot of challenges," Sanko says. "But one of the major advantages is being able to respond to the market and get things done quickly. Here we can respond to a customer requirement."

XEL'S PRODUCTS AND MARKETS

For example, XEL sold products that facilitated the transmission of data and information over phone lines. Driving the need for XEL's products was the fact that "businesses are more and more dependent on the transfer of information," as Bill Sanko noted. In addition, more businesses, including XEL, were operating by taking and filling orders, for example—through electronic data exchanges. Instead of dialing into inside salespeople, businesses often accessed databases directly.

XEL's products performed a number of functions that allowed businesses to incorporate their specific telecommunications needs into the existing telephone "network" functions such as data exchanges. XEL had a diverse product line of over 300 products that it manufactured. Some of its major products included:

Fiber Optic Terminal Products
Coaxial Business Access
Analog Voice Products
Analog Data Products
Digital Data Products
Digital Transmission Products
Telecom Maintenance Products

XEL's products would, for example, translate analog information into digital transmissions. Adapting electronic information for fiber optic networks was another area of emphasis for XEL, as was adapting equipment to international standards for foreign customers.

One of XEL's strengths was its ability to adapt one manufacturer's equipment to another's. Often, it was the bits and pieces of telecommunications equipment that XEL provided to the "network" that allowed the smooth integration of disparate transmission pieces. XEL also sold central office transmission equipment and a full range of mechanical housings, specialty devices, power supplies, and shelves.

"Business customers and their changing telecommunications needs drive the demand for XEL's products. That, in turn, presents a challenge to the company," said Sanko. Sanko cited the constant stream of new products developed by XEL—approximately two per month—as the driving force behind its growth. Industry-wide, product life cycle times were getting ever shorter. Before the breakup of the Bell System in 1984, transmission switches and other telecommunications devices enjoyed a 30-to-40 year life. In 1995, with technology moving so fast, XEL's products had about a three-to-five year life.

In terms of its customers, XEL sold to all of the Regional Bell Operating Companies as well as such companies as GTE and Centel. Railroads, with their own telephone networks, were also customers. XEL's field salespeople worked with engineers to satisfy client requests for specific services. Over a period of time, a rapport was built up with these engineers, providing XEL with new product leads.

With all the consolidations and ventures in telecommunications, one might suspect that the overall market would become more difficult, but Sanko believed "out of change comes opportunity. The worst-case scenario would be a static situation. Thus, a small company, fast to respond to customer needs and able to capitalize on small market niches, will be successful. Often, a large company like AT&T will forsake a smaller market and XEL will move in. Also, XEL's size allows it to design a product in a very short time."

Interestingly, Sanko was watching pending federal legislation proposing to open up local telephone services to companies other than the regional Baby Bells. Consequently, said Sanko, "we need to expand our market and be prepared to sell to others as the regulatory environment changes." Sanko believed legislation would be signed in the near future that would set the groundwork and timetables to open local telephone monopolies to competition. The recent joint venture between Time Warner and U S WEST also signalled that telephone and cable companies would be pooling their resources to provide a broader array of information services.

As for the future, Sanko saw "a lot of opportunities we can't even now imagine."

THE XEL VISION

In addition to developing products and maintaining customer loyalty, XEL also had to deal with a number of important "people" issues. "We had good, sound management practices right from the beginning," Sanko said.[6] "We were competing with small companies who did not have the control systems, discipline, and planning experience that we had gained as part of GTE. Coming from a large arena, we could start from the top down and tailor the procedures to our needs, rather than, as many small businesses do, have to start developing controls from the bottom and then apply them—hopefully in time."

Yet, while bringing such experiences from GTE proved to be quite valuable, there were also a number of thorny issues which emerged. The first one involved people. As with any transition, there were those people that the owners wished to bring on to the new team and those whose future, for whatever reasons, was not with this new organization. "We were fortunate that personnel from GTE worked in tandem with us in this people transition phase," noted Julie Rich. "We spent a great deal of time talking people through it."

There were other critical human resource issues as well. One of the first ones was the design of the benefits package for the people. Under GTE, XEL had a traditional benefits package with little employee selection. To be competitive as well as cost effective, Julie needed to design a package that had to be reduced from 42% of overall payroll costs to 30%. She also wanted to create a package that was flexible and allowed the individual some latitude. "One approach we instituted was to allow individuals to have an allowance for total time off as opposed to so many days for sick leave, vacation, and the like. Its primary purpose was to bring down costs. And while it did succeed in this regard, we did have occasions in which people were coming to work sick rather than use this time."

Another approach was to institute a cafeteria plan of benefits in which the individual would select the specific benefits they would like to receive as part of an overall package. "The cafeteria approach was just beginning to be discussed by organizations at this time (1984)," noted Julie. "We felt there were a great deal of pluses to this approach; and it allowed the employee some discretion."

One critical issue that XEL wanted to address was developing a culture that would distinguish them from others and would also demonstrate that they were no longer a division of a large corporation. So, beginning in 1985 and carrying over into 1986, Julie Rich did a lot of reading and research on changing culture. By 1986, a first draft of these ideas and principles was developed (Exhibit 1). Julie reflected on this initial effort: "Once we developed 'XEL's Commitment to XEL-ENCE,' we printed up a bunch and hung them on the walls. However, nothing changed. You also have to realize that this company is largely comprised of engineers and technicians; and for them, a lot of this visioning was foreign."

By late 1986 and early 1987, the senior management team felt that a change agent was needed to help them deal with the issue of managing culture. An outside party was brought in; his philosophy was that corporate vision should be strategically driven. This approach was warmly received by Bill Sanko and through a series of monthly meetings, he worked with senior management.

Exhibit 1   **XEL's Commitment to Excellence**

XEL Communications, Inc. is a customer-oriented supplier of high quality transmission system products and services to telecommunications service providers with emphasis on the effective application of emerging digital technologies.

XEL provides its customers with products which allow them to offer competitive special service features to the end users while improving system operating efficiencies.

To achieve our commitment to XEL-ENCE:

1. Our customers' needs shall always come first.

2. Profitability ensures a return to our investors, company growth, and team member rewards.

3. High ethical standards are maintained in all corporate relationships.

4. On-time individual commitments are a personal pledge.

5. Superior performance through teamwork achieves rewards and advancement.

6. Customers, employees, and suppliers are team members to be treated with respect and dignity at all times.

His first effort was directed at getting the team to determine what their core values were and what they would like the company to look like in five years. Bill made an effort to develop a first draft of such a statement. In addition, other members of the senior team made similar efforts. "It was interesting," Julie notes. "Even though we each had a different orientation and background, there was a lot of consistency among the group." The team then went off-site for several days and was able to finalize the XEL Vision statement (Exhibit 2). By the Summer of 1987, the statement was signed by members of the senior team and was hung up by the bulletin board. Again, Julie reflects: "The other employees were not required to sign the Vision statement. We felt that once they could really buy into it then they were free to sign it or not."

Julie then described their approach to getting the rest of the organization to understand as well as become comfortable with the XEL Vision:

"Frequently, organizations tend to take a combination top-down/bottom-up approach in instituting cultural change. That is, the top level will develop a statement about values and overall vision. They will then communicate it down to the bottom level and hope that results will percolate upward through the middle levels. Yet it is often the middle level of management which is most skeptical, and they will block it or resist change. We decided to take a "cascade" approach in which the process begins at the top and gradually cascades from one level to the next so that the critical players are slowly acclimated to the process. We also did a number of other things—including sending a copy of the vision to the homes of the employees and dedicating a section of the company newspaper to communicate what key sections of the vision mean from the viewpoint of managers and employees."

Unlike the first vision statement which was hung on the wall but not really followed, this new vision statement has sustained and reinforced a corporate culture. Julie believed that employee involvement in fashioning and building the statement made the real difference, as well as the fact that XEL made signif-

Exhibit 2   **The XEL Vision**

XEL will become the leader in our selected telecommunications markets through innovation in products and services. Every XEL product and service will be rated Number One by our customers.

XEL will set the standards by which our competitors are judged. We will be the best, most innovative, responsive designer, manufacturer, and provider of quality products and services as seen by customers, employees, competitors, and suppliers.*

We will insist upon the highest quality from everyone in every task.

We will be an organization where each of us is a self-manager who will:

- initiate action, commit to, and act responsibly in achieving objectives
- be responsible for XEL's performance
- be responsible for the quality of individual and team output
- invite team members to contribute based on experience, knowledge, and ability

We will:

- be ethical and honest in all relationships
- build an environment where creativity and risk taking is promoted
- provide challenging and satisfying work
- ensure a climate of dignity and respect for all
- rely on interdepartmental teamwork, communications, and cooperative problem solving to attain common goals**
- offer opportunities for professional and personal growth
- recognize and reward individual contribution and achievement
- provide tools and services to enhance productivity
- maintain a safe and healthy work environment

XEL will be profitable and will grow in order to provide both a return to our investors and rewards to our team members.

XEL will be an exciting and enjoyable place to work while we achieve success.

---

*Responsiveness to customers' new product needs as well as responding to customers' requirements for emergency delivery requirements has been identified as a key strategic strength. Therefore, the vision statement has been updated to recognize this important element.

**The importance of cooperation and communication was emphasized with this update of the vision statement.

icant use of teams in all facets of its business, including decision making. For example, in 1990, XEL was experiencing some economic difficulties. The employees were brought into meetings and were told the business was in trouble, and were asked for ideas on how to deal with the downturn. The employees discussed the problem and decided to try a four-day work week rather than lay off anyone. After a few months, the economic difficulties continued and the employees reluctantly decided to lay off 40% of the work force. The work teams were asked if they wanted to be involved in deciding who would be laid off. They declined to participate in these tough decisions, but were still clearly concerned about the decisions themselves. In fact, Julie recalls being visited by a number of production workers during this time. "There was one particular fellow who knew that a coworker had a family, and that he would suffer a great deal of hardship if he was to be laid off," Julie remembers. "This fellow came in to my office and asked that he be laid off instead of his coworker. That's when I knew the employees believed in and shared our vision." Eventually, virtually all of the laid-off production workers were hired back.

In a strange way, the business crisis of 1990 moved the teams along more quickly than they might have developed in times of profit. Like many businesses using work teams and facing downsizing, XEL laid off a number of middle managers who were not brought back when business improved. When tough decisions needed to be made, the work teams no longer had managers to fall back on.

When teams, or managers, are making decisions, it is routine for the XEL Vision statement to be physically brought into the discussion, and for workers to consult various parts of the statement to help guide and direct decisions. According to Julie, the statement has been used to help evaluate new products, to emphasize quality (a specific XEL strategic objective is to be the top quality vendor for each product), to support teams, and to drive the performance appraisal process.

The XEL Vision was successfully implemented as a key first step, but it was far from being a static document. Key XEL managers continually re-visited the statement to ensure that it became a reflection of where they want to go, not where they have been. Julie believed this was a large factor in the success of the vision. "Our values are the key," Julie explains. "They are strong, they are truly core values, and they are deeply held." Along with the buy-in process, the workers also see that the statement is experimented with. This reflected the strong entrepreneurial nature of XEL's founders—a common bond that they all share. They were not afraid of risk, or of failure, and this spirit was reinforced in all employees through the vision itself, as well as through the yearly process of revisiting the statement. Once a year, Bill Sanko sat with all employees and directly challenged (and listened to direct challenges) on the XEL Vision. Since 1987, only two relatively minor additions have altered the original statement (see Exhibit 2).

HUMAN RESOURCE MANAGEMENT AT XEL

Julie Rich was pleased as she scanned the recent article in *Business Week* which mentioned XEL's efforts to use team-based compensation.[7] It mentioned that since they instituted this system, average production time has been slashed from 30 days to 3, and waste as a percentage of sales has been cut in half. "We have certainly come a long way."

Julie was heavily involved in the development of XEL's first vision statement, and she chuckled about the reaction from others: "Being the non-engineer in an outfit that is predominantly made up of technical people, they looked at me like they thought I was crazy. This 'touchy-feely' vision and values statement was about as foreign to them as it could get. Yet, once they saw the linkage to XEL's strategy and direction, it began to catch on." In many ways, Julie was an unusual HR manager. Not only did Julie believe HR to be a strategic issue for XEL, Julie herself was one of the owners of the business. Where HR was often relegated to a "staff" function, Julie was clearly a "line" manager at XEL. Julie felt very comfortable working closely with technical managers, and carried the entrepreneurial spirit as strongly as her colleagues.

Once the vision statement had been finally developed, Julie and others soon turned their attention to the issue of managing the new culture within XEL. A key ingredient of this process was changing the mindset of the employees. In the GTE days, individuals had discrete jobs and responsibilities which were governed by specific policies and procedures. "We wanted to instill a sense of ownership on the part of employees," Julie noted. When asked when she knew that the culture was working, she replied, "One day, a work team was having a meeting. The team leader was agitated, and was speaking harshly to one of the team members. One of the other workers stood up and confronted the team leader, saying that his treatment of the worker was not consistent with The XEL Vision." The worker and her team leader still work on the same team at XEL.

The HR system at XEL was unusually well-integrated. The team-based work system created a great deal of intrinsic motivation, and opportunities for employee voice and influence were in abundance. The workers participated in hiring decisions, and XEL used a 360-degree performance appraisal system. Production workers were appraised by peers and also appraised themselves. The compensation system used a three-pronged approach: profit-sharing to encourage teamwork, individual and team-based merit to encourage quantity and quality of performance, and skill-based pay to encourage continuous improvement. In one quarter in 1994, the 300 production workers were paid an average of $500 each in profit-sharing. When workers mastered a new task, they had the opportunity to earn an additional 50 cents per hour. Finally, each unit shared a bonus based on meeting a quarterly goal, such as improving on-time delivery. The average reward was 4.5% of payroll, with top teams earning up to 10% and lagging groups getting nothing. Employee response to the compensation system was generally positive. "The pay system doesn't stand alone," said Julie. "It's only in support of the teams."[8]

Julie did a lot of background reading in the management literature as well as exploring what other companies were doing. Unfortunately, she found that there was little to go on. "That is when, in working with John Puckett, vice-president for manufacturing, we began to see that self-directed work teams could give them a distinct competitive advantage—resulting in better quality products that could be delivered in a timely manner."

A key step in the development of self-directed teams was to create an open organization. The first step was to take a look at the physical layout of the work environment. One experience remains vivid for Julie: "I remember that on one particular Friday, John was toying with the idea of how to better organize the plant. One worker approached John and told him to take the weekend off and go fishing. John, initially hesitant, decided to do so; and over one weekend, the workers came in and, on their own, redesigned the entire floor. On Monday, John returned and found that they had organized themselves in various work cells—each devoted to a particular product group. Teams were then organized around this cellular production and began to set their own production goals and quality procedures."

XEL'S STRATEGIC PLANNING PROCESS

The business telecommunications market was rapidly changing and evolving in 1996—creating an ideal business climate for XEL.[9] Working with local telephone companies and others, XEL designed and manufactured equipment that "conditioned" existing lines to make them acceptable for business use.

Exhibit 3   **XEL Planning Cycle**

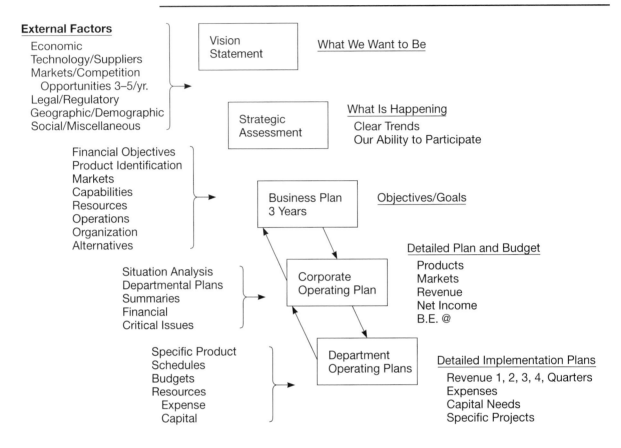

As a means of positioning themselves for products and markets in a rapidly changing environment, XEL engaged in a strategic planning process on an annual basis. Exhibit 3 provides an overview of this process. As Bill Sanko noted: "Since there are such rapid changes taking place and new products being constantly introduced, we needed to tie what we're doing back to the strategic elements—quality, responsiveness, cost."

The strategic planning process began in August of each year with the senior management team listing strategic issues and taking on key assignments. For Bill, his key assignment began with assessing key external factors. Taking on such an assignment provided him an opportunity to step back and look at the bigger picture.

"I hope that legislation pending will deregulate local telephone companies. This will open up local telephone services to companies other than the regional Baby Bell. At present, AT&T has an almost 60% hold in the market with respect to long distance but deregulation will allow the local companies to enter the global market. Major telephone companies have been downsizing in the recent past to cut down on costs by developing products and installing services that require less maintenance and, therefore, fewer people to maintain them. With this trend, we hope to get business from our present customers seeking help to develop such products for them."

Another key industry trend which was constantly monitored is technology. The pace at which the technology was moving had reduced the product life cycle from 40 years to less than 5 years. Bill noted the example of fiber optic products, which is a very hot area in today's market; XEL was trying to compete with other companies with respect to building fiber optic products. Other areas in which it was trying to find opportunities for a small company was the emerging personal communications systems market.

With the industry trend data as a beginning, the senior team then spent the ensuing months in developing plans around the key strategic issues. This would then entail capturing data on key competitors and assessing their strengths and weaknesses relative to XEL. "Some of these data are available due to public disclosure requirements," according to Bill Sanko," but data on private competitors are particularly difficult to get—due to the competitive nature of the business; we get a lot of information through trade show contacts."

Throughout this entire process, the XEL team needed to keep a focus on those critical success factors that would determine their performance. Essentially, they involved innovativeness, a skilled sales force, quality, investing in automation, effective pricing, and, above all, responsiveness.

Another key goal was to achieve a 20% improvement in margin by year end 1994 and to strive to reach 25% by December 1995 and 30% by December 1997. This goal is one that was particularly sensitive among the senior management team since it involved two critical variables: pricing coupled with achieving economies of scale in the manufacturing plant. Previously, achieving such a goal was parceled out among the respective groups: marketing and sales, operations, finance, and the like. Unfortunately, this activity was frequently tabled in the face of day-to-day activities. It was then decided that a cost reduction team needed to be formally structured to address this goal. As such, XEL decided to hire an engineer, a technician, and a buyer from outside the organization to constitute the team. Its primary responsibility was to examine the pricing of products and costs, and to target core products for the purpose of achieving 25% improvement in margin by December of 1995. The team reported primarily to the vice president of manufacturing, John Puckett.

In terms of overall financial performance, XEL has been profitable. Its revenues increased from $16.8 million in 1992 to $23.6 million in 1993 and $52.3 million in 1994—more than a three-fold increase in three years.

Another key issue that was identified in the strategic planning process was how much to invest in R&D—given the rapid pace of technology development that is taking place in this industry. XEL's goal was to invest 10% of its sales in R&D. "We have come to realize that we grew faster than last year's plan," according to Bill Sanko, "and we need to invest more in engineering as a means of keeping pace. Our goal is to have one-third of our revenue in any given year come from products introduced in the past two years." This would also involve investing its R&D efforts into new technologies as cable TV converges with telecommunications.

Aside from investment in new technologies, the other key strategic issue that was identified in the planning process was penetration into international markets. XEL was seeking to do business in Mexico in order to build data networks that are critical in upgrading Mexico's infrastructure. It has also looked for business opportunities in countries such as Brazil, Chile, Argentina, Puerto Rico, and the Far East. As a means of focusing responsibility for this effort, XEL tapped Malcom Shaw, a new hire of XEL who is fluent in Spanish and has prior marketing experience in South America, to lead this international expansion effort.

As all of the above issues indicate, the formal strategic planning process was a critical ingredient of XEL's way of doing business. "Strategic planning makes you think about how to invest for the future," Bill emphasized. "The role of the CEO is really to keep a viewpoint of the big picture—not to micro-manage the operation." To reinforce this last point, it should be noted that Bill Sanko had a personal tragedy in June of 1992, in which he was involved in a serious auto accident—the car in which he was traveling was broadsided by another auto. "Even while I was out of the office for an extended period of time," noted Bill, "the fact that we had a formal strategic plan and an annual operating plan gave us the guidance to continue business as usual." As the planning process moved forward, Bill's goal was to have their 1995 strategic plan ready for the November meeting of the Board of Directors. As Julie noted, "We don't just look for 'programs,' but for ideas for the longterm."

XEL'S MARKETS

The marketing and sales functions for XEL closely reinforced the earlier emphasis on being responsive and oriented to customer's needs. Don Bise, vice president of marketing, came to XEL with diverse experience, having moved around in nine previous firms. "The culture here at XEL is much less structured than some other organizations where I worked before," Don reflected. "I feel much more comfortable in a stand-alone company as opposed to being a branch or subsidiary of a large firm."

Unlike many companies in which the marketing approach is to have product managers dedicated to certain product segments or accounts, XEL's sales managers worked closely with the engineers in addressing customer needs. "The difficulty with having the sales manager or the engineer working solely with the customer is that their particular perspective may differ," noted Don. "By having both the engineer and the sales manager working with the customer, we have cut down on the communications difficulties and have been able to develop a more realistic pricing and delivery schedule. At the same time, by having the engineer present, he is able to understand their specific needs or can steer them towards a reasonable solution to what they are trying to achieve. This has gone a long way to create great customer loyalty and repeat business. In addition, we have been able to manage our overall costs better. Our marketing expenses are typically 6-7% of sales, which is low compared to a number of companies."

In terms of XEL's marketing strategy, a number of external developments have reshaped its approach. "Traditionally, in a market as concentrated as the telecommunications industry, the customer has tremendous buying potential and tries to leverage this as much as possible. With more players coming into this market, coupled with downsizing on the part of the Regional Bell Operating Companies, we are trying to develop a portfolio approach to make us less dependent on a few key accounts. As a result, XEL must introduce new products for traditional as well as new accounts. This means that XEL must pay a great deal of attention to technology."

To meet this goal, marketing worked closely with the engineering group—not only in the sales area but also in new product development. Specific market opportunities included the convergence of telephony with cable, personal communication services based on radio expertise, and business access in developing countries. To reach these market segments, Don Bise noted that XEL was exploring several avenues.

One approach was the OEM (Original Equipment Manufacturer) market in which XEL built the product according to another's specification. GTE's Airfone, which allowed airline passengers to place and receive calls, was a three-way venture in which XEL manufactured the electronics for the phone and did final assembly and test. This venture was quite profitable for XEL; they shipped about 300 Airfones a day out of their plant in 1995. A second approach was to build customized units for voice and data transmission in the industrial market. Exhibit 4 provides an example of XEL's approach to this market.

A third avenue, one that offered a great deal of future potential, is the international market. This is an area that Don was particularly excited about: "Clearly the growth path is international as developing regions are looking to upgrade their telecommunications infrastructure to spur economic growth. To do this, both voice and data transmission are key. What XEL can do is take something that we are familiar with and use it in areas they aren't familiar with. For example, in one particular country, we found that we can take one of our channel units and plug it into their system—providing an instant upgrade to their current capabilities." Yet going international was not without its risks. "We would prefer to begin by developing a niche in international markets with our existing equipment. This would minimize some of the up-front risks. As the international side of the business begins to take off, we realize we will need to have a local in-country partner and will need to have some local manufacturing content."

To compete successfully in the future, Don felt that XEL should "go where they ain't." XEL needed to seek out niches where there was very little or no competition, keep its cost low, and price accordingly. He felt that their traditionally strong customer base, the major telephone companies, was using its buying power to telegraph the prices they would accept. At the same time, they were cutting down their list of vendors quite extensively.

FINANCIAL CONSIDERATIONS

Turning from the ever-present spreadsheet on his desktop computer, Jim Collins, vice-president of finance, reflected on the key financial considerations facing XEL. "Coming from another company to XEL, I soon found out that the culture here is quite different. There is indeed a sense of empowerment and teamwork. People set their own goals, and the engineers make a serious commitment to the customer."

In addition to the formal strategic planning process, financial planning at XEL involved a 3-year top-down plan with input from the bottom up. According to Jim, "I interface a great deal with marketing and sales and develop costs. My goal is to ensure that there aren't a lot of surprises. We also tend to manage by percentages." Jim was asked whether XEL was experimenting with implementing some form of activity-based accounting. He noted that they reviewed it in 1993 and decided that they weren't ready. Yet, they do plan to implement a modified activity-based accounting system in 1995. "We tend to look at the major drivers of cost in this business. There is an overall operations review once a month among the senior management team in which there is open dialogue, and we explore a number of key operational issues."

Yet the financial picture for XEL has not always been rosy. "In addition to the costs associated with the separation from GTE, there were three years where we lost money—part of this was due to our dependency on GTE as it was going through its own consolidation as well as a new product introduction which didn't fly." Again, Jim Collins remarked: "Those two setbacks were a bitter pill to swallow. We now try to make our financial projections more realistic—even somewhat on the conservative side. We also set targets by market segments."

Although there was pressure to raise cash by going public, Jim felt that this wasn't realistic for XEL. "We really don't want analysts setting constraints for our business—rather we tend to look for cash infusions from strategic partnerships and alliances." Both Bill Sanko and Jim Collins were actively involved in negotiating these partnerships, particularly in the international arena. "Above all," Jim commented, "we need to stay focused, develop a plan, and get realistic input."

QUALITY MANAGEMENT AT XEL

One of the critical success factors that was identified in the strategic planning process and was imbedded throughout XEL was the focus on responsiveness to customers. When XEL was in its initial stages, cycle time—the period from start of production to finished goods—was about six weeks. That left customers disgruntled and tied up money in inventory.[10] XEL's chain of command, moreover, had scarcely changed since the GTE days. Line workers reported to supervisors, who reported to unit or departmental managers, who reported on up the ladder to Sanko and a crew of top executives. Every rung in the ladder added time and expense. "If a hardware engineer needed some software help," Sanko says. "He'd go to his manager," Sanko says. "The manager would say, 'Go write it up.' Then the hardware manager would take the software manager to lunch and talk about it. We needed everybody in the building thinking and contributing about how we could better satisfy our customers, how we could improve quality, how we could reduce costs."

Soon after XEL drafted its vision statement, John Puckett, vice president for manufacturing, redesigned the plant for cellular production, with groups of workers building whole families of circuit boards. Eventually, Sanko and Puckett decided to set up the entire plant with self-managing teams. By 1988, the teams had been established, and the supervisory and support staff was reduced by 30%.

The RIF (Reduction in Force) was achieved by a number of avenues. In 1990, there was a downturn in business and workers went to a four-day work week in order to avoid layoffs. Unfortunately, the downturn continued and production workers, supervisors, and support staff were laid off. Workers were asked for cost-saving ideas. Some workers moved to trainer roles. One worker was moved to Industrial Engineering while another became the manager of facilities.

Unlike other plans where workers are given incentives to provide cost-saving ideas and suggestions, there was no such direct financial incentive at XEL. As Julie recalled, "We were in a total survival mode—the only payoff was that the doors stayed open." Eventually, the teams and the quality strategy took hold and a turnaround was achieved. Virtually all laid-off production workers were rehired. The supervisory and support staff were not. This is a testament to the strength of the team system at XEL.

XEL rebuilt itself around those teams so thoroughly and effectively that the Association for Manufacturing Excellence chose the company as one of four to be featured in a video on team-based management. Dozens of visitors, from companies such as Hewlett-Packard, have toured through their facility in search of ideas for using teams effectively.

On the shop floor, colorful banners hung from the plant's high ceiling to mark each team's work area. Charts on the wall tracked attendance, on-time deliveries, and the other variables by which the teams gauge their performance. Diagrams indicated who on a team was responsible for key tasks such as scheduling.

Every week, the schedulers met with Production Control to review what needed to be built as well as what changes needed to be made. The teams met daily, almost always without a manager, to plan their part in that agenda. Longer meetings, called as necessary, took up topics such as vacation planning or recurring production problems. Once a quarter, each team made a formal presentation to management on what it had and hadn't accomplished.

As for results, XEL's cost of direct assembly dropped 25%. Inventory had been cut by half; quality levels rose 30% (Exhibits 5 and 6). The company's cycle time went from six weeks to four days and was still decreasing (Exhibit 7). Sales grew to $52 million in 1994, up from $17 million in 1992. Above all, according to John Puckett, these self-directed work teams must be guided by customer focus (Exhibit 8). In order to facilitate this, customers frequently came in and visited with the team. By clearly understanding their customers' needs the teams were

Exhibit 4   **XEL Communications, Inc.
Customer Returns, Component Level, All Causes**

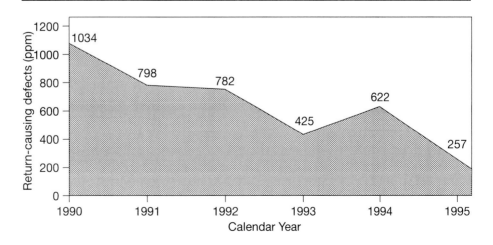

Exhibit 5

XEL Communications, Inc.
Cycle Time Reduction, 1985-94

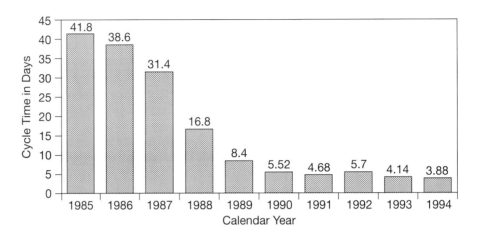

Exhibit 6

XEL Communications, Inc.
WIP Annual Inventory Turns 1986-95

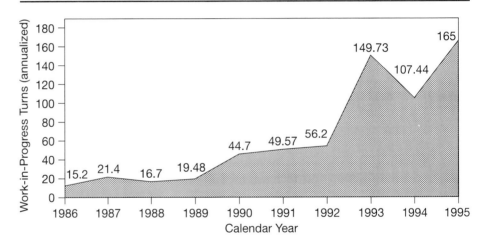

able to respond rapidly with a high quality product. At the same time, XEL team members went and visited with their key suppliers.

Another key issue for manufacturing involved establishing certain procedures while retaining a certain degree of flexibility. Part of this involved the strategic issue of entering global markets. As firms go global, meeting ISO 9000 standards for quality becomes critical. "To meet these standards, several things have to take place," John noted. "We have to have a structure that defines the process; then we need to document and have solid procedures in place." In addition, John felt that manufacturing for international markets would also mean building manufacturing capabilities closer to those markets, which entailed a host of environmental issues and labor laws. Developing alliances would also be critical since XEL could not afford to run it all.

Exhibit 7

**XEL Communications, Inc.
Productivity, 1991-95**

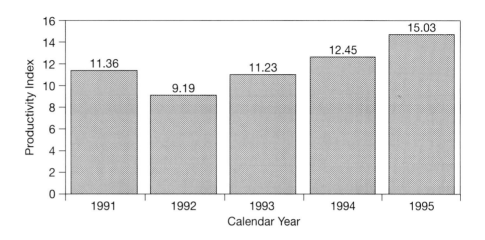

Exhibit 8

**XEL Communications, Inc.
Scrap/Rework (in $Thousands)**

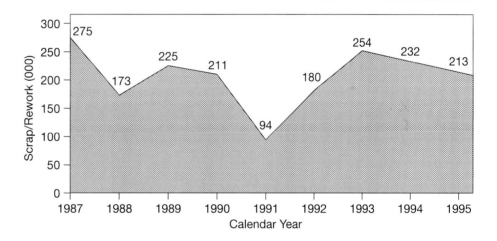

In terms of integration with other parts of XEL, John briefly sketched out the overall process. "Basically, most of manufacturing is driven off of the financial and market plan. We start with a three-year plan which is converted in terms of the demands on facilities. My staff then develops models which reflect product development and product mix. The budget then sets the baseline for new product development. Here, at XEL, we tend to plan on the low side and are fairly conservative. Currently, we target two new products per month and produce in low volume for beta testing. This allows us to carefully manage costs."

As for future issues, John was struggling with the XEL goal of improving margins by 25% by December of 1996. "This is going to be a real challenge for my operation since we have to maintain a short cycle time as the business grows without a lot of excess inventory. We instituted a just-in-time (JIT) system several years ago, and we are currently turning our inventory about 7 or 8 times, which is close to our benchmarks relative to the best in our business (Exhibit 9). Supply chain management is really critical for us."

Another issue John faced was maintaining the culture which had been instituted through the team-based training. "While the current teams have pretty much gelled in terms of feeling comfortable with setting their targets and self-managing, orienting new members becomes a challenge. We are exploring some form of built-in orientation which would involve two weeks of internal training."

John also faced an even greater concern: skilled workers. "I think one of the serious deficiencies in our current U.S. educational system is vocational and occupational education. People have simply not been prepared. There is a misconception that there is a shortage of jobs in this business. They are dead wrong. One of my difficulties is finding qualified workers. As a basic assembler, you aren't going to become rich and put down a deposit on a BMW. But it provides a nice steady income—particularly for two-wage-earning families." John felt that there needed to be a stronger work ethic for those entering the labor force. "We need to understand how to transfer those hard skills that are needed as well as the concept of holding a job. Part of this should involve more industry-level involvement in changing the overall mind-set of what is needed for today's workers. I would like to create an environment in which people really enjoy working here."

The strategic need for skilled workers drove XEL's involvement in a Work Place Learning Skills program, funded by the Department of Education. When XEL began training workers in quality tools, managers noticed that the training was not having as great an effect as it might have. Upon further investigation, the managers discovered that some workers were having difficulty not only in making calculations, but also in reading the training materials. Using the DOE grant, and working with Aurora Community College, which is located near the plant, XEL developed a basic skills training program which is now used as a template by DOE for worker training across the United States. The program, not surprisingly, was designed by an employee task force made up of managers and workers. The task force used a questionnaire to ask employees which courses they would be interested in taking. Participation in the program was not mandatory, but a measure of its success is that 50% of employees participated in the program on their own time. Courses were offered on site for convenience, and included "soft" skills such as communication and stress management. On December 1, 1994, XEL was awarded a three-year DOE grant to expand and continue the training, and to evaluate scientifically the effects of the training on such outcomes as productivity and ROI. Julie believed that these training programs were consistent with other Human Resource policies of XEL, such as skill-based pay. More than that, Julie stated, "The Work Place Learning Skills program is consistent with our XEL vision." As further testament to these efforts, XEL's overall workforce productivity continues to improve.

MAINTAINING INNOVATION

In a climate that is constantly undergoing rapid change, staying ahead of the competition is the name of the game. For XEL, this meant that cross-functional

Exhibit 9   **XEL Communications, Inc.**
Process Solder Defects

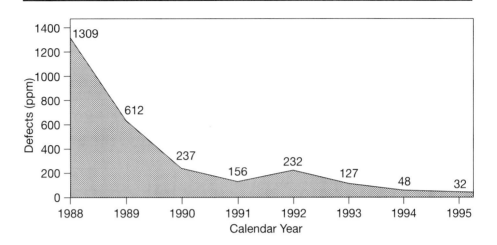

relationships were key. One critical link in this process was the role of new product development. Terry Bolinger, vice-president of engineering, described how this process worked: "Here at XEL, engineering is involved from start to finish. Rather than have a large marketing staff that is out there making calls or picking up new pieces of information, we deliberately have a small group. The engineers do a lot of traveling at XEL—going out in the field and working directly with the customers."

As for its commitment to innovation, XEL allocated approximately 10% to 12% of sales to R&D. Terry noted that, for the current year, he spent below this amount. When pressed why, he commented: "I guess I am hesitant to spend up to this amount since I don't want to grow my engineering group too fast. A few years back, we went through some cutbacks due to a number of factors, and I am somewhat gun-shy about that experience. I know we are running at about the 10% level, and Bill keeps pressing me about this. But I would rather proceed somewhat cautiously."

In order to create a climate to allow his people to innovate, Terry noted that he was careful not to create a management system that bogged everything down. "Our process of setting priorities is fairly free-form. While we are typically running 50 projects at one time, we don't do much formal scheduling. We went through a time in which a lot of formal planning and presentations were done. Unfortunately, we spent too much time in meetings and too little in what I considered the search and discovery process." While Terry was comfortable with this loose form of management, he laughed that others were not so at ease. "I see Bill Sanko stroll the office periodically, and I know that he is often perplexed with how this works—coming from his engineering background. I just say 'trust me' and he is pretty good at accepting it."

In addition to this loose form of project management, Terry tried to motivate his engineers in other ways. "I also try to give them interesting assignments which will challenge them. They are also allowed to work at odd hours—many come to work on weekends or at night. In a number of cases, I will simply send them to work at home where they can be relaxed. If they need some particular equipment, I will get it for them with little or no questions asked. Also, they periodically like to travel just to get out of the office; and field calls to customers or potential customers is a way of getting them charged up." There were also periodic in-house seminars with professors from various universities who would come and brief them on new technological advances. In a sense, Terry was trying to re-create the college environment within XEL.

As XEL continued to grow, Terry saw several issues that were critical for his group: "First is the issue of how do I improve time to market without sacrificing quality; second, how do I speed up product development; and third, how do I respond extremely fast to new technology developments?" As he prepared his departmental plan for the strategic planning meeting, he also shared some concern about the opening of the second building. While he clearly needed more space for his people, the ease with which an engineer could go over to manufacturing or marketing and sales if he or she had a question or needed some information would be hard to replace.

XEL'S FUTURE

Ironically, the most serious current issue for XEL came from its own success, namely growth. XEL had increased its labor force by 50% and had doubled its revenues in the last year, and was experiencing some associated growing pains. Hiring sufficient workers was difficult, and assuring that the new workers will "fit" the XEL culture was hindered because of the pressures to add staff. The teams, who normally hired their own replacement workers, were less able to participate in the hiring process since they were under great pressure to produce and satisfy their customers.

Another example of the pressures of growth occurred in the skills training program. Originally, team members were scheduled to teach the classes. Unfortunately, as pressures for production increased, more and more team members canceled their training classes. As a solution, trainers were hired from local community colleges, and the team members acted as their partners to assure the course content was job-related.

Growth increased pressure to satisfy customer demands, increased pressure on the culture via the increased size and complexity, and created additional financial pressures. As a high-technology company, XEL faced the challenge of using technology to help the company be more effective. XEL would use its annual strategic planning process to determine its priorities, what measures it will use to assess its results, and which feet to hold to the fire.

Having finished reading the *Wall Street Journal* article, Bill Sanko made a note to have a copy made for the next managers' meeting, which was scheduled for every other Thursday. He also wondered what the new session of Congress would bring—now that the Republicans appeared to be in solid control.

Since XEL was in the process of beginning its annual strategic planning process, Bill thought that a useful exercise for the next managers' meeting would be to have everyone list and prioritize the key strategic issues facing XEL over the next three to five years. At the same time, he wondered whether it would be possible for XEL to maintain its entrepreneurial culture while it managed rapid growth.

N O T E S

1. *Financial World*, October 11, 1994.
2. 1994 University of Michigan Economic Forecast
3. *Denver Business Journal*, June 17, 1994, p. 12.
4. *Rocky Mountain Business Journal*, July 1, 1985.
5. *Colorado Business*, July 1990.
6. *Rocky Mountain Business Journal*, July 1, 1985.
7. *Business Week*, November 14, 1994, p. 62
8. *Ibid.*, p. 62.
9. *Denver Business Journal*, April 15, 1994.
10. *Inc.,* September 1993, p. 66.

XEL Communications, Inc. (B): Forming a Strategic Partnership

Cynthia V. Fukami, University of Denver

Robert P. McGowan, University of Denver

I n the fall of 1995, Bill Sanko, President of XEL Communications, Inc., strolled around the new 115,000-square-foot facility with its spacious conference rooms and computer-based skills training center, into which the company had just moved. Their former facility was a 53,000-square-foot building that just couldn't accommodate XEL's growth. During the upcoming round of strategic planning sessions, Bill wondered how XEL and its management team would decide to grapple with the two-edged sword of rapid growth. Would it be possible for XEL to maintain its entrepreneurial culture while it experienced rapid growth? Would they find the resources necessary to sustain their growth without harming their culture? From where?

XEL COMMUNICATIONS, INC.

XEL Communications, Inc.[1]—located in the outskirts of Denver, Colorado—designs and manufactures various telecommunications products for a number of companies—primarily large U.S. telephone operating companies. Originally a division within GTE headed by Bill Sanko, it was in the process of being closed when Bill and a few key managers persuaded GTE to sell the division to them. In July 1984, Sanko and fellow managers from the division signed a letter of intent to buy the division from GTE. Two months later, the bill of sale was signed and XEL Communications, Inc., became an independent company. Ironically, GTE remained as one of XEL's major customer accounts.

In terms of overall financial performance, XEL was doing well. Its revenues increased from $16.8 million in 1992 to $23.6 million in 1993 and $52.3 million in 1994—over a three-fold increase in three years. In 1996, XEL employed approximately 300 people.

XEL designed and manufactured more than 300 individual products which enabled telecommunications network operators to upgrade existing infrastructures and cost-effectively enhance the speed and functionality of their networks, while reducing operating expenses and overhead costs. Its products provided access to telecommunications services and automated monitoring and maintenance of network performance, and extended the distance over which network operators were able to offer their services.[2] For example, XEL produced equipment that "conditioned" existing lines to make them acceptable for business use, and sold products that facilitated the transmission of data and information over phone lines. Driving the need for XEL's products was the fact that "businesses are more and more dependent on the transfer of information," as Bill Sanko noted. In addition, more businesses, including XEL, were operating by taking and filling orders through electronic data exchanges. Instead of dialing into inside salespeople, businesses often accessed databases directly.

One of XEL's strengths was its ability to adapt one manufacturer's equipment to another's. XEL provided the bits and pieces of telecommunications equipment to the "network," allowing the smooth integration of disparate transmission pieces. XEL also sold central office transmission equipment and a full range of mechanical housings, specialty devices, power supplies, and shelves.

In 1995, XEL began developing a hybrid fiber/cable broadband modem for use by cable television firms seeking to provide enhanced data communication services over their network facilities. Cable modems were one of the hottest new products in telecommunications at the time. The devices would enable computers to send and receive information about one hundred times faster than standard modems used with phone lines. Given that 34 million homes had personal computers, cable modems were seen as a surefire way to exploit the PC boom and the continuing convergence of computers and television. Media analysts estimated cable modem users would rise to 11.8 million by the end of 2005 from a handful in 1996.[3]

"Business customers and their changing telecommunications needs drive the demand for XEL's products. That, in turn, presents a challenge to the company," said Sanko. Sanko cited the constant stream of new products developed by XEL—approximately two per month—as the driving force behind the growth. Industry-wide, product life cycle times are getting even shorter. Before the breakup of the Bell System in 1984, transmission switches and other telecommunications devices enjoyed a 30 to 40 year life. In 1995, with technology moving so fast, XEL's products had about a three to five year life.

In terms of its customers, XEL sold to all of the Regional Bell Operating Companies (RBOCs) as well as such companies as GTE and Centel. Railroads, with their own telephone networks, were also customers. In addition to its domestic business, products were sold in Canada, Mexico, and Central and South America.[4] XEL's field salespeople worked with engineers to satisfy client requests for specific services. Over a period of time, a rapport was built up with these engineers, providing XEL with new product leads.

With all the consolidations and ventures in telecommunications, it was often concluded that the overall market would become more difficult, but Sanko believed "out of change comes opportunity. The worst-case scenario would be a static situation. Thus, a small company, fast to respond to customer needs and able to capitalize on small market niches, will be successful. Often, a large company like AT&T will forsake a smaller market and XEL will move in. Also, XEL's size allows it to design a product in a very short time."

Interestingly, Sanko watched federal legislation. The recently signed Telecommunications Act of 1996 which removed numerous barriers to competition clearly changed the rules of the game. Consequently, said Sanko, "we need to expand our market and be prepared to sell to others as the regulatory environment changes." The recent joint venture between Time Warner and U.S. West also signals that telephone and cable companies will be pooling their resources to provide a broader array of information services. As for the future, Sanko saw "a lot of opportunities we can't even now imagine."

THE XEL VISION

A dimension that management thought set it apart from other companies was its strong and healthy corporate culture. Developing a culture of innovation and team decision making was instrumental in providing the results XEL prided itself on.[5] An early attempt to define culture in a top-down fashion was less successful than the management team hoped,[6] so the team embarked on a second journey to determine what their core values were and what they would like the company to look like in five years. The team then went off-site for several days and was able to finalize the XEL Vision statement. By the summer of 1987, the statement was signed by members of the senior team and was hung up by the bulletin board. Employees were not required to sign the statement, but were free to do so when each was ready.

Julie Rich, Vice President of Human Resources, described their approach to getting the rest of the organization to understand, as well as become comfortable with, the XEL Vision: "Frequently, organizations tend to take a combination top-down/bottom-up approach in instituting cultural change. That is, the top level will develop a statement about values and overall vision. They will then communicate it down to the bottom level and hope that results will percolate upward through the middle levels. Yet it is often the middle level of management which is most skeptical, and they will block it or resist change. We decided to take a "cascade" approach in which the process begins at the top and gradually cascades from one level to the next so that the critical players are slowly acclimated to the process. We also did a number of other things—including sending a copy of the vision statement to the homes of the employees and dedicating a section of the company newspaper to communicate what key sections of the vision mean from the viewpoint of managers and employees."

The Vision statement became a living symbol of the XEL culture and the degree to which XEL embraced and empowered its employees. When teams, or managers, made decisions it was routine for the XEL Vision statement to be physically brought into the discussion, and for workers to consult various parts of the statement to help guide and direct decisions. According to Julie, the statement was used to help evaluate new products, to emphasize quality (a specific XEL strategic objective is to be the top-quality vendor for each product), to support teams, and to drive the performance appraisal process.

The XEL Vision was successfully implemented as a key first step, but it was far from being a static document. Key XEL managers continually revisited the statement to ensure that it became a reflection of where they want to go, not where they have been. Julie believed this was a large factor in the success of the vision. "Our values are the key," Julie explained. "They are strong, they are truly core values, and they are deeply held." Along with the buy-in process, the workers also saw that the statement is experimented with. This reflected the strong entrepreneurial nature of XEL's founders—a common bond that they all shared. They were not afraid of risk or of failure, and this spirit was reinforced in all employees through the Vision itself, as well as through the yearly process of revisiting the statement. Once a year, Bill Sanko sat with all employees and directly challenged (and listened to direct challenges to) the XEL Vision. From 1987 to 1995, only two relatively minor additions altered the original statement.

■ Which Path to Choose?

When the 1995 annual strategic planning process got underway, XEL was in good shape on any one of a number of indicators. Profits were growing, new products were being developed, the culture and vision of the company were strong, employee morale was high, and the self-directed work teams were achieving exceptional quality.[7] On the other hand, rapid growth was also presenting a challenge. Would it be possible for XEL to maintain its entrepreneurial culture given rapid growth? Could they sustain their growth without harming their culture? Would they find the resources necessary to sustain the growth? From where?

As the strategic planning retreat progressed, three options seemed apparent to the team. First, they could stay the course and remain privately held. Second, they could initiate a public offering of stock. Third, they could seek a strategic partnership. Which would be the right choice for XEL?

■ Staying the Course

The most obvious option was to do nothing. Bill Sanko indicated that staying the course and remaining privately held was not favored in the discussions by the management team. "We had a venture capitalist involved who, after being with us for 10 years, wanted out. In addition, the founders—ourselves—also wanted out from a financial standpoint. You also have to understand that one of the original founders, Don Donnelly, had passed away, and his estate was looking to make his investment more liquid. So, there were a lot of things that converged at the same time."

Once they determined they would not remain privately held, Bill mentioned that the decision boiled down to two main avenues: either XEL would do an initial public offering and go public, or it would find a strategic partner. "To guide us in this process, we decided to retain the services of an outside party; we talked to about a dozen investment houses. In October 1994, we decided to hire Alex Brown, a long-time investment house out of Baltimore. What we liked about this firm was that they had experience with doing both options— going public or finding a partner."

■ Going Public

One avenue open to XEL was initiating a public offering of stock. Alex Brown advised them of the pluses and minuses of this option. "The plus side for XEL doing an initial public offering was that technology was really hot about this time (October 1994). In addition, we felt that XEL would be valued pretty highly in the market. The downside of going public was that XEL was really not a big firm and institutional investors usually like doing offerings of firms that generate revenues of over $100 million. Another downside was that you had to deal with analysts and their projections become your plan, which really turned me off. Also, shareholders want a steady and predictable rate of return. Technology stocks are not steady—there are frequent ups and downs in this marketplace—caused by a number of factors, such as a major telecommunications company deciding not to upgrade at the last minute or Congress considering sweeping regulatory changes. Finally, Alex Brown felt that the stock would have traded thinly. This, coupled with SEC restrictions on trading, made the option of going public less desirable."

■ Strategic Partnership

"So, we decided to take the third path and look for a potential partner. But you have to also note that there was always the first option available as a safety valve. We could not do anything and stay the way we were. That's the nice thing about all of this. We were not under any pressure to go public or seek a partner. We could also wait and do one of these things later on. So, we had the luxury of taking our time."

"In terms of finding a potential partner, there were certain key items that we wanted Alex Brown to consider in helping us in this process. The first was that we, management, wanted to remain with XEL. We had really grown XEL as a business and were not interested in going off and doing something else. The second key item was that we were not interested in being acquired by someone who was interested in consolidating our operations with theirs, closing this facility and moving functions from here to there. To us, this would destroy the essence of XEL. The third item was that we wanted a partner that would bring something to the table but would not try to micro-manage our business."

THE CASE AGAINST STRATEGIC PARTNERSHIP

In the 1990s, a "merger mania" took place in the United States. In the first nine months of 1995, the value of all announced mergers & acquisitions reached $248.5 billion, surpassing the record full year volume of $246.9 billion reached in 1988. This volume occurred in the face of strong evidence that over the past thirty-five years, mergers & acquisitions have hurt organizations more than they have helped.[8] Included among the reasons for failure in mergers and acquisitions are:

- Inadequate due diligence;
- Lack of a strategic rationale;
- Unrealistic expectations of possible synergies;
- Paying too much;
- Conflicting corporate cultures; and
- Failure to move quickly to meld the two companies.

On the other hand, there were successful mergers and acquisitions. Most notably, small and mid-sized deals have been found to have a better shot at success. Michael Porter argued that the best acquisitions are "gap-filling," that is, a deal in which one company buys another to strengthen its product line or expand its territory, including globally. Anslinger and Copeland argued that successful acquisitions will be more likely when preacquisition managers are kept in their positions, when big incentives are offered to top-level executives so that their net worths are on the line, and when the holding company is kept flat—that is, when business is separated from other operating units and retains a high degree of autonomy.[9]

More often than not, however, the deal has been won or lost after it is done. Bad post-merger planning and integration can doom the acquisition. "While there is clearly a role for thoughtful and well-conceived mergers in American business, all too many don't meet that description."[10]

CHOOSING A PARTNER

"With these issues in mind, Alex Brown was able to screen out possible candidates. In January 1995, this plan was presented to our Board of Directors for approval; and by February we had developed the 'book' about XEL that was to be presented to these candidates. We then had a series of meetings with the candidates in the conference room at our new facility. The interesting side on these meetings was that, often, senior management from some of these firms didn't know what pieces of their business that they still had or had gotten rid of. We did not see this as a good sign."

One of the firms with which XEL met was Gilbert Associates, based in Reading, Pennsylvania. Gilbert Associates was founded in the 1940s as an engineering and construction firm, primarily in the area of power plants. They embarked on a strategy of reinventing themselves by divesting their energy-related companies, becoming a holding company whose subsidiaries operated in the high-growth markets of telecommunications and technical services. Gilbert also owned a real estate management and development subsidiary. After due diligence and due deliberation, Gilbert was chosen by the Management team as XEL's strategic partner. The letter of intent was signed on August 29, 1995, the preliminary document was signed on October 4, 1995, and the deal was closed on October 27, 1995. Gilbert paid $30 million in cash.[11]

Why was Gilbert chosen as the partner from among the six or seven suitors? Not because they made the highest bid, says Sanko. XEL was attracted to Gilbert by three factors: their long-term strategy to enter the telecommunications industry; their intentions of keeping XEL as a separate, autonomous company; and because Gilbert paid cash (as opposed to stock or debt). "It was a clean deal," said Sanko.

The deal was also attractive because it was structured with upside potential. XEL was given realistic performance targets for the next three years. If these targets were achieved, and Sanko had every expectation that they would be, approximately $6-8 million would be earned. Gilbert did not place a cap on the upside.

In spite of the attractive financial package, more was necessary to seal the deal. "At the end of the day," says Sanko, "culture, comfort, and trust—those were more important than money." It was important to XEL's Board that Gilbert presented a good fit. Sanko was encouraged because he felt comfortable with Gilbert's CEO. Vice President of Human Resources Julie Rich also noted, "the management team was to remain intact. Gilbert recognized that the XEL Vision was part of our success and our strength. They wanted to keep it going."

As one way of gaining confidence in Gilbert, Bill Sanko personally spoke with the other CEOs of Gilbert's recent acquisitions. In these conversations, Sanko was assured that Gilbert would keep its promises.

Timothy S. Cobb, Chairman, President, and CEO of Gilbert Associates, commented at the time of the acquisition, "This transaction represented the first clear step toward the attainment of our long-term strategy of focusing on the higher margin areas of telecommunications and technical services. XEL's superior reputation for quality throughout the industry, its innovative design and manufacturing capabilities, and its focus on products aimed at the emerging information highway markets will serve us well as we seek to further penetrate this important segment of the vast communications market."[12]

Mr. Cobb continued, "We see long-term growth opportunities worldwide for XEL's current proprietary and Original Equipment Manufacturer (OEM) products as well as for the powerful new products being developed. These products fall into two families: (1) fiber-optic network interfaces designed specifically to meet the needs of telephone companies, inter-exchange carriers (e.g., AT&T, Sprint, MCI), and specialized network carriers installing fiber-optic facilities; and (2) a hybrid fiber/cable broadband modem for use by cable television firms seeking to provide enhanced data communications services over their network facilities. Going forward, we expect to leverage Gilbert's knowledge and relationships with the RBOCs to significantly increase sales to those important customers, while also utilizing our GAI-Tronics subsidiary's established international sales organization to further penetrate the vast global opportunities which exist. As a result, revenues from Gilbert Associates' growing telecommunications segment could represent over half of our total revenues by the end of 1996."

Timothy Cobb came to Gilbert from Ameritech, an RBOC which covers the Midwest United States. He was President of GAI-Tronics Corporation, an international supplier of industrial communication equipment, a subsidiary of Gilbert, prior to his appointment as CEO.

Bill Sanko offered, "When all the dust had settled, the one firm that we really felt good about was Gilbert—based in Reading, Pennsylvania. Gilbert is an interesting story in itself. Ironically, they had contacted us in August 1994, based on the advice of their consultant who had read about us in an *Inc.* magazine article. Unfortunately, at the time, they did not have the cash to acquire us since they were in the process of selling off one of their divisions. In the intervening period, Gilbert Associates divested itself of one of its companies, Gilbert/Commonwealth. This sale provided needed funds for the acquisition of XEL."

Before the purchase agreement was signed, but once Bill Sanko was confident it would be signed, the pending acquisition was announced to the management team, and a general meeting was held with all employees. SEC regulations prohibit (as does general common sense) sharing particular information, but Sanko and his associates felt it was important to keep employees informed before the letter was signed.

During the meeting, Sanko told the employees that the Board was "seriously considering" an offer. Sanko assured the employees that the suitor was not a competitor, and that he felt that the suitor was a good fit in culture and values. Sanko reiterated that this partnership would give XEL the resources it needed to grow. Questions were not allowed based on SEC regulations. Employees left the meeting concerned, and somewhat nervous, but members of the management team, along with Julie Rich, were positioned in the audience and made themselves available to talk.

During the closing of the deal, Sanko held another general meeting where more detailed information was shared. Managers were informed in a premeeting so that they could be prepared to meet with their teams directly following the general meeting. In addition, Timothy Cobb personally participated in this meeting.

Generally, employees wanted to know about Gilbert. They wanted to know simple information, such as where they were located, and what businesses they were in. They wanted to know strategic plans, such as whether there were any plans to consolidate manufacturing operations. Finally, they wanted to know about the near future of XEL—they wanted to know if their benefits would change, if they would still have profit sharing, and if the management team would stay in place. "We have a track record of being open," says Sanko. "Good news or bad is always shared. This history stemmed much of the rumor mill."

In the next few weeks, Tim Cobb returned to hold a series of meetings with the management team, and with a focus group of thirty employees representing a cross-section of the organization. Cobb also met with managers and their spouses at an informal reception. Sanko wanted to slowly bring the management team to the realization that they were now part of a larger whole in Gilbert. As such, he asked Cobb to make the same presentation to XEL that he was then making to stockholders throughout the country—a presentation that emphasized the role XEL would play in the long-term strategy of Gilbert.

GOING FORWARD

The HR systems remained in place with no changes. The Management bonus would change somewhat since it included stock options which were no longer available. XEL's internal advisory board, the "Management team," remained intact, but XEL's external advisory board was disbanded. Bill Sanko reported to Gilbert's chairman.

XEL's strategic plan was to follow the process then in place. XEL's process was not unlike Gilbert's. The cycle didn't change. Gilbert expected XEL's next strategic plan in early November, 1996.

XEL's strategic objectives didn't change. Nothing was put on hold. Plans were still in place to penetrate Brazil, Mexico, and South America.[13] Sanko hoped to capitalize on the synergies of Gilbert's existing international distribution network. XEL met with Gilbert's international representatives to see if this was an avenue for XEL to gain a more rapid presence in South America. Finally, XEL was planning to move into Radio Frequency (RF) engineering and manufacturing, potentially opening the door for wireless support.

Whether XEL would grow depended on the success of these new ventures. In 1996, slight growth was forecasted. But if these new markets really took off, Julie Rich was concerned that it would be hard to hire enough human resources in Colorado where, at the time, the labor market was approaching full employment. Julie developed more creative ways of attracting new hires—for example, by offering more flexible scheduling, or by hiring unskilled workers and training them internally. A new U. S. Department of Education grant to pilot test computer-based training systems was being implemented. However, employment was strong in the Denver metro area in 1996, and migration to Colorado had slowed. It would be a challenge to staff XEL if high growth becomes the business strategy.

Approximately six weeks after the acquisition, Sanko noted that there were a few changes. Now that they were a publicly held company, there was a great deal more interest in meeting quarterly numbers. "If there has been a change," said Sanko, "it is that there is more attention to numbers." Julie Rich noted that there had been no turnover in the six-week period following the acquisition. She took this as a sign that things were going well so far.

One reason things went well was that the management team had all worked for GTE prior to the spin-off of XEL. They have all worked for a large public company, so the acquisition by Gilbert was not such a terrible culture shock. Time would tell if the remaining XEL employees would feel the same way.

As Sanko awaited Cobb's upcoming visit, he wondered how to prepare for the event, and for the year ahead. He wondered whether XEL would attempt new ventures into RF technology, or how the planned fiber/cable broadband modem would progress. He wondered whether Gilbert's experience in selling in South America would prove valuable for XEL's international strategy. In addition, he wondered how he could encourage XEL and its employees to become members of Gilbert's "team." Would XEL's vision survive the new partnership?

Finally, according to one study of CEO turnover after acquisition, 80% of acquired CEOs turn over by the sixth year after the acquisition, but 87% of those who left did so within two years. The key factor in their turnover was post-acquisition autonomy.[14] After nearly twelve years as the captain of his own ship, Sanko wondered what his own future, and the future of the XEL management team, would hold.

NOTES

1. For additional information on XEL Communications, Inc., and the key strategic issues facing XEL, see "XEL Communications, Inc. (A)" by McGowan and Fukami, 1995.

2. *PR Newsletter*, October 5, 1995.

3. Menezes, Bill, "Modem Times," *Rocky Mountain News*, April 28, 1996.

4. *PR Newswire*, October 5, 1995.

5. Sheridan, John, "America's Best Plants: XEL Communications," *Industry Week*, October 16, 1995.

6. See McGowan and Fukami, XEL Communications, Inc. (A) for a larger discussion of corporate culture at XEL.

7. Sheridan, John, "America's Best Plants: XEL Communications," *Industry Week*, October 16, 1995.

8. Zweig, Philip, "The Case Against Mergers," *Business Week*, October 30, 1995.

9. Anslinger, Patricia, and Thomas Copeland, "Growth Through Acquisitions: A Fresh Look," *Harvard Business Review*, January-February, 1996.

10. Zweig, Philip, "The Case Against Mergers," *Business Week*, October 30, 1995.

11. Bunn, Dina, "XEL to be sold in $30 million deal," *Rocky Mountain News*, October 27, 1995.

12. *PR Newswire*, October 5, 1995.

13. For more information on the global penetration of XEL, see McGowan and Allen, "XEL Communications (B): Going Global."

14. Stewart, Kim A. "After the Acquisition: A Study of Turnover of Chief Executives of Target Companies," Doctoral Dissertation, University of Houston, 1992.

Tootsie Roll, Inc.

Sharon Ungar Lane, Bentley College
Alan N. Hoffman, Bentley College

INTRODUCTION

"Tootsie Roll's good fortunes are an accumulation of many small decisions that were probably made right plus bigger key decisions, such as acquisitions, that have been made right, and a lot of luck."

MEL GORDON, CEO
TOOTSIE ROLL, 1993

Tootsie Roll Industries, Inc., a niche candy maker, has often been voted one of *Forbes* magazine's "200 Best Small Companies of America." A top quality producer and distributor of Tootsie Rolls and other candy, Tootsie Roll Industries maintains a 50% market share of the taffy and lollipop segment of the candy industry, and sales have increased each year for the past nineteen years. The world's largest lollipop supplier, the company produces approximately 16 million lollipops and 37 million individual Tootsie Rolls a day.

EARLY HISTORY

In 1896, Leo Hirschfield, a young immigrant from Austria, set up a small shop in Brooklyn, New York, to make candy from a recipe he had brought from Europe. As he rolled the sweet, chewy chocolate candies, his thoughts wandered to his young daughter, Clara "Tootsie" Hirschfield, and he named his new confection the "Tootsie Roll." He wrapped the Tootsie Rolls individually in paper to keep them clean and sanitary, and priced them at a penny each.

Hirschfield's Tootsie Rolls were an immediate success, and demand quickly outpaced supply. Hirschfield realized he would need more capital to promote and expand his business. After just one year, he merged his operation with a local candy manufacturer, Stern & Saalberg, which incorporated eight years later, and officially changed its name to the Sweets Company of America in 1917.

From 1922 to 1966, the Sweets Company of America set up manufacturing facilities around the United States to meet growing demand for Tootsie Roll products. Having captured America's sweet tooth with the Tootsie Roll, the company expanded its product line in the 1930s, developing a series of companion products such as the first soft-centered lollipop, the Tootsie Pop, which had a Tootsie Roll center and a hard candy outside.

In 1962, Ellen and Melvin Gordon took over as President / Chief Operating Officer and Chief Executive Officer / Chairman of the Board, respectively. In 1966, the Gordons changed the company name to Tootsie Roll Industries, Inc. and opened a large manufacturing facility in Chicago (which subsequently became the company's world headquarters). In the late 1960s, Tootsie Roll began exploring foreign markets, establishing a subsidiary in Mexico and licensing a firm in the Philippines to produce and distribute Tootsie Rolls. After a positive response in both these countries, the company expanded to Canada in 1971.

Amazingly enough, as the Tootsie Roll celebrates its 100th birthday in 1996, the candy still tastes exactly the same as it did when it was first hand-rolled by Leo Hirschfield. The company's success, as 19 consecutive years of record sales and 14 consecutive years of record earnings confirm, is based on strong consumer awareness of the Tootsie Roll brand name, and strategic acquisition of other well positioned and highly recognized brand names to leverage its existing operations. The Gordons own 66% of the voting rights and 47% of the company's stock, and continue to control the company, which remains exclusively a candy company making the very best quality candy for the market it knows best.

THE CANDY INDUSTRY

The United States' largest manufacturing sector, the processed food and beverage industry, is composed of two primary divisions: lower value-added and higher value-added food processors. Higher value-added processors, such as candy manufacturers, make retail-ready, packaged, consumer brand name products which have a minimum of 40% of the industry shipment value added through sophisticated manufacturing. Candy is a $20 billion retail industry worldwide, and accounts for about one third of the dollar-value of the snack-food market (the largest segment of the higher value-added division). Tootsie Roll Industries occupies a niche market within the Standard Industrial Classification (SIC) code 2064 (candy and other confectionery products) which includes taffies, lollipops, and chewing gum. The U.S. confectionery market generates approximately $9.7 billion in annual sales.

Candy is not yet a "mature" industry in the United States. The compound annual growth rate for candy in the past ten years has been close to 6% a year, a very solid gain in an industry that is supposedly mature. In fact, within the chocolate confectionery subcategory, the United States ranks 11th in the world in per capita consumption and fifth in the world in growth since 1980. Based on current demographics, many analysts believe that there will be further growth for confectioneries. A "baby boomlet" is on the way, significantly increasing the teenage population. By the time the population bulge peaks in the year 2010, it will top the baby boom of the 1960s in both size and duration. According to government statistics, the percentage of children between the ages of 5 and 14 will rise during the 1990s, increasing from 14.2 percent of the population in 1990 to 14.5 percent in the year 2000. This trend will serve as a strong foundation for increasing consumption of confectionery products through the end of the century. Nevertheless, spending for food and drink as a percentage of all personal consumption is declining in the United States, and most manufacturers recognize that future opportunities lie in using profits from domestic sales to penetrate foreign markets.

Many U.S. producers now use complex processing methods and efficient, automated manufacturing operations which yield comparable quality at lower cost, and are finding a growing international market for their products. Despite recessionary economic conditions and reduced discretionary income, foreign consumers purchase U.S. higher value-added foods and beverages because U.S. products compare favorably with similar products made elsewhere, offering equal or better quality at a lower price. Today, the top five importers of U.S. products are: Japan, Canada, Mexico, South Korea, and the Netherlands. Foreign demand for U.S.-produced higher value-added products (including candy) has increased since 1993, thanks primarily to the rapid growth of the middle class in developing and emerging nations, and growth in the new markets of the former Soviet bloc nations.

However, the candy industry has recently faced several industry curbs. New nutritional labeling requirements were imposed by the Food and Drug Administration in 1990 to regulate serving size, health messages, and the use of descriptive terms such as "light" and "low fat." The Federal Trade Commission also developed stringent sale-date requirements and strict guidelines for documenting environmental claims on packaging. These new regulations were imposed under costly, disruptive, difficult-to-meet deadlines, and posed a particular threat to many foreign food and beverage processors, who are not accustomed to such extensive product analysis and disclosure. For Tootsie Roll, this major packaging revision was costly, and involved detailed laboratory analysis and package modification of every item the company produces.

Candy is still a treat for all ages. People who loved Tootsie Rolls when they were children often buy them for their children and thus the Tootsie Roll perpetuates itself. The baby boom generation grew up with Tootsie Roll products, therefore name recognition is very high among this group. While parental purchases may increase due to brand recognition, the baby boomers are becoming increasingly more concerned with their health and their children's diet. As a result, baby boomers are purchasing less candy for themselves and their children. Thus, as people become more health and weight conscious, their demand for sugar-based products decreases. Additionally, as this consumer group gets older, their concern for dental health becomes greater. Candy has been identified as a major cause of dental decay, and hard, sticky, or chewy snacks, such as Tootsie Rolls, cannot be eaten by people who have had various kinds of dental work. Also, some parents do not buy candy because they are concerned that sugar causes hyperactivity in some children.

Children are Tootsie Roll's primary target market, since children ages six to seventeen create the greatest demand for confectionery products. According to a study by the Good Housekeeping Institute, candy is the second most requested snack food among six to twelve year olds; only ice cream is higher in demand. This group (ages 6 to 17) spend $60 billion of their own money annually, with two-thirds of this spending on candy, snacks, and beverages.

TOOTSIE ROLL—1996

Tootsie Rolls are unique, and occupy a niche of the candy market which includes taffies, lollipops, and chewing gum. Tootsie Roll Industries' competition is other candy and ready-to-eat snack food manufacturers. Tootsie Roll Industries commands 2–3% of the overall market as the eighth largest candy manufacturer following Hershey (27%), M&M Mars (25%), Nestle (10%), Brach (6%), Huhtamaki (4%), Storck (3%), and RJR Nabisco (3%). Although Tootsie Roll has captured only 2–3% of the total candy market, it continues to be the leader in its own segment, where it maintains a 50% market share. Tootsie Roll's strengths are brand loyalty, established shelf space, state-of-the-art manufacturing facilities, and the fact that there are fixed price ceilings for candy products. Also, as the United States becomes a more nutrition-oriented society, Tootsie Rolls have another advantage because they contain no cholesterol and have less saturated fat than other leading candy bars.

Tootsie Roll uses many suppliers for sugar, corn syrup, cocoa, and milk, and adapts to fluctuations in commodity prices by changing the formula and size of its products to keep total costs relatively constant. For example, Tootsie Roll can substitute corn syrup for some of the necessary sugar, thus decreasing its dependency upon a given commodity or supplier. Tootsie Roll also reduces and controls costs by owning its own refinery. The company can thus buy raw sugar and make, rather than buy, processed sugar, decreasing its dependence on processed sugar suppliers. When natural disasters affect the availability or price of one of its ingredients—for instance, sugar or cocoa—as did floods along the Mississippi River in 1993, the company usually decreases the size of its product to keep the selling price constant.

Tootsie Roll Industries' vertically-integrated structure supports its drive for competitiveness, keeping total costs down and maintaining its leading edge in technology. In addition to the sugar refinery, Tootsie Roll owns its own advertising agency, so that commissions flow back in to it. The company also makes the sticks for its lollipops, has a print shop for color printing, and owns a machine shop where new machinery is built and existing machinery rebuilt. Tootsie Roll Industries also constantly upgrades its manufacturing equipment to maintain the utmost efficiency.

Tootsie Roll's objectives, which have made it one of America's strongest companies, are, and have always been:

1. Run a trim operation
2. Eliminate waste
3. Minimize cost
4. Improve performance

To be competitive in the world candy market, where margins are limited, one must produce top-quality candy very efficiently. Tootsie Roll has spent millions of dollars on state-of-the-art expansion and automation of its five production facilities (Chicago, Massachusetts, New York, Tennessee, and Mexico). Much of its equipment is designed specifically for Tootsie Roll. As Mel Gordon, CEO and Chairman of the Board of Tootsie Roll Industries, explains: "Anybody can buy machinery and in that way become state-of-the-art, but if you develop your own adaptations to the machinery so that it runs faster and runs better for your products, or you develop in-house machinery that does what nobody else in the market can do, then you're ahead of state-of-the-art. We've strived in the last 15 years to be ahead of state-of-the-art." However, the one aspect of its operations the company has not been able to control is the power of its packaging material suppliers. Increased demand has led to dramatic price increases in paper, board, plastics, and foil. To insulate itself from price fluctuations, Tootsie Roll has, whenever possible, negotiated fixed price contracts with its packaging suppliers.

ACQUISITIONS

Tootsie Roll Industries often generates more cash than it needs for internal growth, and can therefore consider complementary acquisitions. Following strict criteria, such as a strong brand name, and a preference for non-chocolate (such as hard candies and chewy candies) over chocolate so as not to compete in its own niche, Tootsie Roll has made several key acquisitions of proven brands to expand its product line, increase its shelf space, and spur growth. As President Ellen Gordon explains, "We add new lines only when it benefits our product in quality and efficiency."

Two of Tootsie Roll's earliest acquisitions (1972) were the Mason Division of Candy Corporation of America, which makes such well-known products as Mason Mints, Mason Dots, Mason Licorice Crows, and Mason Spice Berries; and the Bonomo Turkish Taffy Company. In 1985, Tootsie Roll acquired Cella's Confections, which makes chocolate-covered cherries; and in 1988, it acquired the Charms Company, thereby becoming the world's largest manufacturer of lollipops. Charms' principal product, the Blow Pop, a lollipop with a bubble gum center, makes a nice complement to the highly successful Tootsie Pop. Shortly after the acquisition of the Charms Company, Mel Gordon observed, "We specialize in hard candies such as Tootsie Pops and Blow Pops and all the flat pops that Charms makes. That's a big niche for us, to be the world's largest manufacturer of pops. Also, we're in chewy candy with the Tootsie Roll and the growing Frooties and Flavor Roll lines. We feel that in those two areas we have a certain dominance and we'd like to keep our expertise focused in those areas."

In November 1993, Tootsie Roll purchased the chocolate and caramel division of the Warner-Lambert Company, which makes the popular brands Junior Mints, Charleston Chew, Sugar Daddy, Sugar Babies, and Pom Poms. The acquisition of these new lines places Tootsie Roll Industries in more direct competition with other major chocolate manufacturers such as Hershey and M&M Mars, and provides it with a number of new products which clearly complement its "chewy" candy product lines. Over the years, Tootsie Roll has carefully and selectively acquired 17 popular candy brands, enlarging its niche in the candy and other confectionery segment of the higher value-added products market.

DISTRIBUTION/ADVERTISING

Tootsie Roll Industries uses over 100 public and contract brokers to distribute its products to nearly 15,000 customers. To market the newly-acquired Warner-Lambert brands more effectively, Tootsie Roll created new packaging for them which resembled the packaging of its more established Tootsie Roll products and capitalized on the synergies of Warner-Lambert products with its existing lines.

In addition to using its distribution network to increase sales of Warner-Lambert products, Tootsie Roll is pushing those products generally associated with movie theaters, such as Junior Mints, into mainstream retail outlets: convenience stores, grocery stores, drug chains, and warehouse club stores. Convenience stores and supermarkets have traditionally been the dominant candy retailers, but have recently been losing sales to discount stores and drug store chains. Right now, all four venues share equally in confectionery sales. However, most candy purchases are impulse buys made while waiting in line at a store, and since many supermarkets have switched to candy-free aisles, these impulse sales have been reduced. As impulse sales opportunities are diminished, the customer must search for the product. A consumer is unlikely to undertake a search unless desire is heightened through advertising. Parents are the target market that advertisements must reach. However, marketing efforts often tend to focus on children, who are not always the purchasers. These eager consumers purchase through, and with the acceptance of, a parent.

Tootsie Roll has most recently focused its sales efforts on the more rapidly growing classes of trade such as warehouse clubs. In the candy industry it is difficult to gain shelf space, particularly when competing with large companies such as Hershey and M&M Mars. It appears that Tootsie Roll has begun to make progress toward this objective. Tootsie Rolls are beginning to appear in warehouse stores, such as Sam's, BJ's Warehouse, and COSTCO, with large packages of traditional Tootsie Rolls and bags of multi-colored Tootsie Roll pops.

Candy regularly shows the strongest gains from promotion and merchandising, clearly evident by the significant increases in candy sales during major holiday periods — Valentine's Day, Easter, Halloween, and Christmas. In fact, candy has shown a stronger response to promotions than any other snack category.

The third quarter has always been the strongest for Tootsie Rolls due to increased Halloween sales. However, Halloween is changing. Grocery retailers report that there is a noticeable shift in consumer behavior because of concern for child safety. In the last several years, Halloween celebrations have moved from the streets, with "trick or treating" door to door, to indoor parties sponsored by schools, churches, and, more recently, enclosed shopping malls, thereby reducing purchases for candy that used to be given to trick or treaters. Also, parents have been reluctant to purchase any products that could be easily tampered with, particularly at Halloween. The way Tootsie Roll products are packaged creates a potential concern. Individually wrapped, unsealed products can be tampered with and are thus negatively impacted by an event such as the 1982 Tylenol poisoning. In fact, Tootsie Roll sales suffered in the wake of that national scare.

While Tootsie Roll's 100-year history has contributed to its wide product recognition, a tradition of national advertising begun in the early 1950s on television programs such as "The Mickey Mouse Club" and "Howdy Doody" has successfully made "Tootsie Roll" a household word, establishing its domestic market; and schedules continue to be regularly placed in both electronic and print media. Although the Tootsie Roll and Charms brands are well known, as Ellen Gordon puts it, "It's important to keep them in front of the public." In Tootsie Roll's memorable 1970s advertising campaign, "How Many Licks?", a little boy asks a wise owl, "How many licks does it take to get to the Tootsie Roll center of a Tootsie Pop?" Consumers became actively involved as they tried to answer the question for themselves. Although the company has had several successful advertising campaigns since then, it currently spends very little on advertising (approximately 2% of sales, concentrated on television), relying instead on nostalgia and its 100-year-old brand. Internationally, however, aggressive advertising programs support the brands in Mexico as well as in the Pacific Rim markets and certain Eastern European countries.

THE GORDONS

Tootsie Roll Industries, Inc. has been run since 1962 by the husband and wife team of Ellen Gordon, President and Chief Operating Officer, and Melvin Gordon, Chairman of the Board and Chief Executive Officer. The couple owns 47% of the company stock, most of which was inherited by Ellen Gordon, whose family has been Tootsie Roll's largest shareholder since the early 1930s.

Ellen and Melvin Gordon have been working together since the 1960s. They are quick to state that they have an open door policy, but often do not attend annual meetings, saying that they already know what has happened. Together with five other executives, they plan all of the company's marketing, manufacturing, and distribution strategies, but the Gordons alone determine Tootsie Roll's corporate vision by controlling strategic planning, decision making, and the setting of corporate goals. Ellen, 64, and Melvin, 75, have no immediate plans to retire, and insist they want to continue working, although on a number of occasions they have expressed the desire to have one of their four daughters (none of whom currently works for Tootsie Roll) take over the management of the company. "We hope that our children, or the management that we are building up in the company, will be able to run the company someday," the Gordons claim, but they have no definite strategic plan for passing on the succession.

Tootsie Roll's strong performance and superior balance sheet should make it a prime target for a takeover, but the Gordons' determination to maintain control over Tootsie Roll Industries may be one reason why Wall Street has shown little interest in the company. The majority of Tootsie Roll's voting stock, 66%, is controlled by the Gordons, and the couple says they have no intention of selling the company. Ellen Gordon explains: "We're busy making Tootsie Roll products and selling them. We're kind of conservative and we don't make projections."

Although Tootsie Roll does not intend to sacrifice long-term growth for short-term gains, its strategy has simply been to focus on making Tootsie Rolls, rather than on preparing forecasts or strategic planning. Over the years, several key acquisitions have enhanced Tootsie Roll's product line, but these acquisitions have generally been made as opportunities have presented themselves within its niche market, and not necessarily as part of a well thought out strategic plan. The Gordons remain arrogant in their view of the market, and Ellen Gordon repeatedly states, "No one else can make a Tootsie Roll."

Recently, Tootsie Roll Industries took advantage of an opportunity related to the location of its headquarters in Chicago. The lease on their 2.2 million square foot facility in Chicago was due to expire and the landlord was not willing to renew it. Tootsie Roll faced the possibility of relocating to a less expensive territory because, with a low ticket item like candy, every penny counts, but the company did not wish to relocate. At the same time, the city did not want Tootsie Roll Industries to leave because it feared the resulting rise in unemployment. Thus, Ellen Gordon was able to leverage the firm's 850 jobs into a lucrative package of incentives to stay headquartered in Chicago. The deal signaled a national trend: small companies are more likely to get big tax concessions and other perks as city economies increasingly depend on them. The Gordons' negotiations garnered $1.4 million in state and local tax exemptions over the next fifteen years, a $20 million low-interest-rate loan to buy the Tootsie Roll plant, $200,000 in job training funds, and the creation of a state enterprise zone located in the plant for tax breaks on machinery and utilities. In turn, the Gordons agreed to add 200 workers over five years and start a loan program for employees to buy homes in Chicago.

Tootsie Roll has remained an independent company for its 100-year history and Ellen Gordon feels that its independence has been a great strength: "As we have grown beyond a small entrepreneurial company we have been able to retain some of our entrepreneurial philosophy and way of doing business." The Gordons are determined to continue Tootsie Roll as an independent company "for generations to come," but Ellen claims, finally, that the key to its success is ". . . fun. Whenever I tell people I work in a confectionery company there's always a smile. That's very important—the magic of candy."

GLOBAL OPPORTUNITIES

The United States accounts for 90% of Tootsie Roll's sales; the remaining 10% of Tootsie Roll products are sold in foreign markets. Mexico is Tootsie Roll's second largest market, and Canada is third. However, because U.S. consumer spending for food and drink as a percentage of all personal consumption is declining, Tootsie Roll and other candy manufacturers have begun to recognize that future growth opportunities lie in using domestic profits to penetrate foreign markets.

Tootsie Roll needs to increase its sales and distribution internationally in order to continue to grow as the U.S. market moves toward maturity. As trade barriers decrease, Tootsie Roll's opportunities to expand internationally are growing, especially because foreign demand for U.S.-produced higher value-added products, including candy, has increased significantly since 1993. The predicted reduction or elimination of the European Community confection tariffs and variable levies on ingredient composition may also facilitate export growth into Eastern Europe.

Tootsie Roll Industries has begun slowly and cautiously working toward worldwide market penetration, targeting export growth to the Far East and Europe, where per capita confectionery consumption is 40% higher than in the United States. Tootsie Roll currently holds licenses in several countries and regions including the Philippines, Colombia, Europe, the Far East, and Latin America. In addition, the company opened a sales office in Hong Kong in 1992 for sales to China, Korea, and Taiwan, and exports products to the Middle East, Eastern Europe, and Central and South America. However, this international activity remains a very small percentage of Tootsie Roll's total sales.

Since the Gordons are not getting any younger, the future of Tootsie Roll candy will depend on several key decisions they will make over the next few years. Perhaps the time has come for Mel and Ellen to think ahead while they are still on top.

U.S. Electricar: Zero-Emissions Autos in the 1990s

Robert N. McGrath, Embry-Riddle Aeronautical University

During the 1996 Atlanta Olympics, the General Motors Corporation spent millions of dollars advertising the introduction of a two-seat passenger all-electric automobile called the EV-1, the first truly commercial, mass production electric car that had been announced for sale in decades. Unfortunately, what the TV commercial did not say, but what otherwise was common knowledge among industry followers, was that the car would be priced as high as some luxury automobiles yet travel less than 100 miles before it needed recharging—except, of course, on cold days or in conditions of frequent acceleration and deceleration, in which case the single-charge range could easily be cut in half. GM had created a special division for the design, development, and commercialization of this one automobile, which, despite much acclaim as the most technologically advanced automobile in the world, years of careful prototyping, and an unprecedented level of market testing and analysis, did not have a range much better than its technological brethren of a century before (*Autoweek*, December 13, 1993; *New York Times*, January 28, 1994; *Detroit News*, May 8, 1994).

The Ford Motor Company was either more cautious or farther behind, having in the advanced prototype stage a small, European-style delivery van of similar technology and performance characteristics as GM's passenger car (*Business Week*, May 30, 1994). Chrysler's approach was different still, having already started leasing, for over $100,000 per vehicle, an electric variant of the Chrysler Voyager minivan, which also could not travel more than a hundred miles or so on a charge (*New York Times*, May 6, 1994). Meanwhile, all of the major automobile manufacturers around the world, many of the smaller automobile manufacturers, and many small firms starting up or spilling over from other industries, were also scrambling to develop the best product of this kind that they could (*Automotive News*, June 7, 1993). For a list of the projects being pursued by major players in the industry, see Exhibit 1.

Exhibit 1   **Industry Incumbents' Electric Vehicle Programs Underway in 1993**

Chrysler Corporation
Program: 50 Dodge Caravan/Plymouth Voyager Electric
Battery: Nickel-Iron or Nickel-Cadmium
Range: 80 miles
Top Speed: 70 mph
Partners: Energy Power Research Institute, General Electric, SAFT America, Good-year.
Customers: Utilities

Daihatsu Motor Co. Ltd.
Program: 300 (per year) Hijet vans and Ruggers
Battery: Lead-Acid
Range: Hijet, 81 miles at 25 mph; Rugger, 125 miles at 25 mph.
Top Speed: Hijet, 50 mph; Rugger, 56 mph
Partners: Japan Storage Battery Co., Kansai Electric Power Co.
Customers: Government Units and Electric Power Companies

Fiat Auto SPA
Program: 400 Panda Elettras and Cinquecentros
Battery: Elettra, Lead-Acid; Cinquecentro, Lead-Acid and Nickel-Cadmium
Range: Elettra, 62 miles at 31 mph; Cinquecentro, 62 miles at 31 mph (Lead-Aci); 93 miles at 31 mph (Nicad)
Top Speed: Elettra, 43 mph; Cinquecentro, 50 mph (Lead-Acid); 53 mph (Nicad)
Customers: Utilities, Governments, Individuals

Ford Motor Company
Program: 80 EcoStar vans
Battery: Sodium-Sulfur
Range: 100 miles
Top Speed: 70 mph
Partners: Asea Brown Boveri, Silent Power Ltd., United Technologies Automotive Inc.
Customers: Utilities and governments in U.S., Mexico, Europe

General Motors Corporation
Program: 50 Impact prototype passenger cars
Battery: Lead-Acid
Range: 100 miles
Top Speed: 75 mph
Partners: Hughes Power Control Systems, Delco Remy
Customers: Internal use, contractors seeking defense department grants

Honda Motor Company
Program: planning a ground-up design
Battery: Lead-Acid
Partners: Advanced Lead-Acid Battery Consortium

Isuzu Motors Ltd.
Program: 8 1994 Elf Delivery vans
Battery: Lead-Acid
Range: 56 miles at 25 mph
Top Speed: 62 mph
Partners: Co-op Electric Vehicles Development Corp., Japan Storage Battery Co.
Customers: Local community groups, delivery companies, the Tama zoo

Mazda Motor Corporation
Program: 3 Eunos/Miata roadsters
Battery: Nickel-Cadmium
Range: 112 miles at 25 mph

| **Exhibit 1 (continued)** | **Industry Incumbents' Electric Vehicle Programs Underway in 1993** |

Top Speed: 81 mph
Partner/Customer: Chugoku Electric Power Co.

Mitsubishi Motors Corporation
Program: 28 Libero cargo vans
Battery: Lead-Acid and Nickel-Cadmium
Range: 102 miles at 25 mph (Lead Acid); 155 miles at 25 mph (Nicad)

Nissan Motor Company
Program: 52 1991 Cedric/Glora sedans
Battery: Lead-Acid
Range: 75 miles at 25 mph
Top Speed: 62 mph
Partner: Japan Storage Battery Co.
Customers: Local government units and corporations in urban areas

PSA Group (Peugot and Citroen)
Program: 600 Peugot and Citroen C25 vans
Battery: Lead-Acid
Range: 43 miles
Top Speed: 50 mph
Customers: 17 French cities, 8 European countries, Hong Kong

Renault
Program: 50 to 100 Master and Express vans
Battery: Lead-Acid and Nickel-Cadmium
Customers: Towns, major companies

Suzuki Motor Co.
Program: 1992 Alto, 86 Carry vans
Battery: Lead-Acid
Range: Alto, 80 miles at 25 mph; Carry, 75 miles at 25 mph
Top Speed: Alto, 62 mph; Carry, 47 mph
Partners: Japan Storage Battery Co.
Customers: Government units

Toyota Motor Company
Program: 40 Towne Ace vans
Battery: Nickel-Cadmium
Range: 99 miles at 25 mph
Top Speed: 68 mph
Customers: Governments/municipalities

Volkswagen AG
Program: 70 Jetta CityStromers
Battery: Lead-Acid
Range: 75 miles
Top Speed: 65 mph
Partners: RWE

Source: *Automotive News*, June 7, 1993.

In a more general sense, their aim was to produce an automobile that would not cause any pollution at all, or one that would cause "zero-emissions." Why? In 1990 the California legislature had adopted into law the requirement that, beginning in 1998, all automobile manufacturers which sold significant numbers of vehicles in the state must make available for sale zero-emissions vehicles, in numbers that would account for about 2% of total automobile purchases (Winn, 1994). This figure was grounded in some fairly rough analyses, made by California public officials, which noted that about 2% of all vehicles in the state were owned and operated by organizations with fleets of automobiles of various descriptions. The required percentage rose in the out-years, as California officials seemed resolved to begin, and then carefully nurture, a transition to clean automobiles that, as a bonus, also would not be dependent on imported foreign oil. Pressured by this deadline, most manufacturers decided that "zero-emissions" also meant "all-electric," and a resurrection of the kind of cars that competed fairly well with gasoline models until the invention of the electric starter in 1912. Few experts in the field foresaw the successful development of any other kind of technology as early as 1998.

The large automobile manufacturers faced a tough list of options. They could spend billions, collectively and in some cases individually, developing electric vehicles that virtually all industry officials "knew" would fail because of the ongoing consumer love affair with the performance and cost characteristics of gasoline-powered automobiles. Or, they could simply exit the California market altogether and avoid spending all those billions, but this would leave wide open 15% of the total U.S. automobile market, which was also well-known for its global marketplace leadership. Or, they could ignore the law and be fined $5,000 per vehicle they sold in California starting in 1998. Or, they could find less drastic and more innovative solutions, such as getting credit for zero-emission vehicle sales by licensing other small companies to design and develop zero-emission automobiles, and marketing them under their own names. Exhibit 2 provides a list of some of the recently-formed EV firms in the United States.

In most studies, the economics of production as well as the lack of marketplace acceptance forecast failure, except perhaps in some small niches. The *idea* of zero-emissions automobiles was very popular, of course, but when it came time to actually pay a steep price for an underperforming albeit clean car, consumers voiced reluctance (*J.D. Power Report*, May 1993; *Automotive News*, June 7, 1993; *Automotive News*, December 5, 1994). Worse still, the most environmentally-conscious individuals constituted a segment that in general could ill-afford luxury-priced automobiles. So the vision was appealing, but the reality was daunting.

U.S. ELECTRICAR

■ Company History

U.S. Electricar was a fairly young company and, like many others, experienced a great deal of early change. The firm began in 1976 in Sebastopol, California, as Solar Electric Engineering, Inc., during an era when environmental and energy consciousness became important in the United States. Solar Electric became successful enough at developing solar-powered consumer products to go public in 1980 (*Battery & EV Technology*, May 1994). Later, by acquiring a company called California General Sun, Inc. in 1985, and through a joint venture with a company called Solar Electric Technology, the company found even greater success developing energy-related technologies such as advanced solar cells (*Moody's OTC Manual* 1995).

By the early 1990s it became apparent to management that in light of the California zero-emission statutes, it fortuitously already had some of the key

Exhibit 2   **Electric Vehicle Start-Ups**

AC Propulsion Inc. San Dimas, California.
Founded: 1991
1993 Revenue: $.7 Million   Employees: 6
Profile: AC was founded by Alan Coccioni, who was instrumental in designing the
Impact before leaving GM. His expertise was in electric drivetrains.

Ecoelectric Corp. Tucson, Arizona.
Founded: 1992
1993 Revenue: not available   Employees: not available
Profile: Ecoelectric was founded by former race-car driver and computer software company owner Mary Ann Chapman; she was planning a Phoenix-to-Tucson courier service, conversion of small sedans and pickup trucks, the design of components, and EV
consulting in maintenance and repair.

Renaissance Cars Inc. Palm Bay, Florida.
Founded: 1989
1993 Revenue: $0   Employees: 26
Profile: Renaissance was founded by President Bob Beaumont and was building a
ground-up two seater named Tropica, a sporty, technologically-advanced roadster, but
designed for warm climates and having no roof. Beaumont's first attempt at EVs was the
Citicar, a 38 mph "glorified golf cart"; 2,253 sold from 1974 to 1976.

Rosen Motors Corp. Los Angeles, California.
Founded: 1993
1993 Revenue: not available   Employees: not available
Profile: Rosen Motors was founded by Ben Rosen, Chairman of Compaq Computer Corporation; he was planning a hybrid EV which included a gasoline turbine engine.

Solectria Corp. Arlington, Massachusetts.
Founded: 1986
1993 Revenues: $2 Million   Employees: 25
Profile: James D. Worden was President; Solectria converted GEO Metros and Chevrolet S-10 pickup trucks, and was also working on a ground-up EV called Sunrise.

Unique Mobility Inc. Golden, Colorado
Founded: 1967
1993 Revenues: $2.3 Million   Employees: 45
Profile: Unique was headed by Ray A. Geddes, was developing EV components, and
had contracts with BMW, Ford, and others.

Source: *Business Week*, May 30, 1994; *Inc.*, May 1994.

skills that would probably be necessary to be successful in developing Electric
Vehicles (EVs). In addition to consumer products, the firm had been producing
on-road electric cars since 1983, and, in 1992, started developing custom-built,
original equipment cars and vans (*Business Wire*, August 3, 1993). By 1993, the
firm had sold more than 200 electric vehicles, and began promoting itself as the
country's largest EV manufacturer.

In June of 1993 it was announced that the firm had selected Gates Energy
Product's Genesis lead-acid battery as the featured power source for all of the
electric vehicles it would subsequently produce, at a planned rate of 500 total
vehicles a year. David Brandmeyer, Engineering Vice President and General
Manager, said, "With Genesis batteries powering our EVs, Electricar can provide vehicles today that realize the full potential of existing EV technology. EVs
are an affordable, environmental transportation alternative that are viable now

within the appropriate operations setting" (*Battery & EV Technology*, June 1993). Also that month, Electricar secured exclusive distribution rights to an advanced electronic drivetrain developed by the Hughes Power Control Systems division of General Motors.

On July 30, 1993, Solar Electric acquired Nordskog Electric Vehicles, Inc. for $300,000 in cash and notes payable, $1,900,000 worth of common stock, and $1,000,000 in convertible notes payable. Nordskog had been producing industrial electric vehicles since 1946, and had produced over 55,000 such vehicles over the years. This acquisition gave Solar Electric immediate access to a network of 70 dealers, the largest EV production backlog in the industry, an 11-acre production site in Redlands, California, and the ability to produce a full spectrum of EVs, from in-plant industrial units to automobiles, trucks, vans, and 22-passenger buses.

On October 20th, Solar Electric acquired a Florida company called Consulier Automotive, which was known for its development of lightweight, high-tech materials for use in the construction of automobile bodies, and formed a wholly-owned subsidiary called U.S. Electricar Consulier, Inc. Eleven days later this subsidiary acquired, from a company called Mosler Auto Care Center, the assets it would need in order to develop composite integrated chassis and automobile body systems for lightweight cars. This acquisition was financed with $1,250,000 in shares of unregistered common stock. In November of the same year it acquired the Synergy Electric Vehicle Group, and in December it acquired the Livermore Research and Engineering Corporation. Each acquisition was made for approximately $250,000 in common stock.

■ A Commitment to EVs

On January 12 of 1994, the name U.S. Electricar was formally adopted. This decision was not merely symbolic; it reflected management's decision to devote all the firm's resources to the EV industry and divest all lines of business not dedicated to this purpose.

Four product groups were established: a commercial line which included utility, cargo, passenger, commercial delivery, and airport EVs; a bus group which would concentrate on 22-passenger EVs using existing designs; an Original Equipment Manufacturer (OEM) group which would concentrate on developing new designs for vans, trucks, buses, sedans, utility vehicles, and sports cars; and a mainstay "upfit" group which would concentrate on retrofitting Chevrolet S-10 pickup trucks and GM Geo Prizms with electric powertrains (*Battery & EV Technology*, May 1994). The primary distinction between the commercial, bus, and upfit group and the OEM group was one of how much the product would be produced internally versus externally. The commercial, bus, and upfit group were, to varying degrees, to retrofit other manufacturers' products, or use a lot of other manufacturers' existing designs and components. The OEM group was intended to develop products which would be all new U.S. Electricar design and manufacture. However, it was always assumed the divisions would share resources and work in concert with each other.

The upfit group was to become Electricar's bread-and-butter business, and the idea attracted a great deal of attention from manufacturers looking for short-term solutions to the California mandates. In particular, Ford was interested in supplying Electricar with what the industry termed "gliders": regular automobiles, but without the gasoline-engine components. The concept was simple. It was much easier to *fit* an existing model with electric components than it was to *retrofit* a fully-produced auto by first stripping out the gasoline engine. In this way Electricar could keep costs down, and Ford could get the credit for supplying zero-emissions vehicles in California. Ford was considering the Windstar minivan and Crown Victoria sedan for such a program, but had serious concerns about also being able to maintain the image for quality that it had struggled so hard to achieve. Ford was slow to commit until it could be sure that Electricar could meet the tough standards of being a "qualified vehicle modifier" *(Los Angeles Times*, November 16, 1994; *The Toronto Star*, November 26, 1994).

In any event, in conjunction with management's decision to commit to the EV industry was the establishment of its headquarters in Santa Rosa, California. By this time the firm owned a 14,650 square foot product development facility in Sebastopol, and leased 15,000 square feet of production space, 20,000 feet of warehouse space, and a 1,400 square foot sales office in Los Angeles. The company had about three hundred people on its payroll.

By the end of the year a great debate was underway regarding the California statutes and the EV issue in general. Fortunately, U.S. Electricar was faring well on all sides of the debate. An article in the December 1993 *Motor Trend* read, "Little credence has been given to small-time electric car manufacturers—and for good reason. Their wares have fallen short in too many ways."

Beyond mediocre performance and range, small-time ground-up EV efforts haven't offered the kind of fit and finish expected in new vehicles. Many production cars retrofitted to electric by converters have even failed to provide such basics as smooth and responsive steering, braking, shifting, and clutch operation. Crashworthiness of battery-laden EVs has also been suspect because barrier crash testing of these low-volume vehicles isn't required.

So how can an electric car company possibly overcome these problems? Perhaps by following the lead of Solar Electric Engineering of Sebastopol, California. For years, this company's niche was retrofitting year-old Ford Escorts and similar car models for electric propulsion, a business plan suitable only for small-time success. But significant corporate restructuring and several recent key acquisitions could change that.

Solar Electric's renewed vision began to unfold with the opening of its Electricar Los Angeles facility, the first in a series of planned satellite operations destined to serve regional EV markets. The company then signed with GM Hughes Electronics to buy variants of the high-tech electric powertrain developed for the GM Impact. It followed up with the acquisition of Nordskog Electric Vehicles, an established industrial EV manufacturer and recent electric bus developer, and then Consulier Automotive.

Each of these moves is individually noteworthy, but together they signify a unified plan for the production and sale of purpose-built electric vehicles. GMHE's advanced electric powertrains will provide a level of performance more in line with that of today's gasoline-powered cars. Consulier's expertise in automotive cored-composite technology—showcased in its ultra-lightweight, race-proven composite monocoque Consulier Intruder supercar—will provide advanced body/chassis technology for a ground-up vehicle. The Nordskog operation will supply an existing nationwide network of 70 service centers and potential sales outlets and yet another EV manufacturing site in California.

Much of the praise being given Electricar by the automotive establishment was no doubt deserved. In June of 1994, it was announced that the National Highway Traffic Safety Administration certified Electricar's light pickup truck under all Federal Motor Vehicle Safety Standards. As far as anyone could remember, this was the first EV to ever achieve this certification without exemptions or waivers. Boasted Ted Morgan, Electricar's CEO, "U.S. Electricar's new vehicle safety program establishes a new threshold for the electric vehicle industry comparable to the highest level of passenger car safety," and attributed much of the success to "virtual prototyping" on a special computer program (called DYNA3D) developed over a 15-year period at the Lawrence Livermore National Laboratory (LLL). Electricar had been using LLL's software in a collaborative agreement; in a sense, LLL was a pure R&D lab, and Electricar was a field test. Benefits of this software were similar to the benefits of tools generally called Computer-Aided-Design (CAD). LLL's software allowed much safety engineering to be done by computer simulation, making possible a drastic reduction in the number of actual crash tests needed, and a reduction in the time required to redesign imperfections. This innovation was certainly a coup, as small firms typically are too strapped for cash to fund extensive and massively expensive developmental tasks where complex technologies are involved (*Alternative Energy Network*, June 7, 1994).

On the other hand, there was still poor acceptance in the marketplace, even in the niches that Electricar was targeting. Though the characteristics of Electricar's products were probably best suited to the industrial fleet market, managers of industrial fleets were tough, pragmatic, sophisticated customers (*Automotive News*, April 26, 1993). While advocates could clearly see the advantages of EVs' low maintenance, energy efficiency, relative ease of refueling once a home base was wired for it, and relatively cheap electricity (the cost-per-mile of operating an EV was cheaper than the same measure for gasoline engine autos), they were dissuaded by the exorbitant initial price tags, short range, unproved reliability, service technician re-training costs, service-bay remodeling costs, low payload capacities, and battery replacement costs. Some of these worries presented a paradox for the industry, since EV manufacturers could not work out real-life bugs without first achieving the significant sales volumes that would bring desperately-needed experience. One fleet manager commented, "I tried to get someone from GM to give me a vehicle range. It varied by about 40 miles depending on who you talked to. Let's face it, 40 miles is a considerable distance to walk" (*Automotive News*, August 8, 1994).

In order to improve sales, on August 1, 1994, Electricar established its own credit corporation to help finance sales of EVs in creative ways. Leasing arrangements, for example, would allow potential buyers such as fleet managers the flexibility of trying EVs before (or without) committing to purchase (*Business Wire*, August 1, 1994).

But by the end of 1994 it was apparent that in order to continue to grow as the firm's management wished—in fact, in order to survive as a going concern—further arrangements and some restructuring of operations and financial liabilities would be required. It became obvious the firm needed additional capital, and more moves were necessary.

■ Global Alliances

In one important strategic move, Electricar established an arrangement with the Itochu Corp., which would bring in an immediate $15 million, but would give Itochu 3% of Electricar, and possibly another 5% if Itochu eventually opted to convert debt to equity. Itochu was a large Japanese trading company experienced in distributing automobiles for several Japanese automotive giants. This move was essentially the beginnings of a global alliance, and had associated risks and opportunities.

The deal included the formation of a Tokyo-based joint venture, the Japan Electricar Corporation (JEC), formed to develop EV products targeted at commercial fleet purchasers in that region. The immediate intention was for U.S. Electricar to export fleet vehicles specifically tailored to the Japanese market. JEC would essentially be the marketing arm and would have exclusive distribution rights in all of Asia. Also as part of the deal, Itochu would gain access to Electricar's vehicle designs.

Some critics were skeptical of Itochu's decision, as well as Electricar's long-term technology strategy. Despite Electricar's advances in areas such as manufacturing advanced composite materials and the impressive inroads made in engineering processes, Electricar's designs were still centered on lead-acid battery technology. Many experts seriously doubted that lead-acid technology was the viable, long-term propulsion technology needed to solve the EV range problem and really gain marketplace acceptance, except in very small niches. Its converted Chevrolet S-10s and GEO Prizms still had ranges of only about 60 to 80 miles, and sold (in lots of 30 or more) for about $33,000 and $29,000, respectively (*New York Times,* June 10, 1994). The first S-10 was only delivered to Florida Power and Light on May 31, 1994, however, so production economies were certain to improve. The short-term production goal was 400 conversions a month. Worse, EV subsystems such as the battery, electronic controller, and electric drive motors were so interrelated that the vehicles were centered on the technological characteristics of the battery. In short, Itochu was at risk of buying access to vehicle designs that might well become obsolete, given the likelihood of significant advances in other promising battery technologies (McGrath, 1996).

Nevertheless, the joint venture envisioned the sale of converted Grumman postal vehicles for distribution as light industrial delivery trucks in Japan—U.S. postal vehicles already had right-hand drive, required in Japan on all vehicles. Itocho would also be aided by a third party in the venture—Tokyo R&D, renowned in Japan for automotive design excellence and willing to provide technological services to the venture. Quipped an Itochu Executive Vice President, "We are just buying a ticket to see if it will hit the jackpot or not. . . . We hope we can get a major capital gain" (*Wall Street Journal,* June 10, 1994).

Soon Electricar would announce that much of the firm's production activities would be relocated to a site in Malaysia, due to the generally poor business climate for EVs in the United States. But this decision was no doubt encouraged by the fact that in industrializing Asian countries, one million cars had been sold in 1994—a figure which had doubled in only six years, and was expected to double again by the year 2000 (*World Trade,* August 1995).

Another important alliance was formed on October 6, when Electricar entered into a joint venture with Grupo Industrial Casa of Mexico City. Casa was Mexico's largest bus body manufacturer, and sold buses throughout Latin America. The venture aimed at developing, manufacturing, and marketing several thousand industrial EVs, especially small food delivery trucks and buses, for the heavily congested and polluted cities of North, Central, and South America. Mexico City seemed especially opportune, since a new law there banned gasoline delivery trucks six hours a day, three days a week. "The Mexican side of this venture was exuberant," said Casa's Chairman Ricardo Cornejo. "In the cooperative spirit of NAFTA [the North American Free Trade Agreement], this exciting venture follows a global business strategy to design and manufacture vehicles directly within the customer's market" (United Press International, October 6, 1994). Two jointly-owned corporations were planned, one based in the United States which would handle U.S. and Canadian operations, and one based in Mexico which would handle the remainder of the Western Hemisphere.

Next, a test-market of Electricar EVs was established in Hawaii, inaugurated by a two-year, $1.8 million contract from the Hawaiian Electric Vehicle Development Project. The project was matched by $3.4 million in Federal funds. A total of twenty-nine electric sedans would be furnished to indigenous electric utility companies as well as the U.S. Air Force and Navy (U.S. Electricar News, August 11, 1994). This project would serve as a feasibility test for entry into government fleets, which Federal law mandated must include "alternative fuel" vehicles (i.e., electric, propane, methanol, solar, hybrid, etc.) by 1996. Though alternative fuel vehicles were, technologically speaking, a much more inclusive category than all-electric vehicles, the law created the opportunity for as many as 500,000 EVs to be sold by the year 2000 (Battery & EV Technology, May 1994).

On November 21, Electricar announced that the U.S. Department of Commerce had awarded it funding for a five-year, $21.8 million program for the further development of a cost-effective composites manufacturing process. Electricar was to act as lead company in an extended effort to advance the technology involved in producing lightweight, high-quality, affordable, and safe EVs. The magnitude of the program was impressive: Electricar was commissioned to develop composites fit for use in EV components that would be recyclable, never require painting, and would be cost effective in production runs equivalent to making materials for 1,000 to 25,000 vehicles a year. This government subsidy was a significant step towards making mass-marketable EVs possible, and clearly positioned Electricar at the front. In a similar vein, on December 13, 1994, it was announced that Electricar and Kaiser Aluminum agreed jointly to develop advanced aluminum structures for EVs. The specific focus was improving the Electrolite urban delivery vehicle recently introduced by Electricar, which was intended for international markets. But certainly the knowledge gained would be transferable to other EVs and be useful to both firms.

In terms of actual production, between August 1994 and February 1995, U.S. Electricar produced 190 converted GEO Prizms and Chevrolet S-10 pickups, and seven electric buses. Additionally, it shipped several hundred off-road vehicles, such as forklift trucks and airport service vehicles. Financial data for U.S. Electricar can be found in Exhibits 3 and 4.

Exhibit 3   **Consolidated Income Account, years ended July 31 ($000)**

	1994	1993	1992
Net Sales	5,787	863	1,220
Cost of sales	6,372	802	848
Gross margin	(585)	61	372
R&D	7,724	376	56
Selling, general, and admin. expenses	11,805	1,936	777
Interest expense	339	146	80
Depreciation and amortization	833	17	14
Other expense (income)	17	24	(31)
Loss on disposition of solar home	—	—	55
Market development expense	3,718	—	—
Total other costs & Expenses	24,436	2,499	951
Income (loss) from continuing operations	(25,021)	(2,438)	(579)
Income (loss) from discontinued operations	—	(169)	(203)
Net Income	(25,201)	(2,607)	(782)
Previous retained earnings	(5,050)	(2,443)	(1,661)
Retained earnings	(30,071)	(5,050)	(2,443)
Earnings on common shares	(1.67)	(.45)	(.20)
Common shares: Year-end (000)	15,518	5,839	4,393
Average (000)	9,571	4,487	3,871

Source: *Moody's OTC Industrial Manual*, 1995.

VIEWS FROM THE TOP

■ Ted Morgan: CEO

Ted Morgan had been the President and CEO of Electricar since November of 1992 (Cronk, 1995). He came to the firm having already established himself as something of an expert at managing and financing growth ventures, developing niche strategies, and creating novel methods of distribution. He developed these skills working in sales and marketing positions in the Xerox Corporation for 14 years, and honed them through nurturing The Office Club superstore chain to an eventual merger with Office Depot in 1991, which created a $3 billion company.

From this experience Morgan had a strong appreciation for what institutional investors looked for in a growth company. He was much less expert at acquiring private financing, which was fueling most EV start-ups in the early nineties. The EV industry was fueled mostly by environmental concerns, not the opportunity for short-term gain. But technologies and other factors were evolving rapidly, and professional fund investors were beginning to take serious notice.

To attract large, professionally-managed blocks of funds, Morgan knew that establishing credibility was a critical factor. He believed in establishing

Exhibit 4   **Consolidated Balance Sheet, as of July 31 ($000)**

	1994	1993	1992
Assets			
Cash and equivalents	5,327	617	57
Accounts receivable	1,551	625	26
Inventory	6,716	1,086	214
Other	—	—	20
Prepaid and other current assets	803	269	—
Total current assets	14,397	2,597	317
PP&E	4,945	2,809	54
Intangibles, net	1,355	47	—
Other assets	609	—	—
Total assets	21,306	5,453	371
Liabilities			
Accounts payable and accrued expenses	—	—	267
Accounts payable	5,314	534	—
Accrued payroll and related expenses	406	274	—
Accrued warranty expenses	640	127	—
Other accrued expenses	801	459	—
Customer deposits	1,769	154	204
Notes payable & current portion of long-term debt	18	464	—
Notes payable, other	—	—	165
Notes payable, related parties	—	—	129
Total current liabilities	8,948	2,012	765
Long-term debt	9,980	1,020	30
Royalties payable	773	—	—
Series A preferred stock	7,118	4,408	—
Notes receivable	(1,094)	(1,000)	—
Common stock	25,652	4,063	2,019
Retained earnings	(30,071)	(5,050)	(2,443)
Total shareholder's equity	1,605	2,421	(424)
Total liabilities & stock equity	21,306	5,453	371
Net current assets	5,449	585	(448)
Book value	0.02	0.41	(0.10)

credibility upfront, by putting in place the strongest management team possible, not just at the top but down several layers of management, all the way to the point of purchase. Such a team should be capable of performing its own extensive marketing research and subsequently developing a sound, easily communicable strategy. He felt that the pronouncements made by environmentalists of the benefits of EVs were wild-eyed, and that the hundreds of millions of dollars of needed capitalization would never materialize unless the firm's plans could withstand the tough scrutiny of the venture capital community.

Key to becoming that one-in-ten choice of venture capitalists, then, was the development of a sound business plan. He felt sure that a company should never go to market prematurely. Otherwise a firm could easily wind up spending all its "easy" money foolishly and wastefully and then, after initial failures became evident, find it only that much more difficult to find subsequent investors. Being a small, public company had the advantage of being open to scrutiny, though such visibility was a double-edged sword.

In short, Morgan was a pragmatist and realist who felt unsure about blue-sky terms like "synergy," and felt uneasy about partnering relationships and alliances that did not show economic returns. The nature of the financial environment mandated remuneration to the owners. Hence Electricar had embarked on its acquisition spree when management realized what additional help it would need to succeed. Morgan knew that across-the-board reliance on in-house development of technologies would be too slow, but going outside the firm for help invited much trouble unless control was assured. Morgan felt that acquisitions, patenting, and licensing were viable approaches to keeping developments proprietary.

On the other hand, Morgan did not believe in being too focused, mostly due to the premature nature of so many key technologies. He felt that the "upfit" business was an appropriate entree to the EV industry and had huge national and international potential, but subsequent industry developments were much harder to foresee accurately. There were no rules to this industry yet and many paths were possible. "Fleet operators" was about as specific as he would define Electricar's potential niche, though of course he could cite endless examples of how rapid transit districts, public utilities, and corporations should be attracted to what he had in mind. Generally, Morgan envisioned an Electricar that leased fleets of vehicles and also provided maintenance, warranty, training, and other services. But "in the short term, [success depended on] the ability to raise capital. That's the measure of success. The only measure of success" (Cronk, 1995).

In contrast to the combined wisdom of the Big Three in Detroit, Morgan felt that the key to early success lay not so much in the performance of EVs as it did on price. He noted the obvious difficulty that Chrysler was having leasing its electric Voyager for up to $120,000 apiece. He felt that if volumes could be reached where converted Chevrolet S-10s could be leased for about $20,000, "every utility company in the country" would line up for them. Such an accomplishment might create a 3-to-5 billion dollar "niche," and several hundred million dollars of business by as early as 1997.

With numbers like these in mind, it was no wonder that Morgan rarely thought about the individual consumer, and saw little point in pursuing individual sales, which almost certainly would have to be done through layers of middlemen and independent dealers. He felt that Electricar did not have the capital, tools, and distribution network needed to really crack the mass market. Foreseeable per-unit margins were not nearly inviting enough: "Everybody is attempting to paint grandiose pictures of what's going on here. The reality is that the business-to-business transaction is the only transaction right now in the electric vehicle area. . . . We'll leave others to their dreams of building hundreds of thousands of electric vehicles" (Cronk, 1995).

■ John Dabels: Vice President for Sales

John Dabels was Vice President for Sales, Marketing, and Government Relations. He was fairly new to Electricar, having joined the firm in May of 1994. But from October 1990 to March of 1993, he had served as the Director of Market Development for General Motors' Impact program. Prior to that, he had been Director of Marketing for Buick since 1979.

Naturally, Dabels was intimately familiar with the individual automobile purchaser—the regular consumer. He felt that the 1990s rebirth of the electric automobile concept, constituent technologies, and other broad conditions were such that this time around, the EV was ready to become much more than a fad. He felt that EVs did make consumer sense for short trips in confined communities, for commuting where routes were predictable on a daily basis, for running kids around, for shopping trips, and so forth—EVs were not ready to be "first" cars, but were ready to take their place in many families as second or third cars. However, he too felt that price was a severe problem. But he also had a more encompassing and systematic view of what an automobile was and could be. In particular, he understood that when it came to cars, many people viewed the purchasing experience as obnoxious, and that this simple reality was an important obstruction to sales.

Hence, Dabels felt that the EV was less characteristically like a gasoline automobile than it was like a very large electric appliance or even personal computer, and that lessons could and should be taken from those industries. There, successful marketing innovations included the use of mail-order houses and home shopping networks; certainly, enough managerial ingenuity existed in the neophyte EV industry to adapt the wisdom developed in the electronics and computer industries. No one should be a slave to doing business anything like the way the established auto giants did business.

In fact, Dabels was generally skeptical about the major players' willingness or abilities to succeed in the much-different EV world: "I think there will be some guys wildly successful before the Big Three figure out what to do. . . . Today, if you're not a car guy you don't qualify in the auto industry. You've got to be a car engineer. Those guys hit such small, narrow markets that they have literally forgotten about the consumer. They'll come out with engineering ideas that are not well-executed. They have great disdain for marketing people" (Cronk, 1995).

■ Robert Garzee: Vice President of U.S. Electricar

Robert Garzee was a Vice President of U.S. Electricar, and President of the Synergy EV Group. He came to Electricar with the acquisition of Synergy, Inc., in 1993. There he learned the ropes of learning and profiting through partnering. For example, he was an original member of the CALSTART design team, a quasi-public consortium of several organizations devoted to making the EV movement happen in California. He had previously spent 12 years with IBM, eight in a marketing-management capacity.

Unlike CEO Morgan, Garzee was a big fan of strategic partnering. He had learned through experience that consortia could be extremely effective if the right people were involved and the management was good. At McClellan Air Force Base in California, home of the Air Force's R&D activities in developing advanced/special materials, he had brought together the Sacramento Municipal Utility District, the City of San Jose, California, the FMC Corporation, Pacific

Gas & Electric, and Nordskog in a successful program that advanced the state of the art of composite materials intended for use in buses and automobiles. When Electricar absorbed Synergy and Nordskog, this brought an important subset of this consortium under U.S. Electricar's control, also making it economically accountable for progress. The price for all this control, of course, included not only the costs of acquisition, but continuing administrative oversight.

In any event, Garzee also was committed to the fleet market, and felt that the Big Three would or could not respond well to that niche. Like Morgan, Garzee had a view that seemed pragmatic: " . . . people are buying industrial EVs not because they want to solve the pollution problem, but because it's the best way to solve a business problem. . . . If, for some reason, Detroit decides [to] back out, I [still] don't see the utilities saying that EVs don't make any sense. . . . EVs will cost about 15-20% more than their [gasoline] counterparts, but it doesn't take long to make up that percentage once in operation" (Cronk, 1995).

■ Scott Cronk: Director of Business Development

Scott Cronk was Director of Business Development at Electricar and led its strategic partnering activities. Cronk came to Electricar with a Big Three pedigree. General Motors had sponsored his engineering degree at the General Motors Institute in Flint, Michigan, and he joined GM in 1982. From 1988 to 1991 he managed an avionics product line in northern Europe for Delco Systems Operations, a division of GM. From 1991 to 1994 he worked at Delco Electronics headquarters, leading international business development and planning. He joined Electricar in 1994.

Where Morgan seemed to be the stern pragmatist on the team, Cronk seemed to be more abstract and philosophical. Cronk felt that in order to bring the EV idea to profitable fruition, a "new business theory" would be required—or at least a synthesis of business practices that at the time had not yet been pieced together in traditional American business circles. He felt that it was incumbent upon managers in the new industry to bring together four forces: environment, energy, economy, and education.

The environmental force was straightforward. It seemed imperative that the world find a way out of its dependence on oil, a limited resource and one that was draining the U.S. economy of massive amounts of money each year. But the more important issue was pollution, a problem that affected not only lifestyles but possibly the future of the planet. Managers in the new industry should root themselves in this idea.

The energy force referred not to oil, but to electricity. Industrialized society had created a massive infrastructure that was just as dependent on electricity as it was on oil, and overall capacity had been built to accommodate peak electric-load requirements. This was inefficient on a social scale—an extensive EV industry could absorb the excess, off-peak capacity, make the industry more efficient in the process, and reduce the unit cost of using electricity, which is obviously the energy resource of the future (however it might be generated).

In terms of economic forces, the early 1990s saw the economically painful transition from a defense-oriented, Cold War world economy to one that was market-driven and militarily peaceful in its basic character. The managerial and technical brilliance that won the technological battles of the Cold War was too important a national resource to underemploy; these skills could be applied to a new endeavor—the EV—that had a total potential that rivaled defense spending. Managers had a window of opportunity for acquiring much of this talent (especially in California) that would not stay open for very many years.

In terms of education, managers should feel it their responsibility to convert the environmental, energy, and economic forces into an overall consensus—by advocating EVs through such fundamental marketing and informational campaigns—that basic education was the prime goal. Across the board, grassroots movements needed help from the new industry which it spawned.

However, Cronk felt that a fifth "e"—enterprise structure—was probably the most crucial, since it would require the most ingenuity and effort from industry management. This was the essence of what he foresaw as the new, necessary business theory. He felt that it would be absolutely necessary for management in the EV industry to abandon the old automotive industry model. A century of development had evolved the automobile industry into a giant, hierarchical, oligopolistic structure, oriented towards technologies, not markets.

Cronk's alternative vision was difficult to describe, since what he had in mind had no fully-formed precedent. The "virtual corporation" model that developed in the computer industry was not exactly it, though networks of value-adding firms would be essential. The "lean production" model was incomplete, though production efficiency was a must. The Japanese *keiretsu*, or cluster of closely interconnected firms supplying the parent firm, was the closest single model Cronk could articulate, though he noted two problems: one, he felt that the Japanese model was excellent at developing emerging technologies, but did not make the transition well to a mature industry environment; two, some of the formal relationships found in *keiretsus* were deemed collusive in the U.S. legal system, and were illegal.

Cronk articulated his vision in this way:

> [The term "EV" should] refer to any vehicle which is focused on efficient use of energy predominantly through the use of lightweight structural materials and electric motors that drive the vehicle's wheels. It is important to define EVs in this way because at this time it is far from clear which types of energy storage devices will win out in the end. . . .
>
>   New electric energy storage and delivery systems and new structural materials: this is what EVs are about. [This] moves the discussion away from 'the battery' and allows us to focus on a larger, more multidimensional set of challenges. . . . (Cronk, 1995; p.122)

CONCLUSION

By 1995, management at Electricar decided to focus its resources on what had become core lines of business: electric transit shuttle buses and industrial/commercial vehicles. In order to accomplish this complete corporate conversion, however, some manufacturing operations had to be suspended and/or closed. Facilities in Redlands, California, were temporarily shut down, while operations in Los Angeles and Florida were permanently closed (but planned to be moved to the Redlands, California, facility.) During this moratorium, management looked scrupulously at the continued viability of its electric sedan and light truck conversion business, but in any eventuality decided to continue providing full services to previous purchasers of these wares. As a result of these decisions, the firm's work force was reduced by about 30%, with additional reductions foreseen.

By late 1994 and throughout 1995, the firm was still suffering losses. For the quarter ending October 31, 1994, Electricar reported net sales of $6.18 million, which was greater than its total revenues for all of fiscal year 1994 (Electricar's fiscal year ended on July 31)—but net losses amounted to $8.96 million, or $.54 per share. In the first quarter of fiscal year 1994, sales had been $1.12 million, which yielded a net loss of $1.26 million or $.21 per share. Through the first nine months of 1995, Electricar had suffered a $37 million loss on revenues of $11 million (*World Trade*, August 1995).

While the firm had a number of promising products and development contracts as of early 1995, the volumes were obviously inadequate to break even, much less achieve profitability. The management team now felt it had to attempt to define the direction it intended to go in marketing electric vehicles. They felt they had to anticipate, to the best of their ability, where the demand

Exhibit 5	**Automobile Ownership Costs**	
	1993 Ford Escort	*Hypothetical EV*
Price	$11,387	$11,900
6% sales tax	683	0
Acquisition cost	$12,070	$11,900
Per mile (cents):		
Gasoline and oil	4.8	0
Electricity	0	1.5
Maintenance	2.2	1.0
Tires	.7	.8
Battery	0	8.0
Total	7.7	11.3
Dollars per year:		
Insurance	$784	$784
License/registration	147	100
Depreciation	2,412	1,179
Finance charge	527	517
Total	3,870	2,580
(cents per mile)	25.8	17.2
Total (cents per mile)		
Operation	7.7	11.3
Fixed	25.8	17.2
Operation cost per mile	33.5	28.5

"Table compares costs for a 1993 Ford Escort against a mythical electric vehicle that would compete against it evenly as a choice for a household's second car, based on a four-year, 60,000 mile cycle."

Source: *Automotive News*, June 7, 1993.

for electric propulsion would grow over the next decade. They then needed the financing which would allow U.S. Electricar to take advantage of those opportunities.

REFERENCES

Alternative Energy Network, "U.S. Electricar Announces FMVSS Certification of Volume Production Electric-Powered Truck." June 7, 1994.

Automotive News, "Key Players: Fleet Managers Take Lead Role in Cutting Costs, Testing Use of Alternative Fuels." April 26, 1993.

Automotive News, "California Dreaming." June 7, 1993.

Automotive News, "Electric Utility Fleet Managers Cast Wary Eye at Electric Vehicles." August 8, 1994.

Automotive News, "Conversions Generate Interest in EV Conversions." December 5, 1994.

Autoweek, "Plug In, Turn On, or Drop Out: A Debate Grounded in Reality." December 13, 1993.

Battery & EV Technology, "Electricar Selects Gates Energy Products' Lead-Acid Batteries." June 1993.

Battery & EV Technology, "Electricar Keeps Its Focus on the Road." May 1994.

Business Week, "Electric Cars: Will They Work? And Who Will Buy Them?" May 30, 1994.

Business Wire, "Solar Electric Acquires Nordskog Electric Vehicles." August 3, 1993.

Business Wire, "U.S. Electricar Establishes Credit Corporation to Offer Electric Vehicles Financing for Fleets, Dealers." August 1, 1994.

Cronk, S.A. 1995. *Building the E-Motive Industry: Essays and Conversations About Strategies for Creating an Electric Vehicle Industry.* Society of Automotive Engineers. Warrendale, PA.

Detroit News, "Why Big Three's Electric Car Strategy Backfired." May 8, 1994.

Inc., "Charged Up: Electric Vehicles." May 1994.

J.D. Power Report, "Consumers Aren't Turned on by Electric Vehicles." May 1993.

Los Angeles Times, "Ford in Talks to Sell Frames for Electric Car Production." November 16, 1994.

McGrath, R.N. 1996. *Discontinuous Technological Change and Institutional Legitimacy: A Morphological Perspective.* (Doctoral Dissertation.) University Microfilms, Inc.

Moody's OTC Industrial Manual, 1995. New York: Moody's Industrial Services, Inc.

Motor Trend, "Trends: Environmental Report." December 1993.

New York Times, "Expecting a Fizzle, GM Puts Electric Cars to Test." January 28, 1994.

New York Times, "Chrysler, With Misgivings, Will Sell Electric Mini-Vans." May 6, 1994.

New York Times, "U.S. Electricar Announces a Venture With Itochu of Japan." June 10, 1994.

The Toronto Star, "Electric Gliders." November 26, 1994.

United Press International, "Electricar Pact in Mexico." October 6, 1994.

U.S. Electricar News, "U.S. Electricar, HEVDP to Offer EV Test Drives at Dedication Ceremony in Honolulu." August 11, 1994.

Wall Street Journal, "Itochu Agrees to Take Stake in Car Company." June 10, 1994.

World Trade, "Looking to the ASEAN Market for a Jump Start." August 1995.

Winn, J.L. 1994. "The Role of Government and Industry in the Development of The Electric Vehicle." Society of Automotive Engineers Technical Paper 941035.

Sigcom Inc.

Isaiah O. Ugboro, North Carolina A&T State University

Betty L. Brewer, North Carolina A&T State University

Chi Anyansi-Archibong, North Carolina A&T State University

Ida Robinson-Backmon, North Carolina A&T State University

INTRODUCTION

"Don't bite off too much at a time. Manage cash flow. You can always get qualified people but money is less easy to acquire." This was John Kim's formula for managing the growth of Sigcom Inc. Kim spoke from experience. From 1991 to 1995, his company, Sigcom, had grown at an average annual rate exceeding 100 percent. Its 1995 sales exceeded $28 million and management believed it had the capability of generating $100 million in sales by the year 2000.

Sigcom's rapid growth and the size which it had attained in 5 years had been very gratifying to Kim and his employees. The company's future offered new opportunities and challenges that management had to identify and for which it had to prepare.

Managing this type of growth and maintaining a reputation for on-time project completion and 100 percent customer satisfaction had not been easy for John Kim, who was president and sole owner of the company. His wife had not been particularly happy that Kim brought home work every night and was preoccupied by it. The faster the company grew, the harder Kim worked to keep and maintain his company's reputation. The rapid pace of product and technology innovation generated new market and industry growth opportunities for which Sigcom had to prepare continually.

John Kim, at 62, did not expect to continue at this current pace forever. He wanted to play more golf and spend more time with his grandchildren. However, he had several concerns about Sigcom. First, there was the challenge of positioning the company to be able to keep pace with rapid industry and technology change. There was the need to prepare the future leadership to take over when he decided to retire. Other concerns included management of rapid growth, market strategies, financial strategies, and private or public ownership decisions. Additionally, Kim had to identify ways to harvest the benefits of his risk-taking behavior in creating Sigcom.

BACKGROUND: JOHN KIM

America has been a land of opportunity for John Kim, who came from Korea in 1958 to study engineering at the University of Kentucky. He worked his way though the university with low-paying jobs, such as gas station attendant. He graduated in 1962 and joined GTE Corp. In 1965, Western Electric, a subsidiary of AT&T, hired Kim. During the next 25 years, he moved among various AT&T subsidiaries, rising to the position of Senior Project Manager. In 1990, he took advantage of an early retirement package that AT&T had initiated as part of its downsizing program.

Kim had entrepreneurial aspirations while employed by AT&T. He had established a part-time consulting business in 1985, working out of his home. He provided systems design and development for security and sound systems. The business generated about $300,000 per year in revenues. Kim refers to this part-time business as his "learning stage" for developing Sigcom. He also prepared by reading extensively about entrepreneurs and business leadership. He learned about the opportunities, challenges, successes, and failures of those who created new businesses. From his reading, he identified two key elements he would use to build his own business: strategic planning and cash flow management.

■ Developing Sigcom

In July 1990, John Kim took the first steps toward creating his own business. He had substantial expertise in communications technology, extensive understanding of the contracting process for government agencies, and an extended range of contacts in the communication business. Building on these, he identified the market niche he would serve: designing, assembling, and installing security and audio/video systems. He devoted the last six months of 1990 to developing a business plan and applying for an SBA minority status loan. The SBA denied his original application but Kim persisted. He reapplied and was granted a loan of $250,000.

■ Management

Kim decided that building his executive team was critical for his business venture's success. In January 1991, Sigcom hired its first paid, full-time employee, Elmer Baugess, an AT&T National Account Executive. Baugess had extensive experience in business development and marketing for AT&T and joined the

Exhibit 1   **Organizational Chart**

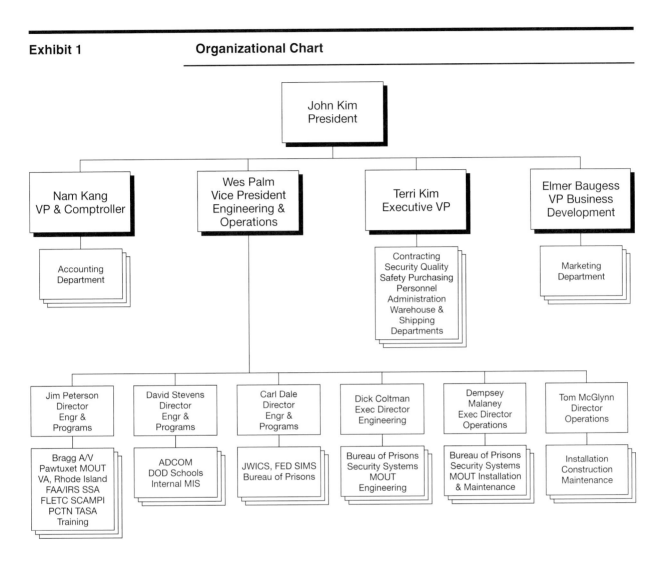

firm as Vice President for Business Development. Over the next few months, Kim recruited two more members to his executive team. Nam Kang, Vice President and Controller, joined Sigcom from Desoto, Inc., where he was corporate treasurer. Wes Palm, Vice President for Engineering and Operations, joined Sigcom from AT&T.

Planning was a cornerstone for Sigcom. Management established a 5-year strategic plan which would undergo quarterly review. These strategic audits enabled management to make revisions and adjustments to take advantage of new opportunities as they arose.

Terri Kim, John Kim's daughter, entered the business in 1992 as Office Manager. Her performance led to rapid promotion to Executive Vice President for Sigcom. Terri Kim was the youngest member of the executive team. However, her family obligations, including 3 young children, were causing John Kim to question the assumption that she would become his immediate successor. The remaining members of the executive team were of comparable ages to John Kim.

■ Strategic Planning and Competitive Strategy

John Kim developed a strategic plan for Sigcom before he established the business. That plan addressed the product, market niche, financing, and operations. He continued to use strategic planning by preparing a 5-year plan which was reviewed and, as necessary, revised by the executive team. The plan was shared with all employees, as a means of keeping them informed about the firm's prospects and encouraging their commitment to Sigcom.

Management performed cost/profit analysis of new opportunities as they arose. Kim ultimately made the final decisions for Sigcom. He noted that he never relied on a single recommendation, preferring to have consensus among his executives before moving into new opportunities. However, he also noted that "regardless of the staff recommendations, final decisions are my responsibility."

"Knowledge is Sigcom's key competitive strength," Kim said. "Our customers are informed about latest technologies and well-prepared to identify their needs. Consequently, Sigcom's employees have to be equally knowledgeable and well-prepared." Another key strength was the organizational expertise in military contracting. This was augmented by the extensive network of professional connections which the executive team brought with it. This network was continually expanded with each new contract on which Sigcom bid. Another strength was the engineering staff, about 50 percent of whom had a masters, doctorate, and/or professional certification. This enabled them to design the interface devices which made vendor equipment compatible with client equipment or the equipment of other vendors.

Kim expected that technology changes would continue to provide new opportunities for Sigcom. He perceived no significant threats to the company at this time. He expected that the company's size and success record would provide momentum for its future growth.

■ Human Resources

By the end of 1991, Sigcom had 10 full-time employees, four of whom were executives. As sales grew to $1.1 million, the company hired additional staff, including engineers and technicians. By the end of 1993, Sigcom had 40 employees with sales of over $11 million. In 1994, Sigcom doubled its sales and employees. By the end of 1995, sales had grown to $28 million and employment to 110.

Sigcom had experienced very low turnover of personnel. Kim attributed this to the competitive salaries and benefits which his company offers. Salaries were higher than those offered by firms of the same size in the Greensboro area. The benefit package was comparable to packages in the top 5 percent of small companies nationwide. Benefits included medical insurance, tuition reimbursement, disability insurance, and the opportunity to participate in a 401(K) matching program. Sigcom contributed a matching 50 percent to the 401(K) plan. Additionally, management fostered a relaxed, "no-tie" environment. The company compensated employees for heavy travel duties with cash awards.

The company rarely advertised for new personnel. Most employees came to Sigcom by referral through the extensive network of contacts maintained by the executive team. Given the nature of the business and the clients it served, Sigcom performed extensive background checks on prospective employees.

According to Kim, "heavy investment in training employees saves money in the long run." Vendors of products used in assembling Sigcom's systems provided factory training for selected employees. The company provided in-house training for its employees, including a project management course taught by Kim.

The latest technology was available for employees to carry out their responsibilities. The company placed lower priority on physical facilities, outfitting office cubicles with furniture from a used office furniture supplier. The salary/benefits package available to employees was supported by the firm's emphasis on cost containment on items management considered to be peripheral to its primary functions.

■ Marketing

Sigcom assembled and marketed teleconferencing, distance learning, telemedicine, simulation instrumentation and control, audiovisual, security, and computer systems. Target customers included private businesses and government agencies, such as the Federal Aviation Administration and U.S. Armed Forces installations and bases. It offered both first-time systems and replacements for technologically obsolete videoconferencing and telecommunication systems. Some of its systems enabled companies to conduct simultaneous job training to potentially hundreds of locations. Sigcom counted on rapid advances in telecommunication equipment technology and the resultant obsolescence of existing equipment to be the source of future market growth. Kim expected demand to continue to grow. The driving force would be the need to improve efficiency through application of technology improvements in videoconferencing and other telecommunication systems.

Government agencies were the initial target market. This was a logical choice, given executive experience with government contracting procedures and processes. The company established offices in Washington, D.C., Providence, Rhode Island, and Canton, North Carolina, to provide access to government agencies and the information network for government contracts.

The company bid on and won several commercial contracts but the bulk of its marketing effort continued to be directed toward U.S. government agencies. By 1995, about 90 percent of Sigcom's contracts were U.S. military and government agencies; the remaining 10 percent were commercial. Over 90 percent of revenues came from domestic markets. (See Exhibit 2 for a list of key clients.) Early foreign contracts included fire alarm, security, and audio systems for the companies in Saudi Arabia, the Philippines, and Thailand.

Sigcom defined its basic marketing strategy as offering the same or better quality products and services as its much larger competitors at a lower price. As Kim noted: "Our strength is in the quality of our products and services, price, and our knowledge of customers' needs."

Management's task was to select those bidding opportunities which provided significant likelihood of securing contracts. Kim said, "We do not compete against small companies. That's deadly. The margin is too small." Conversely, he also noted that "some jobs were too big." This meant that

Exhibit 2

Key Clients

Commercial/International	Department of Defense
AT&T	Defense Intelligence Agency
Royal Saudi Air Force	Department of Energy
Kuwait Air Force	U.S. Air Force
MCI	DECCO/DISA
American Express	U.S. Navy
Sprint	U.S. Army
Federal Government	U.S. Army Corps of Engineers
Department of Labor	
U.S. Bureau of Prisons	
Department of Justice	
Internal Revenue Service	
Dept. of Health & Human Services	

Sigcom was competing against larger firms with greater visibility and more established reputations. Management decided that it would bid on selected contracts as prime contractor. It would also join with larger firms in bidding for contracts. With the latter approach, Sigcom became a sub-contractor. The mix of prime- and sub-contractor roles varied from year to year according to the sizes of available contracts which were up for bid.

Sigcom designed and assembled systems that used products from more than 80 vendors. It developed interfaces to assure that the products from different manufacturers communicated effectively with each other and with customers' existing systems. It installed complete "turnkey" systems and provided maintenance for systems after installation.

Local competitors included two small businesses, American Telecom and Long Communications. Large nationwide competitors included major telecommunication and electronic systems firms.

Kim's pricing philosophy was simple: "We do not gouge the customer." He insisted on giving the customer the highest value for his money because it was the best way to maintain customer loyalty. Sigcom produced to contract. Therefore very little advertising was utilized. The company relied on the bidding process for promotion, advertising, and selling opportunities. It emphasized its performance record on previous contracts as a major promotion and selling mechanism.

■ Production/Operations

According to John Kim, a guiding principle for Sigcom's employees was "Every job should be done right the first time." From design to installation, management emphasized system quality and performance. Sigcom's systems were individually designed to meet customer specifications and requirements. Individually designed, made-to-order systems produced the bulk of its revenues.

Systems included components from a variety of manufacturers. Some of these manufacturers would not make necessary modifications so that their equipment met the needs of Sigcom's customers. Therefore, Sigcom made the necessary modifications, designing appropriate interfaces, and providing its own warranty on the original vendor's equipment. Interface design, manufacturing, and installation comprised the company's proprietary production activity.

When a system had been partially assembled locally, Sigcom employees, using rental trucks, transported the components to each installation site. These employees finished any remaining assembly requirements and installed the system on site, testing it fully and assuring that it was functioning according to contract specifications.

Sigcom had a designated specialist who functioned as a troubleshooter. If a customer was experiencing difficulty with a system, a call to this specialist often provided immediate resolution of the problem. When a more complex problem arose with a system, Sigcom employees were dispatched directly to the site to identify and correct the difficulty.

The firm quickly outgrew its original 300-square-foot headquarters. It relocated to a 17,000-square-foot facility within the city limits of Greensboro in May 1994. Approximately one-half of the space was devoted to offices while the remainder was used for inventory storage and assembly. Kim anticipated that Sigcom would outgrow its current facilities within two years.

■ Finance

John Kim observed that "banks do not lend to business startups." Consequently, he used a number of tactics to raise initial funding for Sigcom in 1991. He sold his investments and home, purchased a mobile home, and transformed his residence into the headquarters for the company. He negotiated an arrangement with suppliers whereby he would pay them after he received payments from his customers. Government agency customers agreed to make progress payments, rather than pay upon contract completion. He secured an SBA loan guarantee which enabled him to secure a bank loan. All earnings were automatically reinvested in the business. Kim did not receive a salary from the firm until mid-1993, when he determined that Sigcom was on a sound financial footing.

Sigcom's original bank provided a $100,000 loan, although it took six months for approval despite the SBA guarantee. As the company grew, it requested a credit line of $250,000 from this bank, which the bank refused. In 1993, Sigcom moved all of its banking business to three other banks which were more amenable to lending to his growing business.

"For any starting company, the most difficult thing to manage is cash flow," Kim commented. Prior to establishing Sigcom, Kim had read extensively about small business planning and management. He noted the emphasis on cash flow control as a determinant of small business survival. When he founded Sigcom, he assigned cash flow monitoring and control as a critical priority. This influenced negotiations with suppliers and customers to establish terms which would support the company's operations. Rapid growth placed significant pressures on cash flow but monitoring procedures enabled management to plan ahead and negotiate bank loans on a timely basis.

Sigcom voluntarily relinquished its SBA loan guarantee in 1994. Kim noted that it was time to let someone else have the opportunity to benefit from the program, as he had done.

By 1995, Sigcom's revenues exceeded $28 million. (See Exhibits 3 and 4 for representative financial statements.) The company was organized as an S-corporation, resulting in the pass-through of before-tax earnings as income to John Kim.

Exhibit 3   **Sigcom, Inc., Income Statement and Retained Earnings for Year Ended December 31, 1995, and Nine Months Ended September 30, 1996**

	1995	*9/30/96*
Contract Revenue	$ 28,864,458	$ 28,584,392
Contract Costs		
Direct Labor	1,456,753	1,780,348
Materials	6,191,049	6,017,105
Freight and Shipping	215,302	93,516
Subcontract	655,571	1,508,022
Subcontract - IBR, Inc.	14,004,545	13,090,405
Consultants	1,960	*****
Travel	953,594	737,302
Equipment Rental	13,621	28,774
Communications	26,502	39,212
Other direct costs	3,267	18,877
Unallowable costs	6,638	*****
Fringe benefits	616,356	618,648
Job site overhead	935,471	781,988
Total Operating Expenses	25,080,628	24,714,198
Gross Profit	3,783,830	3,870,194
General and Administrative Expenses	1,542,434	1,127,955
Net Income From Operations	2,241,396	2,742,239
Other Income (Interest Expense)		
Interest income	16,480	18,094
Interest expense	(57,592)	(64,128)
Gain on disposal of equipment	1,171	—
Miscellaneous	—	(89,287)
	(39,941)	(135,321)
Net Income (Loss)	2,201,455	2,606,918
Retained Earnings, Beginning	1,870,839	2,351,363
Less: Dividends	(1,720,931)	(1,497,550)
Retained Earnings at End of Period	$ 2,351,363	$ 3,460,731

*****Not calculated for nine months ended

Note: S-Corporation - Income Tax Status: The Company has elected, under Internal Revenue Service regulations, to be an S corporation. The S corporation shareholders are taxed on respective shares of the company's taxable income. Accordingly, no liability or provision for income taxes is made in the financial statements.

Source: *Authors' Estimates Based on Actual Figures*

Exhibit 4

Sigcom, Inc., Statement of Financial Position as of December 31, 1995, and Nine Months Ended September 30, 1996

	1995	9/30/96
Assets		
Current Assets		
Cash	$ 65,774	$ 581,713
Accounts Receivable	3,707,950	3,291,126
Cost and estimated earnings in excess of billings on completed contracts	4,577,895	2,020,150
Employee Advances	60,414	16,481
Prepaid Expenses	7,752	25,543
Inventory	3,362	*****
Total Current Assets	8,423,148	5,935,014
Property and Equipment:		
Leasehold Improvements:	3,831	3,831
Land	101,000	101,000
Building	569,107	569,189
Vehicles	153,311	201,952
Equipment	73,353	111,970
Office Equipment	426,722	432,867
Less: Accumulated Depreciation	(289,308)	(401,835)
Total Property and Equipment	1,038,015	1,018,973
Investment in Real Estate		484,716
Total Assets	$ 9,461,163	$ 7,438,703
Liabilities and Stockholders' Equity		
Current Liabilities		
Bank Overdraft	$ 143,156	*****
Current maturities of long-term Debt	19,675	16,541
Note Payable-Line of Credit	2,491,670	*****
Accounts Payable	3,130,440	2,177,242
Accrued expenses	164,524	346,323
Billings in excess of costs and estimated earnings on uncompleted contracts	874,884	1,159,024
Total Current Liabilities	6,824,350	3,699,130
Long-Term Liabilities		
Long-Term Debt, net of current portion	$ 225,187	$ 218,578
Total Liabilities	7,049,536	3,917,708
Stockholders' Equity		
Capital Stock Common	$ 51,510	$ 51,510
(Par Value $1,100,000 authorized, 51,000 Shares Issued and Outstanding)		

Exhibit 4 (continued)   **Sigcom, Inc., Statement of Financial Position as of December 31, 1995, and Nine Months Ended September 30, 1996**

	1995	*9/30/96*
Additional Paid-in-Capital	8,754	8,754
Retain Earnings (Deficit)	2,351,363	3,460,731
Total Stockholders' Equity (Deficit)	2,411,626	3,520,994
Total Liabilities and Equity	$ 9,461,163	$ 7,438,703

*****Not calculated for nine months ended.*
Source: *Authors' Estimates Based on Actual Figures*

INDUSTRY OVERVIEW

■ History

Telecommunications became a regulated industry when Congress enacted the Communications Act of 1934. The legislation created the Federal Communications Commission (FCC) to govern interstate and foreign commerce in communications. The main goal of the act was to ensure affordable and available telephone service. The FCC regulated the industry based on a public interest, rather than antitrust, criterion. During the regulatory period, it was assumed that a monopoly supplier would be more concerned with the public's needs. Accordingly, AT&T became a protected monopoly. For most of the twentieth century, the company provided nationwide telephone connections and the majority of equipment for connections through its regional operating units. AT&T controlled technology development through Bell Labs. Another subsidiary, Western Electric, produced the transmission hardware and telephone equipment. The regulatory policies for various reasons began to change in the mid-1950s.

The initial change was in the equipment market. In 1957, legislation was enacted that permitted individuals and businesses to connect non-AT&T equipment to their phones. By 1970, the FCC was certifying equipment for direct connection with the network. In the service arena, advances in technology resulted in lower costs for services, thus permitting other telecommunication providers, such as MCI, to compete with AT&T. During this time regulatory restrictions were also declining at the state level. In 1984, the monopoly was officially dissolved when a federal court ordered AT&T to divest selected operations. The outcome was that AT&T retained long-distance and enhanced telecommunication services, international operations, equipment manufacturing, customer premises equipment, and the retail equipment sales market. The wholly owned Bell companies were spun off into seven regional holding companies (RHCs). The RHCs, or "Baby Bells," were not permitted to manufacture telecommunications equipment but they were allowed to market equipment produced by other companies.

Exhibit 5 **Trends in Selected Ratios and Factors—Equipment and Service Industry Money amounts in ($000 s)**

	1987	1988	1989	1990	1991	1992	1993	1994	1995	1996
Operating Margin (%)	1.6	0.7	1.1	1.6	1.4	1.1	n/a	n/a	n/a	0.2
Average Net Rec. ($)	2,993	3,757	3,598	3,909	4,246	6,565	5,190	6,602	6,508	6,180
Average Inventories ($)	1,031	1,052	782	701	702	813	641	525	521	411
Average Net Worth ($)	17,460	16,210	17,037	17,917	17,926	21,247	17,528	17,240	18,860	16,099
Current Ratio	0.7	1.2	1.1	1.0	1.1	1.0	1.0	1.0	1.1	1.0
Quick Ratio	0.5	0.9	0.8	0.8	0.8	0.8	0.8	0.8	0.9	0.8
Asset Turnover	0.5	0.5	0.4	0.5	0.5	0.4	0.5	0.5	0.5	0.5
Total Liab./ Net Worth	1.3	1.2	1.1	1.2	1.3	1.3	1.3	1.4	1.3	1.4
Return on Assets	5.2	5.4	5.3	5.7	6.0	6.2	6.3	6.4	6.6	6.5
Return on Equity (%)	2.3	2.6	2.9	3.4	4.3	5.3	5.0	5.3	5.3	6.0
Cost of Labor (%)	7.8	10.9	8.7	6.7	7.1	7.6	8.3	6.6	3.9	3.3

▪ Economic Growth

Since 1987, the economic growth of the equipment and services industry had been significant. As of 1995, the average compounded five-year growth rate in net income was 19 percent for the telecommunications equipment and services industry. The ten-year average growth was approximately 6 percent. There were 12,239 enterprises in this industry in 1993 with total net sales of $215 billion. The estimated number of companies operating in the equipment and service industry in 1995 had grown to 13,493 with net sales of approximately $237 billion. Exhibit 5 uses various ratios and measures to show the industry trend from 1987 to 1995 along with projections for 1996 industry performance.

▪ Anticipated Growth and Products

Telecommunication service providers depended on equipment providers/ assemblers for innovative and more advanced equipment. It was estimated that major U.S. telecommunication companies would spend approximately $125 billion on fiber-optic installations and other infrastructure changes. It was also estimated that the U.S. telecommunications industry would have an annual growth rate of about 5% to 7% over the next five to ten years. The market outside the U.S. was also expected to grow as developing countries expanded their telecommunication infrastructures. The international sector was expected to grow over the same period at an annual rate of 12% to 13%. Fiber-optics equipment was the fastest-growing segment. Network apparatus was composed of switches that connect and route calls and transmission devices that accept, change, or act on a signal. Fiberoptics was a highly favored transmission device.

Many telecommunication industry participants had plans to offer a range of advanced services, such as video-on-demand and distance learning. To provide such services, the companies required extensive capacity or bandwidth, not presently provided by copper wire networks. A greater capacity of brandwidth was also needed because transmission of data through phone lines was growing at a rate approximating 20 percent annually. Fiber-optic cable provided the necessary bandwidth; however, fiber-optic installation was cost prohibitive for most firms. Alternate capacity networks, such as hybrid-fiber coaxial cable and switched digital video, had emerged that were less costly than fiberoptics while offering some of its benefits.

The largest segment of the network equipment industry was the central office switches. The expected annual growth rate for this market was 2.7% over the next two years. The asynchronous transfer mode (ATM) equipment, although expensive, was considered to be the best switching device. The upgrading of networks with ATM equipment was a primary activity of telephone companies.

The customer premises equipment (CPE) or terminal equipment was another significant segment of the equipment industry. Examples of these network devices include private branch exchanges (PBXs), facsimile products, and videoconferencing equipment. Foreign equipment providers, such as Sony and Mitsubishi, tended to dominate the market for such products as telephone sets/answering machines and facsimile devices. Consequently, the growth in the domestic CPE market through 1998 was anticipated to be only 2 percent per year.

Cellular equipment was another fast-growing sector of the equipment industry. In 1995, subscribers increased by 46 percent over the previous year and revenues increased by 34 percent. According to the Cellular Telecommunications Industry Association, total domestic subscribers exceeded 30 million and global subscribers were expected to exceed 200 million by the year 2000. The rapid expansion in the cellular equipment industry growth had an offsetting factor—the emergence of Personal Communications Services (PCS). Although PCS operated like cellulars, these systems had a higher frequency band and used new digital technology. PCS systems would also operate at lower power levels and lower costs.

■ Future Market Opportunities

The fastest-growing product area was videoconferencing systems, which could also be adapted for distance learning and telemedicine. For many years, videoconferencing and distance learning had been little more than dreams because of the high cost of the available technology. Recently, new technological developments had lowered costs and brought video teleconferencing to the desktop. According to industry analysts, the videoconferencing market was expected to increase from $621 million in 1994 to $1.3 billion in 1998. Most of this growth was expected to be in medicine, corporate training, marketing, and education. In medicine, experts in research and diagnosis were joining with telecommunication providers to meet growing health care needs of rural America, where distance was an obstacle to adequate health care. Government agencies, corporations, and universities were searching for telecommunication systems with broadcasting capability that allowed teachers, trainers, and executives to originate satellite-based video broadcasts from their classrooms, offices, or homes using desktop computers or videoconferencing systems.

Globally, the market for telecommunications equipment and services was expected to grow at a rate of 9.2 percent annually during the second half of the 1990s. For 1995, total sales were estimated to be $750 billion. By 2000, the level was expected to reach $1,200 billion. Services were expected to account for approximately 80 percent, and equipment, for the remaining 20 percent. According to industry analysts, North America and Western Europe currently accounted for about 67 percent of the total market. This level was expected to decline slightly over the coming years. Developing economies were expected to provide much of the rapid growth in the future.

SIGCOM'S FUTURE

John Kim had identified several steps that he considered essential for Sigcom's future development. First, he emphasized the continuing need to develop a business plan and update it. He suggested that the company needed to establish specific goals for its markets and for employees. Finally, he suggested that it was essential that Sigcom follow its business plan.

Sigcom was organized as a single-owner S-corporation. This could be a negative influence on its ability to support above-normal growth. Kim noted that the opportunity to become a public firm was among the available options. However, he expressed concern about the effects this would have on the company and on its employees.

While he had considered the issue of management succession, no decisions had been made about the firm's future management and ownership. The natural desire to retain family control of the firm encountered a number of constraints, including (1) qualifications, experience, and motivation of family members; (2) the capacity of a family-owned company to generate sufficient capital, both internally and externally, to support its potential growth; and (3) the appropriate form of family ownership. For Kim personally, there was the issue of providing for his own retirement years. As the sole owner, he had to identify the most effective way to harvest the benefits of his risk-taking in creating Sigcom. He wanted to provide for both his own and the company's future.

AN ENTREPRENEUR'S LIFE

John Kim had taken a calculated risk when he sold his house and used his savings to start Sigcom. That risk had paid off in the form of a thriving company. In 1994, he and his wife had moved from their mobile home to a home overlooking the golf course which hosts the PGA golf tournament in Greensboro. He still did not have as much time to play golf as he would like.

In 1995, Kim received the Greensboro Area Chamber of Commerce "Small Business Person of the Year" award. He had also been recognized for his success at a White House Conference on Small Business.

John Kim believed that four factors had contributed to his success. First, he identified the importance of knowledge and how to apply it. Another factor was his business philosophy: be fair to customers and to your employees. The third component was the role of personal integrity and morality in behavior and decisions. Kim commented: "You have to be able to live with yourself or the outcome is not worth the effort." The fourth element was hard work.

John Kim had found life as an entrepreneur to be exciting, demanding, challenging, and rewarding. He observed that it was a heavy burden to be the leader of a rapidly growing business. "The ultimate responsibility is yours," he says. "And it is a lonely position."

REFERENCES

Arnst, Catherine, "The Last Frontier," *Business Week,* Sept. 18, 1995, pp. 98-114.

Gee, Jack, "A New Age in Global Telecom," *Industry Week,* Vol. 244, No. 14, July 17, 1995, pp. 42-47.

Gross, Andrew, Hester, Edward D., and Javalgi, Rajshekhar G., "Industry Corner: Global Telecommunications: The Market and the Industry," *Business Economics,* Vol. 30, No. 4, Oct. 1995, pp. 55-60.

Harrison, Keith, "Distance Learning the Way Ahead," *Banking World,* Vol. 12, No. 8, Aug. 1995, pp. 39-44.

Kim, John, *Personal interview,* April 1996.

Kramer, Erin Todd, "Going the Distance for Rural Health Care," *Rural Telecommunication*, Vol. 14, No. 6, Nov./Dec. 1995, pp. 52-57.

Laberis, Bill, "Long Distance Race," *ComputerWorld,* Vol. 29, No. 39, Sept. 25, 1995, p. 34.

Mullich, Joe, "Videoconferencing Growth Focuses on Sales, Marketing," *Advertising Age,* Vol. 80, No. 8, Aug. 1995, pp. 21-22.

Neu, Werner, and Schnoring, Thomas, "The Telecommunications Equipment Industry: Recent Changes in Its International Trade Pattern," *Telecommunication Policy,* Vol. 13, No. 1, March 1989, pp. 25-39.

Scism, Jack, "Kim, Chesson to Receive Awards for Small Business." *News and Record,* May 1, 1995, p. 3.

Stewart, Ann, "Going the Distance," *CIO*, Vol. 9, No. 6, Dec. 15, 1995/Jan 1, 1996, pp. 62-70.

NTN Communications, Inc.— Interactive Television: The Future Is Now

Julie Driscoll, Bentley College
Alan N. Hoffman, Bentley College
Alison Rude, Bentley College
Carol Rugg, Bentley College
Bonnie Silveria, Bentley College

Internet site of interest: **www.ntn.com**

"In the next five years, interactive television is going to take off. The whole industry is going to explode."

DANIEL DOWNS,
CO-FOUNDER, NTN
COMMUNICATIONS, INC.

On June 28, 1994, Patrick Downs, Daniel Downs, and Don Klosterman met to decide the future strategic direction of NTN Communications. NTN's interactive television programming products, QB1 and Diamond Ball, designed to run on a variety of platforms including television and personal computers, were big hits. But the continual advent of new technologies, such as direct satellite communication, made it hard to stay current. The three principals needed to decide where to focus their efforts and resources in light of the veritable explosion of new technologies in the marketplace.

QB1—INTERACTIVE FOOTBALL

QB1 is an interactive television game that allows patrons of hotels, taverns, and restaurants to play the role of quarterback during live television coverage of college and professional football games. Patrons watch a live football game on television and predict the quarterback's calls by punching their play of choice (pass, middle, deep is one option) on a portable playmaker box. Once the real action begins, their choices are locked in and beamed by satellite to NTN's Carlsbad, California, headquarters. Viewers win or lose points based on the accuracy of their predictions. Using sophisticated computers and software, the score of each QB1 competitor is tabulated instantaneously and bounced back via satellite to each game site. As the game progresses, QB1 players can track how they are doing against every single individual competing across the country as their scores and results are flashed on the television screen. "QB1 is definitely a game of skill; you cannot be successful at it if you approach it as a game of chance," says Dan Klosterman, co-founder of NTN Communications, who, together with NFL coaches Don Schula, Hank Stram, and Bill Walsh, collective winners of six Super Bowl games, developed QB1 for NTN.

WHAT IS INTERACTIVE TELEVISION?

Interactive communication, a synthesis of television, games, education, and information systems, is potentially the "mega-industry" of the 1990s. Although interactive communication is popular with restaurant/bar owners, educators, business professionals, and home owners, there are many consumers who do not understand the concepts behind it, and some who are not even aware that interactive options exist.

Interactive communication is two-way (or more) communication between a viewer and a device, usually a television screen. A viewer may interact with a television program as if a dialogue were taking place between two people. For example, a person can play "Jeopardy" interactively by answering the questions on the show via a remote control device. While one viewer answers the questions, viewers at any number of other locations may also answer; thus all participating viewers compete against each other simultaneously, making for a more active and enjoyable viewing experience through interactive participation.

THE HISTORY OF INTERACTIVE TELEVISION

The earliest form of interactive communication was the Morse code machine which made two-way communication possible via a transmitter and a receiver. Next, the telephone enabled virtually any two people to be linked; and now more than two people can communicate instantly via sophisticated teleconferencing technology. Companies such as AT&T, Picturetel, and Intel have also developed video-conferencing which enables participants from remote locations to see each other via satellite or long distance telephone lines while they talk. Universities also use video-conferencing to conduct classes for students in inaccessible locations. Now, the development of the "information highway" by companies such as America Online, Compuserve, and Prodigy allows users to communicate with a vast database of information, and with other users, via computer hook-up.

Interactive television is a natural development of current technology. The potential for interactive communications is so great that no single firm will be able to dominate all aspects of the industry. Consequently, many alliances are forming among cable, telephone, and computer firms to develop the necessary technology and infrastructure. Time Warner has joined forces with Silicon

Graphics to develop computer equipment for an interactive television network, and with US West to develop a full-service interactive system. In addition, the Federal Communications Commission has granted regional telephone companies permission to offer audiovisual services, and thus to compete directly with cable companies.

COMPANY HISTORY

NTN was founded in 1983 by three sports executives: Donald C. Klosterman, and Patrick J. and Daniel C. Downs. Pat Downs was vice-president and business manager of the San Diego Padres baseball team from 1964 to 1969 and director of special projects for Time/Life Broadcast Properties in San Diego from 1970 to 1973. Dan Downs began his career in the early 1960s in the Los Angeles Dodgers' management training program. In 1966, he became stadium manager and director of sales for the Houston Oilers football team, and was later promoted to assistant general manager. His interest in interactivity dates back to those Houston Oilers days, when he and his boss, Don Klosterman, were working on ways to get more fans to the Astrodome to watch the Oilers play.

Pat and Dan Downs made ambitious plans, but more than once their interactive ventures teetered on the brink of financial ruin. Nevertheless, they persevered, marketing their first game, QB1, to restaurants and bars. After losing the financial backing of Time Inc.'s Home Box Office, they risked everything to build the interactive network themselves, going without pay for three years, even losing their homes. Still the Downs brothers never considered turning back, though many advised them to quit. "In retrospect, we were ahead of the times. But we hung on long enough to raise enough capital to keep going," said Dan Downs. "At times it felt really lonely out there. But we believed so much in what we were doing, we just kept going." Now people who scoffed at them years ago want to deal. "We've put ourselves in a position to succeed and that's what we intend to do," Pat says. "Deals with the big players (ABC, AT&T, and Sony) are in the works, and when the superhighway comes along, we will be ready to go."

NTN Communications, Inc., an international provider of interactive television games and educational programs, and a pioneer in developing interactive television, was formed from the merger of Alroy Industries, Inc. and National Telecommunicator Network, Inc. The company's revenues presently derive from three sources: broadcasting, the sale of interactive equipment, and the licensing of technology. NTN owns and operates the only interactive television network in North America that broadcasts 24 hours a day, every day of the week.

A number of games are now available through NTN's interactive network. The company began with sports games because it was their area of expertise, and have since broadened their product base to include Diamond Ball (baseball), Power Play (hockey), Passport (an interactive travel game), Spot Light (an entertainment game), and Playback (a music game). NTN's niche is public venues and special event productions such as the Superbowl, the Grammy Awards, the Academy Awards, all game shows on the ABC television network, and trade shows, sales conferences, and charity events. NTN has the capability to allow many people to participate at the same time through the use of their 200 unit playmaker system, which is perfect for large events, and the wide variety of their games is a strength because there is something for everyone.

NTN'S TARGET MARKETS

The NTN network is currently marketed to group viewing locations such as bars and restaurants. There are approximately 700 location subscribers in the United States and 220 in Canada. All NTN network programming is produced at NTN corporate headquarters in Carlsbad, California, and transmitted to subscribers using multiple data transmission techniques including FM radio transmission, direct satellite broadcast, and television transmission via vertical blanking intervals. Using the same technology as that used for pay-per-view movies, NTN can provide simultaneous transmission of up to eight live events for interactive play, allowing the company to broadcast different programs to different geographic locations at the same time. The NTN feed is carried via satellite and each establishment has a decoder which enables it to receive advertisements and games designated specifically for that location.

Bars and restaurants are capitalizing on interactive trends by offering games tied to popular sporting events to increase traffic into their establishments and increase sales. However, observers have noted that the success of their interactive offerings is tied directly to the bar or restaurant's successful promotion of the event. For example, a pub in Chicago gets at least 30 extra people specifically to play NTN's QB1 game, while another bar down the street, although full, may have only a few people using the interactive game.

NTN currently services four domestic markets: the hospitality, home, education, and video games markets. For the hospitality market, NTN has joined with LodgeNet to provide over 14,000 hotel rooms nationwide with an interactive network of games which allows hotel guests to play along with live sporting events. For the home market, NTN has joined forces with Prodigy, AT&T ImagiNation Network, GEnie, and GTE's Main Street to offer interactive computer games. For the interactive education market, NTN provides surveys, academic competitions, and testing capabilities which can be performed within a single classroom at a particular site, or at several different locations, all with instantaneous feedback via satellite networks. And NTN's wholly-owned subsidiary, IWIN, Inc. is a full-service provider of interactive applications and transactions services for the interactive games industry.

NTN also operates internationally. In Canada, NTN has an exclusive license with NTN Interactive Network, Inc. NTN also has an agreement with TWIN, its licensee for Europe (owned by Whitebread Breweries, PLC, and BBC Enterprises) to license the rights to all of NTN's products and services throughout Europe. Australasia became an operational company in November 1993 with a broadcast facility in Sydney, Australia, and NTN is currently pursuing interactive education opportunities in Mexico, and has received some approval from the Mexican Ministry of Education.

NEW PRODUCTS

In 1993, NTN formed a wholly-owned subsidiary, IWIN (I Win), to take advantage of the legalization of home betting on horses. IWIN is a full-service provider of interactive applications and transactions services to the worldwide gaming industry, and is currently testing a new pari-mutuel game called

"Triples" which allows cable TV subscribers in California to wager on the races at the Los Alamitos Race Course. NTN plans further expansion into the gaming industry using a vertical market strategy to break into the lottery and casino gaming markets in the near future.

In January 1994, NTN teamed up with Replica Corporation to offer Replica's interactive investment and Sports Fantasy Games through NTN's distribution system. The agreement boosts NTN's offerings, adding to its appeal to new target markets as well as current customers. In March of the same year, NTN cut a deal with Event Entertainment and Kingvision Pay-Per-View to form the NTN Event Network which will offer interactive boxing for 8-12 fights per year.

Interactive programming has many potential uses beyond allowing players to participate in games—for instance, enlivening training and education. To expand its capabilities in more markets, NTN formed an Interactive Education Division in 1993. Interactive education can provide rural or disadvantaged students with the same opportunities as those from wealthier school districts by allowing students to participate actively in the learning process and communicate with teachers at remote locations as if they were in the same classroom. At the same time, teachers effectively control the process by quickly monitoring student progress and providing instant feedback. NTN has had success in developing and licensing its interactive technology to KET, an education network in Kentucky. NTN has also developed the Interactive Learning System, a unique tool for teaching students in a more enjoyable environment. It operates via satellite and has been used for conducting surveys, academic competitions, and testing. The Interactive Learning System has been used in 19 states for more than five years and regional centers are currently being established in California and Arizona.

NTN is also working with the Mexican government to provide educational services. Field tests were conducted in which Mexican schools received a satellite broadcast transmitted from Mexico City. These tests were successful and NTN anticipates making a final agreement with the Mexican government to provide interactive educational services to approximately 3,000 schools in the near future. Under this arrangement, NTN will receive $695 per month, per system, for the next five years in addition to a one-time installation fee of $250 and a monthly maintenance fee of $150 per system. In addition to the 3,000 schools already targeted, there are 5,700 schools remaining which could benefit from NTN's services. However, NTN has not yet received a signed contract, and if the deal falls through NTN stands to lose millions of dollars in potential revenue.

NTN seeks to expand into the corporate world by using their products for corporate training, product knowledge testing, employee testing, and certification and technical training. They plan to market interactive training as a way to help companies cut their training and development costs by combining training with other branches of the company or by eliminating the need for an on-site trainer.

In 1995, NTN entered into an agreement with America Online to provide 24–hour access to NTN's popular interactive football game "QB1" and their new interactive trivia game "Countdown." NTN also entered into an agreement that will make NTN's interactive programming available to more than 285 TGI Friday's restaurants throughout the United States.

In February 1996, NTN debuted "QB1" on the Internet. NTN was granted early access to Microsoft's new Internet Explorer "Active X" technology to allow NTN more efficient delivery of its interactive games, play along sports, and trivia on the Internet's World Wide Web.

NTN'S COMPETITIVE LANDSCAPE

The competition in the field of interactive television is fierce. Many new entrants are adept at using both current technologies such as television and telephone lines, and state-of-the-art technologies such as satellites, cellular networks, and personal computers. NTN's direct competitor in the interactive television home market is the Interactive Network, Inc. (IN). IN distributes their own interactive network whose programming is very similar to that of NTN. IN's subscriber-based service allows television viewers to play along in real time with televised sporting events, game shows, dramas, news, and talk show programming. Currently testing in Sacramento, California, and Chicago, Illinois, IN's system, like that of NTN, is designed to run on many different delivery platforms. The biggest threat IN poses to NTN, however, is that it is backed by Tele-Communications, Inc., Gannett Co., Cablevision, NBC, and A.C. Nielsen, large media investors with "deep pockets," all of whom are significant players in their respective industries.

Because NTN's services are designed to utilize various already existing delivery mechanisms, their competitors are diverse. Local and long distance telephone companies such as AT&T and Bell Atlantic are recent entrants into the interactive television marketplace, which can use their existing telephone infrastructure and a combination of both television and personal computers to deliver interactive programming.

Many cable-TV companies across the United States are also interested in interactive television both as a future programming alternative and as an opportunity to expand their revenue stream. The cable companies pose a real threat because they have large financial resources, their delivery infrastructure via cable networks is already in place, and they have access to a wide variety of programming possibilities.

In addition, online services such as Prodigy, CompuServe, and America Online pose a competitive risk to NTN. They have been in the interactive marketplace for over ten years; they have the infrastructure in place; and their products already provide high levels of interactivity through interactive chat and gaming capabilities.

As is characteristic of most growth industries, many new players will compete directly with NTN. The threat to NTN is real, especially because competition can take so many different forms. And, because there are so many ways a company wishing to compete can proceed, the current climate in the industry is volatile and unpredictable. In addition, there are no industry standards; thus, a company developing its own technology runs the risk of being side-tracked by an alternative technology. In addition, NTN relies on distribution networks, such as radio stations and telephone and cable companies, to supply their products to customers. Consequently, they are at the mercy of their distributors to get their products to clients. Mergers and alliances are one way to reduce this threat. Alternatively, a concerted effort to offer the best services (those most desired by consumers) would shift the balance of power in NTN's favor by outdoing the competition.

In the home and hospitality segments, NTN relies heavily on information providers (NHL, NFL, Trivia, the Academy Awards) to supply content for their products, which are, in turn, evaluated primarily on the basis of their association with major sporting events or game shows.

THE INFORMATION SUPERHIGHWAY

Technological advances have given consumers access to many services without having to leave home, and it is interactive technology (the ability of the consumer to respond and communicate directly and interactively with a television or computer) that makes it all possible. Because it is so responsive to consumer needs, the growth potential for interactive technology is huge. Cable subscriptions currently represent approximately 61% of the total television household market, and are on the rise; and many consumers spend a significant portion of their time watching movies, playing video or electronic games, or watching sports programs.

Industry experts predict that television and cable services are still in their infancy, and that the near future holds a wider selection of cable channels, the ability to select and watch a movie on demand, and the ability to interact directly with the television. However, television is not the only medium competing for a share of the interactive market. A recent study revealed that the average household spends almost twice as much time using a computer as watching television. Some experts even predict that PCs will replace televisions as the household electronic appliance of choice and that the majority of homes will have a PC by the year 2000, despite the extra expense. Software and cable companies currently offer very similar products such as news services, home-shopping, and electronic games, suggesting that computer and video marketing are beginning to converge in a competition for the same consumers. Microsoft plans to capitalize on this trend by developing software that works with both platforms. The company is currently working on a network which will operate not only on phone networks but on cable-TV networks as well, which could have a tremendous impact on the interactive television segment. For example, Microsoft Baseball, a CD-ROM program which dials into an electronic service to retrieve daily scores, will eventually become a video update program which will allow consumers to scan for the baseball footage they missed the night before. In addition, Microsoft is forming alliances with Hollywood film studios and other software companies to combine computing and video technologies more effectively. As Microsoft's president Bill Gates puts it, "The PC industry has come a long way, but that's nothing compared with what's going to happen."

THE FUTURE

The future of the information superhighway is promising, but uncertain. Because technology is constantly changing there are very few industry standards relevant to the development of interactive television. Companies developing a product must take all the risks and may very well end up with an already obsolete new product. A recent FCC ruling granting permission to telephone companies to offer audiovisual services opens even more doors for players intending to enter the market. However, because it is unclear which avenue or mode of technology will be the wave of the future, cable, telephone, and computer companies are forming alliances which not only combine technologies, but secure markets within the industry. Cable companies, for example, already enjoy concessions such as right-of-ways and legal easements for cable installations, and monopolies on particular service territories which prevent other cable companies from competing directly with them.

The future of the information superhighway becomes even more uncertain when satellite technology is factored in. As satellite technology advances, satellite dishes are becoming smaller and more inexpensive, and will soon be offering greater opportunities for interactive technology. In fact, satellites may very well supersede cable and telephone technology, which would tremendously benefit all involved. For instance, digging permits or right-of-way issues, a large source of aggravation and cost for cable companies today, would be eliminated. In fact, many businesses currently opt for satellite television services instead of cable because cable companies cannot provide access, either because of awkward location or building and right-of-way issues. There are, however, problems with satellite technology, especially with regard to the "line of sight" when satellite signals are obstructed by large buildings or other impediments.

DEMOGRAPHIC TRENDS

One potential problem for NTN is the public's lack of product awareness. In a recent survey, 66% of the population stated they did not have much interest in or awareness of interactive television, although 22% indicated they were interested in subscribing to interactive television in their homes. However, the survey did reveal a rise in interest among consumers between 18 and 34; and as the income levels of those surveyed rose, so did interest in interactive services. Thus consumer education, especially education targeted to particular demographic markets, is crucial to the promotion of interactive products.

The elderly currently represent 13% of the U.S. population, and population growth statistics predict that the group of those over 65 will grow at a faster rate than any other age group between 1994 and 2000. Although the elderly population often have a great deal of leisure time, historically speaking they have not been comfortable with high-tech devices. While interactive television could offer useful services to this age group (e.g., at-home bingo, shopping), it is not clear there is sufficient interest among this demographic group.

The 0-15 age segment currently represents 23% of the total population and although this age segment shows slow growth within the next few years, it will continue to be, proportionately, the largest population segment in the United States through the year 2002.

MARKETING

Within the interactive industry, NTN has positioned itself in an enviable niche: programming and programming distribution. NTN's ongoing marketing objectives include:

- attracting important new sponsors and advertisers
- forming new strategic alliances and securing new contracts
- entering into agreements that expand the distribution of their programs and services.

At the same time, the interactive industry is continually changing and NTN's marketing strategies must reflect this. In 1992, NTN repositioned itself as a leader in interactive communications, rebuilding its core product offerings and recasting NTN's marketing operation.

NTN's primary market focus is hospitality, especially restaurants, bars, and hotels. NTN's plan is to garner expertise in this segment before moving into the home market, their next growth segment. In North America alone, there are approximately 330,000 bars and restaurants NTN can target—a tremendous growth area. Some of NTN's subscribers include: Bennigan's, Steak and Ale, Hooters, TGI Friday's, Chili's, Ground Round, and Chi Chi's. In 1993, NTN added military bases, college campuses, hospitals, country clubs, fraternal organizations, and bowling centers to their list of subscribers. These subscribers are easy markets for NTN products because they can afford them, and it is not necessary to sell them television set-top boxes.

NTN entered the hotel segment of the hospitality industry through an agreement with LodgeNet Entertainment Corporation, which gave NTN access to 14,000 guest rooms. The full hotel segment potential is 250,000 guest rooms in major hotel chains such as Marriott, Hilton, ITT Sheraton, Radisson, Ramada, and Holiday Inn. Interactive marketing to the hospitality industry grew significantly since 1992, the subscriber base nearly quadrupling from 776 to 2,500 locations by the end of 1995. During 1995, the number of interactive participants has increased to 75 million. These increases mark significant growth and are considered reliable indicators of future industry growth.

Advertisers are also finding creative ways to take advantage of interactive television services. Infomercials are using interactive TV to review feedback about their products, and Ocean Spray has teamed up with NTN to create interactive advertisements which sponsor prizes for top-scoring customers. Indeed, the latest challenge for advertisers will be marketing their products effectively using interactive media. Anticipated trends include:

- more sponsor-oriented programs focused on specific interest groups
- product channels which allow for comparison shopping
- increased use of infomercials
- increased availability of commercial spots.

Currently, NTN has national advertisers such as Paddington, Seagrams, Miller Brewing, which has been a sponsor of NTN's game QB1 for the past three years, and American Express, which advertises on NTN's Passport game. Advertisers view the interactive network as a powerful medium and an effective way to target many different segments of their markets at the same time. In addition, advertising on this medium is more cost effective. The flexibility of interactive programming allows advertisers to tailor their product promotions to different geographical areas and age groups, especially the hard-to-reach 21-35 year olds. Advertisers are thus able to reach more than five million players each month, with a year-end 1995 estimate of eleven million per month, a major attraction for many corporate sponsors.

FINANCIAL SITUATION

NTN's financial objectives are: increase shareholder value by reaching profitability; fund future growth from revenues generated by the Company; and contain costs. The company achieved its first objective of reaching profitability in the fourth quarter of 1993, realizing a profit of $160,000. However, NTN reported a consolidated net loss of $3.9 million for 1995 as compared to a consolidated net profit of $707,000 for 1994.

NTN's stock price has fluctuated from a low of 12 cents in 1990 to $11.50 in 1993. As of April 11, 1996, the price was $4.09. One of management's objectives is to "have a stock that can properly reflect both the current results, as well as future potential which entails expenses for which no financial benefits may be available for the short term."

NTN currently has a sale-lease back arrangement for its equipment, which allows for an off-balance sheet financing method. Under this arrangement NTN pays for the equipment, sells the assembled equipment to another company for a higher price to pay for it, then leases it back, an arrangement NTN found necessary because of insufficient working capital to finance the cost of the equipment itself. In the future, NTN will finance the equipment purchases by exercising the warrants and options.

In 1995, sales grew by 33%, a rise attributable to increases in sales of equipment, numbers of subscribers, and in retail sales of products. NTN's other sources of revenue include license fees and royalties from foreign licensees, and the advertising and sponsorship revenues from companies advertising on its games and shows.

LEGAL ISSUES

The legal environment for interactive services is uncertain. The major obstacle to NTN's effort to provide an interactive betting service is that in many states home betting is illegal. Senate Bill 1431 legalizes home betting in California, but mandates blackout areas of 15 miles around satellite facilities and 30 miles around racetracks. The process for legalizing home betting in other states has been slower than expected, hindering penetration of the market. However, there are five states where betting is legal: Kentucky, Pennsylvania, Michigan, Ohio, and New York, making them potential candidates for a home betting service. This number will most likely increase as state governments seek additional revenue through gambling profits.

Other legal hassles include a patent infringement case with Interactive Network, Inc. (IN). The dispute involves NTN's royalty-free use of IN's patent to lock out responses from viewers during a live sports telecast. Under a partial settlement agreement, IN licensed NTN's QB1 trivia game for a fee, but the license expired on March 31, 1993, and has not yet been renewed. As of now, IN is the only other company developing a subscription-based interactive television service, and it has formed powerful alliances that could lock NTN out of certain key markets. For example, Cablevision, an affiliate of Rainbow Programming, Inc., currently services all of Boston, and a great deal of New York's residential and business market. However, NTN does not think that patent technology is key to their success in the interactive industry. Rather, it is NTN's corporate philosophy that they can maintain a competitive edge by differentiating their product and service offerings, and by fostering consumer loyalty.

Licensing arrangements, which are similar to patents, also act as barriers to new firms entering the interactive sports entertainment market, and may allow

NTN to gain a competitive advantage in the marketplace. In September 1995, NTN signed a new multi-year exclusive NFL licensing agreement. Under this arrangement, NTN can also sub-license the use of NFL games for interactive television to other cable service companies and delivery systems.

STRATEGIC DIRECTION?

NTN is at a critical point in its life cycle. NTN faces several opportunities and challenges on the technological and competitive fronts. NTN must confront tremendous competitive pressures from other interactive service providers such as MSN (The Microsoft Network), Prodigy, Compuserve, and the World Wide Web, any of which could, from another perspective, provide opportunities for NTN to cultivate strategic alliances. Given NTN's limited resources, Patrick, Dan, and Don know they need to focus on a particular strategic direction for NTN and concentrate NTN's resources on one or two technologies, either cable, telephone, online, satellite, or wireless communication, if NTN is to survive and prosper in the long run.

REFERENCES

Aho, Debra. "Miller Calls an Interactive Play." *Advertising Age,* October 11, 1993, p. 41.

Armstrong, Larry. "I Have Seen the Future and Its—Urp!" *Business Week,* January 24, 1994, p. 41.

Armstrong, Larry; Sager, Ira; Rebello, Kathy; Burrows, Peter. "Home Computers." *Business Week,* November 28, 1994, p. 88.

Bhattacharya, Sanjoy. "NTN Communications, Inc." *D. Blech and Company,* November 16, 1993, pp. 1-10.

Fawcett, A. W. "Interactive TV's Toughest Question." *Advertising Age,* October 11, 1993, pp. 39-40.

Hartke, James, Tarum Chandra, and Peter Kambourakis. "NTN Communications, Inc." *Laidlaw Equities, Inc.,* June 8, 1993, pp. 1-20.

Hunger, J. David, and Thomas L. Wheelan. *Strategic Management.* Reading: Addison-Wesley Publishing Company, 1993.

Interactive Network. Annual Report, 1993.

Interactive Television Today and Tomorrow. San Francisco: Interactive Services Association, July 18, 1994.

NTN—At a Glance. San Diego: Leedom's San Diego Stock Report, 1994.

NTN Communications. Annual Report, 1993.

NTN Communications. First Quarter Bulletin, 1994.

NTN Communications. Standard American Stock Exchange Stock Reports. New York: McGraw-Hill, Inc., 1994.

"NTN Communications is Teaming with Event Entertainment and Kingvision Pay-Per-View." *Broadcasting and Cable,* March 14, 1994, p. 12.

Quinn, James Brian. *Intelligent Enterprises.* New York: The Free Press, 1992.

Smith, Virginia. "The Consumer Market for Interactive Television: Today and Tomorrow." *AT&T Consumer Video Services,* July 18, 1994, pp. 1-9.

KFC: Doing Chicken Right in the U.S. Fast-Food Industry

Jeffrey A. Krug, The University of Memphis
W. Harvey Hegarty, Indiana University

Internet site of interest: **www.kentuckyfriedchicken.com**

"I think our most critical issue in the future will be our ability to handle change. We have a concept that, in the last two years, has moved us out of the 1960s to perhaps the late 1980s. Unfortunately, it's 1994, and we have a lot more changes that need to take place in our system. Our system is older in terms of facilities and product forms, and our attitudes still don't reflect the realities of our changing business environment.

"One of the great challenges at KFC is that there is a lot that needs fixing. It's like being a kid in a candy store—you don't know where to go first. I think one of the toughest challenges we have had is to stay focused. That is true on the menu side as well. People really see us as being the experts on chicken-on-the-bone. There is so much we can still do with products such as Rotisserie Chicken and different forms like that.

"We also have a significant service problem in a service-driven industry. I think we have got to figure out a way to meet our customer service expectations, which we don't meet today. They come to us really because they love our product in spite of our service. And you can't survive long-term on that trail."

KYLE CRAIG, PRESIDENT, KFC BRAND DEVELOPMENT, APRIL 1994

Through 1994 and 1995, KFC remained the world's largest chicken restaurant chain and the world's third largest fast-food chain. It held almost fifty percent of the U.S. market in terms of sales and ended 1995 with over 9,000 restaurants worldwide. It was opening a new restaurant at a rate of roughly one per day worldwide and was operating in over 65 countries. One of the first fast-food chains to go international during the late 1960s, KFC has developed one of the world's most recognizable brands.

Craig found himself faced with a number of critical issues in 1994. Despite KFC's past successes in the U.S. market, much of KFC's growth was now being driven by its international operations, which accounted for 95 percent of all new KFC restaurants built in 1994. Additionally, intensified competition among the largest fast-food competitors had resulted in a number of obstacles to further expansion in the U.S. market. Further expansion of freestanding restaurants was particularly difficult. Fewer sites were available for new construction and those sites, because of their increased cost, were driving profit margins down. Profit margins were driven down further by the need to promote the brand more rigorously, consumer pressure to reduce prices, the high cost of bringing new products to market, and higher operating costs.

Through the late 1980s, most of KFC's competition was limited to other fried chicken chains such as Church's, Popeyes, and Bojangles. Today, KFC is faced with competition from non-fried chicken chains such as Hardee's and McDonald's, who have introduced fried chicken to their menus. With KFC's menu limited to chicken, it has lost business to chains which offer customers a greater variety of food items that cut across different food segments. In addition, a number of new, upscale chicken chains—for example, Kenny Rogers

Roasters and Boston Market—have entered the market. These new chains have focused on higher-income customers by offering non-fried chicken items. Because KFC is best known for its fried chicken products, these new entrants are reaching out to customer groups which KFC is only now beginning to tap. Even Pizza Hut, a sister company of PepsiCo, introduced buffalo wings to its menu in 1995.

KFC's early entry into the fast-food industry in 1954 allowed KFC to develop strong brand name recognition and a strong foothold in the industry. However, its early entry into the industry has also been the cause of many present-day problems. By the mid-1980s, many of KFC's restaurants had begun to age and were designed mainly for take-out. As a result, KFC had to expend significant financial resources to refurbish older restaurants and to add additional inside seating and drive-thrus, in order to accommodate customers' increasing demands for faster service.

KFC's major problem in 1994 and 1995 was how to transition the old KFC into a new KFC which appealed to consumer demands for more healthy food items at lower prices, greater variety in food selection, and a higher level of service and cleanliness in a greater variety of locations. In effect, this entailed greater reflection over its entire business strategy—its menu offerings, pricing, advertising and promotion, points of distribution, restaurant growth, and franchise relationships.

THE U.S. FOOD SERVICE INDUSTRY

The concept of franchising became well-established by the early 1950s. Colonel Harland Sanders founded Kentucky Fried Chicken in 1954, Ray Kroc opened the first McDonald's restaurant in 1955, and Burger King quickly followed by opening its first restaurant in Miami, Florida. Other franchises founded in the 1950s were Chicken Delight, Burger Chef, Burger Queen, Carol's, and Sandy's. Today, the U.S. restaurant industry is made up of over 550,000 restaurants and food outlets, according to the National Restaurant Association (NRA). Standard & Poor's estimates that U.S. food service industry sales surpassed $289 billion in 1995. Exhibit 1 shows U.S. food service industry sales segmented into eleven categories. The fast-food segment continued to outpace all other segments, with estimated sales of $93.4 billion in 1995. This compared with an estimated $87.8 billion in sales in the full-service segment.

The U.S. food service industry as a whole grew at an estimated compounded annual growth rate of 4.2 percent from 1990 to 1995, compared with an annual growth rate of 5.1 percent in the U.S. gross domestic product. The fast-food segment of the food industry grew at a more healthy rate of 6.0 percent, outpacing all food categories except social caterers and vending, which grew only slightly more quickly. While eleven categories of restaurants make up the food industry, the top three—fast-food, full-service, and institutions—have maintained a constant share of about 73 percent of total industry sales. However, the share of industry sales controlled by the fast-food segment has risen by about 2.6 points over the last five years, mainly at the expense of full-service restaurants and institutions.

EXHIBIT 1   **U.S. Food Service Industry Sales**

($ Billions)	1990	1991	1992	1993	1994	1995	5-Year Growth Rate
Fast-Food	69.8	73.6	75.6	81.4	87.1	93.4	6.0%
Full-Service	75.9	79.2	80.3	83.0	85.3	87.8	3.0%
Institutions	26.4	27.5	28.3	27.7	29.5	30.6	3.0%
Vending	16.3	19.9	20.3	20.7	21.9	22.9	7.0%
Food Contractors	14.1	15.0	15.5	16.0	16.4	17.1	3.9%
Lodging Places	14.9	14.3	15.2	15.5	16.2	16.9	2.6%
Bars & Taverns	8.7	8.6	9.2	8.9	9.1	9.4	1.6%
Cafeterias	4.4	4.6	4.5	4.5	4.7	4.9	2.2%
Social Caterers	2.3	2.4	2.5	2.7	2.9	3.1	6.2%
Ice Cream	2.0	2.1	2.4	2.5	2.5	2.6	5.4%
Military	1.0	1.1	1.1	1.1	1.1	1.1	1.9%
Total Sales	235.8	248.3	254.9	264.0	276.7	289.8	4.2%

Source: Standard & Poor's, Industry Surveys, 1996. 1994 and 1995 sales estimated.

THE U.S. FAST-FOOD INDUSTRY

Financial and other data for the fast-food segment of the U.S. food service industry are most frequently reported for eight separate categories: sandwich chains, pizza chains, family restaurants, dinner houses, chicken chains, steak restaurants, contractors, and hotels. Exhibit 2 shows sales for the largest 100 U.S. fast-food chains over the last five years. The top 100 chains have grown at a compounded annual rate of 4.9 percent over the last five years. Only three of the nine food categories have grown at greater than a 6.0 percent annual rate: family chains (6.1 percent), dinner houses (12.7 percent), and chicken chains (6.8 percent). The growth in the chicken segment has, in recent years, suffered from the health trend away from fried foods. However, new entrants to the chicken segment such as Boston Market and Kenny Rogers Roasters, which have promoted non-fried chicken products—and the addition of non-fried chicken products to KFC's menu—have revived growth within the chicken segment.

Exhibit 2 indicates that the top four fastest growing categories within the fast-food industry control 69 percent of all fast-food sales. During the last six years, the market share held by these four categories has increased from 64.5 percent to 68.8 percent. The most significant improvement in sales has occurred in the dinner house segment. Eight of the fifteen major dinner houses registered double-digit sales growth in 1995, including Lone Star Steakhouse &

Exhibit 2   **Top 100 Fast-Food Chain Sales By Food Segment**

($ Billions)	1990	1991	1992	1993	1994	1995	5-Year Growth Rate
Sandwich Chains	35.6	36.7	39.7	41.0	44.0	47.2	5.8%
Pizza Chains	9.2	9.6	10.4	10.2	10.5	11.2	4.0%
Family Chains	6.4	7.0	7.7	7.6	8.0	8.6	6.1%
Dinner Houses	5.4	6.3	6.9	7.6	8.7	9.8	12.7%
Chicken Chains	4.6	4.5	4.7	5.0	5.6	6.4	6.8%
Steak Chains	3.4	3.5	3.3	3.0	3.0	3.2	-1.2%
Food Contractors	11.2	10.8	11.2	10.6	11.1	11.7	0.9%
Hotels	5.3	5.4	5.5	5.7	5.8	6.0	2.7%
Other	6.7	6.7	6.7	6.8	7.2	7.5	2.4%
Total Sales	87.8	90.5	96.1	97.6	104.0	111.7	4.9%

Source: *Nation's Restaurant News*, National Restaurant Association.

Saloon (55.2 percent), Outback Steakhouse (49.7 percent), Fuddruckers (32.9 percent), Ruby Tuesday (22.6 percent), Hooters (18.6 percent), and Applebee's (15.0 percent).

Much of the improvement in sales among the dinner houses and family restaurant chains during the last decade is partially attributable to demographic trends in the United States. In particular, the number of young people as a percentage of the population is declining. Those in the 18–24-year age group, for example, are of particular importance to fast-food restaurants because they consume about five meals away from home weekly, compared to under four meals for all consumers. While this age group nearly doubled during the 1960–1980 period, it will drop by about 20 percent by the year 2000. Those over the age of 65 tend to eat out less often, about two times per week, and this group is the most rapidly growing age group in the country. Older individuals tend to spend more time eating their meal, prefer sit-down restaurants, and are more likely to choose more upscale restaurants such as dinner houses. The higher price of the average meal in a dinner house is offset by the fewer times that older individuals eat out each week.

The initial high growth rates in fast-food franchising in the United States during the late 1950s and 1960s made the fast-food industry attractive to new entrants. The lack of established market share leaders and brand loyalties meant that there were relatively few companies that could defend against new market entrants. During this period, a number of fast-food chains were acquired by larger, diversified firms. Some of the most notable acquisitions were Pillsbury's acquisition of Burger King, General Foods' acquisition of Burger Chef (which was later sold to Hardee's Food Systems in 1982), Ralston-Purina's acquisition of Jack in the Box, United Brand's acquisition of Baskin-Robbins (which it later sold in 1973), and Great Western's acquisition of Shakey's Pizza.

The acquisition of a number of fast-food franchises by larger, more established marketing firms intensified competition during the 1970s. Not only were many fast-food chains owned by larger companies with resources enabling them to promote and invest heavily in their respective chains, but consumers increasingly demanded more value for their dollar. This further intensified competition and a second wave of acquisitions followed during this period. PepsiCo acquired Pizza Hut in 1977 and Taco Bell in 1978. KFC, which was sold by Heublein to R.J. Reynolds Industries in 1982, was also acquired by PepsiCo, in 1986. Other notable acquisitions during this period were Hardee's acquisition of Roy Rogers, Popeyes' acquisition of Church's, Tennessee Restaurant Company's acquisition of Friendly's Ice Cream, and Gibbons, Green von Amerongen's acquisition of Jack in the Box. Many of these acquisitions were made in order to strengthen the parent company's position within the fast-food industry (e.g., PepsiCo's decision to diversify into fast-food by acquiring Pizza Hut, Taco Bell, and Kentucky Fried Chicken). However, another factor that led to many of these acquisitions was the deteriorating financial position of smaller competitors, brought about by a lack of resources to compete with the market share leaders. A number of chains, therefore, became attractive takeover targets.

An interesting characteristic of the fast-food industry is that, in almost all cases, the leader in each food segment controls a large relative market share when compared to the market shares of its nearest competitors. Exhibit 3 shows the market share leaders in the top six fast-food categories for the industry's leading chains. KFC controls 58 percent of the chicken segment, while McDonald's, Red Lobster, Ponderosa Steak House, Denny's, and Pizza Hut control 34, 19, 23, 21, and 48 percent of their respective segments.

Demographically, consumers became more and more demanding during the 1980s. In 1991, the National Restaurant Association conducted a survey to measure consumer attitudes toward fast-food and moderately-priced restaurants. Of those consumers who said they would rather go to a fast-food restaurant than any other type of restaurant under most circumstances, 48 percent mentioned being in a hurry, being busy, and wanting fast service as the major factor in their choice of a fast-food restaurant. Convenience, expense, "didn't feel like cooking," and quality were less important. This trend was further supported in a 1992 survey by the National Restaurant Association, which found that 66 percent of the respondents felt that their expectations of the value they received at fast-food restaurants for the price paid was generally met. Twenty-four percent of the respondents felt that value fell below their expectations.

By 1994, however, consumers had become more demanding. In addition to demanding faster service, consumers were increasingly demanding a greater variety of menu items, greater value for their dollar, and fast-food available at a greater number of non-traditional outlets, such as airports. This has resulted in a number of fast-food chains (such as McDonald's, Taco Bell, and Wendy's) offering combinations of food items ("value meals") at lower prices and several fast-food chains cutting across food segments by offering products not traditionally offered by other competitors in their food segment (for example, Hardee's offering fried chicken). The latter has affected KFC, which competes exclusively within the chicken segment.

Exhibit 3   **Leading U.S. Fast-Food Chains (ranked by estimated 1995 sales, $000s)**

Sandwich Chains	Sales	Share
McDonald's	15,800	33.5%
Burger King	7,830	16.6%
Taco Bell	4,853	10.3%
Wendy's	4,152	8.8%
Hardee's	3,520	7.5%
Subway	2,905	6.2%
Arby's	1,730	3.7%
Dairy Queen	1,185	2.5%
Jack in the Box	1,082	2.3%
Sonic Drive-In	880	1.9%
Carl's Jr.	562	1.2%
Other Chains	2,658	5.5%
Total	47,156	100.0%

Dinner Houses	Sales	Share
Red Lobster	1,850	18.9%
Olive Garden	1,250	12.8%
Applebee's	1,012	10.4%
Chili's	950	9.7%
T.G.I. Friday's	870	8.9%
Outback Steakhouse	822	8.4%
Ruby Tuesday	545	5.6%
Bennigan's	455	4.7%
Chi-Chi's	340	3.5%
Ground Round	305	3.1%
Other Dinner Houses	1,366	14.0%
Total	9,765	100.0%

Steak Houses	Sales	Share
Ponderosa	741	23.2%
Golden Corral	629	19.7%
Sizzler	625	19.6%
Ryan's	562	17.6%
Western Sizzlin'	349	10.9%
Quincy's	287	9.0%
Total	3,193	100.0%

Family Restaurants	Sales	Share
Denny's	1,810	21.1%
Shoney's	1,277	14.9%
Big Boy	1,010	11.8%
Cracker Barrel	970	11.3%
Int'l House of Pancakes	729	8.5%
Perkins	688	8.0%
Friendly's	656	7.7%
Bob Evans	585	6.8%
Waffle House	294	3.4%
Coco's	279	3.3%
Marie Callenders	261	3.1%
Total	8,559	100.0%

Pizza Chains	Sales	Share
Pizza Hut	5,400	48.1%
Little Caesars	2,050	18.2%
Domino's Pizza	1,973	17.6%
Papa John's	450	4.0%
Sbarros	420	3.7%
Round Table Pizza	374	3.3%
Chuck E. Cheese's	307	2.7%
Godfather's Pizza	260	2.4%
Total	11,234	100.0%

Chicken Chains	Sales	Share
KFC	3,720	58.1%
Boston Chicken	725	11.3%
Popeyes Chicken	689	10.8%
Chick-fil-A	507	7.9%
Church's Chicken	501	7.8%
Kenny Rogers Roasters	263	4.1%
Total	6,405	100.0%

Source: *Nation's Restaurant News,* National Restaurant Association. See current issues for recent figures.

THE CHICKEN SEGMENT OF THE FAST-FOOD INDUSTRY

Only about one-half of all chicken chains had established restaurants outside of the United States by 1995. In contrast, KFC opened its first restaurant outside of the United States in the late 1950s. KFC's early expansion abroad, its strong brand name, and managerial experience operating in international markets partially explains KFC's dominant market share. KFC also leads all chicken chains in sales and units in the U.S. market; however, it faces much stronger competition domestically (see Exhibit 4). During the last five years, KFC's sales have grown at a 2.7 percent annual rate, while the overall chicken segment has grown at an average annual rate of 7.1 percent. With the exception of Church's, Boston Market, Popeyes, Chick-fil-A, and Kenny Rogers have grown at significantly faster rates than KFC. Boston Market and Kenny Rogers, which have focused on non-fried chicken products, have been particularly successful. In addition, while KFC, Popeyes, and Church's have focused on unique fried chicken recipes served to customers in free-standing restaurants, Chick-fil-A serves pressure-cooked and char-grilled skinless chicken breast sandwiches to customers in sit-down restaurants located predominately in shopping malls.

■ Chick-fil-A

Chick-fil-A's relatively high growth rate during the last five years may at first appear surprising, considering the culture at Chick-fil-A and the management style of S. Truett Cathy, Chick-fil-A's founder, chairman, and chief executive officer. Cathy, a strongly religious man, keeps all Chick-fil-A stores closed on Sundays. He also refuses to take the company public, will not franchise, and does not aggressively advertise his product or concept. Cathy is also involved in a variety of community activities which take him away from the day-to-day operations of his business, and he contributes heavily to youth programs, charities, and scholarship funds.

Chick-fil-A's corporate culture and new distribution strategy, however, have helped it maintain a higher growth rate in sales over the last five years compared to the chicken segment as a whole. For example, Cathy is well-known for treating his employees like family members. This has resulted in low turnover rates among both managers and part-time workers. In addition, Cathy has taken the step to expand beyond shopping malls. As many malls have added food courts, often consisting of up to fifteen fast-food units competing side-by-side, shopping malls have become less enthusiastic about allocating separate store space to food chains. In addition to Chick-fil-A's original sit-down mall stores, it has begun opening smaller units in shopping mall food courts, freestanding units, restaurants in hospitals and colleges, and "Dwarf Houses" (full-service restaurants which offer hamburgers and steaks as well as chicken).

■ Church's and Popeyes

Much of the slow growth in sales and units in Popeyes and Church's is a function of financial problems during the last five years. In 1989, the San Antonio-based Church's Fried Chicken was acquired in a hostile takeover by

Exhibit 4		Top U.S. Chicken Chains					
Sales ($ Millions)	*1989*	*1990*	*1991*	*1992*	*1993*	*1994*	*1995*
KFC	3,000	3,249	3,400	3,400	3,400	3,500	3,720
Boston Market	N/A	N/A	N/A	43	152	384	725
Popeyes	510	560	536	545	564	610	689
Chick-fil-A	264	300	325	356	396	451	507
Church's	466	445	415	414	440	465	501
Kenny Roger's	N/A	N/A	N/A	N/A	69	150	263
Total U.S. Market	4,240	4,554	4,676	4,758	5,021	5,560	6,405
Year-End Restaurants	*1989*	*1990*	*1991*	*1992*	*1993*	*1994*	*1995*
KFC	4,937	5,006	5,056	5,089	5,128	5,149	5,200
Boston Market	N/A	N/A	N/A	83	217	937	971
Popeyes	739	778	794	775	764	848	932
Chick-fil-A	411	441	465	487	545	534	825
Church's	1,111	1,059	1,021	944	932	592	702
Kenny Roger's	N/A	N/A	N/A	35	102	187	303
Total U.S. Market	7,198	7,284	7,336	7,413	7,688	8,247	8,933

Source: *Nation's Restaurant News*, National Restaurant Association.

Al Copeland, owner of Popeyes Famous Fried Chicken & Biscuits. The $400 million leveraged buy-out of Church's was financed through Merrill Lynch and the Canadian Imperial Bank of Canada. Most of the financing was achieved through the issue of junk bonds. Merrill Lynch and CIBC's fee was $58 million!

Copeland's strategy was two-fold: (1) to convert Church's restaurants into Popeyes restaurants and (2) to sell off several hundred Church's restaurants in order to cover interest and debt payments arising from the acquisition of Church's. Exhibit 4 shows that both sales and the number of Church's restaurants began to fall in 1990. Sales began to rise again in 1993. Popeyes achieved a five-year growth rate in sales of 4.2 percent, higher than the growth rate of KFC during this period. The growth of Popeyes units grew at a lower 3.7 percent annual rate. Much of this growth, of course, was achieved through the conversion of Church's units into Popeyes units. Church's units have fallen from 1,059 restaurants in 1990 to 702 in 1995, an annual decline of 7.9 percent. In a 1992 court battle, Copeland was forced out as owner of Popeyes and Church's, and the two units became divisions of America's Favorite Chicken Co., a subsidiary of the Canadian Imperial Bank of Canada and Copeland's major financial backer during the 1989 takeover of Church's.

A major issue facing Church's and Popeyes in 1996 is whether they can survive over the long term as they have been unable to make major market share gains over the last ten years. In addition, the chains have been burdened by large debt that accumulated as a result of Al Copeland's acquisition of Church's and subsequent financial problems, which ultimately led to Copeland's downfall. There is also some concern that Church's and Popeyes' current owner, the Canadian Imperial Bank of Canada, does not have the managerial know-how and expertise to operate Church's and Popeyes other than as autonomous units. The Canadian Imperial Bank's eventual takeover of Church's and Popeyes was a court-approved remedy for Al Copeland's inability to repay the bank for the bank's financial support of Copeland's acquisition of Church's. Therefore, there is little strategic fit or opportunity to transfer value from the parent to the newly acquired chicken chains.

■ Boston Chicken

Through the early 1980s, all of the leading chicken chains focused on fried chicken products. However, by the mid-1980s, many fast-food chains began to recognize the need to introduce products which appealed to an increasingly health-conscious consumer. To address these needs, the major chicken chains added more healthful products to their menus, such as grilled chicken sandwiches and rotisserie chicken. However, they continued to emphasize what they did best—fried chicken-on-the-bone.

In 1985, a new restaurant called Boston Chicken was opened in Newton, Massachusetts. Instead of offering a wide range of fried and non-fried chicken products, Boston Chicken chose to build a concept around a single product: marinated, slow-roasted chicken. Part of Boston Chicken's strategy was to differentiate itself from other fast-food restaurants by emphasizing the "home-cooked" nature of its products. The menu was simple. Customers chose a quarter or half chicken, white or dark meat, and two side orders. Side orders were selected from a variety of food items in a delicatessen-like display case. Corn bread was included with every meal. In addition to its roasted chicken meals, the menu included chicken sandwiches, chicken soup, chicken salad, and chicken pot pie. All food items were made from scratch, further enhancing the restaurant's image for "home-cooked" rather than "fast" food. Units were simple and clean and the decor was designed to give the appearance of a delicatessen. While units were designed mainly for take-out, no drive-thrus were used. This further enhanced its delicatessen image. Prices were slightly higher than other chicken chains, but this fit with the "home-cooked" image of the restaurant and appealed to professionals and other higher income customers.

On November 9, 1993, Boston Chicken went public. From an initial offering of $20 per share, the price jumped to $48.50 by the close of the day, a 143 percent increase. According to NASDAQ, it was the largest first-day increase in stock price of any new stock in any industry in over two years. Total market capitalization was $18.6 million. Boston Chicken's first annual report for the year ended December 26, 1993, showed the company's first profit—net income of $1.6 million on revenues of $42.5 million. This represented a 413 percent increase in revenue from the previous year. Boston Chicken later changed its franchise name to Boston Market.

KENTUCKY FRIED CHICKEN CORPORATION

■ Parent-Subsidiary Relationship

When PepsiCo, Inc. acquired KFC from RJR-Nabisco in 1986, KFC's relationship with its parent company underwent dramatic changes. RJR-Nabisco ran

KFC as a semi-autonomous unit, satisfied that KFC management knew the fast-food business better than they. In contrast, PepsiCo acquired KFC in order to complement its already strong presence in fast food. After its acquisition of KFC, PepsiCo had the leading market share in chicken (KFC), pizza (Pizza Hut), and Mexican food (Taco Bell). However, rather than allowing KFC to operate autonomously, PepsiCo undertook sweeping changes. These changes included negotiating a new franchise contract to give PepsiCo more control over its franchisees, reducing staff in order to cut costs, and replacing KFC managers with its own. In 1987, a rumor spread throughout KFC's headquarters in Louisville that the new personnel manager, who had just relocated from PepsiCo's headquarters in New York, was overheard saying that there will be "no more home-grown tomatoes in this organization."

Such statements by PepsiCo personnel, uncertainties created by several restructurings which led to layoffs throughout the KFC organization, the replacement of KFC personnel with PepsiCo managers, and conflicts between KFC and PepsiCo's corporate cultures created a morale problem within KFC. Colonel Sanders' philosophy when he founded KFC was to create an organization with a relaxed atmosphere, lifetime employment, good employee benefits, and a system of relatively independent franchisees. In stark contrast to KFC's culture, PepsiCo's culture was characterized by a strong emphasis on performance. PepsiCo used its Taco Bell, Pizza Hut, and KFC operations as training grounds for its future top managers and rotated its best managers, on average, every two years among its KFC, Taco Bell, Pizza Hut, Frito-Lay, and Pepsi-Cola subsidiaries. Therefore, there was immense pressure for managers to continuously show their managerial prowess within short periods, in order to maximize their potential for promotion. However, KFC personnel were often chosen from outside the KFC organization or hired through executive consultants. This practice left many existing KFC managers with the feeling that they had few career opportunities with the new company. One KFC manager commented that a senior manager told him that "You may have performed well last year, but if you don't perform well this year, you're gone, and there are 100 ambitious guys with Ivy League MBAs at PepsiCo who would love to take your position."

PepsiCo., Inc., headquartered in Purchase, New York, has three major divisions: beverage, snack foods, and restaurants. The two business units within the beverage division, Pepsi-Cola North America and Pepsi-Cola International, are both located in Somers, New York. Frito-Lay, located in Dallas, Texas, is the sole business unit within the snack food division. The restaurant division contains four business units directed by PepsiCo Worldwide Restaurants (Dallas, Texas): Pizza Hut, Inc. (Dallas, Texas), Taco Bell (Irvine, Texas), KFC (Louisville, Kentucky), and PepsiCo Restaurants International (Dallas, Texas).

Officially, PepsiCo managers were given autonomy to make their own decisions. In reality, PepsiCo kept a tight reign on its units. This was partially the result of its policy of continuously evaluating managers for promotion. Accounting, MIS, and financial planning systems were dictated from PepsiCo and much of KFC's capital expenditures were allocated by PepsiCo from other PepsiCo units. In 1995, KFC accounted for a little over one percent of PepsiCo's consolidated operating profit but 9.2 percent of total capital spending. In contrast, Frito Lay accounted for 47.9 percent of PepsiCo's overall 1995 operating profit but 36.3 percent of capital spending.

Asked about KFC's relationship with its parent, Kyle Craig commented:

The KFC culture is an interesting one because I think it was dominated by a lot of KFC folks, many of whom have been around since the days of the Colonel. Many of those people were very intimidated by the PepsiCo culture which is a very high performance, high accountability, highly driven culture. People were concerned about whether they would succeed in the new culture. Like many companies, we have had a couple of downsizings which further made people nervous. Today, there are fewer old KFC people around and I think to some degree people have seen that the PepsiCo culture can drive some pretty positive results. I also think the PepsiCo people who have worked with KFC have modified their cultural values somewhat and they can see that there were a lot of benefits in the old KFC culture.

Even now, though, that is still not universally understood. PepsiCo pushes their companies to perform strongly, but whenever there is a slip in performance, it increases the culture gap between PepsiCo and KFC. I have been involved in two downsizings over which I have been the chief architect. They have been probably the two most gut-wrenching experiences of my career. Because you know you're dealing with peoples' lives and their families, these changes can be emotional if you care about the people in your organization. However, I do fundamentally believe that your first obligation is to the entire organization.

▪ Financial Results

Exhibit 5 shows KFC's corporate sales since 1993. KFC corporate sales continue to grow at a healthy rate. Sales have grown at a compounded annual growth rate of 13.6 percent during the last five years. Sales were up 13.8 and 9.2 percent in 1994 and 1995, respectively, mainly because of new restaurant construction outside the United States, higher pricing in U.S. restaurants, and higher

---

Exhibit 5 **PepsiCo, Inc. Corporate Net Sales ($000s)**

	1993	*1994*	*1995*
Beverages	8,638	9,687	10,548
Snack Foods	7,027	8,264	8,545
Restaurants	9,356	10,521	11,328
Pizza Hut	4,129	4,443	4,828
Taco Bell	2,901	3,431	3,609
KFC	2,326	2,647	2,891
Total	25,021	28,472	30,421
Domestic	18,309	20,246	21,674
International	6,712	8,226	8,747
Total	25,021	28,472	30,421

Source: PepsiCo, Inc. annual reports.

Note: Sales data include sales from company restaurants and royalties from franchises (sales from franchises are excluded).

Exhibit 6   **KFC Worldwide Restaurant Growth**

Year	U.S. Stores	New Builds	%Total	Int'l Stores	New Builds	%Total	Worldwide Stores	New Builds	%Total
1986	4,720	-	71.8%	1,855	-	28.2%	6,575	-	100.0%
1987	4,814	94	64.0%	2,708	853	36.0%	7,522	947	100.0%
1988	4,899	85	63.1%	2,862	154	36.9%	7,761	239	100.0%
1989	4,961	62	62.4%	2,987	125	37.6%	7,948	187	100.0%
1990	5,006	45	61.1%	3,181	194	38.9%	8,187	239	100.0%
1991	5,056	50	59.6%	3,424	243	40.4%	8,480	293	100.0%
1992	5,089	33	58.3%	3,640	216	41.7%	8,729	249	100.0%
1993	5,128	39	56.8%	3,905	265	43.2%	9,033	304	100.0%
1994	5,149	21	54.7%	4,258	354	45.3%	9,407	373	100.0%

Source: PepsiCo annual reports.

franchise royalty revenues. Foreign restaurants represented about 55 percent of KFC's net sales in 1994 and 1995. Exhibit 6 shows KFC's worldwide restaurant growth during the last nine years. Increasingly, most of KFC's new restaurant construction is outside of the United States. Of 373 new restaurants built in 1994, only 21 were constructed in the United States. While international restaurant construction has grown at a compounded annual rate of 10.9 percent, U.S. restaurant construction has grown at a low 0.7 percent annual rate.

Slower restaurant growth and lower profits in the United States reflect a variety of factors. First, new, upscale chicken chains, such as Boston Market and Kenny Rogers Roasters, have attempted to cut out a market niche by marketing non-fried chicken products to higher income consumers. Second, many sandwich chains have introduced fried chicken and chicken sandwiches to their menus. By widening their menus, sandwich chains have appealed to families who need to satisfy different family member preferences. Third, all competitors in the fast-food industry have been under pressure to lower prices while at the same time improving menu offerings and service. All of these factors have made it more difficult for individual KFC restaurants to increase sales from year to year.

■ Business Strategy

Before 1986, KFC's menu offerings were relatively limited. Its major product offerings were its Original Recipe and Extra Crispy fried chicken products. However, by the mid-1980s, slowing per-store sales and increased competition among fast-food competitors led KFC to aggressively develop new products to appeal to a wider variety of consumers. In 1987, Chicken Littles were introduced. Designed as a snack product, Chicken Littles consisted of a small chicken patty in a small bun. One year later, KFC introduced its full-size chicken filet burger. Both products, however, were only modestly successful and ultimately withdrawn from KFC's menu.

Between 1990 and 1993, KFC introduced a variety of products in an attempt to expand its consumer base to lunch and snacks. In 1990, Hot Wings and Spicy

Chicken were introduced. In 1992, Honey BBQ chicken, Oriental Wings, and Pop Corn Chicken were introduced as limited time offerings to attract new customers. And, in 1993, a full-size barbecue sandwich was introduced. All of these offerings were only modestly received. In October 1993, KFC introduced its Rotisserie Gold chicken nationally. The introduction of rotisserie chicken received a tremendous response. During the fourth quarter of 1993, KFC reported a ten percent increase in sales in restaurants which offered the new roasted chicken product. Rotisserie chicken, which was slow-roasted and sold in whole, half, or quarter sizes, was designed to compete with the roasted chicken product that served as Boston Market and Kenny Rogers' major menu item.

In response to competition from sandwich chains and the consumer trend toward increased value, KFC made the decision to test an all-you-can-eat buffet in one of its franchises in Arkansas in 1991. The buffet, which was offered for $4.99 (lunch) and $5.99 (dinner) (1995 prices), offers up to 30 food items including fried chicken, biscuits, a salad bar, vegetable bar, and Pepsi-Cola soft drinks. Ultimately, KFC plans to introduce the buffet into about one-half of its domestic restaurants.

KFC's image as a fried chicken chain and the older age of many of its restaurants led to a new campaign to upgrade its restaurants in the mid-1980s. By 1994, over three-fourths of all KFC restaurants in the U.S. had been refurbished. In addition, KFC outfitted many of its restaurants with additional seating and drive-thrus, in order to accommodate increased consumer demand for both indoor seating and faster take-out service. In 1986, about three-fourths of KFC's sales were take-out. Take-out sales had fallen to about one-third of all sales by 1988 and have continued to fall since that time. In order to help dispel KFC's image as a fried chicken chain, Kyle Craig made the decision in 1990 to change the restaurant chain's official logo from Kentucky Fried Chicken to KFC. While the old Kentucky Fried Chicken signs can still be seen in KFC's older restaurants, its newer restaurants have signs that carry only the initials "K F C" accompanied by the profile of Colonel Sanders, KFC's founder.

One of the most difficult problems for KFC in 1994/95 was distribution. Because KFC's domestic restaurant construction program has slowed during the last five years, KFC has searched for new ways to grow the KFC brand domestically. When asked how KFC planned to grow its brand in the future, Kyle Craig commented:

> You know that McDonald's is still building a couple hundred restaurants a year, but we are not building a lot of traditional (freestanding) restaurants. But the business is changing. It is very expensive to build today, for us it is about a million dollars per restaurant. The returns are not what they once were so as opposed to going in and building traditional million-dollar restaurants, we are saying, hey, does it make more sense to go into other types of distribution centers; does it make sense to set up a delivery unit that may be much less expensive a way to expand both our points of distribution and consumer access to our products? I think we will find much more financially viable ways to grow the brand and we are trying to do it both for ourselves and for our franchisees.

■ Franchising Problems

KFC's ability to expand its distribution base was limited by an on-going feud with its franchisees. Through the mid-1980s, KFC's franchisees had been allowed to operate with little interference from KFC management. This "hands-off" approach could be traced back to the 1950s when Harland Sanders sold his first franchise, and resulted mainly from the Colonel's lack of interest in franchise affairs. Over time, franchise independence became a deeply-rooted part of KFC's corporate culture. As a result of their independence, and the control they had over their day-to-day operations, KFC franchisees developed a strong devotion to both the Colonel and the KFC organization.

When PepsiCo acquired KFC in 1986, one of its first steps was to negotiate a new contract which would give it more control over franchises' menu offerings and operations, allow it to close unprofitable franchises, and allow it to take over franchises that were poorly managed. Such actions were viewed as critical to improving product and service consistency and improving KFC's QSCV (quality, service, cleanliness, value) image. In addition, KFC believed that future growth in the KFC concept would come from smaller KFC units in shopping malls, colleges, and hospitals. In many cases, this meant that KFC would have to build units within close proximity of existing KFC franchises.

The last contract between KFC and its franchisees, prior to KFC's acquisition by PepsiCo, was negotiated in 1976. This contract stipulated that KFC would not build any KFC unit within 1.5 miles of an existing franchise. This stipulation was designed to protect existing franchises from lost sales to new KFC units built within these 1.5 mile protection zones. The 1976 contract also gave franchises power over supplier sourcing and the right of automatic contract renewal. The new contract would eliminate the 1.5 mile protection zone, eliminate automatic contract renewal, and increase PepsiCo's control over supplier sourcing. In 1989, the Association for Kentucky Fried Chicken Franchises (AKFCF) sued KFC over its new contract. In December 1993, KFC guaranteed that they would adhere to the 1.5 mile limit for seven months and Kyle Craig personally pledged not to open new full-service restaurants, home delivery, or take-out units within 1.5 miles of an existing franchise. However, the law suit remained unresolved in a Kentucky federal court in early 1996.

CONCLUSION

KFC faced a variety of problems and issues at the end of 1994 and in early 1995. Still the world's largest chicken chain and third largest fast-food chain, it continued to grow at a healthy rate worldwide. It also continued to control one-half of all chicken chain sales in the United States and had one of the world's most recognized brands. In addition, its new rotisserie chicken and buffet had been tremendously successful in those markets where they had been introduced. However, while prospects for continued growth internationally were bright, continued growth within the domestic market was threatened by a number of industry and societal trends. Competition from sandwich chains and new chicken chains, as well as consumer demand for a wider variety of menu offerings, forced KFC to reanalyze its product strategy. At the same time, KFC and other fast-food competitors were forced to improve product offerings and to serve their product faster and with better service to consumers who increasingly demanded greater value for their money. Asked to comment on KFC's situation, Kyle Craig responded:

> We are in a fairly complex business with lots of agendas. Our franchises want one thing done, PepsiCo wants something else done, and our field operators want

something done differently than the company [does]. There has to be a central location where key decisions are made and a vision for the business is established. I think I or another leader has to be that visionary. Our number one issue is our ability to handle change. We have introduced the Rotisserie product and that's given our franchises some confidence, but this franchise situation has been very difficult. If we can resolve that in the next year or two we really could operate as a unified system as opposed to 3000 franchise stores going one way and 2000 company stores going another way. People do see us now as doing a better job of meeting their variety needs and recognize that we are not solely dependent on fried chicken, but they don't yet see us as contemporary as we would like them to in the long term. This is particularly true of people who do not presently patronize KFC. Today's consumer is less loyal, more value driven, and much more information based. The only thing that I am sure of is that tomorrow's consumer is going to be even more demanding.

Turning Things Around at America's Favorite Chicken

Claire J. Anderson, Old Dominion University

Caroline M. Fisher, Loyola University

I n November 1992, Frank Belatti, a fast-food consultant to the Canadian Imperial Bank of Commerce (CIBC), took over as Chairman and CEO of America's Favorite Chicken, Inc. (AFC). AFC was a new company and part of a reorganization plan which consisted of America's second and third largest fried chicken chains, Church's and Popeyes.

By 1995, AFC, the parent of Popeyes and Church's, had put what was once the fried chicken empire of Al Copeland back in business, showing strong recovery in both brands. One major issue was to de-leverage the company, whose debt stood at $200 million at the end of 1994. Another major challenge was to revitalize the two chains and compete in an increasingly saturated market. A related issue was changing the corporate culture of the former Al Copeland Enterprises (ACE) to the more "business-like" one of AFC. Could Popeyes be the same without its colorful owner? Had negative publicity permanently damaged the two chains? Could AFC restore the confidence of their franchisees?

AMERICA'S FAVORITE CHICKEN

In April 1991, ACE petitioned for bankruptcy. By August 1991, after lengthy closed negotiations, a plan was revealed which called for Al Copeland to step down as owner and CEO of ACE. And, on October 20, 1991, a bankruptcy judge turned ACE over to CIBC, which would operate the firm under a reorganization plan.

Under the bankruptcy plan, Frank Belatti, a former Arby's executive, replaced Al Copeland as Chairman and CEO of ACE, renamed America's

Exhibit 1   **Income Statement, Al Copeland Enterprises**
                           (as of 12/91 in $000)

Net sales	$414,780
Company owned restaurants	370,851
Revenues from franchised units	32,669
Other	11,260
Cost of goods sold	132,381
Gross profit	282,399
Selling, general, & admin. expense	259,919
Income before depreciation & amortization	22,480
Depreciation & amortization	32,344
Interest expense	36,208
Reorganization expense	14,544
Income before tax	(60,616)
Tax benefit	24,834
Net loss	(35,782)
Preferred stock dividends	(531)
Net loss attributable to common stock	($36,313)

Source: *ACE 10K*

Favorite Chicken, Inc. Belatti inherited a firm beset by negative publicity, flattening sales, and a changing market. His central objective was to increase same-store sales 20 percent over the next five years, an increase of more than $100,000 per unit. As of the end of 1991, ACE experienced a $36 million loss, an improvement over the staggering $138.4 million loss in 1990, but much of the 1990 loss was due to a large charge-off of excess cost over fair value of assets acquired in the 1989 takeover of Church's. Total assets were down from $589.3 million as of the end of 1989 (first year of the acquisition) to $396.3 million. The firm was in a negative equity position and sales of the two chains had flattened. (See Exhibits 1 and 2 for 1991 financial statements for ACE.)

CHANGES IN THE INDUSTRY

Many changes were taking place in the fast food industry. The major trend was expansion of menus. Even Domino's Pizza, after almost 35 years of selling only pizza, expanded its menu to offer Buffalo wings, and with smashing success. Diversification became the buzzword in the chicken chains that were operating in a saturated market. In response, chicken restaurants added red meat, salads, meat loaf, and even tacos to menus.

The industry leader in the chicken market, Kentucky Fried Chicken, opened a prototype outlet, The Colonel's Kitchen, that offered chicken and turkey and 19 side dishes, including Santa Fe squash, Cajun rice, green beans, cobbler, and oatmeal cookies.

Exhibit 2

**Balance Sheet, Al Copeland Enterprises
(as of 12/91 in $000)**

Assets

Cash	$ 28,277
Accounts receivable	6,759
Inventory	6,794
Notes receivable	840
Other current assets	13,079
Total current assets	55,749
Property, plant, and equipment	269,431
Other non-current assets	71,140
Total assets	$396,320

Liabilities

Notes payable	$ 18,599
Accounts payable	14,237
Current long-term debt	4
Other current liabilities	21,019
Total current liabilities	53,859
Deferred charges	53,243
Liabilities subject to compromise	450,302
Total liabilities	557,404
Preferred stock	39,404
Accumulated deficit	(200,579)
Total Liabilities & Net Worth	$396,320

Source: *ACE 10K*

Boston Chicken, the nation's fastest growing food chain and darling of the stock market, attempted to position itself against casual dining chains. This was accomplished by changing its name to Boston Market and adding a host of new entrees at its 530 locations. Some wondered why Boston Chicken tinkered with its success. Ron Paul, national restaurant consultant, disagreed: "Chicken chains must broaden their menus to remain competitive—there are so many of them out there now. . . . I think Boston Chicken was smart to change its name. In fact, I would have gone further. People in Atlanta, for instance, don't want to eat anywhere with Boston in the name."

Others were more skeptical of the diversification trend. They held that these chains may learn the same lessons as the burger giants who attempted expansion in the mid-1980s to include pizza, shrimp, and salads. As a fast food menu grows, so does the risk that a chain will blur its identity, and complicate a business whose strength is simplicity. These problems drove several big burger chains back to basics when they began to lose business to narrowly focused upstarts such as Rallys. McDonald's scrapped a test of a sitdown family-style restaurant.

Exhibit 3   **Fried Chicken Is Still King—Trends in Restaurant Chicken Consumption**

	Change in number of orders 1992/1993	Share of total chicken orders
Fried	0.1%	47.0%
Baked/Broiled	51.7%	7.2%
Grilled/charbroiled	5.0%	8.5%
BBQ	−29.9%	3.3%

Source: *Restaurant Business*, March 20, 1994

Still another change in the industry was a shift to nontraditional sites such as retailing establishments, convenience stores, universities, and airports. Some featured buffets that were highly successful in towns and smaller cities and kiosks such as those employed in KFC, Pizza Hut, and Taco Bell.

Perhaps the major industry change was the quest for a tasty, low-fat, fast-food chicken that would appeal to the health conscious. The National Restaurant Association reported that skinless chicken and grilled chicken breasts helped the poultry category grow twice as fast as the rest of the fast-food industry. But the failure of skinless chicken at KFC might have meant that customers didn't really want a tasteless, skinless low-fat chicken. One Church's franchisee said: "Everyone says they want healthier chicken but the customers keep rejecting it. The bottom line is, if the taste is not as good, people won't eat it." A Chicago food consultant said that big chains like Popeyes and KFC ought to be careful lest they offend their core customer base. He said, "These guys have to figure out how much of this movement is real. They have to be careful not to move too fast." Another factor in the baked/broiled market rested on ease of preparation. Restaurant prepared baked/broiled chicken had little advantage over home-cooked versions.

In 1993, rotisseried (cooked on a spit) chicken became the hot new fare for fast-food businesses. Rotisserie was one answer to how to offer a healthier, quick service alternative to fried that was not too easy to duplicate at home. Even KFC promoted a rotisseried product with a "secret" Colonel Sanders recipe in its costliest advertisement ever. The promotion for KFC's Rotisserie Gold held that the product had 42 percent fewer calories and 42 percent less fat than its Extra Tasty Crispy fried product. In 1993, KFC sold more than $200 million of rotisserie product. Still, some in the industry wondered if the rotisserie revolution might be a passing fad. Industry consultant Ron Paul was convinced that "It's a trend, not a fad," and predicted that rotisserie chicken could grow to reach 10%, 15%, or even 25% of the market in the next few years. Moreover, according to Paul, rotisserie chicken was not as easy to manage: "The product doesn't hold as well and takes longer to cook so there are more issues with timing."

Still, 1994 figures showed a 50% increase in orders of baked and roasted chicken served in 1993 compared to 1992. But, the whole category accounted for a mere 7.2% of all restaurant chicken orders in 1993. Fried chicken still accounted for nearly half of all restaurant chicken sold (see Exhibit 3). Nonetheless, KFC franchisees said the addition of non-fried chicken was already bringing in customers who previously shunned the standard fried fare.

The chicken phenomenon was still difficult to project. Per capita consumption rose more than 50% between 1970 and 1990, but chicken entrees as a percent of total restaurant orders remained steady at roughly 10% for several years.

New product introductions were poorly received at Popeyes and Church's. Popeyes tried both roasted and skinless chicken but neither survived a market test. Church's franchisees were especially critical of some new menu items—a chicken sandwich, and pork chop and white bean dishes. AFC announced it was not ready to enter the rotisseried market. In 1993, Dennis Campbell, VP of product research and development of AFC, stated, "We're not convinced that the investment it would take is justifiable long-term."

BELATTI TAKES OVER

While president and CEO of Arby's, Belatti was instrumental in turning around that chain, almost doubling sales from 1985 to 1991. AFC owners hoped that what he did for beef he could do for chicken. He promptly named several former Arby's executives to top management posts. Hoping for a repeat performance, Belatti set out to model AFC after the Arby's triumph.

Belatti had his work cut for him. By June 1992, sales had declined at both Church's and Popeyes. Some franchisees said the problem was a need for new chicken products. At the time competitors were flooding the fast-food market with new chicken items ranging from a grilled chicken breast at McDonald's to skinless chicken at KFC. Phil Klein, who had shut down one of his four Church's restaurants, said: "We desperately need some new chicken products. If we don't see some kind of improvement soon, we are going to have to close the rest of our locations."

At the beginning, AFC remained loyal to the concepts of its two operations. Church's was low-priced and specialized in Tex-Mex and Southern-style chicken and Southern side dishes such as fried okra. Popeyes specialized in spicy fried chicken and Cajun-style side dishes such as red beans and rice. Both Popeyes and Church's centered their operations in the South, primarily in Louisiana and Texas. Church's also had a heavy presence in Georgia, Alabama, and Florida. Exhibit 4 contains the distribution of chicken restaurants in the United States.

■ Corporate Culture

Belatti did not want to build a new organization as much as to make the old one run better. He stated: "My intention largely is to build equity in both brands [Popeyes and Church's] and to grow both brands and make them profitable." He pointed out that his mission was "to solidify those positions, [prevent] the new chicken competitors that are emerging from taking hold, and certainly, to steal some market share from Kentucky Fried Chicken." To do this would require changes in nearly every area of the firm.

Almost as a gesture to underline the change and to distance itself from Al Copeland, AFC announced the move of its headquarters from New Orleans to Atlanta. But, Belatti said that moving away from Copeland "has never really been a concern of mine." Belatti added that the change of location would help the process of change. All employees at the New Orleans headquarters location were offered a job in the gleaming new Atlanta headquarters, but only a handful accepted.

Exhibit 4   **Chicken Restaurant Distribution[a]**
                                 Percent of Total U.S. Chicken Restaurants

Region	Percent
New England	2.8%
Mid Atlantic	10.1
South Atlantic	23.1
East North Central	15.2
East South Central	8.0
South West Central	17.8
North West Central	5.2
Mountain	4.3
Pacific	13.5

[a]By U.S. Census Region
Source: *Restaurant Business*, March 20, 1994

Belatti set out to change the corporate culture: "We really think this company, over the next five years, is going to be a different place. The corporate culture is going to be different, the menu is going to be different, the advertising is going to be different." Belatti stated that he was trying to "create a new orientation and new corporate culture." But, he also understood the strengths of the chain: "I don't want to give up anything that made Popeyes successful."

When Belatti took over he was determined to run AFC like a "real company." Peter Romeo, in a 1994 article in *Restaurant Business*, detailed the changes at AFC. Belatti saw Copeland's corporate culture as one "lacking discipline." According to one franchisee, "The corporate culture *was* Al Copeland— he decided what you were going to do and you did it."

Chris Roush of *The Atlanta Constitution* noted that the changes were dramatic. He described the difference between the two styles as "akin to dining on prime rib at the Commerce Club vs. wolfing 10 wings and a pitcher of beer at Hooters. Under Copeland, all corporate decisions went through his office, but he allowed franchisees a freer hand. . . . Belatti delegates more authority but keeps the franchisees on a short leash."

Belatti effected the change by bringing in longtime friends and associates for his management team. AFC was dramatically restructured with staffers divided into two separate groups: Popeyes and Church's. Each was to have its own management team and even a separate floor at the Atlanta headquarters complete with a "war room" where they strategized away from the other chain.

AFC's executive vice president of marketing, Joe Genovese, contended that "When the war rooms aren't being used, they are locked to prevent any spying by the other brand." At AFC's headquarters, competition between the two chains was not only accepted but encouraged. This wasn't easy. For example, some Popeyes franchisees weren't happy about the spicy wings added by Church's in a short-term promotion. Genovese answered their complaint: "We can't stop Church's from doing it anymore than we could stop KFC from doing it. Go out and find something better."

Despite some disagreements, there appeared to be a consensus that relations with franchisees had improved since AFC took over. One franchisee said, "I haven't been in total agreement with what they have done but how they have done it." He continued, "They came to us with an arsenal of ideas and then invited our input. They listened to what we had to say." Strained relations were placated by creating franchisee steering councils to give licensees real input on their system's direction. Further, AFC helped each chain to set up franchisee-run purchasing cooperatives. The latter addressed one of the major issues in franchisees' dealing with Copeland, whose Diversified Foods was a major supplier. Owners seemed happier that decisions about a new product where not made by the same person who stood to supply it.

■ Debt Reduction

As of the end of 1994, AFC still faced a debt of $200 million. Federal regulation forbids banks from holding an asset for more than five years. To make an initial public offering sufficiently favorable to investors, a major priority was to draw down the debt of the former Al Copeland Enterprises. Further, the chain needed a hefty capital investment to expedite the finishing touches on its overhaul. Belatti admitted that turnaround was difficult. He noted that "A company that has been troubled by bankruptcy has more trouble getting turned around . . . because the investment community still remembers."

■ The Outlook—1995

When he took over, Belatti's high priorities were facilities improvement, menu enhancements, and the addition of restaurants in key markets. Details of the plan included a new advertising campaign, broader menus, and a makeover both inside and outside of all Popeyes and Church's restaurants. Belatti predicted he would open another 1,000 restaurants and double company sales to more than $2 billion in the next five to six years. The growth was to come from franchising that required less company investment.

In mid 1994, in a drive to revitalize the two chains and contend with industry changes, AFC introduced two new brands on a test basis. A 13-item Mexican product line called Chickita Grille was introduced into Church's. Meanwhile, the New Orleans Shrimp brand was introduced in a Popeyes restaurant. The objective was to create dual anchor restaurants, pairing Church's with a Mexican-inspired fast-food restaurant and its Popeyes chain with a New Orleans–inspired restaurant.

Another part of the overall revitalization focused on "re-imaging" both Church's and Popeyes; this included refurbishment, new logos, new unit designs, and new upgraded packaging. Some franchisees grumbled at costly refurbishing plans. In response, makeover of a Church's unit was reduced to $30,000, and less than $45,000 for a Popeyes restaurant.

AFC planned to extend itself past fast food. One plan was for a new restaurant chain, tentatively called Fresh Chef, aimed at aging baby boomers. The new concept called for units of 4,000 square feet (approximately twice the size of fast food establishments) which would feature bakeries, take-home food markets, exhibition cooking, and drive-through windows. Belatti acknowledged that franchisees would not be happy about the third restaurant concept, but there was overall agreement that relationships between franchiser and franchisee had warmed considerably since Copeland days.

Expansion efforts continued. On a regional basis, one AFC target was Arizona's red-hot economy in its search for growth. In 1995, AFC announced its intention to add 30 more Church's restaurants to its current 21 over the next two years in the Phoenix market. But, no plans for growth were announced by AFC for the Popeyes chain in Phoenix, which at the time had only one Popeyes.

Genovese, in an interview published in the *Atlanta Constitution*, suggested that AFC was planning to open between 250 and 300 restaurants in 1995. Half the increase was to be in international growth with franchises and joint ventures in Mexico, China, El Salvador, Korea, and Thailand. The bulk of the domestic growth was to be in traditional locations, but nontraditional locations were to be pursued. AFC operated in nontraditional sites such as aircraft carriers and discount stores such as Wal Mart, Handy Way convenience stores in Florida, and McCrory's, a variety store chain.

In the first full year operating under AFC, Popeyes increased sales $20 million over 1992 to $600 million, with a net increase of only two stores, and Church's sales grew almost 8% in spite of a slight decrease in stores. AFC estimated sales for 1994 to top $1.1 billion and projected sales for 1995 were $1.5 billion with a net income of $51 million.

While the record was healthy, AFC still lagged far behind its major competitor KFC. By 1995, Popeyes operated about 900 restaurants in 38 states and 12 countries, and Church's operated about 1,000 restaurants in 30 states and five countries. AFC's size was still far behind its major competitor KFC, which had approximately 9,000 units, of which slightly over 40% were in international markets. Most KFC units (approximately 70%) were franchised, whereas franchises accounted for roughly 40% of units in the Church's chain.

Belatti's job now was to continue to grow both same-store sales and the numbers of units in his two networks. At the same time, it was important that AFC not be left behind in important product developments. Such issues as moving into baked/broiled products and expanding Church's and Popeyes menus, as well as launching new store formats, would all have to be addressed. It was also critical that he prepare the firm for an initial public stock offering. All of this would have to be accomplished while working down AFC's debt. While AFC had perhaps been resuscitated, it was still a long way from the picture of health. Belatti still faces a number of important challenges.

REFERENCES

"Bamberger Retakes Church's CEO Post after Sherman Quits," *Nation's Restaurant News*, February 23, 1987, p. 55.

Barrett, W. F. "Sick Chicken," *Forbes*, December 26, 1988.

Bruno, K. "Copeland Makes Church's Bid," *Nation's Restaurant News*, November 7, 1988, p. 1.

Casper, C. "The New Spin," *Restaurant Business*, 1994, (5), 95-110.

"Church's Asks for New Hearing in Move to Block Takeover Bid," *New Orleans Times Picayune*, January 18, 1989.

"Copeland Wins Round in Court," *New Orleans Times Picayune*, December 13, 1988, p. C2.

"Depression-era Sandwich Boards Brighten Sales at Church's," *Nation's Restaurant News*, May 9, 1988, p. 11.

Deters, B. "Eatery Chains Adding Valley to their Menus," *Arizona Republic,* May 19, 1995, E1.

Ely, E. S. "Showdown: How Al Copeland May Yet Skunk Wall Street," *Restaurant Business,* January 1, 1992, pp. 60-70.

Faiola, A. "All's Fare in the Chicken Chains' War for Market Share," *Washington Post,* February 7, 1995, B1.

Fisher, C. "Chicken Hawk," *Advertising Age,* November 7, 1988, p. 12.

Howard, T. "New Investors, Cash Infusion Fuel AFC's Overhaul Program," *Nation's Restaurant News,* 28(46), 7, 99.

Pillsbury, R. *From Boarding House to Bistro: The American Restaurant Then and Now,* Boston: Unwin Hyman, 1990, pp. 97-98.

Powers, N. "Copeland Hints at Higher Bid," *New Orleans Times Picayune,* November 4, 1988, pp. C-1, C-2.

Powers, N. "Old Plan Offered to Save Church's," *New Orleans Times Picayune,* January 20, 1989, pp. C1, C2.

Romeo, P. "Is It Fixed Yet?" *Restaurant Business,* January 1, 1992, pp. 60-70.

Roush, C. "Challenging the Pecking Order," *Atlanta Constitution,* January 22, 1995, Section D.

Dayton Hudson Corporation

Marshall Foote, University of North Dakota

Troy Gleason, University of North Dakota

Aaron Martin, University of North Dakota

Brent Olson, University of North Dakota

Brian Wavra, University of North Dakota

Jan Zahrly, University of North Dakota

Internet site of interest: **www.shop-at.com**

Robert J. Ulrich assumed the Chairman and CEO positions of Dayton Hudson Corporation (DHC) in July of 1994 with a multitude of problems. Media coverage was negative and getting worse. Analysts' assessments were negative. Investigations by the U.S. Labor Department, earnings down seriously, key executives resigning, and merger offers from major competitors were some of the problems Ulrich had to face. And each of the divisions seemed to be cannibalizing customers from the others. Ulrich joined the company in 1967 as a merchandise trainee, was one of the managers who built Target into a powerhouse but, so far, has not been able to turn the company around. When would investors and Wall Street analysts give up on DHC? When would the company give up on itself and sell out or merge or divest its poorly performing division?

DHC is the fourth largest discount and fashion retailer in the U.S. behind Wal-Mart, Sears, and K-Mart. J.C. Penney closely trails Dayton Hudson in sales. DHC has retail operations in all segments of the discount and clothing industry. These range from a national upscale discount store chain (Target) to Mervyn's, a moderate-priced family department store chain specializing in non-durable goods. DCH also includes a Department Store Division (DSD), which is a centrally operated full-line, full-service chain of department stores emphasizing fashion leadership (under the names of Dayton's, Hudson's, and Marshall Field's).

A PLETHORA OF PROBLEMS

Dayton Hudson Corporation's problems were so many that stockholders and analysts were beginning to group them into categories. First and foremost, the company could not get profits up. This was reflected in the stock price. Secondly, the problems with the U.S. Labor Department were not only serious but public. Secretary of Labor Robert Reich insisted on talking about the problems on TV talk shows and news shows covered the sweatshop raids (Chandler, 1995c). Finally, the profit and labor problems contributed to personnel problems. Again, the problems became public knowledge when a division CEO resigned unexpectedly.

■ Profitability Problems

On May 16, 1995, Dayton Hudson Corporation (DHC) announced that first quarter earnings fell 72 percent from the previous year's first quarter earnings. The company blamed weakness in its Mervyn's division and weaker than projected sales in its other department stores for the steep decline in profits.

On March 14, 1996, DHC announced that net earnings for fiscal 1995 were down 28 percent from the year before. The company cited a "tough Christmas season" and a bad year in general. Company spokesperson Jill Schmidt contended that Dayton Hudson Corporation did not plan any reorganization. "Right now, there are no plans to sell anything. We're sticking with the plans in place," Schmidt stated (Dayton Hudson Plans No Changes, 1996).

Apparently J.C. Penney did not believe the public statements of DHC and approached the firm about a merger in February 1996. Penneys confirmed that it offered $6.8 billion for DHC but the Dayton Hudson board promptly rejected the unsolicited offer and offered no counterproposal to discuss the possibilities of a merger. See Exhibit 1 for comparative industry data.

The Mervyn's division continued to lag the industry with 1995 profits down 51% from the previous year. Executives at Dayton Hudson maintained that discount and fashion retailing was in an industry slump and there was some evidence to support that argument. Apparel sales were up only 2% in the first half of 1995 and much of that was due to special sales (Chandler, 1995b). Analysts noted that the industry is saturated and some firms such as Target and Sears are expanding.

■ Legal Problems

In August of 1995, Dayton Hudson Corporation found itself in trouble with the U.S. Labor Department when an El Monte, California, sweatshop was raided. Dozens of Thai nationals, illegal aliens, were discovered working in a shop manufacturing clothing. They were enclosed behind barbed wire and were making less than $1 an hour. Also discovered were boxes of clothing with shipping labels for Montgomery Ward and Mervyn's stores. "Two retail stores, from initial evidence, appear to have been dealing directly with the contractors" who managed the sweatshop, according to California Labor Commissioner Victoria Bradshaw (National Retailers Investigated, 1995).

Robert Reich, Secretary of Labor, forced a meeting in September 1995 with executives from Dayton Hudson, Sears, and Montgomery Ward to discuss

Exhibit 1   **Comparative Sales and Earnings Data—1995 Discount and Fashion Retailing Industry (sales and profits in millions of $)**

	Sales	Profits	ROE
Wal-Mart	$90,524	$2827.6	20.1
Sears	$34,925	$1025.0	25.1
K-Mart	$34,572	$ 8.0	– .2
DHC	$22,564	$ 362.0	11.3
J.C. Penney	$22,019	$ 940.0	16.9
INDUSTRY AVERAGE			12.9

Source: *Business Week Corporate Scoreboard*, March 4, 1996

ways the firms could counter the use of sweatshops (Chandler, 1995c). DHC was later excluded from a list of "Fair Labor Fashions Trendsetters" issued by the Labor Department in December 1995. The list of 31 retailers were firms that were actively working to guarantee that clothing sold by the retailers was made in shops and factories that comply with federal wage, labor, and immigration laws (Dayton Is Against Sweatshops, 1995). Secretary Reich wanted the retail industry to take an active role in enforcing fair labor and wage laws and was using public pressure to get retailers to comply.

The negative publicity about Mervyn's contracting directly with sweatshops for clothing hurt DHC's image of being a socially responsible firm. *Hoover's Handbook of American Business* in 1993 listed Dayton Hudson as fifth in the nation for job creation. *Hoover's Handbook* also noted that "Dayton Hudson has a long history as a great place to work. . . . " Because of its high-quality work atmosphere, job creation activities, and corporate charitable policies (5% of net income goes to local charities), Dayton Hudson was included in *The 100 Best Companies to Work For in America* in 1993.

The corporation was recognized in 1993 for its good treatment of working parents, minorities, and those with disabilities. Dayton Hudson was listed in *The 100 Best Companies for Minorities: Employers Across America Who Recruit, Train, and Promote Minorities*. Dayton Hudson was also named to "The 100 Best Companies for Working Women" by *Working Mother* magazine and "The 50 Best Companies for Hispanic Women," compiled by the Vista magazine section of *The Dallas Morning News*. Overall, Dayton Hudson, through its generous contributions and attitudes toward hiring, had made itself one of the more identifiable good corporate citizens—until the news of the sweatshop raid became public.

■ Personnel Problems

In March 1996, Stephen Watson abruptly resigned as President of the Department Store Division. He had been popular with subordinates but had clashed with Chairman Ulrich (Chandler, 1996). Watson was quoted as saying he resigned because he believed the Department Store Division will soon "no longer need" a chief executive officer (Dayton Hudson Executive Resigns, 1996). He was apparently referring to the intervention of Ulrich.

At the same time Watson's resignation was announced, Linda Ahlers, one of the few women in Ulrich's inner circle, was named as the new CEO of the Department Store Division. Many outsiders and analysts believe that Ahlers "does not have much of a chance," even though she has been with Target for 19 years and has been very successful (Chandler, 1996). The department stores' profits were down by 32% in 1995 (compared to profits in 1994), Ahlers is under pressure to cut millions of dollars in costs, and the department stores' product line is being rejected by customers after a 1994 strategy shift to "value" products.

COMPANY HISTORY

The history of DHC dates back to the late 1800's when the J.L. Hudson Company was founded in Detroit, Michigan. The Dayton Company was founded in Minneapolis, Minnesota, in 1902 and later became the Dayton Corporation. In 1956, Dayton's opened the world's first fully enclosed, two-level shopping center in suburban Minneapolis, named Southdale. Meanwhile, Hudson's opened the Northland Center in Detroit, the world's largest shopping center at the time.

The shopping centers gained national attention from other retailers. Dayton's and Hudson's each realized they had market potential and both grew externally through acquisitions and mergers during the 1960's, 70's, and 80's. Dayton's also developed internal growth ventures, hoping to capitalize on low-margin merchandising. The 1962 venture was the opening of three Target stores in the Minneapolis area. Dayton's entered the specialty book retailing market in 1966 through the creation of the B. Dalton Bookseller stores.

In 1969, the Dayton Corporation and the J.L. Hudson Company merged to form the Dayton Hudson Corporation (DHC), making the corporation the 14th largest general merchandise retailer in the U.S. DHC continued its strategy of growth. Department store expansion moved to the West through mergers and acquisitions of specialty stores and fashion retailers. In 1977, Target stores became the corporation's top revenue producer.

DHC merged with Mervyn's, a West Coast department store chain, in 1978 and became the country's seventh largest general merchandise retailer. At the same time, DHC began to shed its less profitable operations by selling regional shopping centers and entire divisions. DHC bought and sold stores in an attempt to strengthen its core business, general and fashion retailing. In 1984, Hudson's and Dayton's department stores combined to form the Dayton Hudson Department Store Company, the largest individual department store company in the nation. B. Dalton Bookseller was sold in the same year.

In 1990, DHC made its final major acquisition—Marshall Field's, a Midwest upscale department store chain founded in Chicago in 1852. Mervyn's initiated a major entry into south Florida by acquiring six Jordan Marsh stores and five Lord & Taylor stores. Target expanded into key Florida markets also and opened its first of many smaller market store formats. By 1993, the Mervyn's stores were losing market share due to heavy competition.

On January 7, 1994, Retailers National Bank, a national credit card bank and a wholly owned subsidiary, was chartered. The bank acquired the outstanding accounts receivable of the Department Store Division and Target. The bank now issues the DSD named credit cards and a Target credit card.

INDUSTRY TRENDS

The general and fashion retailing industry is characterized by intense competition. For most of the 1970s and through the mid-1980s, retailers achieved earnings and growth by adding new units and expanding existing stores. Strong economic growth and vigorous consumer spending made this possible and feasible. With high volume, retailers were able to reduce operating costs as a percentage of sales, producing solid profits year after year.

In the wake of the recession of the early 1990s, however, the retail landscape changed. Slow economic growth, a decrease in consumer spending for nondurable goods, and a surfeit of retail space put American retailers to the test. Successful department stores and general merchandise chains were following corporate level strategies of growth through acquisitions. At the same time, less successful companies were following retrenchment strategies. Successful business level strategies were differentiation and niche.

Retailers and customers alike grew accustomed to innovations in retailing. Upstart competitors were appearing in virtually every segment of retailing. Outlet malls, for example, with their selection of brand-name apparel at value prices, were luring customers away from department stores and off-price retailers. Superstores, carrying a wider variety of goods than the traditional department store, have emerged. Specialty stores evolved into "category killers" that carry a single dominant product. Examples are stores that carry many varieties of office supplies or many computer products. Specialty retail stores do not attempt to carry many different products; they want to carry all products related to a particular product or service.

Catalog retailing is expanding and at-home shopping is growing. Most of these new formats are competing on price or convenience. Different types of competition are becoming more powerful in the marketplace. Technological advances such as television, computer on-line services, and computer databases have opened new doors to reach consumers in their homes. Companies such as The Home Shopping Network (QVC), America On-Line, and Eddie Bauer are all cashing in on this new technology.

While some consumers remain loyal to the stores they patronize, customer loyalty, in general, is eroding throughout the industry. The once powerful and extremely profitable department stores have reached a mature stage in the industry. The only segment of the retail industry that is currently in the growth stage is the discount merchandise retailer.

> The retail life cycle is a natural evolutionary process and executives can do very little to counteract it. What they can do is to plan more efficiently in order to sustain profitability in the different stages. Such planning implies continuous rethinking and revision of operations. This, in turn, means that retailing will continue to be an area of turbulence and uncertainty for some time to come (Bass, Bates, & Davidson, 1976:75).

DAYTON HUDSON CORPORATION DIVISIONS

In 1995, Dayton Hudson Corporation had three divisions, all involved in general merchandise and fashion retailing. Credit operations were consolidated in a wholly owned subsidiary, the Retailers National Bank.

■ TARGET

In 1962, the Target division was created, focusing on discount prices. During the 1970s, Target expanded rapidly with internal development of stores and external acquisitions. In 1977, Target became Dayton Hudson's top revenue producing division. One year later, Target made its first entry into a shopping mall in Grand Forks, North Dakota.

Target was the first mass merchant to use a promotional toy in 1986. More than one and one-half million Kris Kringles were sold during the 1986 holiday season. During the 1990s Target introduced several new strategies, including establishing local flexibility through micro-marketing, initiating a total quality system, and focusing on efficiency through use of advanced communication technology and reduced inventory levels.

Target executives characterize the firm as an upscale discounter in the general merchandise retail industry. The discount segment of the industry is experiencing intense growth. Target is trying to position itself by focusing on the quality of service it offers its consumers. Target stores are described as having high quality at low prices; maintaining clean and attractive stores; stocking plenty of products to avoid stockouts; and offering fast, friendly, and accurate checkout procedures. Many consumers have realized that there is not much difference in the brands they can purchase at Target compared to those they might purchase at Nordstrom's or Dayton's.

The broad product mix is one of the reasons Target has been so successful. Target's emphasis is on basic, family-oriented merchandise. An aggressive fashion strategy enables Target to compete as a lifestyle trend merchandiser in all categories. Apparel and domestics represent approximately one third of the product assortment. The targeted customer is 25-44 years old, typically married with children in a two-wage-earner family with income and education levels higher than the market median.

The perceived value to the consumer has been a key differentiation factor. Another less obvious differentiation factor is the millions of dollars Target and its employees annually donate to local nonprofit organizations. Through these numerous contributions, Target has established goodwill in the communities in which it operates.

At year-end 1995, Target had 611 stores throughout the United States. The only region Target does not operate in is the Northeastern part of the country. Exhibit 2 lists the number of stores in each division.

Target's performance is the strength of DHC. Even though Target is a discounter and most of the products it sells make low profit margins, it is still the most profitable division of the company.

	1992	1993	1994
Revenues ($ in mil.)	10,393	11,743	13,600
Operating Profit ($ in mil.)	574	662	732
Net Profit Margin	5.52	5.63	5.38

Source: *Dayton Hudson 1994 Annual Report*

Exhibit 2   **Number of stores (year-end)—Dayton Hudson Corporation**

	1995	*1994*	*1993*
Target	611	554	506
Mervyn's	286	276	265
Department Stores	63	63	63
TOTAL	960	893	834

Source: *Hoover's Handbook*, 1994, 1995, 1996.

▪ MERVYN'S

Mervyn's is a moderate-priced family department store specializing in soft goods. Based in the San Francisco Bay area, Mervyn's was founded in 1949 and was purchased by Dayton Hudson Corporation in 1978. Retailer Mervyn Morris started the chain with the objective of mirroring J.C. Penney Co. but offering national brands and customer credit. Mervyn's still views its typical stores as smaller versions of J.C. Penney and Sears stores without the hardware and appliance departments.

By year-end 1995, approximately 70% of Mervyn's senior management team was new to Mervyn's. The single purpose of the new management was a turnaround. Mervyn's profitability has been below industry averages for several years. One key addition to the management team was Paul Sauser, formerly senior vice president of merchandising at Target, now Mervyn's president and chief operating officer. Sauser, a highly regarded retail executive, was brought in to help implement Mervyn's turnaround. Mervyn's turnaround included a new pricing strategy, shrinking inventory, sprucing up stores, tailoring merchandise assortments to match the needs of the local customers, and polishing Mervyn's image among customers. The stores are being renovated with wider aisles, knowledgeable associates, less crowding, and improved store graphics.

Mervyn's recent pricing strategy is an improvement on the previous strategy which created large price differentials on many sale items. For example, a cotton blanket was regularly priced at $35.00 but carried a $17.50 sale price one week per month. Consequently, virtually all the purchases occurred when specific items were sale priced. Under the new pricing strategy, the blanket's promotional price is $17.99, with a regular price of $25.00.

Another element of the turnaround was an improvement in its image. This key element involved a return of women's career apparel and dresses, which Mervyn's dropped in 1991. Mervyn's reintroduced its female business apparel product line, which sparked sales of more than $90 million in 1993. Approximately 50% of its offered merchandise is nationally known name brands. The key customer is a 25-44-year-old female, typically married with children, working outside the home. The customer tends to have a moderate household income, and some college education.

Mervyn's operates in 15 states in the Northwest, West, Southwest, Southeast, and Michigan. The vast majority of stores are located in California, where Mervyn's derives about 50% of its revenues. Other major states Mervyn's operates in are Arizona, Florida, Colorado, and Michigan. Mervyn's faces additional threats because of its strong presence in the struggling California economy. Even though Mervyn's profits and profit margin were increasing by 1994, they continued to lag the industry and depress company profits.

"Mervyn's was our major disappointment," the fourth largest U.S. retailer noted in its 1993 year-end earnings report. By 1995, the annual report noted that Mervyn's had "solid improvement" because of improved markdowns, reduced initial retail prices, and improved inventory management.

DEPARTMENT STORE DIVISION

The Department Store Division (DSD) operates stores under the Dayton's, Marshall Field's, and Hudson's names. The division has goals of fashion leadership, quality merchandising, customer service, and dedication to the communities in which it operates.

The Department Store Division focuses on trends in the marketplace and new fashions and products. The emphasis placed on product mix is a strength when competing with rivals. The DSD relies on a broad assortment of trend-right, quality softlines and hardlines, national brands, and private labels to fulfill customer interest and to sustain a competitive advantage. The DSD also invests in fashion and basic merchandise in the moderate-to-better price range to renew focus on "value" offerings across the price spectrum. This broadened their customer base by lowering opening price points in many departments. An example of this value-priced merchandise is its Field Gear line, introduced in 1993. While customers could still purchase higher-priced items like Ralph Lauren and Pierre Cardin, they could also choose from the Field Gear line that prices button-down shirts at $32.

The department stores' target consumer is married, with a median age of 43, and a median family income of $50,000. Approximately 40% have children living at home. Over half have attained at least an undergraduate degree; two-thirds hold white-collar positions.

The DSD is in the business of selling image and maintaining a certain image. Service, human resource management, and community involvement are elements that relate to their image. They uphold the quality of store appearance and remodel when changes are needed or anticipated. The overall image of the DSD is that of a full-service department store, fulfilling the needs and wants of their consumer.

The DSD places a heavy emphasis on full-color tabloids, direct mail, and occasional television and radio advertising. Also, a strong special store events calendar tied to key merchandising trends and/or community events aids in specialty pricing. Finally, a strong emphasis on primary and secondary holiday advertising and promotions is utilized.

The net profit margin for the Department Store Division has been increasing over the last three years. This trend is due to the increase in inventory turnover and the fact that the department stores can command a higher price for products. Higher productivity has also resulted from the introduction of new systems that track and control the purchase and delivery of merchandise.

The Department Store Division's major markets are located in Chicago, Minneapolis/St. Paul, and Detroit. The division continues to grow. A new Dayton's is planned for Minneapolis in 1997, as well as a new Marshall Field's in Columbus, Ohio. The recently resigned CEO of the division, Stephen Watson, said, "We wouldn't build them if we couldn't pencil in a good return" (Chandler, 1995d).

FINANCIAL POSITION

The Dayton Hudson Corporation has two main financial objectives: to produce an average 15% annual fully diluted earnings per share growth rate and to achieve an 18% return on equity. See Exhibits 3 and 4 for financial statements.

Dayton Hudson Corporation had industry average returns on equity but lower than industry returns on assets for 1994. The industry average return on equity was 17.4%. However, this number is inflated due to Wal-Mart's return on equity of 25.3%. The industry, without Wal-Mart, had a return on equity of 15.4%. In addition, Dayton Hudson Corporation generated RDA of 3.9% in 1994, compared to an industry average of 6.6%, including Wal-Mart, and an industry average of 5.1% when Wal-Mart is not included.

CURRENT SITUATION

Target has a strong market position in the industry. The department stores and Target carry recognizable brand-name products which give the stores credibility. Target and the department stores have a strong market image in the markets in which they operate. However, one of Dayton Hudson's main strengths could pose a problem to another aspect of its business. This is the phenomenal growth of Target. Target's growth in stores and customers may lead to cannibalization of the DSD. "After all, why should I shop in Dayton's when I can get almost the same thing for less money in Target?" said a recent Target customer who was applying for a Target credit card. A similar problem which may arise could be the cannibalization of Target by the DSD. Since the DSD is introducing lower-priced product lines to attract a wider consumer base, it might take consumers away from Target. The department stores also use sales, with significant advertising, to attract the budget-conscious shopper.

DHC is considering the introduction of a single consolidated credit card. Currently, the corporation has three cards. The first one can be used in all of the DSD stores as well as Target. A second card is a Mervyn's card and can be used only at Mervyn's. The third card is a Target signature card which is limited to use at Target stores.

Exhibit 3

**Dayton Hudson Corporation
Consolidated Balance Sheets (numbers in millions)**

Assets

	1/95	1/94	1/93
Current Assets:			
Cash and cash equivalents	$ 147	$ 321	$ 117
Accounts receivable	1810	1536	1514
Merchandise inventories	2777	2497	2618
Other	225	157	165
Total Current Assets	4959	4511	4414
Property and Equipment			
Land	1251	1120	992
Buildings & Improvements	5208	4753	4342
Fixtures & Equipment	2257	2162	2197
Construction-in progress	293	248	223
Accumulated depreciation	(2624)	(2336)	(2197)
Net Property & Equipment	6385	5947	5563
Other	353	320	360
Total Assets	$11,697	$10,778	$10,337

Liabilities and Shareholders' Investment

	1/95	1/94	1/93
Current Liabilities:			
Notes payable		$200	$ 23
Accounts payable	$ 1961	1654	1596
Accrued liabilities	1045	903	849
Income tax payable	175	145	125
Current portion L. Term Debt	209	173	371
Total Current Liabilities	3390	3075	2964
Long-Term Debt	4488	4279	4330
Deferred Income Taxes	582	536	450
Convertible Preferred Stock	360	368	374
Loan to ESOP	(166)	(217)	(267)
Common Shareholders' Investment			
Common Stock	72	72	71
Additional paid-in capital	89	73	58
Retained Earnings	2882	2592	2357
Total Common Shareholders' Investment	3043	2737	2486
Total Liabilities & Common Shareholders' Investment	$11,697	$10,778	$10,337
Common Shares Outstanding	71.6	71.5	71.3

Source: *Dayton Hudson Annual Report 1994*

Exhibit 4

**Dayton Hudson Financial and Operating Data
(numbers in millions except share data)**

	1/95	1/94	1/93
REVENUES	$21,311	$19,233	$17,927
Cost of sales, buying	15,636	14,164	13,129
Selling, publicity, & administrative	3,631	3,175	2,978
Depreciation	531	498	459
Interest expense, net	426	446	437
Taxes other than income	373	343	313
Total Expenses	$20,597	$18,626	$17,316
Earnings from continuing operations, net of tax	714	607	611
Income taxes	280	232	228
NET EARNINGS	434	375	383
Earnings per share	$5.52	$4.77	$4.82

Source: *Dayton Hudson Annual Report 1994*

The Corporation says that it is committed to the creation of value for its shareholders, despite a disappointing performance during the past ten years. The stock price has remained flat for the last five years and earnings are "up just 5% in four years despite 45% growth in sales" (Chandler, 1995a). High and low stock prices for the last five years are listed as follows.

	1991	1992	1993	1994	1995
Stock price high	80.25	79.25	85.00	86.88	81.00
Stock price low	53.73	58.00	62.63	64.88	63.00

Source: *Hoover's Handbook*, 1996

Ulrich had his hands full. Stockholders and analysts were truly frustrated with the downward cycle of profits as well as the stock price in light of the recent bull market. The image of the firm was tarnished. Top executives were leaving suddenly. Mervyn's was a burden. Hungry competitors were circling the firm. Divisions were cannibalizing each other. Would things ever get better?

BIBLIOGRAPHY

Bass, S.J., Bates, A.D., & Davidson, W.R. November-December, 1976. The retail life cycle. *Harvard Business Review*: 75.

Chandler, S. March 27, 1995a. "Speed is life" at Dayton Hudson. *Business Week*: 84-85.

Chandler, S. September 18, 1995b. Why clothiers are feeling pinched. *Business Week*: 47.

Chandler, S. October 16, 1995c. Look who's sweating now. *Business Week*: 96-98.

Chandler, S. November 27, 1995d. An endangered species makes a comeback. *Business Week*: 96.

Chandler, S. May 20, 1996. Under the gun at Dayton Hudson. *Business Week*: 69-70.

Corporate Scoreboard. March 4, 1996. *Business Week*: 99-122.

Dayton Hudson Corporation. 1994, 1993. *Annual Reports*. Minneapolis, MN.

Dayton Hudson Corporation. 1994. *DAYTON HUDSON: 1994 At a glance*. Minneapolis, MN.

Dayton Hudson Corporation. 1994, May. *History*. Minneapolis, MN.

Dayton Hudson Corporation. 1994. *Investor's factbook*. Minneapolis, MN.

Dayton Hudson Earnings Fall. May 17, 1995. *Grand Forks Herald*: D7.

Dayton Hudson Executive Resigns. March 26, 1996. *Grand Forks Herald*: D7.

Dayton Hudson Plans No Changes Despite Profit Dip. March 15, 1996. *Grand Forks Herald*: D5.

Dayton Is Against Sweatshops. December 6, 1995. *Grand Forks Herald*: D7.

Department Store Division of Dayton Hudson Corporation. 1991. *Three great stores, one great company*. Minneapolis, MN.

Fearnley-Whittingstall, S. October 13, 1993. Outlook for Field's Northbrook opening. *WWD*: 20.

Hoover, G., Campbell, A., & Spain, P.J. 1995, 1994, 1993. Dayton Hudson Corporation. *Hoover's Handbook of American Business*. Austin, TX: Reference Press, Inc.

Keeton, L.E., & Patterson, G.A. May 17, 1995. Dayton's first-period profit sank 72%: Net fell at Penney but rose at Wal-Mart. *The Wall Street Journal*: A8.

National Retailers Investigated in Forced Labor Case. August 10, 1995. *Grand Forks Herald*: A3.

Patterson, G.A. March 29, 1994. Mervyn's effort to revamp results in disappointment. *The Wall Street Journal*: B4.

Spain, P.J., & Talbot, J.R. 1996. Dayton Hudson Corporation. *Hoover's Handbook of American Business*. Austin, TX: Reference Press, Inc.

Standard & Poor's. 1993, 1994. *Standard & Poor's Industry Surveys*: New York.

Circuit City Stores, Inc.: Plugged Into Growth in a Saturated Market

Donald L. Lester, Union University
John A. Parnell, Texas A&M University
Commerce

C ircuit City Stores, Inc. is a specialty retailer of electronics and appliances headquartered in Richmond, Virginia. The company generated annual sales in fiscal 1994 of $4.13 billion from 294 outlets. Most of the firm's superstores, regular stores, and mall stores operate under the Circuit City name, with some mall stores under the Impulse name. Currently, Circuit City stores are located in twenty-two states. Circuit City is a public company traded on the New York Stock Exchange under the ticker CC.

The company has experienced rapid growth for almost two decades. The key challenge facing the top management team is how to continue that growth in light of the saturation of most major U.S. markets.

BACKGROUND

Circuit City began operations in 1949 when its founder, Samuel S. Wurtzel, opened his first retail store in Richmond. Sam Wurtzel was a visionary who was able to anticipate what was to eventually be labeled the "Age of Consumerism" in America. He taught his employees that every customer contact was an opportunity to make a friend.

Sam Wurtzel also envisioned the growth of the consumer electronics industry. While having his hair cut in a barber shop in Richmond, he noticed the construction of a television station, the first to be built in the South. Deciding that television had a promising future, Wurtzel opened a retail television store named Ward's Company in the front half of a tire store. He also introduced his product to the public by hauling a two-hundred pound television set door-to-door, providing in-home demonstrations.

That same year, 1949, Abraham Hecht joined Ward's as a partner. For the next decade the two men expanded operations to four television and home appliance stores, all located in Richmond. By 1959, annual sales volume had reached approximately one million dollars.

Ward's Company's strategy changed in 1960 with the introduction of licensed departments (approximately 3000 square feet dedicated to electronics and/or appliances, operated by Ward's) in mass merchandising discount stores around the country. The four stores in Richmond continued to operate, but the new licensed departments represented the company's desire to grow. In 1961, the company made its first public offering of 110,000 shares at $5.375 per share. This capital provided seed money for future growth.

In 1962, Circuit City began to offer a new service plan to its customers. If a set could not be repaired in the home, Circuit City would loan the customer a television. This emphasis on service after the sale became an important competitive advantage. In 1964, the fifth television and appliance store was opened in Richmond.

THE ACQUISITION GAME

The company decided to expand through acquisition in 1965 with the purchase of the Richmond Carousel Corporation, a subsidiary of T. G. Stores. This acquisition binge continued until 1970 when Franks Dry Goods was purchased. The following chart details the primary businesses acquired by Circuit City:

Company	Primary Business	# of units	Date Acquired	Date Sold
Richmond Carousel	Mass Merchandisers	1	1965	1975
Murmic of Delaware	Hardware/Housewares	6	1965	1975
Custom Electronics (Dixie Hi-Fi)	Hi-Fi/Audio/Mail Order	13	1969	1977
The Mart	TV/Appliances	4	1969	1975
Certified TV	TVs	3	1969	1972
Zody's (Licensed Departments)	Department Stores	100	1969	1983
Woodville Appliance	TV/Appliances	5	1970	1975
Franks Dry Goods	TV/Appliances	1	1970	1972

By 1970, Ward's was operating over 100 licensed departments and stores, with annual sales of $56 million.

A DECADE OF RETRENCHMENT

Circuit City began a serious retrenchment from the acquisition game during the early 1970s. Alan Wurtzel, son of founder Sam Wurtzel, spearheaded a divestment program that included selling or closing most of the businesses acquired during the mid- to late-1960s. To replace the loss of sales represented by the acquired outlets, Circuit City began implementing a strategy of internal growth, some of which is outlined below.

In 1971, Circuit City opened two specialty audio stores in Richmond under the name of Sight 'N Sound. Five audio stores were opened in 1973 in Washington, D.C., Richmond, Va., Charlotte, N.C., Costa Mesa, Ca., and City of Commerce, Ca. The company also opened nine Dixie Hi-Fi discount audio stores and The Loading Dock, a 40,000 square-foot retail warehouse showroom displaying a vast selection of audio, video, and major appliance products.

In 1976, the company began replacing the Dixie Hi-Fi and Custom Hi-Fi discount stores with the new concept "Circuit City" stores. The first six stores opened in the Washington, D.C., market. This concept featured top brand names in audio and video products, an in-store service department, convenient product pick-up area and knowledgeable sales personnel in a 6,000 to 7,000 square foot Circuit City store. The Circuit City stores reflected a strategic planning program begun by Ward's in 1976, which called for a new type of store for the future and a redeployment of assets. Ward's had been involved in over a dozen different businesses due to the strong wave of acquisitions from the late 1960s, and the new strategic direction was designed to narrow its focus. Sales reached $111 million by 1979.

A DECADE OF GROWTH

In 1981, Circuit City merged with Lafayette Radio Electronics Corporation, which operated eight consumer electronics stores in metropolitan New York. It also began expanding the Loading Dock concept in new markets under the name Circuit City Superstores. The first four superstores opened in Raleigh, Greensboro, Durham, and Winston-Salem, North Carolina. The Richmond Loading Dock stores were renamed Circuit City superstores in 1982. In 1984, the entire company was renamed Circuit City Stores, Inc.

The company also began replacing Circuit City stores with Circuit City Superstores. The first replacements were in Knoxville, Tenn., Charleston, S.C., and Hampton, Va. In 1986, all the remaining non-Circuit City operations, including Lafayette and Zodys licensed departments, were closed and resources diverted into building Circuit City Superstores. In 1987, Circuit City acquired a custom electronics design and manufacturing company—Patapsco Design, Inc., of Maryland—to serve as an in-house engineering firm. In 1988, the first Impulse stores in Baltimore, Md., Richmond, Va., and McLean, Va., were opened. These were operations within malls that handled small electronic gift ideas. In 1989, the advertising concept of "Circuit City—Where Service is State of the Art" was begun. A new graphic automation system was also installed to increase the effectiveness of print advertising.

OUTSTANDING PERFORMANCE

Circuit City Stores, Inc. seeks to maintain a low price image, excellent product selection, and unparalleled commitment to customer service, while maintaining a leadership position in margin and commitment to continuous improvement to maintain its competitive edge.

From 1984 to 1988, Circuit City provided the highest return to investors of any company listed on the New York Stock Exchange. The major company investments leading to this performance included:

1. The point of sale information system;
2. The opening of three automated distribution centers;
3. The development of an intensive sales training program; and,
4. The establishment of a balanced management structure which shifted marketing responsibilities to the operating divisions near the customer and technical and logistical responsibilities in the home office.

Circuit City first reached $1 billion in sales in 1987. By 1990, sales had climbed to over $2 billion.

NEW DIRECTIONS FOR THE NINETIES

Circuit City introduced a private-label credit card program by establishing the First North American National Bank in 1990. By 1996, this venture employed nearly 1,000 people and had expanded operations to include two call centers. In 1991, *Answer City*[SM], a toll-free phone service that assists customers with questions about product installation and operations was opened. In fiscal year 1993, CarMax, a retailing venture selling used cars, was initiated, and a 15,000 square-foot prototype store design was introduced to serve areas too small to support a full superstore. The firm also expanded into the Boston and Chicago markets. In 1994, the company announced plans to open 180 Superstores over the next three years. This expansion plan would place Circuit City in every major metropolitan area in the United States, except New York.

However, the focus of expansion into the major metropolitan markets of the United States has been at the expense of the international arena. This has given the company substantial growth, but it has done so at the expense of smaller markets. Some of Circuit City's competitors have specifically focused on the smaller markets, similar to the strategy of Wal-Mart, and this strategy has allowed them to gain market share.

Circuit City has implemented a point-of-sale system that speeds the customer's shopping experience through automatic inventory checks as well as credit card and check approval. It also allows the customer to receive better service while dealing with one employee. Additionally, the company has a Customer Service Information System which keeps a historical record of individual customer transactions. This system is beneficial in helping customers with future purchases, in helping to ensure that new products can be integrated with existing products in the home, and in facilitating product returns and product repair—even when the customer has lost a receipt (Circuit City Annual Report, 1994).

Circuit City's point-of-sale system is linked to its automated distribution system. This allows the company to keep a close eye on inventories and to provide overnight replenishment of inventories (Annual Report, 1994). The system tracks the shipment of nearly every box traveling to company locations. It is reported that this system adds as much as one percentage point to Circuit City's pre-tax margin (Foust, April 27, 1992).

Throughout its growth, the company has emphasized the need for cost control. Organization of its distribution channel has been instrumental in maintaining a low-cost distribution system. Circuit City operates fully automated distribution centers that service the stores. Each store is less than a day's drive from a distribution center. Using the point-of-sale system, the centers can replenish inventories overnight. The centers utilize laser barcode scanners to reduce labor requirements, prevent inventory damage, and maintain tight inventory control.

Circuit City believes that developments in digital sound and video will generate higher industry growth as the decade progresses. Digital products are becoming popular, and direct broadcast satellite technology transmits digital signals to a variety of U.S. markets. Circuit City will be selling the hardware and programming for this new technology. It is anticipated that in the late 1990s, high-definition television with its clear theater-style screen will spark additional growth as consumers upgrade a variety of existing products to obtain digital quality (Annual Report, 1994). In addition, video CD players, unveiled in 1994, are designed to play both audio CDs and a new generation of video CDs (Gillen, 1994). Analysts believe that this recording system provides a higher quality picture with compact disc quality sound.

Circuit City's advertising layout focuses on a quality image. It emphasizes exceptional service and price guarantees. This focus has given Circuit City strong name recognition throughout its market and helps develop markets prior to stores being opened. In addition, Circuit City currently offers over 300 brands. Each of the product categories has many varying brands to choose from, with large selections within each brand.

Circuit City has also taken a proactive approach to human resource development. Each associate receives extensive training to ensure a thorough understanding of the products before being allowed contact with the consumer. The company has included training for the associates that enables them to offer "one-stop" shopping. This concept allows for the customer to complete the entire transaction with the sales counselor. Sales counselors can accept all forms of payment and process credit applications for Circuit City's private-label credit card. This approach simplifies the transaction for the buyer and has enabled the company to generate considerable labor savings by reducing the support staff at each store. This is a new concept for Circuit City. However, this aggressive sales approach has earned the firm's sales force a "pushy" reputation.

FUTURE GROWTH IN A DIFFERENT INDUSTRY

Historically, top management appears to have demonstrated the strength to make decisions that negatively affect the stock price for the long-term good of the company. The company has also focused its strength of management, customer service, and operating control into the used car industry in a venture known as CarMax. The company feels the same skills it currently uses in the retailing of electronics and appliances can be transferred to the used car business.

Developed as a growth vehicle, CarMax opened its doors in Richmond, Virginia, in late 1993. Richard Sharp, current CEO of Circuit City, and Austin Ligon, senior vice president of corporate planning and automotive, placed the first showroom less than a mile from corporate headquarters. Other locations include Raleigh, Atlanta, and Charlotte.

Retail sales of previously owned vehicles total about $150 billion annually in the United States (Simison, 1996). Industry insiders speculate that the used car market will continue to grow, boosted by the price of a new car, $20,000 on average (Rudnitsky, 1995). During the past five years, the average price of a used car has increased from $6,000 to over $10,000 (Welles, 1996). In 1995, the average price of a used car sold by a franchise was $11,585, compared to $9,188 by independent dealers and $4,316 by private individuals (CNW, 1996). Consumers are finding used cars to be a better value since the typical new car depreciates 28% in the first year (Welles, 1996).

The supply of late model used cars is projected to rise as the popularity of leasing continues to grow. From 1991 to 1995, the percentage of new car acquisitions made under leasing arrangements rose from 15.4% to 31.5% (CNW, 1996). In 1995, 2.4 million leased cars were returned to the leasing company, many of which were resold at auctions (*Newsday*, 1996).

Currently, used auto retailing is a highly fragmented industry without a single market share leader. Used car sales in the United States are roughly split into thirds, with 36% coming from franchised dealers, 33% from independent dealers, and 31% from private parties (CNW, 1996). An estimated 35 million used cars between two and ten years old were sold in the United States in 1995 (McKesson, 1996). The typical used car dealer averages about $2 million in sales annually (Rudnitsky, 1995).

CarMax's offering is highly differentiated. Inventories are stocked with between 500 and 1200 vehicles, each less than five years old with fewer than 70,000 miles. Non-negotiable prices are clearly marked on each vehicle, and each car comes with a complete thirty-day warranty. There is a no-pressure sales philosophy, and consumers can operate the user-friendly computers in each showroom to find the locations of vehicles on the lot that match their make, model, price, and other preferences. CarMax buys its cars at auctions, and from consumers and fleet dealers, but all vehicles must pass a 110-point inspection before being offered for sale.

Circuit City has not publicized the financial results of its early years of used car operations, but Sanford Bernstein's Ursula H. Moran estimates that the Richmond operation turned over about 4,000 vehicles in 1994, for total sales of approximately $55 million (Rudnitsky, 1995). Competition is expected to intensify with the entrance of other used car superstore outlets. Autonation USA plans to open 25 outlets in South Florida and Texas by the end of the decade. CarAmerica has experienced success with its two concept stores in Wisconsin. Driver's Mart plans to open more than ten outlets per year in the late 1990s. Other competitors include HPR Automotive and Car Choice (Mohl, 1996).

CarMax is also looking at the new car industry, having recently signed a franchise agreement with Chrysler Corporation that will allow it to sell new Chryslers in Norcross, Georgia.

KEY PERSONNEL

Chairman of the Board: *Alan L. Wurtzel.* Wurtzel, son of founder Sam Wurtzel, had joined the company in 1966 as vice president for legal affairs. He became President in 1969 and Chairman and Chief Executive Officer (CEO) in 1984. In 1984, he retired as President, and in 1986 he retired as CEO.

President and CEO—*Richard L. Sharp.* Sharp joined the company in 1982 as executive vice president. Sharp had been president of his own software company, and he is credited with the development of the point-of-sale system. In 1984, he was elected President of Circuit City, assuming the CEO duties in 1986.

Senior Vice President and Chief Financial Officer (CFO)—*Michael T. Chalifoux.* Chalifoux came to Circuit City in 1983 from public accounting. In 1989, he became the vice president and CFO. He became a member of the board in 1991.

The Board of Directors consists of ten individuals, including the three individuals already mentioned and a retired vice president. Of the remaining six, two are from the academic world, two are retired presidents of other corporations, one is an attorney, and one is the Executive Vice President of an advertising company.

THE INDUSTRY

The specialty brand-name consumer electronics and major appliance industry in which Circuit City competes is currently faced with a variety of environmental changes. As the population ages, consumer electronics stores will need to determine the customer base they wish to serve and will have to market more aggressively to that target. Retailers will need to segment the data base and offer different promotions to different customers depending on purchase habits and behaviors or on demographics (Abrams, 1993).

As the consumer population becomes more informed about technological innovations and products, consumer electronic retailers will need to offer a more upscale product and improved customer service. Consumers will become more demanding as they spend a larger portion of their disposable income and will expect retailers to be on the same level or above.

Americans have always had an affinity for electronics and gadgets. This affinity has not decreased in the 1990s. The trend has always been to replace outdated electronics with newer models and to purchase add-on products. This trend will continue and consumer electronics retailers will be able to take advantage of this portion of the market.

The recession of the early 1990s provides the best picture of the effect tough economic times could potentially have on the electronics industry. While the industry as a whole has suffered, with Radio Shack closing over 175 stores and Highland Superstores, Inc. filing for Chapter 11 protection (Hewes, 1992), some segments of the industry, particularly the home-office and the television sector, have been extremely strong. However, when white-collar workers lost their jobs due to downsizing, many turned to freelancing or consulting from their homes, fueling a demand for equipment that until recently had been marketed primarily to businesses (Lavoie, 1992).

While worries about a sluggish economy have persuaded many consumers to forgo a trip or other luxury, they tend to adopt a recession mentality. Some buyers feel if they have to give up dinners out and expensive vacations in favor of nights at home, they will at least invest in a decent TV. Many consumers feel that television is an inexpensive way to entertain their families (Therrien, 1992).

Circuit City remained strong during the economic downturn of the early 1990s, maintaining its expansion plans and increasing its sales dramatically. In fiscal year 1992, Circuit City reported sales growth of 28% and earnings growth of 38%. Same-store sales increased by 3% in 1992 and 7% in 1993. Despite the the industry's problems, some of the strong are getting stronger. Circuit City and Best Buy were able to gain market share as other specialty retailers retrenched (Foust, 1992).

Circuit City is the industry leader in sales followed by Silo and Best Buy. Other competitors in the industry include Tandy, Highland, and REX. On the fringe of this industry are discount retailers (Wal-mart, K-Mart, and Target), wholesale clubs, regional chains, and mom-and-pop stores. Sales figures for each competitor for year end 1993 are presented in Exhibit 1. All sales figures are in millions of dollars.

SILO

Reported sales for Silo in 1992 were $1 billion, and sales for 1993 were running 20% higher than those during 1992. President Peter Morris attributed the sales increase to four changes Silo implemented early in 1993: changes in sales' associates compensation so that it is based on gross margin dollars (rather than total sales), changes in store organization, a move to "every day low pricing" and a new emphasis of "every day low pricing" in its advertising (Pinkerton, August 1993).

TANDY

Tandy includes Incredible Universe Superstores, Computer City, The Edge In Electronics, Radio Shack, McDuff Electronics, and Video Concepts. Tandy has a store of some type in literally every town in the United States with 5,000 people or more (Hartnett, May 1993).

Incredible Universe Superstores were designed to be destination stores with broad assortments, rather than convenient, neighborhood Radio Shack stores (Hartnett, May 1993). Computer City stores feature all brands of merchandise. The 5,000-item assortment includes personal computers, printers, telephones, fax machines, copiers, software, and furniture. The Edge in Electronics is Tandy's upscale retail chain.

Exhibit 1   **Sales Figures for Competitors**

Company	Sales—1993 (in millions)
Circuit City	$2,790
Silo	953
Best Buy	929
Tandy	703
Highland	575
REX	$ 202

Radio Shack stores are in convenient neighborhood locations with a unique product mix of gadgets and parts, all sold by a knowledgeable staff. It is estimated that one in four Americans will visit a Radio Shack in the next year.

The two successful consumer electronic superstores for Tandy are McDuff and Video Concept. The stores had estimated sales of $600 million, a 5% improvement over the previous year. All plans for expansion of the two chains are dependent on the performance of the Incredible Universe superstores (Gelfand, January 1993).

BEST BUY CO.

Best Buy Co. recently announced aggressive plans to expand its number of stores by 41% in the next 18 months to 112, with stores in 14 states. The chain reported sales of $929 million for 1992. The no-commission policy it instituted may be the wave of the future for electronics stores, said Peter Hisey, senior editor of *Discount Store News*. Even though Best Buy might have incurred losses during the change, market share has grown consistently (Goerne, 1992).

Best Buy offers more than 2,000 products covering every imaginable category within video/audio equipment, home office equipment, major appliances, and entertainment software. Additionally, the company provides a wide range of customer services, including authorized warranty service on most products, extended service plans, revolving credit, in-home delivery, and installation.

HIGHLAND SUPERSTORES

After peaking at 92 stores in 1991, Highland has been left with only 30 stores in the Great Lakes region and more than $100 million of debt. The chain is seeking a debt reorganization plan with its creditors through Chapter 11.

REX STORES CORP.

REX Stores Corp. was formerly known as Audio/Video Affiliates, Inc. Buying in volume for 100-plus stores while slashing overhead has enabled the Dayton, Ohio-based company to keep its prices low as it targets smaller, less competitive markets (Pinkerton, August 1993). The company's goal is to have 50% more stores within the next two years. All this expansion is taking place in small- to mid-sized cities with populations averaging 50,000. Stores can currently be found in cities with populations ranging from 30,000 to 300,000.

DISCOUNT RETAILERS, WHOLESALE CLUBS, REGIONAL CHAINS AND MOM-AND-POP STORES

According to industry observers, these stores sell consumer electronics, but their primary focus is on entry-level products. They carry step-up and more sophisticated products, but they don't sell them (Glasse, March 1993). For this reason, Circuit City has noted that these competitors exist, but does not feel that Circuit City competes directly with them in terms of products, customer service, service programs, and sales staff.

CIRCUIT CITY'S FINANCIAL POSITION

Circuit City has been successful in achieving growth in its sales and profitability. The company's income statement is summarized in Exhibit 2.

Circuit City has consistently increased its sales and profitability through internal expansion and the continued success of its existing stores. While the company's gross margin has decreased resulting from prices being driven down by competition and the company's more recent sales of lower margin computer/home-office products, Circuit City has been able to keep its operating margin and its net profit margin stable by operating more efficiently. This has been achieved by automating the company's distribution and point-of-sale functions.

Exhibit 2 — **Income Statement for Circuit City**

(In $000s)	FYE93	%	FYE94	%	FYE95	%
Sales	$3,269,769	100.0	$4,130,415	100.0	$5,582,947	100.0
Gross Profit	923,720	28.3	1,105,656	26.8	1,385,000	24.8
Operating Income	179,070	5.5	213,791	5.2	278,630	4.9
Net Profit	$ 110,250	3.4	$ 132,400	3.2	$ 167,875	3.0

Exhibit 3 — **Statement of Fixed Charges**

(In $000s)	FYE 92	FYE 93	FYE 94
Net Profit	$ 78,223	$110,250	$198,457
+Depreciation	117,929	145,742	198,457
+Interest Expense	9,033	3,820	4,791
=Cash Available for Fixed Charges	205,185	259,812	335,648
Interest Expense	9,033	3,820	4,791
+Current Maturities of Long-Term Debt	1,927	1,828	1,819
+Lease & Rent Expense	59,996	72,175	89,579
Total Fixed Charges	$ 70,956	$ 77,823	$ 96,189
Fixed Charge Coverage (%)	2.89	3.34	3.49

Circuit City's financial performance should be analyzed on its own merit, since the direction of the company and that of its industry are opposites. While most of the major players in the industry are in retrenchment, Circuit City is growing.

The most important ratio for banks when considering the financial viability of a company is a typical debt service coverage ratio or a fixed charge coverage ratio, depending on the circumstances. Circuit City has substantial lease and rental expenses since the company has sale-leaseback agreements on many of its stores. Exhibit 3 presents Circuit City's ability to meet its fixed charges.

Circuit City's cash flow is strong, as evidenced by the fixed charge coverage of 3.49 in 1994. Further evidence includes the repayment in 1994 of $60 million in subordinated debt. Exhibit 4 presents Circuit City's consolidated balance sheet.

Exhibit 4   **Consolidated Balance Sheet for Circuit City**

Assets	1995	1994	1993
Cash & cash equivalent	$ 46,962	$ 75,194	$ 141,412
Net accts & notes receivable	264,565	188,890	120,448
Merchandise inventory	1,035,776	721,348	515,771
Deferred income taxes	25,696	26,700	—
Prepaid expense & other assets	14,162	11,476	13,270
Total current assets	1,387,161	1,023,708	790,901
Property & equipment net	592,956	438,096	370,791
Deferred income taxes	5,947	78,688	87,588
Other assets	17,991	14,172	13,650
Total assets	2,004,055	1,554,664	1,262,930
Liabilities			
Current inst of long-term debt	2,378	1,819	1,828
Accounts payable	576,578	419,037	278,348
Accrued expenses & other liabilities	113,631	86,826	66,487
Accrued income taxes	13,533	38,582	26,310
Total current liabilities	706,120	546,264	372,973
Long-term debt excluding current ins	178,605	29,648	82,387
Deferred rev & other liabilities	241,866	268,360	232,054
Total Liabilities	1,126,591	844,272	687,414
Common stock	48,238	48,040	47,835
Cap in excess of par value	72,639	64,485	54,540
Retained earnings	756,587	597,867	473,141
Total stock equity	877,464	710,392	575,516
Total liabilities & stock equity	2,004,055	1,554,664	1,262,930
Net current assets	$ 681,041	$ 477,444	$ 417,928

ORGANIZATIONAL STRATEGY

Circuit City seeks *growth*. Over the life of the company, growth has been and continues to be its major driving force. Through mergers, acquisitions, and opening new types of stores the company has grown to 294 retail outlets in twenty-one states. Over the next three years the company's plans are to open 180 new stores, representing a 61% increase. This expansion will put them in every major metropolitan market area in the United States, except New York.

Circuit City attempts to distinguish itself from the competition through the strength of its merchandising assortment and by consistently delivering exceptional customer service. To maintain margin and not give market advantage to discount competitors, Circuit City has adopted a marketing approach that includes some lower-priced initiatives along with stepped-up advertising and promotions in highly competitive areas. The overall goal remains to differentiate the consumer offer through an outstanding merchandise selection and exceptional customer service. A customer service information system, developed in 1992, maintains an online history of all customers and their purchases.

The company has also adopted an internal strategy of high quality and low cost service to the stores. The point-of-sale computer information system handles the total sales transaction with one associate, maintains detailed records of all purchases, and keeps inventory levels adequate at each store.

THE FUTURE

Circuit City presently has a variety of growth options should it seek to continue to pursue this strategy. The firm could continue rapid expansion plans to reach all major metropolitan markets. Continued growth would allow the company to further improve its market share and increase its sales revenue. In addition, continued expansion into the major markets will give the company the ability to fully utilize the experience and technology it has developed over the past years.

However, growth cannot be pursued without a price. The rate at which the company is presently growing will place burdens on the management to maintain the control it currently has. Many competitors before Circuit City have run into this problem and faced retrenchment to remain viable. As the company opens new stores the infrastructure of the company must expand to handle the increased demand. With the emphasis the management has placed on customer service, the threat of reduced service levels to the stores is possible with rapid expansion. Further, the strain on the financial sources, especially during downturns in the economy, can be damaging.

Circuit City could slow expansion plans and concentrate on maximizing profit in current markets. This would allow the company to emphasize the return to the company from the current markets and absorb the new markets and work them into the system. It would also allow the company to have a feel for what the new market will be like for the company. Slowing expansion will allow management to insure that proper controls are in place and the infrastructure of the company can handle the new markets. If there are problems, they can be addressed with more problems building up.

However, slowed expansion might allow competitors to make inroads into the new markets. This will make it more difficult to enter these new markets once the competition has set up. As this happens, competitors will begin to gain market share on the company. In addition, because the company uses a national advertising campaign, not having stores in every market will not give them full utilization of their ads. The full advertising has helped introduce Circuit City to new markets, and could leave consumers confused as to where their stores are. Circuit City could also lose some of its clout with suppliers. Being in the number one slot with rapid expansion gives the company a strong position with the suppliers. If this is abandoned, suppliers may view this as an indication the company is in trouble.

Circuit City could focus on expansion into Canada. Canada's proximity allows the company to utilize the current operations, while its market is not vastly different from the United States and will allow the company to expand internationally without major problems. However, cross-cultural expansion—even into Canada—requires the learning of a new culture, including such factors as political, legal, and currency differences. This could slow the expansion process and possibly create a learning curve challenge for operations and management.

Circuit City could continue diversification plans into the $150 billion used car market (Lavin, 1994). By gaining only a small part of this market, revenues of the company could increase significantly. However, as the energy is invested to learn the new business, the focus on the core business may suffer. Management will have to balance the resources of the company in the two industries, further straining capital resources.

Chief Financial Officer Mike Chalifoux described the Circuit City executives perspective of their business succinctly: There is not one "right" strategy for a business; there is only a strategy that is right for its time. To that end, the Superstore concept is continually scrutinized and updated, always being redesigned to fit the current merchandising and aesthetic standards of the day. Chalifoux relates that Circuit City's top management team decided in the early 1980s to focus on doing one hundred things 1% better than its competitors, rather than trying to do one thing 100% better.

The company's recent foray into banking and used car sales represents an attempt to capitalize on its retailing, marketing, and management strengths. Chalifoux says there are no plans for global expansion of the Superstore concept.

REFERENCES

Abrams, Judith. "The Power of Private Label Plastic." *Dealerscope*, September 1993, pp. 74-76.

Circuit City Stores, Inc., Richmond, Virginia, *1994 Annual Report*.

CNW Marketing Research Spreadsheet. "At-a-glance data and quick analysis of used car trends." *Used Gold Newsletter*, February 1966, p. 3.

Foust, Dean. "Circuit City's Wires are Sizzling." *Business Week*, April 27, 1992, p. 76.

Gelfand, Michael. "Consumer Electronics Superstores." *Discount Merchandiser*, January 1993, pp. 60-66, 70.

Gillen, Marilyn A. "CES Reflects Industry's Forward Focus." *Billboard*, January 22, 1994, pp. 11, 96.

Glasse, Jennifer. "Speaking Out on Keeping Up." *Dealerscope*, March 1993, pp. 10-11.

Goerne, Carrie. "Customer Friendly Sales Reps Get Tryout." *Marketing News*, October 26, 1992, pp. 1, 3.

Hartnett, Michael. "New Path for Tandy." *Stores*, May 1993, pp. 20-26.

Hewes, Ken. "Weak Economy Makes Hard Times for Hard Lines." *Chain Store Age Executive*, August 1992, pp. 29A-31A.

Lavoie, Francis J. "Spotty Outlook Ahead for Consumer Electronics." *Electronics*, January 1992, pp. 40-42.

Lavin, Douglas. "Cars Are Sold Like Stereos By Circuit City." *Wall Street Journal*, June 6, 1994, pp. B1, B6.

McKesson, Mike. "CarMax concept draws attention of potential customers." *Lafayette Business Digest*, January 8, 1996, p. 3.

Mohl, Bruce. "Superstores move in on used cars." *Boston Globe*, February 19, 1996.

Newsday. "Newer vehicles drive growth of used cars in American market." *Newsday, Money & Careers*. February 4, 1996, p. 1.

Pinkerton, Janet. "Mining the Boondocks." *Dealerscope*, August 1993, pp. 50-53.

Rudnitsky, Howard. "Would you buy a used car from this man?" *Forbes*. October 23, 1995, pp. 52-54.

Simison, Robert L. "New-car dealers form alliance to sell used vehicles in trendy superstores." *Wall Street Journal*, February 7, 1996, p. A3.

Therrien, Lois. "Recession, Hell—Let's Buy Another TV." *Business Week*, October 19, 1992, p. 35.

Welles, Edward. Show and sell, VirtuMall, Internet Resource.

Fingerhut Companies, Inc.

Patricia Feltes, Southwest Missouri
State University

Phillip Hall, St. Ambrose University

Internet site of interest: **www.fingerhut.com**

I t seemed like a good idea at the time but now it was one more breakdown on the information superhighway. Fingerhut Companies, Inc., had tried to enter the promising world of television shopping but things didn't go as planned. The S Channel, which offered all-day product presentation, was canceled and USA Direct, a subsidiary created to do lengthy television commercials called infomercials, was scaled back. These company changes resulted in losses of $19.4M and were reflected in Fingerhut's financial returns for 1994. In addition, the slowdown in consumer spending in the first part of 1995 was causing bottom line problems and a 21.9% drop in the stock price (*The New York Times*, 1995).

Fingerhut, a direct marketing company, recognized the maturity of an industry based on paper and the postal service. It already used a limited telemarketing approach targeting its own customers for repeat business. Like its competition, Fingerhut was faced with the continual problems of enticing new customers. Mailing lists were the bane and boon of direct advertisers. When purchased lists were combined, 80% of the names could already be present on an existing mailing list (Levin, 1994), resulting in very few new prospective customers.

Ted Deikel, Chairman and Chief Executive Officer, and the other executives at Fingerhut would have to go back to the strategic "drawing board" to answer some important questions. Where would new customers be found? How could they reach those potential customers who were not committed to catalogs? How could they take advantage of the projected wonders of the information age? How does a company continue to grow while faced with the increasing maturity of its industry?

BACKGROUND

Fingerhut Companies, Inc., was a direct merchandiser of brand-name and private label goods, including electronics, housewares, domestics, jewelry, and apparel. The company was based in Minnetonka, Minnesota, near the Twin Cities. Many of the products were specifically manufactured or packaged to appeal to its target market. In addition, it sold financial service products (especially its in-house credit plans) to its direct marketing customers.

Principal subsidiaries at the end of 1994 included Fingerhut Corporation, Figi's (bought in 1981), and USA Direct, Inc. During 1993, Fingerhut sold the assets of COMB Corporation, a remaindered goods subsidiary, and the assets of FDC, a subsidiary of Figi's. A planned sale of Figi's was abandoned in late 1994 when the purchaser was unable to complete its financing.

In March 1995, USA Direct allied itself with Guthy-Renker Corporation. Guthy-Renker took over the production, media placement, and market distribution of infomercials, while USA Direct provided the merchandising functions of product development, sourcing, and customer service. The company also participated in a catalog joint venture with Montgomery Ward & Co., Inc.

OWNERSHIP

Fingerhut began as a partnership in 1948, became a publicly held corporation in 1970, and was acquired by the Travelers, Inc., in 1979. In May 1990, the company again became publicly held as Travelers sold off its shares. By 1993, Travelers no longer held any stock in Fingerhut. As of February 28, 1995, there were 696 holders of record of Fingerhut common stock. Stock prices in 1993 ranged from a low of $14 7/8 at the beginning of the year to a high of $30 5/8 at the end. In 1994, the stock slipped to $14 at the close of the year (Exhibit 1). By March 22, 1995, the stock price had fallen to $11 1/8.

STRATEGY

The primary mission of Fingerhut Companies, Inc., was the profitable growth of the corporation through a focus on the core business. To accomplish this goal, the firm intended to 1) institute increased operational efficiencies, 2) expand the company's customer list, 3) develop new product and service categories and proprietary merchandise, and 4) utilize an improved database marketing system to create a competitive edge.

SUBSIDIARIES

■ Figi's, Inc.

Figi's sold specialty food gifts through a mail order retail operation. It was one of the largest direct mail food gift marketing firms in the United States, with net sales of $70M in 1994. The business was highly seasonal, with 82% of net sales being made in the fourth quarter.

Exhibit 1		Stock Data for Fingerhut Companies, Inc., and Subsidiaries								
1994		**First**		**Second**		**Third**		**Fourth**		**Year**
Common stock price:										
High	$	33¼	$	32	$	29½	$	23⅞	$	33¼
Low	$	25¼	$	22⅝	$	21⅝	$	14	$	14
Dividends paid	$	.04	$	.04	$	.04	$	.04	$	.16
1993		**First**		**Second**		**Third**		**Fourth**		**Year**
Common stock pice:										
High	$	20⅜	$	22½	$	29⅛	$	30⅝	$	30⅝
Low	$	14⅞	$	19⅛	$	21⅛	$	24	$	14⅞
Dividends paid	$	.04	$	.04	$	.04	$	.04	$	.16

The Company's common stock is traded under the symbol "FHT" on the New York Stock Exchange. As of February 28, 1995, there were 696 holders of record of the Company's common stock.

Customers were similar to Fingerhut's target market and were found in similar ways. Unlike Fingerhut, however, only 78% of the customers used the in-house credit plan of interest-free purchases with three monthly payments. Other customers preferred to use their own credit cards.

▪ USA Direct, Incorporated

USA Direct marketed specific products through 30-minute television advertisements known as infomercials. These commercials were formatted as entertainment as well as product demonstrations and often featured a well-known entertainer or celebrity. These products could then be marketed through Fingerhut catalogs and presented as "as seen on TV" items. USA Direct sold $59M of product in 1994.

In November 1994, Fingerhut announced it would reduce USA Direct's involvement with the production of the infomercials themselves and instead focus its efforts on the merchandising aspect of the business. This was done in connection with the cancellation of "S: The Shopping Network" which was to support the operations of USA Direct.

▪ Montgomery Ward Direct

Montgomery Ward Direct was the result of the joint venture limited partnership between Montgomery Ward & Co. and Fingerhut. Each partner held a 50% interest in the operation. In 1994, the joint venture mailed 124 million catalogs primarily to Montgomery Ward credit card holders, generating net sales of $188M.

MARKETING

In early 1995, Fingerhut Companies, Inc., was one of the Big Three in general merchandise catalog retailing. It was second to J.C. Penney Corp. but larger than Spiegel. During 1994, approximately 558 million catalogs were sent to existing and prospective customers. This included 154 different catalogs and promotions, including a 448-page holiday edition (see Exhibit 2).

■ Fingerhut 1994 Annual Report

Fingerhut offered a broad mix of nearly 15,000 different general merchandise products (see Exhibit 3). Along with merchandise, the company provided various financial service products including credit insurance, extended property

---

Exhibit 2   **Revenues by Media**

General Merchandise Catalogs	46%
Specialty Catalogs	26%
Print Media and Direct Mail	17%
Telemarketing and Television	11%

Exhibit 3   **Fingerhut Corporation 1994 Product Mix**

	Percent of Gross Retail Sales
Electronics	20%
Home Textiles	18
Housewares	17
Furniture/Home Accessories	11
Apparel	9
Jewelry	8
Leisure	8
Tools/Automotive/Lawn & Garden	6
Financial Service Products	3
Total	100%

Source: Fingerhut 10K for 1994.

Exhibit 4   **Gross Sales per Customer**

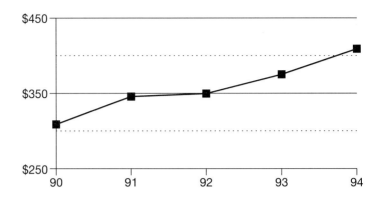

insurance, accidental death, hospital income, whole and term life insurance, and merchandise service contracts. Fingerhut planned to introduce a co-branded MasterCard and a Fingerhut MasterCard in 1995 and created a special purpose bank, Direct Merchants Credit Card Bank in Salt Lake City.

TARGET MARKET

Fingerhut targeted a market of moderate-to middle-income consumers. The median age of its customers tended to be slightly lower than the national average, therefore young families were a significant portion of its customer base. That base consisted of approximately seven million established customers who accounted for 80% of the company's net sales (see Exhibits 4 and 5).

Customers passed through three specific stages as part of Fingerhut's marketing program: 1) new customer acquisition, 2) transitional customer, and 3) established customer base. Fingerhut sought to gain new customers through rented mailing lists, magazine and newspaper advertisements, television, catalog requests, and mailings. New customers accounted for close to 20% of net sales. After an initial successful order, new customers were added to a transitional group who would be offered additional products. The additional catalogs and other promotions presented to these customers depended upon their individual creditworthiness. Finally, through their continued reliability and payment history a customer could be promoted to more Fingerhut offerings and benefits. Fingerhut believed that developing long-term repeat buyers and balancing customer response with relevant losses and returns were the key strategies to fulfill their goal of maximizing profitability.

CREDIT EXTENSION

Substantially all of Fingerhut's sales were made on credit, utilizing its own closed-end credit. The company held the dominant position in the general merchandise-for-credit market.

Exhibit 5   **Average Frequency of Purchases**
                       (purchases last 12 months)

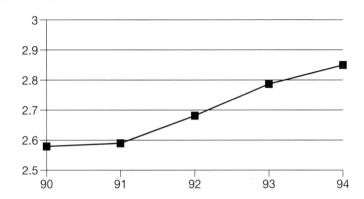

Fingerhut extended credit to customers in the form of fixed term, fixed payment installment contracts. Customers would make monthly payments based on coupon books which were delivered with each order shipped. Terms ranged from 4 to 32 monthly payments, with a majority of customers making use of a deferred payment option which extended the date of the first payment up to four months.

Credit management and loss containment relied on automated proprietary techniques for evaluating the new and ongoing creditworthiness of customers. It was also used to qualify customers with regard to which category of mailing they received. After an order was placed, the system aided in the identification of those individuals whose orders could be immediately shipped, those for whom more information was needed, and those who did not have the appropriate credit standing. After an order was shipped, customer payment was continuously monitored to provide an early warning of possible credit problems.

The goal of credit management was to provide a cost and benefit analysis of each customer in terms of credit losses, return rates, and orders to optimize profitability rather than sales. The company believed that its 45 years of mail order experience, its data base, and its proprietary analytical models gave it a competitive advantage in its industry.

The company relied on Minnesota's "time-price" doctrine in establishing and collecting installment payments on products sold in many of the states. Under this doctrine, the difference between the time price and the cash price charged for the same goods was not treated as interest subject to regulation under laws governing the extension of credit. Other states regulated and limited the maximum finance charges that could be applied and required refunding of finance charges to customers under certain circumstances (Fingerhut 10K).

OPERATIONS

In 1994, Fingerhut processed approximately 25 million orders, 53 million customer payments, and shipped 30 million packages (Fingerhut 1994 10K). A state-of-the-art distribution center operated by another Fingerhut subsidiary, Tennessee Distributing Inc., started operations in 1992 with a capacity of 20 million packages a year in its 1 million-square-foot plant. Fingerhut also expanded its St. Cloud, Minnesota, distribution center to 1.5 million square feet (*Packaging Digest*, 1993).

Postage and paper costs increased over the period. In 1994, Fingerhut spent an aggregate of $256M on postage including the cost of parcel shipments that were passed on to customers. Of the total cost, 45% was attributable to parcel shipments, 47% to the mailing of catalogs and other promotional material, and the remaining to miscellaneous communication with customers and suppliers. The postal increases put into effect on Jan. 1, 1995, were expected to raise overall postage costs 12%. To reduce the effects of both postage and paper increases, Fingerhut began printing catalogs and other material on lighter paper.

ELECTRONIC MARKETING

Fingerhut canceled the December 1994 launch of their planned home shopping service, S: The Shopping Network, two weeks before it was operational. The network was designed to attract a more upscale market to Fingerhut products. The company took a $19.4M fourth quarter after tax write-off as a result of this attempted expansion (Fingerhut 1994 Annual Report).

Originally, the company planned to operate the channel itself. Then as start-up costs increased, it hoped to sell a 70% to 75% stake in the operation to a group of unidentified investors. Fingerhut intended to maintain a minority interest in the shopping network (*Advertising Age*, 1994). The deal fell apart and the company was unwilling to accept the financial risk on its own. The company had commitments from cable operators for only four million households when at least ten million was considered a minimum threshold for a financial breakeven (Levin, 1994).

Unlike entertainment-type networks which cable operators pay for their programming, shopping channels pay operators to carry them. Competing new shopping channels were offering cable operators as much as $9 per cable subscriber to convince the cable systems to carry them, hoping that returns would cover the costs. Theodore Deikel, Fingerhut Chair and CEO, responded to the bidding trend by saying, "When people started talking $9 per subscriber, we just didn't know how you make money doing that" (Robichaux, 1994).

The S channel was also planned to utilize infomercials produced by the company's subsidiary USA Direct. As a result of the elimination of the television expansion, Fingerhut cut back and repositioned the subsidiary as a merchandising rather than program production operation. Fingerhut still remained involved in MTV Network's test of a home shopping channel, The Goods (*Mediaweek*, 1994).

MANAGEMENT

Theodore Deikel had a long history with Fingerhut. He was Chief Executive Officer from 1975 until 1983, when he became Executive Vice-President of the American Can Company, a predecessor of Travelers, the former parent company of Fingerhut. From 1985 until 1989, Deikel served as Chairman and CEO of CVN Companies, a direct marketing company which operated the

Exhibit 8 (continued)   **Consolidated Statements of Cash Flows for Fingerhut Companies, Inc., and Subsidiaries (in thousands of dollars)**

	For the fiscal year ended		
	December 30, 1994	*December 31, 1993*	*December 25, 1992*
Supplemental noncash investing and financing activities:			
Fixed assets retired under capital lease	$ —	$ —	$ 11,064
Capital lease retired	$ —	$ —	$ 12,214
Noncash retirement of common stock	$ —	$ —	$ 7,851
Noncash exercise of stock options	$ —	$ —	$ 7,851
Tax benefit from exercise of non-qualified stock options	$ 1,508	$ 2,305	$ 5,248
Accrued stock repurchase	$ 4,695	$ —	$ —

The Company included in cash and cash equivalents liquid investments with maturities of fifteen days or less.

Exhibit 9   **Highlights of Operations**

	For the fiscal year ended		
	1994	*1993*	*1992*
Percent of net sales			
Finance income, net	12.6%	10.6%	9.2%
Product cost	49.7	50.3	48.4
Administrative and selling expenses	40.8	37.9	38.0
Provision for uncollec- tible accounts	13.3	11.9	12.7
Percent of revenues			
Discount on sale of accounts receivable	2.8%	1.5%	1.4%
Interest expense, net	1.3	1.9	2.1
Earnings before taxes	3.7	6.2	5.8
Provision for income taxes	1.3	2.0	2.0
Net earnings	2.4	4.2	3.8

FINGERHUT COMPANIES, INC.

Exhibit 10

Five Year Summary of Selected Consolidated Financial Data for Fingerhut Companies, Inc., and Subsidiaries (in thousands of dollars, except per-share data)

	For the fiscal year ended				
	December 30, 1994	December 31, 1993[c]	December 25, 1992	December 27, 1991	December 28, 1990
Earnings data:					
Revenues	$1,934,385	$1,807,908	$1,606,114	$1,428,428	$1,247,997
Earnings before taxes [b]	$ 70,926	$ 111,879	$ 93,930	$ 81,398	$ 74,139
Net earnings [b]	$ 45,925	$ 75,328	$ 61,806	$ 53,558	$ 47,715
Net earnings as a percent of revenues [b]	2.4%	4.2%	3.8%	3.7%	3.8%
Per share:					
Earnings [a] [b]	$ .91	$ 1.50	$ 1.19	$ 1.07	$ .98
Dividends declared	$ .16	$ .16	$ .16	$ .16	$ .08
Financial position data:		At fiscal year-end			
Total assets	$1,097,933	$ 988,302	$ 925,649	$ 801,999	$ 651,162
Total current debt	$ 336	$ 313	$ 333	$ 62,853	$ 87,284
Long-term debt and capitalized lease, less current portion	$ 246,516	$ 246,852	$ 247,190	$ 119,164	$ 15,015
Total stockholders' equity	$ 500,950	$ 472,389	$ 399,591	$ 384,149	$ 318,600

[a] Based on a weighted average of 50,270,419; 50,101,739; 51,937,936; 49,960,546, and 48,565,694 shares of common stock and common stock equivalents for the fiscal years ended December 30, 1994; December 31, 1993; December 25, 1992; December 27, 1991; and December 28, 1990, respectively.

[b] 1994 results included a $29.9 million charge ($19.4 million after tax) relating to unusual items. See Note 3 to the Consolidated Financial Statements.

[c] In 1993, the Company sold certain assets of COMB Corporation and FDC, Inc., a subsidiary of Figi's, Inc.

Exhibit 11   **Quarterly Financial Data for Fingerhut Companies, Inc., and Subsidiaries**

Quarterly Financial—Fiscal Year Summaries

1994	First	Second	Third	Fourth [b]	Total
Revenues	$ 362,144	$ 446,031	$ 429,445	$ 696,765	$1,934,385
Gross margin [a]	$ 162,292	$ 191,487	$ 193,695	$ 314,712	$ 864,186
Net earnings	$ 9,973	$ 16,192	$ 7,087	$ 12,673	$ 45,925
Earnings per share	$ .20	$ .32	$ .14	$ .26	$ .91
1993	First	Second	Third	Fourth	Total
Revenues	$ 371,807	$ 420,835	$ 379,313	$ 635,953	$1,807,908
Gross margin [a]	$ 169,371	$ 187,269	$ 162,944	$ 293,068	$ 812,652
Net earnings	$ 7,764	$ 12,976	$ 13,759	$ 40,829	$ 75,328
Earnings per share	$ .16	$ .26	$ .27	$ .81	$ 1.50

[a] Gross margin is equal to net sales less product cost.

[b] Fourth quarter 1994 results included an after-tax charge of $19.4 million from unusual items, as well as the results of Figi's for the year. See Note 3 to the Consolidated Financial Statements.

Exhibit 12   **Revenues From Continuing Operations (billions)**

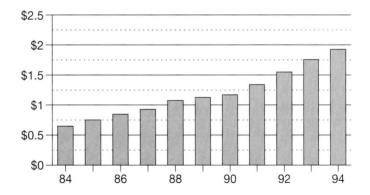

Exhibit 13   **Operating Income From Continuing Operations (millions)**

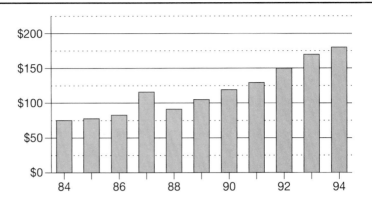

Exhibit 14   **Revenue Growth Industry Comparison**

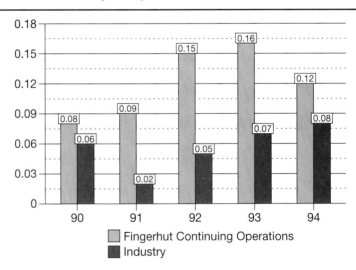

DIRECT MAIL INDUSTRY

Total catalog sales in 1994 were almost $53 billion in an almost $2 trillion retail market. This total reflected sales by all retail organizations offering catalogs, including computer specialty outlets, department stores, specialized retailers, and others, as well as those operations using catalogs as their sole marketing tool (Rigdon, 1995).

The catalog industry was negatively affected in 1994 by overall weak retail demand and by higher paper costs and postage rates (*Value Line*, 1995, p. 1699). Those establishments specializing in women's apparel were also affected by stagnant clothing sales throughout 1994 and the early part of 1995.

Exhibit 15   **1993 Marketing Expenditures–Catalog and Media**

	Catalog	*Media*	*Total*	*Revenue[b]*
J.C. Penney Co.	$560.0	[a]	$560.0	$3,500.0
Fingerhut Cos.	363.0	$ 4.4	367.4	1,650.0
Spiegel	285.0	12.2	297.2	1,500.0
The Limited	183.2	7.9	191.1	916.0
Lands' End	154.8	9.4	164.2	860.0
Hanover Direct	134.9	0.3	135.2	642.5
L.L. Bean	126.7	4.3	131.0	754.0
J. Crew	125.0	0.3	125.3	625.0
Blair Corp.	83.2	1.9	85.1	520.0
Chadwick's	71.4	2.7	74.1	420.0

Dollars in millions (Levin, 1994)

[a]J.C. Penney spent $265.8M on media but this promoted their retail stores rather than their catalog operations.

[b]Catalog sales only. Does not include retail stores.

The retirement of Sears, Roebuck & Co. from the list of catalog retailers in 1993 provided an opportunity for remaining industry members. The Sears Big Book merchandise catalog alone ordinarily generated $3.3 billion in annual revenues. J.C. Penney Co. and Fingerhut proved the biggest beneficiaries (Levin, 1994).

MARKETING

The top ten catalog marketers sold $11.4 billion in catalog merchandise in 1993. They spent more than $2.1 billion of that revenue on marketing. This amount included spending on creative, production, and mailing costs for catalogs and for media coverage purchased to support catalogs (see Exhibit 15).

J.C. PENNEY

J.C. Penney was the fourth largest retailer in the U.S., with 1,246 stores located in all fifty states and Puerto Rico in 1994. It also operated an extensive catalog business serviced by six distribution centers, 526 drugstores under the "Thrift" or "Treasury" name, mail order pharmacies, and financial services including credit card, insurance, and real estate sales. Revenues totaled $20.38 billion during the year (see Exhibit 16).

| Exhibit 16 | **Key Annual Financial Ratios for J.C. Penney** | | | |

Fiscal year ending	*1/28/95*	*1/29/94*	*1/30/93*
Current ratio	2.11	2.21	2.63
Quick ratio	1.21	1.25	1.39
Receivables turnover	4.09	4.18	4.94
Inventory turnover	5.44	5.52	5.68
Total debt/equity	0.59	0.61	0.67
Net income/net sales	0.05	0.05	0.04
Net income/total assets	0.07	0.06	0.06
Net income/common equity	0.21	0.20	0.19

Disclosure 1995.

SPIEGEL

Spiegel, Inc., had revenues of $3.012 billion in 1994, with approximately $1.5 billion coming from direct mail operations. It was the third largest major catalog retailer in the U.S., serving 6.4 million customers in 1994. It sent over 235 million catalogs, including the 600-page core catalog and over 80 specialty catalogs, to those customers during the year (*Value Line,* 1995, p.1721). Spiegel also operated 353 retail stores under the name "Eddie Bauer." Spiegel went international in 1994 with the opening of Eddie Bauer stores in Tokyo and the introduction of Eddie Bauer catalog sales in Germany and Japan (Disclosure 1995).

| Exhibit 17 | **Key Annual Financial Ratios for Spiegel** | | | |

Fiscal year ending	*12/31/94*	*12/31/93*	*12/31/92*
Current ratio	3.04	2.54	2.63
Quick ratio	1.84	1.67	1.66
Receivables turnover	2.68	2.60	2.72
Inventory turnover	5.05	5.92	5.40
Total debt/equity	2.38	1.87	1.83
Net income/net sales	0.01	0.02	0.02
Net income/total assets	0.01	0.02	0.02
Net income/common equity	0.04	0.09	0.09

Disclosure 1995.

Spiegel's primary product focus was ladies apparel, which accounted for 68% of sales while home furnishings and other goods were 32%. Catalog credit sales totaled 75% which provided 7.7% of total revenues (*Value Line*, 1995).

As a reflection of its belief in the future of electronic marketing, Spiegel introduced a video catalog and three separate CD-ROM tests as a joint venture with Time Warner Entertainment. It was also exploring interactive TV shopping and the introduction of a Catalog 1 offering on the Internet in 1995 (see Exhibit 17).

LANDS' END

Lands' End sold high-quality merchandise primarily through mail order. It also operated twelve outlet stores. In fiscal 1994, its sales totaled $870M. Its product line focused on traditionally styled clothing for men, women, and children; accessories; soft-sided luggage; and bath and bedding items. During the year it also expanded its catalog operations to the United Kingdom and introduced a corporate sales line of team or company embroidered garments (*Value Line*, 1995, p. 1710) (see Exhibit 18).

OTHER COMPETITORS

The catalog industry also faced continued competition from other forms of retail organizations. Rural areas which historically were the key sources of direct mail customers were served more and more by the growing number of Wal-Mart stores and other discounters. Wal-Mart operated 1,990 stores in 49 states besides 198 foreign-based stores and 143 supercenters. The average community served by a Wal-Mart in 1994 consisted of 15,000 people.

Exhibit 18   **Key Annual Financial Ratios**

Fiscal year ending	1/27/95	1/28/94	1/29/93
Current ratio	1.93	2.11	2.04
Quick ratio	0.10	0.28	0.34
Inventory turnover	5.88	5.81	6.92
Net income/net sales	0.04	0.05	0.05
Net income/total assets	0.12	0.16	0.16
Net income/common equity	0.19	0.25	0.24

Disclosure 1995.

ELECTRONIC SHOPPING

■ Computer On-line Shopping

In 1994, there were an estimated 35,000 vendors on the Internet's World Wide Web. The companies ranged from Gottschalks department store to Salsa Express. Sales were not as evident as the number of vendors might imply. Forecasters say it will be the year 2000 before annual sales on the Web will reach $6 billion.

Merchants blamed technology for the lack of revenue, citing unavailable security software and too-slow transmission speeds. Technology experts expect these problems to be solved in a year or two. They insisted that the real difficulty was the reluctance of sellers to adapt to the different marketing demands made by Net users. Substantial discounts on prices were expected, since electronic selling could save merchants up to 50% of their marketing costs. Lands' End executives rejected discounts because the lower prices would offer an advantage to one group of customers over another, violating its one-price-for-all policy. Other companies objected to the growing role of consumer-software agents who do global comparison shopping to inform customers of the best prices available. Other merchants did not understand how to make their product line appealing in the new medium (Rigdon, 1995). CompuServe and Prodigy insisted that their services would see an expansion in the Electronic Mall over time. They were particularly interested in expanding their business with catalog merchandisers. A representative of the Interactive Services Association estimated that 1994 shopping services totaled approximately $250 million, with most of that concentrated in computer-related goods (McConnell, 1994).

■ Television Home Shopping

The market for home shopping and infomercial television channels began to stabilize and lose the high-growth image it had in the past. Mergers of existing infomercial channels began to be the norm in 1994. Cox Cable Communications, the country's third largest cable operator and owner of the one million subscriber Consumer Information Network, and Jones International Networks, parent company of the one million plus subscriber Product Information Network, agreed to merge the two channels into one 24-hour infomercial network in November 1994 (*Mediaweek*, 1994). QVC was combining two new TV shopping services to cut costs while Spiegel's Catalog 1 didn't grow as fast as expected. Federated Department Stores, Inc., put off introducing the TV Macy show (Robichaux, 1994). The television home-shopping industry produced more than $2 billion in sales in 1994. However, the percentage of home-shopping viewers was only about 12% of cable households in 1993, which was down from a high of 16% in 1991.

Limited channel capacity also proved to be difficult to overcome. Cable operators couldn't fit more new services on their systems. New cable channels needed approximately 15 million or more subscribers to break even. The proposed new shopping channels entered a bidding war to get carried by a cable system. Home-shopping channels must pay cable operators to be on their system and the new channels are offering operators as much as $9 a subscriber. QVC, one of the two dominant shopping channels, offered $5 and a long-term commitment (Robichaux, 1994).

Other analysts say the mergers, rollbacks, and setbacks in the industry were temporary effects. The cable environment was seen as uncertain due to the dynamics of past growth and potential changes in the government's regulation of the industry.

DEMOGRAPHICS

The U.S. population totaled about 262 million at the end of 1994. In the 1990s, population gains have exceeded 1% a year. The gains have come from both higher-than-expected birth rates, with an average of 4.1 million annually, and the highest level of immigration in 100 years. Between 1990 and 1994, 4.6 million immigrants joined the United States population (*Industry Surveys*, 1995).

In 1993, there were 96 million households in the United States. Approximately 46 million earned between $25,000 to $75,000 annually and were considered to be in the middle to moderate income category. Almost 11 million households had income over $75,000, and were considered in the upper income level. Real median income rose only 3.8% from 1970 through 1992 (*Industry Surveys*, 1995).

ECONOMY

Renewed economic growth was expected for the second half of 1995 and 1996. Real gross domestic product increases of 1.5% to 2% and 2.25% to 2.75% were projected for 1995 and 1996, respectively. The dollar was also expected to stabilize.

The unemployment rate was reported at 5.6% in the early part of 1995. Capacity utilization was at the relatively high level of 83.5%. Inflation remained moderate in the fifth year of the economic expansion (Sherman, 1995).

Increased interest rates were reported in the early part of 1995 and were expected to continue to climb at least in the short term. Consumer debt as a ratio of disposable income reached 81% in 1994, an all-time high. Consumer confidence ratings in 1995 continued to remain high while consumer spending remained flat. The insecurity of the public regarding jobs and the ongoing cost-cutting practices of U.S. corporations was considered a major factor in the confused retail industry results (*Value Line*, 1995, p. 1641).

CONCLUSION

Theodore Deikel and Fingerhut face a totally changed environment. Forty-five years of experience in direct mail have made Fingerhut a strong competitor. Now direct sales entails far more than paper and stamps. Computers, television, and the far-reaching network of the Internet will become a mainstay of direct marketing. Fingerhut must transfer its core competencies to the new situations in order to continue to succeed in the next forty-five years.

BIBLIOGRAPHY

Advertising Age. 1994. Fingerhut TV shopping businesses on the block. *v65. n43*. Nov. 14, p. 2.

Broadcasting and Cable. 1994. Fingerhut cans shopping service. *v124. n48*. Nov. 28, p. 13.

FINGERHUT. 1995. Notice of annual meeting of shareholders.

FINGERHUT. 1995. Quarterly Report (10Q). March 31, 1995.

FINGERHUT. 1995. Annual report (10 K). December 30, 1994.

FINGERHUT. 1995. Annual Report. December 30, 1994.

Gose, Joe, & Dan Margolies. 1994. Catalog giant considers KC. *The Kansas City Business Journal. v12. n19*. Jan. 28, p. 1(2).

HFD-Home Furnishings Newspaper. 1994. Eye On: Fingerhut. *v68. n42*. Oct. 17, p. 67.

HFD-Home Furnishings Newspaper. 1992. NBB&L names three best retailers. *v66. n11*. March 16, p. 74.

Industry Surveys. 1995. Retailing. June 15, 1995.

Levin, Gary. 1994. Fingerhut cuts plans for shopping net. *Advertising Age. v65. n50*. Nov. 28, p. 22.

Levin, Gary. 1994. J.C. Penney tops list of catalog spenders. *Advertising Age. v65. n43*. Oct. 10, p. 52.

McConnell, Chris. 1994. On-line services blossoming. *Broadcasting & Cable. v124. n23*. p. 60.

Marks, Robert. 1994. Catalogs grow, add more RTA products. *HFD-Home Furnishings Newspaper. v68. n43*. Oct. 24, p. 22.

Mediaweek. 1994. Cable TV. *v4. n46*. Nov. 28, p. 12.

Neal, Mollie. 1992. Marketers develop a new climate. *Direct Marketing. v54. n10*. p. 26(3).

Neal, Mollie. 1993. Marketers develop a green consciousness. *Direct Marketing. v55. n10*. p. 35(4).

New York Times. 1995. Fingerhut Shares Dive on Lower Earnings Outlook. *v144*. March 23, p. D4.

Packaging Digest. 1993. Fingerhut's distribution center conveys efficiency. *v30. n7*. p. 46(4).

Patterson, Gregory. 1994. Catalog shares draw interest of analysts. Dec. 5, p. C1(E).

Rigdon, Joan E. 1995. Blame retailers for Web's slow start as a mall. *Wall Street Journal*. August 16, p. B1.

Robichaux, Mark. 1994. TV shopping losing its shine for retailers. *Wall Street Journal*. Nov. 22, p. B1(E).

Shapiro, Eben. 1991. Coming back to catalogues. *The New York Times. v141*. Oct. 27, p. F12(W).

Sherman, Eugene J. 1995. With economy humming, the Fed will probably resume tightening in 1996. *American Banker. v160. n141*. July 25, p. 22.

Value Line. 1995. Fingerhut Co. May 26, p. 1699.

Value Line. 1994. Fingerhut Co. Nov. 25, p. 1684.

Wall Street Journal. 1994. Fingerhut Co.: Marketer to launch service for cable home-shopping. March 23, p. B6(E).

Wall Street Journal. 1995. Marketer to cut 200 jobs in cost-reduction program. Jan. 4, p. A8(E).

Wall Street Journal. 1995. Fingerhut Cos. July 17, p. B5.

Four Seasons Regent Hotels and Resorts

Angela R. Lanning, University of Guelph
Robert C. Lewis, University of Guelph

I n March of 1995, the Four Seasons Regent (FSR) corporate marketing team had reviewed their plans for the remainder of the year. Collectively, the team agreed that their plans and objectives should remain intact, that their strategies were working, and that Four Seasons Regent would continue to strengthen its domination in the luxury hotel market.

Individually, however, each member of the team had unresolved questions about the past, present, and future of the company. Things had been so hectic over the past two years that nobody had really had time to analyze the effectiveness of past marketing strategies. There were indications that the consolidation of Regent and Four Seasons had been successful, but was there anything that had been overlooked? Were they making legitimate, informed, and realistic decisions in their 1995 Marketing Plan? Were there any potential threats to their position as the leading luxury hotel chain that they had not yet considered?

Perplexed by many of these issues, members of the marketing team wondered to themselves ". . . can we wait until next year to think about it—nobody has time for this right now."

It was at that point that John Richards' secretary interrupted the meeting to ask him to take an urgent phone call from John Sharpe, Executive VP of Operations. "Have you seen today's *Wall Street Journal?*" said Sharpe. "No," said Richards. "Then listen," said Sharpe.

"Ritz-Carlton Hotels has been 49% acquired, with a right to buy the rest, by a group of investors, including Marriott International Inc., which intends to transform it into a high-growth international chain. Richard Rainwater, a Texas millionaire and one of the investors, is quoted as saying, `With the additional capital and the potential for efficiencies provided by Marriott, this company could be five to ten times the size it is today in five to ten years.'"

"Well folks," said Richards, as he hung up the phone. "In light of this new development, it would be a good idea for us to re-evaluate all our corporate strategies. Let's start thinking about how this will affect our competitive situation. Does anyone have any thoughts on this?"

■ Background

In May of 1993, Isadore Sharp, Chairman and President of Four Seasons Regent Hotels and Resorts, concluded his oration at the annual shareholders meeting:

> The last two years have been extraordinarily difficult and all these difficulties are not yet behind us. We have every confidence that we have invested wisely, consolidating our leadership and assuring our future. We have only to keep our focus to continue to improve what we are already doing well, and profits and shareholder equity will rise with our reputation.

The acquisition of Regent Hotels in mid-1992 had been a great source of turmoil for Four Seasons Hotel Company. The integration of the two luxury hotel chains and the high debt load resulting from the transaction had left the company in a strained financial position. The global economic downturn that began in 1990 had also been a significant obstacle and had affected profits throughout the tour and travel industry. It wasn't until the end of 1993, however, that indications of an economic recovery finally appeared.

All of this had presented an enormous challenge for John Richards, Senior Vice President of Marketing. By the end of 1994, however, there were indications that the efforts of the corporate marketing team were paying off. Cost efficiencies were being realized and there were noticeable improvements in occupancies and average room rates for many of the Regent properties.

In light of these trends, preparation of the 1995 marketing plan appeared elementary. Four Seasons Regent management saw itself as able to maintain its leadership in the luxury hotel market by continuing to focus on its long-time principal marketing objectives.

The key objectives that would continue to drive the company's marketing initiatives for 1995 had been established:

1. Leverage the Four Seasons Regent combination,
2. Increase individual business worldwide, and
3. Improve global sales network efficiencies.

John Richards had wondered, however, if it was as simple as all that or whether more strategic thinking and direction were necessary from the corporate level before the marketing plan was actually developed. And now there was this Ritz-Carlton thing!

COMPANY BACKGROUND

Four Seasons Regent Hotels and Resorts, headquartered in Toronto, Canada, was the world's largest luxury hotel operator. Founded in 1960 by Isadore Sharp, the company in 1995 managed 39 medium-sized luxury urban and resort hotels in 16 countries under management contracts with their owners, containing approximately 13,000 guest rooms, and had 11 other management contracts on properties under construction or development in nine countries. Four Seasons Regent held a minority equity interest in 20 of these hotels. Exhibit 1 shows a list of hotels operated by Four Seasons Regent, its equity interest, some occupancy details, and their hotel locations—many of which would be virtually impossible to duplicate.

▪ The Founder

In 1992, honored for being the driving force behind the international success of Four Seasons, Isadore (Issy, pronounced Izzy) Sharp received the prestigious Canadian award of CEO of the Year. An article in *The Financial Post* (Toronto) attributed the growth of Four Seasons to largely the result of one man's vision. "Isadore Sharp has created a company that friends and foes alike agree is a model for how Canadian companies compete globally in an increasingly interconnected world economy."

Issy Sharp completed his studies in architecture in 1952 and immediately joined his father in the construction business. His hotel empire began with a small motel he built in a seedy downtown area of Toronto. Its doors opened in 1961 and its rapid success inspired Issy to continue in the hotel business but only in the upscale end of it. After four hotels, he decided to go public with Four Seasons as a way to finance his expansion plans.

Four Seasons first went public with a 25% ownership offering on the Toronto Stock Exchange during a new issue boom in the late 1960s. The original investors, all of whom were still members of the board of directors in 1995, maintained 75% ownership. Due to the instability and high discounting of the stock, they repurchased and took the company private again in 1978. Philosophically, Issy didn't want to sacrifice his long-term quality objectives for quarterly results that would please short-term investors.

Four Seasons went public again in 1985 but, to ensure that fractional ownership would not delete his singular vision, Issy maintained 80% control of the voting shares. His absolute control of the company was considered an asset by market analysts because it meant that Issy would be able to maintain the culture of Four Seasons.

▪ The Regent Acquisition

In August 1992, wishing to expand quickly in the Far East, Four Seasons completed a (US) $122 million deal to acquire the luxury Regent Hotels Company from its Hong Kong owners. The transaction included the addition of 15 management contracts (including four hotels under construction), the Regent International Hotels trademark and trade names, and a 25% ownership interest in the Regent Hong Kong hotel. The purchase was financed by a combination of existing working capital lines, additional bank indebtedness, and a (Cdn) $58.5 million new equity issue (in early 1995, one Canadian dollar equalled approximately 72 U.S. cents). The structure of the company underwent significant changes after the acquisition, resulting in a complicated web of holding companies designed to satisfy the interests of all parties involved in the agreement.

Some of the benefits and risks associated with the acquisition were identified in the *Four Seasons Regent 1992 Annual Report*:

Exhibit 1	Properties Managed by Four Seasons Regent Hotels and Resorts (1994)					
Hotel and Location	Date of Opening Change/latest renovation in Yield	Equity Interest	Number of Rooms	Term to Initial Expiration of Management Contract (years from 1993)	1993 Occupancy	Change from 1992
North America						
Austin, Texas Four Seasons Hotel	1986 +0 to 10%	19.9% **	292	18	high 70s	up
Beverly Hills, CA Regent Hotel	1927/1990 +11 to 20%	0	295	31	mid 60s	up
Boston, MA Four Seasons	1985/1992 +11 to 20%	15% **	288	16	high 70s	up
Chicago, IL Ritz-Carlton	1975/1991 +0 to 10%	25%*	429	31	mid 70s	up
Chicago, IL Four Seasons Hotel	1989 +11 to 20%	7.7%	343	30	low 80s	up
Dallas, Texas FS Resort & Club	1979/1994 +0 to 10%	0	357	8	high 70s	up
Houston, Texas Four Seasons Hotel	1982/1992 +0 to 10%	0	399	23	high 60s	down
Los Angeles, CA Four Seasons Hotel	1987 +11 to 20%	0	285	48	mid 70s	up
Mexico City, Mexico Four Seasons Hotel	1994 N/A	0	239	20	N/A	N/A
Nevis, West Indies Four Seasons Resort	1991 Over 20%	15%	196	27	mid 60s	up
Newport Beach, CA Four Seasons Hotel	1986/1994 +11 to 20%	0	285	22	high 60s	up
New York, NY Four Seasons Hotel	1993 N/A	14.9%	367	19	N/A	N/A
New York, NY The Pierre Hotel	1981/1991 +0 to 20%	19.9%	205	18	mid 70s	up
Palm Beach, FL FS Resort Ocean Grand	1989 N/A	0	234	40	N/A	N/A
Philadelphia, PA Four Seasons Hotel	1983/1993 +0 to 10%	5%	371	19	mid 60s	up

Exhibit 1 (continued)   Properties Managed by Four Seasons Regent Hotels and Resorts (1994)

Hotel and Location	Date of Opening Change/latest renovation in Yield	Equity Interest	Number of Rooms	Term to Initial Expiration of Management Contract (years from 1993)	1993 Occupancy	Change from 1992
San Francisco, CA Four Seasons Hotel	1976/1990 +0 to 10%	0	329	12	high 60s	down
Santa Barbara, CA FS Biltmore Resort	1929/1988 +0 to 10%	10%	234	18	low 70s	down
Seattle, Washington FS Olympic Hotel	1982/1992 +0 to 10%	3.4%	450	46	mid 70s	flat
Wailea, Maui, HI Four Seasons Resort	1990 +11 to 20%	0	380	16	low 60s	up
Washington, DC Four Seasons Hotel	1979 +11 to 20%	15%	196	15	low 80s	up
Minaki, Ontario Four Seasons Resort	1986 N/A	100%**	142	18	N/A	N/A
Toronto, Ontario Four Seasons Hotel	1974/1992 +11 to 20%	19.9%	380	18	high 60s	up
Toronto, Ontario FS Inn On The Park	1963/1985 +0 to 10%	19.9%	568	18	high 40s	up
Vancouver, BC Four Seasons Hotel	1976/1990 +0 to 10%	19.9%	385	18	mid 70s	up
Montreal, Quebec** Le Quatre Saisons	1976 N/A	0	300	10	N/A	N/A
Asia						
Bangkok, Thailand Regent Hotel	1983/1994 +0 to 10%	0	400	1	mid 50s	up
Chiang Mai, Thailand Regent Hotel	1995 N/A	0	67	to 2024	N/A	N/A
Hong Kong Regent Hotel	1980/1993 +0 to 10%	25%	602	6	mid 70s	down
Jakarta, Indonesia Regent Hotel	1995 N/A	5%	384	to 2015	N/A	N/A
Kuala Lumpur, Malaysia Regent Hotel	1989 Behind	0	469	15	mid 70s	up

Exhibit 1 (continued)   **Properties Managed by Four Seasons Regent Hotels and Resorts (1994)**

Hotel and Location	Date of Opening Change/latest renovation in Yield	Equity Interest	Number of Rooms	Term to Initial Expiration of Management Contract (years from 1993)	1993 Occupancy	Change from 1992
Singapore Four Seasons Hotel	1994 N/A	0	257	to 2014	N/A	N/A
Singapore Regent Hotel	1982/1991 +10 to 20%	0	441	14	mid 60s	up
Taipei, Taiwan Regent Hotel	1990 Behind	0	553	4	high 70s	up
Tokyo, Japan Four Seasons Hotel	1992 +11 to 20%	0	286	8	mid 60s	up
South Pacific/ United Kingdom/Europe						
Auckland, New Zealand Regent Hotel	1985/1995 Behind	0	332	12	high 50s	down
Bali, Indonesia Four Seasons Resort	1993 N/A	0	147	19	N/A	N/A
Melbourne, Aust. Regent Hotel	1981/1986 Behind	0	363	1	low 60s	down
Nadi Bay, Fiji Regent Hotel	1975/1993 +10 to 20%	18%	294	18	high 60s	up
Sydney, Australia Regent Hotel	1982/1990 Behind	0	594	29	mid 50s	down
London, England Four Seasons Hotel	1970/1991 +0 to 10%	50%	227	17	low 60s	down
London, England Regent Hotel	1992 N/A	0	309	17	N/A	N/A
Milan, Italy Four Seasons Hotel	1993 N/A	19.9%	98	19	N/A	N/A
Under Construction or Development						
Aviara, CA Four Seasons Resort	Unknown	5%	337	to 2085		
Berlin, Germany Four Seasons Hotel	1996	23%	204	to 2071		

Exhibit 1 (continued) Properties Managed by Four Seasons Regent Hotels and Resorts (1994)

Hotel and Location	Date of Opening Change/latest renovation in Yield	Equity Interest	Number of Rooms	Term to Initial Expiration of Management Contract (years from 1993)	1993 Occupancy	Change from 1992
Bombay, India Four Seasons Hotel	1997	0	300	N/A		
Cairo, Egypt Four Seasons Hotel	1997	0	105	N/A		
Goa, India Four Seasons Hotel	1997	0	295	N/A		
Hualalai, Hawaii Four Seasons Resort	1996	0	250	to 2066		
Istanbul, Turkey Four Seasons Resort	1996	0	65	N/A		
Prague, The Czech Republic Four Seasons Hotel	1997	0	185	to 2072		
Punta Mita, Mexico Four Seasons Hotel	N/A	20%	100	N/A		
Royal Sentul Highlands, Indonesia Regent Hotel	1996	0	171	N/A		
Riyadh, Saudi Arabia Four Seasons Hotel	1998	0	231	N/A		

*The 25% ownership in the Ritz-Carlton Chicago is the result of an arrangement that was made with the owners of the hotel at the commencement of the management contract. The details of this agreement are unknown, but it has no significance to this case.

**Interest sold or management contract terminated as of December 31, 1994, or early 1995 (San Francisco).

Sources: Occupancy and yield figures from Deacon Barclays de Zoete Wedd Research Ltd. All other information is excerpted from the FSR 1993 Annual Report. Four Seasons Regent defines yield as occupancy times average rate.

■ Benefits

1. Geographic diversification of the company's revenue sources, which helps to moderate the effects of regional economic downturns.
2. Leveraging the Corporate cost base by utilizing the existing base of management to oversee a significantly larger business.
3. Enhanced marketing opportunities through the integration of distribution networks, resulting in a more cost-effective organization.
4. The elimination of a direct luxury hotel competitor in both present and future locations.

■ Risks

1. The potential of owner conflicts regarding breaches of radius restriction in their management contract related to the acquisition. Namely, The

Regent Singapore, The Regent Taipei, and the Four Seasons Los Angeles properties are predisposed to strained relationships between the owners and Four Seasons for this reason.

2. Foreign currency matters, e.g., Regent earns fees from hotels operating in ten different countries thus increasing the element of risk associated with the rapid fluctuation of international exchange rates.

3. In 1997 the Chinese government [took] control of Hong Kong. The effects that this event will have on the Hong Kong business community are difficult to predict.

After considering a number of options, the corporation decided to maintain the head office of Regent in Hong Kong, and to continue to operate Regent as an independent subsidiary. Initially, Four Seasons planned to flag the entire chain of hotels under the Four Seasons trade name to establish the worldwide presence of a single brand. After further consideration, however, it was decided that the newly acquired hotel management contracts would be kept under the Regent trade name, but any new developments would be flagged as Four Seasons hotels, regardless of geographical location. This decision led to the designation of their new developments in New York, Bali, and Milan as Four Seasons hotels.

FSR management subsequently reviewed this approach and decided that new hotels in Asia and the South Pacific would be more successful with the Regent brand name because of higher customer awareness in those markets. Apart from a few major international destinations, new developments in North America and Europe would continue to be flagged as Four Seasons.

The decision of how to flag a new hotel was also influenced by the owners of the hotel properties. The owner's choice of brand name was often a stipulation of new management contracts. This added another element of complexity to the branding issue.

■ Getting Out

In June of 1994, Issy Sharp announced plans to relinquish his controlling interest in Four Seasons Regent. The announcement stunned the hotel world and his own staff. Recognizing the inevitability of change in the ownership of the company, Mr. Sharp, then 62, said that he wanted to control the process and commit his personal involvement and leadership to achieving a smooth transition over a period of 3 to 5 years. "Every good leader should know when to step down and how to ensure the continuing good health of the company. It's tempting to stay on too long, but at Four Seasons Regent I believe the time to act is now."

One of the many implications associated with the possible sale of Four Seasons Regent was the fact that many of the existing management contracts provided that they could be terminated by the owners in the event of a change in control of the company. Putting the company up for sale clearly jeopardized many properties in the portfolio of hotels under FSR management.

On November 10, 1994, a partnership was commenced with Prince Al-Waleed Bin Talal Bin Abdulaziz Al Saud, an international investor with previous heavy investments in EuroDisney and Fairmont Hotels of San Francisco, other companies needing a capital infusion. The Prince bought 25% of Four Seasons' shares for (Cdn) $165 million from Issy and other shareholders. Issy Sharp's voting stake dropped to about 65 percent from his previous 80 percent. Referring to the investment as a "long-term strategic alliance," the Prince said that "It is consistent with my strategy to invest significant amounts of capital with superior management teams throughout the world." In addition to his investment, the Prince was working closely with the company to identify opportunities to acquire and develop luxury hotels for Four Seasons Regent to manage. He had allocated $100 million to this program. As a first step, Four Seasons Regent would manage a luxury hotel being developed by the Prince in Riyadh, Saudi Arabia.

Analysts said there was some disappointment that the offer wasn't for 100 percent of the shares. But the deal solved a critical problem for Sharp. "If something happens to me, my estate doesn't have to act. They'll have adequate liquidity because of this transaction." Sharp also said that he was not considering stepping down for at least three years. Further, Sharp indicated there was plenty of management depth ready to continue his leadership and management agenda as most in the corporate office had been with the company for many years.

THE INDUSTRY

The hotel industry was generally divided into five categories: budget, economy, mid-price, upscale, and luxury. In the U.S. market, luxury hotels, which included Four Seasons, had the brightest outlook for 1995 with forecasted occupancies as high as 75% according to Smith Travel Research, an industry research firm. Projected operating performance figures for the U.S. market are presented in Exhibit 2.

The World Travel and Tourism Council reported in 1993 that travel and tourism was the world's largest industry, accounting for more than 6% of Gross Domestic Product (GDP) and 13% of consumer spending worldwide. Travel growth, according to Boeing's 1993 Current Market Outlook (an industry newsletter), was expected to increase an average of 6% per year through the year 2000. Travel to, from, and within Asia accounted for 25% of world air travel but, by the year 2010, was expected to account for 42% of travel growth (Four Seasons Annual Report, 1993).

The World Tourism Organization tracks the arrivals and tourism receipts for six regions. The preliminary findings for 1994 indicated that Asia was the dominant growth leader in tourism. These findings are presented in Exhibits 3a, 3b, and 4 along with the 1994 average occupancies and room rates for Asia's top five destinations.

Growth of hotel supply was slow to moderate in most parts of the world, while GDP in all markets was expected to grow. Other reports, however, drew different conclusions. It was generally agreed that east and southeast Asia would remain the focal point of economic growth over the next several years, as well as the fastest growing area of travel, fueled primarily by intra-regional activity which was not necessarily in the luxury category.

At the same time, there were new trends apparent in the luxury market: While luxury segments were increasing demand, it was on a different scale than before the recession. What complicated the rebirth of upscale hotels was price. For example, in the U.S., room rates were averaging around $113 in the luxury segment and $77 in the upscale segment—lower than they should be to support replacement costs.

While the hotel industry as a whole was operating at 65% of replacement costs, the luxury market was trading at 45%. In addition, 70% of all hotels were

Exhibit 2   **Projected Operating Performance Figures for the U.S. Hotel Market (1994-1995)**

Occupancy Percent	1995	1994	% Change
Price Level			
Luxury	75.3	72.2	4.3
Upscale	69.2	67.9	1.9
Mid-price	65.5	65.1	0.6
Economy	63.4	62.1	2.1
Budget	62.4	61.3	1.8
Location			
Urban	69.1	67.1	3.0
Suburban	67.1	65.3	2.8
Airport	72.8	70.6	3.1
Highway	63.5	62.4	1.8
Resort	69.7	68.3	2.0
Average Rate (US$)	**1995**	**1994**	**% Change**
Price Level			
Luxury	113.49	109.88	3.3
Upscale	77.58	74.25	4.5
Mid-price	59.31	56.79	4.4
Economy	46.33	44.04	5.2
Budget	35.98	34.00	5.8
Location			
Urban	93.79	89.42	4.9
Suburban	59.86	57.57	4.0
Airport	66.61	63.61	4.7
Highway	47.10	45.40	3.7
Resort	96.95	94.04	3.1

Source: *Four Seasons Regent*

profitable in 1994, but only 50% of luxury hotels were in the black that year. Most industry experts predicted it would be several years before more upscale brands traded at a profitable rate. They also agreed that the current business climate was all part of a natural pattern: a segment gets overbuilt, overfinanced, debt is restructured, and properties get repositioned.

Significant trends were also occurring in the luxury resort market. To meet growing customer demand for "enrichment" holidays, resort hotels were moving from "service providers" to "experience managers" where guests become alumni. MRA, a hospitality industry consulting firm based in Philadelphia, cited five major shifts in tourists' motivation that were causing resorts to shift focus to organized, interactive programs of "experiential learning."

Exhibit 3a   **1994 Tourism Arrivals and Growth Rate by Region**

Region	Arrivals (millions)	% Total	% Change (from 1993)	Receipts (billions)	% Total	% Change (from 1993)
World	**528.4**	**100.0**	**3.0**	**$321.5**	**100.0**	**5.1**
Europe	315.0	59.7	1.9	153.3	47.7	0.6
Americas	108.5	20.5	4.1	97.4	30.3	8.9
East/Asia/ Pacific	74.7	14.1	7.6	59.0	18.3	14.0
Africa	18.6	3.5	1.5	5.7	1.8	-4.0
Middle East	7.9	1.5	-4.0	3.7	1.1	-12.0
South Asia	3.7	0.7	7.0	2.4	0.8	11.2

Source: 1994 Tourism arrivals from *Tourism in 1994 Highlights (January 1995)*, World Tourism Organization, Madrid.

Exhibit 3b   **1994 Occupancy and Room Rates at Asia's Top Destinations**

City	Occupancy Percent	Avg. Room Rate (US$)	Type of Hotel
Bangkok	61	75	4-Star
	50	139	5-Star
Beijing	73	92	4-Star
Hong Kong	82	130	4-Star
	72	239	5-Star
Singapore	82	130	4-Star
	70	128	5-Star
Tokyo	69	200	4-Star
	67	280	5-Star

Note: Rates based on 1994 year-end exchange rate. Rating based on international standard.

Source: 1994 occupancy and room rates from *Travel Business Analyst, Hong Kong*, February 1995.

In Asia, Four Seasons was exploring the fertile fields of Thailand and Indonesia to make its mark on the hottest luxury segment: boutique hotels. Their newest, with 67 suites, was the Regent, Chiang Mai, Thailand. Meanwhile, in the Americas, Situr and its partner Grupo Plan, a Mexican development firm, had teamed up to start Hoteles Bel-Air Mexico, a chain of posh boutique hotels along Mexico's Pacific Coast.

Reports out of the U.S. showed resorts were showing steady improvement as Americans emerged from the recession with pent-up desires to get away.

Analysts assessed what resort travelers wanted:

- Vacationers favored shorter trips closer to home.
- They showed preferences toward all-inclusive pricing that included transportation, transfers, lodging, meals, and recreations.

Exhibit 4   **Hotel Market Business Cycles, 1995**

Downturn	Slump	Recovery	Growth
Asia Pacific			
Seoul	Jakarta	Shanghai	Brisbane
Melbourne	Kuala Lumpur	Beijing	Sydney
Taipei	Bangkok	Bali	Tokyo
	Manila		Hong Kong
Europe			
Hungary	Austria	Spain	United Kingdom
Poland	Germany	Italy	Turkey
Czech Republic	Belgium	Switzerland	Greece
	Netherlands	Sweden	
	France	Norway	
		Denmark	
United States			
	Honolulu	Los Angeles	Atlanta
	San Diego	Miami	Houston region
		Orlando	New Orleans
		Washington, DC	Denver
		Boston	Phoenix
		New York	Las Vegas
		Chicago	
Canada			
	Montreal	Halifax	Vancouver
		Edmonton	
		Calgary	
		Toronto	
		Ottawa	
Central, South America and the Caribbean			
	Venezuela	Peru & Mexico beaches	Colombia
	Bahamas	Brazil	Chile
	US Virgin Islands	Other Caribbean islands	Costa Rica
		Argentina	Nevis & St. Kitts
		Aruba	Puerto Rico
			Mexico's commercial markets
Middle East and Africa			
	Egypt	Kenya	South Africa
		Jordan	United Arab Emirates
		Saudi Arabia	
		Morocco	
		Bahrain	
		Tunisia	

Source: *Hotels*, January 1995, p. 29.

- They were interested in fitness programs and amenities geared to children.
- They included companies, which are turning to resorts as places to combine business with a vacation retreat for executives and their families.

Knowing the resort industry was improving, if not set to soar, international chains including Radisson, ITT Sheraton, and Hilton were preparing for the millennium.

Gaining a share of the resort market was key to the global strategies of many upscale chains, which needed elegant resorts to complement more well-known city hotels. "The luxury market is clearly headed toward resorts with more privacy and exclusivity," according to John Richards. "You will not see big single-style buildings in this segment nor will you see boutique hotels built in the U.S. or Hawaii," he said. Labor is just too costly to build and run small resorts in these areas. Instead, Four Seasons is looking at Asia and also at Mexico, areas where construction and labor costs are dramatically lower, to build its boutiques.

FOUR SEASONS CORPORATE STRATEGY

Four Seasons Regent had a clear set of corporate objectives that was driven by two primary goals: to be the first choice as manager of luxury hotels and resorts world-wide, and to operate the finest hotel or resort in each destination where it locates by creating a positive experience for its guests. Four Seasons' annual reports consistently referenced a set of key objectives that had been adopted as part of its core mission:

1. Market Leadership: to achieve and maintain leading market share in major markets;
2. Operational Strength: to operate the finest urban hotel or resort in each destination;
3. Motivated people: to maintain the industry's most motivated employee group, a factor inextricably linked to building customer value;
4. Earnings growth: to increase trend line EPS by 10% to 15% per annum from the fiscal 1985 base—the year prior to becoming a public company; and
5. Leverage: to achieve a long-term targeted debt-to-equity ratio, net of cash, of 1:1.

A long-range strategy was to improve the company's earnings by concentrating on hotel management rather than on the ownership of hotels. This permitted expansion without assuming significant additional capital risks. The company's stated position was to have no more than a 10% to 20% equity interest in any of its projects. Future growth expansion was planned only in locations that satisfied Four Seasons Regent's objectives of better servicing the travel needs of its existing customer base and attracting new international business travelers. Management expected that future expansion would focus on Europe, China, and Southeast Asia.

■ Financial Performance

Four Seasons Regent earned revenues from hotel management and hotel ownership operations. Management revenues were derived from a combination of fee categories, the terms of which are listed in Exhibit 5. Earnings from hotel ownership were derived from cash flow participation and the realization of capital appreciation upon the sale of the ownership interest.

Exhibit 5	Hotel Management Contracts—Fees and Terms

a) Basic management fee and other related fees
Percentage of annual gross operating revenue of the hotel or percentage of defined profit, calculated and payable monthly, or, in one case, a lump-sum amount payable annually.

b) Incentive Fees
Percentage of defined profit or of annual net cash flow of the hotel after specified deductions, payable monthly, quarterly, or semi-annually, subject to adjustment at year-end, or payable annually, or, in one case, a lump sum payable annually.

c) Pre-opening development and purchasing fees
Negotiated amounts, payable in monthly installments prior to the opening of the hotel.

d) Centralized purchasing fees
Percentage of cost of purchases of food and beverage inventories, operating supplies and furniture, fixtures and equipment.

e) Refurbishing fees
Percentage of total cost of approved refurbishing programs or negotiated amounts.

f) Corporate sales and marketing charge and corporate advertising charge
Percentage of annual budgeted gross operating revenue or gross rooms revenue of the hotel, payable monthly and calculated on the basis of the cost of providing the services, or a flat charge.

g) Centralized reservation service charge
Monthly charge per hotel room, calculated on the basis of the number of hotel rooms or the number of reservations made, or a flat charge.

Source: *Four Seasons 1994 Annual Report*

Financial results for hotel management operations and hotel ownership operations, from 1990 to 1994, as well as pro forma results for 1995 to 1997, are shown in Exhibit 6. Exhibit 7 shows consolidated balance sheets for 1993 and 1994.

▪ 1992 and 1993 Financial Summary

Approximately 75 percent of the total fees for both 1992 and 1993 were basic management fees and other related fees, and 25 percent were from a combination of the other six fee categories. Of the fee revenues generated by Four Seasons Regent in 1993, 52 percent were attributable to hotels in which Four Seasons Regent owned an equity interest, exactly half of the hotels at that time.

Fee revenues from hotel management operations increased 42 percent in 1993. Of the $17.8 million increase in fee revenues, $10.8 million related to the 11 Regent hotels acquired and operating in 1993 as opposed to those earned in 1992 from the date of acquisition on August 14. The balance of the increase resulted from the growth in fees from newly opened properties in New York, Milan, Bali, Nevis, and London and from the growth in incentive fees earned at several other properties.

Operations of all Four Seasons Regent's North American hotels improved their financial performance in 1993, with an average growth in gross operating profit of more than 25 percent. This was primarily the result of increases in occupancies and room rates; the average yield rose by over 11 percent in 1993.

Exhibit 6

Four Seasons Regent Hotels Statement of Earnings 1990-1997*
(In thousands of Canadian dollars except per share amounts)

	1990	1991	1992	1993	1994	1995*	1996*	1997*
Total Revenues of *Managed Hotels*								
Four Seasons	66092	631023	728000	916700	1188708	1296886	1437750	1563200
Regent	0	0	151000	435200	509447	523595	569125	614655
Total	66092	631023	879000	1351900	1698155	1820481	2006875	2177855
Hotel Management Ops. Fee Revenues								
Four Seasons	37820	34849	35600	42500	58315	60305	67574	74252
Regent	0	0	6900	17779	21569	21467	23334	25201
Total	37820	34849	42500	60279	79884	81772	90908	99453
General & Admin. Exps.	(22820)	(20763)	(23865)	(32359)	(34000)	(35676)	(37460)	(39333)
EBITD Mgt. Ops.	15000	14086	18635	27920	45884	46096	53448	60120
Hotel Ownership Ops. Revenues	157214	137365	93099	38019	43093	53500	56000	59000
Dist. from Hotel Investments	0	0	1845	3839	6795	5000	5000	5000
Cost of Sales	(136069)	(136945)	(97736)	(33675)	(34464)	(44940)	(46760)	(49265)
Fees to Management	(6878)	(5539)	(3501)	(1021)	(1271)	(3300)	(3300)	(3300)
EBITD Ownshp. Ops.	14267	(5119)	(6293)	7162	14153	10260	10940	11435
Total EBITD	**$29,267**	**$8,967**	**$12,342**	**$35,082**	**$60,037**	**$56,356**	**$64,388**	**$71,555**
Investment Income	3494	2021	3202	4770	510	0	0	0
Depreciation/Amort.	(8138)	(10830)	(12840)	(13216)	(15702)	(14250)	(15000)	(15325)
Interest Expense	(1208)	(40)	(8604)	(17855)	(27239)	(19900)	(16900)	(15000)
Provision for Loss from Disposed Hotels	(2240)		(13789)	(110000)				
Provision for (Loss)Recovery on Mortgages Receivable			12906	(17000)	(6828)	**		
Tax (Expense)/Recovery								
Current	(225)	125	875	(1482)	(2297)	(2500)	(3800)	(3000)
Deferred	(3614)	2514	13662	468	(459)	(831)	(1073)	(1284)
Net Profit	**$17,336**	**$2,757**	**$7,754**	**($119,233)**	**$8,022**	**$18,875**	**$27,615**	**$36,976**
EPS ($)	.84	0.13	0.32	(4.30)	0.29	0.68	1.00	1.27
Cash Dividend/Share	.11	.11	.11	.11	.11			
Share Price Year-end	16.00	17.50	19.38	13.00	16.25			
Common Stock Outstanding (Millions)	20.1	22.2	27.7	27.8	28.4	27.8	27.6	29.1
Debt, Net of Cash	60.7	121.3	290.2	345.6	299.2			
Shareholders' Equity	112.4	139.6	247.8	126.8	140.5			
Debt-to-equity Ratio, Net of Cash	.5	.9	1.2	2.7	2.13			

Source: 1992-1994 Four Seasons Annual Reports and, projections for 1995-1997, RBC Dominion Securities

*Regent revenues only August 14-December 31.

**Costs associated with sale of shares. Investment banking costs primarily to Goldman Sachs, engaged to seek a strategic investor.

The term "yield," as defined by Four Seasons Regent, is hotel occupancy multiplied by achieved room rate. A substantial loss was reported, however, for 1993. This was due to a decision to dispose of interest in seven hotel properties

Exhibit 7   **Consolidated Business Sheets, 1993-1994**
December 31, 1994 and 1993 (In thousands of Canadian dollars)

	1994	*1993*
Assets		
Current Assets		
Cash and short-term investments	$9,436	$11,926
Receivables	39,182	25,975
Inventory	814	750
Prepaid expenses	1,440	1,795
Total Current Assets	50,872	40,446
Notes and mortgages receivable	25,098	37,475
Investments in hotel partnerships	151,256	171,873
Fixed assets	68,052	72,606
Investment in management contracts	116,486	114,323
Investment in trademarks and trade names	64,238	65,889
Other assets	21,534	20,288
Total Assets	**$497,536**	**$522,900**
Liabilities and Shareholders' Equity		
Current Liabilities		
Bank indebtedness	$ -	$825
Accounts payable and accrued liabilities	44,904	36,253
Long-term debt due within one year	876	3,821
Total Current Liabilities	45,780	40,899
Long-term debt	307,721	352,898
Deferred income taxes	3,530	2,316
Shareholders' equity		
Capital stock	175,729	169,810
Contributed surplus	4,784	4,784
Deficit	(38,076)	(43,007)
Equity adjustment from foreign currency translation	(1,932)	(4,800)
Total Shareholders' Equity	140,505	126,787
Total Liabilities and Shareholders' Equity	**$497,536**	**$522,900**

Source: *Four Seasons Regent 1994 Annual Report*

and a provision of $110 million on possible real estate loss and $17 million on the company's loan portfolio on their prospective sales.

The average total management fee revenues received by Four Seasons Regent from each hotel group, per available room, was expected to increase significantly through 1997. This was primarily due to the additional rooms added or to be added in the resort and Asian markets, which have higher average revenues per room.

■ 1994 Financial Summary

The strong recovery in occupancies and room rates, combined with effective cost control measures implemented since 1992, resulted in an increase of over 45 percent in 1994 in the average gross operating profit of managed hotels. Operating earnings from hotel management increased 64 percent while hotel ownership earnings increased 98 percent, from 1993 levels, reflecting strong recovery in the London, Hong Kong, and Chicago markets which generated virtually all the revenues and earnings from hotel ownership operations, from the company's equity interests. This improvement positively affected growth in the company's management incentive fee revenues, which were tied to the profitability of certain managed hotels. Incentive fees represented 15 percent of total management fee revenues for 1994 as compared to ten percent in 1993.

Four Seasons hotels that opened in 1994 included Mexico City and Singapore, plus assumption of the management contract at The Ocean Grand in Palm Beach, Florida. One management contract, for Le Quatre Saisons property in Montreal, was discontinued on January 1, 1994.

New hotels opened in 1993 (Milan, London, New York, Bali) made a strong contribution to overall improvements in 1994. The Four Seasons Boston, Regent Sydney, and Regent Hong Kong also had strong performances in 1994. Average rooms performance figures for Four Seasons and Regent hotel groups are presented in Exhibit 8.

Significant gains in room revenues were realized in many Four Seasons and Regent hotels between 1993 and 1994. Fourteen properties had yield performance gains greater than ten percent, five of which were Regent hotels.

In November 1993, the company implemented a disposition program to sell seven of its significant real estate interests with the objective of substantially eliminating its hotel ownership segment and reducing debt levels by approximately one-third ($120 million). This would also allow the company to reduce its exposure to future real estate cycles and to reduce ongoing capital and operational funding requirements. As of December 31, 1994, it had completed the sale of its interest in three hotels (Austin, Minaki Lodge, and Boston) and used $51.7 million generated from these sales for debt reduction. The company continued to manage the Austin and Boston hotels under long-term management agreements. Notes receivable related to the hotel in San Francisco were sold in early 1995 and

---

Exhibit 8   **Rooms Performance**

	Occupancy %	Average Rate	Yield
Four Seasons			
1993 Actual	68.7%	$183.58	$126.12
1994 Actual	70.2%	$208.16	$146.13
Regent			
1993 Actual	66.0%	$152.96	$100.95
1994 Actual	71.4%	$162.23	$115.83

Source: *Four Seasons Regent Hotels*

the management contract terminated. Other hotels in the program were in Santa Barbara, Vancouver, Toronto, and London. Sale of these interests was expected to generate about $50 million in 1995 after asset-related debt payments.

CORPORATE MARKETING

The overall marketing strategy of the corporation was to serve the luxury segment of the market for business and resort travel worldwide. The corporate office was responsible for the development of overall sales and marketing strategies. These included establishing broad international awareness for both Regent and Four Season brands, as well as developing local market potential for specific hotels.

Four Seasons also provides an international corporate advertising program which develops and places advertising for the Four Seasons hotels and oversees the individual hotel's programs. Regent coordinates the advertising programs for the individual Regent hotels. In 1994, Four Seasons Regent implemented a standard policy of identifying Four Seasons Regent Hotels and Resorts with all corporate and hotel advertising programs.

The corporate marketing staff of Four Seasons Regent also oversees the planning and implementation of hotel marketing programs, and organizes the training and development programs for local sales and marketing staff. The local marketing strategy concentrated on developing rooms and food and beverage business for hotels locally and regionally, and promoting the hotel as a center of community activity with a view to developing local revenues, particularly from catering. Four Seasons Regent generally recovered the costs associated with providing all of these services.

■ Sales Mix

The corporation estimated that business travel and leisure travel represented approximately 66 percent and 34 percent, respectively, of Four Seasons and Regent's combined occupancy. Approximately 37 percent of occupied rooms at the seven resort properties were sold to vacationers. Other major markets for resorts were corporate groups and incentive groups, representing 29 percent and 16 percent, respectively, of all occupied rooms. Approximately 40 percent of urban business and virtually all of resort business was booked through travel agents.

Forty-nine percent of hotel revenue, overall, was derived from the sale of guest rooms and 41 percent from the sale of food and beverages. The other ten percent was attributable to the sale of other services to hotel guests. Asian hotels generally had a higher contribution of food and beverage sales than North American hotels. Food and beverage business for the Four Seasons Tokyo, for example, represented approximately 65 percent of total revenues. This was typical of upscale Asian hotels, especially in Japan.

■ Worldwide Reservations Systems

As a further means of more effectively securing global business, Four Seasons Regent upgraded its international reservations network in 1992. This system provided reservation services in the local language at a total of 22 locations worldwide in major European and Asian cities. Separate toll-free reservations telephone numbers were designed to preserve and enhance the individual Four Seasons and Regent brand identities, while integration enabled the reservations network for each hotel group to sell the other hotel group in cities or countries where its hotel group did not operate, or to sell rooms at a second hotel in the same city if one hotel was full. Central systems booked 35-40 percent of individual reservations for the company.

■ Sales Office Network

Four Seasons Regent operated 13 worldwide sales offices to develop group and corporate business for hotels. Since the 1992 acquisition of Regent, sales operations had been integrated worldwide to provide larger and more diversified sales and marketing coverage for both brands.

COMPETITION

Competition from large hotel chains was vigorous in all Four Seasons Regent markets and was primarily comprised of the Ritz-Carlton, Peninsula, Mandarin, Shangri-La Westin, Inter-Continental, and Hyatt hotel chains. Four Seasons management strategically considered these five hotel chains to be their only real competition at or near their level of quality. Other major international hotel chains such as Sheraton, Marriott, Le Meridien, and Kempinski of Germany, were considered secondary competition as most properties were not at the same luxury level. Individually owned luxury hotels were also a source of competition in certain markets.

Ritz-Carlton was considered the leading competitor, with seven city hotels positioned in direct competition with Four Seasons or Regent hotels in 1995. Ritz-Carlton hotel locations are shown in Exhibit 9.

Peninsula, Shangri-La, and Mandarin Oriental were located in virtually all major Asian destinations. Westin and Hyatt were present in major cities and resort destinations worldwide. Inter-Continental hotels were located in most major world capitals and gateway cities. Most of the other chains mentioned were in just about all Four Seasons Regent locations. Most of Four Seasons Regent competitive analysis was based on comparisons with Ritz-Carlton.

Ritz-Carlton, after three years of endeavor, had received in 1992 the prestigious Malcolm Baldrige National Quality Award, which recognized American companies for their commitment to service, consistency, and reliability. Four Seasons and Regent hotels, however, have individually gathered more accolades than Ritz-Carlton hotels.

THE OUTLOOK FOR 1995

Performance projections for 1995 suggested 11.5 percent and 6.9 percent yield increases for Four Seasons and Regent Hotels, respectively (see Exhibit 10). In light of continuing performance improvements throughout the company, the marketing team decided to focus on the same priorities:

Exhibit 9   **Ritz-Carlton Hotel Locations**

United States	Hawaii/Pacific/Asia	Europe	Mexico
Boston	Double Bay, Australia	Barcelona	Cancun
New York	Kahana, Maui		
Pentagon City (DC)	Big Island of Hawaii		
Philadelphia	Sydney		
Tysons Corner (DC)	Hong Kong		
Washington, DC	Seoul		
Amelia Island, FL	Bali, Indonesia		
Atlanta	Osaka, Japan		
Buckhead, GA			
Naples, FL			
Palm Beach, FL			
Cleveland			
Dearborn, MI			
Kansas City			
St. Louis			
Houston			
Phoenix			
Aspen			
Pasadena, CA			
Rancho Mirage, CA			
Marina del Rey, CA			
San Francisco			
Laguna Niguel, CA			

- Growing individual business worldwide
- Improving the quality and nature of group business
- Striving for greater marketing efficiencies
- Strengthening individual brands and hotels
- Leveraging the Four Seasons Regent combination
- Focusing on special situations
- Focusing on *'Unique Service = Value = Worth More'* as the main communications message throughout the world

From these priorities, three collective objectives were identified as the main focus of marketing efforts in 1995.

Growing individual business worldwide.

The company identified this market as its greatest opportunity to support its growing international portfolio. While the majority of group sales take place relatively close to a hotel's location, and require heavy local sales involvement, individual travel decisions can be made anywhere and can be effectively influenced by the efforts of a worldwide sales organization, regardless of location.

Exhibit 10

1995 Budgeted Hotel Performance

	Four Seasons	Regent
Occupancy %	73.4%	72.2%
Average Rate	$221.81	$169.83
Yield	$162.81	$122.62

Source: Four Seasons Regent Hotels

Four Seasons introduced three company-wide initiatives to influence and attract global individual business travel:

1. A hotel guest recognition program to provide basic information to each hotel on the top 100 individual customers for all other properties. According to the 1995 Marketing Plan, this focus was on what was believed to be the primary need for the high-end individual traveler— that of recognition during a first stay in a Four Seasons or Regent hotel.

2. Development of a promotional database to sell and communicate directly with individual customers who voluntarily were willing to be contacted. This would also allow for increased cooperation with promotional partners who wished to cross-market with Four Seasons Regent.

3. Reshaping of direct sales efforts in the North American sales offices to focus more on individual travel segments. In the past, worldwide sales offices had focused on the lucrative group and incentive markets but, now that the company portfolio ranged across many continents, sales efforts would have to be diversified to support growth in both individual and group-travel segments.

Leveraging the Four Seasons Regent Combination.

Four Seasons Regent planned to continue to ensure that "cross-selling" of the Four Seasons and Regent brands was the rule rather than the exception. Given the increasingly global nature of both the competition and target customers, Four Seasons Regent was committed to using combined human resources and systems to represent the entire company regardless of brand or location.

Improving Global Sales Network Efficiencies.

Two primary initiatives were put in place to facilitate faster and more cost-effective communications.

1. Wherever possible, individual hotels would soon be electronically linked to worldwide reservations systems, allowing each hotel to communicate directly and easily with reservations outlets.

2. By mid-1995, 17 Four Seasons and 8 Regent hotels would have a database software program for the management of group rooms and function space. The next objective was to link up the individual hotels to worldwide sales offices, allowing for more consistent timely information on key accounts and eliminating the manual/voice exchange of information.

LOOKING TO THE FUTURE

Continued improvement from existing operations as a result of the worldwide economic recovery, combined with additional fee income from recently opened hotels and hotels opening in Chiang Mai, Thailand (mid 1995), Jakarta (mid 1995), Istanbul and Royal Sentul Highlands, Indonesia (mid 1996), and Berlin (mid 1996) were expected to contribute to further increases in the company's operating margins in 1995 and 1996.

Four Seasons Regent would continue to serve the luxury segment of the market for business and leisure travel and intended to maintain and improve upon the standards established in existing properties, as well as those in the hotels and resorts presently under development or construction. Four Seasons Regent would continue to review opportunities to manage newly constructed and existing hotels and resorts. They planned to seek development opportunities aggressively worldwide and their goal was to have a combined portfolio of 50 hotels and resorts within five years.

The corporate marketing team's discussion continued for many hours as it contemplated the issues that the Ritz-Marriott marriage had introduced. Many questions were still left unanswered. Would Ritz-Carlton stay exclusively in the luxury market? Would the Ritz-Carlton name be enhanced or jeopardized by their association with a worldwide mid-market hotel chain? Would Marriott put its name on Ritz-Carlton hotels? Should Four Seasons Regent position against Ritz-Carlton, Marriott, or both? What if Marriott started stealing Four Seasons Regent employees for its Ritz-Carlton operations? Most of all, how will any of these issues affect Four Seasons Regent and should Four Seasons Regent devise strategies to deal with any of these eventualities?

Richards pondered the possibilities. If strategies needed to be devised, what would they look like? Do we respond to the threat, do we preempt, fortify, defend? When, and at what point? How does the Regent acquisition fit into this? Are we in a better or worse position? Do we have the right organization to handle this?

"It looks like we all have quite a lot to think about tonight" said Richards as the conversation came to a tiresome end. "Let's meet again tomorrow to prepare our contingency plans."

Shortly after this incident, John Sharpe, a 20-plus-year veteran of Four Seasons was named President of the company and heir apparent to Issy Sharp. John Richards, among others, was promoted to Executive Vice President.

Airborne Express: The Domestic Air Express Industry

Robert J. Mockler, St. John's University

Dorothy Dologite, CUNY-Baruch College

Internet site of interest: **www.airborne-express.com**

Airborne Express has been exciting many shippers with its competitive pricing and technological achievements since 1991. Prior to 1994, Airborne had taken the monopolistic control away from rival and industry leader Federal Express by staying within its corporate goal of being the low-cost operator in the domestic air express industry. By directing its sales strategies at large national accounts and large business to business shippers and away from small and residential shippers, Airborne achieved its goal of being the low-cost operator in the industry. This enabled Airborne to grow from about 14 percent the size of its top competitor in 1985, to the 1993 level of 40 percent Federal Express's size. In terms of total number of shipments handled, Airborne Express was the third largest carrier in the industry behind Federal Express and United Parcel Service in 1994. In 1985, the number of domestic shipments handled by Airborne Express was 19,277,000. That number skied to 64 million by 1989 and was over 160 million by 1993. On a percentage basis, Airborne has been the fastest-growing air express company in the United States from 1984 to 1993. As shown in Exhibit 1, the domestic shipment growth has been tremendous since 1980 and twelvefold since 1984. As shown in Exhibit 2, domestic revenue has quadrupled since 1985, and has nearly doubled from 1989 to the 1993 level of $1.48 billion.

Exhibit 1   **Airborne Express's Domestic Shipments 1980–1993**

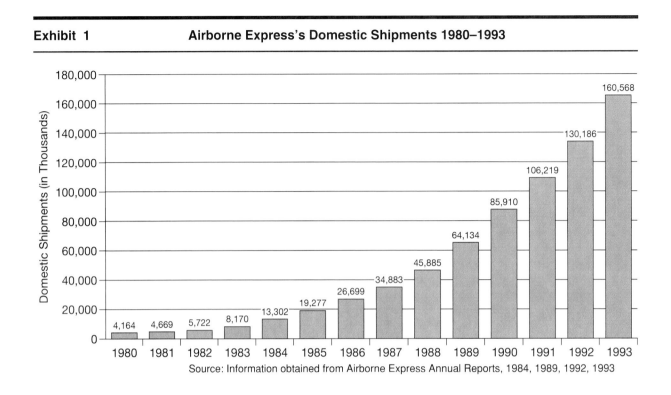

Source: Information obtained from Airborne Express Annual Reports, 1984, 1989, 1992, 1993

Exhibit 2   **Airborne Express's Domestic Revenue 1980–1993**

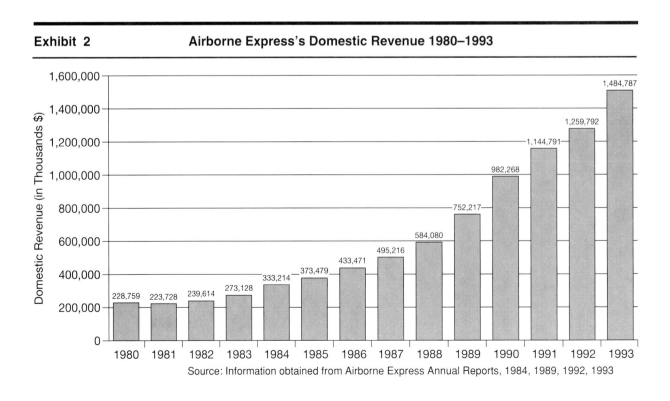

Source: Information obtained from Airborne Express Annual Reports, 1984, 1989, 1992, 1993

The shipment rate for the industry has been steadily increasing since the air express industry was introduced in 1973. The industry has been growing by an average of 15.6% per year from 1980 to 1992. Even during the economic downturn of the late 1980s and the early 1990s, the number of shipments tendered has increased. But revenues have decreased steadily. One series of numbers shows that the air courier industry, "with $20 billion or 60 percent share of the $33 billion worldwide market for air cargo," is more glamorous than most believe. In 1991, as seen in Exhibit 3, Federal Express accounted for $7.8 billion, Airborne Express $1.4 billion, and United Parcel Service $3.8 billion of the air express industry.

In light of the positive growth Airborne has had since 1980, the company was faced with some key strategic decisions in early 1994. Should it maintain the current Select Delivery Product of letter to 5 pounds, or should Airborne modify the top weight limit of the Select Delivery Product from 5 pounds to the competitive level of 150 pounds? Should Airborne maintain its present Priority Service, which guarantees delivery by 12:00 noon to all major metropolitan areas, or should it modify its Priority Service to meet competitors' guarantees of 10:30 a.m. delivery? Should Airborne continue with its present customer mix, consisting mainly of national account and small business segment shippers, or should the company target a different customer mix to include more customers that ship mainly to residential areas, such as the catalogue shipping segment?

Exhibit 3   **Worldwide Breakdown of the $33 Billion Air Freight & Express Industry (in billions) (1991)**

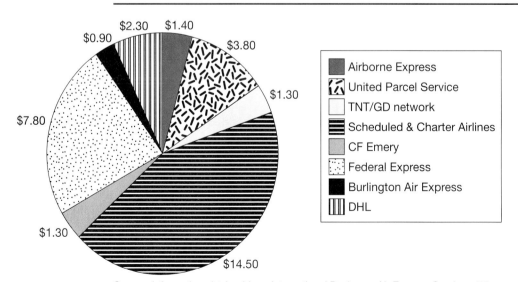

Source: Information obtained from International Business, Air Express Services, '92

INDUSTRY AND COMPETITIVE MARKET

■ Cargo Industry

The cargo industry consists of companies and individuals shipping small and large, heavy and light packages through a variety of transportation modes. As shown in Exhibit 4, the transportation modes are through the air (freight or cargo), on the ground (trucking), by rail (railways) and across the water (maritime).

Air freight (or air cargo) is grouped into four classifications. The air freight groups are domestic air express, domestic air heavyweight (i.e., domestic air freight), international air express, and international air heavyweight, i.e., international air freight. Air freight is considered shipments that weigh over 150 pounds (*Traffic Management*, March 1993).

Domestic air express consists of small letters, packages, and boxes designed for delivery within a couple of days within the United States. Domestic air heavyweight includes shipments over 150 pounds that require delivery within one week throughout the United States. International air express shipments are those shipments that require expedited delivery anywhere worldwide. These shipments can be in any form, dutiable (those destined for resale) or non-dutiable. Finally, international air heavyweight involves large shipments, usually in multiple-piece lots that do not require expedited delivery. This case study focuses on the domestic air express industry. Exhibit 5 shows the structure of the domestic air express industry.

DOMESTIC AIR EXPRESS INDUSTRY

In 1994, the domestic air express industry was dominated by five companies: Airborne Express, Federal Express, United Parcel Service, DHL, and the United States Postal Service. There were many other express companies that delivered regionally, but nationally, the above five covered the market, servicing national accounts, small business, individual shippers, and catalogue shipping.

Exhibit 4   **Structure of the Cargo Industry**

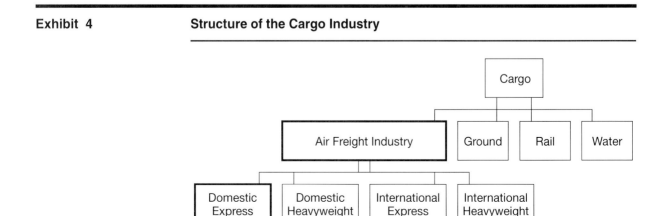

Exhibit 5   **Structure of the Domestic Air Express Industry**

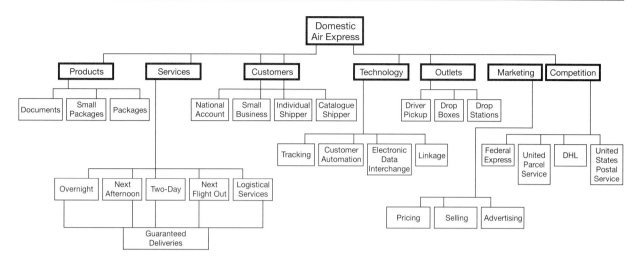

In 1973, Federal Express introduced American business to a new concept of on-time delivery of important packages. Fred Smith, CEO of Federal Express, developed a new product and created a market that encompassed the delivery of over three million air express packages daily in the 1990s. The market he created was for the delivery of time-sensitive materials, originally including mostly legal documents, but later composed of everything from stocks and bonds to heavy computers and parts.

■ Hub-and-Spoke System

When Federal Express was born in 1973, it instituted a shipping system called the hub-and-spoke system. This revolutionized the shipping industry. Packages destined for locations anywhere in the United States would find themselves in a centralized hub for redistribution back throughout the United States. This simplified the movement of packages. It also reduced the cost of package redistribution for companies seeking entrance into the industry. The air express industry came into prominence with the introduction of the hub-and-spoke system.

The majority of the air express companies used this system of sorting and distributing their packages in 1993. A few, such as Airborne Express and Federal Express, also utilized regional sort hubs to handle packages within a local delivery area. A regional sort hub is a smaller version of the national sort hub, for packages being delivered within the regional area or those marked as two-day shipments by the shipper.

PRODUCT

The domestic air express industry consists of all shipments picked up in the United States on a daily basis for delivery in the next two business days within the United States. Most overnight packages in the air express industry are transported by airplane at some time during the journey, though some are trucked during the whole route. The domestic air express industry was composed of three types of shipment classifications in 1993. They were *documents* that weighed under four pounds, *small packages* that weighed from four to 70 pounds, and *packages* that weighed between 70 and 150 pounds (*Traffic Management*, March 1993). Detailed descriptions of these three categories can be found in Appendix B.

The air express industry has changed society's perception of the importance of having something the next day. From 1984 to 1992, the industry grew nearly tenfold, and continued growth was expected. The industry also saw continuous price reduction in shipping, and the price for large shippers in the industry was coming down near the level of ground shipping services. Many shippers determined that they could enhance their shipping service to many of their customers and keep prices relatively steady. Therefore, they were more inclined to switch to overnight air. Tracking of packages had given the air express industry increased popularity since the introduction of positive tracking in 1988. Picking up packages at the shipper's office also enhanced the industry's growth. There was no need for dropping off packages at a post office, mailbox, or at drop centers in the 1990s. This little convenience enhanced the growth of the overnight industry. Finally, customers have been offered the flexibility of many different products to choose from, and air express carriers have shown a great ability to conform to their customers' needs.

Exhibit 6 shows that overnight, next afternoon, and two-day packages made up 72.2 percent of the shipping industry in 1990, compared to 71.4 percent in 1991. This is directly related to the recession that the United States was experiencing. The nearly 2 percent decrease in the shipment of overnight envelopes and letters shows that companies were becoming more conscious of their shipping costs and cutting back where possible.

Exhibit 6   **Domestic Package Mix 1990–1991**

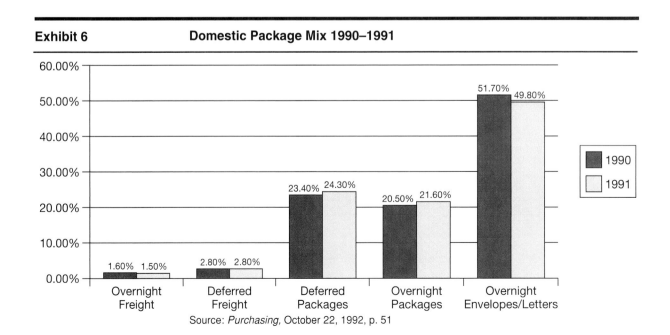

Source: *Purchasing*, October 22, 1992, p. 51

SERVICES

Services offered by air express companies were *overnight*, *next afternoon,* and *second-day* (a.k.a. two-day) air service. A fourth type of service that many express companies offered in 1993 was a *next-flight-out* (NFO) premium service for extremely important items. A fifth type of service was an on-demand service that became Just-In-Time service, called *Logistical Services. Guaranteed delivery* was also very important for air express companies.

The industry consists of both overnight and deferred deliveries. Deferred packages (those shipments under 150 pounds) and deferred freight (those packages over 150 pounds) refer to those shipments that are shipped through the array of trucking, railway, and waterway shipping systems in the United States that are not as time sensitive as their overnight counterparts. Due to limited funds availability in the late 1980s and into the early 1990s, corporations were diverting overnight and two-day packages to slower and less costly modes of shipping. For example, books were shipped via ground as opposed to an air express courier.

■ Overnight Delivery

Overnight delivery is used for those packages that are picked up for delivery the next business morning. It was the heart of this industry. With the recent expansion into next-afternoon and second-day services, overnight packages have decreased in volume since 1989. Overnight consists of the highest cost for the customer and the best service offered by the carrier. Since 1992, customers have begun using more of the deferred services of the Air Express industry for those items that they need to have timely deliveries on, but do not necessarily need premium service on. Exhibit 7 shows a comparison of the overnight price offered by Federal Express and Airborne Express.

■ Next Afternoon Delivery

Next afternoon delivery is used for those packages that are scheduled for delivery during the next business afternoon. Next-afternoon deliveries are derived from customers who want their packages to arrive the next business day, but it is not necessary in the morning. The air express companies offering this service used a 3:00 p.m. guaranteed delivery time in 1993. The cost for this type of package was roughly 65–70 percent of overnight delivery. Exhibit 8 shows what a customer with no discount would pay if they were shipping a package using Airborne Express's or Federal Express's next-afternoon delivery services (letter to 5 pounds only) in 1993.

With substantial savings (about 30 percent) and delivery the next business day, many companies were switching all essential but noncritical shipments to this service in 1993.

■ Two-Day Delivery (a.k.a. Second-Day Delivery)

Two-day delivery is used for those packages that are scheduled for delivery within two business days. This service is for noncritical packages that are important none-theless. These packages would cost approximately 40–50

Exhibit 7   **ABX Overnight vs FEDX Overnight**

Wt	FEDX P1	ABX 1408	$ Savings	%Savings	Wt	FEDX P1	ABX 1408	$ Savings	%Savings
LEX	$13.00	$8.75	$4.25	32.69%	36	$76.25	$51.14	$25.11	32.93%
1	$20.00	$11.00	$9.00	45.00%	37	$77.50	$52.08	$25.42	32.80%
2	$21.75	$12.13	$9.62	44.23%	38	$78.75	$53.02	$25.73	32.67%
3	$24.50	$13.63	$10.87	44.37%	39	$80.00	$54.09	$25.91	32.39%
4	$27.25	$15.50	$11.75	43.12%	40	$81.25	$55.40	$25.85	31.82%
5	$30.00	$17.25	$12.75	42.50%	41	$82.50	$56.59	$25.91	31.41%
6	$32.75	$18.75	$14.00	42.75%	42	$83.75	$58.13	$25.62	30.59%
7	$35.50	$20.50	$15.00	42.25%	43	$85.00	$59.38	$25.62	30.14%
8	$38.25	$22.00	$16.25	42.48%	44	$86.25	$60.63	$25.62	29.70%
9	$41.00	$23.44	$17.56	42.83%	45	$87.50	$61.88	$25.62	29.28%
10	$43.75	$24.50	$19.25	44.00%	46	$88.75	$63.13	$25.62	28.87%
11	$45.00	$25.50	$19.50	43.33%	47	$90.00	$64.13	$25.87	28.74%
12	$46.25	$26.50	$19.75	42.70%	48	$91.25	$65.07	$26.18	28.69%
13	$47.50	$27.50	$20.00	42.11%	49	$92.50	$66.07	$26.43	28.57%
14	$48.75	$28.50	$20.25	41.54%	50	$93.75	$67.07	$26.68	28.46%
15	$50.00	$29.50	$20.50	41.00%	51	$95.25	$67.43	$27.82	29.21%
16	$51.25	$30.50	$20.75	40.49%	52	$96.75	$68.61	$28.14	29.09%
17	$52.50	$31.50	$21.00	40.00%	53	$98.25	$69.80	$28.45	28.96%
18	$53.75	$32.50	$21.25	39.53%	54	$99.75	$70.98	$28.77	28.84%
19	$55.00	$33.38	$21.62	39.31%	55	$101.25	$72.17	$29.08	28.72%
20	$56.25	$34.38	$21.87	38.88%	56	$102.75	$73.35	$29.40	28.61%
21	$57.50	$35.25	$22.25	38.70%	57	$104.25	$74.29	$29.96	28.74%
22	$58.75	$35.82	$22.93	39.03%	58	$105.75	$75.22	$30.53	28.87%
23	$60.00	$36.51	$23.49	39.15%	59	$107.25	$76.16	$31.09	28.99%
24	$61.25	$37.70	$23.55	38.45%	60	$108.75	$77.09	$31.66	29.11%
25	$62.50	$38.88	$23.62	37.79%	61	$110.75	$78.03	$32.72	29.54%
26	$63.25	$40.19	$23.06	36.46%	62	$112.75	$78.96	$33.79	29.97%
27	$65.00	$41.50	$23.50	36.15%	63	$114.75	$79.90	$34.85	30.37%
28	$66.25	$42.81	$23.44	35.38%	64	$116.75	$80.83	$35.92	30.77%
29	$67.50	$44.12	$23.38	34.64%	65	$118.75	$81.77	$36.98	31.14%
30	$68.75	$45.50	$23.25	33.82%	66	$120.75	$82.70	$38.05	31.51%
31	$70.00	$46.69	$23.31	33.30%	67	$122.75	$83.64	$39.11	31.86%
32	$71.25	$47.76	$23.49	32.97%	68	$124.75	$84.57	$40.18	32.31%
33	$72.50	$48.70	$23.80	32.83%	69	$126.75	$85.51	$41.24	32.54%
34	$73.75	$49.51	$24.24	32.87%	70	$128.75	$86.44	$42.31	32.86%
35	$75.00	$50.33	$24.67	32.89%	Total			$1,756.01	34.77%

Exhibit 8

ABX Select Delivery vs FEDX Standard

Wt	FEDX STD	ABX 492	$ Savings	%Savings
LEX	$9.00	$8.00	$1.00	11.11%
1	$13.00	$8.00	$5.00	38.46%
2	$14.00	$9.00	$5.00	35.71%
3	$15.00	$11.00	$4.00	26.67%
4	$16.00	$12.00	$4.00	25.00%
5	$17.00	$13.00	$4.00	23.53%
TOTAL			$23.00	26.75%

percent of the cost of delivering overnight. A price comparison of United Parcel Service's two-day Blue Label Service to Airborne Express's Select Delivery Service is shown in Exhibit 9.

With the discount from overnight delivery to two-day service in the range of 40–45 percent, shippers were able to get reliable, timely, and cost-effective service for urgent but noncritical merchandise while still having the comfort of a reasonable price.

From 1991 to 1992, for example, Airborne Express's delivery of overnight packages declined from 83% of total packages handled to 74% of all packages handled (Airborne Annual Report, 1992). Shippers that have been hit hard by the recession have been scaling back the delivery requirement of their non-critical packages. This has hurt the revenue margins of all large air express carriers. This has occurred because the price difference between overnight and next-afternoon delivery varied from one dollar per package for the large national accounts to 7–8 dollars for a smaller shipper sending a small package (3–4 pounds) in 1993. There was even another drop of the price from next-afternoon delivery to two-day delivery.

Overall, in 1993, using Federal Express's Economy versus Priority Shipping provided savings of 45.35 percent; with United Parcel Service, Blue Label versus Red Label service provided savings of 42.16 percent; and with Airborne Express, Select Delivery versus Express Service provided savings of 26.11 percent. These numbers are the average savings on weights of letters to thirty pounds.

■ Next Flight Out (NFO)

The industry also encompasses those companies that deal expressly next-flight-out (also known as NFO) business. Next-flight-out is a premium service for extremely time-sensitive packages. Prices generally range from $200 to $300 per piece. Sky Courier and Sonic Courier were two of the larger NFO couriers.

■ Logistical Services

Logistical services enables air carriers to ship from their own warehouses merchandise that is stored there for their customers. This enables shipments that are of an extremely critical nature to be shipped on demand. This type of

Exhibit 9   **ABX Select Delivery vs UPS Blue Label**

Wt	UPS Blue	ABX 8753	$ Savings	%Savings	Wt	UPS Blue	ABX 8753	$ Savings	%Savings
LEX	$5.75	$5.25	$0.50	8.70%	36	$43.75	$38.25	$5.50	12.57%
1	$6.00	$5.50	$0.50	8.33%	37	$44.75	$39.25	$5.50	12.29%
2	$7.00	$6.25	$0.75	10.71%	38	$45.75	$40.25	$5.50	12.02%
3	$7.75	$7.00	$0.75	9.68%	39	$46.75	$41.25	$5.50	11.76%
4	$8.25	$7.50	$0.75	9.09%	40	$47.75	$42.25	$5.50	11.52%
5	$9.00	$8.25	$0.75	8.33%	41	$48.75	$43.25	$5.50	11.28%
6	$10.25	$8.25	$2.00	19.51%	42	$50.00	$44.25	$5.75	11.50%
7	$11.50	$9.25	$2.25	19.57%	43	$51.00	$45.25	$5.75	11.27%
8	$12.75	$10.25	$2.50	19.61%	44	$52.00	$46.25	$5.75	11.06%
9	$14.00	$11.25	$2.75	19.64%	45	$53.00	$47.25	$5.75	10.85%
10	$15.25	$12.25	$3.00	19.67%	46	$54.25	$48.25	$6.00	11.06%
11	$16.25	$13.25	$3.00	18.46%	47	$55.25	$49.25	$6.00	10.86%
12	$17.50	$14.25	$3.25	18.57%	48	$56.50	$50.25	$6.25	11.06%
13	$18.75	$15.25	$3.50	18.67%	49	$57.50	$51.25	$6.25	10.87%
14	$20.00	$16.25	$3.75	18.75%	50	$58.50	$52.25	$6.25	10.68%
15	$21.25	$17.25	$4.00	18.82%	51	$59.50	$53.25	$6.25	10.50%
16	$22.50	$18.25	$4.25	18.89%	52	$60.25	$54.25	$6.00	9.96%
17	$23.75	$19.25	$4.50	18.95%	53	$61.25	$55.25	$6.00	9.80%
18	$24.75	$20.25	$4.50	18.18%	54	$62.25	$56.25	$6.00	9.64%
19	$26.00	$21.25	$4.75	18.27%	55	$63.00	$57.25	$5.75	9.13%
20	$27.25	$22.25	$5.00	18.35%	56	$63.75	$58.25	$5.50	8.63%
21	$28.25	$23.25	$5.00	17.70%	57	$64.50	$59.25	$5.25	8.14%
22	$29.25	$24.25	$5.00	17.09%	58	$65.25	$60.25	$5.00	7.66%
23	$30.00	$25.25	$4.75	15.83%	59	$66.00	$61.25	$4.75	7.20%
24	$31.00	$26.25	$4.75	15.32%	60	$66.75	$62.25	$4.50	6.74%
25	$32.00	$27.25	$4.75	14.84%	61	$67.50	$63.35	$4.15	6.15%
26	$33.00	$28.25	$4.75	14.39%	62	$68.25	$64.45	$3.80	5.57%
27	$34.00	$29.25	$4.75	13.97%	63	$69.00	$65.55	$3.45	5.00%
28	$35.00	$30.25	$4.75	13.57%	64	$69.75	$66.65	$3.10	4.44%
29	$36.00	$31.25	$4.75	13.19%	65	$70.50	$67.75	$2.75	3.90%
30	$37.00	$32.25	$4.75	12.84%	66	$71.25	$68.85	$2.40	3.37%
31	$38.25	$33.25	$5.00	13.07%	67	$72.00	$69.95	$2.05	2.85%
32	$39.50	$34.25	$5.25	13.29%	68	$72.75	$71.05	$1.70	2.34%
33	$40.75	$35.25	$5.50	13.50%	69	$73.75	$72.15	$1.10	1.50%
34	$41.75	$36.25	$5.50	13.17%	70	$73.75	$73.25	$0.50	0.68%
35	$42.75	$37.25	$5.50	12.87%	Total			$298.50	11.93%

service is provided to the shipper for a fee. The carrier takes responsibility for warehousing, picking, packaging, and shipping the items as orders come in, any time of the day or night. These locations are usually based near or between large cities so that a large coverage area can be maintained.

■ Guaranteed Delivery

Guaranteeing a delivery is offering money-back or, in some instances, free service for packages which do not reach their destination by the delivery time promised. When a package is guaranteed to be delivered by 10:30 a.m., 12:00 noon, or 3:00 p.m., shippers become more careful to ensure that the commitment time has been met. This is a money-back issue that the air express companies must be sure to keep track of. If guaranteed delivery times are not met consistently, and a customer feels unsatisfied with their current carrier, they can make a switch to another carrier fairly quickly.

In the 1993–94 market, United Parcel Service and Federal Express guaranteed a 10:30 a.m. delivery to all the major metropolitan areas in the United States for their overnight service; Airborne Express guaranteed delivery by noon for the same service. For the afternoon services offered by Federal Express and Airborne Express, 3:00 p.m. was the guaranteed delivery time. The guarantee for a two-day package was by 5:00 p.m. the second business day for all the major carriers.

CUSTOMERS

The three main customer segments in the air express market were the national account, small business, and individual shipper segments. A fourth was the catalogue merchandise shipper. Catalogue companies became an emerging customer segment in the air express industry in the 1990s.

■ National Account Segment

The *national account segment* consists of corporations and organizations that have multiple shipping locations throughout the United States. This was the segment of business that air express companies targeted. Although the revenue per package was usually lower than other types of shippers, customers of this type were desirable due to the large volume of packages that were picked up from one stop. The revenue per package was lower because these types of shippers had discounted rates due to the volume of packages shipped locally or throughout the entire company or organization.

Large corporations generally made the more lucrative business-to-business type of shipment. In this case the dollar amount of the packages was not key; it was the number of packages being shipped from one location that made the overall customer coveted. Business-to-business shipments were more desirable because the chance of a business having more than one package being delivered or picked up from it in one day was great. Businesses were usually clumped together in buildings or office parks, which enabled one driver to make more than one delivery or pickup without having to move the truck too far. In contrast, deliveries to residences did not usually come in multiples.

The keys to success in the national account segment are threefold. First, the rates charged the national account customer were expected to be either the lowest bid received or priced very aggressively. National account companies were very interested in cost savings. Second, the air express carrier was expected to be technologically flexible. More and more companies wanted to integrate their own computer system with the carrier's system. Third, upper management must be approachable, because management played a large role in major sales.

■ Small Business Segment

The *small business segment* comprises companies that have one or a few shipping locations. This segment of business was necessary because this is where a higher revenue per package is realized. This type of shipper usually had discounted rates, but not as much as at the national account level. However, since the revenues per shipment from this segment were quite high, it was cost effective to pursue these types of businesses. Servicing this type of customer properly was essential because these were the customers who would stay with a courier because of a personal attachment to the courier's personnel. National accounts usually come and go due to national agreements signed out of their national headquarters, where price is generally the deciding factor. The small business account can be swayed by the customer service offered.

■ Individual Shipping Segment

The *individual shipping segment* comprises individuals shipping one package every once in a while. These shipments were very high in revenue, but not extremely desirable. Individuals usually ship one package at a time, and it is expensive to transport since one driver must pick up one package. This is not as cost effective as if the driver were picking up many packages at one stop. If the individual shipper were able to drop off the package at a shipping terminal, then this type of shipper would become more desirable. These shipping terminals were available in most major cities, but they were expensive to run due to rent and other costs that were not usually associated with a driver picking up packages.

■ Catalogue Shipping Segment

The *catalogue shipping segment* consists of companies that warehouse and ship merchandise from locations that are not part of a retail sales establishment. Generally, customers of catalogue shippers were given the choice as to the method of shipping—overnight or by ground shipper. Due to the relatively high volume of shipments coming from one catalogue shipper location, the cost to the catalogue shipper was low; this cost savings was passed on to its customers. Thus there were many catalogue shippers using air express companies. Many of these packages were for residential delivery and thus were not cost effective to the courier.

Residential deliveries were more expensive than business-to-business deliveries. They usually take the delivery driver off the natural route of the business district, where the majority of the deliveries are made, into the residential area, where very few deliveries are made; rarely will there be more than one delivery to any one location. Thus the cost per package to deliver would be higher.

TECHNOLOGY

Technology in the industry included customer automation, tracking, electronic data interchange, and linkage. Although pricing and service are the two main factors in securing new business, technology has become extremely important since the price and services provided by all of the companies in the industry have become similar across the board.

■ Customer Automation

All of the major domestic air express services offered large customers the option of using carrier-owned computer equipment for the purposes of shipping their domestic packages. This equipment was supplied free of charge in order for the customers to ship, invoice, and track their own packages. The benefits for the carrier included self-invoicing, self-tracking, and an automated means for transmitting package pickup information. Customers can audit themselves by printing daily, weekly, and monthly reports for the purpose of proper departmental charge-backs. United Parcel Service called their machine MaxiShip, Federal Express had the PowerShip, DHL had EasyShip, and Airborne Express supplied customers with its Libra System.

■ Tracking

Knowing where a customer's package is at every step of the way is essential. This could be done with the use of telephone couplers and satellites. This technology allowed air express carriers immediate access to delivery and scan information all along the route of the package (see Exhibit 6). When an inquiry was made about the status of a package by the shipper, the carrier could detect immediately where the package was. This technology also offered customer service agents up-to-the-minute information for use on calls about specific shipments.

Customers equipped with carrier-supplied hardware, automation systems, or software, tracking-only systems possessed the ability to retrieve this information without the assistance of customer services. The more customers who have this technology at their disposal, the fewer customers who will have to call customer service. This offered customer service agents more time to work with customers who did not have this technology available.

In 1993, Federal Express and United Parcel Service used satellites and radio waves to transmit their delivery and pickup information to their corporate computers. This transmission was done from their delivery trucks and the information on their pickups. Deliveries were transmitted each time they returned to their trucks. This was also known as "real time information." Two other methods of transmitting delivery information were through phone lines or through downloading from a driver's scanner to the corporate main computer system at the end of the delivery day.

The cost of setting up a truck with a transmitting system was in the range of $3,500 to $4,000 in 1993.

▪ Electronic Data Interchange (EDI)

EDI gives customers the ability to receive and pay their bills without receiving any paper invoices. This transaction uses disk, tape-to-tape or phone-line computer to computer transmission technology to transmit all billing and delivery information to the shipper. This information is verified by the shipper and payment is then completed through a wire transfer of money.

▪ Linkage

Linkage allows the shipper to be directly on-line with the courier. All shipments tendered by the shipper are directly fed into the courier computer for the purposes of billing and tracking. This is the wave of the future for all large-and medium-sized mass distribution companies and mail order houses. A mass distribution company is a company that distributes like merchandise to recipients of their packages.

Linkage is an order entry mode of shipping. When a shipper's customer service agent takes an order for an item, he or she enters the type of item that needs to be shipped. The same information that is being entered for the customer's invoice also creates a record of what is to be shipped. This record of what is to be shipped in turn creates a waybill (airbill) for the shipping room to use to ship the package. Therefore, the one set of information that is entered by the order entry clerk does three tasks: invoicing the purchaser of the merchandise, creating a manifest for the shipping room, and creating a waybill for the package. The sum total of all entered shipments for that day can then be combined for inventory records.

OUTLETS

There are three major types of outlets for overnight shipping services: Customers can have a driver pick up their packages, drop packages in drop boxes, or drop packages at drop stations or retail stores.

▪ Driver Pickup

A *driver pickup* occurs when a driver for the air express company stops by the company shipping the packages to pick them up. These services come in two forms. First, some customers have daily scheduled pickups that are performed at approximately the same time each day. Second, there are those customers that do not ship every day. These customers would call on the day that they have packages being shipped. With some courier companies, having a driver stop by to pick up packages costs a little more than dropping off packages in either drop boxes or drop stations.

▪ Drop Boxes

Drop boxes are courier-owned boxes that allow local shippers to drop their packages off conveniently without having a scheduled pickup or after their own pickup has occurred. These are usually located in areas that are convenient to many potential shippers.

■ Drop Stations

Drop stations are either retail storefronts or courier stations that enable shippers to provide multiple locations where their packages can be dropped. High traffic areas are the most common locations for these storefronts and courier stations.

MARKETING

Marketing consists of not only advertising, but also pricing techniques, customer service, shipping enhancements such as a computer software for tracking, and calendar and promotional giveaways during the holiday season. Trade show attendance is another form of marketing.

Of the five major overnight companies in the industry, four advertised via newspaper and television ads. DHL advertised its international service more than its domestic service, and Airborne Express advertises sparingly, and only in industry magazines. United Parcel Service highlights its overnight-by-10:30 service as well as its international services. United States Postal Service highlights its Express Mail Overnight service and its Priority Mail 2-pound service. Federal Express, on the other hand, focuses on its 10:30 a.m. guarantee. It has also brought its name into the sports world by sponsoring two major sporting events, including the Federal Express Orange Bowl of College Football on January 1st and the Federal Express Golf Tournament in its hometown of Memphis, Tennessee.

All major carriers offer pricing discounts to large shippers, sometimes noted as a percentage off of the base rates for the carrier. Pricing not only depended on the volume of the shipper, but also on the industry type, affiliations (such as organizations and associations), and whether the pricing was for a single location of a company or as part of a national account.

Service was the largest part of the industry, that is, delivering the packages, but customer service was extremely valuable, too. Helpfulness and responsiveness could make the difference between a satisfied customer and a dissatisfied customer.

COMPETITION

Competition in the domestic air express industry included internationally known companies such as Federal Express, United Parcel Service, DHL, and the United States Postal Service (USPS). There were also dozens of regional companies, such as Burlington Air Express and Twilight Express. Exhibit 10 gives the breakdown of the worldwide air courier market. Another competitor to air express is telecommunication systems that include E-mail, fax machines, and in-computer fax boards. These systems enable small documents to be sent via a modem easily and quickly, and they challenge the need for overnight services.

Exhibit 10   **Percentage Revenue for Domestic Air Express Companies, 1992**

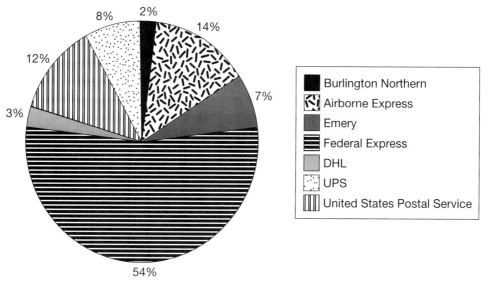

Source: Information obtained from Presentation by Jerry Hempstead, VP Airborne Express, October 25, 1993

■ Federal Express

Federal Express is the largest domestic air express carrier in the United States. It handled 54 percent of the packages in the industry in 1993. As well as being the original player in the industry, Federal Express has become one of the industry's technological leaders. Federal Express was the first company in the industry to transmit delivery information of packages using satellite transmission from company trucks to their main computer, as opposed to having the data entered back at the delivery stations. This enabled customers to have an 'up-to-the-minute' status on their packages.

Federal Express offered three services in 1993. First was the Priority Service for packages delivered the next morning by 10:30. Second, there was the Standard Service for packages that were to be delivered by 3:00 p.m. the next afternoon. Finally, there was the Economy Service for those packages destined to be delivered within two business days. All of these service levels were chosen by the shipper and were money-back guaranteed.

Federal Express was the largest and most effective company in the industry. In fiscal year 1993 alone it had domestic revenues of nearly $5.67 billion. Using these funds, it was able to be one of the heaviest advertisers in the industry, with an easily identified name, colors, and reputation. With this type of name recognition, the Federal Express moniker, or the abbreviated term FedEx, has become the generic term in the shipping industry.

Federal Express was the first company with a hub-and-spoke system. It had its main hub based out of the Memphis Airport, along with more than twelve regional hubs, including a hub in Indianapolis for packages being delivered via its two-day Economy service.

As the number one company in the industry, Federal Express had the ability to demand a higher price for its services. While prices have been coming down in the industry since 1989, Federal Express has still been able to maintain a yield of $14.99 per package, higher than the competition. Federal Express boasted extremely reliable service with a high degree of technological experience to enhance its service. With a well-known name, an extremely competitive advertising budget, and comprehensive service, Federal Express was expected to remain the industry leader.

■ United Parcel Service (UPS)

United Parcel Service has just recently entered the air express industry full force. UPS was the leader in ground transportation in the United States, handling nearly 3 billion packages per year in 1993. In 1991, UPS had overall revenues of $13.6 billion. In the early 1980s, UPS entered the air cargo market and in 1993 it had about 12 percent of the industry. Early in 1993 UPS followed Federal Express and began transmitting delivery data from its more than one hundred thousand trucks via satellite transmission. UPS had two air express services in 1993: 'red label' service (overnight by 10:30) and 'blue label' service (two-day). Both of them were money-back guaranteed. UPS was based out of Atlanta, Georgia, but had its main sorting hub in Louisville, Kentucky.

Being the largest ground transportation company in the United States, UPS conducted business with virtually all shippers within the United States via its ground service. Using over 100,000 delivery vehicles in its ground fleet, UPS had immersed itself in the overnight industry. UPS did business with so many of the companies that when these companies had an overnight package to ship, they could easily give the package to the UPS delivery person instead of making arrangements for another carrier. This "foot in the door" enabled UPS to get business they otherwise would not normally receive. Since the end of 1991, UPS has been aggressively advertising its overnight service. This marketing campaign along with its national name and color recognition enabled UPS to become an aggressive player in the industry.

■ DHL

DHL was known more for its international delivery service than for its domestic service. It was the number one carrier in the international express delivery industry. In the United States it delivered about 3 percent of the air express packages in 1993. Many of the packages it delivered in the United States were from abroad destined for the United States, not packages originating in the United States. Tracking was not automated for customer use at DHL, and was generally found to be slower than UPS, Federal, and Airborne Express. DHL offered only one level of service in 1993, that was overnight service. No form of deferred service was offered by DHL. DHL had its United States hub in Columbus, Ohio.

Being the leader in the international shipping industry, DHL got much of its domestic business as residuals from its international services. Customers who did the majority of their shipping in the international market would send their domestic packages through DHL for reasons of convenience. DHL also maintained its domestic hub and trucking facilities mainly to accommodate packages being shipped from overseas for distribution in the United States.

▪ United States Postal Service (USPS)

The United States Postal Service handled about 8 percent of the air express business in 1993. It had a distinct advantage over all the other couriers in that it was the only company that could deliver to a P.O. Box and thus much of its business is based on that fact. P.O. Boxes are Government property and other courier services cannot deliver packages to them. The USPS also boasted the convenience of having mailboxes and post offices in virtually all the towns and localities within the United States, thus giving it drop areas all throughout the United States. The USPS had its hub in Indianapolis, Indiana.

The USPS had two service levels in 1993. First was its Express Mail, guaranteed by 10:30 the next business morning, and second was its priority mail service for delivery in two days. Given that the USPS is a government-run organization, prices are fixed and not flexible. Thus, the USPS did not solicit new business.

THE COMPANY

As the fastest growing air express carrier in the United States for the tenth consecutive year, Airborne Express has built a reputation for providing reliable next-morning delivery of small packages and documents in a cost-effective manner for businesses throughout the United States. This has been led by a shipment growth rate of over twenty percent for each of the years from 1984 to 1993. With the promising market condition in 1994, Airborne Management expected this to continue its growth into the late 1990s.

▪ History

Airborne Express was created through a merger of Airborne Freight Corporation of California and Pacific Air Freight of Seattle, Washington, in 1968. Keeping the name of Airborne Freight Corporation (known in the industry as Airborne Express) and its headquarters in Seattle, Airborne was exclusively a freight forwarder until 1980 when it ventured into the overnight air express industry.

In 1993, with its own fleet of airplanes and its own airport (formerly Wilmington Airport, but now Airborne Air Park) in Wilmington, Ohio, Airborne Express was the third largest air express carrier in the United States, handling about 14 percent of the business, behind Federal Express and United Parcel Service.

With its fleet of 144 airplanes (90 were company owned and operated, and 54 chartered), its trucks, its 10 regional sort centers, and one main national sort center, Airborne Express delivered packages to every zip code in all 50 states, the District of Columbia, Puerto Rico, Guam, and the U.S. Virgin Islands through its domestic operations.

Airborne's airport hub in Wilmington, Ohio, was the nation's largest category II airport in 1993. The Wilmington hub had a sort capacity of 862,000 pieces per night. At the end of 1993, Airborne Express was averaging 685,900 shipments per night. Airborne also had related services to handle shipments destined overseas, covering over 200 countries worldwide.

Airborne Express was broken down into 12 different operating regions in the continental United States with over 240 delivery stations which housed the delivery and sales personnel.

MANAGEMENT

Airborne Express was a multidimensional company, legally known as Airborne Freight Corporation. Airborne Freight Corporation was the sales, customer service, and operational division of Airborne Express. Three subsidiaries constituted the remaining portion of Airborne Express.

ABX Air, Inc., headquartered in Wilmington, Ohio, was the airline division of Airborne Express responsible for moving the over half a million packages handled every evening. Sky Courier, the same-day delivery division of Airborne Express, worked out of Reston, Virginia. Advanced Logistics Services (ALS), also located in Wilmington, Ohio, was the newest addition to Airborne Express. ALS was the division responsible for the warehousing and shipping of goods for many companies that stored their merchandise in Airborne's Commerce Park at the Airborne Hub in Wilmington, Ohio.

Airborne management were extremely encouraged by the numbers posted at the end of 1993. In the 1993 Annual Report, Chairman and Chief Executive Officer Robert S. Kline and President and Chief Operating Officer Robert G. Brazier expressed enthusiasm about the future and the projects underway at Airborne in 1993. As the fastest-growing air express company in the United States for the tenth consecutive year, management had much to be proud of.

Since the middle of 1992, the company had undergone an intense push to reduce waste throughout the company. Costs were reduced in every facet of the company, from downsizing the secretarial pool in the sales offices, to automating more data input functions, and to cutting time doing major maintenance checks on the airplanes. This type of cost consciousness has allowed Airborne to continue to be the low-cost operator in the industry.

Officers of the company made themselves available to everyone, from people who worked within the company to customers who could reach the president through a 1-800 'hot-line' that rang in his office.

EMPLOYEES

Headquartered in Seattle, Washington, Airborne employed over 15,000 people worldwide in 1993. Outside of the headquarters in Seattle, and the airport in Wilmington, Ohio, Airborne had predominately three types of positions available: sales, operations, and customer service.

The sales force was split up into 12 regional sales teams, with regional managers in the following cities: Atlanta; Charlotte; Philadelphia; New York, NY; Norwalk, CT; Boston; Detroit; Chicago; Houston; Los Angeles; Seattle; and Denver. Sales teams were then split into different districts, usually following the patterns of the delivery stations within that region.

District managers usually handled from one to three different operating stations in densely populated areas, but might service more in the sparsely populated areas. Each district manager then had between one and six sales reps working for him or her, depending on the dollar volume of the district.

Operationally, things were different. In the over 240 domestic operating stations throughout the country, there was a mix of unionized and nonunionized locations. The majority of the nonunion stations were operated by what were called owner/operators, whose sole task was to pickup and deliver Airborne packages. Many of these were franchised. Using Airborne vehicles and Airborne clothing, these locations were paid a per-piece percentage of the packages they handled.

The managers who ran the stations were all Airborne employees, regardless of whether they were union or nonunion stations. This gave Airborne a handle on the responsibilities and priorities within the stations.

Customer service was another area that was split in 1993: some customer service centers were unionized while others were not. In all unionized areas, management and the unions respected each other so that the chance of a strike was minimal.

PRODUCT

Airborne Express handled all products, from letter-size envelopes to large, freight shipments. Domestically, Airborne focused its marketing on the small-package shipper (those customers shipping up to 70 pounds). Airborne handled international express shipping as well as international freight shipping. The international freight consisted of those items that weighed over 150 pounds. The domestic air express industry consisted of over 3 million packages being shipped each day. Since Airborne handled only 14 percent of the market in 1993, and they were adept in keeping the expenses down, they were expected to have a great opportunity for growth.

Airborne had been able to keep expenses down since the early 1980s, by limiting outside interference. Most work needed to be accomplished was done by internal sources, from printing business cards to repairing airplanes. With internal cost much less than potential external cost, money was saved. Those savings were then passed on to the consumer. With this Airborne had been consistently able to offer lower prices than the competition. Low cost has been the number one cause for the growth of Airborne Express.

SERVICES

Airborne Express offered three services in its domestic air express business, including overnight, next afternoon, and second-day (i.e., two-day) air service. All shipments had a printed, guaranteed delivery time, either in an Airborne Express customer service guide, or through a specialty contract set between the shipper and Airborne Express.

Each evening over 140 airplanes moved into action to bring the nearly 700,000 packages into the Airborne system for sorting and redistribution back to the appropriate airplane destined to the appropriate city. For example, Airborne currently had six airplanes flying out of the New York Metropolitan area. Two fly from Newark Airport, two from Kennedy Airport, one from Stewart Airport in Newburgh, NY, and one from a small airport in western New Jersey.

■ Overnight

Overnight shipments, which are those packages shipped for delivery the next business morning, had increased nearly tenfold from 1984 to 1993. Since 1979, when Airborne Express came out with its next afternoon and two-day services, the percentage of overnight packages handled by Airborne has declined.

■ Select Delivery Service (under 5 pounds)

Airborne Express's policy was that all shipments shipped via the Select Delivery Service route, the deferred service for Airborne, would have a different guaranteed delivery time than the overnight shipments. If the weight of the package was under five pounds, Airborne would deliver those packages by 3 p.m. the next business afternoon.

■ Select Delivery Service (over 5 pounds)

Airborne Express's third service was only for packages weighing over 5 pounds that were marked for Select Delivery Service. These packages were considered two-day packages in 1993. The delivery guarantee for these packages was for 5 p.m. on the second business day.

In 1991, Select Delivery packages accounted for 17 percent of all shipments tendered by Airborne; in 1992, that number rose to 25 percent; and in 1993, that number totaled 31 percent of the total shipment volume. This brought down the revenue per shipment due to the lower prices paid per package with the deferred level of shipping, but management believed that much of the gain in the SDS service was at the expense of ground carriers and not at the expense of their own higher-yield overnight service.

■ Next Flight Out (NFO)

Sky Courier was an independently operated, wholly owned subsidiary of Airborne Express. Its responsibilities were to deliver packages that customers urgently needed. These packages were considered next-flight-out packages and were expensive to the shipper. Sky Courier was open every day of the year, 24 hours a day. Important packages such as law documents and organs for transplant were shipped via this premium service. This emergency service, even with the cost of a few hundred dollars a package, grew by 27 percent in 1993.

■ Logistical Services

In early 1993 Airborne Express introduced a new subsidiary called Advanced Logistics Services (ALS). This group enabled Airborne to manage inventory, order replacement equipment or parts, print plane tickets, and offer the best possible solutions to customers' logistics needs.

Attached to Airborne's hub airport facility in Wilmington, OH, Airborne's Commerce Park facility was completed with access to Airborne's 900,000- square-foot stock exchange in 1992. The stock exchange warehoused merchandise that enabled customers to access their merchandise until 2:00 a.m. eastern time for delivery the next morning in the United States and Canada. Airborne's own employees oversaw, shipped, and tracked the packages. [*Airborne Express News,* Summer 1993].

Within the commerce park was a central print facility that enabled customers to print digitized images, plane tickets, or any printed materials as late as 2:00 a.m. for delivery that same day. The commerce park was located within one hour's driving time from Cincinnati, Dayton, and Columbus so if it was necessary to get a particular part or item out on the same day that the request was made, there were hundreds of flights available to get them there. In addition to the stock exchange located at the commerce park, Airborne also had regional stock exchanges located in major cities throughout the United States.

CUSTOMERS

Airborne Express was an interesting case in that they did not advertise. This made selling to small customers a little more difficult due to lack of name recognition. Therefore, Airborne and its sales representatives generally worked on larger customers where recognition came from industry knowledge, not advertisement. The customer segments that Airborne specialized in were the national account and small business segments. Catalogue shippers, specifically those that shipped their products to commercial establishments, were also aggressively pursued.

■ National Account Segment

Airborne Express was a leader within the national account segment. There were a number of different types of national account customers, including those that had multiple shipping locations throughout the country, banks such as Chemical Bank, and insurance companies such as American International Group. They all qualified as national account due to the large number of shipping locations and also the great number of shipments they tendered on a monthly basis. Large corporations such as IBM and General Motors also qualified as national account customers due to their high volume, although they were shipping from a limited number of locations. The dollar cutoff in 1993 for a national account was any customer that shipped over one hundred thousand dollars in one month.

Airborne also recognized companies that did not have many locations through a special mini-national account program. These companies shared the same characteristics of larger national accounts, but they only had a dollar volume amount of between five thousand and one hundred thousand dollars a month. Companies such as Waldbaum's Food Stores qualified as a mini-national account.

■ Small Business Segment

Airborne Express made the small business market a target through its unique PACE program. This program was developed by Airborne Express to give small customers an alternative over the higher-priced competition. This program was available to all customers regardless of shipping volume and could result in savings of up to 40 percent off of published shipping rates.

PACE customers enjoyed the same high service standard given to Airborne's larger customers, without having to pay the higher prices of the competition. This savings could be substantial for customers who shipped twenty to twenty-five packages a week. The program was run through the sales reps of Airborne, all of whom were required to send kits (called PACE kits) to fifteen different new/prospective customers per week. These customers were found through cold-calling and knocking on door-to-door selling.

■ Individual Shipping Segment

Airborne did not cater to the individual shipping market. The main issue here was not price, but service requirements. Most individuals ship only one package at a time. This becomes costly. When a driver is dispatched to pick up one package, the cost is the same as if he/she were picking up many. Thus the cost per package is too high for Airborne. This shipping segment was also not a high growth market, thus the profit potential was not significant. Unlike its competition, Airborne did not have retail stores available for convenient drop off of packages for individual shippers. And without this convenience, many individual shippers were turned off. The price of the package, although probably less with Airborne than with its competition, was not generally a major concern for this market.

Finally, since Airborne Express did not advertise, many individual consumers had never heard of Airborne Express. Although this image problem was not good, since this was not the target market, the impact on Airborne was not substantial.

■ Catalogue Shipping Segment

Airborne Express was not the major player with the catalogue shipping segment. Although they were a large force in the overnight air express industry, Airborne Express selected its customers very carefully. There were two types of catalogue shipper. One was the cataloguer that catered to businesses. The other was the cataloguer that catered to individual/residential customers. Airborne coveted and worked closely to acquire the business of the first type, the business-to-business catalogue shipper. The cost of delivering the package was simply less expensive than shipping to a residence.

Many residential catalogue shippers realized this problem and tried to work with carriers to help bring the cost down by finding out from the purchaser whether an item they were buying could be delivered to their place of business as opposed to their home. A lower delivery price was given to the consumer for those packages going to businesses. Two major cataloguers that shipped with Airborne in 1993 were two computer-related giants, MacWarehouse and Microsoft.

TECHNOLOGY

As delivery costs were dropping, and services became less differentiated, technology was becoming a point of competition among the major carriers in the 1990s.

■ Customer Automation

Airborne supplied its volume shippers with hardware and software for use in shipping their packages. The program was called Libra II. This program gave customers the ability to store repetitive consignees, create daily shipping reports, invoice themselves daily, and also track incoming, outgoing, or any package for which they had the shipment number.

■ Tracking

Airborne Express had state-of-the-art technology for tracking shipments. Packages could be tracked from a customer's office if they had their own computer or an Airborne-supplied computer system (for large-volume customers) along with Airborne's on-line tracking software. They could also call Airborne customer services for tracking information.

There were three ways that Airborne drivers transmitted their daily delivery information to the corporate mainframe in 1993. First, drivers could download their scanners into a scanner board at the delivery station. This sent a record of what packages had been scanned to the main computer in Seattle. Second, telephone couplers allowed drivers to transmit data from regular telephones to the mainframe. The driver could call a 1-800 number from a pay phone, attach a small, hand-held attachment to his scanner, wait for a hissing tone on the phone, and put the coupler over the mouthpiece of the phone. This transmitted the data through the phone line. This was especially helpful for those drivers whose routes took them far from their home station. All drivers were required to do this phone coupler download by 11:00 a.m. and again by 1:00 p.m. to record delivery times. When a driver returned to his home station, his scanner was then downloaded completely to verify the original transmission. Finally, the technology was available for Airborne drivers to plug themselves into Airborne-supplied computers situated at strategic locations for dial-up and transmittal purposes only. This third type of technology was becoming obsolete due to the expanding use of the telephone couplers.

■ Electronic Data Interchange (EDI)

Airborne Express was the industry leader in Electronic Data Interchange (EDI) technology. By connecting with the customer through a disk to disk or tape to tape transfer, Airborne could eliminate hours of research by accounts payable personnel. The EDI procedure provided the customer with invoice information in a format that met the requirements of the customer. This type of transfer eliminated the need for paper invoices and re-keying by the accounts payable department. Airborne also supported EDI electronic remittance, which automated the payment process through an electronic transfer of funds. In 1993 alone, Airborne had an increase of 30 percent in the number of customers doing business through EDI.

■ Linkage

Airborne was also the industry leader in linkage programs. The linkage programs not only enabled customers who used order entry as their main internal invoicing system, but also enabled Airborne to integrate that information into its system for creating package labels and an invoicing system. This procedure worked well with catalogue companies that did order entry. This enabled the order entry, customer invoicing, and label printing to be completed in one procedure, as opposed to having different departments duplicating the work.

OUTLETS

There are three major types of outlets for overnight shipping services: Customers can have a driver pick up their packages, drop packages in drop boxes, or drop off packages at delivery stations.

■ Driver Pickup

Airborne Express supplied driver pickups for all customers free of charge. Pickups could be set up in two ways. First, the driver could be scheduled for a daily pickup from any customer that shipped on a daily basis. Pickups would generally be scheduled at the same time each day. The second type of pickup would be for customers that did not ship on a daily basis. These customers could call in for a driver to stop by to pick up their packages. Both of these services were free of charge.

■ Drop Boxes

Airborne had drop boxes located at strategic locations within major cities, at airports, hotels, and at large gathering places in more rural areas. They were used by those customers who wanted to drop their packages at a convenient location, and allowed local shippers to drop their packages off without waiting on a scheduled pickup, or drop off additional packages after the original daily pickup. Drop boxes could be picked up later than customer office pickups due to the roadside location of these boxes.

■ Drop Stations

Customers could also drop packages at Airborne Express delivery stations. These stations were located in all major cities and some smaller towns throughout the country. These stations offered the latest drop-off times for any packages within the respective areas. Most of the drop stations were located near or on the premises of the airport to reduce travel time between the unloading and loading of trucks and the loading and unloading of the airplanes.

■ Marketing

Management at Airborne had always stressed customer service and a close contact with clients as the way to ensure that a customer's desires were met to the fullest. Customer service was where Airborne excelled. Price and national contracts were always important, but management believed personal contact was extremely important. Airborne's sales strategy used telephone sales reps whose sole responsibility was to cold-call customers to solicit business. This worked very well when soliciting the smaller, low-volume shipper.

■ Finance

Overall, Airborne Express enjoyed a good performance in 1994 (see Exhibit 11). The final numbers for Airborne Express's domestic services in 1993 are shown in Exhibit 12.

Accounting changes in 1993 accounted for another $.20 per share to be added to the net earnings, bringing the earnings per common share to $1.86. Total shipment count was up by 23 percent in 1993, once again allowing Airborne Express to be the industry leader in that category. Overall capital expenditures were down nearly $140 million. This, along with the improved earnings, produced a stronger cash flow and allowed for a $31.8 million reduction in debt.

Exhibit 11	Airborne Express Selected Consolidated Financial Data				
	1994	*1993*	*1992*	*1991*	*1990*
			(in thousands except per share data)		
Operating Results:					
Revenues					
Domestic	$1,660,003	$1,484,787	$1,259,792	$1,144,791	$982,268
International	310,756	235,194	224,524	222,256	199,622
Total	1,970,759	1,719,981	1,484,316	1,367,047	1,181,890
Operating Expenses	1,881,821	1,636,861	1,456,450	1,307,790	1,117,594
Earnings From Operations	88,938	83,120	27,866	59,257	64,296
Interest, Net	24,663	24,093	18,779	10,842	8,857
Earnings Before Taxes	64,275	59,027	9,087	48,415	55,439
Income Taxes	25,440	23,738	3,930	18,416	21,862
Net Earnings Before Changes in Accounting	38,835	35,289	5,157	29,999	33,577
Cumulative Effect of Changes in Accounting	—	3,828	—	—	—
Net Earnings	38,835	39,117	5,157	29,999	33,577
Preferred Stock Dividends	894	2,760	2,760	2,760	2,548
Net Earnings Available to Common Shareholders	$37,941	$36,357	$2,397	$27,239	$31,029
Net Earnings Per Common Share					
Primary	$1.81	$1.66*	$.12	$1.40	$1.76
Fully Diluted	$1.74	$1.64*	$.12	$1.40	$1.76
Dividends Per Common Share	$.30	$.30	$.30	$.30	$.30
Average Primary Shares Outstanding	21,001	19,596	19,423	19,471	17,626

Exhibit 12	Airborne Express Financial Picture		
	1993	*1992*	*1991**
Operating Results			
Revenues			
Domestic	$1,484,787	$1,259,792	$1,144,791
International	$235,194	$224,524	$222,256
Total	$1,719,981	$1,484,316	$1,367,047
Operating Expenses	$1,636,861	$1,456,450	$1,307,790
Earnings from Operations	$83,120	$27,866	$59,257
Interest, Net	$24,093	$18,779	$10,842
Earnings Before Income Taxes	$59,027	$9,087	$48,415
Income Taxes	$23,738	$3,930	$18,416
Net Earnings before Changes in Accounting	$35,289	$5,157	$29,999
Cumulative effect of Changes in Accounting	$3,828	$0	$0
Net Earnings	$39,117	$5,157	$29,999
Preferred Stock Dividends	$2,760	$2,760	$2,760
Net Earnings Available to Common Shareholders	$36,357	$2,397	$27,239
Net Earnings Per Common Share			
Primary	$1.66	$0.12	$1.40
Fully Diluted	$1.64	$0.12	$1.40
Dividends Per Common Share	$0.30	$0.30	$0.30
Average Primary Share Outstanding	$19,596	$19,423	$19,471
Financial Structure			
Working Capital	$60,564	$50,276	$26,618
Property and Equipment	$733,963	$730,937	$613,149
Total Assets	$1,006,909	$964,739	$823,647
Long-Term Debt	$269,250	$303,335	$153,279
Subordinated Debt	$122,150	$125,720	$129,290
Redeemable Preferred Stock	$40,000	$40,000	$40,000
Shareholders' Equity	$318,824	$285,639	$287,344

*In thousands except per share data

LOOKING TOWARD THE FUTURE

Airborne Express, in 1994, handled packages destined for delivery by the next afternoon or by 3 p.m. Only packages under five pounds were eligible for this next afternoon service. The management at Airborne was wondering if they should modify the next afternoon service to handle packages of all weights, or should it continue with its current setup.

One group of management argued that with some more hands-on management, Airborne could manipulate its current system to accommodate more packages. These packages, which would be for afternoon delivery, would give Airborne some more leverage in the overnight/next afternoon shipping environment in relation to its chief competitor Federal Express. Airborne had in place a procedure to handle all packages up to 150 pounds for overnight delivery in 1993. Adding an additional all-encompassing service would require some creativity in the operational area, but it was possible.

Another group of management argued that using the current equipment available, planes could fly during the day to alleviate some of the nighttime congestion and possible freight overload. Additional personnel could be hired to do the sorting, loading of planes, and delivery of packages. Additions to the existing sort center could be made to increase the maximum capacity.

Telling customers about the service could be done by flyers sent in invoices. Those customers with Airborne-supplied computers could receive a message on the screen to explain about the new service. Prices could be kept in check through the same cost-reduction procedures currently in place.

There would be no competition from UPS with this new service. UPS did not provide customers with a next afternoon service in 1993. The competition with Federal Express would be similar to that with the Priority Overnight Service. Since the service would be identical (both guaranteeing delivery by 3:00 p.m.), Airborne would have better rates available because costs were lower at Airborne.

Cost would be a large problem in getting this service started. The initial cost of more equipment (both airplanes and trucks) would be tremendous. The planes would be necessary because the 1993 capacity utilization on the Airborne airplanes was about 85–90%. With the conditions in 1994, Airborne had only one runway to work with; even if flights would be making more than one trip in a day, runway space would be needed to handle these extra flights. The budget would also be a major concern. After having a tough year in 1992, stockholders might be troubled by additional large expenditures and low earnings two years so close to each other. Faced with such arguments, Airborne executives were wondering how to approach the evolving industry and market conditions in 1995.

REFERENCES

"A Third-Party Analysis of Service and Pricing for Overnight Deliveries," *What to Buy for Business*, March 1993, pp. 1–10.

"Aerospace and Air Transport Basic Analysis," *Standard & Poor's Industry Surveys*, July 1, 1993, pp. A40–A41.

Air Express Services/'92, International Business.

Airborne Express Annual Report, 1992 & 1993.

"Airborne Introduces New Subsidiary: Advanced Logistics Services," *Express News*, Summer 1993, p. 1.

Aviation Week & Space Technology, April 26, 1993, p. 38.

Bradley, Peter, "Buyers take all in Package Slugfest," *Purchasing*, Oct. 22, 1992, pp. 48–51.

"FedEx Updates Tracking System," *Air Transport World*, March 1993, p. 48.

History of Airborne Express, Brochure.

Hoffman, Kurt, "Setting New Sites," *Distribution*, December 1992, pp. 58 & 61.

"Looking Ahead: Freight Transport," *Gifts and Decorative Accessories*, May 1992, p. 38.

"Third Quarter '93 Earnings Reported, Right Now," *Airborne Express Special News Bulletin*, October 25, 1993.

Traffic Management, March 1993, pp. 85–124.

"United Parcel Service: The Air Cargo Industry," *Strategic Management*, 1993, pp. 881–903.

Appendix A: An Example of the Hub-and-Spoke System

Formerly, a package picked up in New York destined for San Francisco was bundled together with other packages destined for the San Francisco Area. They were sent via commercial airline to San Francisco. This sounds fine on a one city to one city transport, but there were also packages every night going from New York to hundreds of other cities. That would mean that packages in New York would have to be sorted and loaded onto a plane to each of those locations. This is not very practical.

Thus, the success of the *hub-and-spoke* system of shipping is its practicality. A package, picked up in New York, going to Los Angeles will now be flown from New York with all packages from the New York Metropolitan Area to the carrier's hub airport. There, these packages are combined with packages from all over the country and sorted by destination and redistributed to the airplane going to the packages' ultimate destination. Using this procedure, only one sort process is necessary.

Packages are then delivered by van or light truck to the appropriate destinations. (See Exhibit 6)

Appendix B: Products
in the Domestic Air Express Industry

Documents are a combination of Letters and Envelopes. Examples of documents are payroll, proxy statements, and negotiable securities.

Small packages range in weight from four to 70 pounds. These consist of inter-office paperwork shipped weekly from one office to another, computer parts, and drug samples.

Packages are shipments that weigh between 70 and 150 pounds. Packages are items such as computers, boxes of books, and retail store merchandise.

Dakota, Minnesota & Eastern Railroad: A Light at the End of the Tunnel

Paul Reed, Sam Houston State University
Carol J. Cumber, South Dakota State University

John C. "Pete" McIntyre caught himself shaking his head as he thought back over his almost nine years as President of the Dakota, Minnesota & Eastern Railroad (DM&E). Pete remembered the railroad's first days in 1986: no working capital, track and roadbed that had not been properly maintained in 20 years, old locomotives, and a lack of freight cars. Over the years, droughts, blizzards, wild fire, record rains, and subsequent flooding had contributed to DM&E's woes. To add to the company's problems was an unfriendly Chicago & NorthWestern Railroad (C&NW), the DM&E's major customer and supplier.

The DM&E had been a survivor, Pete thought. Over time, $60 million had been put into track rehabilitation, locomotive purchase, and freight car leasing. The railroad was now better prepared to meet the uncertainty of the elements. Even the C&NW had loosened, somewhat, its stranglehold on the DM&E.

Most of the events of the past year appeared to bode well for the DM&E. In July 1994, the railroad refinanced its long-term debt at considerable savings. In March 1995, the State of South Dakota had agreed to issue $35 million in state revenue bonds to finance the rebuilding of the western 266 miles of the railroad. In April 1995, the powerful, and hopefully more friendly, Union Pacific Railroad (UP) purchased the C&NW. Pete knew that the next few years would be all important to the DM&E. When and how the railroad would get to the light at the end of the tunnel would occupy Pete's thoughts for some time.

INDUSTRY BACKGROUND

In the 160-year history of railroading in the United States, the industry traveled through some of its most profound changes during the past 25 years. The combination of deregulation in the transportation arena, basic changes in the nature and output of American heavy industry, the loss of local business, the use of Continental United States as a bridge for cargo that formerly passed through the Panama Canal, and the dramatic increase in long-distance coal movement for power generation have caused the railroads of today to be far different from the traditional railroads of yesterday. In essence, railroads were once responsible for hauling almost everything and everybody into and out of every city and village, and accounted for 75 percent of all United States intercity freight ton-miles in 1929.[1] The volume of freight handled by today's railroads is some 260 percent of that of 1929, although modal share has been lost to trucks, river carriers, and pipelines. In 1993, railroads handled 38 percent of all freight ton-miles.[2] Thus, railroads have evolved from general freight carriers to specialized freight carriers primarily handling large-volume bulk commodities, oversized or bulky loads, and general products and merchandise when combined into container or trailer-sized lots (intermodal).

The Interstate Commerce Commission (ICC) classifies all of the common carrier railroads operating within the United States into one of three categories based primarily on annual operating revenue. The major rail freight carriers are defined as Class I railroads and must meet an adjustable revenue threshold for a period of three continuous years. In 1993, this threshold was $253.7 million. Regional railroads are those carriers that operate at least 350 miles of track and/or earn revenue between $40 million and the Class I threshold. The DM&E is classified as a regional railroad, the second largest of 34 such mid-sized carriers in the United States. Local railroads are all those that fall below the regional railroad criteria and include Switching and Terminal railroads. A comparison of these three types of railroads is shown in Exhibit 1.

THE BEGINNINGS

During the 1970s and into the 1980s, the railroad industry in the upper Midwest had felt drastic changes stemming from the deregulation of both trucking

Exhibit 1	**Types of Railroad in the United States: 1994**			
Type of Railroad	*Number*	*Miles Operated*	*Employees*	*Annual Revenue ($000,000)*
Class I	12	123,738	189,086	$27,990
Regional	34	21,581	11,642	1,543
Local	463	23,645	12,530	1,241
Totals	**509**	**168,964**	**213,258**	**30,774**

Source: Association of American Railroads, *Railroad Facts: 1994*, p. 3

and railroads, the decline of heavy industry, the loss of local railroad business, the growth of coal traffic, and mergers. During this period, many lines merged, were downsized, or disappeared with pieces purchased by former competitors or, in many cases, entrepreneurs desiring to operate their own railroad.

The C&NW was particularly active during this time frame, purchasing and then abandoning major portions of competitors—Chicago GreatWestern (1,450 miles) and Minneapolis and Saint Louis (1,300 miles)—plus acquiring the Minneapolis-Kansas City line of the Rock Island (600 miles). By the late 1980s, the C&NW had also sold or abandoned some 4,500 miles of its own trackage. Included in this downsizing was the vast majority of its lines in Minnesota and South Dakota.

Most of the trackage of what is now the DM&E (Exhibit 2) was unprofitable for the C&NW for several years. In 1983 and again in 1985 the C&NW petitioned to abandon the line from five miles west of Pierre to Rapid City. This action would leave South Dakota with no centrally located east-west rail transportation. C&NW's requests were met with unusually strong opposition from the State and U.S. Senator Larry Pressler, R-South Dakota. Realizing that abandonment was no longer a wise move, the C&NW was faced with either continued operations or sale. All parties agreed that the former was not feasible and therefore the C&NW initiated actions to find a buyer.

Lengthy negotiations ended in September 1986, with the sale of what is now the DM&E to a group of investors. The $26 million agreement was heavily leveraged, with Westinghouse Credit Corporation the primary lender and the C&NW assuming a $4 million subordinated note.

Exhibit 2   **DM&E Dakota, Minnesota & Eastern Railroad**

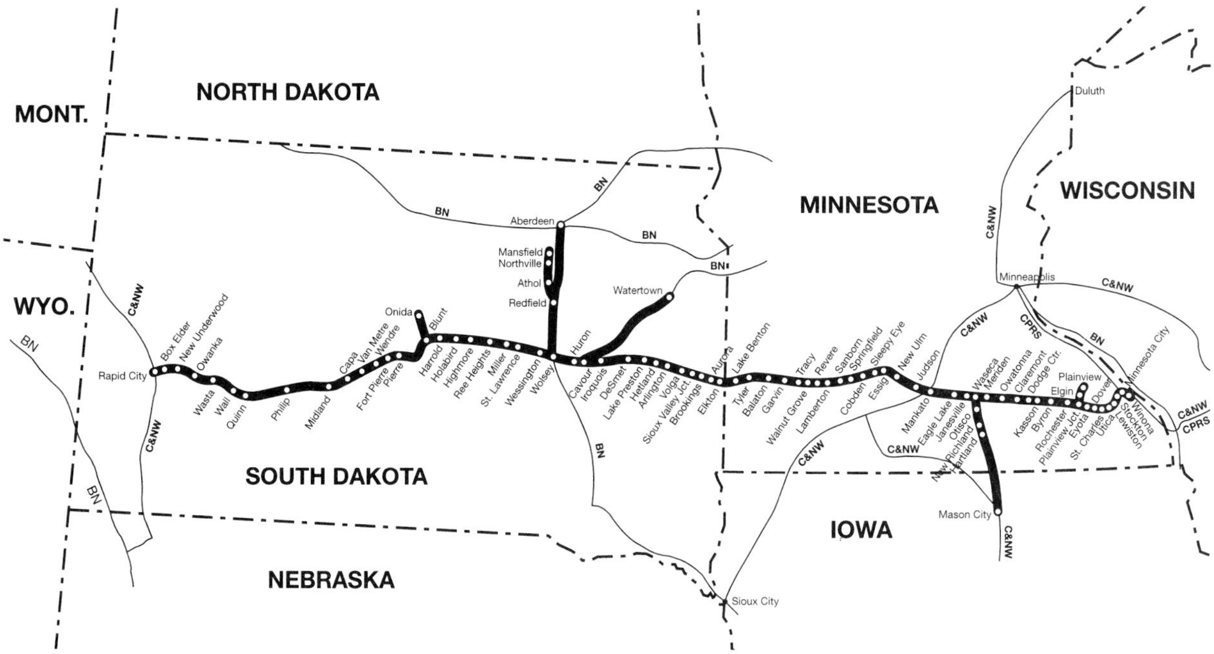

The buyers acquired 826 miles of track and rights to operate on an additional 139 miles. Included were 18 C&NW locomotives, averaging 35 years old, and maintenance and repair equipment. The C&NW retained ownership of the tracks at the DM&E's main interchanges at Winona and Mankato, MN, Mason City, IA, and Rapid City, SD. It also could exercise veto power over DM&E's rates and route proposals or any changes in existing financing. The new line also had to agree to pay substantial monetary penalties unless 89 percent of DM&E's originated traffic was loaded in C&NW freight cars.[3]

Of additional concern to newly hired President "Pete" McIntyre were the assumptions others had used in entering the purchase agreement, and the agreement itself. Traffic projections had been overstated. The physical condition of track was far worse than estimated. Revenue projections were based on an unrealistic level of business. The DM&E was seriously undercapitalized. Many were of the opinion that the C&NW had been paid far too much for the property. Also, the negotiators had, in effect, severely limited McIntyre and his subordinates' ability to operate the road efficiently by agreeing to the aforementioned C&NW restrictions.

INTERNAL ENVIRONMENT

■ Description of the Railroad

The DM&E is headquartered in Brookings, SD, and operates mainly in South Dakota and Minnesota. A 69-mile branch line serves Mason City, Iowa. Exhibit 3 shows that the Winona-Rapid City main line and the trackage to Mason City carry the greatest freight tonnages. It also indicates that most traffic is

Exhibit 3　　**DM&E Railroad 1994 Freight Density Map Shown in Million Gross Tons per Mile (no scale)**

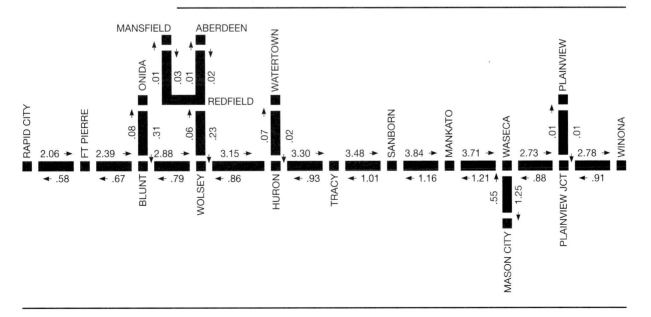

east-bound. West-bound trains consist mainly of empty cars being returned for loading. Track conditions on most of the line prevent freight train speeds in excess of 25 mph and approximately 40% of the line can only support 10 mph.

The DM&E serves the main line with a minimum six day per week commercial train (See Glossary) service between Rapid City and Winona. A similar schedule handles freight between Waseca, MN, and Mason City. During peak months (June-October) two trains per seven day week are often scheduled. Extra trains also originate at points between Pierre and Waseca to handle grain and other tonnage. Branch lines see trains on an as-needed basis. Local freights provide service to many on-line customers, thus relieving commercial trains from making numerous stops between Rapid City and Winona.

Freight cars are sorted and blocked at the division points at Waseca and Huron, S.D. The DM&E must turn over most of its traffic to the UP(C&NW) at its four principal gateways. This forces the DM&E to pay the UP(C&NW) switching charges in excess of $100 per car or share revenue on all through traffic. Exhibit 4 indicates the size of the largest cities (1990 Census) along the DM&E route and the ownership of the trackage.

The company owns and operates car and locomotive repair shops at Huron. Major repairs and overhauls are performed on the road's 59 locomotives. Similar services are provided, on an as-needed basis, to freight cars of other railroads. All active locomotives have been rebuilt or received major overhaul since start-up. The availability rate for locomotives is over 96 percent and approaches 100 percent during the winter months, when many units are stored due to lower traffic requirements. During the summer-fall season, the DM&E is often required to lease a few locomotives to handle increased traffic.

Grain and grain-derived products make up 45 percent of the DM&E's carloads. Grain shipments include South Dakota wheat and corn and soybeans

---

Exhibit 4   **Largest Cities and Track Ownership**

State	City	Size	Track Ownership
Minnesota	Winona	47,828	UP(C&NW)
	Rochester	70,745	DM&E
	Owatonna	19,386	UP(C&NW)
	Waseca	18,079	DM&E
	Mankato	31,477	UP(C&NW)
Iowa	Mason City	29,040	UP(C&NW)
South Dakota	Brookings	16,270	DM&E
	Huron	12,448	DM&E & BN
	Watertown	17,592	BN & DM&E
	Aberdeen	24,927	BN & DM&E
	Pierre	12,906	DM&E
	Rapid City	54,523	UP(C&NW)

Source: U.S. Government—1990 Census

from eastern South Dakota and the western two-thirds of Minnesota. The second major item of traffic is bentonite clay (used in foundry operations, oil drilling, iron ore pelletizing, and cat litter) which is turned over by the UP(C&NW) at Rapid City for delivery by DM&E to its lines farther east. Other major traffic sources include industrial sand, cement, wood chips, lumber, and kaolin clay (used in the manufacturing of cement). Exhibit 5 shows the traffic mix.

■ Mission

In the words of President Pete McIntyre, to provide rail users in the upper Midwest with consistent, damage-free, on time, wholesale and retail transportation service with the intent of moderate growth and profitability, recognizing its employees as valuable assets and with the aim of being customer driven.[4]

■ Senior Management

The DM&E maintains a lean organization throughout its entire structure. Senior management appears relatively young, well qualified, and highly motivated.

John C. McIntyre—Director, President, and Chief Executive Officer. His thirty-seven year railroad career includes 29 years with the C&NW where he advanced from clerk to Assistant Vice President and Division Manager—Chicago. McIntyre also has an equity position in the railroad.

Lynn A. Anderson—Director, Vice-President of Marketing and Public Affairs. He is responsible for marketing, pricing, sales and serves as liaison to various federal, state, and local governments. Spent 15 years with the C&NW,

Exhibit 5	Historical Carloadings by Category (1989-1994)					
Categories of Traffic	*1989*	*1990*	*1991*	*1992*	*1993*	*1994*
Wheat	6,664	8,949	10,532	9,883	11,319	10,353
Bentonite Clay	740	6,756	9,054	9,666	9,545	10,737
Woodchips	3,450	3,768	3,232	3,353	2,369	2,359
Corn	8,436	10,443	8,045	8,469	4,281	4,601
Cement	3,321	1,976	2,171	2,853	2,581	2,514
Industrial Sand	4,055	5,040	2,369	3,407	3,040	3,276
Lumber/Boards	109	825	656	546	458	454
Soybeans	1,902	2,915	2,766	2,973	1,921	2,275
Kaolin Clay	0	663	1,036	1,295	2,321	466
Soybean Oil	1,458	1,566	1,969	1,971	2,231	2,005
Wheat Flour	434	966	974	930	891	1,124
All Others	9,644	8,721	8,658	9,814	9,813	10,429
Totals	**40,024**	**52,588**	**51,462**	**55,160**	**51,040**	**50,593**

Source: Company records

rising to the position of general manager of grain marketing and pricing. Anderson also has an equity position on the railroad.

Robert F. Irwin—Vice-President Transportation. He is responsible for scheduling, train operations, dispatching, personnel (engineers, conductors, and brakemen) and division point operations. Irwin spent 22 years with the C&NW where he held various operating positions in the Midwest.

James H. Appleman—Chief Mechanical Officer. He oversees providing operational maintenance for locomotive and freight cars so that the DM&E can meet projected traffic levels and customer service requirements. He spent 20 years with CONRAIL, where he rose from welder to Manager of Yards & Productivity.

Kurt V. Feaster—Chief Financial Officer. He is involved in finance, personnel, accounting, and computer information activities. Has served in various financial capacities for three different railroads during the past 25 years. Last served as Chief Financial Officer for the Wheeling & Lake Erie Railway.

Douglas G. DeBerg—Chief Engineer. He is responsible for upgrading and maintaining the railroad infrastructure, including track, bridges, signals, and buildings. Has spent over 30 years working in various engineering capacities for five different railroads. DeBerg joined the DM&E July 1, 1995.

■ Corporate Philosophy

DM&E has made a long-term commitment to provide reliable freight service and not diversify into nonrail efforts. Overall, DM&E believes in strengthening its position as a rail freight carrier in the upper Midwest by making its existing system more efficient and serving its present territory better. Accordingly, DM&E increased revenues by enlarging its market share of freight shipped by existing customers, by regaining customers who had shifted to trucks when the railroad was operated by previous owners, by serving new shippers in its territory, and by improving relations with other railroads. The railroad continues to employ a strategy of strengthening its existing traffic base and increasing its market share within the territory it serves rather than expanding much beyond South Dakota and Minnesota. The DM&E has also shown great interest in better controlling its main traffic interchanges such as the UP(C&NW) Colony Line that delivers over 20,000 cars a year to the DM&E at Rapid City. Also, ownership of UP's (C&NW) Winona freight yard would permit direct interchange with Mississippi River barge traffic and the Canadian Pacific Railroad (CP).

■ Marketing

The DM&E has the freedom to set rates within a relevant range of pricing and has aggressively gone after traffic from both large and small shippers. It has initiated long-term agreements with large shippers to stabilize its traffic base; given eight to 10 percent discounts to grain shippers who make unit train shipments of 25 cars or more; and has initiated pricing and service packages to provide South Dakota and Minnesota farmers markets in Texas, the Eastern United States, the Pacific west coast, and the gulf coast via the Mississippi River. The DM&E adds or reschedules train service and has opened a computerized Customer Service Center to improve rail-customer interface.

The DM&E knows the importance of the customer and has done considerable research and planning to identify customer needs and packaging services to satisfy them. Marketing V.P. Lynn Anderson feels that the Customer Service Center has enabled the DM&E to better determine customer expectations in terms of car supply, transit times, loss or damage, billing, switching, car tracing, response time, etc.[5] While DM&E's innovative ideas affect shippers and receivers of all categories of traffic, the marketing of grain is of particular interest. The DM&E took advantage of the Winona end of track on the Mississippi River by developing a rail-barge service that opened up new markets to shippers and receivers at prices that took advantage of cheaper barge rates. Going in the opposite direction, DM&E has been dispatching unit grain trains to the Pacific Northwest via the Burlington Northern Railroad (BN). In March 1995 alone, the DM&E originated eleven 54 car grain trains.

The DM&E has also been successful in gaining some new industry along its lines. For example, a new soybean processing facility in Volga, S.D., will add approximately 1,500 carloads annually.

DM&E's innovative efforts, however, are often offset by the weather. The rains and floods of 1993 greatly reduced corn and soybean production and resulted in the DM&E moving 4,500 fewer carloads in 1993 and 1994. High water closed down the Winona rail-barge operation for several weeks in both years. Conversely, 1994 was an excellent year for all crops and the DM&E anticipates large shipments of all types of grain in 1995.

Lynn Anderson's department also faces other challenges: the demographics of the DM&E service area limit the size and nature of the railroad's target markets; occasional freight car shortages, particularly during peak demand; some difficulty in interchanging traffic with the UP(C&NW); and prior agreements precluding car interchange with the CP at Winona impact on shippers, receivers, and the DM&E itself.

■ Transportation

Providing accident-free, timely service that meets customer needs is a never-ending challenge to the DM&E. Poor track, interchange difficulties, lack of adequate passing sidings to permit train meets, locomotive and train crew shortages, and the weather have too often equated to high operating costs, train derailments, and unsatisfied customers. The DM&E inherited trackage that, in the main, had not received adequate maintenance in 20 to 30 years. A great portion of the line west of Huron, for example, is the original 72 pound (per yard) rail laid in the early 1900s. Eighty odd years of pounding have made the track and the supporting grade increasingly unable to support 100 ton railcars moving at speeds much above 10 mph.

DM&E tracks end short of the yards at Mason City, Rapid City, and Winona and, as a result, entry, car switching, and exit are controlled by the UP(C&NW). DM&E trains were often forced to idle for several hours waiting for the C&NW(UP) yard crews to put outgoing trains together or clear tracks for incoming cars.

Lack of adequate sidings (6,000 ft.) often causes one DM&E train to wait several hours for a meet with a train coming from the opposite direction. Additional time is lost when there is a shortage of rested train crews or a lack of locomotives.

The weather adds its toll. Winter may cause trains to take 120 hours to make the Rapid City-Winona trip rather than the ideal 60 hours. Heavy rains result in unstable track and, coupled with deferred maintenance, ultimately causes 80 percent of the derailments that annually cost the DM&E $3 million. (Individual derailment costs varied from a few thousand dollars to over $1 million.)

Some or all of the above factors cause train crew overtime, extra crews, higher freight car rental expenses, and increased locomotive fuel and maintenance costs. These items can easily add $1 million to operating expenses. Vice President Bob Irwin and his Transportation Department continually fight to improve service while lowering costs. Yard engine crews now assemble trains, conduct air tests, and often take the train a mile or two out of town. All the commercial train crew has to do is climb aboard and depart. This division of duties saves the commercial crew two to three hours, thus reducing overtime and improving transit time. Irwin also has added three local freight trains that pick up and deliver freight cars to the many grain elevators and businesses along the line. This enables the commercial train to travel from Rapid City to Winona or Mason City without performing switching duties.

In December 1994, Bob Irwin and his C&NW(UP) counterpart reached agreement on improving the interchange of traffic. The C&NW(UP) began expediting yard switching in Winona by adding a second engine crew, increased emphasis on timely delivery of traffic to the DM&E at Rapid City, and moved the congested Mason City interchange north to Albert Lea, MN. This move now permits a DM&E train crew to complete the traffic interchange in six hours. Before, this operation often required in excess of 12 hours and a second train crew.

As Vice President of Transportation, Irwin leads a team of 61 locomotive engineers and 32 conductors plus a management and administrative staff of 15. The DM&E trains its own conductors and has a 70 day cross-training program, in conjunction with the Santa Fe Railroad, where senior conductors are qualified as engineers. This dual qualification has added job stability by permitting conductors to serve as engineers during peak season and return to their former duties during slack time. The increased number of operating crews and the addition of nine locomotives has given the DM&E needed flexibility in train make up and scheduling.

▪ Engineering

This department has the Herculean task of maintaining track, bridges, and other physical plant in a safe condition commensurate with DM&E requirements. This charge includes cross-tie replacement, rail replacement, rock ballasting, surfacing (cleaning, leveling, and smoothing of track), sub-grade and bridge improvements.

As mentioned earlier, the DM&E inherited a poorly maintained railroad. Added to these woes was the discovery that the native clay (Pierre shale) sub-grade on the Pierre-Rapid City (PRC) section would prove very unstable during periods of heavy rains. In effect, the water becomes trapped between wet clay and track structure and the wet clay itself often proves unable to support the weight of 100 ton car trains. Frequently, the end result is that water, clay, ballast, etc., are squeezed to both sides of the railbed, thus causing the track to sink. Some of these soft spot areas extend for 500 feet. Unseasonably wet weather in four of the last five years has played havoc on the PRC section and by late June 1995 had washed out roadbed in eastern South Dakota and at many places across Minnesota. Repair costs for the "flood of 1993" approximated $2.1 million and were paid for by a Federal emergency relief grant. The

Exhibit 6   **Dakota, Minnesota & Eastern Railroad Corp.**
                   Capital Expenditures ($000)

Capital Expenditures	1987-89	1990	1991	1992	1993	1994	Total
SD Track—West of Pierre	$5,629	$2,614	$955	$2,221	$1,421	$2,019	$14,949
SD Track—East of Pierre	5,843	3,429	219	1,120	797	2,216	13,624
Total SD Track	$11,562	$6,043	$1,174	$3,341	$2,218	$4,235	$28,573
MN Track	6,250	2,969	1,374	1,713	3,811	4,350	20,467
Total All Track	$17,812	$9,012	$2,548	$5,054	$6,029	$8,585	$49,040
Locomotive & All Other	2,618	1,410	1,267	1,454	2,280	3,803	12,832
Total	$20,430	$10,422	$3,815	$6,508	$8,309	$12,388	$61,872
Funded by							
SD Grant (FRA Funds)*	626	0	0	89	264	467	1,446
SD Grant (State Funds)	1,502	345	278	567	0	0	2,692
SD State Loan	0	0	75	0	0	0	75
SD Industry	346	0	48	76	0	0	470
SD FRA Loan	4,870	2,720	60	0	0	0	7,650
MN Grant (FRA Funds)	228	70	21	49	868	494	1,730
MN Grant (State Funds)	1,301	408	334	509	0	0	2,552
MN State Loan	3,161	967	5	0	1,833	1,229	7,195
MN Industry	465	210	0	40	361	200	1,276
DM&E Cash	7,931	5,702	2,994	5,178	4,983	9,998	36,786
Total	$20,430	$10,422	$3,815	$6,508	$8,309	$12,388	$61,872

*FRA—Federal Rail Administration

Source: Company records

costs associated with the wet spring of 1995 have yet to be totaled but will add up to several hundred thousand dollars.

The DM&E had spent in excess of $49 million on track and bridge-related capital projects by the end of 1994. Over 59 percent of this was from cash generated from operations and the remainder came from federal and state loans and grants plus loans from customers. The DM&E also performs normal maintenance and maintenance-support activities that are not included in capital expenditures. Exhibit 6 shows capital expenditures for 1987–1994.

Budgeted capital track expenditures for 1995 approximate $7.2 million. Included are installation of 59,000 cross ties, 150,000 tons of rock ballast (2,000 car loads), surfacing 270 miles of track, installing 13 miles of longitudinal drain plastic pipe, upgrading 12 bridges, replacing 780 feet of wooden bridging with culvert and earthen fill, constructing a 6,000 ft. passing track near Wendte, S.D., and installing five miles of continuous welded rail west of Wolsey, S.D.

The railroad has long recognized that a targeted main line average speed of 25 mph will never be attained until a solution is found to the PRC subgrade problems, and replacement of the lightweight rail between Wolsey and Pierre, S.D. After extensive study, the DM&E determined that those two projects would require an estimated $35 million to accomplish. Included in the project are replacement of 96 miles of 72 lb. rail, 85 miles of ditching, surfacing of the entire 170 mile PRC subdivision with a total of 6,800 cars of ballast, and installation of 35 miles of waterproof fabric between ballast and clay. Also, over 4,500 perforated lateral drain pipes and 20 miles of perforated longitudinal piping will be used to remove trapped pockets of water.

The need for the upgrading of this section of the DM&E and the resultant benefits to the state resulted in the signing of legislation authorizing the issuance of up to $35 million in revenue bonds. Under terms of the bill, South Dakota will acquire ownership of the western 266 miles of track, leasing it back to the DM&E on an exclusive basis until the bonds are paid off by the railroad. At that time, ownership will revert to the DM&E. The Wolsey to Pierre section will require $20 million and take approximately three years to finish. The PRC will need $15 million to complete and will take an additional three years. There are several underwriters interested in handling the bond offering and a nine or 10 percent interest rate is expected. The DM&E hopes to receive the proceeds for the Wolsey to Pierre portion in late fall 1995.

The Engineering department is staffed with 30 section personnel who are equally spread along the 10 sections of 850 mile owned rail. Each three-man section is responsible for maintaining a safe railroad across its section. The department's other 37 non-management personnel install and maintain signals, repair bridges, inspect track, and operate a variety of equipment. This 67 man base work force is augmented by temporary hires in the spring and summer. Also, the railroad uses contractors for all major capital projects.

■ Mechanical

This department is tasked with maintaining the DM&E locomotive fleet, repairing all on-line railcars owned by other railroads, and providing similar service to nearly 300 newly-leased covered hoppers. James Appleman's 36-member department has the equipment and expertise to perform almost any type of maintenance or repair requirement. The fact that locomotive availability remains 96 percent or higher with units manufactured between 1952 and 1974 and averaging 39 years in age is a testament in itself. The department is currently covering 100 percent of its entire budget from foreign railcar (i.e., railcars owned by others) repairs.

■ Human Resources

Human Resources Management (HRM) is not centrally administered. Hiring and training are done at the department level, while pay, benefits, performance appraisal, and administrative recordkeeping are performed by the Finance and Accounting Department. Human resources, however, take a back seat to no functions on the DM&E. President Pete McIntyre continually stresses the importance of all employees, both as people and as the real cause of the railroad's success.[6] Most key managers seem to echo this philosophy, though some seem to have difficulty adjusting from the too typical railroad confrontational leadership style.

Communications

Pete McIntyre schedules "Employee Appreciation Dinners" in the summer and during the Christmas season at major locations. The employees seem to enjoy the "give and take" during these festivities and many feel relatively free to express their views. McIntyre and other rail officials get out on the line as often as possible but acknowledge that their hectic jobs keep them from getting needed feedback.[7] Face-to-face communication is supplemented by a quarterly newsletter *DM&E Enroute*, which keeps employees, customers, and supporters informed of current operations and future plans. One innovation is an open invitation to employees to phone McIntyre direct, or in his absence, leave a message. Overall, employees have a positive attitude toward these efforts, although some feel they need more one-on-one contact and a few wonder if they are really listened to.

Stable Work Force

The DM&E recognizes the importance of job security to employee morale, turnover, and possible increased productivity. The use of temporary employees and contract labor serve to minimize layoffs greatly in the seasonal transportation, engineering, and mechanical departments. In addition, cross training affords flexibility needed to move employees efficiently where needed.

Pay

The DM&E pays its craft, clerical, and non-union employees very competitively versus local rates. The DM&E has admitted from the beginning that it could not match the train crew pay of unionized Class I railroads. Rates of pay are 15 to 25 percent below comparable wages on the C&NW(UP). Extensive overtime on the DM&E plus profit sharing and year-round employment (Class I railroads often have winter layoffs) undoubtedly narrow this gap.

The DM&E also uses bonus and merit pay to reward non-union employees further. Bonuses for all non-managerial employees averaged $1,700 in 1990, $2,200 in 1991, $2,700 in 1993, and $2,300 in 1994. All but operating United Transportation Union (UTU) non-managerial employees are eligible to receive performance appraisal-based merit pay. This incentive averaged 3 percent in 1990, 2 percent in 1991, 3 percent in each year from 1992 to 1994, and 4 percent in 1995. In addition, this category of employees received 3 percent across the board increases in 1990, 1992, and 1993.

Benefits

The benefits package offered DM&E employees equals or exceeds those provided by the major union railroads. Exhibit 7 gives a sample comparison.

Unions

Although the initial DM&E work force was comprised, in large part, of former union members, there was little sentiment for unionization. Many employees knew that for the railroad to survive in the short run, all costs had to be kept to a minimum. Also, some employees blamed the union for the loss of their former jobs with major Class I carriers and were willing to forgo some wages just to get

Exhibit 7

Sample Benefits Comparison

Benefit	DM&E	Unionized National Railroad Plan
Life Insurance	$50,000	$10,000
Accidental D&D	$50,000	$8,000
401(K)	Yes	Not Provided
Profit Sharing	Yes	Not Provided
Maximum Medical	$1,000,000	$500,000
Deductible	$100-each individual	$100-each individual
Maximum out-of-pocket	$500-individual $1,000-family	$2,000-each person covered

Source: DM&E Benefits Brochures

back in their profession. The DM&E remained non-union until June 1990 when train crew, railcar repairmen, and electricians began being represented by the UTU. One of the major complaints against the DM&E was its failure to improve wages as compared to major railroads.

The American Train Dispatchers Association attempted to organize the dispatchers in 1989 but failed. The UTU attempted to organize engineering employees in 1991 but was rejected by a vote margin of 2 to 1. In August 1992, the car repairmen voted to decertify the UTU and formed their own local union. In November of 1992, the International Association of Machinists (IAM) failed in their attempt to organize the Mechanical Department. The IAM has renewed its organization efforts and an election is upcoming.

Morale

Employee attitudes are generally good across the various categories of workers. Turnover is within limits and a "can do" spirit seems fairly prevalent. The lack of scheduled time off for train crews, however, appears to be an unsolvable problem for both union and management. Train crews often find themselves called back to work 10 hours after completing a trip, or spending a day away from home waiting for a train to complete the round trip. This leaves little time with family, and planned outings are a rarity. Some consideration had been given to a six-day-on, two-off work cycle but variables in demand, schedule interruptions, and the unwillingness of many to lose overtime pay have made this proposal impractical. Many train crew members use vacation or "sick" time for days off.

■ Summary of Financial Performance 1992–1995

The DM&E has continued to improve its financial condition since start-up and particularly from 1992 to date. The railroad generated $40.4 million in operating revenues in 1992, while traffic volume was 55.1 thousand carloads. Operating revenues for 1993 were $41.9 million and traffic volume 51 thousand carloads, a 3.7 percent increase in revenues and a 7.5 percent decline in carloads. In 1994, operating revenue was $43.3 million while carloads stood at 50.6 thousand, an increase of 3.3 in revenue and a .07 percent decrease in carloads over comparable 1993 levels. Dur-

Exhibit 8   **Dakota, Minnesota & Eastern Railroad Income Statements 1992–1994 ($000)**

	1992	1993	1994
Revenues			
Freight	40,377	41,969	43,283
Other	577	454	715
Net Revenue	40,954	42,423	43,998
Operating Expenses:			
Car Hire & Car Leases	5,723	6,308	6,439
Fuel	3,381	3,492	3,606
Accident Expense + Insurance	3,831	3,559	4,354
Transportation	7,288	8,232	8,174
Maint. of Way (Inc. Prop. Tax)	3,515	3,711	3,849
Maint. of Equipment	1,952	1,959	1,964
Total Operating Expenses	25,690	27,261	28,386
Gross Profit	15,264	15,162	15,612
General & Admin. Expenses:			
Wages & Benefits	2,049	2,113	2,284
Professional Fees (Inc. Audit)	599	1,400	984
Other	382	186	151
Other Expenses (Income)	(164)	(689)	(366)
EBITDA	12,398	12,152	12,559
Adjustments	(1,029)	0	7,484
Adjusted EBITDA	11,369	12,152	20,043
Depreciation & Amortization	3,314	3,482	3,945
EBIT	8,055	8,670	16,098
Interest-Revolver(net of int. income)	(10)	108	92
Interest-Westinghouse	2,319	1,924	823
Interest-CNW	991	1,350	742
Interest-Government Loans	249	273	207
Interest-First Bank/Tifco/Etc.	148	151	175
Interest-New Debt	0	0	1558
EBT	4,358	4,864	12,501
Income Tax	895	1,800	4,715
Net Income	3,463	3,064	7,786
Less Preferred Dividends-Reg	186	187	187
Net Income Available to Common	3,277	2,877	7,599

Source: Company records

ing the first five months of 1995, operating revenues were $16.7 million or $72,000 over budget. At the same time, carloadings increased slightly over the same period in 1994.[8] Exhibit 8 presents income statement data for years 1992–1994.

Revenues

Traffic volume during 1992–1994 decreased in seven of 12 commodity groups with an overall decrease of 8.3 percent. The largest increases were in bentonite clay, wheat, wheat flour, woodchips, and soybean oil. Major decreases in corn and soybeans are attributable to weather and market conditions rather than to loss to other transportation modes. Higher gross revenues were due to increased traffic in commodities that command higher per car charges such as bentonite clay, lumber, wheat, and wood chips.

Operating Expenses

These expenses rose 10.4 percent between 1992 and 1994. Increased traffic coupled with roadbed problems increased expenses in all six categories. Expenses during the first five months of 1995 exceeded budget by $600,000. This overrun was due to accident costs.[9]

Liquidity and Capital Resources

Cash generated from operations is the DM&E's primary source of liquidity and is used principally for debt service, capital expenditures, and working capital requirements. The DM&E was highly leveraged at start-up and has been forced to ask continually for federal, state, and local financing to assist in roadbed maintenance. Governmental loans are at approximately three percent and have a delayed principal payment feature. The July 1994 private placement of 13 year 10.13 fixed rate senior secured notes totaling $32 million enabled the DM&E to refinance older senior obligations, some carrying a 13 percent interest rate. The DM&E recorded a gain of $4,660,813 net of tax on this transaction and it is carried as an extraordinary item in the 1994 income statement. The DM&E continues to pay down its senior debt and as of April 1, 1995, had reduced its debt to equity ratio to 2.4 to 1. The ideal railroad debt to equity ratio is 2 to 1. The South Dakota revenue bond issue requires the DM&E to not exceed a 3 to 1 debt to equity ratio. See Exhibit 9 for balance sheet information for 1992–1994.

EXTERNAL ENVIRONMENT

■ Competition

The DM&E's operations are subject to competition from railroads and trucks.

Rail

There are several local and three major railroads that have lines in or near the DM&E service area.

C&NW.   As mentioned earlier, the C&NW has played a sort of Jekyll and Hyde role during most of DM&E's existence. One of the most unusual twists in

Exhibit 9

**Dakota, Minnesota & Eastern Railroad
Balance Sheets 1992–1994 ($000)**

	1992	1993	1994
Assets			
Cash	1,231	575	5,316
Accounts Receivable	6,555	8,582	7,530
Materials & Supplies Inventory	417	590	1,634
Prepaid Expenses	574	1,043	888
Total Current Assets	8,777	10,790	15,368
PP&E-Net	53,369	56,545	63,848
Capitalized Leases-Net	0	0	0
Deferred Fin. & Other Assets	1,062	4,579	3,167
Total Assets	63,208	71,914	82,383
Liabilities and Stockholders' Equity			
Accounts Payable-Trade	1,834	2,522	1,210
Accts Pay-Intnl+Contract Allow	1,158	1,664	1,618
Car Hire Payable	591	985	890
Notes Payable	286	257	257
Wages & Benefits Payable	1,519	1,835	1,946
Interest Payable	495	252	1,560
Other Accrued Liability	2,858	2,401	2,497
Total Current Liabilities	8,741	9,916	9,978
Deferred Income Tax Liability	4,784	6,450	10,904
Revolving Loan	2,000	2,000	2,650
Westinghouse Term Loans	16,105	12,849	0
CNW Term Loan	7,388	8,947	0
Government Loans-Net	10,652	13,930	7,317
First Bank	313	435	220
New Debt	0	0	33,393
Other Liabilities	874	1,972	258
Total Liabilities	50,857	56,499	64,720
Preferred Stock	2,025	2,212	2,399
Senior Preferred Stock	0	0	0
Common Stock	3,290	3,290	2,758
Retained Earnings	7,203	10,080	12,673
Treasury Stock	(167)	(167)	(167)
Total Stockholders' Equity	12,351	15,415	17,663
Total Liab. & Stockholders' Equity	63,208	71,914	82,383

Source: Company Records

this saga occurred in July 1992 when the C&NW unexpectedly backed out of an earlier agreement to sell the "Colony Line" to the DM&E for $6.3 million.

A possible reason for C&NW's action took place a month later when UP requested Interstate Commerce Commission (ICC) approval to acquire ownership of the C&NW. The addition of the most powerful railroad in the United States to the C&NW equation would, in the DM&E's opinion, severely restrict its already limited operational freedom. As a result, the DM&E intervened in the ICC proceedings requesting:[10]

1. Enforcement of the sale of the Colony Line.
2. Removal of interchange restrictions at Winona, Mankato, Owatonna, and Mason City.
3. Allowing direct service to shippers at Winona and access to shippers via reciprocal switching agreement at the other three cities.
4. Modifying the car supply agreement which requires the DM&E to use C&NW cars while at the same time not requiring the C&NW to furnish them. The DM&E could use cars from any source without C&NW penalty.

Later DM&E-C&NW negotiations resulted in an agreement whereby the C&NW relinquished its financial investment in the DM&E, thus enabling DM&E to refinance under more favorable terms; guaranteed all "Colony Line" traffic would be turned over to the DM&E; relaxed interchange restrictions in Mason City and agreed to the establishment of a committee to resolve operating disputes. Unresolved problems would be subject to binding arbitration. There would be monetary penalties if DM&E trains were unduly delayed operating over C&NW track. Lastly, DM&E would retain right of first refusal should the "Colony Line" be offered for sale. Also, C&NW would be given preference in any proposed sale of DM&E.[11] As a result of this December 1993 agreement, DM&E withdrew its opposition to UP gaining control of C&NW.

Subsequent ICC approval led to UP's purchase of C&NW on April 1995 and the beginnings of a new relationship for DM&E. A late May meeting between the two roads went well and UP promised to honor the agreements that C&NW had made with DM&E. The topic of future line sales to DM&E was discussed. UP has traditionally avoided owning lines that were separated from the rest of its rail system. This fact may enhance the DM&E's chances of buying the Colony Line and the former C&NW railyard in Winona. These purchases would give the DM&E ownership of both ends of its rail line and permit better control of soliciting, scheduling, and routing of freight. Resultant revenue increases would be substantial. McIntyre feels that there will be no quick resolution to these line purchases.[12]

Other. Conversely, as major carriers continue selling off ancillary lines, there remains the opportunities for smaller railroads to pick up complementary trackage. The UP(C&NW)'s Minneapolis-Sioux City Iowa branch (277 miles), the CP's corn lines across southern Minnesota (112 miles) and northern Iowa to the Mississippi River (253 miles), and BN's Sioux City to Aberdeen, South Dakota, route (265 miles) may fit this category for the DM&E.[13]

Trucks

Trucks carry a greater share of intercity traffic than do railroads. Their innate flexibility, relatively low capital requirements, and huge network of tax-supported highways gives them great advantage in smaller volume and under

500-mile shipments. Railroads are very competitive in bulk shipments over long distances. Intermodal shipments (truck or container on rail flatcar) often offer the advantages of both modes to shippers.[14] The DM&E faces the strongest truck competition in Minnesota.

■ Weather

DM&E's location in the upper Midwest will always subject the railroad to weather extremes. While the "flood of 1993" caused extensive crop damage, the moderate temperatures and rainfall in 1994 resulted in bumper crops in both South Dakota and Minnesota. The spring of 1995 was the wettest on record for South Dakota. As planting deadlines for small grains such as wheat and oats passed, farmers switched planting plans to include more corn and soybeans. Given a normal growing season with no early frost, harvest yields are expected to be average.[15] While the DM&E does not expect the level of traffic that resulted from the 1994 crop, they do not anticipate a significant decrease in traffic revenue due to the wet spring.

■ Economic

South Dakota

Agriculture remains the economic mainstay of the state, while agribusiness, processing of forest products, and mining make significant contributions. Due to this industry mix combined with the absence of a strong manufacturing base, South Dakota's economy tends to be affected less than the national average during times of both economic upswings and downturns. Per capita personal income percent change in 1993–94 found South Dakota, at 9.5%, to be one of the fastest growing states. Although per capita personal income is growing, at $19,577 in 1994, it remains below the national average of $21,809. Increases in both farm and nonfarm income were near or above average and the state enjoyed above average increases in earnings in both durables and nondurables manufacturing.[16] Noteworthy is that although the state had the number one increase in average annual pay in 1994, it continues to rank last in overall average annual pay.[17] South Dakota is forecasted to experience the region's fastest job growth in 1995, due primarily to gains in manufacturing, business, and financial services.[18]

Minnesota

Minnesota is a leading agricultural state with a strong industrial base. It is becoming increasingly urban and is considered the commercial center of the upper Midwest. The state's economy revolves around a steady flow of products from factories, forests, and farms, supplemented by income from mining and marketing.[19] Per capita personal income percent change in 1993–94 found Minnesota, at 7.0%, to be one of the fastest growing states. The average per capita personal income in 1994 was $22,453, above the national average of $21,809. Increases in both farm and nonfarm income were near or above average, and the state enjoyed above average increases in earnings and in both durables and nondurables manufacturing.[20]

■ Legal/Political

The DM&E is subject to various federal, state, and local laws and regulations pertaining, in varying degrees, to almost every phase of its operations.

Federal

Government programs and policies which influence the strength of the dollar, export enhancement, crop support prices, and interest rates greatly affect the agricultural sector of the economy and therefore the DM&E. Major federal legislation aimed specifically at rail industry enhancement includes:

1. The 1976 Railroad Revitalization and Regulatory Reform Act (4Rs)—freed the railroads of 75 year old regulations that may have been appropriate before the coming of the truck and airplane. Railroads were permitted greater flexibility in rate making, abandonments, mergers, and line sales. Federal funds were provided through state agencies to rehabilitate needed rail trackage. Individual states were required to become involved in rail planning.

2. The Staggers Rail Act of 1980 furthered the work of the 4R's Act. It further streamlined the mechanics of restructuring the physical rail system and rail rate structure. It allowed railroads either to increase net revenues on unprofitable branchlines or to redirect traffic and abandon them.

3. Rural Rail Infrastructure Act of 1995 has been introduced by South Dakota Senator Pressler. The act would mandate $25 million a year in matching fund grants to the states and provide for $500 million in funded loan guarantees. These monies are aimed principally for secondary rail lines like the DM&E.

Other pertinent federal legislation is:

1. Highway Trust Fund—Has subsidized truck use of the highway network. Over $125 billion is to be spent exclusively on highways over the next five years while railroad support under the 4R's Act is running at $8–10 million a year.

2. Federal Employees' Liability Act—Is a form of workers' compensation mandated for the railroad industry. Unlike workers' compensation, it is an adversarial system rather than no-fault. As a result, average cost per employee hour worked is $1.51 for railroads and $0.27 for the rest of American industry.

3. Railroad Retirement Act—Requires larger contributions from railroads than from employers under the social security system.

4. Safety User Fees—Railroads must fund federal safety inspections of their track and equipment ($32 million in 1992) while truck and barge competitors do not have this requirement.

South Dakota

The state has a history of support for the rail industry. In 1973, the governor appointed a task force to recommend changes in state taxation and regulation of railroads in order to lessen their financial plight. It was hoped this would reduce the need for branch line abandonment. The state later used 4R's Act funding to help rehabilitate critical branch lines. In 1979, the state legislature moved rail regulatory authority to the Department of Transportation and authorized the use of state funds to purchase rail properties from private companies. The state subsequently purchased over 1,000 miles of track of what became known as the state core system. Since then, several hundred miles have been sold to BN or leased to local rail operators. The BN is under contract to operate the 368 miles remaining in the state core system.

The DM&E has used state 4R's Act funding to refurbish the RedfieldMansfield branch and 12 miles of the Huron to Watertown line. The DM&E enjoys strong political support in both states. In South Dakota, the governor's office, state senators, and representatives have all taken a positive and active role. The 1995 act authorizing $35 million of state revenue bonds has been mentioned elsewhere. U.S. Senator Pressler is a powerful advocate at the federal level.

Minnesota

Minnesota has been politically supportive, particularly monetarily through its Rail Service Improvement Program. The State Rail Plan is the principal legislative vehicle for supporting the rail industry. This plan uses the 4R's Act and state funds to assist in the acquisition and rehabilitation of rail lines and subsidization of continued rail service. The state has used over $25 million of its own monies to supplement 4R's Act grants. Funds are distributed to approved rail rehabilitation projects via the Minnesota Rail Service Improvement Program. Project funding is as follows:

70%	State Funds	(Some of which are federal dollars. This is a low-interest loan program. Typical is 3% interest, 10 year payback.)
10%	Shippers	(Loan—no interest, negotiable payback. DM&E bases payback on number of carloads shipped. A 3-4 year payback period is typical. Shippers are paid back first, then the state.)
20%	Railroad	(Is the minimum they must contribute—it may be the balance of the project, in the case of cost overruns).

The DM&E used over $6.3 million to fund projects through 1990. During 1993–1995, it will utilize an additional $5.7 million for track rehabilitation.

▪ Planning For The Future

Pete McIntyre's day was soon filled with the normal business of a busy executive. He spent several hours gathering and dispersing information, making decisions, and checking on the progress of previous ones. It was late afternoon before he got back to his earlier thoughts of the railroad's future. Pete reached in his lower left drawer, pulled out his copy of the 1995 DM&E Strategic Audit and Plan, and began searching for a pencil.

GLOSSARY

Bridge route A railroad that serves as a connection that joins two or more non-contiguous rail lines.

Car hire The renting of freight cars from another railroad. Charges are computed on a daily basis.

Commercial trains DM&E terminology for thru freights. A thru freight is a train that makes infrequent stops along its assigned route. Such stops are normally for changing operating crews.

Gateway A rail center where freight cars from connecting railroads are interchanged.

Intermodal Freight that is moved by differing modes of transportation enroute to its destination.

Local traffic Freight that originates and terminates on the trackage of the same railroad.

Local freight A train that services customers along the rail line. Such service includes the delivery and pick up of empty or loaded freight cars. This type of train relieves the commercial or thru freight of such duties.

Originating traffic Freight that originates on one railroad but is interchanged with another in order to reach its final destination.

Overhead traffic Freight received from one railroad for delivery to a second railroad.

Sort and block The arranging of freight cars so they will be in order for delivery to individual customers, destinations, or connecting railroads.

Terminating traffic Freight that is received from another railroad for delivery to its final destination.

Trackage rights A right to use the tracks of another railroad. A rights fee is normally charged.

Waybill A document, prepared by the carrier of freight, that contains details of the shipment, route, and charges.

REFERENCES

1. Association of American Railroads, *Railroad Facts: 1994 Edition*, Economics and Finance Department, Washington, D.C., p. 32.

2. *Ibid.*, p. 32.

3. "DM&E Seeks Access to C&NW Track," *DM&E Enroute*, May 1993, p. 1.

4. Interviews with President John C. "Pete" McIntyre, Dakota, Minnesota & Eastern Railroad Corporation, May-June 1995.

5. Interviews with Vice President Marketing Lynn A. Anderson, Dakota, Minnesota & Eastern Railroad Corporation, May-July 1995.

6. McIntyre, Interviews, May-June 1995.

7. Interviews with numerous DM&E officials, August 1992, May-June 1993, May-June 1995.

8. "DM&E Meets Revenue Goal, Expense Up," *DM&E Enroute*, June 1995, p. 2.

9. *Ibid.*, p. 2.

10. "DM&E and NorthWestern Face Off," *Trains*, August 1993, p. 18.

11. "DM&E, C&NW Sign Colony Line Pact," *DM&E Enroute*, January 1994, p. 1.

12. McIntyre, Interviews, July 1995.

13. South Dakota Bureau of Finance and Management, *Economic and Revenue Forecast*, February 9, 1993, p. 1.

14. Helming, Bill. "The U.S. and Global Economy Outlook," prepared for the Annual Agricultural/Commercial Credit Conference Meeting of the South Dakota Bankers Association, April 7, 1995.

15. South Dakota Bureau of Finance and Management, *Economic and Revenue Forecast*, February 15, 1995, p. 2.

16. Bureau of Economic Analysis, "Per Capita Personal Income Growth in 1994," Economics and Statistics Administration, US Department of Commerce News, April 27, 1995, p. 3.

17. "Business Climate Rated: South Dakota's Economy Gets Average Grades," *Brookings Register*, May 25, 1995, pp. A1-2.

18. South Dakota Bureau of Finance and Management, *Economic and Revenue Forecast*, February 15, 1995, p. 2.

19. Bureau of Economic Analysis, "Per Capita Personal Income Growth Picked Up in 44 States in 1992," Economics and Statistics Administration, US Department of Commerce News, April 27, 1993, Table 2.

20. Bureau of Economic Analysis, "Per Capita Personal Income Growth in 1994," Economics and Statistics Administration, US Department of Commerce News, April 27, 1995, p. 1.

Wisconsin Central: Continuing Success in the Railroad Industry

Paul R. Reed, Sam Houston State University

Otto P. Dobnick, SouthEastern Wisconsin Regional Planning Commission

President Ed Burkhardt glanced again at the favorable article in the *Milwaukee Sentinel* concerning the July 28, 1994, announcement that the Wisconsin Central Transportation Corporation (WCTC) had agreed to purchase the Algoma Central Corporation's railway.[1] This action would add 320 miles of track running north between Sault Ste. Marie and Hearst, Ontario. The agreement also included 966 rail cars and 23 locomotives. More importantly, it would enhance the U.S.-Canada movement of iron ore, paper, and wood pulp, plus provide connections to the main lines of the Canadian National (CN), Canadian Pacific (CP), and Ontario Northland (ONT) railways.

Ed had led the WCTC since its start-up in 1987 and was pleased with its progress. Traffic had grown year after year, mushrooming in late 1993 and 1994 to date. Resultant revenues had continued to climb, net income improved, and debt to equity reduced. Yet, not all was well; the company was in some danger of being a victim of its own success. With the influx of business came the continual need for more track, more railcars, more locomotives, more trains, and more people. A Herculean effort by all seemed to leave the company, on occasion, a quarter step behind demand. A few customers had begun to complain about service and operating employees about long hours. Was it time for WCTC to consider changing strategies? How would current and potential on-line customers react? Would attractive investment opportunities wait? Life was never dull in the railroad business, Ed thought.

INDUSTRY BACKGROUND

In the 160-year history of railroading in the United States, the industry has traveled through some of its most profound changes during the past two decades. The combination of deregulation in the transportation arena, basic changes in the nature and output of American heavy industry, the loss of local business, and the dramatic increase in long-distance coal movement for power generation have caused the railroads of today to be far different from the traditional railroads of yesterday. Railroads were once responsible for hauling almost everything and everyone into and out of every city and village. For example, in 1929 they accounted for 75 percent of all United States intercity freight ton-miles.[2] The volume of freight handled by today's railroads is more than double that of 1929, although the railroad industry's share of freight has been greatly reduced by trucks, river carriers, and pipelines. In 1993 railroads handled 37 percent of all freight ton-miles.[3] Thus, railroads have evolved from general freight haulers to specialized freight carriers, primarily handling large volume bulk commodities and oversized loads. In addition, intermodal traffic—which is the movement of containers and truck trailers on rail cars—has enabled railroads to recapture general products and merchandise formerly lost to the trucking industry. In 1994 United States freight railroads are regarded as being more profitable and efficient and in better physical condition than at any other time in recent history.

The Association of American Railroads (AAR), the principal industry organization for the freight railroad industry, classifies all of the common carrier railroads operating within the United States into one of three categories based primarily on annual operating revenue. The first category includes the major rail freight carriers, which are defined as Class I railroads and must meet an adjustable revenue threshold, which in 1992 was $251.4 million. The next category includes regional railroads which are those carriers that operate at least 350 miles of track and/or earn revenue between $40 million and the Class I threshold.[4] The WCTC's Wisconsin Central (WC) subsidiaries are classified as a regional railroad, the largest of 33 such mid-sized carriers in the United States. Most regional railroads were formed during the 1980s from systems of secondary and branch lines no longer wanted by larger Class I railroads. The third category includes local—or "short line"—railroads which are all those that fall below the regional railroad criteria and include Switching and Terminal railroads. A comparison of these three types of railroads is shown in Exhibit 1.

Exhibit 1

Types of Railroads in the United States: 1992 (000,000)

Type of Railroad	Number	Miles Operated	Employees	Annual Revenue
Class I	12	126,237	194,120	$27,508
Regional	33	20,697	11,600	1,514
Local	464	22,730	12,885	1,242
Totals	509	169,664	218,605	$30,264

Source: Association of American Railroads, *Railroad Facts: 1993 Edition* (Washington, D.C., August 1993), p. 3.

■ Beginnings

During the 1970s and into the 1980s, the railroad industry in the upper Midwest had felt drastic changes stemming from the deregulation of both trucking and railroads, the decline of heavy industry, the loss of local railroad business, the growth of coal traffic, and mergers. During this period, many lines merged, were downsized, or disappeared, with pieces purchased by former competitors or, in many cases, entrepreneurs desiring to operate their own railroad.

It was during this time that the Soo Line Railroad Company (Soo), a long-established conservative railroad serving a seven-state area of the Upper Midwest, decided that its fiscal viability would be best assured by selling off much of its network throughout Wisconsin and the Upper Peninsula of Michigan. The successful bidders for this trackage, which became the Wisconsin Central, were a five-man entrepreneurial team headed by Ed Burkhardt and Tom Power, both seasoned railroad executives. The sale price of $122 million was largely debt financed and purchased 2,134 miles of track or trackage rights plus associated buildings and adjoining property.[5]

The new regional railroad was not bound by Soo union labor agreements and was therefore not required to have a union work force. Beginning salaries were pegged anywhere between 28 and 33 percent below comparable jobs on unionized railroads but were well above the average Wisconsin wage earners income. Work rules were designed to permit far more flexibility than was the case on the Soo Line.[6]

■ Success to Date

In its first seven years of operation, Wisconsin Central qualifies as a success by just about all measures. From 1988, the first full year of operation, through 1993, annual operating revenue increased from $94 million to $152 million and net income from $3 million to $15 million. Annual revenue carloads increased from 145,000 in 1988 to 257,000 in 1993. Between start-up in October, 1987, and July, 1994, the number of employees rose from about 660 to 1,370; regularly scheduled daily trains increased from 36 to 86; the number of locomotives from 98 to 179; freight cars from 2,900 to 10,200. An initial stock offering in 1991 and a follow-up in 1992 were favorably received in the marketplace and, along with debt, were used to fund large equipment and physical plant improvements.

The Wisconsin Central has earned an excellent reputation in what is generally regarded as a conservative industry. In recognition of the Company's excellent service, trade publications such as *Distribution and Railway Age*, and major customers such as Consolidated Papers and 3M have presented awards to the Wisconsin Central. The railroad has also been the focus of many news items and stories in both the general and industry media. Wisconsin Central has become a textbook example of a successful leveraged buyout.[7]

DESCRIPTION OF THE COMPANY

■ Corporate Structure

The corporation is organized as a holding company, Wisconsin Central Transportation Corporation (WCTC), doing business through five wholly owned and consolidated subsidiaries. These include: Wisconsin Central Ltd. (WCL), which carries out all U.S. railroad operations and is the largest and most prominent subsidiary of the corporation; Fox Valley & Western, Ltd. (FV&W), which was formed basically for financing purposes in order to purchase other regional railroads in Wisconsin and is indistinguishable from WCL; WCL Railcars, Inc. (Railcars), which owns locomotives and freight cars and leases them to the railroad; Sault Ste. Marie Bridge Company (Bridge), which owns the international rail bridge connecting Michigan with Ontario; and Wisconsin Central International, Inc., which enables the company to invest in railroad ventures outside the United States. For purposes of clarity and simplicity, WCL-FVW, Railcars, and Bridges are collectively called Wisconsin Central, or WC in this case.

■ Mission

Wisconsin Central's mission is summarized by its pledge that liberally appears in company marketing and other materials: "to offer superior transportation consisting of more frequent, dependable train service, at competitive prices, with proper equipment, accomplished by customer-minded employees."

■ Routes and Hubs

The WC owns or operates 2,507 route miles of track and trackage rights in Wisconsin, the Upper Peninsula of Michigan, eastern Minnesota, northeastern Illinois, and Sault Ste. Marie, Ontario. Main lines extend from Chicago, through Fond du Lac, to Stevens Point, and then on to Duluth-Superior at the head of Lake Superior, and to Minneapolis-St. Paul, as shown in Exhibit 2. A main line also extends from Neenah-Menasha north to Gladstone and Sault Ste. Marie. The majority of the main line permits freight train speeds of 40 to 50 m.p.h., which is comparable with many Class I railroads, and better than most regional railroads. The main line between Chicago and Owen is equipped with a Centralized Traffic Control (C.T.C.) system which enables sidings, junctions, and signals to be controlled by dispatchers in Stevens Point. A system of secondary and branch lines are located throughout eastern, central, and northern Wisconsin, and northern Michigan. Most of these permit freight train speeds of 25 m.p.h. to 35 m.p.h., typical of such lines on all sizes of railroads.[8]

Freight cars are sorted and blocked at four major hubs—the classification yards at Fond du Lac, Stevens Point, Neenah, and Gladstone. Principal gateways are at Chicago, Minneapolis-St. Paul, Duluth-Superior, and Sault Ste. Marie, where direct interchange is made with all major connecting rail carriers. Access to its interchanges with other railroads at Chicago and Minneapolis-St. Paul is via trackage rights on other railroads. The company owns and operates car and locomotive repair shops at Fond du Lac, Stevens Point, and Gladstone for its own equipment and offers repair service to other railroads and clients.[9]

■ Traffic

At the end of 1993, about 60 percent of the railroad's traffic was paper industry related, as it has been since start-up in 1987. Much of the traffic consists of inbound raw and partially processed materials and supplies destined for the numerous on-line pulp and paper mills. A variety of commodities make up paper industry carloadings. Inbound shipments to the mills include pulpwood

Exhibit 2   **Wisconsin Central Map**

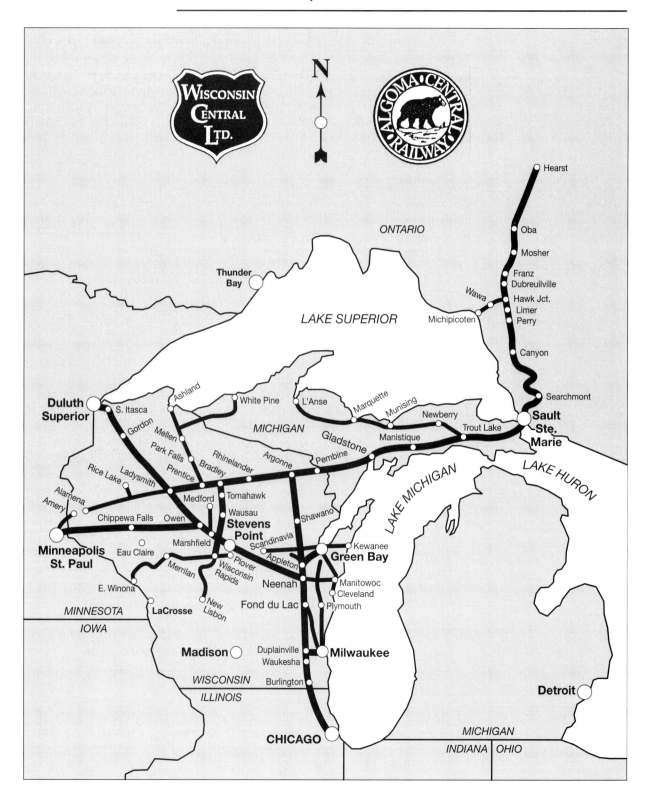

logs, wood chips, wood pulp, clay, chemicals, coal, machinery, and waste paper. Outbound shipments include wood pulp, light and heavy papers, paperboard, boxboard, corrugated stock, and some byproducts such as lignin. The 25 largest customers accounted for about 64 percent of the volume and about 71 percent of gross revenues in 1993. Of the ten shippers that accounted for over 50 percent of the railroad's gross revenues in both 1992 and 1993, six were paper and pulp mills. The paper producers located in Wisconsin and Upper Michigan are diverse, producing many types of paper products, including magazine stock, writing papers, packaging papers, and sanitary products.

The remaining traffic represents various markets that are typical sources of carloadings on most United States freight railroads. The railroad had made a habit of tracking these markets for additional business, since they are likely to shift from time to time depending on the demand and price for raw materials and products worldwide. Other commodities transported include: chemical and petroleum products; sand, stone, and minerals, including iron ore; clay products and granules; and general merchandise hauled in truck trailers and shipping containers (referred to as intermodal traffic).

Intermodal traffic represents a significant portion of WC's traffic, handling truck-competitive and time-sensitive commodities. This business represented about 12 percent of the railroad's volume in 1993. Major intermodal loading facilities are located in Green Bay, Neenah, and Stevens Point. All have been improved recently. In 1994, the railroad also began loading containers in Arcadia, Wisconsin. In 1992, WC commenced joint intermodal services with J. B. Hunt and Schneider International, the two largest truck load motor carriers in the country to offer shippers door-to-door truck/rail service to and from northeastern Wisconsin.

■ Equipment

At the end of June 1994, the railroad's fleet of rolling stock included 179 diesel-electric locomotives, and approximately 10,200 freight cars for revenue service.[10] The locomotives and a majority of the cars were acquired through the used equipment market, a typical procedure for newly formed railroads. Since start-up, WC has continued to acquire additional locomotives and new or reconditioned cars either through purchase or lease, to meet traffic demands and to upgrade the fleet. The company has placed a heavy emphasis on reconditioning and maintenance. For example, the most recently acquired set of mainline freight locomotives are being upgraded and equipped with wheel-slip control equipment to improve tractive effort.

MANAGEMENT

Exhibit 3 sets forth information about each person who serves as one of the Company's executive officers.

Burkhardt has served as a director, President and Chief Executive Officer of WCTC and its subsidiaries since its formation in 1987. From 1967 to 1987, Burkhardt was employed by Chicago & North Western Railroad (CNW), most recently as Vice President, Transportation. Burkhardt has 33 years of railroad management experience.

Exhibit 3   **Key Management**

Name	Age as of 5/1/94	Title
Edward A. Burkhardt	55	President and Chief Executive Officer
Thomas F. Power, Jr.	53	Executive Vice President and Chief Financial Officer
Walter C. Kelly	50	Vice President, Finance
Glenn J. Kerbs	53	Vice President, Engineering, WCL and FV&W
William R. Schauer	49	Vice President, Marketing, WCL and FV&W
J. E. Terbell	41	Vice President and General Manager, WCL and FV&W
Robert F. Nadrowski	47	Vice President, Mechanical, WCL and FV&W
Susan H. Norton	41	Treasurer

Source: Wisconsin Central Transportation Corporation, 1994, *Form 10K*, pp. 16-17.

Power has served as a director, Executive Vice President and Chief Financial Officer of WCTC and its subsidiaries since its formation in 1987. Power was employed by the Chicago, Milwaukee, St. Paul and Pacific Railroad Company, most recently as Chief Financial Officer. Power has over 26 years of railroad management experience.

Kelly has served as Vice President, Finance, of WCTC since September 1988. Prior to joining the Company, Kelly served as Corporate Controller for Speigel, Inc. (a catalog retailer) from 1987 to 1988, as an independent consultant during 1986, and as Vice President, Finance, for Wilton Enterprises, Inc. (a distributor of housewares) during 1985.

Kerbs has served as Vice President, Engineering, of WCL and FV&W since their respective start-ups. From 1974 until 1987, Kerbs was employed by CNW, most recently as Director of Maintenance Operations.

Schauer has served as Vice President, Marketing, of WCL since October 1988 and FV&W since its inception. From 1986 until 1987, Schauer was employed by CNW as General Marketing Manager.

Terbell has been employed as Vice President and General Manager of WCL and FV&W since November 1993. Prior to that time, Terbell served as WCL's Eastern Division Transportation Manager since the original acquisition. From 1973 until 1987, Terbell was employed by CNW, most recently as Assistant Division Manager, Engineering.

Nadrowski has been employed as Vice President, Mechanical, of WCL and FV&W since their respective start-ups. From 1966 to 1985, Nadrowski was employed by the Chicago, Milwaukee, St. Paul and Pacific Railroad Company, most recently as Assistant Vice President and Chief Mechanical Officer.

Norton has been employed as Treasurer of WCTC and its subsidiaries since October 1993. From the original acquisition through October 1993, Norton served as Assistant Treasurer of the Company. From 1978 until 1986, Norton held various positions with the Chicago, Milwaukee, St. Paul and Pacific Railroad Company, most recently as Manager, Strategic Planning.

Exhibit 4   **Principal Owners**

Name	Shares Beneficially Owned	Percent of Outstanding Shares
Janus Capital Corporation	840,575	10.2
Jennison Associates Capital Corp.	670,500	8.1
Kemper Financial Services, Inc.	669,700	8.1
Fidelity Management & Research Company	587,300	7.1
Edward A. Burkhardt	583,956	7.1
Strong/Corneliuson Capital Management, Inc.	473,800	5.7
Thomas F. Power, Jr.	164,403	2.0
Robert H. Wheeler	100,000	1.2
Directors and executive officers as a group (13 persons)	1,415,267	17.1

Source: Wisconsin Central Transportation Corporation, 1994, *Annual Report,* p. 9.

From the original acquisition through October 1993, John L. Bradshaw served as Vice President and General Manager of WCL and FV&W, and Ronald G. Russ served as the Company's Treasurer. Bradshaw and Russ are currently employed by New Zealand Rail (NZ Rail) pursuant to a management services agreement between the Company and NZ Rail.

The executive officers of the Company are elected annually by, and serve at the discretion of, the Company's Board of Directors.

■ Ownership of Stock

The principal owners of the company's common stock are as listed in Exhibit 4.

CORPORATE STRATEGY

■ Overall Philosophy

The goal of WC since inception has been to maximize returns to shareholders by: increasing carloads and revenues; improving freight car utilization and transit times; upgrading fixed plant, facilities, and equipment; paying off debt; increasing contributions to employee profit sharing; and earning a good return on investment. To achieve these goals, WC aims to do what a railroad does best: moving carloads fast and in a way that best suits the customer's needs. The officers have continued a commitment to providing rail freight service and not diversifying into non-rail areas. The company's overall philosophy is to continue strengthening its position as a rail freight carrier in the upper Midwest by making its existing system more efficient and better serving its present territory. It continues to concentrate on this approach by: strengthening its system of railroad lines; taking a proactive approach to marketing; making physical plant improvements; working with state and local government units and public agencies; and becoming involved with other railroad-related investment opportunities.

■ Strengthening the System

WC's approach to strengthening its system is based, in part, on recent studies that have indicated the railroad mode share of Wisconsin's freight traffic to be about 10 percent compared to the truck mode share of between 70 and 80 percent.[11] Thus, its competition is primarily not other railroads, but trucks. Accordingly, the railroad has embarked on a program of acquiring other lines in the area and combining them with the existing system to allow for more efficient train operation, eliminate duplicative facilities, and enable much faster—and thus more competitive—single carrier service to major gateways such as Chicago.

One of the two most important system expansions was the Superior Line acquisitions. In December 1991, a 102-mile railroad line extending from Ladysmith to Superior was purchased from the Soo. Prior to this acquisition, WC operated over this line under an agreement that prohibited the handling of overhead traffic. Overhead traffic is through traffic received from one railroad and delivered to another. Ownership of this line allows the WC to compete for all types of traffic in the Duluth-Superior to Chicago corridor. In July 1992, a 98-mile line extending from Cameron to Superior, which runs generally parallel to the former Soo Line route, was purchased from the Chicago and North Western (CNW) Transportation Company. The best portions of each line have been combined and upgraded. The remaining unused portions were retired with much of the excess track materials reused elsewhere.

The other of the two important system expansions was purchase of the operating assets of two smaller regional railroads, the Fox River Valley Railroad (FRVR) and the Green Bay and Western Railroad (GBW) in August 1993 from Itel Corporation through a newly created WCTC subsidiary, Fox Valley & Western, Ltd (FV&W). The purchase included about 480 miles of rail lines, along with attended property, agreements, rolling stock, equipment, and materials. The FV&W and WCL subsidiaries share locomotives, freight cars, shop facilities, rail yards, and administrative support. Savings are realized from the coordinated operations through consolidation of duplicative trackage, facilities, equipment, and operating and management staffs. Also, the coordination allows former FRVR and GBW traffic to have single line movement to Chicago and other gateways, with improved delivery times.

Attempts have been made to acquire the operations of smaller connecting links to serve nearby customers directly. For example, a six-mile branch serving a Kimberly-Clark paper mill at Munising, Michigan, was purchased from a local railroad in 1989. In 1992, an unsuccessful bid was made for purchase of the 14-mile Tomahawk Railway, which serves two mills and connects exclusively with the WC.

There exist other opportunities for further fine-tuning the system. The CNW still operates two isolated sections of railroad line in Wisconsin, both of which connect solely with the WC. One is a five-mile stretch in the Wausau area and the other is a 180-mile segment from Green Bay to Ishpeming, Michigan, near Marquette. The latter segment offers an opportunity for the WC to eliminate a lengthy circuitous route into the Marquette area.

■ Proactive Marketing

At the start-up in 1987, the business plan relied primarily on originating, terminating, and local traffic, and not on overhead traffic as a base for revenues. Overhead traffic is susceptible to diversion over other railroads, making it very competitive, and usually having small profit margins. Accordingly, initial increases in carloadings and revenues were made by enlarging the market share of freight shipped by existing customers, by regaining customers who had shifted to trucks when the railroad was operated by previous owners, and by serving new shippers in its territory. The railroad continues to build on its existing traffic base and increase its market share within the territory it serves rather than expanding much beyond Wisconsin and Michigan. Long-term multi-year agreements or contracts with major shippers such as the Mead Corporation have been made to help stabilize the traffic base. Maintaining a high level of service to paper industry customers and increasing the volume of intermodal traffic have received particular attention.

With a stable base of originating, terminating, and local traffic in existence, the company has begun targeting certain overhead traffic markets where conditions are favorable. In 1993, originating traffic accounted for 23 percent, terminating 37 percent, overhead 23 percent, and local traffic 19 percent of total carloads.

The acquisition and fine-tuning of the Superior line without the traffic restrictions imposed by the Soo opened two potentially large markets to build overhead traffic. The first market is attracting traffic which originates in western Canada, and then is routed to Duluth-Superior via the Canadian National (CN) rail system before continuing on to Chicago. This is a sizable market, estimated to be at least 75,000 carloads annually in the Duluth-Chicago corridor.[12] While CN announced a joint haulage agreement with the Burlington Northern (BN) railroad for this traffic in 1992, freight routings remain the customers' choice. The WC, which has the shortest route of any rail carrier between Chicago and Duluth-Superior, has aggressively gone after this traffic, including opening its first off-line sales office in Vancouver, British Columbia. The WC's share of Duluth-Chicago rail traffic has been estimated to have increased from nothing in 1990 to 15 to 20 percent in 1993.[13]

The second market is the handling of iron ore, largely in the Duluth-Superior to Chicago corridor. Traditionally, the economics of transporting iron ore dictated that lake boats handle the long haul of the ore from northern Minnesota and Upper Michigan to steel mills primarily in Indiana, Ohio, West Virginia, and Pennsylvania. During the 1980s, following deregulation, rail carriers had become more competitive. The Wisconsin Central serves both of the major iron ore ranges that are active today in the United States. In 1987 and 1988, no iron ore was handled. In 1989, 17 trains containing 1,200 carloads were handled for the first time from Superior to Chicago. In 1993, 19,000 carloads of iron ore were handled, much of it on a year-round basis rather than only during the winter season when Great Lakes shipping is closed.[14]

In 1994, WC won a five-year contract with the Southern Pacific Railroad to move 26,000 carloads of ore from Minnesota's Mesabi iron range to the Geneva Steel mill in Utah. This traffic will ride the WC from Superior to Chicago. John Carey, Assistant Vice-President, Marketing, has predicted that ore may be the railroad's number one commodity someday. WC has begun marketing itself as "America's year-round all-rail route for ore," including placing advertisements in mining industry magazines.[15]

▪ Physical Plant Improvements

As part of the railroad's commitment to dependable service, investments have been made in upgrading and expanding facilities. Cross tie replacement, new ballast and rail, and general trackwork have been a major portion of each year's capital improvement budget. Also, acquisition of the Superior lines, the former Fox River Valley, and Green Bay and Western Railroads has enabled parts of several other railroad companies to be combined, while eliminating some bottlenecks and slow segments. Capacity-related improvements have also been made, such as expansions of critical yard facilities at North Fond du Lac and Neenah, and changing mainline turnouts (switches) from manual operation to remote control.

▪ Cooperative Efforts With Public Sector

An unusual proactive approach has been taken toward cooperating with the public sector along various avenues. For example, Metra—the commuter passenger train operator in the Chicago area—will be inaugurating a new commuter rail line in 1996 from downtown Chicago to Antioch, Illinois, of which 40 miles will be on the WC. Significant improvements to the existing track and signals that are required to operate this service are being funded from federal, state, and local public sources.

▪ Other Investments

The company has reviewed other rail-oriented investments and looks to seizing such opportunities, if appropriate. In 1993, Wisconsin Central successfully participated as part of a consortium in a bidding process to acquire the New Zealand national railroad system (NZ Rail) from the New Zealand government. The total purchase price for the NZ Rail system was about $222 million (in U.S. dollars) for 2,500 route-miles of track, 270 locomotives, 6,000 freight cars, and ferry and freight forwarding operations. WC has a 29 percent interest in this rail operation and an option to purchase $3^1/_2$ percent more. This investment is expected to enhance the financial performance of WC and enable the exchange of expertise, technology, and ideas between the WC and NZ Rail.

HUMAN RESOURCES

The WC stresses the importance of the human factor in its operations. Again, President Ed Burkhardt: "When we formed this railroad we decided on a three-point program for dealing with our employees: stress good communications, reduce layoff fears, and treat everyone as if they were a part of management."[16]

▪ Good Communications

Burkhardt formally schedules employee meetings several times a year at the railroad's major locations. Rank and file attendance at some of these meetings, however, has recently been rather light. In addition, he holds informal gatherings during his many visits across the system. His open communications

Exhibit 5   **Average Number of Employees**

| | Year Ended December 31, | | |
	1991	1992	1993
General and Administrative	91	92	101
Marketing	25	27	35
Engineering (maintenance of way)	254	287	379
Mechanical (maintenance of equipment)	199	219	284
Transportation (Engineers, Conductors, Brakemen)	362	408	568
Totals	931	1033	1367

Source: Company Records.

philosophy has percolated down through the hierarchy, and management and corporate staff visits out on the line are the rule rather than the exception. This face to face interchange is supplemented by a quarterly newsletter, the *Waybill*, which keeps employees informed of the current status of operations. One innovation is an 800 number which allows WC employees to call any one at corporate headquarters, including Burkhardt. Many calls are aimed at solving problems but several are just to say "thanks."[17]

■ Reduced Layoff Fears

The WC places great emphasis on creating a stable work force. Judicious hiring to meet actual or forecast increased traffic demand minimizes subsequent layoffs during slack periods. Also, being non-union permits the assignment of employees to where they are needed rather than to where work rules require. An active cross-training program also permits this desired flexibility. The end result is that furloughs are a rarity.

Exhibit 5 shows the general increase in average employment during the last three years of operations.

■ Pay and Benefits

The company admitted from the beginning that it would be unable, at least in the short run, to match the pay of its unionized competitors. Pay ranges from 15 to 20 percent below comparable jobs and the work week often runs several hours longer. To partially offset this, the WC has placed all employees on salary and instituted a profit-sharing plan. There are also pay raises when conditions warrant. The benefit package offered WC employees generally exceeds that provided by the unionized rail lines.

Train crew pay on the WC is based upon hours worked rather than distance traveled. Yard switching crews normally have an eight-hour day while road crews work an average of 10 to 11 hours. If required, crews perform both switching and over-the-road duties in the same day. On unionized roads the 116-mile workday (often performed in three to four hours), coupled with ubiquitous work restrictions, severely limits flexibility. Compensation increases in the last three years can be seen in Exhibit 6.

Exhibit 6

Compensation Increases

Year	Percent Profit Sharing	Percentage Pay Raise
1991	2.3	4.5
1992	5.2	3.5
1993	6.0	3.25

Source: Company Records.

■ Training

The WC training program serves several purposes. First, it enables many employees to prepare themselves for better-paying jobs. For example, those interested in the transportation area can apply to attend the one-week train conductors' program or the eight-week train engineers' course held in Stevens Point. These programs, coupled with seniority and increased business, permit temporary work as extra train crews and possible later movement to full-time transportation status. In the interim, such employees continue to work in their original jobs.

As mentioned earlier, cross-training permits employees to perform multiple tasks, thus increasing their productivity and offering job protection. Line managers and key staff are kept current by attending American Management Association courses and university seminars.[18]

■ Hiring and Promotion

Job vacancies are posted and the WC's active training and development programs permit promotion from within whenever possible. The railroad also actively recruits and encourages employee referrals. The work force is predominately white and male but an increasing number of females are beginning to fill key positions throughout the hierarchy.

■ Unions

The WC saw little union activity during its first five years of operations. The United Transportation Union (UTU) seemed to express some interest in early 1988 but never made a concerted effort to begin organizing. The Brotherhood of Locomotive Engineers' (BLE) attempt in 1990 to represent engineers and, separately, trainmen (conductors and brakemen) failed when only 21 percent of the former and 15 percent of the latter voted affirmatively.

The acquisition of the GB&W and FRVR brought with them a January 1994 National Mediation Board (NMB) requirement that their former unions be recognized as the collective bargaining representative of FV&W's employers. The WC has since countered that the WC-FV&W are operated as a single system and that any unionization activity must apply to both equally. The NMB currently has this matter under advisement.

In March 1994 the NMB notified the company that the UTU had claimed it had enough authorization cards to have a representation election among WC engineers and conductors. Late July 1994 finds the NMB investigating the accuracy of the union count.

SERVICE AND MARKETING

The marketing of services is guided by WC's goals of providing frequent and dependable freight service at competitive prices by customer-minded employees. To accomplish this, all regular freight trains are scheduled so that they can connect in an efficient manner with each other as well as with other carriers' trains. WC trains adhere to their schedules, allowing for a high degree of schedule predictability for individual cars, fast transit times, and reliable arrival estimates for shippers. This is in contrast to many in the railroad industry operations wherein trains operate as unscheduled extras that depart only after certain tonnage requirements are filled. Keeping the cars moving and not waiting at intermediate yards also helps minimize car-hire expenses, typically a large operating expense on any railroad. The strict scheduling of trains also improved car utilization. For example, some cars that used to make three or four round trips per month on the previous carrier now make eight on the WC.[19]

■ Dependent Upon National System

Because most rail freight carriers in the United States must cooperate and function together as a nationwide system, problems with one railroad may affect others. Nowhere is this more obvious than at Chicago, which remains the busiest and most important gateway for the national rail system as well as the WC. For example, major snowstorms and subzero temperatures during the winter of 1993-1994 caused delays for all railroads, disrupted interchanges, and caused factory shutdowns. As a result, trains became difficult to move and yards in Chicago became plugged, making it impossible for the WC to deliver and pick up cars until yard tracks could be cleared. Like other railroads, the WC found itself short of crews and locomotives. This situation came on the heels of the additional traffic generated by the FV&W acquisition, which the railroad had not fully adjusted to.[20]

■ Customer Communication

Constant communication between the railroad and its 500-plus customers is emphasized. Unlike other railroads, WC operating personnel, to include train crews, are responsible for day-to-day contact with customers. Shippers also have direct access to an assigned marketing representative who knows their products, markets, and shipping requirements. This person is responsible for pricing and marketing assistance for both inbound and outbound shipments.

■ TCS

An important tool is a state-of-the-art system of integrated computer programs known as the Transportation Control System (TCS), which covers train and terminal operations, car scheduling, exchanging data with other carriers, waybill and billing functions, car accounting and distribution, equipment maintenance, marketing data, and operations status reports. TCS also allows customers to do their own billing and car tracing functions. To keep customers informed of railroad activities and progress, a professionally produced bimonthly newsletter is widely distributed.

■ Summary of Financial Performance 1991–1994

As previously mentioned, the WC has continued to improve its financial condition since start-up in 1987. The railroad generated $113.7 million in operating revenues in 1991, while traffic volume was 179.7 thousand carloads. Operating revenues for 1992 were $124.4 million and traffic volume 205.5 thousand carloads, a 9.4 percent increase in revenues and a 14.4 percent rise in traffic volume. In 1993 WCL had $151.7 million in operating revenue with 257.3 thousand carloads, an increase of 21.9 and 25.2 percent over comparable 1992 levels. During the first six months of 1994 operating revenues were $101.3 million compared to $67.6 million for the same period in 1993, a 49.8 percent increase. At the same time, carloadings increased 50 percent as compared to a similar period in 1993. Net income during the last three full years of operation increased from $8.2 million in 1991 to $15.4 million in 1993. Net income during the first six months of 1994 increased $14.1 million. Undoubtedly the greatest indicator of success has been expressed by the investors, who have bid the WCTC stock from an initial May 1991 offering of $16.50 per share to the low $70s in late Spring 1994. A July 5th, 1994, two-for-one stock split was followed by a $41 per share price by early August. Supporting data plus other comparisons can be found in Exhibit 7 (Condensed Consolidated Statements of Income).

■ Revenues

Traffic volume during the period increased in all 14 commodity groups with an overall increase of 78 thousand carloads, a 43.5 percent increase. Approximately half of this growth is due to the acquisition of FV&W and the Ladysmith line. While gross revenues increased, per-carload averages decreased in all groups. Exhibit 8 compares the WCL's 1991-1993 traffic volume, gross, and average revenues for carload by commodity group.

■ Operating Expenses

Expenses were $116.8 million in 1993, as compared to $98.9 million in 1992 and $91.2 million in 1991. Exhibit 9 provides a comparison of WC's expenses during this time period.

Labor expenses increased some $11.7 million during the period. These increases were due to an enlarged work force, pay raises, and employee bonuses plus associated fringe benefit costs.

Diesel fuel expenses rose $2.3 million, or 29.8 percent, during the period as consumption increased by 38.9 percent on a 52.8 percent increase in gross ton miles. The decline in fuel consumption per ton-mile was due to operating efficiency improvements. Fuel expenses were also kept in check because of hedge arrangements and a decline in per-gallon prices. Materials expenses rose as increased business levels required additional locomotives, freight cars, and track materials. Equipment rents increased due to additional car hire and equipment lease requirements. The remaining expense increases were attribut-

Exhibit 7

**Wisconsin Central Transportation Corporation and Subsidiaries
Condensed Consolidated Statements of Income
($ in thousands, except per share data)**

	Six Months Ended June 30,		Year Ended December 31,		
	1994	1993	1993	1992	1991
	(Unaudited)		(audited) ($ in thousands, except as indicated)		
Income Statement Data:					
Operating revenues	$101,347	$67,586	$151,691	$124,364	$113,657
Operating expenses	(76,588)	(54,412)	(116,843)	(98,008)	(91,229)
Income from operations	24,759	13,174	34,848	26,356	22,428
Gains on Sales of excess assets	—	—	1,735	2,383	3,120
Rental income	—	—	847	955	1,132
Other income (expense), net	698	607	(342)	(1,972)	(1,648)
Interest expense	(4,866)	(3,559)	(7,798)	(9,886)	(10,946)
Income (loss) before income taxes and extraordinary items	20,591	10,222	29,290	17,836	14,086
Provision for income taxes	(8,135)	(3,987)	(11,944)	(6,955)	(5,494)
Income (loss) before extraordinary items	12,456	6,235	17,346	10,881	8,592
Equity in Net Income of Affil.	4,464	—		1,490	—
Income before Extraordinary Item and Cumulative Effect of Accounting Change	16,920	6,235	18,836	10,881	8,592
Extraordinary item—early extinguishment of debt, net of income taxes	—	(1,398)	(1,398)	—	(341)
Cumulative effect on prior years of change in methods for income taxes	—	(2,067)	(2,067)	—	—
Net income (loss)	$ 16,920	$ 2,770	$ 15,371	$ 10,881	$ 8,251
Net income (loss) per share (dollars)	$ 1.02	$ 0.17	$ 1.86	$ 1.68	$ 1.52

Sources: Wisconsin Central Transportation Corporation, 1993, *Annual Report*, p. 28.
Wisconsin Central Transportation Corporation, 1994, *2nd Quarter Form 10-Q*, p. 3.

able to the FV&W and Ladysmith line acquisitions. The company's operating ratio (operating expenses divided by operating revenues) decreased from 80.3 percent in 1991 to 78.8 percent in 1992, 77.0 percent in 1993, and was at 73.1 percent as of July 1, 1994.

■ Liquidity and Capital Resources

Cash generated from operations has historically been the WC's primary source of liquidity and is used principally for debt service, capital expenditures, and working capital requirements. The company also acquires cash from sale of assets and financing activities. During the five-year period (1989–1993) the company's sources and uses of cash included those listed in Exhibit 10.

Exhibit 8   **Carload and Gross Revenue Comparison by Commodity Group 1991–1993**
($ in thousands, except per carload amounts)

Commodity Group	Carloads 1993	1992	1991	Gross Revenues 1993	1992	1991	Average Revenue Per Carload 1993	1992	1991
Paper	26,844	23,420	22,038	$ 25,466	$ 21,938	$ 21,340	$ 949	$ 937	$ 968
Woodpulp	27,368	19,091	18,270	21,519	17,376	17,911	786	910	980
Pulpboard	15,453	13,196	14,290	8,095	7,446	8,080	524	564	565
Lumber products	15,229	9,642	7,021	9,555	6,403	4,407	627	664	628
Wood fibers	18,387	18,176	15,467	9,229	8,544	7,802	502	470	504
Chemical and petroleum products	25,553	19,668	16,817	21,553	17,622	15,186	843	898	903
Intermodal	31,710	30,791	28,343	4,402	5,421	5,664	139	176	200
Sand, stone and minerals	29,133	19,358	8,402	12,715	7,613	4,316	436	393	514
Clay products and granules	17,461	14,738	13,231	16,322	14,031	12,696	935	952	960
Coal	14,145	10,799	13,663	7,062	5,567	7,240	499	516	530
Food and grain	18,288	14,341	11,479	11,928	9,519	7,475	652	664	651
Waste and scrap	10,990	7,802	6,748	6,932	5,492	4,981	631	704	738
Steel	3,568	2,657	2,144	4,210	3,376	2,823	1,180	1,271	1,317
Miscellaneous	3,197	1,833	1,810	1,760	1,423	1,158	550	776	640
Totals	257,326	205,512	179,723	$160,748	131,811	121,079	$ 625	641	674

Source: Wisconsin Central Transportation Corporation, 1993, *Annual Report,* pp. 16-20.

Exhibit 9   **Operating Expense Comparisons 1991–1993**

	1993	1992	1991
		($ in thousands)	
Labor expense (including payroll taxes and fringe benefits)	$ 49,951	$41,875	$38,265
Diesel fuel	10,194	8,204	7,852
Materials	10,968	9,688	8,698
Equipment rents, net	18,268	16,719	14,144
Joint facilities, net	792	1,369	2,395
Depreciation	6,838	5,783	5,480
Casualties and insurance	4,771	4,103	3,852
Property taxes	3,224	2,173	2,315
Other	11,837	8,094	8,228
Operating expenses	$116,843	$98,008	$91,229

Source: Wisconsin Central Transportation Corporation, 1993, *Annual Report,* pp. 17-21.

Exhibit 10

**Wisconsin Central Transportation Corporation and Subsidiaries 1989–1993
Selected Sources and Uses of Funds
($ in millions)**

Source		Use	
Operations	$129.6	Capital Expenditures	$145.0
Asset Sales	52.2	Asset Acquisition	96.6
Debt Issue	186.4	Debt Retirement	192.3
Equity Issue	86.0	Railroad Investment	16.0
		Working Capital	4.3
Total	$454.2	Total	$454.2

Source: Wisconsin Central Transportation Corporation, 1993, *Annual Report,* p. 23.

Exhibit 11

Roadway and Structure Improvements

	Year Ended December 31,		
	1993	1992	1991
Track miles surfaced[1]	749	592	456
Track miles of rail laid	24.5	27.2	22.2
Tons of ballast applied (thousands)	311.3	219.2	167.4
Ties installed (thousands)	149.4	122.5	81.5

[1] Surfacing is the process by which track was aligned and cross-leveled in conjunction with the application of ballast and the installation of ties.

Source: Wisconsin Central Transportation Corporation, 1993, *Annual Report,* p. 24.

The three years (1991–1993) saw the company invest some $32 million to purchase additional locomotives and freight cars. An additional $57.6 million was spent on roadway and structure improvement, as indicated in Exhibit 11.

By late July, the WC had passed the halfway mark of the 1994 planned laying of 220 thousand tons of ballast and 35 miles of welded rail, and installing 165 thousand ties.

At December 31, 1993, the WC had $134.2 million of debt outstanding, which constituted 47.3 percent of total capitalization. The railroad has an aggregate borrowing capacity of $150 million under various bank loan facilities and at year-end had $75.8 million unused. Cash flows from operations plus bank loan facilities should more than satisfy liquidity and capital expenditure requirements. Exhibit 12 on the following page gives recent consolidated balance sheet data.

Exhibit 12

Wisconsin Central Transportation Corporation and Subsidiaries Condensed Consolidated Balance Sheets ($ in thousands)

Assets			
	June 30, 1994 (Unaudited)	December 31, 1993 (Audited)	1992
Current Assets			
Cash and cash equivalents	$ 4,823	$ 4,677	$ 37,979
Receivables	39,796	32,839	23,480
Materials and supplies	15,881	12,846	9,055
Other current assets	2,289	2,513	1,154
Total current assets	62,789	52,875	71,668
Investment in Affiliate:	23,428	17,532	—
Properties			
Roadway and structures	—	300,036	205,550
Equipment	—	45,174	20,385
Total properties	363,119	345,210	225,935
Less accumulated depreciation	(35,722)	(31,010)	(23,544)
Net properties	327,397	314,200	202,391
Other Assets			
Deferred financing & organization costs, net	4,039	4,575	3,995
Deferred acquisition costs	—	—	2,768
Total other assets	4,039	4,575	6,763
Total assets	$417,653	$389,182	$280,822

EXTERNAL ENVIRONMENT: ECONOMIC

■ National

Railcar loadings have lagged gross domestic product, falling 2.5 percent in 1991 and increasing 1.1 percent in 1992 and 2.4 percent in 1993. Through June 4, 1994, commodity freight carloadings were up 3.8 percent and intermodal ahead by 13.2 percent as compared to a like time period in 1993. Increases in traffic for the remainder of 1994 are expected in such areas as intermodal, chemicals, lumber, paper, metallic ores, motor vehicles, stone, clay, and glass.

■ Regional

The State of Wisconsin is characterized by a variety of diversified and productive manufacturers supported by a highly educated labor force with a strong work ethic. According to a recent study on the state's economy by the University

Exhibit 12 (continued) **Wisconsin Central Transportation Corporation and Subsidiaries Condensed Consolidated Balance Sheets ($ in thousands)**

Liabilities and Stockholders' Equity

	June 30, 1994 (Unaudited)	December 31, 1993 (Audited)	1992
Current liabilities			
Long-term debt due within one year	$ —	$ —	$ 146
Accounts payable	27,441	27,653	16,727
Accrued expenses	40,511	33,917	21,531
Interest payable	2,006	1,544	1,544
Total current liabilities	69,958	63,114	39,948
Long-term debt	131,555	134,155	81,428
Other liabilities	4,923	6,414	2,798
Deferred income taxes	36,895	29,263	18,002
Deferred income	6,269	6,562	4,961
Total liabilities	249,600	239,508	147,137
Stockholders' equity			
Preferred stock par value $1.00; authorized 1,000,000 shares; none issued and outstanding	—	—	—
Common stock, par value $0.01; authorized 40,000,000 shares; issued and outstanding 8,276,983 shares in 1993 and 8,244,707 shares in 1992	—	83	82
Paid in capital	—	101,006	100,389
Retained earnings	—	48,585	33,214
Total stockholders' equity	168,053	149,674	133,685
Total liabilities and stockholders' equity	$417,653	$389,182	$280,822

Sources: Wisconsin Central Transportation Corporation, 1993, *Annual Report*, pp. 26-27.
Wisconsin Central Transportation Corporation, 1994, *2nd Quarter Form 10-Q*, p. 2.

of Wisconsin School of Business, the state has been particularly strong in durable goods production, especially industrial machinery, primary and fabricated metals, lumber, and instrumentation.[21]

The paper industry is of prime importance to Wisconsin, employing about 50,000 people, or nine percent of the state manufacturing employment. In 1992, Wisconsin ranked first among all states in paper industry employment and in paper production, producing over 4.6 million tons of paper, or 11 percent of the nation's total output.[22] Of the over 82 active pulp and paper mills in Wisconsin and the UP of Michigan, 69, most of them large capacity, are directly served by WC. Of the other 13 mills, 9 are located on railroad lines whose only interchange is with the Wisconsin Central. The railroad also serves a mill in Sault Ste. Marie, Ontario.

Large capital expenditures for expansion and modernization at these mills during the 1980s and continuing into the 1990s is expected to help maintain Wisconsin's dominant position as a papermaker. These investments are going not only toward expansion, but also to increase the plants' ability to utilize wastepaper and to meet tighter environmental standards. Wisconsin forest resources are plentiful. Although the harvesting of timber has been increasing, only about 60 percent of the forest growth has been cut in recent years. Eight major paper converting mills are also located on WC in Wisconsin.

Printing and publishing are also a big business in Wisconsin. One of the state's largest, Quad/Graphics, has three plants located on WC's lines, all of which were designed to receive printing paper by rail. Other major manufacturing concerns directly served by the railroad include firms that produce food products, lumber and wood products, chemicals, fabricated metals, electrical machinery, and plastics.

Mining is expected to remain a relatively small industry in Wisconsin, mostly engaged in the extraction of sand, gravel, and stone. Some metallic minerals including copper and gold are mined in the state near Ladysmith. The WC has begun hauling carloads of ore from this mine to Sault Ste. Marie for interchange to Canadian destinations. Copper and zinc deposits have also been found in northeastern Wisconsin near Crandon. It is anticipated that a mine will eventually become operational in this area once economic and environmental reviews have been satisfied. In Michigan, the White Pine Copper Mine, near Ironwood, is increasingly using WC for delivery of copper concentrates, grinding media, and coal, and shipment of copper cathodes.

■ Competition

WC's operations are subject to competition from other railroads, trucks, and water carriers. Railroad competition is primarily in the Duluth-Superior to Chicago market. The WC competes for interchange traffic at Duluth-Superior with the Burlington Northern, Soo Line/CP Rail System, and Chicago and North Western railroads. Both general freight coming down from Canada and iron ore from northern Minnesota can be hauled by any of these railroads to Chicago.

Trucks dominate the transportation market area of the WC. In the all-important paper industry, WC handles the majority of inbound raw materials, chemicals, coal, and clay. Outbound paper products transported by rail consisted of printing paper, kraft (brown) paper, and pulpboard. The WC has won back some sheet paper, consumer, and sanitary products business but the majority of this traffic remains with trucks due to relatively low product weight and off-line delivery requirements.

The WC competes with water carriers primarily for the movement of iron ore from northern Minnesota to Indiana, Ohio, Pennsylvania, and West Virginia. Movement of iron ore by boat is seasonal and cannot occur when the Great Lakes ports and locks are frozen during the winter. Coal deliveries to a copper mine in White Pine, Michigan, can be shipped by rail but have traditionally been handled by boat. The WC is generally too far north to be greatly affected by barges operating on inland waterways.

EXTERNAL ENVIRONMENT: POLITICAL/GOVERNMENT

■ Legal/Political

The WC is subject to numerous federal, state, and local laws and regulations pertaining, in varying degrees, to almost every phase of its operations.

■ Federal

Government programs and policies which influence the strength of the dollar, export/import, crop support prices, and interest rates greatly affect most sectors of the economy and therefore WC.

Major federal legislation aimed specifically at rail industry enhancement includes:

1. The 1976 Railroad Revitalization and Regulatory Reform Act (4Rs) freed the railroads of 75-year-old regulations that may have been appropriate before the coming of the truck and the airplane. Railroads were permitted greater flexibility in rate making, abandonments, mergers, and line sales. Federal funds were provided through state agencies to rehabilitate needed rail trackage. Individual states were required to become involved in rail planning.

2. The Staggers Rail Act of 1980 enhanced the work of the 4Rs Act. It further streamlined the mechanics of restructuring the physical rail system and rail rate structure. It allowed railroads to either increase net revenues on unprofitable branchlines or redirect traffic and abandon them.

3. Rural Rail Infrastructure Act of 1993 has been introduced by Congress and would mandate $100 million a year in matching fund grants to the states and provide for $500 million in funded loan guarantees. These monies are aimed principally for secondary rail lines.

4. North American Free Trade Agreement (NAFTA) of 1993 eliminates or greatly reduces trade barriers among the U.S., Canada, and Mexico. It is estimated that this agreement will create a $6 trillion tariff-free market within a decade. The railroads of the three countries are coordinating operating practices and streamlining border crossing procedures.

Other pertinent federal legislation includes:

1. Highway Trust Fund—Has subsidized truck use of the highway network. Over $125 billion is to be spent exclusively on highways over the next five years, while railroad support under the 4Rs Act is running $8–10 million a year.[23]

2. Federal Employees Liability Act—Is a form of workers' compensation mandated for the railroad industry. Unlike workers' compensation, it is an adversarial system rather than no-fault. As a result, average cost per employee hour worked is $1.51 for railroads and $0.27 for the rest of American industry.[24]

3. Railroad Retirement Act—Requires heavier railroad contributions than for employers under the Social Security system.[25]

4. Safety User Fees—Railroads must fund federal safety inspections of their track and equipment ($32 million in 1992) while truck and barge competitors do not have this requirement.[26]

▪ State and Local Activities

State and local government interaction with the railroad industry has traditionally centered only on selected issues such as safety, grade crossings, branchline abandonments, and freight service preservation. To a large degree, this is due to railroads being for-profit concerns that own and operate over their own rights-of-way, unlike trucks and barges, which have operated over publicly owned and maintained rights-of-way. During the 1970s and 1980s, the State of Wisconsin's rail programs and policies—like most states—focused on preservation of certain light-density branch lines and service provided by major railroads facing bankruptcy. Thus, Wisconsin's rail policies and programs were able to address preservation of endangered rail line segments; track rehabilitation assistance on light density lines; and mitigation of abandonment impacts on rail-using businesses.

WC has participated in several of these programs. For example, in 1990, the railroad completed rehabilitation of the 46-mile-long Manitowoc branch using a $1.25 million grant and a $750,000 low-interest loan from the State. Also, in 1989 the State of Michigan approved a $300,000 loan to WC to upgrade 19 miles of mainline track.

More recently, Wisconsin officials recommended that the state's rail freight policies and programs be modified to change their focus from that of service preservation to economic development. In a recently completed Freight Rail Policy Plan,[27] the Wisconsin Department of Transportation suggested a series of actions which include revising the state constitution's "internal improvements" clause to allow the state to make rail improvements directly; allowing the state to have the ability to manage the use of state-owned rail lines directly; and expanding the requirements in the track rehabilitation program to include a broader range of eligible rail lines. Other recommended actions included additional legislative items dealing with grade crossings and right-of-way fencing.

In 1993, Wisconsin's governor and the state legislature approved a freight railroad infrastructure improvement program which made up to $11 million in loans available from a revolving fund for upgrading rail lines. WC officials have indicated an interest in using funds from this program for such projects as rehabilitating the Ashland to Prentice line, constructing new pulpwood log loading centers in northern Wisconsin, expanding the yard at Neenah, and eliminating other operational bottlenecks.

▪ The Immediate Challenge

Ed Burkhardt's thoughts were interrupted by a report detailing a derailment that had left both locomotives and 28 freight cars on the ground. Ed was relieved to hear that the crew was unharmed. The main line into Chicago, however, would be blocked for several hours. Ed visualized the forthcoming traffic jam that would cause reverberations along the entire railroad. More missed connections, more late trains, more customer complaints, and longer hours for already tired crews. Ed wondered if greater emphasis on strengthening the infrastructure was the answer to the railroad's capacity problems? Or was it something more fundamental?

GLOSSARY

Bridge route   A railroad that serves as a connection between two or more non-contiguous rail lines.

Car hire   The act of renting freight cars of another railroad. Charges are computed on a daily basis.

Gateway   A rail center where freight cars from connecting railroads are interchanged.

Intermodal   Freight that is moved by differing modes of transportation en route to its destination.

Local traffic   Freight that originates and terminates on the trackage of the same railroad.

Originating traffic   Freight that originates on one railroad for delivery to a second railroad.

Terminating traffic   Freight that is received from another railroad for delivery to its final destination.

Trackage rights   A right to use the tracks of another railroad. A rights fee is normally charged.

Waybill   A document prepared by the carrier of freight that contains details of the shipment, route, and charges.

ENDNOTES

1. "Wisconsin Central Will Buy Canadian Rail Routes." *Milwaukee Sentinel*, July 29, 1994, Sec D, pp. 1–3.

2. Association of American Railroads, *Railroad Facts: 1993 Edition*, Economics and Finance Department, Washington, D.C., August 1993, p. 32.

3. Ibid., p. 32.

4. Ibid., p. 3.

5. Otto P. Dobnick, "The Wisconsin Central Story, Part 1: Acting Like a Class I, But Not Always Thinking Line One," *Trains*, September 1990, pp. 32–47.

6. "Another Route to Railroading." *The Chicago Tribune*, 25 January 1988, Sec. 4, p. 7.

7. Kevin P. Keefe, "Wisconsin Central on a Winning Streak," *Trains*, February 1993, p. 6.

8. Otto P. Dobnick, "The Wisconsin Central Story, Part 2: A Hub-and-Spoke System for Trains," *Trains*, October 1990, pp. 40–53.

9. Ibid.

10. Wisconsin Central Transportation Corporation, "Facts About WC and FV&W," July 11, 1994, p. 2.

11. Wisconsin Central Transportation Corporation Press Release dated April 28, 1992, referencing study of transportation competition in Wisconsin conducted by Reebie Associates, Greenwich, Connecticut.

12. Wisconsin Central Transportation Corporation, *1992 Annual Report*, p. 6.

13. William R. Schauer, Vice President-Marketing, Wisconsin Central Transportation Corporation, Presentation at Customers Shippers and Associates Reception, November 10, 1993, Wauwatosa, Wisconsin.

14. Wisconsin Central Ltd. and Fox Valley & Western Ltd., *Waybill* (Employee Newsletter), April 1994, pp. 4–5.

15. Ibid., pp. 4–5.

16. Interviews with President Edward A. Burkhardt, Wisconsin Central Transportation Corporation, 16–19 July 1991.

17. Interviews with Assistant Vice President-Human Resources, Wisconsin Central Transportation Corporation, David M. French, 25–26 July 1994.

18. French, interviews, 25–26 July 1994.

19. Dobnick, "Part 1," pp. 32–47.

20. Wisconsin Central Limited and Fox Valley & Western Ltd., *Waybill*, April 1994, pp. 1, 6.

21. John P. Klus and William A. Strang, *Wisconsin's Economy In the Year 2000* (Madison: University of Wisconsin Press, 1991), pp. 58–85.

22. Wisconsin Paper Council, *Fact Sheet for 1993*, Neenah, Wisconsin.

23. Interviews with Vice President-Marketing Lynn A. Anderson, Dakota, Minnesota & Eastern Railroad Corporation, May–July 1993.

24. "The 103rd Congress . . . Elected to Make Changes, and These Laws Need Changing." Regional Railroads of America, Washington DC, 1993.

25. Ibid.

26. Ibid.

27. Wisconsin Department of Transportation, Division of Planning and Budget, Freight Rail Policy Plan, Madison Wisconsin, January 1992, pp. 1–6, 47–69.

HealthSouth Corporation

W. Jack Duncan, University of Alabama at Birmingham

Peter M. Ginter, University of Alabama at Birmingham

Michael D. Martin, HealthSouth Corporation

Kellie F. Snell, HealthSouth Corporation

R ichard M. Scrushy, chairman and CEO of HealthSouth Corporation, was not surprised by many things when it came to his business. The April 22, 1996, issue of Forbes magazine, however, surprised even him. Forbes listed HealthSouth as the nation's fourth-largest company in market value growth in 1995 and as the two hundred thirty-third largest U.S.-based company in terms of market value. HealthSouth grew by 298 percent in market value in 1995 surpassed only by Ascend Communications, U.S. Robotics, and FORE Systems. Scrushy stated that he "was just surprised because I would have thought there would be more than three companies that outgrew us in market value growth." He was elated that the company he founded only thirteen years ago was now on lists with "big conglomerates we've known about our entire life."

HealthSouth Corporation was the nation's largest provider of outpatient and rehabilitative health care services, as well as the largest ambulatory surgery center provider. The company changed its name from HealthSouth Rehabilitation Corporation to HealthSouth Corporation (HC) to indicate clearly that it was not just a rehabilitation company anymore. HealthSouth, listed on the New York Stock Exchange, was second only to Columbia/HCA in the health care industry. At the close of 1995, HealthSouth operated over 700 locations throughout the United States and Canada. Its goal was simple: "To be the dominant outpatient health care provider in the nation's top 300 cities with 100,000 or more population."

HealthSouth Corporation was one of the most successful business ventures in modern health care. The Corporation's growth can be described as nothing less than "explosive" since its acquisition of National Medical

Enterprise's rehabilitation business in December 1993. Yet, growth involves its own challenge and explosive growth involves even greater challenges. As Scrushy reviewed selected operating results at the end of 1995 (Exhibits 1-3), and reflected on the company's position as it neared the end of its first decade of growth, he wondered about HealthSouth's future.

The ultimate direction of health care reform remained uncertain. Would there be significantly more competition in the rehabilitation market? Scrushy realized that, to sustain growth, continued hard work was even more necessary than during the startup period. Additionally, he realized that some key strategic decisions would have to be made: What was the optimum mix of businesses for HealthSouth Corporation? How far should HealthSouth go with its integrative "virtual hospital" model? What pitfalls lie ahead? Can success continue?

BEGINNING OF SUCCESS

HealthSouth Rehabilitation Corporation was organized in 1983 as AMCARE, Inc., but in 1985 changed its name to HealthSouth Rehabilitation Corporation (HRC). The company was founded by a group of health care professionals, led by Scrushy, who were formerly with LifeMark Corporation, a large publicly held, for-profit health care services chain that was acquired by American Medical International (AMI) in 1984.

In 1982, Richard Scrushy reflected on how he first recognized the potential for rehabilitation services: "I saw the TEFRA (Tax Equity and Fiscal Responsibility Act) guidelines and the upcoming implementation of Medicare's prospective payment system as creating a need for outpatient rehabilitation services. It was rather clear that lengths of stay in general hospitals would decrease and that patients would be discharged more quickly than in the past. It became obvious to me that these changes would create a need for a transition between the hospital and the patient's home." Medicare provided financial incentives for outpatient rehabilitation services by giving comprehensive outpatient rehabilitation facilities (CORFs) an exemption from prospective payment systems, and allowed the services of these facilities to continue to be reimbursed on a retrospective, cost-based basis.

"I also saw that LifeMark, my current employer, would suffer significant reductions in profitability as the use of the then-lucrative ancillary inpatient services was discouraged under the new reimbursement guidelines. I discussed my concerns about the upcoming changes in Medicare with LifeMark management and proposed that we develop a chain of outpatient rehabilitation centers. I saw that the centers I proposed were LifeMark's chance to preserve its profitability under PPS, and when they rejected my proposal, I saw cutbacks and a low rate of advancement in the future," Scrushy confirmed.

"I repeated my proposal for AMI's management when it acquired LifeMark, but AMI could not implement the program immediately after such a major acquisition. I resigned and founded HealthSouth Rehabilitation Corporation in conjunction with three of my colleagues from LifeMark."

Exhibit 1

HealthSouth Corporation and Subsidiaries
Consolidated Balance Sheets

Assets	December 31, 1994 ($000)	December 31, 1995 ($000)
Current Assets:		
Cash & Cash Equivalents	$ 73,438	$ 104,896
Other Marketable Securities	16,628	4,077
Accounts Receivable, Net of Allowances for Doubtful Accounts & Contractual Adjustments of $147,435,000 in 1994 and $212,972,000 in 1995	246,983	336,818
Inventories	27,398	33,504
Prepaid Expenses & Other Current Assets	69,092	70,888
Deferred Income Taxes	3,073	13,257
Total Current Assets	436,612	563,440
Other Assets:		
Loans to Officers	1,240	1,525
Other	41,834	60,437
Property, Plant, and Equipment—Net	872,795	1,100,212
Intangible Assets—Net	426,458	734,515
Total Assets	$ 1,778,939	$ 2,460,129
Liabilities & Stockholders' Equity		
Current Liabilities:		
Accounts Payable	$ 88,413	90,427
Salaries & Wages Payable	34,848	59,540
Accrued Interest Payable & Other Liabilities	57,351	58,086
Current Portion of Long-Term Debt	19,123	27,913
Total Current Liabilities	199,735	235,966
Long-Term Debt	1,032,941	1,253,374
Deferred Income Taxes	9,104	15,436
Other Long-Term Liabilities	9,451	5,375
Deferred Revenue	7,526	1,525
Minority Interests-Limited Partnerships	15,959	20,743
Commitments & Contingent Liabilities		
Stockholders' Equity:		
Preferred Stock, $.01 Par Value—1,500,000 Shares Authorized; Issued and Outstanding—None		
Common Stock, $.01 Par Value—150,000,000 Shares Authorized; Issued 78,858,000 in 1994 and 97,359,000 in 1995	789	974
Additional Paid-In Capital	388,269	740,763
Retained Earnings	138,205	208,653
Treasury Stock, At Cost (91,000 Shares)	(323)	(323)
Receivable from Employee Stock Ownership Plan	(17,477)	(15,886)
Notes Receivable from Stockholders	(5,240)	(6,471)
Total Stockholders' Equity	504,223	927,710
Total Liabilities & Stockholders' Equity	$ 1,778,939	$ 2,460,129

Exhibit 2

HealthSouth Corporation and Subsidiaries
Consolidated Statements of Income
(in thousands except for per share amounts)

	December 31, 1994	December 31, 1995
Revenues	$ 1,274,365	$ 1,556,687
Operating Expenses:	930,845	1,087,554
Operating Units Corporate General & Administrative	48,606	42,514
Provision for Doubtful Accounts	27,646	31,637
Depreciation & Amortization	89,305	121,195
Interest Expense	66,874	91,693
Interest Income	(4,566)	(5,879)
Merger & Acquisition Related Expenses	6,520	34,159
Loss on Impairment of Assets	10,500	11,192
Loss on Abandonment of Computer Project	4,500	—
	1,180,230	1,414,065
Income Before Income Taxes & Minority Interests	94,135	142,622
Provision for Income Taxes	34,778	48,091
	59,357	94,531
Minority Interests	8,864	15,582
Net Income	$ 50,493	$ 78,949
Weighted Average Common & Common Equivalent Share	86,461	94,246
Net Income Per Common and Common Equivalent Share	$ 0.58	$ 0.84
Net Income Per Common Share Assuming Full Dilution	$ 0.58	$ 0.82

▪ Early Development

HealthSouth Corporation began operations in January 1984. Its initial focus was on the establishment of a national network of outpatient rehabilitation facilities supported by a rehabilitation equipment business. In September 1984, HC opened its first outpatient rehabilitation facility at Little Rock, Arkansas, followed by another one at Birmingham, Alabama, in December 1984. Within five years, the Company was operating twenty-nine outpatient facilities located in seventeen states throughout the Southeastern United States. By the end of 1995, HealthSouth operated in more than 700 locations—from California to New Hampshire, from Florida to Wisconsin, and into Canada. Business was booming. In June 1985, HC started providing inpatient rehabilitation services with the acquisition of an 88-bed facility in Florence, South Carolina. During the next five years, the company established eleven more inpatient facilities in nine states, with a twelfth under development.

Exhibit 3   **HealthSouth Corporation and Subsidiaries**
Consolidated Statements of Stockholders' Equity

	Common Shares	Common Stock	Add. Paid-In Capital	Retained Earnings	Treasury Stock	Receivable ESOP	Notes Received from Stock-holders	Total Stock-holders' Equity
Balance - December 31, 1994	$ 78,767	$788.6	$ 388,269	$ 138,205	$(323)	$ (17,477)	$(5,240)	$ 504,223
Adjustment for ReLife Merger	2,732	27.3	7,114	(3,734)	0	0	0	3,407
Proceeds from Issuance of Common Shares	14,950	149.5	330,229	0	0	0	0	330,379
Proceeds from Exercise of Options	819	8.2	8,499	0	0	0	0	8,507
Income Tax Benefits Related to Incentive Stock Options	0	0	6,653	0	0	0	0	6,653
Reduction in Receivable from Employee Stock Ownership Plan	0	0	0	0	0	1,591	0	1,591
Increase in Stockholders' Notes Receivable	0	0	0	0	0	0	(1,231)	(1,231)
Purchase of Limited Partnership Units	0	0	0	(4,767)	0	0	0	(4,767)
Net Income	0	0	0	78,949	0	0	0	78,949
Balance - December 31, 1995	$ 97,268	$ 973.6	$ 740,764	$ 208,653	$ (323)	$ (15,886)	$ (6,471)	$ 927,710

■ South Highlands Hospital

A key development in HealthSouth's growth strategy was the December 1989 acquisition of the 219-bed South Highlands Hospital in Birmingham, Alabama. Although South Highlands had been marginally profitable, its inability to obtain financing meant that it was unable to meet the needs of its physicians, particularly James Andrews and William Clancy, both world-renowned ortho-pedic surgeons. As Scrushy noted: "My immediate concern was to maintain the referral base that Drs. Andrews and Clancy provided. HC had benefited from the rehabilitation referrals stemming from the extensive orthopedic surgery performed at South Highlands. The surgeons needed a major expansion at South Highlands to practice at maximum effectiveness and Drs. Andrews and Clancy would seek the facilities they needed elsewhere if something wasn't done. On the surface our acquisition of South Highlands was defensive."

The purchase of South Highlands Hospital for approximately $27 million was far from a defensive move. Renamed HealthSouth Medical Center (HMC), this hospital was developed into a flagship facility. HC immediately began construction of a $30 million addition to the hospital. Even during construction, referrals continued to flow from HMC to other HC facilities. The construction created interest in the medical community, which in turn created business. The emergency facility at HMC eliminated the necessity of delaying evaluation and treatment of athletic injuries that could be quickly transferred to the facility through HC's extensive linkages with 396 high school and college athletic programs.

The acquisition of additional medical centers is an outgrowth of HealthSouth's rehabilitative services. The medical centers provide general and specialty health care services emphasizing orthopedics, sports medicine, and rehabilitation. In each market where a medical center has been acquired, HealthSouth enjoyed well-established relationships with the medical communities serving the facility. Following each acquisition, it has been HealthSouth's goal to provide resources for improving the physical plant and expanding services through the introduction of new technology. All HealthSouth medical centers are JCAHO accredited and participate in the Medicare prospective payment system. At the end of 1995, the company's inpatient facilities achieved an overall bed utilization rate of just over 70 percent.

■ Surgery Centers

As the result of the acquisition of Surgical Health Corporation (SHC), Sutter Surgery Centers, Inc. (SSCI), and Surgical Care Affiliates, Inc. (SCA), HealthSouth became the largest operator of outpatient surgery centers in the United States. At the end of 1995, HC operated over 100 free-standing surgery centers, with others under development. Most of these facilities were located in markets served by the company's outpatient and rehabilitative service facilities, creating the potential for significant synergies through cross-referrals between surgery and rehabilitative facilities as well as centralization of administrative services. The entry of the outpatient surgery market provided an important ingredient in the realization of HealthSouth's integrated service model illustrated in Exhibit 4. In light of developments in managed care, this integrated service model offered payers convenience and cost-effectiveness because they could deal with a single provider for a variety of services (one stop shopping). With this model, Scrushy noted: "We are laying the foundation for HealthSouth to be the health care company for the twenty-first century. We are establishing the platform on which we will build. Health care in the next century will not be based on the traditional hospital model. Rather, the emphasis will be less intrusive surgical interventions, more efficient diagnostic procedures, and less restrictive environments." According to Scrushy, "Health care in the future will develop around the virtual hospital — an integrated service delivery model that replaces many of the functions of the acute-care hospital with lower-cost outpatient facilities."

Exhibit 4   **Integrated Service Model**

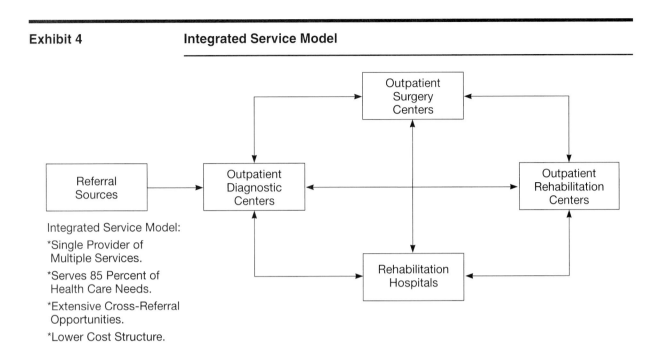

Integrated Service Model:

*Single Provider of
Multiple Services.

*Serves 85 Percent of
Health Care Needs.

*Extensive Cross-Referral
Opportunities.

*Lower Cost Structure.
  *Higher Margins and Returns.
  *Greater Flexibility.

INDUSTRY OVERVIEW

Every year more than 4 million people need rehabilitative health care services as the result of automobile and industrial accidents, sports and recreational injuries, crime and violence, or cardiac, stroke, and cancer episodes. It is estimated that at any particular time, 13 percent of the U.S. population and almost one-half of Americans over 75 years of age require some form of rehabilitative health services. With the population aging, this suggests even higher demand for rehabilitative health services in the future.

Medical rehabilitation involves the treatment of physical limitations through which therapists seek to improve their patients' functional independence, relieve pain, and ameliorate any permanent disabilities. Patients using medical rehabilitation services include the handicapped and those recovering from automobile, sports, and other accidents; strokes; neurological injuries; surgery; fractures and disabilities associated with diseases; and conditions such as multiple sclerosis, cerebral palsy, arthritis, and heart disease. Over 80 percent of those people receiving rehabilitative health care services return to their homes, work, schools, or active retirement.

■ Rehabilitation Services

Medical rehabilitation provider services include inpatient rehabilitation in dedicated freestanding hospitals and distinct units of acute-care hospitals; comprehensive outpatient rehabilitation facilities; specialty rehabilitation programs (such as traumatic brain injury and spinal cord injury); pediatric rehabilitation; occupational and industrial rehabilitation; and rehabilitation agencies.

The availability of comprehensive rehabilitation services was limited in the United States. Provision of rehabilitation services by outpatient departments of acute-care hospitals was fragmented because services were provided through several departments, and private practice therapists rarely provided a full-range of comprehensive rehabilitation services. Often, patients requiring multidisciplinary services would be treated by different therapists in different locations, which could result in uncoordinated care.

Comprehensive inpatient rehabilitation services were provided by free-standing rehabilitation hospitals, distinct units in acute-care hospitals, and skilled nursing facilities. Analysts with Solomon Brothers estimated that the rehabilitation services segment of the health care industry in the United States would grow at a rate of 13 to 15 percent in 1996 and that HealthSouth Corporation should increase its earnings per share by 20-22 percent over the next three years, therefore significantly outperforming the rehabilitation market in general. A number of factors would drive industry growth and ultimately affect HC's performance.

The incidence of major disability increases with age. Improvements in medical care have enabled more people with severe disabilities to live longer. Data compiled by the National Center for Health Statistics showed that, in 1995, 35 million people in the United States (one out of every seven people) had some form of disability. The National Association of Insurance Commissioners pointed out that seven out of ten workers would suffer a long-term disability between the ages of 35 and 65. Increases in leisure time among the middle age population resulted in more physical activity and thus more sports injuries, a major portion of HealthSouth's business. At the same time, the greater proportion of the population in the elderly age group increased the demand for rehabilitation services associated with the elderly, such as treatments for strokes and amputations. As a direct result of improved technology, three million people a year survive automobile crashes, sports injuries, strokes, and heart attacks and require rehabilitation services to restore normal functions.

Purchasers and providers of health care services, such as insurance companies, health maintenance organizations, businesses, and industry were seeking economical, high-quality alternatives to traditional health care services. Rehabilitation services, whether outpatient or inpatient, represented such an alternative. Often early participation in a disabled person's rehabilitation prevented a short-term problem from becoming a long-term disability. Moreover, by returning the individual to the work force, the number of disability benefit payments was reduced, thus decreasing long-term disability costs. Independent studies by companies such as Northwestern Life have shown that of every dollar spent on rehabilitation a savings of $30 occurred in disability payments. Insurance companies generally agreed that every rehabilitation dollar spent on patients with serious functional impairments saved from $10 to $30 in long-term health care costs such as nursing care.

As noted previously, inpatient rehabilitation services, organized as either dedicated rehabilitation hospitals or distinct units, were eligible for exemptions from Medicare's prospective payment system. Outpatient rehabilitation services, organized as comprehensive outpatient rehabilitation facilities or rehabilitation agencies, were eligible to participate in the Medicare program under cost-based reimbursement. Inpatient and outpatient rehabilitation services were typically covered for payment by the major medical portion of commercial health insurance policies. Moreover, Medicare reimbursement and the policies of private insurance companies encouraged early discharge from acute care hospitals, thereby providing opportunities for outpatient rehabilitation, home health, and long-term-care facilities.

Advances in medical science and trauma care made it possible to save the lives of numbers of victims of accidents, greater violence, and serious sports injuries. These victims were provided with therapeutic options that offered opportunities for inpatient and outpatient rehabilitation facilities. Although HealthSouth is no longer simply a rehabilitation company, rehabilitative services remained the core of its integrated systems model. Expansion into medical centers and outpatient surgery augment and capitalize on the company's reputation and relationships in the markets it served.

■ Rehabilitation and Outpatient Surgery

At the close of 1992, HealthSouth's primary rehabilitation services competitors were National Medical Enterprises, Inc., Continental Medical Systems, ReLife, NovaCare, and AdvantageHealth. By the beginning of 1996, HealthSouth had acquired all of these competitors except CMS. It is estimated that HealthSouth presently controls about 40 percent of the rehabilitation beds and approximately 12 percent of the outpatient rehabilitation beds.

Within one year of entry into the market, HealthSouth became the industry leader in ambulatory surgical centers. According to Alex Brown & Sons, of the roughly 2,100 freestanding ambulatory surgery centers approximately 75 percent were single-site and physician owned. This market, in other words, was highly fragmented and represented a major opportunity for HealthSouth. The company owned about ten percent of the freestanding surgical centers.

As illustrated in Exhibit 5, HC's operating units were located in forty-two states, the District of Columbia, and Canada and consisted of 15 medical centers, 15 diagnostic centers, 497 outpatient clinics, and 112 outpatient surgery centers. The competition faced in each of these markets was similar although unique aspects did exist, arising primarily from the number of health care providers in specific metropolitan areas. The primary competitive factors in the rehabilitation services business were quality of services, projected patient outcomes, responsiveness to the needs of the patients, community and physicians, ability to tailor programs and services to meet specific needs, and the charges for services.

HealthSouth's rehabilitative facilities competed on a regional and national basis with other providers of specialized services such as sports medicine, head injury rehabilitation, and orthopedic surgery. Competitors and potential competitors included hospitals, private practice therapists, rehabilitation agencies, and so on. Some of the competitors had significant patient referral support systems as well as financial and human resources. HealthSouth centers competed directly

Exhibit 5

Location of HealthSouth Facilities as of January 1, 1996

State	Outpatient Centers	Inpatient Centers	Medical Centers	Surgery Centers	Diagnostic Centers
Alabama	19	9	1	5	4
Alaska	0	0	0	1	0
Arizona	17	3	0	2	0
Arkansas	2	1	0	2	0
California	46	1	0	18	0
Colorado	21	0	0	4	0
Connecticut	1	0	0	0	0
Washington, DC	1	0	0	0	1
Delaware	4	0	0	0	0
Florida	47	8	2	20	1
Georgia	8	3	0	4	1
Hawaii	3	0	0	0	0
Idaho	0	0	0	1	0
Illinois	46	0	0	2	0
Indiana	13	1	0	2	0
Iowa	3	0	0	0	0
Kansas	3	0	0	0	0
Kentucky	2	1	0	2	0
Louisiana	2	1	0	1	0
Maine	2	0	0	0	0
Maryland	15	1	0	5	3
Massachusetts	1	0	0	1	0
Michigan	1	0	0	1	0
Mississippi	3	0	0	0	0
Missouri	30	4	0	6	0
Nebraska	2	0	0	0	0
Nevada	2	0	0	0	0
New Hampshire	7	1	0	0	0
New Jersey	18	2	0	2	0
New Mexico	3	1	0	1	0
New York	12	0	0	0	0
North Carolina	13	1	0	3	0
Ohio	24	0	0	1	0
Oklahoma	9	1	3	1	0
Ontario, Canada	1	0	0	0	0
Pennsylvania	19	8	5	0	0
South Carolina	6	5	2	0	0
Tennessee	13	6	0	6	1
Texas	42	13	1	14	3
Utah	1	1	0	1	0
Virginia	10	3	1	1	1
Washington	23	0	0	1	0
West Virginia	1	4	0	0	0
Wisconsin	1	0	0	4	0
Total	497	79	15	112	15

Exhibit 6   **HealthSouth Corporation Market Share**

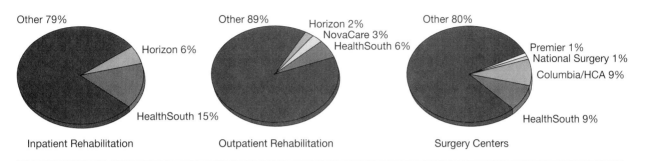

Inpatient Rehabilitation   Outpatient Rehabilitation   Surgery Centers

Inpatient Rehabilitation Services acquisitions include NME, RELife, NovaCare, and Advantage.
Outpatient Rehabilitation Services include Caremark and Advantage Acquisitions.
Surgery Center includes Surgical Care Affiliates, Sutter, and Surgical Health Acquisitions.

with local hospitals and various nationally recognized centers of excellence in orthopedics, sports medicine, and other specialties.

HealthSouth's surgery centers competed primarily with hospitals and other operators of free-standing surgery centers in attracting patients and physicians, in developing new centers, and in acquiring existing centers. The primary competitive factors in the outpatient surgery business were convenience, cost, quality of service, physician loyalty, and reputation. Hospitals had a number of competitive advantages in attracting physicians and patients.

The company faced competition every time it initiated a certificate of need project or sought to acquire an existing facility. The competition would arise from national or regional companies or from local hospitals that filed competing applications or that opposed the proposed CON project. Although the number of states requiring CON or similar approval was decreasing, HC continued to face this requirement in several states. The necessity for these approvals, which was somewhat unique to the health care industry, demanded that organizations planning to open new facilities or purchase expensive and specialized equipment convince a regulatory or planning agency that such facilities or equipment were really needed and would not merely move patients from one provider to another. They served as an important barrier to entry and potentially limited competition by creating a franchise to provide services to a given area.

The market for outpatient rehabilitation services was estimated to be approximately $7.9 billion. In-patient rehabilitation services were estimated to be another $7.7 billion, and the market for outpatient surgery centers was estimated at approximately $6 billion. HealthSouth's estimated market share in each of these markets is shown in Exhibit 6.

■ Reimbursement

Aggressive acquisition and managed care marketing efforts have radically altered the payer mix of HealthSouth over the past five years. Reimbursement for services provided by HC were divided into four distinct categories: commercial or private pay including HMOs, PPOs, and other managed care plans; workers' compensation; Medicare; and "other," which included a relatively insignificant amount of Medicaid. The percentage of each varied by business segment and facility. As illustrated in Exhibit 7, commercial or private pay-

Exhibit 7   **HealthSouth Corporation Revenue Sources**

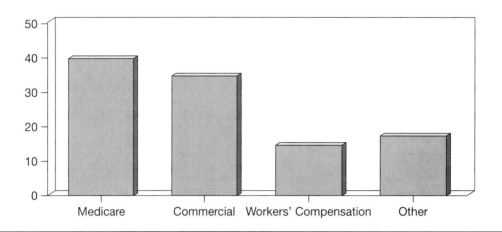

ment represented about 34 percent of total company receipts, Medicare accounted for 41 percent of overall HC revenues, workers' compensation comprised 11 percent of overall revenues, and all "other" sources accounted for 14 percent.

■ Commercial or Private Pay

Approximately 80 percent of the population under age 65 had medical insurance coverage. The extent of the coverage varied by location. Generally, charges for inpatient rehabilitation were completely (100 percent) reimbursed under general hospitalization benefits, and outpatient rehabilitation was reimbursed 100 percent similar to other outpatient services. Studies conducted by the Life Insurance Marketing and Research Association found that more than 70 percent of the employers in their sample provided some financial assistance for employees who participated in company-approved rehabilitation programs. Northwestern National Life Insurance Company reported that complete rehabilitation was possible in 66 percent of the light-industry injuries and in 62 percent of heavy-industry injuries. Of particular significance is the fact that HealthSouth's size and leadership made possible an aggressive managed care contracting strategy. In 1993, for example, HC had 265 managed care contracts. In 1995 the number increased to 1,200. Almost two-thirds of all HC's commercial revenues were under managed care contracts compared to only one-third in 1995.

■ Medicare

Although the rehabilitation services market had grown significantly, it continued to represent a relatively small portion of Medicare expenditures. Since 1983, the federal government had employed a prospective payment system as a means of controlling general acute-care hospital costs for the Medicare program. In the past, the Medicare program provided reimbursement for reasonable direct and indirect costs of the services furnished by hospitals to beneficiaries, plus an allowed return on equity for proprietary hospitals. As a result of the Social Security Act Amendments of 1983, Congress adopted a prospective payment system to cover the routine and ancillary operating costs of most Medicare inpatient hospital services.

HC is generally subject to PPS with respect to Medicare inpatient services. However, as of 1995, Medicare continued to pay certain defined units, freestanding rehabilitation facilities, and certified outpatient units on the basis of "reasonable costs" incurred during a base year (the year prior to being excluded from Medicare's prospective payment system or the first year of operation) adjusted by a market basket index. As a result, PPS has benefited the rehabilitation segment of the health care industry because the economic pressure on acute-care hospitals to discharge patients as soon as possible with the resulting demand for increased outpatient rehabilitation services which are currently exempt from PPS. Even inpatient rehabilitation units in acute-care facilities can obtain exemption from PPS upon satisfaction of certain federal criteria.

■ Workers' Compensation

Increasingly, managed care attempts to include workers' compensation into seamless products. About 40 percent of the costs associated with workers' compensation claims are medical costs and many of these can be reduced through discount purchasing, utilization management, and outcomes-based treatment programs. Much of HealthSouth's expansion over the past several years has been motivated by the need to attack managed care as an opportunity rather than retreat from it as a threat. By becoming the largest rehabilitation services provider and building a network of inpatient and outpatient facilities nationwide, HC has been able to sign national contracts with payers, gain market share, and offset any erosion in margin. At the present time, workers' compensation is estimated to be about 15 percent of HC's rehabilitation business.

■ Regulation

The health care industry was subject to regulation by federal, state, and local governments. The various levels of regulatory activity affected organizations by controlling growth, requiring licensure or certification of facilities, regulating the use of properties, and controlling the reimbursement for services provided. In some states, regulations controlled the growth of health care facilities.

Capital expenditures for the construction of new facilities, addition of beds, or acquisition of existing facilities could be reviewed by state regulators under a statutory scheme, usually referred to as a *CON program*. States with CON requirements placed limits on the construction and acquisition of health care facilities as well as the expansion of existing facilities and services.

Licensure and certification were separate but related regulatory activities. The former was usually a state or local requirement, and the latter was a federal requirement. In almost all instances, licensure and certification would follow specific standards and requirements set forth in readily available public documents. Compliance with the requirements was monitored by annual on-site inspections by representatives of various government agencies.

To receive Medicare reimbursement, each facility had to meet the applicable conditions of participation set forth by the U.S. Department of Health and Human Services relating to the type of facility, equipment, personnel, and standards of medical care, as well as compliance with all state and local laws and regulations. In addition, Medicare regulations generally required entry into such facilities through physician referral.

HEALTHSOUTH TODAY

HealthSouth's primary objective is to be the provider of choice for patients, physicians, and payers for outpatient and rehabilitative health care services throughout the United States. Its growth strategy is based on four interrelated elements: (1) implementation of the Company's *integrated service model* in appropriate markets; (2) successful marketing to managed care organizations and other payers; (3) provision of high-quality, cost-effective health care services; and (4) expansion of its national network.

- *Integrated Service Model.* HealthSouth attempts to offer an integrated system of health care services including outpatient rehabilitative services, inpatient rehabilitative services, ambulatory surgery services, and outpatient diagnostic services. The Company believes that such an integrated model offers patients and payers convenience and offers substantial referral opportunities. HealthSouth estimates, for example, that one-third of its outpatient rehabilitative patients have had outpatient surgery, virtually all inpatient rehabilitation patients will require some form of outpatient rehabilitation, and almost all inpatient rehabilitation patients have some type of diagnostic procedure.
- *Marketing to Managed Care Organizations and Other Payers.* For almost 20 years HealthSouth has focused on the development of contractual relationships with managed care organizations, major insurance companies, large regional and national employers, and provider alliances and networks. The Company's documented outcomes with thousands of patients and its reputation for quality have given it a competitive advantage over smaller competitors.
- *Cost-Effective Services.* An important corporate goal is to provide high-quality, cost-effective health care services. The Company has developed standardized clinical protocols which resulted in "best practices" techniques throughout all HealthSouth facilities. The Company's reputation for its clinical programs is enhanced by its relationship with major universities and its support of clinical research facilities. The Company believes that outpatient and rehabilitative services are inherently less expensive than comparable services delivered in an inpatient environment. To this end HealthSouth is committed to the "virtual hospital" or "hospital without walls" concept, whereby services are delivered more cost-effectively without the heavy overhead burden of the acute-care hospital.
- *Expansion of National Network.* As the largest provider of outpatient and rehabilitative health care services in the United States, HealthSouth is able to realize economies of scale and compete successfully for national contracts with national payers and employers while retaining the ability to respond to the unique needs of local markets. The national network offers payers the convenience of dealing with a single provider, to utilize greater buying power through centralized purchasing, to achieve more efficient costs of capital and labor, and to recruit and retain physicians more efficiently.

FUNCTIONAL CONSIDERATIONS

HC's management was a group of young energetic professionals. In 1995, HealthSouth was formally organized around four operating divisions, each with its own president. All presidents reported to Scrushy, who remained as chairman of the board and chief executive officer. The operating divisions were HealthSouth Inpatient Operations, HealthSouth Outpatient Centers, Health-South Surgery Centers, and HealthSouth Imaging (diagnostic) Centers (see Exhibit 8). The average age of the executive officers was 43 years, with a range from 55 to 36. Despite the relative youth of the executive officers, the team as a whole had an average tenure with the company of slightly over eight years. The range is one year to 12 years. Four of the 12 executive officers had been with HealthSouth from the time of its inception.

The corporate climate was characterized by a sense of urgency that was instilled in all of HealthSouth's employees directly by the chairman and CEO. Scrushy founded HealthSouth at the age of 32. As with many entrepreneurs, he was a visionary, but had the ability to make things happen. He worked virtually 365 days a year, 16 to 20 hours a day for the first five years, waiting until 1989 before taking his first vacation. His pace remained furious, working over 75 hours a week.

As a result of Scrushy's "hands-on" style, HC was run; it did not drift. This was not likely to change with the operating divisions reporting directly to the chairman and CEO. One of the company's most effective tools was a weekly statistical report, compiled every Thursday and distributed on Friday. The report included weekly statistics and trends such as payer mix, census, and revenue. It was reviewed over the weekend; and, if there was a negative trend, it was corrected. Thus, any problem was short lived. In this manner the management team was focused on real and developing problems.

Another tool was effective communications. Every Monday morning at 7:00 A.M. there was a meeting of the company's officers that included personnel from operations, development, finance, and administration. In this meeting each employee made a presentation, detailing what he or she accomplished in the previous week and what was planned for the current week. Questions were answered and problems were resolved. One additional benefit was that each employee was held accountable for his or her actions. Although this could be perceived to be overkill, it was believed to be necessary and helpful to the participants. At one time the meetings were stopped for about six weeks. After the company experienced a slight dip in performance and coordination, the meetings were immediately reinstated.

■ Staffing and Compensation

Unlike many other health care companies, HealthSouth had not experienced staffing shortages. Clinicians were in short supply, but HC was able to recruit and maintain excellent personnel. The ability to offer a challenging environment was a key factor. A HealthSouth inpatient facility in a metropolitan location typically competed favorably against other hospitals and nursing homes for the skills of new therapists. HealthSouth's outpatient facilities offered an attractive alternative to the clinician by offering eight-hour workdays with weekends and holidays off.

Exhibit 8   **HealthSouth Corporation Operations**

Outpatient Rehabilitation	Medical Centers (not an operating division)	Surgery Centers	Inpatient Rehabilitation	Diagnostic Centers
Services Include:	Services Include:	Services Include:	Services Include:	Services Include:
Aquatic therapy	Cardiology	ENT	Aquatic therapy	Computed tomography
Audiological screenings	Day surgery	Gastroenterology	Amputee	Electromyography
Biofeedback	Diagnostic imaging	General surgery	Arthritis	Magnetic resonance imaging
Driving assessments	Dial-a-nurse	Gynecology	Brain injury	Mammography
Family education	Emergency room	Lithotripsy	Burns	Nerve conduction velocity
Foot and ankle	Foot and ankle	Ophthalmology	Cardiac	Nuclear medicine
Functional capacity evaluations	Gastroenterology	Oral surgery	Cerebral palsy	Radiographic fluoroscopy
General orthopedics	General surgery	Orthopedics	Community re-entry	Ultrasound
Hand therapy	Hand surgery	Pain management	General rehabilitation	
Headache	Joint replacement	Plastic surgery	Joint replacement	
Injury prevention	Lithotripsy	Podiatry	Multiple sclerosis	
Neurology	Neurological sciences	Urology	Neurobehavioral	
Neuropsychology	Occupational health		Orthopedics	
Occupational therapy	Oncology		Orthotics/ Prosthetics	
Pain	Orthopedics		Pain management	
Physical therapy	Pain management		Pediatrics	
Speech therapy	Plastic surgery		Pulmonary	
Spine rehabilitation	Spine		Renal dialysis	
Sports therapy	Sports medicine		Spinal injury	
Urinary therapy	Urology			
Vision therapy				
Work hardening				
WCA/FCA				

All of the company's employees were competitively compensated. One compensation tool used was employee incentive stock options, which were granted to key corporate and clinical personnel. The options required a vesting period of four years with 25 percent of the amount being vested annually. If the employee left for another job, the options were lost. With the tremendous success of the company, the stock options had created "golden handcuffs." Some employees had options that could be exercised at prices less than $18 a share. Although HC stock was trading for $29 per share in December 1995, throughout 1995 it traded in a range of $16 to $32 per share. Additionally, in 1991 the company created an employee stock ownership plan (ESOP) for the purpose of providing substantially all employees with the opportunity to save for retirement and acquire a proprietary interest in the company.

■ Development

In order to realize these objectives, HealthSouth initiated an aggressive acquisition strategy. During 1995, HealthSouth finalized pooling-of-interest mergers with Surgical Health Corporation (37 outpatient surgery centers in 11 states) and Sutter Surgery Centers, Inc. (12 outpatient surgery centers in three states), as well as stock purchase acquisitions of the rehabilitation hospitals division of NovaCare, Inc. (11 inpatient rehabilitation facilities, 12 other health care facilities, and two CONs in eight states), and Caremark Orthopedic Services, Inc. (120 outpatient rehabilitation facilities in 13 states). In addition, the company entered into agreements to acquire Surgical Care Affiliates, Inc. (67 outpatient surgery centers in 24 states) and Advantage Health Corporation (150 inpatient and outpatient rehabilitation facilities in 11 states). Advantage Health is a particularly important acquisition not only because of its size but because it was the largest provider of rehabilitation services in the Northeast.

■ Marketing

The company's marketing efforts were similar for each business segment. The demand was controlled by physicians, workers' compensation managers, insurance companies, and other intermediaries. HC administrators and clinicians were all involved in the marketing effort. The company hired a number of individuals who were formerly case managers with local intermediaries, such as insurance companies and HMOs. Every outpatient clinic had its own marketing director.

HC entered into contracts to be the exclusive provider for rehabilitation services directly to industry. Firms such as General Motors were excellent targets because they had many employees in various markets that HealthSouth served. In such cases, significant new business could be generated and in return HealthSouth could afford to discount its charges. HC expanded its marketing efforts to include a focus on national contracts with large payers and self-insured employers.

HealthSouth established a national marketing effort with training programs, national account managers, case managers, and a carefully developed marketing plan for each facility based on a number of factors, including population demographics, physician characteristics, and localized disability statistics. The objective was to put into place a consistent sales methodology throughout HealthSouth and take advantage of its national system of rehabilitation facilities. This national coverage enabled HealthSouth to provide services for national as well as regional companies.

Marketing programs were directed toward the development of long-term relationships with local schools, businesses and industries, physicians, health maintenance organizations, and preferred provider organizations. In addition,

HC attempted to develop and enhance its image with the public at large. One example was the company's joint promotional arrangement with the Ladies Professional Golf Association, whereby HC provided and staffed a rehabilitation van for the players while they were on tour.

HealthSouth's pricing was usually lower than that of the competition. However, this was not used as a major selling point, but rather a bonus. HealthSouth focused mainly on quality of services and outcomes as the best marketing tool.

■ Financial Structure

HealthSouth's growth was funded through a mix of equity and debt. The company raised $13 million in venture capital before going public in 1986. Because of the company's startup nature in its early years, commercial banks were reluctant to lend significant funds for development. After the company's initial public offering, commercial bankers were more responsive to financing growth plans. HC continued to use a conservative mix of equity and debt and believed its cost of capital was the lowest in the health care industry. A decision to give up ownership was an easy one. The founders understood that a smaller percentage ownership of a larger company would be worth more and would not carry as much risk.

Earnings increases were significant, with compounded earnings growth of 416 percent from 1986 to 1990. During the 1990 to 1993 period growth rates declined, as expected, but remained impressive by industry standards. Operating revenues for 1995 increased about 22 percent over 1994. Revenues are estimated to grow between 10-15 percent from 1996-1999. The large ($7.9 billion) outpatient rehabilitation market is fragmented and HC is one of the few providers that has the ability to develop a powerful network. In 1995 it was estimated that HC's outpatient revenue grew about 32 percent (34 percent in visits and two percent in pricing). Surgery center growth is expected to be about 15-20 percent, which should result from a combination of continued acquisitions and same-store volume and price increases. Inpatient services will continue to be the cash cow for HC. Currently, inpatient rehabilitation and specialty medical centers account for about 46 and 11 percent of 1995 revenues, respectively. The outlook for these businesses remains encouraging.

WHERE DOES HEALTHSOUTH GO FROM HERE?

Richard Scrushy was reviewing company projections for the continued success of HealthSouth Corporation. He could not help but wonder if it were possible for HC to continue such rapid growth. All the questions raised earlier were in his thoughts. What will I need to do to make it happen? Are there things we should be doing differently? How can I ensure that HealthSouth does not outgrow its resources (capital and management)? Does the market provide ample opportunity to grow at 20 to 30 percent per year? What external factors do we face? What should we do to ensure that medical rehabilitation continues to be favorably reimbursed? What is the real number of facilities needed, and how many acquisition targets are there? Are our current strategies what they should be?

Scrushy focused on answering the questions. He knew that he could formulate a plan to ensure HealthSouth's success. In fact, in a probing interview in *Rehabilitation Today* (May 1991), Scrushy was careful to state that he would consider any acquisition where he believed "value could be added" and dismissed the possibility that the company's "regional name" implied that his aspirations were regional. Clearly, he was willing to go anywhere, anytime he believed opportunities existed. To date, nothing had changed his mind.

REFERENCES

Sources used for quotes and information to supplement public documents of HealthSouth include the following.

Brown, Alex & Sons, Inc. Research Report, Health Care Group, December 28, 1995.

Brown, Alex & Sons, Inc. Research Report, Health Care Group, February 16, 1996.

Hansen, Jeffrey. "HealthSouth Finishes Deal Doubling Size." *Birmingham News* (January 6, 1994), pp. 6D and 10D.

"HealthSouth Wins Notice of *Forbes,* Wall Street," *Birmingham News* (April, 19, 1996), pp. 1E-4E.

Hicks, W. G., M. Willard, K. Miner, and M. Sullivan. "Consolidation Steamroller Continues to Move Ahead." *Gowen Perspectives* (February 28, 1996).

Securities and Exchange Commission. HealthSouth Corporation. Form 10-K. Washington, DC, March 15, 1996.

United States Equity Research. *Health Services.* Solomon Brothers. March 13, 1996.

U.S. Investment Research. *Healthcare Services.* "Trailblazing into the Northeast." Morgan Stanley. January 2, 1996.

Wilder, Marvin. "The Powerhouse Behind HealthSouth." *Rehabilitation Today* (May 1991), pp. 22-31.

Compass Bancshares, Inc.

Douglas L. Smith, University of Alabama at Birmingham

John Noland, University of Alabama at Birmingham

Patrick Asubonteng Rivers, University of Alabama at Birmingham

Dr. Woodrow D. Richardson, University of Alabama at Birmingham

Three and a half months of stress and anxiety in Bill Swan's life would hopefully come to an end today. Today, April 11, 1995, was the annual shareholders' meeting of Compass Bancshares, where Bill, age 27, had been an employee for 5 years. Many employees would be at the annual meeting because a major issue was up for vote. Most employees were shareholders because they participated in a payroll deduction stock purchase plan offered by the bank. Bill had participated in the plan since he first came to work and owned 350 shares with a market value of approximately $9,100. Like most employees, Bill viewed his stock investment as a nest egg for retirement.

The major issue revolved around a battle which had been going on for several months between Harry Brock, the founder and retired CEO of the bank, and Paul Jones, the present CEO. The stockholders would vote on whether the bank appointed three new directors who supported a merger with a larger bank or directors who supported remaining independent.

As Bill got dressed to attend the meeting, he picked up the two proxy cards off his dresser. White proxy cards from Compass and blue cards from Brock's Committee to Maximize Shareholder Value had been mailed to all shareholders. Bill could not decide which way to vote, so instead of mailing his card, he planned to take them to the annual meeting. He was still not comfortable with how to vote. Should he vote for a group of directors who will most assuredly take action to sell the bank, or should he vote for directors who favor remaining independent? He began to think back over the events of the last three and one-half months.

THE CURRENT SITUATION

Although Harry Brock retired as CEO of Compass Bancshares in 1991, he was still on the board of directors and continued to be interested in the performance of the bank. He also was aware of the changes looming on the horizon in the banking industry. In the summer of 1994, Brock communicated to Jones that the bank should merge with another bank. Brock informed the board that he would, on his own, investigate potential buyers, with both Brock and the board realizing that he did not have the authority to finalize an offer. He found a buyer in First Union for $30.70 a share and brought the offer to the board for consideration. Jones did not support the proposal and asked the board for permission to contact First Union and terminate any idea of a sale. Jones and the majority of the board of directors disagreed with Brock and felt the bank should remain independent. This matter was confined to private board discussion until January 1995. At that time, Brock publicized that he wanted the bank to merge with a larger bank to take advantage of national interstate banking. The battle between Jones and Brock became a public spectacle. At one point, Brock was actually evicted from his Compass office and had to find other office space from which to run his operation. Brock felt so strongly about his position that he, along with two other board members, formed a committee labeled the "Committee to Maximize Shareholder Value" to pursue the merger idea.

Along with most other Compass employees, Bill first heard about the battle in January and was initially shocked to hear that Mr. Brock wanted to sell the bank. Bill's reaction was to side with Jones because he thought not selling the bank would preserve his job. Then Bill heard that Jones was talking about selling the bank to Regions, a large bank in town. Maybe Brock's plan would result in fewer jobs lost because an out-of-town purchaser would want to retain most of the employees; however, Regions might want to eliminate duplicate jobs in Birmingham. So, what is the best answer for Bill personally?

Under Brock's leadership, the "Committee to Maximize Shareholder Value" started a proxy fight to elect a board of directors who would support the merger. He produced a videotape to "set the record straight," including clipped excerpts of Jones' court depositions that indicated Jones had personal motives for power and greed and had been in contact with Regions to discuss a potential merger. Brock's rationale was that "nationwide banking" would bring great changes to the banking industry. He stated that the competition heretofore had been minimal by saying "if we think we have had competition in the past, it has been a picnic compared to the future." Brock was successful in involving Compass in statewide banking. He felt that consolidation was going to be fast paced and that the best thing to do was "pick your partner first" to get maximum advantage for the stockholders and protection for employees. A March 28 Birmingham News article reported that "Jones said in his testimony that he and Stanley Mackin, CEO of Regions Financial, had a 'wide ranging conversation about a number of issues,' including the possibility that he might succeed Mackin as the CEO of the merged banks."

Jones stated that he disagreed with Brock's idea and that he did not think the time was right. He said that a merger with a larger bank could cost the local Birmingham area anywhere from 850 to 1,000 jobs. Jones had also produced a video for employees to calm their fears about the possible merger when the information became public. He attempted to discredit Brock's rationale about the benefits of a merger. In his comments to employees, Mr. Jones stated that in the three-year business plan adopted by the board, there was no plan to sell the bank, but instead the plan was for the bank to remain independent. Bill was not knowledgeable about all the workings of the board, but he was confused about some of the statements. He wondered why the company plan was for only three years. He also wondered about the relationship between Jones and Stanley Mackin, CEO of Regions Financial. Jones' court deposition stated that Mackin was planning to retire in two or three years and that Jones might be the CEO of the merged banks.

Since January, Bill had not known what to do. His uncertainty related to two questions: 1) should he be looking for another job since long-term employment at Compass may be uncertain, and 2) how to vote his shares. He was getting reports from Bloomberg Investment Services every day and talking to his co-workers. Rumors that some executives were sending out their resumes accentuated the stress of the situation. He also wondered if the bank would be sold after the three-year pledge elapsed, thereby resulting in job losses. His boss had been to some information meetings and had suggested that employees vote for Jones and support the board. Was she just saying that to please the executives or did she really feel that way? Bill also heard that voting for employee shareholders who are investing through the monthly investment plan will not be confidential, so executives will know how he votes. Managers are jokingly saying there will be a list of those who vote a certain way.

The infighting had an impact on the public's view of the company. The price of the stock increased from $22 a share, prior to the Brock public announcement of his proxy fight plans, to as high as $28 on March 2. The day before the board meeting the stock closed at $26.63. The normal trading volume for the stock on the Nasdaq was less than 100,000 shares a day. However, since the public announcement, the volume had been much higher, reaching as high as 1.9 million shares a day. At least one major investment firm, which provided services for several hundred institutional investor clients, recommended a vote for Jones' position. Institutions held about 20% of Compass' shares. Employees, like Bill, owned approximately 30% of the shares.

Key events related to the current tense situation are described in Exhbit 1.

THE PROXY PROCESS

Compass will hold its annual meeting on April 11, allowing shareholders to vote for board members who will determine the company's future. Three board members up for election—Jones, Charles Daniel, and George Hansberry (see Exhibit 2 for a list of Compass' Board of Directors)—were supportive of maintaining Compass' independent status.

In publicly held companies, a proxy process is utilized to obtain votes from shareholders on issues to be handled at the annual meeting. Compass used this process for its April 11 meeting. However, unlike the normal process, Harry Brock and his group of supporters also implemented a proxy process to solicit support for their list of nominees for directors. The steps taken by the Committee, as stated in the proxy statement, were "because it is their strong feeling that directors of the company owe an obligation to you, the stockholders of the Company, to maximize your investment in every way." It further stated that

Exhibit 1	Prelude to a Proxy Fight
Summer 1994	Compass Bank founder Harry B. Brock Jr. tells his successor, Chairman and CEO D. Paul Jones Jr., that Compass should merge with a larger bank. His rationale is that under the new legislation which allows interstate branching, Compass will face intense competition. They should take advantage of the situation and merge with a larger bank, realizing a good stock sale price for shareholders.
Sept. 26	Brock says he plans to contact regional banks to gauge their interests in Compass. Jones replies that Brock does not speak for the board of directors.
Sept.-Oct.	Brock contacts several banks about a merger, including (1) Sun Trust in Atlanta, (2) Wachovia in Winston-Salem, N.C., (3) Barnett in Jacksonville, Fla., and (4) First Union in Charlotte, N.C.
Oct. 17	Brock tells Compass board that he has a merger proposal from First Union Corp., which is a bank with assets of $72.3 billion. The offer is for $1.14 billion.
Dec. 1	Compass hires CS First Boston as its investment adviser.
Jan. 1995	Jones privately visits J. Stanley Mackin, chairman and CEO of Regions Financial Corp., to discuss a possible merger of their banks.
Jan. 27	Brock announces proxy fight to elect a board of directors that favor merging Compass with a larger regional bank. Two Compass directors, G.W "Red" Leach and Stanley M. Brock, align with Brock.
Jan. 30	Compass directors Charles W. Daniel, Marshall Durbin Jr., and Goodwin L. Mryrick announce they are backing Jones.
Jan. 31	Compass director Tranum Fitzpatrick announces his support for Jones.
Feb. 13	Compass board of directors adopts three-year strategic plan based on CS First Boston's recommendation that Compass remain independent.
Feb. 25	Compass director Thomas D. Jernigan, who favors a merger, resigns from Compass' board, leaving the board with 11 directors. Two more directors, John S. Stein and William E. Davenport, publicly back Jones.
Mar. 1	Compass announces it will hold its annual meeting on April 11. Proxies mailed to shareholders of record.
Mar. 17	Compass' biggest shareholder, the Daniel Foundation, backs Jones. Brock files a civil suit against Compass, accusing Jones of securities rules violation to sway shareholders. The accusation revolved around the mailing of proxy materials before rules permitted and not giving more than 20 days' notice of the annual shareholders' meeting.
Mar. 24	Institutional Shareholder Services Inc. recommends to its clients that they vote for Jones' position.
Mar. 28	Federal Judge Sam Pointer rules in Compass' favor, dismissing Brock's lawsuit. A Court deposition disclosed that Jones held discussions in January with Regions Financial to discuss a possible merger. Jones dismissed the meeting as "very tentative," although Jones admitted he was being considered as the head of the new merged company. Regions is the parent of First Alabama, a major bank in Alabama.
Apr. 3	Coal magnate Garry N. Drummond, a Compass director, throws his support to Brock. Four directors have announced support for Brock, while seven have announced support for Jones.
Apr. 11	Stockholders' meeting.

Source: Rupinski, *Birmingham Post-Herald*.

"the members of the Committee and their nominees intend to take other appropriate steps to maximize the value of the company's stock." Brock also stated that it is the opinion of the committee that directors should act independently of the CEO, keeping the interests of stockholders in mind. Steps to this end would include "soliciting offers or proposals from suitable potential merger

Exhibit 2

Board of Directors

Name	Dir. Since	Shares Held	Occupation
Nominees to serve until 1998:			
D. Paul Jones Jr.	1978	512,911	Chairman of the Board, CEO, and President, Compass Bank. Age 52.
Charles W. Daniel	1982	197,445	President, Dantract, Inc. (real estate investments). Age 54.
George W. Hansberry		15,214	Physician. Age 67.
Directors to serve until 1996:			
William Eugene Davenport	1993	20,121	President and CEO, Russell Lands, Inc. (resort land development). Age 54.
Marshall Durbin Jr.	1971	591,407	President of Marshall Durbin & Company, Inc. (poultry processing). Age 63.
Tranum Fitzpatrick	1989	148,447	Chairman of Guilford Company, Inc. and President of Guilford Capital and Empire-Rouse, Inc. (real estate investment and development). Age 56.
Goodwin L. Myrick	1988	915,014	President and Chairman of the Board of Alabama Farmers Federation, Alfa Corporation, Alfa Insurance Companies, and Alfa Services, Inc. (agriculture and insurance), and a dairy farmer. Age 69.
John S. Stein	1989	43,758	President and CEO of Golden Enterprises, Inc. (snack food and metal fastener production and distribution). Age 57.
Directors to serve until 1997:			
Harry B. Brock Jr.	1970	789,829	Retired since March 31, 1991, as Chairman of the Board, CEO, and Treasurer of the Corporation and Compass Bank. Age 68.
Stanley M. Brock	1990	171,866	Attorney. Age 44.
Garry N. Drummond Sr.	1990	64,872	CEO of Drummond Company, Inc. (coal and coke production, real estate investment). Age 56.

partners. This is the reason the members of the Committee have undertaken to solicit proxies to elect three new and independent directors." The proxy statement was sent to shareholders on March 16. Brock and "Red" Leach also submitted Shareholder Proposals through proxy statements, recommending addition of the following proposals, which would:

1. require the Company, within 10 days after its receipt of certain proposals for the purchase of the assets or stock of the Company or for the merger of the Company, to mail to the stockholders of the Company the details of such proposal.

2. require prior approval by the holders of a majority of the shares of the Company's Common Stock before any of the following plans or agreements with "principal officers" of the Company may be agreed to : (1) any employment contract for a principal officer in excess of one year; (2) any "golden parachute" contract providing for severance pay or continued compensation in excess of one year's salary; (3) any non-qualified stock option agreement or supplemental retirement plan for a principal officer; and (4) any other plan or agreement providing for post-retirement benefits for a principal officer greater than would be payable under agreements now in effect.

This process was most assuredly confusing to shareholders. For example, Compass issued a proxy which contained white cards to be marked and submitted by shareholders. Brock's proxy contained blue cards for shareholders to mark and submit. Each side reported spending $500,000 on soliciting support for their plan. Both sides sent follow-up and replacement proxies which inundated Bill with piles of paper and added to the uncertainty of the situation. With each package he received, more negative information about the opposing side was included which caused him to feel he could trust neither Jones nor Brock.

THE COMPANY AND ITS BUSINESS

Compass Bancshares Inc. was a multi-state bank holding company with headquarters in Birmingham, Alabama. The company had assets of $9.1 billion as of Dec. 31, 1994, with 204 bank offices in Alabama, Texas, and Florida, employing 4,100. Performance in 1994 included profits of $99,671,000 or $2.68 per share, compared with $89,718,000 or $2.37 per share in 1993. The company was publicly owned, with 37,940,000 shares outstanding. Exhibit 3 contains financial results for Compass from 1992–1994.

Compass Bancshares and Compass of Texas were multi-bank holding companies, as defined by the Banking Holding Company Act (BHC Act) and were registered with the Federal Reserve. Under the BHC Act, a bank holding company was required to obtain prior approval of the Federal Reserve before it acquired all the assets or ownership of any bank.

Alabama, Florida, and Texas, where Compass Bancshares operated its banking subsidiaries, each had laws relating to acquisitions of banks, bank holding companies, and other types of financial institutions. Compass Bank, organized under the laws of the State of Alabama, was regulated by the Alabama State Banking Department. Compass Bank-Florida was regulated by the Florida Department of Banking and Finance. Compass Bank-Dallas and Compass Bank-Houston were regulated by the Department of Banking of the State of Texas and the Federal Deposit Insurance Corporation (FDIC). All these banks, except the Texas banks, are members of the Federal Reserve System.

Since the time Bill had come to work at Compass, one of the things he had enjoyed was the feeling among employees of being part of a family. For example, employees were recognized for achievements, given Thanksgiving dinner, and publicized in company newsletters. This past closeness of employees had made the current turbulent environment even more unsettling for Bill.

Exhibit 3   **Financial Highlights ($000, except per share data)**

	1994	1993	1992
Period End Balances:			
Assets	$9,123,253	$7,333,594	$7,004,506
Loans, net of unearned income	5,761,511	5,197,464	4,627,530
Earnings assets	8,381,434	6,842,111	6,466,511
Deposits	7,062,404	5,625,097	5,349,279
Shareholders' equity	600,613	545,584	506,426
Average Balances:			
Assets	$8,019,343	$7,047,256	$6,737,664
Loans, net of unearned income	5,355,755	4,889,217	4,227,721
Earnings assets	7,420,117	6,514,959	6,197,150
Deposits	6,209,041	5,417,890	5,095,987
Shareholders' equity	574,549	533,526	477,891
Income/Expense:			
Net interest income	331,368	329,013	313,334
Provision for loan losses	3,404	36,306	52,885
Noninterest income	85,631	103,186	95,613
Noninterest expense	261,966	257,703	242,262
Pre-tax income	151,629	138,190	113,800
Net income	99,671	89,718	75,390
Per Common Share Data:			
Net income	$ 2.68	$ 2.37	$ 2.01
Cash dividends declared	0.92	0.76	0.67
Book value	16.25	14.93	13.28
Profitability Ratios:			
Return on average assets	1.24%	1.26%	1.12%
Return on average common shareholders' equity	17.35	16.90	16.12
Noninterest expense to average assets	3.27	3.62	3.60
Net yield on average earning assets	4.46	5.00	5.06
Net yield on average earning assets—taxable equiv.	4.54	5.11	5.19
Asset Quality ratios:			
Allowance for loan losses to net loans	1.86%	2.13%	1.80%
Loan loss provision to average net loans	0.06	0.74	1.25
Net charge-offs to average net loans	0.15	0.22	0.59
Nonperforming loans to loans	0.21	0.37	0.61
Nonperforming assets to loans and ORE	0.33	0.77	1.41
Asset Structure Ratios:			
Shareholders' equity to total assets	6.58%	7.52%	7.23%
Total qualifying capital	13.06	13.23	11.61
Net loans to total deposits	81.58	92.40	86.51
Average net loans to average total deposits	86.26	90.24	82.96

Source: *Compass Bancshares Annual Report.*

GOVERNMENT REGULATION

The banking industry had been highly regulated for many years, mainly to protect the economy from bank failures. Controls included the interest rates charged customers, plus the cost and quantity of money available to banks from the Federal Reserve System. The most significant early legislation included The McFadden Act of 1927, which prohibited expansion of banks across state lines, and The Glass-Steagall Act of 1933, which put in place many tight restrictions, including inhibiting interstate branches and limits on consolidations. A summary of banking legislation is shown in Exhibit 4.

Because states had much authority in banking operations, a group of ten states in the southeast formed a "regional compact" in the early 1980s to allow regional banks to do business across state lines among the ten states. This effort was an attempt to avoid any future interstate activity by powerful banks from large financial centers such as New York. The compacts were challenged in the U. S. Supreme Court but upheld, thus allowing banks to merge across state lines.

The Interstate Banking Bill of 1987 further opened up competition in the industry by allowing interstate banking on a national basis. Under this bill, approval by the individual states was still required. Recently, President Clinton signed into law the Riegele-Neal Interstate Banking and Branching Efficiency Act of 1994 (Interstate Act), which went into effect in 1996 and permitted bank holding companies to acquire banks located in another state without regard to whether the transaction is prohibited under state law.

The Federal Reserve Act imposed certain limitations on extensions of credit and transactions between banks that were members of the Federal Reserve System. Banks that were not members of the Federal Reserve System were also subject to these limitations. Federal law prohibited a bank holding company from engaging in certain arrangements in connection with any credit or sale of property. Generally, federal and state banking laws and regulations governed all areas of the operations of the bank. Federal and state banking regulatory agencies also had the general authority to limit the dividends paid by insured banks and bank holding companies if such payments were deemed to constitute an unsafe and unsound practice.

COMPETITIVE ENVIRONMENT

The Alabama banking industry consisted of five dominant banks: AmSouth Bancorporation, SouthTrust Corporation, Regions Financial Corporation, Compass Bancshares, Inc., and Colonial BancGroup. Exhibit 5 compares Compass' financial performance to the other dominant Alabama banks. Over the past few years, these banks have grown primarily through acquisitions. Each of these entities is discussed in the following paragraphs.

■ Amsouth Bancorporation

In 1995, AmSouth was the largest bank holding company in the State of Alabama. Headquartered in Birmingham, Alabama, AmSouth had 369 offices in Alabama, Florida, Tennessee, and Georgia. AmSouth had grown significantly

Exhibit 4 **Summary of Legislative Activity**

Year	Regulation Activity	Content
1913	Federal Reserve Act of 1913	Imposed limitations on the extension of credit and other transactions by and between banks which are members of the Federal Reserve System.
1927	The McFadden Act of 1927	Prohibited bank expansion across state lines. Gave states authority to set branching standards for banks in their jurisdiction.
1933	The National Banking Act of 1933 (Glass-Steagall Act)	Essentially excluded U.S. banks from non-Treasury securities markets. Banned affiliation between commercial and investment banking functions. Inhibited interstate branch operations, limited consolidation of banks. Prohibited banks from paying interest on demand deposits and placed ceilings on rates of other accounts. "Regulation Q" fixed prices for deposits and gave thrifts a slight advantage in rates they could pay.
1956	Bank Holding Company Act of 1956 (The BHC Act)	Required a bank holding company to obtain prior approval of the Federal Reserve before it can acquire substantially all the assets or ownership or control of voting share if afterwards it would direct or control > 5% of the voting shares of such bank. To restrict single and multibank holding companies by prohibiting acquisitions of banks in other states, unless other states' laws allow so. A 1975 Act closed the loophole that actually encouraged the growth of BHCs.
1977	The Community Reinvestment Act of 1977 (The CRA)	Encouraged regulated financial institutions to help meet the credit needs of their local community, including low and moderate income neighborhoods.
1980	The Depository Institution Deregulation and Monetary Control Act of 1980 (DIDMCA)	The first to allow increased competition in banking environment. Interest rate ceilings phased out by 1986, interest-bearing checking allowed, thrifts' lending power expanded.
1980	Congressional Acts (various)	Phased out interest rate ceilings, lessened the regulatory differences between banks and non-banks, reduced some regulatory burdens.
1982	Bank Holding Company Act	Major deregulation left banks free to set own rates in interest-bearing accounts and charge as desired for services.
1982	Depository Institutions Act	Authorized money market accounts, expanded thrifts' lending powers, made provisions for aiding failing thrifts, interest rate differentials paid by banks and thrifts to be phased out by 1984.
1984-1985	Supreme Court Actions	1984: Upheld acquisitions of discount brokerage firms by banks. 1985: Upheld constitutionality of the regional interstate banking pacts, allowing states to enact interstate banking legislation, usually in the form of reciprocal agreements - and merge. This negated the 1933 McFadden Act.
1986	DIDMCA (continued)	Final provisions of 1980 Act enacted. Minimum balance requirements on money market accounts eliminated. Interest rate ceilings on passbook savings accounts lifted.
1987	Interstate Banking Bill of 1987	Allowed for reciprocal banking between states.
1991	Federal Deposit Insurance Corporation Improvement Act of 1991	Recapitalized the Bank Insurance Fund and Saving Association Insurance Fund. Required federal banking agencies to take prompt action concerning banks that fail to meet minimum capital requirements; mandated new disclosure rules, tougher auditing and underwriting standards.
1993	National Depositor Preference Statute	Losses will fall more completely on unsecured, non-deposit general creditors, and both insured and uninsured domestic depositors will receive preference in claims against a receivership estate over the creditors of the bank.
1993	Federal Reserve System overhaul (pending)	Proposed increasing accountability of the central bank.

Exhibit 4 (continued)   **Summary of Legislative Activity**

Year	Regulation Activity	Content
1994	Bankruptcy Reform Act of 1994	Altered the Bankruptcy Code to include creation of Bankruptcy Review Commission to evaluate the bankruptcy system.
1994	Riegle-Neal Interstate Banking & Branching Efficiency Act of 1994 (The Interstate Banking Act)	Permitted bank holding companies to acquire banks located in any state without regard to whether the transaction is prohibited under any state law, however, states may establish the minimum age of a local bank subject to acquisition by an out-of-state holding company. Minimum age is limited to maximum of 5 years. Law passed 1995; commenced July 1996.

over the past decade through an aggressive acquisitions strategy and offered extensive consumer, trust, and investment services. For example, in July 1993, AmSouth announced its intent to take over Florida Bank of Jacksonville, Florida. In keeping with its tradition of offering bids up to two times book value, AmSouth offered Florida Bank 1.81 times its book value. In August 1993, AmSouth announced plans to purchase First Federal Savings Bank of Calhoun, Georgia, for $14 million in stock. AmSouth chose First Federal because of its strategic location between its Chattanooga offices and the Georgia State Bank of Rome, which AmSouth was also in the process of acquiring. Also, in August 1993, AmSouth announced plans to acquire Citizens National Corporation of Naples, Florida, for $48.8 million in stock, giving AmSouth $289.6 million more in Florida assets. AmSouth's offer was 2.74 times the adjusted book value of the thrift, but was seen as justified because of its attractive location in the southwest Florida area. In September 1993, AmSouth filed a plan with the SEC to issue $300 million in debt to help pay for some of its recent acquisitions throughout Florida. In December 1993, AmSouth completed its acquisition of First Sunbelt Bancshares, which also owned Georgia State Bank of Rome. This merger was achieved through a stock swap. In total, AmSouth added 145 banking offices in 1993, a 70 percent increase in assets. This expansion continued in 1994 with five acquisitions in Florida, Tennessee, and Georgia.

■ Southtrust Corporation

The second largest bank in Alabama, SouthTrust was considered the most aggressive of the group. The retail leader had substantially out-branched the other banks, competing head-to-head with small community banks across the state. As soon as Alabama law allowing interstate banking went into effect in mid-1987, SouthTrust began seeking growth through out-of-state acquisitions. It was the first of Alabama banks to branch into the Florida panhandle. In 1988, SouthTrust bought banks in South Carolina and Tennessee and moved into Georgia in 1989. In 1990, SouthTrust bought banks in central Florida and moved northeast with purchases in North Carolina (Cantrell, 1992).

In 1991, SouthTrust expanded its presence in Atlanta and central Georgia with its purchase of 22 former Fulton Federal Savings & Loans offices. In 1992, SouthTrust purchased First American Bank of Georgia, which boosted its presence in Atlanta to a total of $2 billion in assets with some 70 offices in 11

Exhibit 5   **Performance Indicators for the Five Largest Alabama Banks (1990–1994)**

Bank	1990	1991	1992	1993	1994
SouthTrust Corporation					
EPS	1.71	2.13	2.49		
DPS	0.46	0.48	0.52	0.60	
NI	69,708	90,006	114,246	150,535	
AmSouth Bancorporation					
EPS	1.97	2.07	2.51	3.10	2.25
DPS	0.94	0.98	1.07	1.22	1.43
NI	75,000	83,000	108,000	146,720	127,290
Regions Financial Corporation					
EPS	1.91	2.16	2.60	3.01	
DPS	0.84	0.87	0.91	1.04	
NI	68,894	78,256	95,048	112,045	
Compass Bancshares, Inc.					
EPS	1.51	1.74	2.01	2.37	2.68
DPS	0.53	0.59	0.67	0.76	0.92
NI	52,605	63,374	76,003	89,718	99,671
Colonial BancGroup					
EPS	1.19	1.45	1.97	2.35	2.74
DPS	A=0.60	A=0.63	A=0.67	A=0.71	A=0.80
	B=0.20	B=0.23	B=0.27	B=0.31	B=0.40
NI	9,143	10,430	13,793	18,709	27,671

EPS = Earnings per Share

DPS = Dividends per Share

NI   = Net Income ($000)

counties in central Georgia. Through acquisitions, SouthTrust's assets more than doubled by 1992 and were in excess of $17.6 billion at the end of 1994. In 1995, SouthTrust owned 396 banks in Alabama, Florida, Georgia, North Carolina, South Carolina, and Tennessee.

■ Regions Financial Corporation (First Alabama Bancshares, Inc.)

First Alabama, one of the South's most conservative banks, had increased its earnings and dividends consecutively for the past 21 years. First Alabama's growth had occurred primarily through acquisitions when J. Stanley Mackin assumed control in 1990 with a strategy intended to build market share through the purchase of savings and loans throughout Alabama and then move into neighboring states. In 1993, the parent company changed its name from First Alabama Bancshares to Regions Financial Corporation in recognition of its expansion outside of Alabama. Banks outside Alabama operated under the name of Regions Bank, while those within Alabama retained the First Alabama name. Mackin's five-year profitability goals included raising

Region's return on equity (ROE) to 15% and its asset base to $12 billion by 1995. As a result of Mackin's strategy, Region's ROE was up to 15 % by the end of 1992 and up to 16.6 percent by the end of second quarter 1993, with operations expanding into Florida, Georgia, Louisiana, Mississippi, South Carolina, and Tennessee.

■ Colonial Bancgroup

Colonial was established in 1981 with one bank and $166 million in assets. Colonial was the fifth largest bank holding company in Alabama. Through acquisitions, Colonial had grown to a $2+ billion bank holding company with 100 offices across the Southeast. Colonial's strategy was to build market share by acquiring other financial institutions, add profitable new lines of business or product, and expand to other growth markets. In 1994, Colonial purchased two banks in Alabama, Brundidge Banking Company and Colonial Mortgage Company.

HISTORY OF COMPASS BANK

Harry B. Brock Jr., 69, co-founded Central Bank & Trust Co. in Birmingham, Alabama, in 1964. His background was primarily in sales, which resulted in his aggressiveness in pursuing other markets. He initiated state-wide branching, expanding the bank outside its home county. He was also responsible for the bank's entrance into the Texas market, which was unique in that the bank skipped over several neighboring states to pursue a new market. Following his retirement in 1991, he continued as a director until 1997. Exhibit 6 presents a list of key events in the history of Compass Bancshares, Inc., formerly Central Bank & Trust Co. Under Brock's leadership, Central Bank enjoyed continuously improving performance and was recognized as a fast-growing company. It was also a low-cost producer, having an efficiency ratio, as measured by noninterest expenses relative to net operating revenues, lower than any of the other major Alabama banks.

Brock's past actions had instilled a strong sense of loyalty in employees. They had come to trust his decisions based on performance results. While employees felt that Brock had the best interests of the bank in mind, they were also worried about the consequences of a bank merger on their future with the company.

COMPASS AND PAUL JONES

Upon Brock's retirement in 1991, his handpicked successor, D. Paul Jones, took the reins of Compass as President and CEO. Jones joined Compass Bank in 1978 at the request of Brock. Jones, a lawyer by background, was with the firm which handled legal matters for Compass. Since taking over as CEO of Compass in 1991, Jones, 52, had continued the record of increasing profits and earnings per share. Under his leadership, Compass has also further expanded into new markets in Texas and Florida.

Exhibit 6	**Brief History of the Rise of Compass Bank**

1964	Harry B. Brock Jr. co-founded Central Bank & Trust Co. in Birmingham, Alabama.
1971	Bank acquires the larger State National Bank in Decatur, becoming one of the first Alabama banks to move beyond its home county.
1972	D. Paul Jones Jr., an attorney with the Birmingham law firm of Balch & Bingham, becomes Central's legal counsel.
1973	Central Bancshares of the South Inc. becomes the new name for the bank holding company.
1977	*American Banker* ranks Central as one of the country's fastest growing banks.
1978	Jones leaves Balch & Bingham, joining Central as a senior vice president, general counsel, and a member of the board of directors.
1980	Brock, with Jones' assistance, is instrumental in pushing the Statewide Bank Merger Bill through the Alabama Legislature. It allows banks to branch across county lines. Jones is named executive vice president.
1981	Statewide branch banking takes effect.
1984	Jones is named vice chairman, with responsibility for financial, human resources, trust, legal, and credit departments.
1987	Central skips across several Southern states to acquire its first out-of-state bank in Houston. In later years it acquires more banks in Houston, Dallas, and San Antonio, eventually getting 69 banking offices in the state. Central moves its administrative operations to the newly built Brock Center on Birmingham's Southside.
1989	Jones is named Central's president and chief operating officer.
1991	Brock retires as Central's chairman and chief executive officer and is succeeded by his handpicked choice, Jones. Later in the year, Central buys its first bank in Florida.
1993	Central Bank of the South changes its name to Compass Bank to reflect its expansion in all directions.

Source: Rynecki, *Birmingham Post-Herald.*

In July 1991, Central entered the Florida market with the acquisition of Citizens & Builders Federal Savings Bank, Pensacola. In 1987, Central became the first out-of-state bank to enter the Texas market with the purchase of a Houston bank. At that time, the Texas economy had taken a severe beating from collapsing oil and real estate prices. In May 1993, Central signed an agreement to purchase Spring National Bank in Houston, Texas, which was holding $75 million in assets and $67 million in deposits. This increased Central's assets in Texas to $1.8 billion. During this same period, Central also announced its intent to purchase First Federal Savings Bank of Northwest Florida for $14.4 million. This was Central's third acquisition in the Fort Walton Beach, Florida, area, increasing its Florida asset base to $223 million. In August of 1993, Central signed an agreement to purchase First Performance National Bank in Jacksonville, Florida, Central's first expansion into the northeastern region of Florida.

On November 8, 1993, Central changed its name to Compass Bancshares, Inc. in order to make the bank more marketable outside the State of Alabama.

Exhibit 7

Compass Bank Mergers & Acquisitions (1991–1994)

Acquisitions	Date Acquired	Assets Acquired (In 000s of Dollars)
Plaza National Bank Dallas, Texas	1-31-91	50,000
River Oaks Bancshares, Inc. Houston, Texas	3-28-91	427,000
Gleneagles National Bank Plano, Texas	5-9-91	20,000
Bank of Las Colinas, N.A. Irving, Texas	5-9-91	30,000
Citizens & Builders Federal Savings, F.S.B. Pensacola, Florida	7-12-91	39,000
Promenade Bancshares, Inc. Dallas, Texas	7-31-91	170,000
Ameriway Bank, N.A. Houston, Texas	12-11-91	40,000
Interstate Bancshares, Inc. Houston, Texas	6-18-92	66,000
City National Bancshares, Inc. Carrollton, Texas	10-28-92	62,000
FWNB Bancshares, Inc. Plano, Texas	12-22-92	161,000
Cornerstones Bancshares, Inc. Dallas, Texas	1-19-93	239,000
First Federal Savings Bank of Northwest Florida Ft. Walton Beach, Florida	10-14-93	101,000
Peoples Holding Company, Inc. Ft. Walton Beach, Florida	10-21-93	43,000
Spring National Banking Houston, Texas	11-3-93	75,000
First Performance National Bank Jacksonville, Florida	12-7-94	278,000
Security Bank, N.A. Houston, Texas	5-1-94	76,000
Anchor Savings Bank Jacksonville, Florida	5-12-94	100,000
First Heights Bank, F.S.B. Houston, Texas	10-1-94	68,000

Source: Compass Bancshares Annual Report

All offices throughout Alabama, Florida, and Texas were united under one name. Compass was the name chosen for Central's Texas offices because another Texas bank was already operating under the name of Central Bank.

Central also chose the name "Compass" because of its compatibility with the company's already established logo.

Compass had been expanding into the Florida and Texas markets, which were both growing faster than the Alabama market. By 1994, Compass had one-fourth of its assets based in these markets. Because Compass was a low-cost provider, it was able to offer very competitive prices on its products and services targeted at small business and consumer niches. Even with all the acquisitions made during the last few years, Compass consistently increased its return on equity.

In November 1993, Compass signed an agreement to purchase Security Bank of Houston, increasing its assets in Texas to $2 billion and its banking offices from 3 to 39. Compass completed the purchase in May 1994, and began to acquire First Heights Bank of Houston, giving Compass 22 more offices in the Houston area, $885 million in deposits, and $47 million in consumer loans. This was Compass' largest Texas transaction.

From 1991 to 1994, Compass acquired 18 financial institutions in Florida and Texas. A list of the mergers and acquisitions completed from 1991 to 1994 with their asset size and closing dates is shown in Exhibit 7.

THE ISSUE

As Bill thinks about the situation, he tries to determine his options. Is Harry Brock rationally motivated to want to sell the bank, or is he just trying to regain control of a company he founded? Even if he loses this battle, Brock will still have other opportunities to raise other issues since he will still be serving on the Board of Directors for two more years. Jones seems to believe that a higher price for the shareholders could be realized when stock prices are not so depressed. Bill would like to know the future as to mergers in the industry.

The employees, as shareholders, will heavily influence the outcome of this battle when they vote today. As Bill enters the door of the Birmingham-Jefferson Civic Center at 9:15 A.M., the questions are still swirling in his mind. What should he do?

REFERENCES

"Brock's Review and Critique of His Lawsuit Against Compass Bancshares, Inc." Videotape.

Cantrell, W. (July 1992). "Bama's Big Four Are Booming." *Bank Management,* 68: 36–43.

Compass Bancshares, Inc. Annual Report, 1994.

Rupinski, Patrick, "End of fight will be relief for Jones," *Birmingham News,* April 11, 1995, p. A1, A3.

Rynecki, David, "Shootout at the Compass corral," *Birmingham News,* April 12, 1995, p. F1, F5.

Southwest Airlines Company

John J. Vitton, University of North Dakota
Charles A. Rarick, Transylvania University
Ronald P. Garrett, United States Air Force

Internet site of interest: **www.iflyswa.com**

Wall Street was stunned when Southwest Airlines announced fourth-quarter earnings for 1994 that were far below analysts' expectations! Financially, the 1990s had been devastating for the domestic passenger airline industry. Southwest was the sole exception among the major air carriers, having rung up 22 years of consistent profitability, while other carriers hemorrhaged red ink. It was the only major carrier to achieve net and operating profits in 1990, 1991, and 1992. Yet here in black and white, Southwest stated in its 1994 annual report that it experienced a 47 percent decline in earnings in 1994's fourth quarter as compared to fourth quarter 1993. Also, as compared to 1993 levels, load factors and passenger revenue yields were depressed. Load factors, which measure an airline's percentage of seats occupied by paying passengers, fell to 57.8 percent in January 1995, down from 63.1 percent for January 1994.

Harassed by low fares offered by newly aggressive carriers such as United's "U2" and Continental's Lite, Southwest responded by slashing its already ultra-cheap fares. Southwest was particularly provoked by United's apparent targeting of the California market with "U-2," a Southwestern style, low-cost, no-frills operation. Gary Kelly, Southwest's Chief Financial Officer, "noted that intra-California traffic accounts for 10-15% of Southwest's total business." He also stated that "Since we're already on a competitive stance with United, we'll simply confine our efforts, particularly our long-haul service to markets where United dominates."[1] These fare wars came at a rather inopportune time, when Southwest was digesting the acquisition of Salt Lake City-based Morris Air. While the acquisition gave Southwest a presence in the Pacific Northwest, the one-time acquisition cost of $10 million and the conversion of the Morris operation into that of the parent company hurt Southwest's bottom line. Southwest's 13% increase in capacity in 1994 was also provoking a competitive response.

Herb Kelleher, Southwest's ebullient CEO, was identified as "Commander-in-Chief" in the aircarrier's first-ever national TV ad campaign. Speaking from a mocked-up war room, with "Wild Blue Yonder" playing in the background, Herb said: "It's not a gimmick, it's not a promotion with us. It's something we believe in with all of our fiber. It's every seat, every flight, everywhere we fly. Other airlines try to copy Southwest, but they're just facsimiles of the real thing. Southwest is THE low-fare airline. If there's a fare war, they're gonna get nuked."[2]

COMPANY HISTORY

The Southwest Airline operation is truly a Horatio Alger story! During a 1967 luncheon meeting, Herbert D. Kelleher, a young San Antonio lawyer, was discussing with his client Rollin King, a Texas entrepreneur and pilot, the bankruptcy of a small air carrier, which had served small Texas towns. Later in the meeting, King broached the concept of a low-fare, no-frills, short haul airline with frequent flights between major Texas cities. Three points of a napkin were labeled—Dallas, Houston, and San Antonio.

Initially skeptical and later intrigued by King's plan, Kelleher raised $560,000 to back the venture. An application was filed with the Texas Aeronautics Commission in November 1967; however, starting up an airline was very difficult as the airline industry was heavily regulated. The burden of proof was on King and Kelleher to convince the Texas regulators that a new airline was needed. In February 1968, the Commission approved and issued a certificate to Air Southwest Company to fly from Love Field, Dallas, to Houston and San Antonio. Braniff, Continental, and Trans Texas obtained a restraining order to block Southwest's certificate from taking effect, claiming that the Texas market could not possibly support another air carrier. Investors urged Kelleher to give up the fight after losing the first two of three courtroom battles. Kelleher persevered and won the third battle when the Texas Supreme Court ruled in Air Southwest's favor. This allowed the airline to begin service with a fleet of three aircraft. Lamar Muse was hired to run the airline, which was renamed Southwest Airlines. Muse, as the former president of several airlines, brought extensive airline knowledge to the new company. His initial actions included buying four 737-200 aircraft and hiring veterans from Braniff, American Airlines, and Trans Texas to help mold and create an innovative approach to operations which is still prevalent today.[3] On June 18, 1971, the first Southwest flight took off from Love Field in Dallas headed for Houston.

In 1971, one-way Southwest fares were $20 for the flights from Dallas to San Antonio and from Dallas to Houston. The company lost $3.7 million in its first eleven months in operation. Southwest added a fourth plane to its fleet in September 1971, and two months later opened service on the third leg of the triangle, Houston to San Antonio. On February 1, 1973, Braniff initiated price wars on the flights between Dallas and Houston and Southwest countered by offering half-fare tickets. Despite fare wars, Southwest proudly proclaimed 1973 as its first profitable year.[4] The airline also announced that it was expanding its routes into the Rio Grande Valley (Harlingen), Texas.

There were more battles to be fought, however. A hearing was held in U.S. District Court on whether Southwest would be allowed to remain at Dallas Love Field, or be forced to move with other airlines to the new Dallas-Fort Worth Regional Airport. Judge W.M. Taylor Jr. ruled in April 1973 that Southwest could operate out of Love Field as long as it remained open as an airport.[5] Southwest gained a virtual monopoly position at Love Field, which was much closer to downtown Dallas than the Dallas-Forth Worth airport. This monopoly proved to be limiting, however, when the Wright Amendment became law in 1979. This law, championed by Texas U.S. representative James Wright, who later was forced out of office for misuse of funds, prevented airlines operating out of Love Field from providing direct service to states other than those neighboring Texas. Southwest's customers could fly from Love Field to Arkansas, Louisiana, New Mexico, and Oklahoma, but had to buy new tickets and board different Southwest flights to points beyond.

Braniff was fined the maximum of $100,000 on December 27, 1978, for using illegal tactics designed to force Southwest Airlines out of business. As a result of this settlement, Southwest was able to add to its Boeing fleet.

The Airline Deregulation Act of 1978 allowed Southwest to enter markets outside the state of Texas. This expansion will be described in the Operations Section.

In the 1980s, Southwest's annual passenger traffic count tripled. Nearly bankrupt Muse Air Corporation, founded by one-timer Southwest Executive, Lamar Muse, was sold to Southwest in 1985, which operated that Houston-based airline as TranStar. TranStar was liquidated in 1987 when profits fell, due to competition from Houston-based Continental Airlines.

Air Transport World magazine named Southwest the 1992 "Airline of the Year," stating that "Southwest has demonstrated excellence over the years in disciplines required for safe, reliable, and fairly priced air transportation."[6] The airline also won the first annual Triple Crown for the best on-time performances, best baggage handling record, and best customer satisfaction in 1992 and repeated again in 1993.

In 1994, Southwest expanded its service into the Northwest and California by acquiring Salt Lake City-based Morris Air on December 31, 1993.

THE AIRLINE INDUSTRY

The dawn of U.S. commercial aviation occurred on January 1, 1934. Passengers could fly one-way between Tampa and St. Petersburg, Florida, for $5.00 in a open-cockpit Benoist flying boat. The day-long trip by land took only 20 minutes by air. Financial troubles resulted in bankruptcy for the airline only four months later.[7]

The formative years and even the more mature stage of the airline industry life cycle were characterized by heavy government regulation of private carriers. Economists frequently identify protection of a fledgling industry from destructive competition and national defense as two of the primary justifications for governmental intervention in a market-driven economy. Regulation by the U.S. government of the airline industry began with a series of air mail acts beginning with the Kelly Act of 1925, which authorized airmail contracts between the U.S. Post Office and private carriers and made the postmaster general "the czar of the industry without competitive bidding."[8] Air mail contracts were extremely important to the fledgling airlines to supplement meager passenger revenue. The Air Mail Act of 1934 severed aircraft manufacturers' linkage to the airline industry. Boeing had to divest itself of United Airlines, Pratt & Whitney engines, and Sikorsky helicopter. General Motors sold its stock in Eastern and Western airlines, AVCO gave up American, and North American Aviation sold its TWA holdings. The Post Office, Interstate Commerce Commission, and Department of Commerce were all involved in developing weather information, navigational aids, and airport facilities. Also, in 1934, the nation's 24 domestic airlines were placed under the Railway Labor Act.[9]

By 1936, airline income from passengers surpassed that from airmail. The stretched-out, incredibly strong DC-3, designed by Jack Northrup, increased the speed and comfort of air travel. It operated reliably and profitably, and made the Ford Trimotor obsolete. Pan American pioneered Pacific flights in 1935, spanning the sea in Clipper Ships that pampered their passengers in airborne grand hotels.

By 1938, the airline industry was in critical financial shape and several major airlines faced bankruptcy. In response, Congress passed the McCarren-Lea Act (better known as the Civil Aeronautics Act) in 1938, which superseded all previous civil aviation legislation. The new Act created the Civil Aeronautics Board (CAB) to administer the Act. The CAB set fares, awarded domestic airline routes, and also determined which airlines would fly them. The Board also approved mergers, and forbade any airline from operating without being certified by CAB. This in effect established barriers to entry and curbed destructive competition. The Act also enabled the CAB to determine subsidy levels, write consumer regulations concerning overbooking, establish lost luggage policies, and regulate air safety.

In 1956, the jet age was ushered in by the 600-mph Boeing 707 and Douglas DC-8, which marked the end of an era of propeller-driven airliners such as the DC-4 and the pressurized Lockhead Constellation. That same year a TWA Super Constellation and a United DC-7 collided over Grand Canyon, killing 128 people. This led to a reorganization of governmental regulatory agencies. The Civil Aeronautics Act was superseded in 1958 by the Federal Aviation Act, which established the Federal Aviation Agency (FAA) as the watchdog of air safety. The FAA responsibilities were for safety rules, use of navigable air space, and development of air navigation facilities. The CAB was left intact to administer airline pricing and routing policies and was responsible for accident investigations. In 1967, Congress created the Department of Transportation (DOT) and abolished the Federal Aviation Agency. Safety came under the Department of Transportation's jurisdiction within the Federal Aviation Administration.

While real gross national product grew by 3.6 percent between 1949 and 1980, constant dollar domestic airline passenger revenue increased by 9.0 percent per annum. . . . Domestic air passenger miles rose by 11.4 percent annually from 1949 to 1980. During the same period, intercity rail and bus passenger counts were declining by 1.8 percent a year. Air transport volume exceeded the rail and bus total in 1964 and by 1981, 65 percent of the U.S. adult population had flown at least once.[10]

Air carrier profits plummeted during the recessionary period 1957–58 and the CAB approved domestic price increases on passenger rates. From 1962 through 1968, "the price of an average airline ticket declined by more than 13 percent. . . . By 1968 productivity gains began to be outpaced by rising costs—

of labor, landing fees, and interest charges. The CAB approved of several small increases but in 1970, the airline industry recorded the largest loss in its previous history. Fuel costs soared during the 1970s, rising from 13 percent of airline operating expenses to 31% by 1980, due to OPEC cartel pricing policies in 1974 and again in 1979."[11]

The deregulation movement began in 1974. Many economists and consumer advocates, such as Ralph Nader, cited the lower fares of the unregulated intrastate air carriers in California and Texas (22-26% lower than interstate carriers) and called for the abolishment of the CAB. In 1974, the airline industry could be described as an oligopoly with the "Big Four" being American, Eastern, Trans World, and United. In earlier years, the airlines established fares at approximately the level of standard railroad passenger fares plus Pullman car charges. Under the CAB, airline management did not have to manage finances carefully, as the CAB would allow a 10-12% return on assets (ROA) to be tacked on to labor, fuel, and other costs. This was then passed on to customers in the form of higher prices. Many also felt that the economies of jet aircraft were not reflected in lower prices to the customer.

The Airline Deregulation Act was passed by Congress on October 24, 1978. The CAB was phased out in a "twilight zone" with domestic routing decisions coming under the jurisdiction of the airlines. The CAB lost authority over domestic rates and fares on January 1, 1983, and the CAB was out of existence on December 31, 1984. On January 1, 1985, the CAB's authority over foreign air transportation matters was transferred to the Department of Transportation in consultation with the Department of State. The CAB's authority over mergers, intercarrier agreements, and antitrust immunities for foreign transport was turned over to the Department of Justice. However, in the twilight years, DOT was given approval over mergers. Safety responsibilities remained with DOT's Federal Aviation Administration.

Immediately after the Deregulation Act of 1978, the second OPEC oil shock hit the aviation industry with hurricane force. This was followed by the illegal strike by the Professional Air Traffic Controllers Organization (PATCO). Eleven thousand FAA controllers, who had signed an employment oath not to strike against their government, went out on strike and were subsequently fired after a warning by President Reagan to return to work within 48 hours. Despite soaring interest rates, the 1979-1982 recession, and escalating oil prices, more than 120 new airlines appeared, with most being small commuter lines.[12] As of 1988, over 200 airlines went bankrupt or had been acquired in mergers since deregulation; only 74 carriers remained.[13] Among the casualties since 1978 were Braniff, Eastern, Pan American, Peoples Express, Air Florida, Midwest, Frontier, and a host of smaller carriers.

Major airlines, unshackled from the North-South or East-West air routes required by CAB edicts, have gone to a hub-and-spoke flight structure which uses feeder aircraft operating on the spokes to consolidate passengers at the hubs. In 1988, "450 million passengers boarded commercial airlines, compared to 275 million in 1978. However, with nine of ten airline passengers traveling on some sort of discounted fare, the average cost of travel on an airliner has dropped 13 percent over the last decade if inflation is taken into account, according to the Transportation Department."[14]

The airline industry recently chalked up its greatest growth: 56% more passengers crammed aboard its planes in 1990 than a decade before. The 1980s was a time of heady expansion, of billion-dollar aircraft orders, and rapid addition of international routes. Horizontal mergers were allowed and eight carriers swallowed 11 others. Economists viewed the industry as a highflier across a business landscape marred by the declining auto, steel, and energy industries.[15]

"In the ten years (1978-1988) since deregulation, the Department of Transportation presided over 21 mergers. During that era, the ten largest airlines controlled 93 percent of the domestic market, compared with 89 percent in 1977, in part as a result of major airlines gobbling up regional and other smaller carriers."[16] Two of the Department of Transportation mergers, Northwest/Republic and USAir/Piedmont, were challenged by the antitrust division of the Department of Justice to no avail.

In 1988, at last count, the eight largest airlines had gained effective control over 48 of the 50 largest regionals. The Department of Transportation allowed the major airlines to acquire numerous commuter airlines. Alfred Kahn, now a Cornell University professor and formerly the chairman of the Civil Aeronautics Board, was the principal architect of airline deregulation. Noting the flurry of mergers and acquisitions, Kahn stated that "consumers are more likely to be exploited."[17]

In the early 1990s, the airline industry was confronted with a bath of red ink, excessive leverage often twice what is considered prudent, and a business turndown that reduced revenue. More than 100,000 airline employees have been laid off since 1989. Many others have taken pay cuts. In addition, the U.S. Justice Department has been investigating airline price fixing. The concern involves anticompetitive price signaling using the computerized reservation systems. Also, computer bias—giving an advantage to the computer owner's by listing their flights prior to leasee flights—and other "dirty tricks," such as computer screens showing competitor's flights filled when they were not, were other concerns.

Deep discount for the discretionary (leisure) traveler, while the business traveler pays higher fares, created another problem area. In 1993, 92% of airline passengers bought their tickets at a discount, paying on average just 35% of full fare. Frequent flyer programs are extensively used to promote customer loyalty.

High concentration, resulting in a few airlines controlling landing slots and gates, is a major concern at many hub airports. Some studies have shown the routing through hubs has increased air fares rather than reducing them.

Major airlines are concerned that weak competitors in Chapter 11 bankruptcy are permitted to disregard creditor short-term claims and their subsequent low prices make competition destructive. Between 1989 and 1993, the industry lost $12 billion and Southwest alone showed a profit.[18] Air safety is at an all-time high. The industry is heavily unionized but has been cutting costs through layoffs, reduction in food items offered, and two-tier pay schemes. Delta, United, American, US Air, and Northwest were the leading firms in an industry confronted with huge losses.

By 1995, the airlines recovered from their financial swoon, with Northwest and others registering significant profits. "Low cost airlines generated about $1.4 billion in revenue in 1994, up from $450 million in 1992 and next to nothing in 1989," according to Paul Karos, an airline analyst at CS First Boston. John Dasburg, Northwest Airlines CEO, says that the new low cost, short haul carriers "are viable products, they will endure, for the same reason Motel 6 endures. This product will be defined. It will be located in the top hundred markets that are 750 nautical miles or less from each other."[19]

HUMAN RESOURCES

■ Management

Herbert D. Kelleher is Chairman of the Board, President, and Chief Executive Officer and the driving force behind Southwest's success. Son of a Campbell Soup Company manager, Herb Kelleher's formative years were spent in Haddon Heights, New Jersey. Herb was star athlete and student body president at Haddon Heights High School. He graduated from Wesleyan University in Connecticut where he studied English literature. Later, he attended New York University Law school. Herb and his wife moved in 1961 to San Antonio, Texas, where he entered his father-in-law's law firm. During Southwest's early years, Kelleher served as general counselor and director of the firm. When Lamar Muse, Southwest's president, resigned in 1978 because of differences with Rollin King, Kelleher became president. Three years later Kelleher took over as CEO and president of Southwest Airlines Company.

Herb is a 62-year-old Irishman, a workaholic, who smokes five packs of cigarettes a day and is considered to be one of the zaniest CEOs in America. He loves to party and drink and has been known to sing "Tea for Two" while wearing bloomers and a bonnet at a company picnic. One Easter, he walked a plane's aisle clad in an Easter bunny suit and on St. Patrick's day, he dressed as a leprechaun.[20] Behind all of this is a leader who works 14-hour days, seven days a week, and leads by example. His management style—referred to as "management by insanity"—is far from any textbook style and it has worked extremely well. He has made work at Southwest fun for its employees and customers. He encourages flight attendants to organize trivia contests, delivering instructions to customers in rap fashion and awarding prizes to customers with the biggest holes in their socks.[21] Kelleher uses the "Management By Walking Around" (MBWA) concept. He regularly helps flight attendants serve drinks and peanuts when he flies. Every quarter, Kelleher and other top managers work a different job within the company for a day.[22] They have been observed doing tasks ranging from serving as counter agents, to loading baggage, to serving drinks. Southwest has fostered the practice of trying to breed leaders, not managers or administrators. Kelleher's span of control was reduced from 13 executives earlier to only four or five to free him up to monitor long-term developments, promote growth, and also to maintain good employee and customer relations. Some critics claim Kelleher holds power very tightly and he is the only one who makes major decisions. Some of the decisions were not so good, such as the acquisition of Muse Air. Others say Herb is the type of manager who will drink at a bar in the early hours of the morning with a mechanic just to find out what is wrong. Then he will fix the problem.

Until 1991, Southwest was the only major airline without an incentive stock-option plan for management personnel. There are no other management perks and executives receive the same percentage of pay increases as other employees. Southwest officers, with the exception of Kelleher, are in the 35- to 48-year-old bracket. On March 23, 1993, Herb Kelleher was appointed to a highly visible congressional commission entitled the National Commission to Ensure a Strong Competitive Airline Industry.

■ EMPLOYEES

Herb Kelleher proudly proclaimed that "The people who work here don't think of Southwest as a business. They think of it as a crusade."[23]

Southwest's personnel department is called the "University of People," to reflect top management's attitude toward its employees. Southwest generally recruits only in cities into which it flies in order to obtain employees who are familiar with Southwest. Recruiters are looking for that "Southwest Personality" of friendliness, warmth, and kindness. They search for people who are extroverts with a sense of humor. Recruiters ask prospective employees questions such as: "Tell me how you recently used your sense of humor in a work environment" and "Tell me how you used humor to defuse a difficult situation." Job candidates who can't answer these questions satisfactorily are automatically disqualified. Only one in ten applicants fits the company's image and is hired. Southwest looks for extroverts with a team attitude. One flight attendant played "The Eyes of Texas" on his harmonica over the loudspeaker after touchdown and sang cautions about remaining seated until coming to a full stop at the terminal. A customer reported the attendant received "three ovations from the passengers and would have had a standing ovation except that the seat-belt sign was on." Southwest does not hire anyone from other airlines as it does not want to inherit their problems.[24] The motto at Southwest is: "Do it right, but keep it light."

Levering and Moskowitz also found that "Southwest also put a lot of money into training. Its University for People, located in a terminal building at Dallas's Love Field, not far from the corporate headquarters, runs quarterly leadership training programs that are required for all supervisors and managers. Customer-care programs are run by line-level employees. For example, flight attendants teach other flight attendants. Pilots get customer-care training, a very rare practice in the airline industry. This is in keeping with Herb Kelleher's answer to the question why his low-fare carrier had been posting profits: 'We dignify the customer.'"

Training is emphasized in part because Southwest promotes from within. The airline fills roughly 80 percent of higher-level jobs through internal promotion.

While almost 90% of Southwest's employees are unionized, they do not exhibit the adversarial roles found in many major corporations. Contract agreements allow very flexible work rules. Pilots and flight attendants are often seen cleaning the aircraft between flights.[25] New contracts have been signed recently with the Southwest Airlines Pilot Association; the Teamsters, which represents mechanics, aircraft cleaners, and stock clerks; the IAM, which represents customer-service and reservations employees; the Ramp, Operations, and Provisioning Association and Southwest Airlines Professional Instructors Association. In January 1995, Standard & Poor's noted that Southwest Airlines took a major step to reinforce its market share when it reached an innovative, ten-year agreement with its pilots. The contract maintains current pay rates for five years, with 37% raises in three of the final five years. Stock options are offered in lieu of pay increases.

With an average salary of $47,000, Southwest's work force is among the airline industry's best paid and its productivity is also higher than the industry's average.[26] Southwest was the first carrier to offer a profit-sharing plan to employees (1973) and some early participants have become millionaires. Employees can collect only when they leave. Other benefits include unlimited space-available travel for employees and their families and fully transferable passes for accomplishments such as perfect attendance. Southwest also offers a flexible health-benefit program under which employees can choose coverage suitable to their individual circumstances, and a stock-purchase plan under which employees can acquire stock at 90% of market value via payroll deductions.[27] Employees own about 10% of the company's outstanding shares.

Kelleher has delegated to the lowest level the authority to make decisions on the spot without having to wade through layers of management and waste valuable time. Says Kelleher: "The bigger we get, the smaller I want our employees to think and act." The 1993 edition of *The 100 Best Companies to Work For In America* chose Southwest as one of the ten best. "Last year, Southwest's turnover was about 7% including retirements—half the industry average."[28] In 1990, when fuel prices skyrocketed, one-third of the Southwest employees contributed $130,000, unbeknownst to upper management, to offset some of the increased operating costs.

Herb Kelleher, in the company's 1991 annual report, attributed the airline's success to its business strategy and "because our people have the hearts of lions, the strength of elephants, and the determination of water buffaloes."

OPERATIONS

Southwest runs one of the most impressive operations in the airline industry. Its 203 aircraft make over 1,900 flights a day. In 1994, Southwest generated 624,476 flights, carrying 42,742,602 customers in perfect safety to their destinations. (SWA, 1994 Annual Report)

Southwest's gates average 10.5 departures a day, whereas the industry average is only 4.5 departures. Southwest's aircraft are airborne for an average of eleven hours and ten minutes per day, compared to the industry average of only eight hours. The airline's philosophy is that it can make money only when the aircraft are in the air. Seventy percent of the time, Southwest is able to off-load a group of passengers, service the aircraft, and board a new group of passengers in 15 minutes (see Exhibit 1).[29] Ten percent of the turnarounds are under ten minutes. Most airlines require an hour's ground time to turnaround a flight. This feat is made possible by "guaranteeing seats" but not reserving them with only one class of seat. Groups of thirty are given plastic chips at the gate and board in a first come, first on board operation. Not having to load meals onboard also speeds up the turnaround as does aircrew help in cleaning the aircraft (See Exhibit 1). In 1994, only 0.86 percent of the airline's flights were canceled or delayed due to mechanical incidents. (SWA, 1994 Annual Report, p. 8)

Operating only Boeing 737 series jet aircraft, Southwest simplifies its training, maintenance, and inventory costs. The company's fleet of aircraft averaged only 7.7 years of age at the end of 1994. "At year's end 1994, Southwest owned 97 of the 199 aircraft in the fleet. Of the remaining 102 aircraft, 72 were operated pursuant to long-term leases with various renewal and purchase options at the end of the lease periods and 30 of the older 737s were under short-term leases expiring over the next several years."[30] Southwest contracts out all heavy engine maintenance plus most component work to firms that can do the work for less than doing it in-house. Almost 75 percent of Southwest's fleet have Stage 3 engines which are quieter and more fuel efficient. Twenty-five

Exhibit 1	Anatomy of a 15-Minute Turnaround

7:55	Ground crew chat around gate position.
8:03:30	Ground crew alerted, move to their vehicles.
8:04	Plane begins to pull into gate; crew moves toward plane.
8:04:30	Plane stops; jetway telescopes out; baggage door opens.
8:06:30	Baggage unloaded; refueling and other servicing underway.
8:07	Passengers off plane.
8:08	Boarding call; baggage loading, refueling complete.
8:10	Boarding complete; most of ground crew leaves.
8:15	Jetway retracts.
8:15:30	Pushback from gate.
8:18	Push-back tractor disengages; plane leaves for runway.

On a recent weekday a Southwest Airlines flight arrived at New Orleans from Houston. The scheduled arrival time was 8:00 A.M., and departure for Birmingham, Alabama, was 8:18 A.M. *Forbes* clocked the turnaround, half-minute by half-minute.

Source: "Hit'em Hardest with the Mostest," *Forbes*, September 16, 1991.

737-300 aircraft are scheduled for delivery in 1997, 16 in 1998, and ten in 1999. Between 1997 and 2001, 63 Boeing 737-700 aircraft will be delivered to Southwest. This series is more fuel efficient, easier to maintain, and is expected to be quieter.

In 1989, Southwest became a major airline when it exceeded the billion dollar revenue benchmark. The airline has grown to become the sixth largest U.S. air carrier in terms of domestic customers it transported. Southwest flies to 45 cities in 22 states. (SWA, 1994 Annual Report)

Southwest's strategy is to provide high-frequency, short haul, point-to-point, not hub-and-spoke—low-fare flights. All of Southwest's flights are under two hours in flying time and under 750 nautical miles. Airports near city centers are used whenever possible—e.g., Dallas' Love Field, Chicago's Midway, Detroit Municipal Airport, etc. In an interview with a *Forbes* reporter in 1991, a Southwest executive defended Southwest's slow growth, saying "We attack a city with a lot of flights, which is another form of aggression in the airline industry. We don't go in with just one or two flights—we'll go in with ten or twelve. That eats up a lot of airplanes and capacity, so you can't open a lot of cities. Call it a kind of guerrilla warfare against bigger opponents. You hit them with everything you've got in one or two places instead of trying to fight them everywhere."[31] (See Exhibit 2.) Southwest held a 65% market share in its top 100 markets, as of second quarter 1994, and its passenger load factor was 67.3 percent.

Southwest's rock-bottom fares are often a third below those of its competitors. For example, "In the first quarter of 1991, Southwest's fares were 15% lower than those of its nearest competitor, American West, 29% lower than Delta's, 32% lower than United's, and 39% lower than US Air's."[32] To promote those remarkably low ticket prices, Southwest has to control costs tightly. Its operating costs per available seat mile were 2.3 percent lower in 1994 than in

Exhibit 2

Airline Efficiency Measures

	Airline Passengers Per Employee	Cost Per Available Seat - Mile (Cents)
AMR	863	8.25
Delta	1,181	9.26
Northwest	1,015	9.51
Southwest	2,523	7.20
UAL	837	9.30
USAir	1,141	11.09
Continental	850	7.91
TWA	731	9.64

Source: Commercial Aviation Report, 1993 Data, "Southwest's New Deal," *Fortune*, January 16, 1995, p. 94.

1993. Labor and fuel costs are the most significant, with each ranging as high as 35% of costs. Travel agent fees range between 8% and 14%, with an average of approximately 10%.

As of 1994, Southwest Airlines operated eight reservation centers located in Albuquerque, Chicago, Dallas, Houston, Little Rock, Oklahoma City, Phoenix, and Salt Lake City. "Southwest in recent months (July 1994), was dropped by the major computer reservation systems owned by competitors such as United, US Air, and Continental, which have been hurt by Southwest's expansion into East Coast markets. The reservation system owners maintained that since Southwest refused to pay fees for having its flights listed in their systems, it should not enjoy the same benefits as paying carriers. Southwest has refused to pay these fees, and is listed now only on American Airline's Sabre system." Travel agents currently sell 80% of U.S. airline tickets. Their commissions ranged from 12.96% (1990), 14.08% (1991), 14.31% (1992), to 14.36% (1993). To counter these escalating fees, Southwest is using ticketless systems. Passengers are given confirmation numbers over the telephone for their flights and present identification to airline personnel at airport gates. Also, the growth of on-line systems, which provide access to travel-related information, is causing a growth spurt in personal computer sales. Southwest has added more agents and new reservations centers to iron out the problems that still exist in its over-loaded reservation system.

MARKETING

From the beginning, Southwest has been dedicated to offering point-to-point service in short haul markets with low fares; frequent, conveniently timed flights; and friendly, reliable customer service. This market niche strategy has helped the airline become the sixth largest, and one of the strongest. It has heavily promoted these benefits to consumers. Until recently, Southwest was the only airline of this type. As Donald Valentine, Southwest's Vice President of Marketing and Sales, states, "While we make no pretense at being every-thing for everyone, we constantly strive to improve our convenient, depend-able service for travelers who want to get to their destinations on time, inexpensively—with no hassles." As a result of its marketing strategy, South-west has consistently ranked first in market share in more than 90 percent of its top 50 city-pair markets and is currently holding an overall market share exceeding 65 percent. (SWA, 1994 Annual Report)

Southwest established an innovative frequent flyer program which is based on trips flown, not total miles. Valentine orchestrated this plan to appeal to business and other short haul customers. Passenger contests are held in flight with winners obtaining frequent flyer miles and vacations.[33] The unique frequent flyer program is called "Company Club." After membership is attained with ten round-trip flights, Southwest awards a free trip to the club member and from then on, it takes only eight round-trip flights for each additional free trip. It is the only program by a major airline that rewards a person for short trips.

Southwest does answer the 1,000 or so letters it receives each week with a personal response. It takes up to 1,500 man-hours a week from 45 employees and two departments. Kelleher believes that the letters are the best system he has found to monitor airline performance.

The *product* Southwest Airlines Company is trying to sell can be described as follows, according to the 1991 Southwest Airlines Annual Report: "Southwest is the nation's low fare, high customer satisfaction airline. We primarily serve short haul city pairs, providing single class air transportation which targets the business commuter as well as leisure traveler." Air transportation is the prod-uct that can be served or sold to two types of travelers, business and leisure (discretionary).

Southwest's *prices* are purposefully low because its principal competition in short haul markets is often ground transportation. The airline wants to make flying more cost effective than driving a car or taking a train between two points. According to Southwest's annual report, it recognizes that the leisure market, which is highly price sensitive, is very large and can be stimulated with low fares. As a result, Southwest tends to grow its own markets, often stimulating traffic three- and four-fold versus traffic levels previously existing. "As is typical for Southwest when it's battling for market share, its fares are cheap. For instance, the airline said tickets for any intra-California routes will cost $69 each. Two types of discount fares are offered. The average fare nation-wide for a Southwest ticket is $58. Southwest's fares are approximately one-third lower than the prices of its competitors."[34]

Southwest has the lowest operating costs in the industry. This enables the air carrier to offer low fares which are vital to the short haul customer. One reason Southwest's operating costs are so low is because of its point-to-point travel system, compared to the hub-and-spoke systems other airlines use. This gives Southwest the ability to provide high frequency flights between city-pairs. This results in lower ticket fares compared to competitors. South-west would like an average of ten or more trips per day along these routes, each averaging two hours of flight time or less. For example, Southwest used this strategy in the highly traveled California market. As a result, Southwest is able to offer the lowest fares along any major route, getting travelers (business as well as pleasure) out of their cars and into Southwest jets. Major airlines such as United or American are either forced out of the market or have to compete on Southwest's terms. Competitors often call Southwest's niche strategy the "through-the-legs philosophy," avoiding head-on competition with the giants by going around them.[35]

The fact that Southwest Airlines does not have a reserved seating system is another reason operating costs are low. A potential traveler calls the airline directly for a reservation or can use one of Southwest's innovative ticket machines at the airport to purchase a ticket. This reduces the cost of a reservation system and also makes it more convenient for the customer.

Finally, Southwest has only one type of aircraft in its fleet. The Boeing 737 is the principal aircraft. This significantly simplifies maintenance, flight operations, and training activities. The 737 has been recognized as one of aviation's most successful aircraft. It is attractive, comfortable, and is cost-effective to operate in the short- to medium-range markets.

Southwest Airlines uses a variety of *promotions* to market its *product* to the flying public. Southwest will sponsor major sporting events such as the Southwest Conference basketball tournament or competitive athletic teams, using its logo as an attraction. The airline promotes its frequent flyer program. Southwest rewards customers with the shortest route to free trips—a frequent flyer program based on a few short trips, not long mileage. Southwest will also sponsor many charity events in an effort to help those who are less fortunate. In an effort to celebrate its partnership with Sea World of Texas and California, Southwest painted three of its aircraft to look like Shamu, the famous whale at Sea World. The airline also painted an aircraft with the Texas State Flag on it in tribute to its home state of Texas. Southwest was also the official airline for San Antonio's "Viva Fiesta 1993."

Southwest makes it a point to give customers the most flights available to destinations so they can better plan their schedules. This, coupled with Southwest's use of convenient downtown airports, makes flying easier and—most importantly—cost-effective for its customers.

The *place* portion of the marketing mix is very important to Southwest. Currently, Southwest operates 203 planes flying to 45 cities in the midwestern, southwestern, and western regions of the United States. Southwest tends to stay away from areas in which its short turnaround times would be in jeopardy. This makes flights along the New York, Boston, and Washington, D.C., corridors nearly impossible to penetrate. Southwest also wants to fly in areas where it doesn't have to go head-to-head with the major carriers. For example, airlines such as American and United used to fly frequent routes along the Dallas, San Antonio, and Houston triangle. But, this market was prime for Southwest's short haul, low cost philosophy. As a result, Southwest, with its no-frills approach compared to the full service approach of the other carriers, was able to carve its own niche in this market and go around the competition. Currently, Southwest has the largest market share in the Texas, California, and Phoenix regions due to this philosophy.

FINANCE

Southwest's 21 years of continued profitability began in 1973, the airline's second full year of operation. Only two quarters have been marred by red ink. In 1987, the first quarter loss was attributed to Southwest's ill-fated 1985 acquisition of Muse Air. By 1987, Muse was draining $2 million a month from Southwest, so Kelleher shut down the operation. Its $4.6 million, 1990 fourth-quarter net loss was only the second in 71 quarters.[36]

In 1989, Southwest's annual operating revenues exceeded $1 billion. This made Southwest a major airline, according to Department of Transportation definitions. Only ten domestic carriers presently earn revenues of over $1 billion annually. Southwest Airlines has one of the strongest financial statements in the airline industry. It continues to have the highest profit margins, the lowest operating costs, and a high credit rating. The absence of a huge debt load sets it apart from other major airlines. At a time when other airlines have up to 275% of their assets financed, Southwest has approximately 54%.

In 1990, Salomon Brothers ranked Southwest second among the major airlines in financial strength. Only two U.S. major carriers posted 1990 operating profits, with Southwest racking up $81.9 million and American $68 million. Net profits were generated by only two airlines. United's net income was $95.8 million and Southwest's $47.1 million in 1990. Gary Kelly, the Vice President of finance for Southwest, stated, "We emphasize cost controls, sound marketing, and growth at a reasonable rate. That makes the finance official's job easy." Southwest has never missed a dividend payment since dividends were initiated in 1976.

Between 1991 and 1992, Southwest's passenger revenues increased 28.3%, its freight revenues jumped 25.5%, and other revenues rose 46.6%. Even more impressive, Southwest's net income increased from $27 million in 1991 to $91 million in 1992, and its cash position was $303.1 million. On the other side of the coin, operating expenses increased 20.1% from 1991 to 1992. The primary factors contributing to the increases were the addition of seventeen 737 aircraft, higher travel agency commissions, increased contributions to profit sharing, higher aircraft leasing charges, and increased maintenance costs. (SWA Annual Reports) According to Kelleher, "Hard times come on a regular basis. Our secret is that we manage in good times as if it were hard times, and then we are ready for hard times."[37]

Because of the company's astute leadership, conservative expansion, and sound financial condition, it is able to access the capital markets to acquire new aircraft, expand operations, and continue the patient development of new short haul city pairs. Southwest has an impressive unrestricted, revolving credit of $250 million from a number of domestic banks. For further financial information see the Consolidated Balance Sheet (Exhibit 3) and the Consolidated Statement of Income (Exhibit 4).

THE FUTURE

Wall Street analysts, institutional investors, and financial reporters are standing by to hear "the rest of the story!" Will Southwest reverse the 1994 plunge in earnings of 47%? Will load factors improve? Has Southwest expanded too rapidly and will it enter bankruptcy as did Braniff, in the years following enactment of the Airline Deregulation Act? Can Southwest maintain its distinctive culture as it grows? With the delivery of the new Boeing 737-x aircraft set for 1997, will Southwest make good on its threats to offer transcontinental flights?

Exhibit 3   **Southwest Consolidated Balance Sheet**
(in thousands except/share and per share amounts)

| | Years Ended December 31, | | | |
	1995	1994	1993	1992
Assets:				
Current assets:				
Cash and cash equivalents	$ 317,363	$ 174,538	$ 295,571	$ 437,989
Accounts receivable	79,781	75,692	70,484	57,355
Inventories of parts and supplies, at cost	41,032	37,565	31,707	30,758
Deferred income taxes	10,476	9,822	10,475	—
Prepaid expenses and other current assets	24,484	17,281	23,787	15,792
Total current assets	473,136	314,898	432,024	541,894
Property and equipment, at cost				
Flight equipment	3,024,702	2,564,551	2,257,809	1,874,085
Ground property and equipment	435,822	384,501	329,605	294,458
Deposits on flight equipment purchase contracts	323,864	393,749	242,230	214,584
	3,784,388	3,342,801	2,829,644	2,383,127
Less allowance for depreciation	1,005,081	837,838	688,280	559.034
	2,779,307	2,504,963	2,141,364	1,824,093
Other assets	3,679	3,210	2,649	2,869
	$ 3,256,122	$ 2,823,071	$ 2,576,037	$ 2,368,856
Liabilities and Stockholders' Equity				
Current Liabilities:				
Accounts payable	$ 117,473	$ 117,599	$ 94,040	$ 82,023
Accrued liabilities	348,476	288,979	265,333	208,357
Air traffic liability	131,156	106,139	96,146	65,934
Income taxes payable	—	—	7,025	6,744
Current maturities of long-term debt	13,516	9,553	16,068	16,234
Total current liabilities	610,621	522,270	478,612	379,292
Long-term debt less current maturities	661,010	583,071	639,136	735,754
Deferred income taxes	281,650	232,850	183,616	136,462
Deferred gains from sale and leaseback of aircraft	245,154	217,677	199,362	224,645
Other deferred liabilities	30,369	28,497	21,292	13,167
Commitments and contingencies				
Stockholders' equity				
Common stock, $1.00 par value: 500,000,000 shares authored; 143,255,795 shares issued and outstanding in 1994 and 142,756,308 shares in 1993	144,033	143,256	142,756	96,047
Capital in excess of par value	162,704	151,746	141,168	177,647
Retained earnings	1,120,581	943,704	770,095	605,928
Less treasury stock, at cost (2,904 shares in 1992)	—	—	—	879,586
Total stockholders' equity	1,427,318	1,238,706	1,054,019	879,622
	$ 3,256,122	$ 2,823,071	$ 2,576,037	$ 2,368,856

Exhibit 4   **Southwest Consolidated Statement of Income**
                   (in thousands except for share amounts)

	1995	1994	1993	1992
		Years Ended December 31,		
Operating Revenues:				
Passenger	$ 2,760,756	$ 2,497,765	$ 2,216,342	$ 1,623,828
Freight	65,825	54,419	42,897	33,088
Charter and other	46,170	39,749	37,434	146,063
Total operating revenues	2,872,731	2,591,933	2,296,673	1,802,979
Operating Expenses:				
Salaries, wages, and benefits	867,984	756,023	641,747	512,983
Fuel and oil	365,670	319,552	304,424	257,481
Maintenance materials and repairs	217,259	190,308	163,395	122,561
Agency commissions	123,380	151,247	144,941	113,504
Aircraft rentals	169,461	132,992	107,885	77,472
Landing fees and other rentals	160,322	148,107	129,222	105,929
Depreciation	156,771	139,045	119,338	101,976
Other operating expenses	498,373	437,950	382,945	317,269
Merger expenses	—	—	10,803	—
Total operating expenses	2,559,220	2,275,224	2,004,700	1,609,175
Operating Income	313,531	316,709	291,973	193,804
Other Expenses (Income):				
Interest expertise	58,810	53,368	58,460	59,084
Capitalized interest	(31,371)	(26,323)	(17,770)	(15,350)
Interest income	(20,095)	(9,166)	(11,093)	(10,672)
Nonoperating (gains) losses, net	1,047	(963)	2,739	3,299
Total other expenses	8,391	17,186	32,336	36,361
Income Before Taxes and Cumulative Effect of Accounting Changes	305,140	299,523	259,637	157,443
Provision For Income Taxes	122,514	1120,192	105,353	55,816
Income Before Cumulative Effect of Accounting Changes	182,826	179,331	154,284	101,627
Cumulative Effect of Accounting Changes	—	—	15,259	12,538
Net Income	$ 182,626	$ 179,331	$ 169,543	$ 114,165
Per Share Amounts:				
Income before cumulative effect of accounting changes	$ 1.23	$ 1.22	$ 1.05	$ .71
Cumulative effect of accounting changes	—	—	.10	.09
Net Income	$ 1.23	$ 1.22	$ 1.15	$ .80

Gary Kelly, Southwest's Chief Financial Officer, expects that "Some of Southwest's difficulties will take the first half of '95 to get fully sorted out."[38]

"Long-range planning is a thing of the past at Southwest Airlines, where Kelleher approvingly quotes Klausewitz: 'No battle plans survive contact with the enemy.' Southwest sets its basic construct, niche, and adopts new tactics everyday."[39]

Michael Boyd, an aviation systems research analyst, believes United, saddled with higher costs, is likely to lose any head-to-head battle with Southwest. Aaron Gellman, director of the Transportation Center at Northwestern University, admires how Kelleher manages to stay ahead of his rivals and said: "Whatever other airlines do, Herb is going to eat them up in ways they haven't even thought of. The hardest thing for rivals to copy seems to be Kelleher's secret weapon—the trust and respect of his employees."

REFERENCES

1. McKenna, James T., "Southwest to Raise Ante in United Markets," *Aviation Week & Space Technology,* July 18, 1994, p. 22.

2. Garfield, Bob, "Commander Kelleher Eyes Future in New Southwest Ads, "*Advertising Age*, Vol. 65, No. 42, October 3, 1994, p. 3.

3. "The Southwest Story," Southwest Airlines Company, Dallas, Texas, 1990, p. 2.

4. Southwest Airlines Annual Report, Southwest Airlines Company, Dallas, Texas, 1990, p. 6.

5. "The Southwest Story," Southwest Airlines Company, Dallas, Texas, 1990, p. 6.

6. Southwest Airlines, "Fact Sheet," 1992.

7. Wells, Alexander T., *Air Transportation: A Management Perspective*, Wadsworth Publishing Company, Florence, Kentucky, Third Edition, 1994, p. 38.

8. Kane, Robert, and Allan Vose, *Air Transportation*, Kendall & Hunt Publishing Company, Dubuque, Iowa, 1971, p. 25.

9. Clark, Lindley H., "Airlines and Railroads: A Weird Marriage," *The Wall Street Journal*, Wednesday, March 15, 1989, p. A16.

10. Biederman, Paul, *"The U.S. Airline Industry: End of an Era,"* Prager Publishers, 1982, p. xiii.

11. Hamilton, Martha M., "Airline Mergers to Land on Other Desks," *Washington D.C. Post*, December 22, 1988, Section One, p. A23.

12. Wells, p. 302.

13. Ibid, pp. 76-77.

14. Ibid.

15. Ibid.

16. Hamilton, Martha M., p. A23.

17. Rose, Robert L., "Major U.S. Airlines Rapidly Gain Control Over Regional Lines," *The Wall Street Journal,* Wednesday, February 17, 1988, p. A-1.

18. Smith, Timothy K., "Why Air Travel Doesn't Work," *Fortune,* April 3, 1995, p. 46.

19. Ibid., pp. 49-50, & 56.

20. Levering, Robert, and Milton Moskowitz, *The 100 Best Companies To Work For In America*, Doubleday Press, 1993, p. 413.

21. Woodbury, Richard, *"Prince of Midair,"* Time, January 25, 1993, p. 55.

22. Jaffe, Charles A., "Moving Fast by Standing Still," *Nation's Business*, October 1991, p. 59.

23. Teitelbaum, Richard S., "Where Service Flies Right," *Fortune*, August 24, 1992, pp. 115.

24. Levering and Moskowsitz, p. 412.

25. Chakravarty, Subrata N., "Hit'em Hardest With The Mostest," *Forbes*, September 16, 1991, p. 50.

26. Wells, Edward O., "Captain Marvel," *Inc.*, January 1992, p. 46.

27. Henderson, Danna K., "Southwest Luvs Passengers, Employees, Profits," *Air Transport World*, July 1991, p. 32.

28. Zeller, Wendy, et al., "Go-Go Goliaths," *Business Week*, February 13, 1995, p. 69.

29. Chakravarty, p. 50.

30. Southwest Airlines Annual Report, Southwest Airlines Company, Dallas, Texas, 1994, p. 8.

31. Chakravarty, p. 49.

32. Ibid., p. 50.

33. Lawrence, Jennifer, "Don Valentine Is At The Heart of Southwest's Success," *Advertising Age*, January 25, 1988, p. 57.

34. Teitelbaum, p.115.

35. Zeller, Wendy, and Eric Schine, "Striking Gold in the California Skies," *Business Week*, March 30, 1992, p. 48.

36. Kelly, Kevin, "Southwest Airlines: Flying High with 'Uncle Herb,'" *Business Week*, July 3, 1989, p. 83.

37. Donlan, Thomas G., "The State Bird of Texas, Southwest Airlines' Herb Kelleher Has The Right Stuff"' *Barrons*, October 19, 1992, p. 10.

38. O'Brian, Bridget, "Southwest Air Says First-Half Results Are Likely To Be Hurt by Competition," *The Wall Street Journal*, February 13, 1995, p. A2.

39. Donlan, p. 14.

Cuchara Valley Ski Resort

Gary Bridges, University of Southern Colorado

Donna M. Watkins, University of Southern Colorado

William D. Chandler, University of Southern Colorado

"This is not going to be an easy job," Gary White muttered to himself as he began to spread out worksheets, financial statements, snowfall reports, and other data. He had been associated with Cuchara Valley Ski Resort in a variety of capacities for about 10 years and had witnessed all of its ups and downs. Gary was currently a professor at the business school of a nearby university. His roles at the ski resort had included two stints as controller, informal consultant, ski instructor, member of the ski patrol, owner and operator of three base area shops, and a home owner in the ski area's residential neighborhood. Now, as a consultant for another prospective buyer, he was being asked to give an opinion on whether the resort could ever be financially viable, and if so, to recommend specific actions.

Gary had made some hard decisions in his life—as an Air Force pilot and in his prior corporate position as an auditor. He had moved his family to this rural, mountain area 10 years ago in the hope that this lifestyle would be better for raising a family. They had become involved in community, church, and school activities, and were as much "locals" as outsiders could be. He had watched the valley residents band together and provide the support services that the ski area needed. But more times than anyone was willing to admit, the result had been disappointment and even financial ruin for some of the residents. Yet, every year carried a new hope that the ski area would open and provide much-needed jobs to the valley.

Gary thought back to when the resort first opened. Located in the southern part of Colorado, Cuchara Valley Ski Resort (CVSR) was a small ski area tucked away in the Sangre de Cristo mountain range in the shadows of the towering Huajatallos (known locally as the Spanish Peaks). Two miles away was the unincorporated village of Cuchara, Colorado. The resort was developed by local entrepreneurs and Texas developers, and opened in December 1981 under the name Panadero Ski Resort. (The name had been changed as the result of a dispute between one of the original developers and a new owner.)

The resort property covered 335 acres. The ski trails and terrain covered about 50 acres, 90 percent of which was public land for which the resort had acquired a use permit from the U.S. Forest Service. Because of the resort's distance from major lodging facilities, five different sets of condominiums had been built early in the ski area's history. In addition, approximately 37 acres of the original land had been sold as individual half-acre lots at an average price of $30,000. Twenty homes had been built; the average value of these homes was $500,000. Except for the ten acres that had been designated as green space, the remaining land was available for further development as single- or multi-family dwellings.

Because of its Southern Colorado location, Cuchara Valley Ski Resort had always been attractive to skiers from Texas, Oklahoma, and Kansas, especially those who drove. It was much closer than other Colorado ski areas and didn't require crossing any mountain passes (see Exhibit 1).

Exhibit 1   **CVSR Distances to Major Cities**

Even before the ski resort was built, the area had attracted visitors at other times of the year. The Cuchara area had been a popular summer resort for many years, with many of its summer residents being from this same market. Summer visitors enjoyed fishing, camping, horseback riding, and hiking. In the fall, visitors would come to see the brilliant color changes of the valley's spectacular aspen forests. Hunters from many states also came in search of the area's wildlife—bear, mule deer, elk, and mountain lion.

An additional draw to the area was an 18-hole, championship golf course, Grandote, which was located approximately 14 miles from the ski resort in the community of La Veta. The golf course normally operated from May through September and had been recognized as one of the 10 best golf courses in Colorado by a national golf publication. Despite its excellent design, the golf course seemed to flirt constantly with financial disaster; it was currently plagued by litigation, IRS liens, and a duel between past and present owners.

Until 1986, the CVSR partnership/management group had stayed basically intact, but, as Gary was fond of saying, the owners now changed as often as the fall leaves. The itinerant ownership was partly the result of considerable uncertainty in the Texas investment community brought about by the collapse of oil prices in the early 1980s. Collectively, the owners' lack of experience in ski resort management resulted in well-intentioned but often inappropriate expectations. During the 1985-86 ski season, the resort's Texas lender (Summit Savings) balked at advancing more money for operations. In a fit of brinkmanship, the resort's owners closed the resort in mid-February, a full six weeks ahead of schedule. The early closure left area businesses struggling to dispose of excess inventory. The resort's early and sudden closure badly damaged its reputation as several out-of-state church groups and other guests with confirmed reservations for Spring Break had to scramble to make last-minute arrangements.

The lender began foreclosure proceedings and the owners sued. Gary, along with the resort's mountain manager, was asked to work with a court-appointed receiver who supervised the 1986 summer maintenance operations. Eventually, the parties reached a settlement whereby the partners escaped financial liability and the lender took possession of the resort in the fall of 1986.

The loan to develop and open the ski resort amounted to approximately $22 million. Appraisals done shortly after foreclosure estimated a total value of between $8 million and $10 million. The lender/owner realized that the value of a ski resort resided in a business that was operating and generating revenue rather than in the assets themselves; so Summit Savings agreed to provide operating funds for the 1986-87 ski season while it tried to sell the resort.

The 1986-87 ski season saw the most snowfall in the resort's history but because of the prior year's early closure, the slow start in advertising, and a general uncertainty about the resort's future, the skier count was disappointing.

Not long after the 1986-87 season ended, the lender (Summit Savings) was merged with seven other marginal S&Ls in Texas, as part of a restructuring effort known as the Southwest Plan. The newly formed S&L was called Sunbelt Savings. From Gary's perspective, this turned out to be an "unholy alliance" as it resulted in yet another top management group: Soon after Sunbelt Savings was formed, a different group of S&L executives in Texas assumed responsibility for the Cuchara Valley Ski Resort. Their first action was to hire a management company called Club Corporation of America (CCA) from Dallas, Texas, to operate the ski area for the 1987-88 ski season. Gary remembered the local residents questioning the reasons for hiring an out-of-state management group. Their fears were confirmed when they learned that CCA's expertise was managing golf courses.

The organization chart of CVSR's ownership/management became even more complicated when the Resolution Trust Corporation (RTC) assumed control of this S&L behemoth (Sunbelt Savings). Now, all decisions had to be cleared through RTC officials. After dismissing CCA in 1988, the new and improved RTC-managed S&L, Sunbelt Savings, agreed to fund Cuchara's operations for the 1988-89 ski season, during which they attracted the third highest skier count (25,055) in Cuchara's operating history. Despite this relatively successful season, Sunbelt Savings decided that it would not provide operating funds for the 1989-90 season nor for the foreseeable future. They made this announcement three weeks before the scheduled opening. Sunbelt retained a skeleton crew to answer telephones and to show the property to prospective buyers.

The resort remained closed for three seasons (89-90, 90-91, and 91-92). During this time, local resort management entertained an array of "lookers" professing their desire to buy the ski resort. Finally, in 1991, a Texas businessman who owned a summer home in Cuchara began serious negotiations with the RTC. The sale was finalized in 1992 with the RTC financing a little over half of the purchase price.

Gary had liked the new owner and felt that he started his ownership with the best interests of the resort and the surrounding area in mind. The new owner believed that with the relatively low cash investment, CVSR could generate positive cash flow in the short term and eventually become profitable

After two seasons (1992-93 and 1993-94), it was clear that the owner's expectations were overly optimistic. At the end of a slower-than-expected 1993-94 season, during which the owner had to provide additional cash for operations, he accepted a new investor's offer to assume financial and operating responsibility for the ski operations for the 1994-95 ski season.

Had someone been telling this story to Gary, he knew he would have laughed out loud and said "preposterous" to what happened next. But he had been there and he knew it was all true: The new investor ran out of money before the first snowfall and never opened the resort. He not only failed to open the resort for business, but he also made off with the funds from pre-season ticket sales and left many employees and local merchants unpaid for their services. With legal help, the earlier Texas owner regained full control; but doing so took several months, and the 1994-95 ski season was over by then. It was safe to say that it had not been a good winter for the valley.

■ Snow and Water

Cuchara's southern location had to be considered a mixed blessing in that its snowfall was always consistently inconsistent. The original developers realized this and constructed a snow-making system which, in theory, could cover 75 percent of the skiable terrain with man-made snow. But because of faulty installation, occasional unseasonably warm temperatures during the ski season, and technological advances, the snow-making system was, although operable, inefficient and bordering on obsolescence. Nevertheless, man-made snow had been what kept the resort open during its frequent dry periods (see Exhibit 2).

Snow-making was almost always done at night when the temperatures were colder; effective snow-making required temperatures below 28 degrees

Exhibit 2   **CVSR Snowfall in Inches 1985-86 to 1995-96**

Season	Sept	Oct	Nov	Dec	Jan	Feb	Mar	Apr	May	Total
1985-86	2.50	10.00	25.00	10.00	18.00	21.00	41.50	47.00	15.00	190.00
1986-87	1.50	16.75	33.74	21.00	39.50	74.75	126.10	30.50	21.25	365.09
1987-88	0.00	0.00	50.00	36.00	29.50	19.00	83.25	25.00	18.00	260.75
1988-89	1.00	0.00	33.75	32.50	35.75	52.75	12.00	14.75	0.00	182.50
1989-90	3.00	20.00	7.00	39.50	30.25	43.00	33.00	35.75	22.25	233.75
1990-91	0.00	25.25	36.00	30.25	17.75	32.25	70.00	37.00	2.50	251.00
1991-92	0.00	15.50	74.50	7.00	27.75	59.50	40.75	3.50	0.00	228.50
1992-93	0.00	5.75	85.50	39.75	13.00	47.50	55.25	56.00	19.00	321.75
1993-94	6.75	19.88	31.75	31.25	28.00	22.00	66.00	70.50	5.00	281.13
1994-95	0.25	14.50	27.25	10.50	21.25	16.50	47.50	113.00	10.75	261.50
1995-96	16.00	1.00	14.25	24.75	24.25	22.25	58.25	10.00	0.00	170.75
Avg	2.82	11.69	38.07	25.68	25.91	37.32	57.60	40.27	10.34	249.70
Min	0.00	0.00	7.00	7.00	13.00	16.50	12.00	3.50	0.00	170.75
Max	16.00	25.25	85.50	39.75	39.50	74.75	126.10	113.00	22.25	365.09

Fahrenheit. Snow-making systems rely on a system of pumps and compressors to move the water great distances up very steep terrain and then spray it through guns (actually high-pressure nozzles with fan blades) under pressure. Cuchara's system was all electrical and operated off a separate electric meter. Each night (eight to ten hours) of snow-making operation cost approximately $1,500 in electricity usage.

Management usually started making snow in November, well before the resort opened, so as to have a sufficient base for the resort's traditional mid-December opening. December's natural snowfall alone usually was not sufficient to accommodate skiing. It was extremely important to have good snow (a 30" to 45" base was considered adequate) at Christmas because December and March were always the biggest months of the season.

Temperature and utility costs were critical determinants of the resort's snow-making strategy, but the most limiting constraint to short-term snow-making ability and long-term planning had always been the availability of water. Baker Creek flowed from a source high in the peaks of the Sangre de Cristo range and was the resort's only source of water for snow-making and domestic use (homes, condos, and restaurants). The resort owned water rights under Colorado water law allowing it to divert a specified volume (measured by cubic feet per second) out of Baker Creek. Water for domestic use was pumped to a 100,000 gallon storage tank. In addition, the resort stored approximately one-and-a-half acre-feet (1 million gallons) of water in a small pond.

Without this pond as a storage facility, it would have been impossible to make snow. Heavy snow-making would empty the pond in about eight hours and it took twelve hours to refill under most conditions. The County Water Commissioner would constantly monitor the metered usage of snow-making water to ensure that the resort did not use more than its legal entitlement.

Water rights represent the "right" of the owner to divert water from a stream, in this case Baker Creek, or a river for agricultural use (irrigation) or commercial use (watering the golf course or making snow). The water rights concept is fairly rare and occurs only in the Western states. It is based on historical and original usage of the respective waterway which may date back to the original settlement of the state.

Gary felt that additional water (and storage) was a must. Snow-making needed expanding and, eventually, additional housing would be required if CVSR were to become a true destination resort. He knew that water rights could be bought and sold on an open market basis, with higher priority rights (lower numbers) costing more than lower priority rights (higher numbers). Each residential unit required the water right for one Equal Quantity Ratio (EQR) or enough water to supply the annual needs of a typical family of four (estimated at about 88,000 gallons). This arbitrary unit of water right sold for between $1200 and $2000. Since CVSR already used its entire allotment of 347 EQRs, the resort would need to buy additional EQRs (which it then would make available to homeowners or hotel developers) if it hoped to develop additional lots. EQRs for another 50 units could cost as much as $100,000.

"Of course," Gary thought, "owning the rights and actually getting the water could be two different things." He knew that owning the water rights to a stream such as Baker Creek would not guarantee that the actual volume of water in that stream (determined by snowfall) would be enough to fulfill an owner's legal water rights, especially the demand a fully developed resort might create. Could Mother Nature be counted on to ensure that Baker Creek would always have enough water to meet the resort's growing needs? Gary had never seen Baker Creek dry, but beyond that, he didn't have an answer. He made a note to recommend a water resource expert.

■ Resort Services

Next Gary took a look at the resort's services. He wanted to present a clear picture of what the resort had to offer skiers. "Good people" was the first item he wrote down. Most of the employees were year-round valley residents, and they had always done their best to be friendly and helpful to resort visitors. The resort's wages had always been below the Colorado ski industry's averages, though, and it was getting harder and harder to lure quality, skilled employees back for the see-saw ride.

■ Skiing Terrain

The skiing terrain at CVSR was considered moderate, with 40 percent beginner, 40 percent intermediate, and 20 percent expert runs. The U.S. Forest Service had recently allowed Cuchara to open an additional 45 acres of expert terrain called The Burn, but it was ungroomed and was not served by a lift (see Exhibit 3).

■ Lift Tickets, Ski Rental, and Ski School

The resort's moderate ticket prices, ranging from $15 to $25, placed Cuchara near the lowest of Colorado's and New Mexico's lift ticket prices (see Exhibit 4).

Exhibit 3   **Resort Credentials**

Ski Resort	Elevation Top	Elevation Base	Number Lifts	Vertical Drop	Number of Trails
Cuchara	10810 ft	9248 ft	4	1562 ft	24
Monarch	11900 ft	10790 ft	4	1160 ft	54
Taos, N.M.	11819 ft	9207 ft	11	2612 ft	72
Wolf Creek	11775 ft	10350 ft	6	1425 ft	50

Ski rentals were available at the base area and in the village of Cuchara. The equipment was acceptable, although not in top-notch shape. Prices were standard for the industry.

The ski school offered basic group and private lessons. As with rentals, ski school prices were competitive. Ski instructors were typically local residents who knew the mountain well.

■ Food and Lodging

At the base area, CVSR had available a snack bar, the Warming Hut, where skiers could purchase food and drinks from morning until late afternoon. A full service dining facility, Baker Creek Restaurant, was also located in the base area and served lunch and dinner. A limited number of other restaurants and bars were located in the village of Cuchara and in La Veta.

Although cabins and condos were located within the resort's "borders," none was currently owned by CVSR. Consequently, resort employees reserved lodging for all overnight skiers through local property managers who had contracted with the owners of condos and cabins to provide reservation and cleaning services. When the resort was busy, especially during Christmas vacation and Spring Break, the housing on the resort property would be filled; the resort would then direct overnight guests to the limited local hotels in Cuchara and La Veta. Almost all of the ownership groups had recognized the need for more beds in the resort, but no one had the money to build additional facilities.

CVSR did not provide transportation to and from Cuchara or La Veta. Gary knew that the larger ski areas in the state had ski-in/ski-out lodging adjacent to their slopes. At CVSR, skiers could drive from the condos to the base area in a matter of minutes, although slippery, steep roads and limited base area parking might be considered by some to be problematic. Other resorts had

Exhibit 4   **Selected Lift Ticket Prices**

Resort	Adult Full Day	Child Full Day	Adult Half Day
Cuchara	$25	$15	$18
Monarch	$27	$16	$22
Taos, N.M.	$37	$22	$24
Wolf Creek	$31	$19	$22

solved such problems by providing bus service from the lodging facilities to the base area; Cuchara had no transportation services within the resort property. Was lodging a problem for CVSR? Gary wondered if the lack of rooms near the base area should be considered a major constraint on the resort's long-term viability.

■ Other Services

CVSR tried to behave as much like a larger resort as it could. A few times during the season there would be a dance band or a concert at the restaurant or the Warming Hut. Outside of these typically peak periods, the base area was closed down at night except for the restaurant.

The base area had a small shopping area with six retail spaces open during the day that sold T-shirts, sweatshirts, and ski-related gear such as goggles, gloves, etc. Child care could also be arranged for either the day or night.

MARKET DATA

■ Target Customers

Cuchara's management had consistently marketed the resort to families and groups (mostly church groups) who were beginner and intermediate skiers and who typically drove to Colorado. Gary remembered meeting a chaperone for a group from Texas who told him that somewhat isolated places were, in her mind, a great destination for middle school and high school kids. She had said that it was much easier to "chaperone" when you didn't have to worry about the kids out walking up and down the streets of an unfamiliar ski town. Gary was not sure that was the "marketing theme" the resort wanted to use.

In fact, Gary's years of watching the numbers had led him to the conclusion that church groups were usually break-even business at best and were often loss leaders, at least where lift tickets, ski rentals, and ski lessons were concerned, because of the sizable discounts given. However, management generally felt that at least during slower periods (January and February), groups helped pay the bills until March. Because Spring Break schedules were not as standardized as Christmas vacation dates, the resort was generally busy throughout the month of March. There was also a glimmer of long-term strategic thinking that members of these groups would return with their families or in smaller groups and pay the regular prices.

CVSR did not totally ignore the southeastern Colorado market. The resort focused on the same beginner/intermediate skier, especially those who might want to "try out" skiing but didn't necessarily have the money or want to spend the money to go to the larger ski areas or destination resorts such as Aspen or Vail. In fact, it was typical of skiers in this market to arrive in the morning and drive home after a day's skiing, thereby avoiding the cost of lodging.

■ Location

Gary got out a map and began to look at various distances. CVSR was 114 miles south of Colorado Springs, the closest airport with substantial commercial air service. Pueblo was 35 miles closer but it was served only by commuter service that connected in Denver. La Veta, located 15 miles from CVSR, had an unattended runway that could accommodate small jets but had no scheduled air service and had no instrument landing capability.

The resort was 31 miles west of Interstate Highway 25, Colorado's only north-south interstate. Residents of large cities in Texas, Kansas, and Oklahoma could drive to Cuchara in eight to ten hours (see Exhibit 1).

■ **Competition**

The nearest competitors to Cuchara were Wolf Creek Ski Area, a Colorado ski area approximately three hours' driving time west; Monarch Ski Area, a Colorado ski area approximately three hours' driving time north and west; and Taos Ski Area, a New Mexico ski area approximately two hours' driving time west and south. Getting to any of these three ski areas from any eastern or southeastern destination required not only additional hours on the road but also substantial mountain driving over high mountain passes. For someone who was not used to this kind of driving, snow-packed or icy mountain roads could be most unnerving.

As Gary sifted through the industry data and brochures he had on these competitors, he noted that ticket prices were anywhere from $1 to $12 higher than those at Cuchara (see Exhibit 4). But if a group were coming from outside the state, would a few dollars a day per person really matter? Gary wasn't sure. Ski rental and ski school prices weren't an issue: Unless you went to Aspen or one of the other destination resorts, prices for rentals and ski lessons were about the same everywhere.

Next he took a look at the terrain and snowfall. All of the competitors had more skiable terrain than did Cuchara. Each also had considerably more expert runs. Since Gary and his family had been skiing for years, that was especially appealing to him. Then he looked at the snowfall charts. "No comparison," he thought. All three competitors had more snowfall than Cuchara had. In fact, Wolf Creek typically received more snowfall than any other ski area in Colorado.

And what about the night life, the restaurants, and all those other things skiers liked to do when they weren't skiing? Gary thought that, in general, the competing ski areas were as isolated as Cuchara. None had significant development surrounding the base area as some of the destination resorts did. But Gary had to admit that each of the competitors had larger towns and more entertainment within 20 to 30 miles.

The last thing that Gary considered was off-season activity. Most large ski areas in the state had found ways to use the slopes or other facilities during the summer. Some resorts had installed alpine slides. An alpine slide was a concrete bobsled-like path that was placed on the slopes; visitors rode to the top on the ski lifts and then came down the concrete slide on a cart with wheels that had limited steering and braking capability. Some resorts groomed their trails for mountain biking and let biker and bike ride the ski lifts up the mountain. Concerts, fairs, and other types of gatherings were also typical. These types of activities were supported, of course, by the resorts' abundance of lodging and shopping.

CVSR and its competitors did not typically have summer activities. Summer activity in Taos was certainly big because of its Native American influence and its artist community. But most of this activity occurred in the city of Taos, not at the ski area. Gary thought that CVSR probably had the most potential of the four ski areas because of the lodging that was reasonably close to the base area and because of the well-established summer resident/visitor clientele that had been visiting the Cuchara Valley annually for many years. Throughout the changing ownership of CVSR, Gary had seen various events organized such as both classical and popular music concerts, art shows, etc. Attendance had been acceptable for first-time events, but none had been continued from year to year so as to build a reputation.

MARKETING ACTIVITIES

Gary knew that Cuchara primarily used direct mail to reach previous guests and group leaders. In addition, management had occasionally put employees on the road to make direct contact with church groups in Texas, Oklahoma, and Kansas.

For the southeastern Colorado market, CVSR usually bought TV and radio spots in Pueblo and Colorado Springs which emphasized low prices and no lift lines. The resort would also sell discount tickets to the military and through various retail outlets such as convenience stores and supermarkets. For skiers from Pueblo and Colorado Springs, it was about the same distance away as Monarch Ski Resort.

Gary had learned from resort employees who had worked at other ski areas that ski shows were generally an important marketing tool in that travel agents attended them and could provide important group business. He knew that shows were held in Wichita, Kansas; in Dallas and Amarillo, Texas; and, of course, in Denver. Typically, two or three attractive and enthusiastic marketing representatives from each ski resort would attend these shows and set up attractive booths highlighting their resorts' strengths. CVSR's attention to ski shows has been spotty at best.

From what Gary knew, it cost only between $125 and $200 to set up a booth at one of these shows, and it seemed to him that traveling to regional shows would be cheaper than visiting individual groups and would result in far more contacts. But what about personal service? Gary knew that the friendliness of the valley people was an appealing feature of Cuchara. Traveling to cities and making personal visits with church groups was a nice touch. Unfortunately, no data had been kept on these issues. So Gary could not determine if direct mail, personal visits, or ski shows resulted in the most "bang for your buck."

COLORADO SKI INDUSTRY

Gary thought he had better have a look at the big picture also. He found that data from Colorado Ski Country USA showed the Colorado ski industry to be maturing; it had increased its skier visits only .5 percent in the 1993-94 season and then had suffered a similar percentage decline in the 1994-95 season (see Exhibits 5 & 6). A skier visit or skier day represents one skier buying one lift ticket on a given day; if a particular skier skis more than one day, the skier is counted each of these days. The larger Colorado ski resorts had been attacking the stagnant growth by expanding their skiable terrain and adding high speed

Exhibit 5   **Cuchara and Colorado Skier Days 1981-82 to 1994-95**

Season	Colorado	Cuchara
1981-82	7,616,699	12,567
1982-83	8,200,442	22,263
1983-84	8,617,318	35,337
1984-85	9,052,345	31,232
1985-86	9,110,597	12,998
1986-87	9,453,359	16,495
1987-88	9,557,002	16,383
1988-89	9,981,916	25,055
1989-90	9,703,927	Closed
1990-91	9,788,487	Closed
1991-92	10,427,994	Closed
1992-93	11,111,290	22,775
1993-94	11,011,290	17,203
1994-95	11,105,106	Closed

Source: Information for Colorado obtained from Colorado Ski Country, USA.

lifts and other amenities. In fact, Colorado ski resorts had spent $44.5 million on capital improvements during 1992-93 and $43.5 million during 1993-94.

While the statewide skier visit count was holding its own, summer and winter vacation air travel into Denver International Airport (DIA) had declined. In addition, winter overnight lodging figures in the ski areas were down. Industry experts had interpreted this to mean that many of the skiers were coming from the Front Range (Boulder, Denver, Colorado Springs, etc.). Gary knew that for several years these Front Range cities had been experiencing a significant population migration from other states. Perhaps that increase had created a set of new Colorado residents who were interested in skiing.

Other data showed that tourism (winter and summer visitors) in Colorado was becoming more of a regional activity. The number of visitors statewide that arrived by car had increased significantly.

FINANCIAL DATA

The final item on Gary's list was the financial data. He knew that Cuchara earned revenue from lift ticket sales, ski equipment rentals, ski lessons, child care, and food service. First he looked at the revenue and expense data for the two seasons (1992-93 and 1993-94) the resort had been operating under the current owner (see Exhibits 7 and 8). The owner had given the ski shop to a local resident rent free. In return, the shopkeeper had stocked a small amount of CVSR merchandise as well as the merchandise she sold. The shopkeeper's only

Exhibit 6

Colorado Skier Visits

Destination Resorts	1993-94	1994-95
Aspen Highlands	106,197	159,288
Aspen Mountains	359,848	329,535
Buttermilk	172,948	168,439
Crested Butte	530,088	485,840
Cuchara Valley	17,300	Closed
Howelson Hill	16,171	14,095
Monarch	158,148	162,982
Powderhorn	61,202	80,241
Purgatory	302,103	382,839
Ski Sunlight	88,251	93,952
Snowmass	814,852	767,509
Steamboat	1,021,149	1,013,606
Telluride	300,388	301,748
Wolf Creek	140,456	157,995
Total	4,089,101	4,118,069
Front Range Destination Resorts		
Arapahoe Basin	257,358	262,240
Arrowhead	23,721	28,641
Beaver Creek	504,516	538,897
Breckenridge	1,215,013	1,227,357
Copper Mountain	842,210	770,973
Keystone	1,095,857	1,042,171
Silver Creek	93,516	92,547
Vail	1,527,698	1,568,360
Winter Park	1,008,040	986,077
Total	6,567,929	6,517,263
Front Range Resorts		
Eldora	145,011	145,370
Loveland Basin	295,000	258,000
Ski Cooper	67,193	66,404
Totals	507,204	469,774
Grand Totals	11,164,234	11,105,106
Number Increase/Decrease	52,942	-59,128
Percent Increase/Decrease	0.48	-0.53

Source: Colorado Ski Country USA.

Exhibit 7   **Cuchara Valley Ski Resort Financial Summary**

Season	Skier Count	Revenue						Totals
		Lift Tickets	Ski School	Ski Rental	Baker Creek	Warming Hut	
1981-82	12,567	Unknown	Unknown	Unknown	Unknown	Unknown	
1982-83	22,263	Unknown	Unknown	Unknown	Unknown	Unknown	
1983-84	35,337	$312,696	$32,679	0	$ 85,304	$73,921	$504,600
1984-85	31,232	315,264	34,666	65,880	139,035	96,397	651,242
1985-86	12,998	113,946	21,771	62,766	53,239	59,589	311,311
1986-87	16,495	145,442	17,918	52,727	29,783	52,704	298,574
1987-88	16,383	114,848	17,689	50,031	35,162	48,247	265,977
1988-89	25,055	260,660	52,960	106,696	0	76,178	496,494
1989-90	Closed	0	0	0	0	0	0
1990-91	Closed	0	0	0	0	0	0
1991-92	Closed	0	0	0	0	0	0
1992-93	22,775	323,053	41,140	97,646	Closed	Leased	461,839
1993-94	17,300	$195,305	$54,898	$ 94,397	$ 67,528	$57,998	$470,126

obligation was to remit sales dollars from the resort's merchandise to the resort.

Gary also noted that during the first season (92-93), the restaurant had been closed and the Warming Hut had been leased out. Only a rent amount was collected. In the following season, both food establishments had been operated by the resort.

Overall, the report showed a small profit in the neighborhood of $36,000 over the two-season period. At least that's what it said on paper. But Gary knew that the spreadsheet covered only the two seasons, the four months each year during which skiers could use the mountain. It didn't reflect the expenses of the other eight months of each year. Summer maintenance of the equipment and lifts was required, and someone had to be around to answer the phones. In addition, the fall months (usually beginning in October) always saw a flurry of activity as the resort geared up for the coming season. Marketing activities increased markedly, equipment was readied, and employees were hired and trained.

Next he looked at the list of assets (see Exhibit 9). Some of these assets were "the originals"—snow cats, chair lift motors and assemblies, etc. Some major replacements were due. While depreciation amounts had always been included in expense records, he knew that no real cash existed to make the kind of capital improvements that were going to be necessary in the near future.

Exhibit 8 — Cuchara Valley Ski Resort Summary of Earnings 1992-93 and 1993-94

	Dec 92	Jan 93	Feb 93	Mar 93	Dec 93	Jan 94	Feb 94	Mar 94	Total
Ski Operations									
Revenue	58649	102397	3328	96578	78555	21479	49695	54478	465159
Expenses	61603	76731	37157	37157	70494	69414	45184	32267	430007
Profit/Loss	-2954	25666	-33829	59421	8061	-47935	4511	22211	35152
Ski School									
Revenue	6907	18108	544	18405	25197	4981	13239	12034	99415
Expenses	13467	23099	1332	1332	9082	14128	9448	17412	89300
Profit/Loss	-6560	-4991	-788	17073	16115	-9147	3791	-5378	10115
Ski Rental									
Revenue	18756	37417	1068	36758	33433	10672	23179	28904	190187
Cost of Sales	0	0	0	0	658	0	0	0	658
Gross Margin	18756	37417	1068	36758	32775	10672	23179	28904	189529
Expenses	9006	14606	4406	4406	18720	10767	6148	8964	77023
Profit/Loss	9750	22811	-3338	32352	14055	-95	17031	19940	112506
Ski Merchandise									
Revenue	3245	3805	249	0	3898	1628	2362	4516	19703
Cost of Sales	3630	3492	149	0	1652	6996	1777	886	18582
Gross Margin	-385	313	100	0	2246	-5368	585	3630	1121
Expenses	0	0	0	0	326	0	0	0	326
Profit/Loss	-385	313	100	0	1920	-5368	585	3630	795
Food & Beverages									
Revenue	2151	2448	2134	0	41746	22087	30711	27642	128919
Cost of Sales	0	0	0	0	24953	12049	13006	5561	55569
Gross Margin	2151	2448	2134	0	16793	10038	17705	22081	73350
Expenses	1249	2296	2121	2121	40750	23356	12345	12777	97015
Profit/Loss	902	152	13	-2121	-23957	-13318	5360	9304	-23665
Property Management									
Revenue	3945	12422	-6	1224	9340	54342	28701	22447	132415
Cost of Sales	0	0	0	0	325	44276	15157	36841	96599
Gross Margin	3945	12422	-6	1224	9015	10066	13544	-14394	35816
Expenses	0	0	0	-15500	9394	3819	3243	4099	5056
Profit/Loss	3945	12422	-6	16724	-379	6247	10301	-18493	30761
General & Administrative									
Expenses	6988	10038	6134	322	12214	15233	7443	6390	64762
Marketing									
Expenses	9692	15576	3087	583	11929	8766	8041	6237	63911
Total Revenue	93653	176597	7317	152965	192169	115189	147887	150021	1035798
Total Cost of Sales	3630	3492	149	0	27588	63321	29940	43288	171408
Total Gross Margin	90023	173105	7168	152965	164581	51868	117947	106733	864390
Total Expenses	102005	142346	54237	30421	172909	145483	91852	88146	827397
Total Profit/Loss	-11982	30759	-47069	122544	-8328	-93615	26095	18587	36993

Exhibit 9　　　　**CVSR Assets as of August 1, 1994**

Assets	Cost
Warming Hut	
Equip	$55,574
Improvements	10,193
Total	65,767
Vehicles	9,428
Operations Equipment	207,761
Snow-Making Equipment	
Compressor Line	172,903
Improvements	2,267
Total	175,170
Lifts	212,766
Rental Equip	
Skis, Boots & Poles	10,294
Bindings	24,964
Skis	31,168
Total	66,426
Baker Creek	
Kitchen Equip	13,582
Cooler	6,150
Improvements	2,050
Cash Registers	5,114
Total	26,896
Office Equip	20,216
Grand Total	$784,430

CONCLUSION

Gary decided that the key to preparing a financial pro-forma was a good estimate of skier visits. Unfortunately, the frequent closures and erratic marketing efforts and inconsistent snow made this a daunting task. He felt that the large corporate-owned ski areas would continue to spend heavily on expansion plans to increase market share and there were even rumors of major consolidations. Gary also remembered the fate of a small ski area called Conquistador, located at Westcliffe, Colorado, about 60 miles from Cuchara. Conquistador had almost mirrored Cuchara's experience and its most recent owners had

Exhibit 10   **CVSR Ticket Sales 1993-94 by Type**

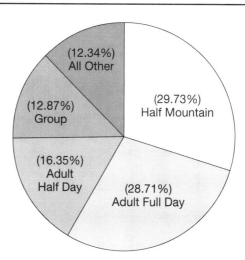

decided to sell off all of its assets and abandon efforts to operate a ski area. Was Cuchara doomed to this fate? On the other hand, Wolf Creek and Monarch ski areas had experienced growth in their skiers during 1994-95, 3 percent and 12 percent, respectively. Gary felt that an increase in lift ticket prices was certainly appropriate and he realized that promotional discounts and the variety of less-than-full price tickets sold reduced the average revenue per lift ticket to something less than the price charged for an adult, full-day ticket. He believed that an increase to $28 for an adult, full-day ticket was warranted. Using historical data (Exhibit 5), he could determine an average revenue-per-skier for each of the departments including lift tickets. This would be a starting point for estimating future revenues.

Beloit Poland S.A.

Zbigniew Malara, Technical University
of Wroclaw, Poland

Mark Kroll, The University of Texas
at Tyler

John Holm, The University of Texas
at Tyler

INTRODUCTION

On June 4, 1989, the Polish Communist system was abolished and Poland held
its first truly democratic parliamentary elections in 50 years. The mere broadcast of election returns over national television captivated the population, most
of which had never experienced the power of democracy. That day also represented the beginning of a great experiment—the Polish people's attempt to
transition their very tightly controlled, centrally planned economy into a
market-driven one in which individuals are free to pursue their own dreams of
economic prosperity.

It was inevitable that the transition process was going to be very difficult.
The Nationalization Act of 1946 transferred ownership of all businesses with
more than 50 employees to the central government. Forty-three years later, the
Polish economy was comprised of about 15,000 state-owned enterprises, each
of which had been operated under extremely tight regulations and controls.
Heretofore, enterprise managers essentially responded to directives from government and Communist Party officials who were far removed from the enterprise. The management of these organizations received orders from central
planners, tried to meet expectations, and continuously fed their higher-ups
streams of reports and documentation justifying their activity. Suddenly, however, the directives, detailed instructions, and purchase orders ceased, and the
enterprise managers and their workers found themselves on their own.

Managers were immediately faced with both the opportunities and threats a
free market holds. Without guaranteed demand for their products, many failed

immediately. Unemployment rose dramatically. Within a few months three million workers were unemployed, representing about fifteen percent of the workforce, and the situation was not about to improve. The unemployment rate was calculated at 13.5, 16.7, and 14.7 percent in 1992, 1994, and 1995, respectively.

However, many organizations prospered. Despite the many business failures, others—especially those with long histories—were determined to survive and prosper in their new environments. One such business was the century-old State Paper-Making Machine Factory (known as FAMPA), located in the southwestern city of Jelenia Góra (see Exhibit 1). FAMPA was the only firm in the former communist bloc capable of producing a full line of paper and paper board manufacturing equipment. Before the transition, FAMPA employed about a thousand people. FAMPA was an important employer in the city of 100,000 and one of the few firms in the area which had exported throughout the communist world.

HISTORY OF THE COMPANY

FAMPA was founded in Jelenia Góra in 1854 as Fullner Werke and was managed and owned exclusively by the Fullner family for about 90 years. From the company's founding until the end of the Second World War the city of Jelenia Góra

Exhibit 1   **Geographical location of Beloit Poland S.A.**

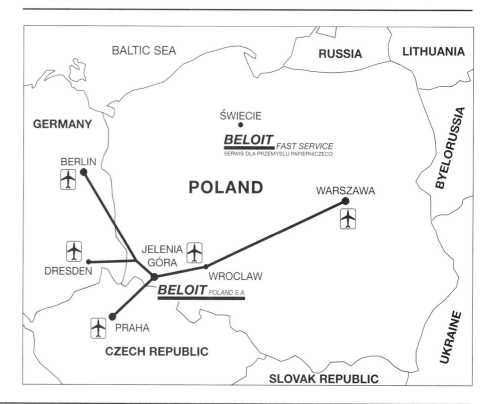

was a part of Germany, just across the southwest border from Poland. After the war, this land was ceded to Poland, and the firm came under the control of a newly Soviet-installed, centralized Polish communist government. The name was changed to the Factory for Paper-Making Machinery, (FAMPA).

Under the direction of the firm's new government-appointed management, the early post-war years were spent rebuilding the plant and training workers using pre-war documentation and pre-war technology. Later, efforts were made to update the company's technology and modernize its procedures. One constant however was the firm's mission, that of making specialized equipment for use in the paper and cellulose industries both in Poland and abroad.

Since Europe's manufacturing base—including the paper industry—was in ruin after the war, there was plenty of work for FAMPA. During the period from 1946 to 1964 FAMPA manufactured and installed equipment for 36 complete paper mills. Additionally, FAMPA completed modernizations and rebuilds of several existing plants which had a combined capacity of 400,000 tons a year. In 1964 FAMPA entered a technology licensing agreement with Beloit Walmsley, Ltd., the British subsidiary of the U.S.-based Beloit Corporation. With access to new technology FAMPA installed 100 new paper plants in 25 countries from 1964 to 1991. From 1946 to 1990 FAMPA had refurbished or installed enough paper mill capacity to produce three million tons of paper annually.

INTO THE UNKNOWN

In December 1989, the Polish government set out principles by which state-owned firms could engage in joint venture projects with foreign investors. In July 1990, the Privatization of State-Owned Enterprises Act outlined the process Poland's state-owned firms would follow in their conversion to privately-owned firms. Both of these steps engendered a certain amount of excitement in the ranks of the younger members of state-owned enterprises' engineering and management teams.

On September 27, 1990, FAMPA was restructured into a state-owned joint-stock company. Although shares were initially owned by the state, they were expected to be distributed to the employees and joint venture partners (if any) in the near future. The new president of the board of directors was Miroslaw Miroslawski, who was very much a representative of the younger, change-oriented element of FAMPA. As the transition proceeded, Miroslawski recognized the need to undertake immediate steps to stabilize the company. One of the major problems FAMPA faced was tremendous overstaffing. Under Communist control, excess employment was acceptable. FAMPA now had to prepare to meet the competition in the international papermaking machinery market, which required a thorough analysis of costs and break-even points.

Miroslawski and the board came under tremendous pressures from the trade unions when the firm began to lay off workers who were not needed or not willing to change. The unions charged that pursuit of the best interests of stockholders—some of whom would be the employees—was not inherently bad, but that long-term employees should not be sacrificed in the process. They questioned whether the pursuit of lower costs, higher sales, and profits would really benefit union memberships.

However, not everyone resisted the change, believing instead that FAMPA must change in order to survive. To them, Miroslawski became something of a latter-day Moses, leading the new company on its perilous journey into the unknown. For his part, Miroslawski simply recognized the extent of the over-staffing problem in every part of the firm. This made the firm a "colossus on clay feet" in terms of its ability to respond to change and compete. Between 1988 and 1994, the workforce shrank from about 1500 to about 500.

Miroslawski had come to understand some of the fundamentals of strategic planning, and recognized that to chart its course effectively, the company needed to define its mission, objectives, and goals. He was also painfully aware of the goal conflict that existed among various FAMPA employee groups, among both the management and non-managerial ranks. While older managers wanted to take a go-slow, status quo approach, the younger managers were eager to pursue rapid change. These conflicting goals were manifest on the board of directors, with substantial divisions between groups of board members.

The president also recognized that his firm was going to be making its transition in a very unstable political and economic environment. The new democratically elected government was very unstable, with annual changes in prime minister. Although the electorate and the politicians knew change was necessary, the pain of the transition to a free market economy was proving to be very severe for many who had relied on the old system for so long. The political instability in turn led to changes in social and economic policy and regulatory instability.

Meanwhile, inflation was rampant in Poland, running at an annual rate of 170 percent in 1990. Coupled with the increase in unemployment, it became clear that the government would have to control its own spending and the expansion of the money supply it was using to pay for it. However, to do so would require balanced budget discipline, necessitating deep cuts in spending and/or higher taxes on an economy which had little ability to pay more. The government would also have to adopt a sound monetary policy which, at least in the short run, would cause significant additional unemployment.

Miroslawski also recognized that his market environment—especially the competitive nature—would be quite different from the past. Both its domestic and foreign sales were controlled by bureaucrats in Poland and in the Soviet Union. Domestic sales consisted of simply receiving orders from central planners. Sales to other Soviet Bloc nations were made through ministries, and did not require a substantial marketing effort. Now the company would have to meet Western competitors head on. He wondered how it would be possible to attract the capital and technological infusion his firm so desperately needed. He was also quite concerned how the firm would mount an effective marketing effort with little or no expertise in this area.

With little money, antiquated technology, no marketing expertise, a host of new competitors to deal with, and the great expectations of his firm's workforce, Miroslawski recognized the absolute necessity for the board to integrate the expectations of FAMPA's stakeholders around some common goals. He knew in the end that the firm would have to emerge committed to providing quality products at competitive prices and high levels of customer support, production without high pollution, opportunities for its current workforce and the economy of Poland, and a reasonable return for its shareholders. He thought the task at first overwhelming, but FAMPA had no choice but to proceed.

■ Beloit Corporation's New Polish Subsidiary

In 1991, 80 percent of FAMPA's common stock was put up for sale in an open bidding process. Most of the world's major manufacturers of paper-making equipment submitted bids. The winning bid was submitted by the Beloit Corporation, parent of FAMPA's long-time partner Beloit Walmsley and one of the three largest firms in the industry. Beloit is 80 percent owned by Harnischfeger Industries (a U.S.-based firm) and 20 percent owned by Mitsubishi Heavy Industries (a Japanese-based firm). In 1995, Beloit had sales of approximately $970 million which accounted for about 45 percent of Harnischfeger Industries' total sales. In addition, Beloit had units in virtually every region of the world. Financial statements for Harnischfeger Industries are provided below, as well as information on the firm's papermaking segment. Exhibit 2 provides a list of Beloit's operating units, Exhibit 3 lists the locations of its facilities around the world, and Exhibit 4 provides a map of these locations.

The twenty percent of FAMPA's stock purchased by the employees was purchased at one-half the per-share price paid by Beloit. Employees were allowed to purchase whatever quantity of shares they wished. Because Beloit's parent Harnischfeger Industries' stock is traded on the New York Stock Exchange and only 20 percent of Beloit Poland's shares are now publicly held, they are not traded on the new Polish National Stock Exchange. Hence, employees wishing to trade shares must do so on an informal basis.

Beloit's winning bid for 80 percent of FAMPA's common stock was $7 million. Beloit also committed to a $15 million investment over the ensuing seven years. The new owners immediately changed the name of the firm to Beloit Poland S.A. (S.A. designating an incorporated entity in Poland) and it became one of a family of Beloit subsidiaries. Beloit planned to refocus its new division's sales efforts from that of being a global competitor to serving primarily the Central and Eastern European markets, leaving other regions to Beloit's

---

Exhibit 2   **Beloit Subsidiaries**

Subsidiary	Location
Beloit Corporation	Delaware
Beloit Canada Ltd./Ltee	Canada
Beloit Industrial Ltda.	Brazil
Beloit Poland S.A.	Poland
BWRC, Inc.	Delaware
Beloit Asia Pacific Pte. Ltd.	Singapore
Beloit Italia S.P.A.	Italy
Beloit Lenox GmbH	Germany
Beloit Walmsley Ltd.	United Kingdom
J&L Fiber Services, Inc.	Wisconsin
Optical Alignment Systems and Inspection Services, Inc.	New Hampshire
Sandusky International, Inc.	Ohio

Exhibit 3	Beloit's Worldwide Facilities	
Plant and Location	**Floor Space (Sq. Ft.)**	**Principal Operations**
Beloit, Wisconsin	928,000	Papermaking machinery and finished product processing equipment
Beloit, Wisconsin	230,000	Castings, pattern shop
Waukesha, Wisconsin	57,000	Castings, pattern shop, and finished product processing
Waukesha, Wisconsin	76,000	Refiner plate machining, finished product processing and warehousing
Rockton, Illinois	469,000	Papermaking machinery, finished product processing equipment and R&D center
South Beloit, Illinois	163,000	Castings
Dalton, Massachusetts	277,000	Stock and pulp preparation equipment and specialized processing systems
Lenox, Massachusetts	127,000	Winders
Pittsfield, Massachusetts	36,000	Research and development facility and pilot plant for process simulation
Aiken, South Carolina Columbus, Mississippi Federal Way, Washington Neenah, Wisconsin Clarks Summit, PA Renfrew, Canada	92,000 133,000 55,000 77,000 88,000 145,000	Rubber and polymeric covers for rolls; rubber blankets; rubber and metal roll repairs
Kalamazoo, Michigan	23,500	Filled rolls for supercalenders and specialty rolls
Portland, Oregon	41,000	Bulk materials handling and drying systems
Rochester, New Hampshire	15,650	Specialty services provide principally to the paper industry
Pensacola, Florida	7,250	Specialty services provide principally to the paper industry
Sandusky, Ohio	254,000	Centrifugal castings
Glenrothes, United Kingdom	56,000	Centrifugal castings
Campinas, Brazil	202,000	Papermaking machinery and finished product processing equipment; stock and pulp preparation equipment; wood-yard and pulp plant equipment
Bolton, United Kingdom Pinerolo, Italy Jelenia Góra, Poland	465,400 517,400 522,000	Papermaking machinery and finished product processing equipment; stock and pulp preparation equipment
Świecie, Poland	37,000	Components and parts for papermaking machinery equipment
Cernay, France	35,200	Roll-covering service

other divisions. Where it could, Beloit Poland would participate with other company units in filling international orders. For Beloit Poland the acquisition meant it could access the latest technology available and its parent's financial resources.

The financial and technological resources of Beloit are considerable. Sales of the parent company, Harnischfeger Industries, exceeded $1.5 billion in 1991. In addition, the company had a history of investing heavily in research and development, injecting about $30 million annually. This has resulted in Beloit

Exhibit 4   **Worldwide Beloit Group Locations**

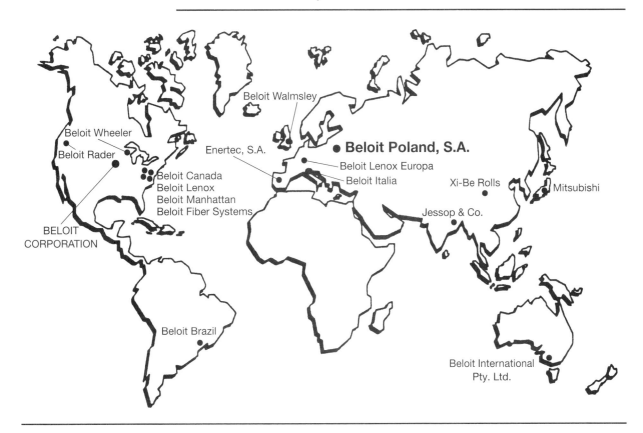

enjoying patented technological advantages in an industry in which they are critical.

The papermaking machinery segment of Harnischfeger had sales of $970 million in 1995, a thirty-six percent increase over 1994. Foreign sales accounted for about 41 percent of total sales. The market for this kind of equipment is cyclical and currently demand is slowly rising. Beloit earned a profit of $87.5 million in 1995. Exhibits 5a, 5b, and 5c provide financial information on Harnischfeger and its various business segments.

Beloit Poland fell under the terms of Poland's new Polish Commercial Code, enacted in June 1991. Under this code, Beloit Poland would be designated as a joint-stock company which, for the most part, possessed the same legal rights and responsibilities as corporations in Western nations. As it was considered a joint-stock company headquartered in Poland, it would be required to work under Poland's labor, taxation, and penal codes.

THINKING GLOBALLY, ACTING LOCALLY

The market for papermaking equipment involves very large capital commitments and highly sophisticated technology; an average-sized paper plant costs $25 million to equip. Beloit is the largest of a three-firm oligopoly, also includ-

C-394   BELOIT POLAND S.A.

Exhibit 5a

Harnischfeger Industries, Inc. Consolidated Statement of Income (000)

	Year Ended October 31, 1995*	1994**
Revenues		
Net sales	2,152,079	1,551,728
Other income	61,865	23,301
Total	2,213,944	1,575,029
Cost of sales	1,671,932	1,195,851
Product development, selling and administrative expenses	330,990	279,016
Operating income	211,022	100,162
Interest expense – net	(40,713)	(47,366)
Income before Joy merger costs, provision for income taxes and minority interest	170,309	52,796
Provision for income taxes	(59,575)	(13,979)
Minority interest	(7,230)	(2,224)
Income from continuing operations before Joy merger costs	103,504	36,593
Joy merger costs	(17,459)	—
Income taxes applicable to Joy merger costs	6,075	—
Income from continuing operations after Joy merger costs	92,120	36,593
Income (loss) from and (net loss) on sale of discontinued operations net of applicable income taxes	(31,235)	(3,962)
Extraordinary loss on retirement of debt, net of applicable income taxes	(3,481)	(4,827)
Cumulative effect of accounting change, net of applicable income taxes and minority interest	—	(81,696)
Net income (loss)	57,404	(53,912)
Earnings (loss) per share		
Income from continuing operations before Joy merger costs	2.23	0.84
Income from continuing operations after Joy merger costs	1.99	0.84
Income (loss) from and (net loss) on sale of discontinued operations	(0.67)	(0.09)
Extraordinary loss on retirement of debt	(0.08)	(0.11)
Cumulative effect of accounting change	—	(1.87)
Net income (loss) per share	1.24	(1.23)
Average shares outstanding	46,218	43,716

* FY 1995 amounts reflect Joy Environmental as a discontinued operation.

** FY 1994 amounts are restated to include the results of Joy Technologies Inc. and to reflect Joy Environmental as a discontinued operation.

Exhibit 5b

Harnischfeger Industries, Inc. Condensed Balance Sheet (000)

	October 31, 1995	October 31, 1994*
Assets		
Current assets:		
Cash and cash equivalents	239,043	196,455
Accounts receivable - net	499,953	421,871
Inventories	416,395	357,847
Net current assets of discontinued operations	—	20,047
Other current assets	57,999	47,181
Total	1,213,390	1,043,401
Property, plant and equipment - net	487,656	490,237
Intangible assets	214,739	213,628
Investment in Measurex Corporation	—	66,347
Noncurrent assets of discontinued operations	—	43,251
Other assets	124,982	125,089
Total Assets	2,040,767	1,981,953
Liabilities and Shareholders' Equity		
Current liabilities:		
Short-term notes payable, including current portion of long-term obligations	22,802	16,540
Trade accounts payable	263,750	237,618
Employee compensation and benefits	100,041	75,679
Advance payments and progress billings	154,401	121,212
Accrued warranties	43,801	33,529
Other current liabilities	138,508	127,498
Total	723,303	612,076
Long-term obligations	459,110	568,933
Liability for postretirement benefits	101,605	118,610
Deferred income taxes	34,805	20,751
Other liabilities	73,057	73,648
Minority interest	89,611	85,570
Shareholders' equity	559,276	502,365
Total Liabilities and Shareholders' Equity	2,040,767	1,981,953

*FY 1994 amounts are restated to include Joy Technologies Inc.

Exhibit 5c

Harnischfeger Industries, Inc. Business Segment Summary for the Year Ended October 31, 1995 (000)

	Net Sales		Operating Profit	
	1995*	1994**	1995*	1994**
Papermaking Machinery and Systems	970,418	712,778	85,719	32,195
Mining Equipment	941,779	729,521	122,116	82,541
Material Handling Equipment	239,882	109,429	22,850	12,094
Total Business Segments	2,152,079	1,551,728	230,685	126,830
Corporate Administration	—-	—	(19,663)	(26,668)
Interest Expense - Net	—-	—	(40,713)	(47,366)
Income before Joy Merger Costs, Provision for Income Taxes and Minority Interest	—-	—	170,309	52,796

	Orders Booked		Backlog at End of Period	
	1995*	1994**	10/95*	10/94**
Papermaking Machinery and Systems	1,016,273	795,888	679,625	633,770
Mining Equipment	972,419	703,354	221,540	190,900
Material Handling Equipment	263,649	137,689	130,879	107,112
Total Business Segments	2,252,341	1,636,931	1,032,044	931,782

*FY 1995 amounts reflect Joy Environmental as a discontinued operation.

**FY 1994 amounts are restated to include the results of Joy Technologies Inc. and to reflect Joy Environmental as a discontinued operation.

ing the German firm Voith Sulzer Papertech and the Finnish company Valmet Paper Machinery, Inc. These two firms each control a percentage of the market slightly smaller than that held by Beloit. In 1993 and 1994, Beloit won judgments for patent infringement against both of its major competitors for copying its paper drying process, a critical component in paper production.

Valmet is the world's second leading supplier of printing paper machines, accounting for more than fifteen percent of the world's paper output. Since 1858, more than 1200 machines have been delivered around the world, including recent deliveries to Korea, South Africa, and the U.S. Printing and specialty paper plants are located in Finland and Canada, pulp drying lines are made in Finland, and paper finishing machines are manufactured in Finland, Italy, France, and the U.S. Demand for paper is strong in North America, Asia, and Great Britain, contributing significantly to Valmet's success.

Exhibit 6   **Annual Sales for FAMPA/Beloit Poland (in millions of dollars)**

Year	Sales
1990	10.7
1991	14.5
1992	8.7
1993	15.1
1994	12.5
1995	34.0

Like Beloit, Valmet places a great emphasis on research and development. The company has seven research centers, each of which specializes in a different area of the papermaking process. Other segments of Valmet include an automotive division which manufactures the Saab Cabriolet and the Opel Calibra as well as other vehicles; an aviation division which maintains the aircraft and engines of the Finnish Air Force; and Valmet Power Transmissions, a manufacturer of gears, couplings, and mechanical drives.

BELOIT'S INITIAL RESPONSE

It was clear to the Polish management team that in order to be competitive, Beloit would not only have to utilize an initial $15 million injection from its parent firm effectively, but would also have to streamline the organization in order to be responsive to the market. The strategic goal agreed to by the Polish team and Beloit was for the plant's capacity to rise from $20 million in annual sales to $35 million within two years and $50 million by the year 2000. This would raise Beloit Poland's capacity to a level sufficient to produce the equipment needed to furnish two typical paper mills annually. Exhibit 6 lists annual sales figures for FAMPA and Beloit Poland from 1990–1995.

Beloit also inserted its own people into two key management roles. While Miroslawski remained the president of the board of directors, Richard Endicott was named general manager. A new outside financial director, Mark McFarland, was also added to the management team. The firm was reorganized into what was essentially a functional structure, illustrated in Exhibit 7. Aside from the Americans holding senior positions, the rest of the management team remained Polish. The 500 employee level achieved after the restructuring was expected to meet the company's needs for the foreseeable future, with no major additions or layoffs anticipated.

Both Beloit's $15 million infusion and its plans for rapid sales growth assuaged many of those who had opposed FAMPA's sale to a foreign firm. The initial fear was that Beloit was buying FAMPA to obtain its market share and would reduce or close FAMPA's operations and supply its former customers from other Beloit units. However, after the investment and growth plans were initiated, such anxieties disappeared.

Beloit Poland S.A. was to specialize in supplying equipment capable of manufacturing paper and paper board sheet up to twenty feet wide and tissue up to twelve feet wide. It would remain responsible for marketing turn key installa-

Exhibit 7   Organizational structure of Beloit Poland S.A.

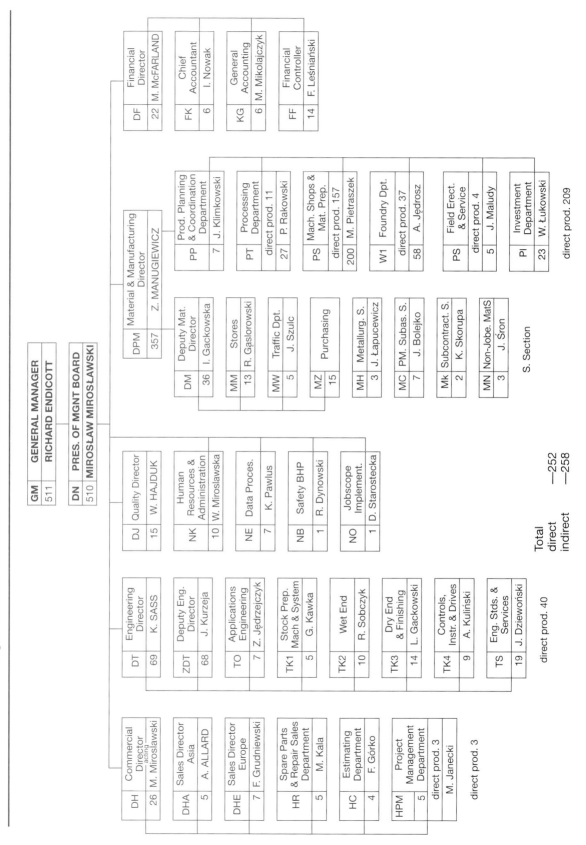

tions, involving design of a new facility's equipment to meet the customer's production requirements, manufacture of the equipment, installation of the entire production process at the customer's plant site, conducting test runs, trouble-shooting problems and making final adjustments, and servicing the equipment after the sale. This process also involves licensing the use of the technology by the customer. Much of the Beloit technology is proprietary and an effort is made to protect it.

Beloit normally provides training for production technicians before and during startup, as well as planning assistance to the customer throughout the process to insure the customer's specifications will result in a plant which actually meets the customer's needs. Beloit also provides consulting services in the areas of construction engineering of the plant, and plant management. Beloit usually supplies its customers with spare parts, specialty supplies, and maintenance following the sale.

BELOIT POLAND'S PRESENT STRATEGY AND POSITION

By 1994 Beloit Poland had not reached its anticipated targets, but was generating sales of about $12.5 million, two-thirds of which were exports. However, after losing money each year since the acquisition, Beloit Poland turned its first profit on sales of $35 million in 1995, an accomplishment widely attributed to its association with Beloit. Total employment has grown to slightly more than the original 500 figure. Employees generally feel circumstances have improved during the last few years, having received pay raises in excess of the rate of inflation and other newfound benefits, such as one-hour lunch breaks.

In many ways, the firm's goals and objectives remain unchanged:

1. to grow the firm and modernize it so it can continue to be a world-class competitor,
2. to continuously improve the quality and technical sophistication of the product,
3. to win new markets for its products and services, and
4. to diversify its activities by entering new, but related, fields.

These were the intentions behind privatization of FAMPA, as pursuing these goals allowed the business to survive and even prosper.

However, as a division of a much larger organization, in addition to the goals of the past, Beloit Poland must continue to focus its efforts toward integrating with the parent organization. For instance, rather than being a global competitor, Beloit Poland is expected to focus on that region of the world not adequately served by Beloit's other divisions. Beloit Poland must also learn to capitalize on the capabilities of its sister units and outsource those products and services it is not in a position to offer, or represent a strategic weakness when it attempts to compete alone. Beloit's various global units normally market its products within the geographic region they are designated to serve. However, Beloit USA maintains centralized marketing and financing units which also pursue global opportunities and coordinate the work of various divisions when especially large orders are involved.

Additionally, Beloit Poland faces a much more dynamic market environment than when under Communist control. During that period, sales were made at predetermined, relatively constant exchange rates and profit was not an issue. Now both the Polish currency as well as the currencies of the neighboring countries in which it sells float in terms of their relative values. Additionally, as Eastern European countries move toward free-market economies, they become subject to the same kinds of economic cycles as occur in the West. Such volatility results in significant changes in the relative attractiveness of Beloit Poland's products. For instance, while Germany was attempting to incorporate East Germany, its economy cooled dramatically, resulting in a 30 percent decline in Beloit Poland's sales.

A major competitive advantage Beloit Poland has is its entrée into a host of formerly state-owned paper manufacturers in what used to be the Soviet Bloc. These firms, many of which are no longer state-owned, are familiar with Beloit's products, and switching costs in this industry are typically high as the components of papermaking systems sold by suppliers are not typically compatible with competitors' equipment. Beloit Poland has recently been working very hard to maintain and expand its market share in the former Soviet Republics, especially Russia and the Baltic States.

Beloit Poland has also been working closely with Beloit USA to enter the Turkish, Korean, Southeast Asian, and Chinese markets. All of these nations are expanding their paper and cellulose products production in step with their relatively rapid economic growth rates. In the Korean, Southeast Asian, and Chinese markets, Beloit faces high-quality competition from Japanese and European firms but has enjoyed good market penetration in these areas. Unfortunately, Beloit has lacked capacity to meet the demand in these emerging markets. It is hoped Beloit Poland will be able to meet some of the unsatisfied demand. Beloit USA manages bid preparation and marketing efforts and usually helps arrange financing in these more distant markets.

Additionally, Beloit's parent, Harnischfeger Industries, hopes Beloit Poland might provide an opening for products of its other major divisions: Harnischfeger Heavy Equipment Group and Joy Manufacturing. These divisions produce materials handling equipment, construction and excavation cranes and draglines, and underground mining and surface mining equipment. Perhaps it is thought that it might be possible for Beloit Poland to grow through diversification into these product areas. As Poland's economy expands, its consumption of energy in the form of coal will likely increase, thereby expanding its need for mining equipment. As the economy expands, Poland's need for construction and materials handling equipment will also likely grow.

Other possibilities Beloit Poland is exploring include the application of its technical expertise and production capacity to new, related, select product-markets in Poland. Areas of interest include equipment used in agricultural and food products processing. FAMPA and Beloit Poland both produced parts used by manufacturers in both of these industries, although such sales have always been a minor part of the firm's total volume. Beloit Poland is presently exploring the possibility of forward integration and expansion into these markets. The firm's management knows little about the total demand for these products other than they are expected to grow as Poland's economy expands and consumers demand more processed foods and more energy is consumed. Even so, it is important to the management of Beloit Poland, especially the Polish management, to grow the firm and create opportunities for people in the local community.

Beloit Poland has also invested considerable energy in its efforts to achieve the same level of product and service quality for which Beloit USA has become known. The firm's quality motto has become "Quality gained now is a guarantee for the future of the firm and its employees." Beloit Poland's workforce is encouraged to see each new order as a challenge to be met and an opportunity to ensure future orders.

The quality assessment and assurance program at Beloit Poland is a complex but coherent mosaic of activities which revolve around three basic tenets. First, individual employees' efforts are concentrated and integrated to achieve high quality. Each employee is to become a true master at the job he/she performs and do it right the first time, while recognizing and working to ensure his/her individual efforts will flow efficiently toward the completion of each contract. Second, Beloit Poland emphasizes implementation of consistent quality assessment programs which are not unduly burdensome and costly. Finally, the company seeks to create an environment in which high levels of product quality can be achieved to ensure customers that no other competitor could have delivered the quality of products and services provided by Beloit Poland. Hence, management must work to develop an environment in which the pursuit of quality is reinforced, not discouraged, and that employees understand the firm's commitment to product quality. As evidence, both ISO 9000 and ISO 9001 certifications were achieved in 1993, covering design, construction, production, assembly and installation, and services.

LOOKING BACK AT THE TRANSITION

The state-owned enterprise FAMPA in Jelenia Góra was one of the first firms in Poland to enter the hazardous path to privatization. At that time, confusion and uncertainty were high as neither the government nor the management of FAMPA really knew what they were doing and how the transition was to unfold. As one of the first East Bloc nations to undertake the transition, there were few if any tested models for converting an economy from one which was centrally planned to one based at least in large part on free-market principles. No one had any experience at dismantling the inefficiencies originally integrated into the system when centralized planning began.

The Euro Disney Case: Early Debacle

Albert J. Milhomme, Southwest Texas State University

Internet site of interest: **www.disney.com**

INTRODUCTION

On an early February morning in 1994, a mix of rain and snow was falling over the Euro Disney Theme Park. . . . Ten thousand miles away, sitting comfortably in his chair, Michael Eisner, the 53-year-old chairman of The Walt Disney Company, was feeling a strange but undeniable desire to lock his office door and hide for the rest of the day. "Wouldn't it be nice if someone else could take care of the mess!" he thought. . . . Euro Disney was at the agony stage.

Events began to flash back and forth in Eisner's mind: his studies at Denison University (Ohio) where he majored in drama and literature in 1950; his first job as an usher at NBC; then his shift to CBS, with a technician's job, before landing at ABC, where he was in charge of Saturday morning programming. Under his control, ABC went from last to first place on Saturday morning, a success which propelled Eisner into primetime where he oversaw the development of an impressive roster of big hits including *Happy Days, Barney Miller, Laverne and Shirley, Rich Man, Poor Man,* and *Roots.* In the late 1970's he left television to join Paramount and his former ABC boss Barry Diller; during eight years together they teamed to produce several box office smashes.

■ Joining The Walt Disney Company

At Roy Disney's request, Eisner received his golden opportunity to join The Walt Disney Company as chairman of the board in 1984. The management contract put a lot of incentives on profit, and favored short-term profitability over the long-term flexibility, safety, and independence of the firm. But this was not his problem. He signed the contract. (Eisner's 1993 earnings of $203,010,590 ranked him as number one among the top-paid chief executives.)

Eisner thought about the history of Disney. When Walt Disney died in December 1966, he left his company at the pinnacle of its success up to that date. Walt's brother Roy took over management of the company and supervised the building of Walt Disney World.

WALT DISNEY WORLD

The first step in the plan had been to purchase a huge tract of land outside Orlando, Florida. Disney had not liked the situation that had developed outside Anaheim after the opening of Disneyland. There the Disney company owned only the area on which the theme park and its parking lot are built. As a result, development around the park proceeded unchecked, and the surrounding area became overgrown with hotels and motels which detracted from the Disney image. Moreover, the profits earned by businesses in the vicinity of the park were vastly greater than the revenues that the company received from park attendance.

Determined to prevent the same outcome in Orlando, Roy arranged through subsidiary companies the purchase of 28,000 acres of undeveloped land, an area of 34 square miles, large enough to hold a multitude of hotels and amusement parks. When Disney made the announcement of the park in 1965, the value of the land increased dramatically overnight. In 1984, however, chains such as Hyatt and Hilton were opening luxury hotels at the borders of Disney World. Potential Disney revenues were, once more, lost to these chains, and the situation which had developed at Disneyland was indeed recurring in Orlando, in spite of the three Disney-owned hotels with over 2,000 rooms.

Eisner remembered going against the conventional wisdom that higher prices would reduce attendance, and he raised the admission prices substantially. The result was a small drop in attendance and a huge increase in revenues. Essentially, Eisner had discovered that the Disney theme parks have a captive audience and a price inelastic demand. When Eisner raised the admission price by 45% in two years, the increase in theme-park price caused a 59% growth in company revenues and accounted for fully 94% of earnings growth in 1986.

Eisner realized that what was needed was more kinds of attractions and more rides inside existing theme parks, as well as additional theme parks or "gates," which would have new collections of attractions and new sources of fees. Disney looked for new "gate" ideas to capture tourists' imaginations. The Disney-MGM park opened to enthusiastic crowds in 1989.

In the effort to wrest tourist dollars from the Orlando competition, Disney did not ignore shopping and night-time entertainment. At night, many Disney guests used to leave the park to eat and play in the entertainment district of Church Street Station in Orlando. To keep patrons on the site, Disney built Pleasure Island, an entertainment complex featuring restaurants and night clubs. Also, the company looked at the food concession business. Eisner realized that the food concessions represented another source of revenue loss; as leases expired, the Disney company began to take over all the food operations at the theme parks.

Meanwhile, new attractions were constantly announced. In developing attractions, Eisner and his team had other money-making ventures in mind. Disney's guests needed somewhere to stay. Here was the opportunity. Disney got into the hotel business on a large scale by building luxury hotels, each of which offered a different kind of experience to Disney guests. Disney found the ideal formula for building hotels without putting a financial debt burden on the company. Management arranged limited partnerships to finance the hotel-building program and the convention centers.

■ Eisner's Midas Touch

The company's earnings jumped by more than 500% during his first four years. Jim Henson, the creator of the Muppets, sold his library of characters to Disney. Kermit and Miss Piggy became part of the Disney family, helping the company to move forward exponentially. Everything was going great; an article in the September 4th, 1989, *Adweek's Marketing Week* had a headline that read "Everything Eisner Touches Turns to Gold." "Eisner's sense of what will and won't work might have been tied to his nature. He is a tremendous evaluator," said journalist Betsy Sharkey.

TOKYO DISNEYLAND

When Eisner joined Disney in 1984, Tokyo Disneyland was completing its first year of operations. After Disney's agreement with the Oriental Land Company in Japan, it took five years of planning and construction. More than 10 million people (9% from other Asian countries) visited the park that year, spending $355 million. This was $155 million more than had been expected, and was partially attributed to the average expenditure per visitor being $35, rather than the estimated $21. Thus, Tokyo Disneyland quickly became profitable. Growth continued, and by 1990 more than 14 million people visited the park, a figure slightly larger than the attendance at Disneyland in California and about half the attendance at Walt Disney World in Florida. The timing of the Tokyo Disneyland opening coincided with a rise in income and leisure time among the Japanese. A Disney executive said that a similar rise in income and leisure had contributed to the successful opening of the first park near Los Angeles.

The Tokyo park was in some ways a paradox. Tokyo Disneyland is nearly a replica of the two parks in the U.S. Signs are in English, and most food is American style. The Oriental Land Company demanded this because it wanted visitors to feel they were getting the real thing, and because they had noted that franchises such as McDonald's had enormous success in Japan as Japanese youth embraced American-style culture. That the park is nearly identical to the ones in the U.S. masks the fact that there have been numerous operational adjustments. Some changes were necessary, such as the addition of a Japanese restaurant. Where Disney uses its own staff to prepare advertising in the U.S., it has relied on outside agencies in Japan to adapt to cultural differences.

Though Disney was not a financial partner in the Tokyo venture, it was reaping the profit from its franchisee (10% royalty from admission and 5% from merchandise and food sales). At last, Disney had in hand the perfect global product, and had to take advantage of it quickly.

EURO DISNEY

Eisner remembered that the dream to expand this perfect global product started in 1984, a few months after his arrival at Disney, with his decision to create a Disney Resort in Europe. Two teams began to work: one to select the ideal location, the other to design the most exciting park ever imagined. In 1985, Disney announced that it had narrowed its locational choice to two countries, Spain and France.

■ France or Spain?

The park was scheduled to open in 1992 at either location. Since the park was estimated to provide about 40,000 permanent jobs (a gross exaggeration; 12,000 jobs have been created up to now) and would draw large numbers of tourists, the two countries courted Disney. Disney openly played one country against the other in an attempt to get more incentives. Spain offered two different locations and 25% of the construction cost, and claimed it could attract 40 million tourists a year! The French claimed that they could attract 12 million customers a year, a number Disney estimated as the break-even point, and agreed to extend the Paris subway to the park's location and to create a station for the high speed train connecting the Benelux countries to the Mediterranean shores, at a cost of about $350 million. In addition, the French government offered 4,800 acres of land at about $7,500 per acre (a bargain price for the area), loaned 22 percent of the funds needed, and accepted a decrease of the value-added tax on the entrance fees from 18.6% to 7%.

If Disney opted for a Spanish location, the park would be like the ones in the U.S., where visitors are outside for almost all amusements. However, Disney had learned from the Tokyo experience that colder weather does not necessarily impede attendance. The colder climate in the Paris area would require more indoor shows, strategically located fireplaces, a glass dome over the teacup ride, and some protected waiting lines.

■ Paris Selection

After three years of discussions with land planners, lawyers, and government officials, the search culminated with the selection of a site at the heart of Europe: Marne-la-Vallée, France. Euro Disney was officially born. The negotiations resulted in Disney's agreement to own at least 16.7%, but no more than 49%, of Euro Disney, which includes satellite investments around the park for hotels, shopping centers, a campground, and other facilities. The total investment by 1992 was estimated at between 2.4 to 3.0 billion U.S. dollars. Disney, through EDL Holding Company, a wholly owned indirect Disney subsidiary, opted for a 49% stake in Euro Disney S.C.A. (Société en Commande par Action), a master limited partnership. Euro Disney S.A., another wholly owned indirect Disney subsidiary, was created to manage Euro Disney S.C.A. Remaining shares of Euro Disney S.C.A. were sold through an international syndicate of banks and securities dealers, with 50% going to investors in France, 25% in Britain, and the remainder elsewhere in Europe.

■ Shareholders' Equity and Liabilities

The share capital was FF1,700,000,000, the equivalent of about $300,000,000 at FF5.67/$1 rate of exchange. Shares were acquired by Disney at their face values, namely FF10, but sold without difficulty to other investors at FF72, creating a share premium (goodwill) of more than FF4,878,000,000, a large contribution to the shareholders' equity.

Euro Disney S.C.A. developed and financed the Euro Disneyland theme park as phase 1A of the project, and six hotels as phase 1B of the project. The theme park was then sold to Euro Disneyland S.N.C. (17% Disney, 83% French companies) and the hotels to six financing companies.

Euro Disney S.C.A., with Euro Disney S.N.C., was one of the "Owner Companies" provided for in the "Agreement on the Creation and the Operation of Euro Disneyland in France" signed in 1987, but indeed Euro Disney S.C.A. was not keeping many fixed assets in its books. Euro Disneyland S.N.C. (a type of general partnership) will own the "Euro Disney Theme Park" and lease it back to Euro Disney S.C.A.; ultimately, it will resell the theme park at a predetermined nominal price, 30 years after. Euro Disneyland S.N.C. is also managed by a wholly owned indirect Disney subsidiary corporation named "Société de Gérance d'Euro Disneyland S.A." The six financing companies which own the hotels will lease the land on which these hotels are built from Euro Disney S.C.A. and will lease the hotels back to six wholly owned Euro Disney S.C.A. subsidiary corporations. These hotels will be managed by E.D.L. Service S.A., a wholly owned Euro Disney S.C.A. subsidiary corporation (see Exhibit 1).

Disney's confidence was due in large part to the fact that 2.5 million Europeans visited the U.S. parks in 1990. It was also due to the fact Disney believed that it was at last, in the position to capture all the dollars in theme park related entertainment activities, a monopolistic situation often searched for, but never achieved by Walt or Roy. Michael Eisner will be the first one to apply the "magic" formula: "If someone can make a living at it, so can we!"

Euro Disney was indeed at the threshold of two formidable coups: first, a long-term real estate coup, the French government having sold to the firm some very expensive land at a bargain price; second, a short-term profit coup, with the potential earnings from the management contract being tremendous (see Exhibit 2). France was in full economic crisis. Job creation was the number one priority, and Disney was taking advantage of this crisis. No one considered the possibility of Disney falling prey to the same crisis . . . no one thought about it. As Euro Disney Chairman Fitzpatrick said, "Disney was determined to change Europe's chemistry."

■ Construction's Excitement

In 1988 the Disney "Imagineers" completed their design and construction began. Four million cubic meters of earth were moved to create a landscape of lakes, rivers, and hills. Most of 1989 was spent underground—laying foundations for the attractions and hotels, putting in place miles of conduit and cable, and preparing an infrastructure which could serve a city of 200,000 people.

By 1990, contractors, manufacturers, and suppliers had been mobilized across Europe. In a dozen different countries, show sets, ride vehicles, and

Exhibit 1 **Euro Disney's Organizational Web**

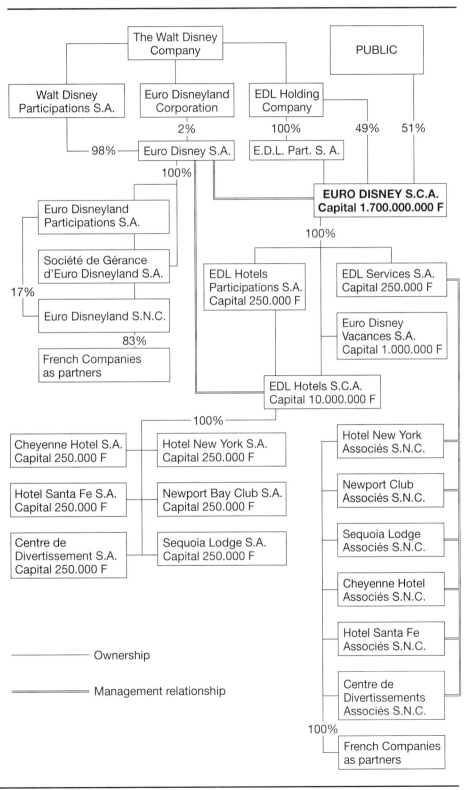

——————— Ownership

═══════════ Management relationship

Exhibit 2   **Management Incentives**

Royalties (30-year agreement), paid directly to Walt Disney Company

10% of gross revenues generated by ticket sales,

  5% of gross revenues from food, beverage, and merchandise sales,

10% of fees due from participants who sponsored some rides,

  5% of gross revenues of theme hotels.

Base Fee, paid directly to EDL Participations S.A., a corporation wholly-owned by Walt Disney Company through EDL Holding Co. S.A.

3% of the Euro Disney S.C.A.'s total revenues in a year, less 0.5 percent of the S.C.A.'s net after-tax profits, until the later of 1) the expiration of five financial years of operations, or 2) the end of the financial year in which the company satisfied certain financial tests under the bank-loan agreement.

Thereafter, the base fee would be 6% per year, less the 0.5% of the S.C.A.'s net after-tax profits.

This base fee is part of the operating expenses.

Incentive Fee paid to EDL Participations

0.5% of Euro Disney S.C.A.'s net after-tax profit.

35% of any pre-tax gain on sales of hotels.

If the Operating Cash Flow (OCF) exceeds FF1.4 billion, Disney will collect:

  30% of the OCF in the FF1.4-2.1 billion range,

  40% of the OCF in the FF2.1-2.8 billion range,

  50% of the OCF above FF2.8 billion range.

Audio-Animatronics figures were being fabricated. Trees were being tagged and transplanted, and the first costume designs were being sent to the manufacturers. On the site, more than 80 cranes reached over bare steel and raw concrete to bring the Resort's structures out of the ground.

In 1991, all efforts converged. More than 10,000 workers from 900 European companies were on the site and the Resort and Theme Park began to take on its definitive character and personality. At the Hotel New-York, one of the park's hotels, the silhouette of Manhattan emerged along the waterfront and the Hotel Cheyenne almost looked like a scene from "High Noon." In the Park, carpenters aged the rough-hewn storefront of Frontierland, turn-of-the-century cobblestones were laid along Main Street, and gold-leaf was applied to the sixteen turrets of the Château de la Belle au Bois Dormant. Over 30,000 props, 4,000 different signs and graphics, and 7,000 specially designed light fixtures were installed. The largest wardrobe in Europe was stocked with a half million costumes. The final phase of preparations had clearly begun.

■ Cultural Adjustments

In spite of the economic benefits that the park was expected to bring, many people in France feared that the park would be just one more step toward the replacement of the French culture with that of the U.S. Critics called Euro Disney "a cultural Chernobyl." Eisner was pelted with eggs in Paris, and a magazine, *Le Nouvel Observateur,* showed a giant Mickey Mouse stepping on the rooftops of Parisian buildings.

THE DREAM BECOMES REALITY

The Euro Disney cast had grown to 2,555 when Euro Disney opened the Casting Center on September 2, 1991. Each day, out of the 500 to 700 candidates interviewed, 60 to 70 were selected for their commitment to quality service, their enthusiasm, and their genuine liking of people, in addition to their professional skills. Eisner recalled the beginning of his marketing campaign with the Rendez-Vous au Château on October 12, 1991: "Over two-thousand journalists and guests joined us as we unveiled the Château de la Belle au Bois Dormant." The result was a great leap in awareness of the Euro Disney Resort throughout Europe.

This event served as the kick-off not only for the marketing and sales efforts, but also for the complete Pan-European promotional campaigns. Simultaneously, the Sales Division began ambitious programs to inspire European families to mark the Euro Disney Resort on their vacation agendas. The sales division established a strong presence in all major markets through special partnerships with leading companies in the travel industry. P & O European Ferries, the SAS Leisure Group, and Belgian Rail joined Disney as Travel Alliance Partners. Agreements with more than twenty tour operators had made the Euro Disney packages available in travel agencies throughout Europe. Disney also launched a tour subsidiary, Euro Disney Vacances, to promote the Resort throughout France, Germany, Italy, and the Netherlands.

■ Inauguration

On April 12, 1992, Euro Disney hosted the biggest event in Disney history, the official opening of the Euro Disney Resort. After five years as a design and construction company, Euro Disney became an operating resort management company literally overnight. The dream became a reality. But the overall cost did not remain within the FF22 billion budget. Instead, it reached FF23.7 billion.

Eisner remembered Disney's letter to the shareholders in the first annual report, saying that ". . . 1992 was a year of satisfaction, challenge, and change. First, satisfaction at having met the objectives. The Euro Disney Resort opened on the day planned. An extraordinary theme park, six splendid hotels, a campground, and Festival Disney came alive with guests from all over Europe. Satisfaction because Euro Disney hosted 7,000,000 guests in its first six months of operation and achieved an average hotel occupancy of 74%. The overwhelming majority of our guests stated their intent to make a return visit and to recommend Euro Disney to their family and friends."

It went on to say, "Satisfaction, as well, because of the tribute paid to the creation of Euro Disney by the French state, when Prime Minister Pierre Beregovoy bestowed the insignia of Chevalier de la Légion d'Honneur to Michael Eisner. Challenge, because the financial results were not as strong as hoped. During the first six months of operation, fear of giant traffic jams and RER strikes for Parisians, truckers blockading the highways of France for foreign tourists, and especially the very difficult economic environment contributed to not meeting the more ambitious objectives."

To build greater awareness of the product, Eisner remembered, the sales-marketing teams moved aggressively to develop new campaigns and to define new agreements with tour and travel operators. The entertainment team had created a multitude of special shows and festivities so that the Euro Disney Resort was an ever-changing celebration for each season and holiday. Disney also had new attractions planned for 1993, which, when combined with seasonal events, were designed to encourage repeat visits.

The Company was also actively pursuing phase 2 of development of the Euro Disney Resort with the French public parties. Given the sluggishness of the real estate market, Euro Disney had proposed reductions in the scale of the Second Detailed Program. It did postpone office development to concentrate on the core of the business—providing the best leisure facilities in Europe—and planned to add a second theme park, the Disney MGM Studios-Europe, and a water park. This expansion would have attracted a substantial number of additional visitors, and greatly increased the guest length of stay on Disney property. Disney was so optimistic that they were simultaneously negotiating a separate agreement which would have ensured the possibility of creating a third theme park at the beginning of the next century.

The financial structure of Euro Disney was extremely elaborate (see Exhibit 1). The leverage effect resulting from a large amount of borrowed money and a small amount of equity was at its center. This strategy would have been workable if the park was generating a return on investment above the mean interest rate on the debt, but it would be a disaster if the return on investment could not reach that level.

WHEN THE DREAM TURNED INTO A NIGHTMARE

Disney had disastrous financial results for the first two years ($36 million in losses in 1992, and more than $900 million in 1993; see Exhibits 3 and 4)—although two-thirds of that was a write-off of pre-opening costs and a change in the accounting procedures. After these disastrous results, the financial restructuring of Euro Disney was under consideration, with the stockholders' equity melting down like snow in sunshine. The gravity of the situation became apparent when attendance in 1993 was down by 15% from the previous year. The share's value was really plunging (see Exhibit 5). Disney was taking a lot of heat for making what appeared to be some hasty marketing decisions.

■ Reactive Management Decisions

A series of price adjustments was made from the very beginning. A premium pricing strategy was initially employed. However, as soon as August 1992, three months after the inauguration, the 1,098-room Newport Bay Club Hotel was downgraded from first class to moderate category and in October 1992, was closed until the summer of 1993. Peak season, when highest prices apply, was shortened by a full month. Two other 1,000-room hotels were then demoted from first class to moderate. The park admission fee cost U.S. $40 for an adult and $26 for a child under 11, a price about 30% higher than the corresponding Disney World price. When the first financial results became known (October 1992), Disney decided to increase the entrance fee from FF225 to FF250. The U.S. Disney park's formula in terms of price elasticity of demand did not apply and the demand fell sharply (a 15% decrease in attendance for a 10% increase in price). Attendance figures were kept secret, but this approach

Exhibit 3   **Euro Disney S.C.A. Group Financial Statements 1990,1991,1992, and 1993**

Condensed Consolidated Statement of Income (Millions of French Francs)

	9/30/93	9/30/92	9/30/91	9/30/90
Revenues	5725	8463	6201	3241
Theme park and Resorts	4874	3819	0	0
Construction sales	851	4644	6201	3241
Costs and Expenses	7542	9145	6215	3385
Cost of Construction Sold	846	4644	5826	3235
Other Operating Expenses	3382	2427	0	0
Operating Income before Fixed and Administrative Expenses	1497	1392	375	6
Depreciation allowance	227	316	48	21
Lease rental expense	1712	716	0	0
Royalties	262	197	0	0
General and Administrative	1113	845	341	129
Operating Income	(1817)	(682)	(14)	(144)
Financial Income	719	541	521	457
Financial Expense	(615)	(307)	(115)	(75)
Income before Exceptional Income and Income Taxes	(1713)	(448)	392	237
Exceptional Income	(3624)	109	4	144
Income before Taxes	(5337)	(339)	396	381
Income after Taxes	(5337)	(188)	249	381

Condensed Consolidated Statements of Cash Flows (Millions of French Francs)

	9/30/93	9/30/92	9/30/91	9/30/90
Cash Flows from Operations	(716)	1228	1984	(754)
Cash Flows from Investment	974	(4484)	(2213)	(1236)
Cash Flows from Financing	608	(474)	2660	4451
Change in cash	1082	(3730)	2431	2461

Condensed Consolidated Balance Sheet (Millions of French Francs)

Assets	9/30/93	9/30/92	9/30/91	9/30/90
Intangible Assets	173	1491	79	34
Tangible Assets	5111	4788	2722	1297
Long-term receivables	5223	3988	1564	7
Total Fixed Assets	10507	10267	4365	1338
Construction in-progress				587
Deferred Charges	510	2001	1716	1075
Inventories	221	387	42	485
A/R Financing Companies		585	1915	1394
A/R Trade	313	456	11	953
A/R Other	966	1248	1903	

Exhibit 3 (continued)	**Euro Disney S.C.A. Group Financial Statements 1990,1991,1992, and 1993**			
Assets	*9/30/93*	*9/30/92*	*9/30/91*	*9/30/90*
Short-term Investments	861	1726	5947	3569
Cash	343	560	69	16
Total Current Assets	2704	4962	9887	5932
Total Assets	13721	17230	15968	8933
Liabilities	*9/30/93*	*9/30/92*	*9/30/91*	*9/30/90*
Capital	1700	1700	1700	1700
Share Premium	4880	4880	4878	4884
Retained earnings	(5063)	447	636	389
Shareholders' equity	1517	7027	7214	6973
Deferred Income Tax			151	5
Deferred Revenues	160	316	265	152
Long-Term Debt	8278	6222	4226	
A/P to Related Companies	1525	796	421	361
A/P Accounts Payable	1640	2869	3691	1442
Current Liabilities	3766	3665	4112	1803
Total Equity Liabilities	13721	17230	15968	8933

reinforced the belief that even in terms of attendance, the objectives were not being reached. Thousands of discounted tickets were issued for many organizations. Free passes were even offered to many officials.

Eisner recalled the letter to the shareholders prefacing the 1992 Annual Report. In it, Robert Fitzpatrick, the Euro Disney chairman, said "that looking at the future, Euro Disney had two primary objectives: to achieve profitability as quickly as possible, and to better integrate Euro Disney into its European environment while reinforcing our greatest asset—our Disney heritage."

■ Who Is Guilty?

As Michael Eisner stated in an interview with Larry King (11/11/93), "Everybody is giving us 42 reasons why we've made a mistake, because we have financial problems. The fact of the matter is, I am totally confident we made the right decision." Then he went on to say: "I am an inveterate salesman—can't help myself. I am sure we made the right decision geographically. Paris is a great city for tourism. Of course, it has not been a great city for tourists with families and kids, because it's been more an adult place. But we will overcome this obstacle."

Then in another interview Eisner said "I don't believe that the Company can reproach its management for the terrible recession (see Exhibits 6, 7, and 8) that is hurting Europe, and which is, to a greater extent, at the origin of today's situation. We are responsible for neither the real estate crisis nor the high French interest rate, which are dreadfully penalizing us. Not a single manager, whomever he be, could manage so many uncontrollable forces."

Exhibit 4	Forecast and Reality				
	3/31/93 forecast	3/31/93 reality	3/31/94 forecast	3/31/94 reality	3/31/95 forecast
Revenues					
Magic Kingdom	4,246	3,800	4,657	3,100	5,384
Second Theme Park	0	0	0	0	0
Resort & Property Dev.	1,236	1,813	2,144	1,462	3,520
Total Revenues	5,482	5,613	6,801	4,562	8,904
Expenses					
Operating Expenses					
Magic Kingdom	2,643	3,745	2,836	3,371	3,161
Second Theme Park	0	0	0	0	0
Resort & Property Dev.	796		1,501		2,431
General & Adm. Expenses		1,427		961	
Start-up Cost First Park	0	340	0	340	0
Total Operating Expenses	3,439	5,512	4,337	4,672	5,592
Total Operating Income	**2,043**	**101**	**2,464**	**(110)**	**3,312**
Other Expenses					
Royalties	302	290	33	239	387
Pre-Opening Cost Amortization	341	125	341	300	341
Depreciation	255	258	263	238	290
Interest Expenses	567	650	575	937	757
Interest Income	(786)	(986)	(788)	(564)	(768)
Lease Expenses	958	1,603	950	1,545	958
Management Incentive Fees	55	0	171	0	477
Total Other Expenses	1,692	1,940	1,545	2,695	2,442
Exceptional Income	0	179	0	(2,740)	0
Profit Before Taxation	351	(1,660)	919	(5,545)	870
Taxation	147	0	389	0	366
Net Profit	**204**	**(1,660)**	**530**	**(5,545)**	**504**

■ Euro Disney Rescue Package Wins Approval

On March 15, 1995, Walt Disney Co. agreed to spend about $750 million to bail out its 49%-owned and fully-operated Euro Disney S.C.A. affiliate, apparently ending the threat that the gates of the troubled Magic Kingdom in France would close forever. A preliminary deal struck with representatives of Euro Disney's lead banks will cut the park's debt in half and is aimed at making Euro Disney profitable in its fiscal year ending Sept. 30, 1995, far earlier than many analysts had expected. The banks would kick in about $500 million and make other concessions.

Exhibit 5   **Euro Disney: Evolution of Share Value**

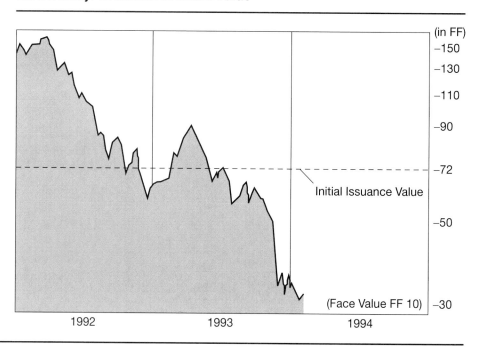

The plan calls for a rights offering of six billion francs, or about $1.02 billion. Such an offering consists of rights to purchase shares, usually at below-market prices, to existing shareholders, in the same proportion as their present ownership. Disney will spend three billion francs, or about $508 million, to buy 49% of the offering. The company also agreed to buy certain park assets for 1.4 billion francs, or about $240 million, and lease them back on terms favorable to Euro Disney.

The plan would halve Euro Disney's debt to about 10 billion francs, or $1.69 billion, from the current 20 billion francs. The banks agreed to forgive 18 months of interest payments and will defer all principal payments for three years. Analysts estimated that the elimination of the interest payments will save Euro Disney about 1.9 billion francs.

The banks will also underwrite the remaining 51% of the rights offering that Disney is not buying. The offering is structured to maintain Disney's existing ownership interest in Euro Disney. "This will ensure that the resort, which has been the best-received park ever in Europe, will operate on a sound financial basis as well," said Eisner, who called the restructuring "fair and economically sensible." The agreement, endorsed by Euro Disney's lead banks, now must be accepted by all 63 creditor banks and the public shareholders.

As part of the package, Disney said it would eliminate for five years the lucrative management fees and royalties (Exhibit 2) it receives on ticket sales and merchandise. The royalties will be reintroduced at lower levels gradually over an unspecified period of time. Disney will still receive an "incentive fee" based on any profit made by the Euro Disney resort, which cost $3.68 billion to build. Disney and the banks said that prior to the rights offering, there will be a reduction in the capital of Euro Disney by reducing the par value of the

Exhibit 6

Adjusted Gross Domestic Product, Using Purchasing Power Parity by Country, from 1985 to 1991 (dollar per capita)

	1985	1989	1990	1991
Belgium	11,805	15,194	16,301	17,454
France	12,875	16,310	17,301	18,227
Germany	13,525	17,020	18,307	19,500
Italy	11,585	15,046	16,012	16,896
Luxembourg	13,703	18,657	19,923	21,372
Netherlands	11,949	14,821	15,951	16,530
Spain	7,953	10,880	11,738	12,719
Switzerland	15,884	19,111	21,020	21,747
United Kingdom	11,473	15,177	15,866	15,720
United States	16,786	20,920	21,866	22,204

Sources: *Statistical Abstract of the United States 1994. The National Data Book,* p. 864, table no.1370. U.S. Department of Commerce. Economics and Statistics Administration. Bureau of Census.

Exhibit 7

Discount and Currency Rates

Central Bank Discount Rates

	U.S.	France	Germany	Italy	Netherlands	U.K.
1985	7.50	9.50	4.00	15.00	5.00	10.78
1990	6.60	9.50	6.00	12.50	7.25	14.68
1991	3.50	9.50	8.00	12.00	8.50	11.75
1992	3.00	9.50	8.25	12.00	7.75	9.55
1993	3.00	9.50	5.75	8.00	5.00	5.60
1994	3.00	5.00	4.50	7.25	4.50	12.00

Foreign Exchange Rate: Average National Currency Units/One dollar

	France	Belgium	Italy	Netherlands	Spain	Switz.	Germany	U.K.
1988	5.95	36.78	1.302	1.97	116.52	1.46	1.75	.561
1989	6.38	39.40	1.372	2.12	118.44	1.63	1.88	.610
1990	5.44	33.42	1.198	1.82	101.96	1.43	1.61	.560
1991	5.64	34.19	1.241	1.87	104.01	1.43	1.66	.565
1992	5.29	32.14	1.232	1.75	102.38	1.40	1.56	.566
1993	5.66	34.58	1.573	1.85	127.48	1.47	1.65	.665
1994	5.54	33.42	1.611	1.81	133.88	1.36	1.62	.652

Sources: *Statistical Abstract of the United States 1994. The National Data Book,* p. 881, table 1402, and p. 882, table 1404. U.S. Department of Commerce. Economics and Statistics Administration. Bureau of Census.

Exhibit 8   **Selected International Economic Indicators 1980 to 1993**

Gross National Product Growth Rate

	U.S	France	Germany	Italy	Netherlands	U.K.
1980	− 0.5	1.6		4.1	0.9	− 2.2
1985	3.2	1.9		2.6	2.6	3.8
1990	1.2	2.5		2.1	4.1	0.4
1991	− 0.7	0.8	1.0	1.3	2.1	− 2.2
1992	2.6	1.2	2.1	0.7	1.4	− 0.6
1993	3.0	− 1.0	− 1.2	− 0.7	0.2	1.9

Ratio of Savings to Disposable Personal Income

	U.S	France	Germany	Italy	Netherlands	U.K.
1980	7.9	17.6		21.9	11.0	13.1
1985	6.4	14.0		18.9	13.1	10.7
1990	4.2	12.5		18.4	16.5	8.6
1991	4.8	13.1	13.8	18.6	12.5	10.1
1992	5.3	13.9	13.9	18.7	13.2	12.3
1993	4.0	14.2	13.2	–	–	11.5

Ratio of Gross Fixed Capital Formation to G.D.P.

	U.S	France	Germany	Italy	Netherlands	U.K.
1980	20.4	23.0		24.3	21.6	17.9
1985	19.4	19.3		20.7	19.7	17.0
1990	16.8	21.4		20.3	20.9	19.4
1991	15.4	21.1	23.2	19.7	20.5	16.8
1992	15.5	20.0	23.4	19.2	20.4	15.5
1993	16.0	18.9	22.7	17.1	19.7	14.9

Source: *The National Data Book*, No. 1369, p. 863.

company's shares. While the price of the offering will be set later, the parties said it is currently estimated to be close to the present par value of Euro Disney stock, or about 10 francs a share.

The new agreement also calls for the banks and Disney to subscribe to bonds with 10-year warrants to purchase Euro Disney shares at 40 francs a share. That could raise up to 2.8 billion francs for the resort company. Disney also agreed to arrange for a 1.1 billion franc standby line of credit at market rates to provide for Euro Disney's liquidity. "If the markets are strong enough to absorb three billion francs of new equity, then it is a good long-term fix," said Jack Hersch of MJ Whitman in New York. "But officials close to the talks say the real work is now in persuading creditor banks to agree to the deal. And approval by Euro Disney shareholders is not a foregone conclusion."

Exhibit 9

Long-term Borrowings and Interest Rates

Currency FF in millions	Interest rate	1993	1992
10-year Convertible Bonds [a]	6.75%	4,327	4,343
Caisse des Dépôts Loan [b]	7.85%	1,442	1,442
Phase 1A Credit Facility [c]	9.75%	2,071	
Credit Foncier Loan [d]	10.04%	35	35
Others		104	
		7,979	5,820

At September 30, 1993, and 1992, total borrowings include accrued interest of FF 358 million and FF 368 million, respectively.

[a] 10-year convertible bonds: 6.75% fixed rate redeemed on October 1, 2001, at 110% of their principal amount, unless converted, redeemed, or purchased by the Company.

[b] Caisse des Dépôts loan: 40% is senior debt, 60% is subordinated debt, maturing 20 years from the drawing date. This loan bears interest at a weighted average rate of 7.85%. Principal repayments begin six years from the drawing date.

[c] Phase 1A Credit: Euro Disney S.C.A. borrowed in December 1992 FF 1,025 million at PIBOR plus 1%, and FF 270 million at fixed rate 8.35%. Principal repayments begin in 1998 through 2006. In March 1993, new borrowing at PIBOR plus 1.1%. Principal repayments begin in 1997 through 2006.

[d] Credit Foncier loan: originated in June 1992, bears interest at a rate of 3-month PIBOR minus 0.3%. Principal repayments begin in 1994 through 2017.

Nevertheless, things went smoothly. The Euro Disney resort was renamed Disneyland Paris. The rescue plan was approved by the shareholders on June 8, 1994. Offset of accumulated losses of approximately FF 4,863 million at September 30, 1993, against existing share premium provided by the small shareholders was approved by the shareholders.

Reduction of the stated capital of the company by 50% was also approved. Each initial shareholder holding two shares was allowed to subscribed to seven new shares at 10 francs a share. Euro Disney raised 5.79 billion francs through the rights offering, but this did not decrease the company's indebtedness by half, but only by 23%, from 21 to 16 billion francs. The equity increase brought a major new shareholder, Saudi Prince Alwaleed Bin Talal Abdulaziz Al Saud, who now holds 24.6% of the theme park. The ownership of Disney in Euro Disney was decreased from 49% to 39%, a sign that Disney did not believe it had a winner on its hands.

The lenders waived aggregate interest charges having a net present value of FF 1.6 billion (discounted at a rate of 7.5% to October 1, 1993) (see Exhibit 9). The waivers will result in estimated reductions of aggregate financial charges to the Group and the Financing SNCs of FF 400 million, FF 600 million, FF 450 million, and FF 220 million in fiscal years 1994, 1995, 1996 and 1997, respectively. The lenders also deferred payments of principal on all outstanding loan indebtedness of the Group and the Financing SNCs for three years from the time that each payment was originally due. This deferral will result in reductions of approximately FF 13 million, FF 50 million, FF 90 million, and FF 220 million in payments under the Group's financial leases in 1995, 1996, 1997, and 1998, respectively.

Royalties, which in fiscal year 1993 totaled FF 262 million, were being waived from October 1, 1993, to September 30, 1998, then reduced to 50% of their pre-restructuring levels thereafter until October 1, 2003. Base management fees were being waived from October 1, 1993, to September 1998. Management fees for fiscal years 1992 and 1993 for FF 113 million and FF 145 million, respectively, which were previously deferred, were waived permanently as well as accrued fees (FF 45 million) for fiscal year 1994.

The Walt Disney Company cancelled receivables due from Euro Disney of approximately FF 1.2 billion for services rendered in connection with the second phase of development of the Resort which was put on hold. At the end of the 1994 fiscal year, in spite of all the concessions, the net losses amounted to 1.8 billion francs, or $346.7 million. Operating revenue fell 16%. The number of visitors dropped from 9.8 million in 1993 to 8.8 million in 1994.

It was announced that the target break-even year is now 1996. Commenting on the financial results, new Euro Disney Chairman Philip Bourguignon said "1994 has been a difficult year. . . . But we still aim to break even by 1996."

At the end of fiscal 1995, for the first time in its history, Euro Disney proudly announced a small profit, resulting mostly from some exceptional gains. But this is hardly a definitive victory when one remembers that the company is temporarily not charged for any interest on its huge debt. Disneyland Paris has a long way to go, and it cannot continue its downward spiral in attendance.

REFERENCES

Bancroft, Thomas, and Tatiana Pouschine. "Why not buy the real thing?" *Forbes* 1 October 1990: 208.

Benson, Tracy E. "America's best CEOs." *Industry Week* 2 December 1991: 28-29.

"Bonjour, Mickey." *Fortune* 20 January 1986: 8.

Cohen, Roger. "Euro Disney in danger of shutdown." *The New York Times* 23 December 1993, late ed.: D3.

Cohen, Roger. "Mickey lacks a soupçon of charm." *The New York Times* 11 July 1993, national ed.: E2.

Cohen, Roger. "When you wish upon a deficit." *The New York Times* 18 Jul. 1993, national ed.: H1.

Coleman, Brian, & Thomas R. King. "Euro Disney Rescue Package Wins Approval." *The Wall Street Journal* 15 March 1994, A3, A5.

Daniels, Bill. "Eisner outlines Disney decade of growth and soothes concerned stockholders." *Variety* 28 February 1990: 9.

Drozdiak, William. "Cheers, Jeers Greet Disney Debut in Europe." *The Washington Post* 13 April 1992: A1.

Drozdiak, William. "Euro Disney posts loss of $900 Million." *The Washington Post* 11 November 1993: B11.

Drozdiak, William. "L'Etat C'est Mouse." *The Washington Post* 2 March 1992: A12.

"Euro Disney adding alcohol." *The New York Times* 12 June 1993, late ed.: 42.

"Euro Disney affirms it will remain open for winter." *The New York Times* 25 August 1993, late ed.: D3.

"Euro Disney posts deficit." *The New York Times* 14 August 1993, late ed.: 35.

"Euro Disney Annual Report Fiscal Year 1991."

"Euro Disney Annual Report Fiscal Year 1992."

"Euro Disney Annual Report Fiscal Year 1993."

"Euro Disney S.C.A. Offering of 85,880,000 Shares of Common Stock." Prospectus. October 1989.

"Euro Disney S.C.A. Offering of 595,028,994 Shares of Common Stock." Prospectus. 17 June 1994.

"France, Disney ink $2-bil contract to construct Euroland." *Variety* 25 March 1987: 156.

Freedland, Jonathan, & Peter Clarke. "Mighty Mouse in Magic Kingdom." *The Guardian* 31 January 1994: 10-11.

Galbraith, Jane. "Farm Near Paris Picked As Site Of Euro Disneyland; Disney Co. Plans To Be Equity Investor." *Variety* 25 December 1985: 8.

Green, Peter. "Euro Disneyland nails construction for 1st phase; gets $1.3 billion in credit." *Variety* 13 July 1988: 61.

Grover, Ronald. "Thrills and chills at Disney." *Business Week* 21 June 1993: 73-74.

Gumbel, Peter. "Euro Disney Posts Wider 1st-Period Loss as Creditors Hold Inconclusive Talks." *The Wall Street Journal* 3 February 1994: A10.

Ilott, Terry. " Disney defers payment to help ED stock price." *Variety* 19 October 1992: 54.

Jaffe, Thomas. "Euro FantasyLand." *Forbes* 2 April 1990: 204.

Kamm, Thomas. "Euro Disney's Loss Narrowed in Fiscal 1994." *The Wall Street Journal* 4 November 1994: A10.

Kindel, Stephen. "Michael Eisner; at Walt Disney, the boast is, 'You ain't seen nothing yet.'" *FW* 3 April 1990: 76.

Lawday, David. "Where all the dwarfs are grumpy: Euro Disneyland may give Paris a run for the money." *U.S. News & World Report* 28 May 1990: 50-52.

Martin, Mitchell. "Mob pelts Disney chiefs." *The Washington Post* 6 October 1989: D2.

"Mickey goes to the bank." *The Economist* 16 Sep. 1989: 78-79.

"Mickey hops the pond." *The Economist* 28 Mar. 1987: 75.

Milhomme, Albert J. "Pricing Strategy at Euro Disney." *Advances in Marketing* Spring 1993: 302-307.

Milhomme, Albert J. "Culture, Economic Anthropology, and Theme Parks." *Journal of International Marketing* Vol. 2 No. 2, 1994: pp 11-21.

Oster, Patrick. "Vive Le Mouse!" *The Washington Post* 24 January 1993: E1-E5.

Riding, John. "Banks clear way for Euro Disney rescue." *Financial Times* 20 May 1994: 19.

Schwartz, Amy E. "Good, Clean . . . Flop?" *The Washington Post* 18 August 1993: A21.

Shapiro, Stacy. "Disney risk management learns French." *Business Insurance* 30 October 1989: 32-33.

Sharkey, Betsy. "Michael Eisner: Disney's big thinker is free of guile." *Adweek's Marketing Week* 4 September 1989: 3-4.

Toy, Patrick. "The mouse isn't roaring." *Business Week* 24 August 1993.

Toy, Patrick. "Is Disney Headed for the Euro-Trash Heap?" *Business Week* 24 January 1994: 52.

Thomas, Dana. "Mickey Mouse's School of Manners." *The Washington Post* 11 August 1992: B1.

Tully, Shawn. "The real estate coup at Euro Disneyland." *Fortune* 28 April 1986: 172.

Vaughan, Vicki. "Euro Disney designers work to avoid culture clash." *Journal of Commerce and Commercial* 2 May 1991: 1B.

Waxman, Sharon. "In Europe, can Mickey be the mouse that soared?" *The Washington Post* 14 August 1993: B1.

Waxman, Sharon. "The key to the Magic Kingdom." *The Washington Post* 13 October 1992: C1.

Will, George F. "In Europe, Mickey Mouse." *The Washington Post* 16 April 1992: A23.

Williams, Michael. "Eisner calls Euro Disney estimates 'Aggressive.'" *Variety* 21 October 1991: 58.

Kentucky Fried Chicken and the Global Fast-food Industry

Jeffrey A. Krug, The University of Memphis

Internet site of interest: **www.kentuckyfriedchicken.com**

D uring the 1960s and 1970s, Kentucky Fried Chicken Corporation (KFC) pursued an aggressive strategy of restaurant expansion, quickly establishing itself as one of the largest fast-food restaurant chains in the U.S. (see Exhibit 1). KFC was also one of the first U.S. fast-food restaurant chains to expand overseas. By 1990, restaurants located outside of the U.S. were generating over 50 percent of KFC's total profits. By the end of 1994, KFC was operating in 68 foreign countries and was one of the three largest fast-food restaurant chains operating outside of the United States.

Japan, Australia, and the United Kingdom accounted for the greatest share of KFC's international expansion during the 1970s and 1980s. However, as KFC entered the 1990s, a number of other international markets offered significant opportunities for growth. China, with a population of over one billion, and Europe, with a population roughly equal to the U.S., offered such opportunities. Latin America also offered a unique opportunity because of the size of its markets, its common language and culture, and its geographical proximity to the United States.

By 1995, KFC was operating successful subsidiaries in Mexico and Puerto Rico. A third subsidiary was established in Venezuela in 1993. The majority of KFC's restaurants in Mexico and Puerto Rico were company-owned. However, KFC had established 29 new franchises in Mexico by the end of 1995, following enactment of Mexico's new franchise law in 1990. KFC anticipated that much of its future growth in Mexico would be through franchises rather than company-owned restaurants. KFC was only one of many U.S. fast-food, retail, and hotel chains to begin franchising in Mexico following the new franchise law. In addition to Mexico, KFC was operating franchises in 20 other countries throughout the Caribbean and Central and South America by 1995.

COMPANY HISTORY

Fast-food franchising was still in its infancy in 1954 when Harland Sanders began his travels across the United States to speak with prospective franchisees about his "Colonel Sanders Recipe Kentucky Fried Chicken." By 1960, "Colonel" Sanders had granted KFC franchises to over 200 take-home retail outlets and restaurants across the United States. He had also succeeded in establishing a number of franchises in Canada. By 1963, the number of KFC franchises had risen to over 300 and revenues had reached $500,000.

By 1964, at the age of 74, the Colonel had tired of running the day-to-day operations of his business and was eager to concentrate on public relations issues. Therefore, he sought out potential buyers, eventually deciding to sell the business to two Louisville businessmen—Jack Massey and John Young Brown Jr.—for $2 Million. Massey was named chairman of the board and Brown, who would later become Governor of Kentucky, was named president. The Colonel stayed on as a public relations man and goodwill ambassador for the company.

During the next five years, Massey and Brown concentrated on growing KFC's franchise system across the United States. In 1966, they took KFC public and the company was listed on the New York Stock Exchange. By the late 1960s, a strong foothold had been established in the United States, and Massey and Brown turned their attention to international markets. In 1969, a joint venture was signed with Mitsuoishi Shoji Kaisha, Ltd., in Japan, and the rights to operate 14 existing KFC franchises in England were acquired. Subsidiaries were also established in Hong Kong, South Africa, Australia, New Zealand, and Mexico. By 1971, KFC had 2,450 franchises and 600 company-owned restaurants worldwide, and was operating in 48 countries.

▪ Heublein, Inc.

In 1971, KFC entered negotiations with Heublein, Inc., to discuss a possible merger. The decision to seek a merger candidate was partially driven by Brown's desire to pursue other interests, including a political career (Brown was elected governor of Kentucky in 1977). On April 10, Heublein announced that an agreement had been reached. Shareholders approved the merger on May 27, and KFC was merged into a subsidiary of Heublein.

Heublein was in the business of producing vodka, mixed cocktails, dry gin, cordials, beer, and other alcoholic beverages. It was also the exclusive distributor of a variety of imported alcoholic beverages. Heublein had little experience in the restaurant business. Conflicts quickly erupted between Colonel Sanders, who continued to act in a public relations capacity, and Heublein management. In particular, Colonel Sanders became increasingly distraught over quality control issues and restaurant cleanliness. By 1977, new restaurant openings had slowed to about twenty per year (in 1993, KFC opened a new restaurant on average every two days). Restaurants were not being remodeled and service quality was declining.

In 1977, Heublein sent in a new management team to redirect KFC's strategy. Richard P. Mayer, who later became chairman and chief executive officer, was part of this team (Mayer remained with KFC until 1989, when he left to become president of General Foods USA). A "back-to-the-basics" strategy was

Exhibit 1   **Leading U.S. Fast-Food Chains**

Chain	Parent	U.S. Sales ($M) 1995*	1994	% CHG	1995 Units*
McDonald's	McDonald's Corporation	15,800	14,951	5.7%	10,175
Burger King	Grand Metropolitan PLC	7,830	7,250	8.1%	6,400
Pizza Hut	PepsiCo, Inc.	5,400	5,000	8.0%	8,725
Taco Bell	PepsiCo, Inc.	4,853	4,200	15.5%	6,565
Wendy's	Wendy's International Inc.	4,152	3,821	8.6%	4,263
KFC	PepsiCo, Inc.	3,720	3,500	6.3%	5,200
Hardee's	Imasco Ltd.	3,520	3,511	0.3%	3,405
Subway	Doctor's Associates Inc.	2,905	2,518	15.4%	10,351
Little Caesars	Little Caesar Enterprises	2,050	2,000	2.5%	4,720
Domino's Pizza	Domino's Pizza Inc.	1,973	1,911	3.3%	4,245
Red Lobster	Darden Restaurants Inc.	1,850	1,798	2.9%	700
Denny's	Flagstar Cos. Inc.	1,810	1,672	8.3%	1,578
Arby's	TriArc Corp.	1,730	1,770	−2.3%	2,678
Dunkin' Donuts	Allied Domecq PLC	1,426	1,332	7.0%	3,074
Shoney's	Shoney's Inc.	1,277	1,317	−3.0%	907
Olive Garden	Darden Restaurants Inc.	1,250	1,146	9.1%	479
Dairy Queen	International Dairy Queen	1,185	1,160	2.2%	4,935
Jack in the Box	Foodmaker Inc.	1,082	1,036	4.4%	1,240
Applebee's	Applebee's International	1,012	881	15.0%	551
Big Boy	Elias Bros. Restaurants	1,010	1,050	−3.8%	858
Long John Silver's	Long John Silver's Rest.	986	931	5.9%	1,564
Cracker Barrel	Cracker Barrel	970	787	23.3%	257
Chili's	Brinker International Inc.	950	885	7.35%	446
Sonic Drive-In	Sonic Corp.	880	756	16.45%	1,500
T.G.I. Friday's	Carlson Hospitality Worldwide	870	774	12.4%	310
Outback Steakhouse	Outback Steakhouse Inc.	822	549	49.8%	279
Ponderosa	Metromedia Co.	741	751	−1.3%	680
IHOP Restaurants	IHOP Corp.	729	631	15.5%	684
Boston Market	Boston Chicken Inc.	725	384	88.9%	825
Popeye's	America's Favorite Chicken	689	610	13.0%	932
Total		74,196	68,872	7.7%	88,526

Source: *Nation's Restaurant News.*
*1995 sales estimated.

immediately implemented. New unit construction was discontinued until existing restaurants could be upgraded and operating problems eliminated. Restaurants were refurbished, an emphasis was placed on cleanliness and service, marginal products were eliminated, and product consistency was reestablished. By 1982, KFC had succeeded in establishing a successful strategic focus and was again aggressively building new units.

■ R.J. Reynolds Industries, Inc.

On October 12, 1982, R.J. Reynolds Industries, Inc. (RJR) announced that it would merge Heublein into a wholly-owned subsidiary. The merger with Heublein represented part of RJR's overall corporate strategy of diversifying into unrelated businesses. RJR's objective was to reduce its dependence on the tobacco industry, which had driven RJR sales since its founding in North Carolina in 1875. Sales of cigarettes and tobacco products, while profitable, were declining because of reduced consumption in the U.S., due mainly to the increased awareness among Americans regarding the negative health consequences of smoking.

RJR's diversification strategy included the acquisition of a variety of companies in the energy, transportation, and food and restaurant industries. RJR had no more experience in the restaurant business than did Heublein when Heublein purchased KFC in 1971. However, RJR decided to take a hands-off approach to managing KFC. Whereas Heublein had installed its own top management at KFC headquarters, RJR left KFC management largely intact, believing that existing KFC managers were better qualified to operate KFC's businesses than were its own managers. By doing so, RJR avoided many of the operating problems that Heublein had experienced during its management of KFC. This strategy paid off for RJR, as KFC continued to expand aggressively and profitably under RJR's ownership.

In 1985, RJR acquired Nabisco Corporation for $4.9 billion. Nabisco sold a variety of well-known cookies, crackers, cereals, confectioneries, snacks, and other grocery products. In October 1986, Kentucky Fried Chicken was sold to PepsiCo, Inc.

PEPSICO, INC

■ Corporate Strategy

PepsiCo, Inc. (PepsiCo) was first incorporated in Delaware in 1919 as Loft, Inc. In 1938, Loft acquired the Pepsi-Cola Co., a manufacturer of soft drinks and soft drink concentrates. Pepsi-Cola's traditional business was the sale of its soft drink concentrates to licensed independent and company-owned bottlers, which manufactured, sold, and distributed Pepsi-Cola soft drinks. Today, Pepsi-Cola's best known trademarks are Pepsi-Cola, Diet Pepsi, Mountain Dew, and Slice. Shortly after its acquisition of Pepsi-Cola, Loft changed its name to Pepsi-Cola Co. On June 30, 1965, Pepsi-Cola Co. acquired Frito-Lay Inc. for three million shares, thereby creating one of the largest consumer companies in the United States. At that time, the present name of PepsiCo, Inc. was adopted. Frito-Lay manufactures and sells a variety of snack foods. Its best-known trademarks are Fritos brand Corn Chips, Lay's and Ruffles brand Potato Chips, Doritos and Tostitos Tortilla Chips, and Chee-tos brand Cheese Flavored Snacks. Eight of the top ten snack chips in the U.S. market during 1995 were Frito-Lay brands. In 1994, 63 percent of PepsiCo's net sales were generated by its soft drink and snack food businesses (see Exhibit 2).

Exhibit 2   **PepsiCo, Inc.—1994 Operating Results ($ millions)**

	Beverages	*Snack Foods*	*Restaurants*	*Total*
Net Sales	$9,687.5	$8,264.4	$10,520.5	$28,472.4
Operating Profit	1,217.0	1,376.9	730.3	3,324.2
% Net Sales	12.6%	16.7%	6.9%	11.7%
Assets	$9,566.0	$5,043.9	$7,202.9	$24,792.0
Capital Spending	677.1	532.1	1,072.0	2,288.4

(1) Assets include corporate assets of $2,979.2 million.
(2) Capital spending includes corporate allocation of $7.2 million.

Source: PepsiCo, Inc. Annual Report, 1994.

Beginning in the late 1960s, PepsiCo began an aggressive acquisition program. Initially, PepsiCo pursued an acquisition strategy similar to that pursued by RJR during the 1980s, buying a number of companies in areas unrelated to its major businesses. For example, North American Van Lines was acquired in June 1968. Wilson Sporting Goods was merged into the company in 1972 and Lee Way Motor Freight was acquired in 1976. However, success in operating these businesses failed to live up to expectations, mainly because the management skills required to operate these businesses lay outside of PepsiCo's area of expertise.

In 1984, then-chairman and chief executive officer Don Kendall decided to restructure PepsiCo's operations. Most importantly, PepsiCo would divest those businesses which did not support PepsiCo's consumer product orientation. PepsiCo sold Lee Way Motor Freight in 1984. In 1985, Wilson Sporting Goods and North American Van Lines were sold. Additionally, PepsiCo's foreign bottling operations were sold to local businesspeople who better understood the cultural and business conditions operating in their respective countries. Lastly, Kendall reorganized PepsiCo along three lines: soft drinks, snack foods, and restaurants (see Exhibit 3). All future investment would be directed at strengthening PepsiCo's performance in these three related areas.

When Wayne Calloway became chairman of the board and chief executive officer of PepsiCo in 1986, he expanded PepsiCo's soft drink segment to include non-soft drink beverages such as tea, sports drinks, juices, and bottled water. These included, among others, ready-to-drink Lipton Tea; All Sport, which has become the nation's second best-selling sports drink; and Aquafina Bottled Water. In addition, several new organizations were created to maximize synergies across PepsiCo's related businesses. These included PepsiCo Foods and Beverages International, designed to coordinate efforts between PepsiCo's beverage and snack food segments, and PepsiCo Worldwide Restaurants, created to maximize synergies across PepsiCo's restaurant companies (see Exhibit 3).

■ Restaurant Business and Acquisition of Kentucky Fried Chicken

PepsiCo first entered the restaurant business in 1977 when it acquired Pizza Hut's 3,200-unit restaurant system. Taco Bell was merged into a division of

Exhibit 3   **PepsiCo, Inc.—Principal Divisions (Executive Offices: Purchase, NY)**

Beverage Segment	Snack Food Segment	Restaurants
Pepsi-Cola North America Somers, New York	Frito-Lay, Inc. Plano, Texas	PepsiCo Worldwide Restaurants Dallas, Texas
PepsiCo Foods and Beverages International Somers, New York		PepsiCo Restaurants International Dallas, Texas
		Kentucky Fried Chicken Corporation Louisville, Kentucky
		Pizza Hut Inc. Dallas, Texas
		Taco Bell Corp. Irvine, California
		PepsiCo Food Systems Dallas, Texas

Source: PepsiCo, Inc. Annual Report, 1994.

Exhibit 4   **PepsiCo, Inc.—Number of Units Worldwide**

Year	KFC	Pizza Hut	Taco Bell	Total
1989	7,948	7,502	3,125	18,575
1990	8,187	8,220	3,349	19,756
1991	8,480	8,837	3,670	20,987
1992	8,729	9,454	4,153	22,336
1993	9,033	10,433	4,921	24,387
1994	9,407	11,546	5,846	26,799
Five-Year Compounded Annual Growth Rate				
3.4%	9.0%	13.3%		7.6%

(1) Taco Bell data include 178 Hot 'n Now and 53 Chevy's restaurants.
(2) Pizza Hut data include 25 East Side Mario's restaurants and 197 D'Angelo Sandwich Shops.

Source: PepsiCo, Inc. Annual Report, 1994.

PepsiCo in 1978. The restaurant business complemented PepsiCo's consumer product orientation. The marketing of fast-food followed much of the same patterns as the marketing of soft drinks and snack foods. Therefore, PepsiCo's management skills could easily be transferred among its three business segments. This was compatible with PepsiCo's practice of frequently moving managers among its business units as a way of developing future top executives. PepsiCo's restaurant chains also provided an additional outlet for the sale of

Pepsi soft drink products. In addition, Pepsi soft drinks and fast-food products could be marketed together in the same television and radio segments, thereby providing higher returns for each advertising dollar.

To complete its diversification into the restaurant segment, PepsiCo acquired Kentucky Fried Chicken Corporation from RJR-Nabisco in 1986 for $841 million. The acquisition of KFC gave PepsiCo the leading market share in three of the four largest and fastest-growing segments within the U.S. quick-service industry. At the end of 1994, Pizza Hut held a 28 percent share of the $18.5 billion U.S. pizza segment, Taco Bell held 75 percent of the $5.7 billion Mexican food segment, and KFC held 49 percent of the $7.7 billion U.S. chicken segment. (See Exhibits 2 and 4 for business segment financial data and restaurant count.)

PepsiCo's success during the late 1980s and early 1990s can be seen by its upward trend in *Fortune* magazine's annual survey of "America's Most Admired Corporations." By 1991, PepsiCo was labeled the fifth most admired corporation overall (of 306 corporations included in the survey). However, PepsiCo's ranking fell to 14th place in 1993, 26th place in 1994, and 72nd place in 1995. PepsiCo's fall in the rankings is partially the result of changes made in *Fortune*'s survey methodology in 1994. In particular, it increased the number of industry groups from 32 to 42 (e.g., by adding computer services and entertainment) and divided some industry groups into their components (e.g., by dividing the transportation group into airlines, trucking, and railroads). Home Depot, Microsoft, and Walt Disney, which were added to the survey in 1994, were all ranked in the top ten most admired corporations in America that year.

However, part of PepsiCo's decline in the *Fortune* rankings is the result of a decline in operating profits among its restaurant chains, which declined $48 million in 1994. Much of the decline was the result of increased administrative and support costs, international development costs, and higher store operating costs. In fact, a nearly two-year decline in earnings led PepsiCo to move the international operations of KFC, Pizza Hut, and Taco Bell to the newly-formed PepsiCo Restaurants International (PRI) group in Dallas, Texas, in 1994.

PepsiCo Ranking

Year	Rank
1995	72
1994	26
1993	14
1992	9
1991	5
1990	6
1989	7
1988	14
1987	24
1986	25

FAST-FOOD INDUSTRY

■ U.S. Quick-Service Market

According to the National Restaurant Association (NRA), 1995 food-service sales will hit $289.7 billion for the approximately 500,000 restaurants and other food outlets making up the U.S. restaurant industry. The NRA estimates that sales in the fast-food segment of the food industry will grow 7.2 percent to approximately $93 billion in the United States in 1995, up from $87 million in 1994. This would mark the second consecutive year that fast-food sales exceeded sales in the full-service segment, which are expected to grow to $87.8 billion in 1995. The growth in fast-food sales reflects the long, gradual change in the restaurant industry from an industry once dominated by independently-operated sit-down restaurants to an industry fast becoming dominated by fast-food restaurant chains. The U.S. restaurant industry as a whole is projected to grow by 4.7 percent in 1995.

Sales data for the top 30 fast-food restaurant chains are shown in Exhibit 1. Most striking is the dominance of McDonald's. Sales for 1995 are estimated at $15.8 billion, which would represent 17.3 percent of industry sales, or 21.3 percent of sales of the top 30 fast-food chains. McDonald's strong per-restaurant sales are more striking given that McDonald's accounts for under 12 percent of the units of the top 30 fast-food chains. U.S. sales for the PepsiCo system, which includes KFC, Pizza Hut, and Taco Bell, are estimated to reach $14.0 billion in 1995, which would represent 15.0 percent of the fast-food industry and 18.8 percent of the top 30 fast-food chains. The PepsiCo system will grow to an estimated 20,490 restaurants in 1995. McDonald's holds the number one spot in the hamburger segment, while PepsiCo holds the leading market share in the chicken (KFC), Mexican (Taco Bell), and pizza (Pizza Hut) segments.

■ Major Business Segments

Six major business segments make up the fast-food market within the food service industry. Exhibit 5 shows sales for the top 64 fast-food chains in the six major segments for the years 1993 through 1995, as compiled by *Nation's Restaurant News*. Sandwich chains make up the largest segment, with estimated sales of $41 billion in 1995. Of the 18 restaurant chains making up the sandwich segment, McDonald's holds a 34 percent market share. Sandwich chains, faced by slowed sales growth, have turned to new menu offerings, lower pricing, improved customer service, co-branding with other fast-food chains, and have established units in non-traditional locations to beef up sales.

Hardee's and McDonald's have successfully introduced fried chicken in many of their restaurants. Burger King has introduced fried clams and shrimp to its dinner menu in some locations and Jack in the Box has introduced chicken and teriyaki with rice in several of its California units, in order to appeal to its Asian-American audience. In order to broaden its customer base, McDonald's has installed 400 restaurants in Wal-Mart stores across the country. In addition, it has cut its building costs for its conventional stand-alone units from $1.6 million to $1.1 million in order to counter reduced profit margins resulting from lower pricing. Co-branding is also a potential source of

Exhibit 5	U.S. Sales of the Top Fast-Food Chains by Business Segment ($ billions)			
Business Segment	**Total Chains**	**1993**	**1994**	**1995***
Sandwich Chains	18	41.0	44.0	47.2
(McDonald's, Burger King, Taco Bell, Wendy's,				
Hardee's, Subway, Arby's, Dairy Queen,				
Jack in the Box, Sonic Drive-In, Carl's Jr.,				
Roy Rogers, Whataburger, Checker's Drive-In,				
Rally's, Blimpie Subs & Salads, White Castle,				
Krystal)				
Pizza Chains	8	10.2	10.5	11.2
(Pizza Hut, Little Caesars, Domino's, Papa John's,				
Sbarro The Italian Eatery, Round Table Pizza,				
Chuck E. Cheese's, Godfather's Pizza)				
Family Restaurants	11	7.6	8.0	8.6
(Denny's, Shoney's, Big Boy, Cracker Barrel,				
IHOP, Perkins, Friendly's, Bob Evan's, Waffle				
House, Coco's, Marie Callender's)				
Dinner Houses	15	7.6	8.7	9.8
(Red Lobster, Olive Garden, Applebee's,				
Chili's, T.G.I. Friday's, Outback Steakhouse,				
Ruby Tuesday, Bennigan's, Chi-Chi's,				
Ground Round, Lone Star, Fuddruckers,				
Hooters, Red Robin Burger & Spirits,				
Stuart Anderson's Black Angus)				
Chicken Chains	6	5.0	5.6	6.4
(KFC, Boston Market, Popeyes, Chick-fil-A,				
Church's, Kenny Rogers Roasters)				
Steak Restaurants	6	3.0	3.0	3.2
(Ponderosa, Golden Corral, Sizzler, Ryan's				
Western Sizzlin', Quincy's)				
Total	64	$74.4	$79.8	$86.4

* 1995 sales figures estimated.

Source: *Nation's Restaurant News.*

expansion for many fast-food chains. PepsiCo plans to add Taco Bell signs and menus to approximately 800 existing KFC restaurants over the next few years. This would increase Taco Bell's 4,500-unit U.S. system by almost 18 percent.

The second largest fast-food segment is pizza, long dominated by Pizza Hut. Pizza Hut expects sales to top $5.4 billion in 1995, which would represent a 53 percent market share among the eight competitors making up the pizza segment. Two years ago, Little Caesars overtook Domino's as the second largest pizza chain, despite the fact that Domino's operated more outlets. Little Caesars is the only pizza chain to remain predominately a take-out chain. Home delivery, which has been successfully introduced by Domino's and Pizza Hut, was a driving force for success among the market leaders during the 1970s and 1980s (Pizza Hut has also recently begun home delivery). However, the success of home delivery has driven competitors to look for new methods of increasing their customer bases. Increased competition within the pizza segment and pressures to appeal to a wider customer base have led pizza chains to diversify into non-pizza menu items, to develop non-traditional units (e.g., airport kiosks), and to offer special promotions. Among the many new product offerings, Domino's has introduced chicken wings, Little Caesars Italian cheese bread, and Pizza Hut stuffed crust pizza.

The highest growth segment in 1995 was the chicken segment. Sales are estimated to increase by 14.3 percent in 1995 over 1994. Dinner houses, which have outgrown the other five segments over the last few years, are expected to increase sales by 12.6 percent in 1995. Both the chicken and dinner house segments are growing at almost twice the rate as the sandwich, pizza, and steak restaurant segments. Red Lobster remains the largest dinner house and is expected to surpass $1.8 billion in sales for its fiscal year ending May 1995. This would make Red Lobster the eleventh largest chain among the top 100. Olive Garden is expected to hit the $1.3 billion sales mark for 1995. Olive Garden is currently a strong second behind Red Lobster within the dinner house segment.

The dinner house segment should continue to outpace most of the other fast-food segments for a variety of reasons. Major chains still have low penetration in this segment, though Darden Restaurants Inc. (Red Lobster and Olive Garden) and PepsiCo, Inc. (Fresh-Mex) are poised to dominate a large portion of this segment. A maturing population is already increasing demand for full-service, sit-down restaurants. Eight of the fifteen dinner houses in this segment posted growth rates in sales of over 12 percent in 1995. Lone Star Steakhouse & Saloon, Outback Steakhouse, Fuddruckers, Applebee's Neighborhood Grill & Bar, T.G.I. Friday's, Red Robin Burger & Spirits Emporium, Ruby Tuesday, and Hooters grew at rates of 65, 50, 32, 23, 19, 15, 15, and 12 percent in 1995, respectively.

KFC continues to dominate the chicken segment, with projected 1995 sales of $3.7 billion. Its nearest competitor, Boston Market (formerly Boston Chicken), is a distant second with projected sales of $725.0 million. Popeyes Famous Fried Chicken and Chick-fil-A follow with projected sales of $689.2 and $507.2 million, respectively. KFC holds a market share of 58 percent in the chicken segment, while Boston Market and Popeyes hold shares of 11.3 and 10.8 percent, respectively. Other competitors within the chicken market include Church's, Kenny Rogers Roasters, Bojangle's, El Pollo Loco, Grandy's, and Pudgie's.

Despite KFC's continued dominance within the chicken segment, it has lost market share over the last two years to both Boston Market and Kenny Rogers Roasters, new restaurant chains which have emphasized roasted chicken over the traditional fried chicken offered by other chicken chains. Boston Market has been particularly successful at creating an image of an upscale deli offering healthy, "home-style" take-out products. Early in 1995, it changed its name from Boston Chicken to Boston Market. It thereafter quickly broadened its menu beyond rotisserie chicken to include ham, turkey, and meat loaf. KFC has quickly followed by introducing its $14.99 Mega-Meal, which is designed to compete with Boston Market as a home-replacement alternative. It is also aggressively pushing home delivery to support its home-replacement strategy. KFC has also introduced its "Colonel's Kitchen" in Dallas and is testing a full menu of home-meal replacement items.

■ Industry Consolidation

Although the restaurant industry has outpaced the overall economy in recent years, there are indications that the U.S. market is slowly becoming saturated. According to the U.S. Bureau of Labor, sales of U.S. eating and drinking establishments increased by 2.7 percent in 1992. Following a period of rapid expansion and intense restaurant building in the U.S. during the 1970s and 1980s, the fast-food industry has apparently begun to consolidate. In January 1990, Grand Metropolitan, a British company, purchased Pillsbury Co. for $5.7 billion. Included in the purchase was Pillsbury's Burger King chain. Grand Met has already begun to strengthen the franchise by upgrading existing restaurants and has eliminated several levels of management in order to cut costs. This should give Burger King a long-needed boost in improving its position against McDonald's, its largest competitor in the U.S. market. In 1988, Grand Met purchased Wienerwald, a West German chicken chain, and the Spaghetti Factory, a Swiss chain. In addition, General Mills spun off its Red Lobster, Olive Garden, and China Coast franchises in early 1995 in order to concentrate on its core businesses.

Perhaps most important to KFC was Hardee's acquisition of 600 Roy Rogers restaurants from Marriott Corporation in early 1990. Hardee's immediately began to convert these restaurants to Hardee's units and quickly introduced "Roy Rogers" fried chicken to its menu. By the end of 1993, Hardee's had introduced fried chicken into most of its 3,313 domestic restaurants. While Hardee's is unlikely to destroy the customer loyalty that KFC has long enjoyed, it has cut into KFC's sales as its widened menu selection appeals to a variety of family eating preferences.

The effect on the industry of these and other recent mergers and acquisitions has been powerful. The top ten restaurant chains now control over 55 percent of all fast-food sales in the U.S. The consolidation of a number of these firms within larger, financially more powerful firms should give these restaurant chains the financial and managerial resources they need to outgrow their smaller competitors.

■ Demographic Trends

Intense marketing by the leading fast-food chains will likely continue to stimulate demand for fast-food in the U.S. through the year 2000. However, a number of demographic and societal changes are likely to affect the future demand for fast food in different directions. One such change is the rise in single-person households, which has steadily increased from 17 percent of all U.S. households in 1970 to approximately 25 percent today. In addition, disposable household income should continue to increase, mainly because more women are working than ever before. According to Standard & Poor's *Industry Surveys*, Americans will spend 55 percent of their food dollars at restaurants in 1995, up from 34 percent in 1970. In addition to the effect of a greater number of dual-income families and less time for home food preparation, growth of fast-food sales has been stimulated by an increase in the overall number of fast-food chains, easier access to fast-food chains in non-traditional locations such as department stores and airports, and the greater availability of home delivery and take-out service.

In addition to these demographic trends, a number of societal changes may also affect future demand for fast food. For example, microwaves have now been introduced into approximately 70 percent of all U.S. homes. This has already resulted in a significant shift in the types of products sold in super-markets and convenience restaurants, which have introduced a variety of products that can be quickly and easily prepared in microwaves. In addition, the aging of America's Baby Boomers may change the frequency with which people patronize more upscale restaurants. Therefore, these various demo-graphic and societal trends are likely to affect the future demand for fast food in different ways.

■ International Quick-Service Market

Because of the aggressive pace of new restaurant construction in the U.S. dur-ing the 1970s and 1980s, future growth resulting from new restaurant construc-tion in the U.S. may be limited. In any case, the cost of finding prime locations is rising, increasing the pressure on restaurant chains to increase per-restaurant sales in order to cover higher initial investment costs. One alternative to contin-ued investment in the U.S. market is expansion into international markets, which offers large customer bases and comparatively little competition. How-ever, few U.S. restaurant chains have yet defined aggressive strategies for pen-etrating international markets.

Three restaurant chains which have established aggressive international strategies are McDonald's, Pizza Hut, and KFC. McDonald's currently operates the most units within the U.S. market. McDonald's also operates the largest number of fast-food chains outside of the United States (4,710), recently over-taking KFC, which long dominated the fast-food industry outside of the U.S. KFC ended 1993 with 3,872 restaurants outside of the U.S., 838 fewer than McDonald's. However, KFC remains the most internationalized of all fast-food chains, operating 43 percent of its total units outside of the U.S. In comparison, McDonald's operates 34 percent of its units outside of the U.S. Pizza Hut pres-ently operates in the most countries (80); however, over 88 percent of its units are still located in the U.S.

Exhibit 6 shows *Hotels'* 1994 list of the world's thirty largest fast-food restau-rant chains. Several important observations may be made from these data. First, seventeen of the thirty largest restaurant chains (ranked by number of units) are headquartered in the U.S. This may be partially explained by the fact that U.S. firms account for over 25 percent of the world's foreign direct invest-ment. As a result, U.S. firms have historically been more likely to invest assets abroad. However, while both KFC and McDonald's operate over 3,800 units abroad, no other restaurant chain, U.S. or foreign, has more than 1,500 units outside of the U.S. In fact, most chains have fewer than 500 foreign units and operate in fewer than twenty-two countries.

There are a number of possible explanations for the relative scarcity of fast-food restaurant chains outside of the U.S. First, the U.S. represents the larg-est consumer market in the world, accounting for over one-fifth of the world's gross domestic product (GDP). Therefore, the U.S. has traditionally been the strategic focus of the largest restaurant chains. In addition, Americans have

Exhibit 6   **The World's 30 Largest Fast-Food Chains (year-end 1993, ranked by number of countries)**

Franchise	Location	Units	Countries
1 Pizza Hut	Dallas, Texas	9,500	80
2 McDonald's	Oakbrook, Illinois	13,993	70
3 KFC	Louisville, Kentucky	9,000	68
4 Burger King	Miami, Florida	7,121	50
5 Baskin Robbins	Glendale, California	3,557	49
6 Wendy's	Dublin, Ohio	4,168	38
7 Domino's Pizza	Ann Arbor, Michigan	5,238	36
8 TCBY	Little Rock, Arkansas	7,474	22
9 Dairy Queen	Minneapolis, Minnesota	5,471	21
10 Dunkin' Donuts	Randolph, Massachusetts	3,691	21
11 Taco Bell	Irvine, California	4,800	20
12 Arby's	Fort Lauderdale, Florida	2,670	18
13 Subway Sandwiches	Milford, Connecticut	8,477	15
14 Sizzler International	Los Angeles, California	681	14
15 Hardee's	Rocky Mount, North Carolina	4,060	12
16 Little Caesar's	Detroit, Michigan	4,600	12
17 Popeye's Chicken	Atlanta, Georgia	813	12
18 Denny's	Spartanburg, South Carolina	1,515	10
19 A&W Restaurants	Livonia, Michigan	707	9
20 T.G.I. Friday's	Minneapolis, Minnesota	273	8
21 Orange Julius	Minneapolis, Minnesota	480	7
22 Church's Fried Chicken	Atlanta, Georgia	1,079	6
23 Long John Silver's	Lexington, Kentucky	1,464	5
24 Carl's Jr.	Anaheim, California	649	4
25 Loterria	Tokyo, Japan	795	4
26 Mos Burger	Tokyo, Japan	1,263	4
27 Skylark	Tokyo, Japan	1,000	4
28 Jack in the Box	San Diego, California	1,172	3
29 Quick Restaurants	Berchem, Belgium	876	3
30 Taco Time	Eugene, Oregon	300	3

Source: *Hotels*, May 1994.

been more quick to accept the fast-food concept. Many other cultures have strong culinary traditions which have not been easy to break down. The Europeans, for example, have long histories of frequenting more mid-scale restaurants, where they may spend several hours in a formal setting enjoying native dishes and beverages. While KFC is again building restaurants in Germany, it previously failed to penetrate the German market because Germans were not accustomed to take-out food or to ordering food over the counter. McDonald's has had greater success penetrating the German market because it has made a number of changes in its menu and operating procedures in order to better appeal to German culture. For example, German beer is served in all of McDonald's German restaurants. KFC has had more success in Asia, where chicken is a traditional dish.

Aside from cultural factors, international business carries risks not present in the U.S. market. Long distances between headquarters and foreign franchises often make it difficult to control the quality of individual franchises. Large distances can also cause servicing and support problems. Transportation and other resource costs may also be higher than in the domestic market. In addition, time, cultural, and language differences can increase communication and operational problems. Therefore, it is reasonable to expect U.S. restaurant chains to expand domestically as long as they can achieve corporate profit and growth objectives. However, as the U.S. market becomes more saturated, and companies gain additional expertise in international business, we should expect more companies to turn to profitable international markets as a means of expanding restaurant bases and increasing sales, profits, and market share.

KENTUCKY FRIED CHICKEN CORPORATION

■ Management

One of PepsiCo's greatest challenges when it acquired Kentucky Fried Chicken in 1986 was how to mold two distinct corporate cultures. When R.J. Reynolds acquired KFC in 1982, it realized that it knew very little about the fast-food business. Therefore, it relied on existing KFC management to manage the company. As a result, there was little need for mixing the cultures of the two companies. However, one of PepsiCo's major concerns when considering the purchase of KFC was whether it had the management skills required to successfully operate KFC using PepsiCo managers. PepsiCo had already acquired considerable experience managing fast-food businesses through its Pizza Hut and Taco Bell operations. Therefore, it was anxious to pursue strategic changes within KFC which would improve performance. However, replacing KFC managers with PepsiCo managers could easily cause conflicts between managers in both companies, who were accustomed to different operating procedures and working conditions.

PepsiCo's corporate culture has long been based heavily on a "fast-track" New York approach to management. It hires the country's top business and engineering graduates and promotes them based on performance. As a result, top performers expect to move up through the ranks quickly and to be paid well for their efforts. However, this competitive environment often results in intense rivalries among young managers. If one fails to perform, there is always another top performer waiting in the wings. As a result, employee loyalty is sometimes lost and turnover tends to be higher than in other companies.

The corporate culture at Kentucky Fried Chicken in 1986 contrasted sharply with that at PepsiCo. KFC's culture was built largely on Colonel Sanders' laid-back approach to management. As well, employees enjoyed relatively good employment stability and security. Over the years, a strong loyalty had been created among KFC employees and franchisees, mainly because of the efforts of

Colonel Sanders to provide for his employees' benefits, pension, and other non-income needs. In addition, the Southern environment of Louisville resulted in a friendly, relaxed atmosphere at KFC's corporate offices. This corporate culture was left essentially unchanged during the Heublein and RJR years.

When PepsiCo acquired KFC, it began to restructure the KFC organization, replacing most of KFC's top managers with its own. By the summer of 1990, all of KFC's top positions were occupied by PepsiCo executives. In July 1989, KFC's president and chief executive officer, Richard P. Mayer, left KFC to become president of General Foods USA. Mayer had been at KFC since 1977 when KFC was still owned by Heublein. PepsiCo replaced Mayer with John Cranor III, the former president of Pepsi-Cola East, a Pepsi-Cola unit. In 1990, PepsiCo named Kyle Craig, a former Pillsbury executive, as president of KFC's USA operations.

Most of PepsiCo's initial management changes in 1987 focused on KFC's corporate offices and USA operations. In 1988, attention was turned to KFC's international division. During 1988, PepsiCo replaced KFC International's top managers with its own. First, it lured Don Pierce away from Burger King and made Pierce president of KFC International. However, Pierce left KFC in early 1990 to become president of Pentagram Corporation, a restaurant operation in Hawaii. Pierce commented that he wished to change jobs partly to decrease the amount of time he spent traveling. PepsiCo replaced Pierce with Allan Huston, who was formerly senior vice president of operations at Pizza Hut. However, by the end of 1995, most of KFC's new top management team had either left the company or moved on to other positions within the PepsiCo organization. John Cranor III resigned in 1994, Kyle Craig resigned in 1994 to join Boston Marketing, Allen Huston (president of KFC International) became president and chief executive of Pizza Hut, and Robert Briggs (vice president of international finance for KFC International) left to become the president of Arby's International.

An example of the type of conflict faced by PepsiCo in attempting to implement changes within KFC occurred in August 1989. A month after becoming president and chief executive officer, John Cranor addressed KFC's franchisees in Louisville, in order to explain the details of a new franchise contract. This was the first contract change in thirteen years. The new contract gave PepsiCo management greater power to take over weak franchises, to relocate restaurants, and to make changes in existing restaurants. In addition, existing restaurants would no longer be protected from competition from new KFC restaurants. The contract also gave management the right to raise royalty fees on existing restaurants as contracts came up for renewal. After Cranor finished his address, there was an uproar among the attending franchisees, who jumped to their feet to protest the changes. The franchisees had long been accustomed to relatively little interference from management in their day-to-day operations. This type of interference, of course, was a strong part of PepsiCo's philosophy of demanding change.

As a result of sluggish performance in its restaurant businesses and a desire to consolidate restaurant operations in order to maximize synergies, PepsiCo created two new divisions to oversee its restaurant businesses in late 1994: PepsiCo Worldwide Restaurants and PepsiCo Restaurants International. Both are based in Dallas, Texas. David Novak was named president of KFC (see Exhibit 7). Roger Enrico, vice-chairman of PepsiCo and former CEO of Frito-Lay, was named chairman and CEO of PepsiCo Worldwide Restaurants. Laurence Zwain, formerly president of KFC International, was named presi-

Exhibit 7   **KFC Organizational Chart**

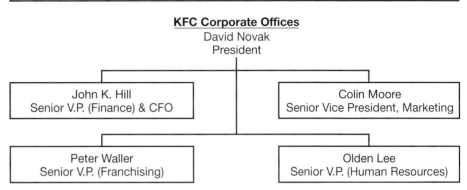

Source: PepsiCo, Inc. Annual Report, 1994.

dent and chief operating officer of PepsiCo Restaurants International. Then in October 1995, James H. O'Neal, who had been president of PepsiCo Foods International–Europe, was named to the new position of chairman and CEO of PepsiCo Restaurants International. Zwain retained his title and would report to O'Neal. O'Neal would report directly to Enrico (see Exhibit 3).

■ Operating Results

KFC's recent operating results are shown in Exhibit 8. In 1994, worldwide sales, which represent sales of both company-owned and franchised restaurants, reached $7.1 billion. Since 1987, worldwide sales have grown at a compounded annual growth rate of 8.2 percent. KFC's domestic market share remained at about one-half of the $7.7 billion U.S. market in 1994. KFC corporate sales, which include company-owned restaurants and royalties from franchised units, reached $2.6 billion, up 14 percent from 1993 sales of $2.3 billion. New restaurants and higher volume contributed $193 and 120 million to corporate sales, respectively.

KFC's worldwide profits increased by 8 percent to $165 million in 1994. KFC's operating profits from international operations represented about 40 percent of worldwide profits in both 1993 and 1994. Profits rose as the result of additional units, higher volume, and increased franchise royalties, which were partially offset by a sales mix shift to lower-margin products, lower pricing, and higher administrative and support costs. Growth in international profits were highest in Australia (now KFC's largest international market) and New Zealand. Profits were lowest in Mexico and Canada.

BUSINESS LEVEL STRATEGIES

■ Marketing

As KFC entered 1996, it grappled with a number of important issues. During the 1980s, consumers began to demand healthier foods and KFC was faced with a limited menu consisting mainly of fried foods. In order to reduce KFC's

Exhibit 8   **KFC Operating Results**

	Worldwide Sales ($B)	KFC Corp.* Sales ($B)	KFC Corp.* Profit ($M)	Percent of Sales
1987	$4.1	$1.1	$90.0	8.3%
1988	5.0	1.2	114.9	9.5%
1989	5.4	1.3	99.4	7.5%
1990	5.8	1.5	126.9	8.3%
1991	6.2	1.8	80.5	4.4%
1992	6.7	2.2	168.8	7.8%
1993	7.1	2.3	152.8	6.6%
1994	7.1	2.6	165.2	6.2%
7-Year Growth Rate	8.2%	13.6%	9.1%	

*KFC corporate figures include company restaurants and franchise royalties and fees.

Source: PepsiCo, Inc. annual reports for 1988-1994.

image as a fried chicken chain, it changed its logo from Kentucky Fried Chicken to KFC in 1991. In addition, it responded to consumer demands for greater variety by introducing a variety of new products. Consumers have also become more mobile, demanding fast food in a variety of non-traditional locations such as grocery stores, restaurants, airports, and outdoor events. This has forced fast-food restaurant chains in general to investigate non-traditional distribution channels and restaurant designs. In addition, families continue to seek greater value in the food they buy, further increasing the pressure on fast-food chains to reduce operating costs and prices.

Many of KFC's problems during the late 1980s arose from its limited menu and its inability to bring new products to market quickly. The popularity of its Original Recipe fried chicken allowed KFC to expand through the 1980s without significant competition from other chicken competitors. As a result, new product introductions were never an important part of KFC's overall strategy. However, the introduction of chicken sandwiches and fried chicken by hamburger chains has changed the make-up of KFC's competitors. Most importantly, McDonald's introduced its McChicken sandwich in the U.S. market in 1989 while KFC was still testing its new sandwich. By beating KFC to the market, McDonald's was able to develop a strong consumer awareness for its sandwich. This significantly increased KFC's cost of developing consumer awareness for its chicken sandwich, which was introduced several months later.

The increased popularity of healthier foods and consumers' increasing demand for better variety has led to a number of changes in KFC's menu offerings. In 1992, KFC introduced Oriental Wings, Popcorn Chicken, and Honey BBQ Chicken as alternatives to its Original Recipe fried chicken. It also introduced a dessert menu which included a variety of pies and cookies. In 1993, KFC rolled out its Rotisserie Chicken and began to promote its lunch and dinner buffet. The buffet, which includes 30 items, had been introduced into almost 1,600 KFC restaurants in 27 states by the end of 1993.

One of KFC's most aggressive strategies was the introduction of its "Neighborhood Program." By mid-1993, almost 500 company-owned restaurants in New York, Chicago, Philadelphia, Washington, D.C., St. Louis, Los Angeles, Houston, and Dallas had been outfitted with special menu offerings to appeal exclusively to the Black community. Menus were beefed up with side dishes such as greens, macaroni and cheese, peach cobbler, sweet-potato pie, and red beans and rice. In addition, restaurant employees have been outfitted with African-inspired uniforms. The introduction of the Neighborhood Program has increased sales by five to 30 percent in restaurants appealing directly to the Black community. KFC is currently testing Hispanic-oriented restaurants in the Miami area, which offer such side dishes as fried plantains, flan, and tres leches.

As the growth in sales of traditional, free-standing fast-food restaurants has slowed during the last decade, consumers have demanded fast food in a greater variety of non-traditional locations. As a result, distribution has taken on increasing importance. KFC is relying on non-traditional units to spur much of its future growth. Distribution channels which offer significant growth opportunities are shopping malls and other high-traffic areas which have not traditionally been exploited by fast-food chains. Increasingly, shopping malls are developing food areas where several fast-food restaurant chains compete against each other. Universities and hospitals also offer opportunities for KFC and other chains to improve distribution. KFC is currently testing a variety of non-traditional outlets, including drive-thru and carry-out units; snack shops in cafeterias; kiosks in airports, stadiums, amusement parks, and office buildings; mobile units that can be transported to outdoor concerts and fairs; and scaled-down outlets for supermarkets. In order to help its KFC, Taco Bell, and Pizza Hut units expand more quickly into these non-traditional distribution channels, PepsiCo acquired a partial share of Carts of Colorado, Inc., a manufacturer of mobile merchandising carts, in 1992. Additionally, KFC and Taco Bell plan to add the Taco Bell menu to existing KFC restaurants in 1996 and 1997. This "dual branding" strategy would help PepsiCo improve economies of scale within its restaurant operations and enable KFC restaurants to improve its customer base by widening its menu offerings.

■ Operating Efficiencies

While marketing strategies traditionally improve a firm's profit picture indirectly through increased sales, improved operating efficiencies can directly affect operating profit. As pressure continues to build on fast-food chains to limit price increases in the U.S. market, restaurant chains continue to search for ways of reducing overhead and other operating costs in order to improve profit margins. In 1989, KFC reorganized its U.S. operations in order to eliminate overhead costs and to increase efficiency. Included in this reorganization was a revision of KFC's crew training programs and operating standards. A renewed emphasis has been placed on improving customer service, cleaner restaurants, faster and friendlier service, and continued high-quality products. In 1992, KFC reorganized its middle management ranks, eliminating 250 of the 1,500 management positions at KFC's corporate headquarters. More responsibility was assigned to restaurant franchisees and marketing managers and pay was more closely aligned with customer service and restaurant performance.

▪ Restaurant Expansion and International Operations

While marketing and operating strategies can improve sales and profitability in existing outlets, an important part of success in the quick-service industry is investment growth. Much of the success of the top ten competitors within the industry during the late 1980s and early 1990s can be found in aggressive building strategies. In particular, a restaurant chain is often able to discourage competition by being the first to build in a low population area which can support only one fast-food chain. Additionally, it is equally important to beat a competitor into more largely-populated areas, where location is of prime importance. Internationally, KFC was operating 4,258 restaurants in 68 countries at the end of 1994. KFC is now the third largest quick-service, and largest chicken, restaurant system in the world. In the future, KFC's international operations will be called on to provide an increasing percentage of KFC's overall sales and profit growth as the U.S. market continues to saturate.

MEXICO AND LATIN AMERICA

KFC was one of the first restaurant chains to recognize the importance of international markets. In Latin America, KFC was operating 205 company-owned restaurants in Mexico, Puerto Rico, Venezuela, and Trinidad & Tobago as of November 1995. In addition, KFC had 173 franchisees in 21 countries throughout Latin America, bringing the total number of KFC restaurants in operation in Latin America to 378 (see Exhibit 9).

Through 1990, KFC concentrated its company operations in Mexico and Puerto Rico and focused its franchised operations in the Caribbean and Central America. However, by 1994, KFC had altered its Latin American strategy in a number of ways. First, it began franchising in Mexico, mainly as a result of Mexico's new franchise law, which was enacted in 1990. Second, it expanded its company-owned restaurants into the Virgin Islands and Trinidad & Tobago. Third, it reestablished a subsidiary in Venezuela in 1993. KFC had closed its Venezuelan operations in 1989 because of the high fixed costs associated with running the small subsidiary. Last, it decided to expand its franchise operations beyond Central America. In 1990, a franchise was opened in Chile and in 1993, a new franchise was opened in Brazil.

▪ Franchising

Through 1989, KFC relied exclusively on the operation of company-owned restaurants in Mexico. While franchising was popular in the United States, it was virtually unknown in Mexico until 1990, mainly because of the absence of a law protecting patents, information, and technology transferred to the Mexican franchise. In addition, royalties were limited. As a result, most fast-food chains opted to invest in Mexico using company-owned restaurants rather than through franchising.

In January 1990, Mexico enacted a new law which provided for the protection of technology transferred into Mexico. Under the new legislation, the franchisor and franchisee are free to set their own terms. Royalties are also allowed under the new law. Royalties are currently taxed at a 15 percent rate on

Exhibit 9   **KFC (Latin America) Restaurant Count (as of November 30, 1995)**

Countries	Company Restaurants	Franchise Restaurants	Total Restaurants	Countries
Mexico	129	29	158	1
Puerto Rico	64	0	64	1
Venezuela	4	0	4	1
Virgin Islands	8	0	8	1
Trinidad & Tobago	0	26	26	1
Franchises	0	118	118	19
Total	205	173	378	24

Source: PepsiCo, Inc. Annual Report

technology assistance and know-how and 35 percent for other royalty categories. The advent of the new franchise law has resulted in an explosion of franchises in fast-food, services, hotels, and retail outlets. In 1992, franchises had an estimated $750 million in sales in over 1,200 outlets throughout Mexico.

At the end of 1989, KFC was operating company-owned restaurants in three regions: Mexico City, Guadalajara, and Monterrey. By limiting operations to company-owned restaurants in these three regions, KFC was better able to coordinate operations and minimize costs of distribution to individual restaurants. However, the new franchise legislation gave KFC and other fast-food chains the opportunity to expand their restaurant bases more easily to other regions of Mexico, where responsibility for management could be handled by individual franchisees.

■ Economic Environment and the Mexican Market

Many factors make Mexico a potentially profitable location for U.S. direct investment and trade. Mexico's population of over 91 million people is approximately one-third as large as the U.S. This represents a large market for U.S. goods. Because of its geographical proximity to the U.S., transportation costs from the United States are minimal. This increases the competitiveness of U.S. goods in comparison with European and Asian goods, which must be transported at substantial cost across the Atlantic or Pacific Ocean. The United States is, in fact, Mexico's largest trading partner. Over 65 percent of Mexico's imports come from the U.S., while 69 percent of Mexico's exports are to the U.S. market (see Exhibit 10). In addition, low wage rates make Mexico an attractive location for production. By producing in Mexico, U.S. firms may reduce labor costs and increase the cost competitiveness of their goods in world markets.

Despite the importance of the U.S. market to Mexico, Mexico still represents a small percentage of overall U.S. trade and investment. Since the early 1900s, the portion of U.S. exports to Latin America has declined. Instead, U.S. exports to Canada and Asia, where economic growth has outpaced growth in Mexico, have increased more quickly. Canada is the largest importer of U.S. goods. Japan is the largest exporter of goods to the U.S., with Canada close behind. While the value of Mexico's exports to the U.S. has increased during the last two

Exhibit 10	Mexico's Major Trading Partners (% total exports and imports)					
	1988		1990		1992	
	Exports	*Imports*	*Exports*	*Imports*	*Exports*	*Imports*
USA	72.9	74.9	69.3	68.0	68.7	65.2
Japan	4.9	6.4	5.8	4.5	3.2	6.3
West Germany	1.3	3.5	1.4[1]	4.2[1]	N/A	5.1
France	1.8	2.0	3.5	2.3	2.0	2.7
Other	19.1	13.2	20.0	21.0	26.1	20.7
Total	100.0%	100.0%	100.0%	100.0%	100.0%	100.0%
Value ($M)	20,658	18,903	26,773	29,799	46,196	62,129

[1]Data include East Germany.

Source: *Business International*, 1994.

decades, mainly because of the rise in the price of oil, Mexico still represents a small percentage of overall U.S. trade. U.S. investment in Mexico has also been small, mainly because of government restrictions on foreign investment. Instead, most U.S. foreign investment has been in Europe, Canada, and Asia.

The lack of U.S. investment in and trade with Mexico during this century is mainly the result of Mexico's long history of restricting trade and foreign direct investment in Mexico. In particular, the Institutional Revolutionary Party (PRI), which came to power in Mexico during the 1930s, has traditionally pursued protectionist economic policies in order to shield its people and economy from foreign firms and goods. Industries have been predominately government-owned or -controlled and production has been pursued for the domestic market only. High tariffs and other trade barriers have restricted imports into Mexico, and foreign ownership of assets in Mexico has been largely prohibited or heavily restricted.

In addition, a dictatorial and entrenched government bureaucracy, corrupt labor unions, and a long tradition of anti-Americanism among many government officials and intellectuals has reduced the motivation of U.S. firms for investing in Mexico. As well, the 1982 nationalization of Mexico's banks led to higher real interest rates and lower investor confidence. Since then, the Mexican government has battled high inflation, high interest rates, labor unrest, and lost consumer purchasing power (see Exhibit 11). Total foreign debt, which stood at $125.9 billion at the end of 1993, remains a problem.

Investor confidence in Mexico has, however, improved since December 1988, when Carlos Salinas de Gortari was elected President of Mexico. Following his election, Salinas embarked on an ambitious restructuring of the Mexican economy. In particular, Salinas initiated policies to strengthen the free market components of the economy. Top marginal tax rates were lowered to 36 percent in 1990, down from 60 percent in 1986, and new legislation has eliminated many restrictions on foreign investment. Foreign firms are now allowed to buy up to 100 percent of the equity in many Mexico firms. Previously, foreign ownership of Mexican firms was limited to 49 percent. Many government-owned companies have been sold to private investors in order to eliminate government bureaucracy and improve efficiency.

Exhibit 11	Economic Data for Mexico				
	1989	*1990*	*1991*	*1992*	*1993*
Population (Millions)	84.5	86.2	87.8	89.5	91.2
GDP (Billions of New Pesos)	507.6	686.4	865.2	1,019.2	1,127.6
Real GDP Growth Rate (%)	3.3	4.4	3.6	2.8	0.6
Exchange Rate (New Pesos/$)	2.641	2.945	3.071	3.115	3,106
Inflation (%)	20.0	26.6	22.7	15.5	8.6
Current Account ($ Billions)	(5.8)	(7.5)	(14.9)	(24.8)	(23.4)
Reserves (Excl Gold $ Bil)	6.3	9.9	17.7	18.9	25.1

Source: *International Financial Statistics*, International Monetary Fund, 1995.

■ Privatization

The privatization of government-owned companies has come to symbolize the restructuring of Mexico's economy. On May 14, 1990, legislation was passed to privatize all government-run banks. By the end of 1992, over 800 of some 1,200 government-owned companies had been sold, including Mexicana and Aero-Mexico, the two largest airline companies in Mexico, and Mexico's 18 major banks. At least 40 more companies were scheduled to be privatized in 1993. However, more than 350 companies remain under government ownership. These represent a significant portion of the assets owned by the state at the start of 1988. Therefore, the sale of government-owned companies, in terms of asset value, has been moderate. A large percentage of the remaining government-owned assets are controlled by government-run companies in certain strategic industries such as steel, electricity, and petroleum. These industries have long been protected by government ownership. As a result, additional privatization of government-owned enterprises until 1993 was limited. However, in 1993, President Salinas opened up the electricity sector to independent power producers and Petroleos Mexicanos (Pemex), the state-run petrochemical monopoly, initiated a program to sell off many of its non-strategic assets to private and foreign buyers. This was motivated mainly by a desire by Pemex to concentrate on its basic petrochemical businesses.

■ North American Free Trade Agreement (NAFTA)

Prior to 1989, Mexico levied high tariffs on most imported goods. In addition, many other goods were subjected to quotas, licensing requirements, and other non-tariff trade barriers. In 1986, Mexico joined the General Agreement on Tariffs and Trade (GATT), a world trade organization designed to eliminate barriers to trade among member nations. As a member of GATT, Mexico is obligated to apply its system of tariffs to all member nations equally. As a result of its membership in GATT, Mexico dropped tariff rates on a variety of imported goods. In addition, import license requirements were dropped for all but 300 imported items. During President Salinas' administration, tariffs were reduced from an average of 100 percent on most items to an average of 11 percent.

On January 1, 1994, the North American Free Trade Agreement (NAFTA) went into effect. The passage of NAFTA, which included Canada, the United States, and Mexico, created a trading bloc which has a larger population and gross domestic product than the European Union. Over the next several years, all tariffs on goods traded among the three countries will be phased out. Given that Canada is the United States' largest trading partner and Mexico the United States' third largest trading partner, the absence of tariffs and reduced restrictions on investment should result in increase trade and investment among the three countries. In particular, Mexico should benefit from the lower cost of imported goods and increased employment from higher investment from Canada and the United States. Canada and the United States should benefit from lower labor and transportation costs from investing in Mexico.

■ Foreign Exchange and the Mexican Peso Crisis of 1995

Between December 20, 1982, and November 11, 1991, a two-tiered exchange rate system was in force in Mexico. The system consisted of a controlled rate and a free market rate. A controlled rate was used for imports, foreign debt payments, and conversion of export proceeds. An estimated 70 percent of all foreign transactions were covered by the controlled rate. A free market rate was used for other transactions. On January 1, 1989, President Salinas instituted a policy of allowing the peso to depreciate against the dollar by one peso per day. The result was a grossly overvalued peso. This lowered the price of imports and led to an increase in imports of over 23 percent in 1989. At the same time, Mexican exports became less competitive on world markets.

Effective November 11, 1991, the controlled rate was abolished and replaced with an official free rate. In order to limit the range of fluctuations in the value of the peso, the government fixed the rate at which it would buy or sell pesos. A floor (the minimum price at which pesos may be purchased) was initially established at Ps 3056.20 and remained fixed. A ceiling (the maximum price at which the peso may be sold) was initially established at Ps 3,056.40 and allowed to move upward by Ps 0.20 per day. This was later revised to Ps 0.40 per day. On January 1, 1993, a new currency was issued—called the new peso—with three fewer zeros. The new currency was designed to simplify transactions and to reduce the cost of printing currency.

When Ernesto Zedillo became Mexico's president in December 1994, one of his objectives was to continue the stability in prices, wages, and exchange rates achieved by ex-president Carlos Salinas de Gortari during his five-year tenure as president. However, Salinas had achieved stability largely on the basis of price, wage, and foreign exchange controls. While giving the appearance of stability, an overvalued peso continued to encourage imports which exacerbated Mexico's balance of trade deficit. Mexico's government continued to use foreign reserves to finance its balance of trade deficits. According to the Banco de Mexico, foreign currency reserves fell from $24 billion in January 1994 to $5.5 billion in January 1995. Anticipating a devaluation of the peso, investors began to move capital into U.S. dollar investments. In order to relieve some of the pressure placed on the peso, president Zedillo announced on December 19, 1994, that the peso would be allowed to depreciate by an additional 15 percent per year against the dollar, compared to the maximum allowable depreciation of 4 percent per year established during the Salinas administration. Within two days, continued pressure on the peso forced the Zedillo administration to allow the peso to float against the dollar. By mid-January 1995, the peso had lost 35 percent of its value against the dollar and the Mexican stock market plunged 20 percent. By November 1995, the peso had depreciated from 3.1 pesos per dollar to 7.3 pesos per dollar.

The continued devaluation of the peso resulted in higher import prices, higher inflation, destabilization within the stock market, and higher interest rates, as Mexico struggled to arrange continued payment of its dollar-based debts. In order to thwart a possible default by Mexico on its dollar-based loans, the U.S. government, International Monetary Fund, and World Bank pledged $12.5, $11.4, and $1.0 billion, respectively (a total of $24.9 billion) in emergency loans to Mexico. In addition, President Zedillo announced an emergency economic package called the "pacto," which included reduced government spending, increased sales of government-run businesses, and a freeze on wage increases.

■ Labor Problems

One of KFC's primary concerns is the stability of Mexico's labor markets. Labor is relatively plentiful and cheap in Mexico, though much of the work force is still relatively unskilled. While KFC benefits from lower labor costs, labor unrest, low job retention, absenteeism, and punctuality continue to be significant problems. A good part of the problem with absenteeism and punctuality is cultural. However, problems with worker retention and labor unrest are mainly the result of workers' frustration over the loss of their purchasing power due to inflation and past government controls on wage increases. *Business Latin America* estimated that purchasing power fell by 35 percent in Mexico between January 1988 and June 1990. Though absenteeism is on the decline due to job security fears, it is still high, at approximately eight to fourteen percent of the labor force. Turnover also continues to be a problem. Turnover of production line personnel is currently running at five to twelve percent per month. Therefore, employee screening and internal training continue to be important issues for foreign firms investing in Mexico.

Higher inflation and the government's freeze on wage increases has led to a dramatic decline in disposable income since 1994. Further, a slowdown in business activity, brought about by higher interest rates and lower government spending, has led many businesses to lay off workers. By the end of 1995, an estimated one million jobs had been lost as a result of the economic crisis sparked by the peso devaluation. As a result, industry groups within Mexico have called for new labor laws giving them more freedom to hire and fire employees and increased flexibility to hire part-time rather than full-time workers.

RISKS AND OPPORTUNITIES

The peso crisis of 1995 and resulting recession in Mexico left KFC managers with a great deal of uncertainty regarding Mexico's economic and political future. KFC had benefited greatly from the economic stability brought about by President Salinas' policies during his 1988-1994 tenure. Inflation was brought down, the peso was relatively stable, labor unrest was relatively calm, and Mexico's new franchise law had enabled KFC to expand into rural areas using franchises rather than company-owned restaurants. By the end of 1995, KFC had built 29 franchises in Mexico. KFC planned to continue to expand its franchise base and to rely less heavily on company-owned restaurants as a cornerstone of its strategy to maintain its market share against other fast-food restaurants, such as McDonald's and Arby's, which were pursuing high growth strategies in Mexico.

The foreign exchange crisis of 1995 had severe implications for U.S. firms operating in Mexico. In particular, the devaluation of the peso resulted in higher inflation and capital flight out of Mexico. The Bank of Mexico estimated that $7.1 billion fled the country during the first three months of 1995. In order to bring inflation under control, the Mexican government instituted an austerity program in early 1995 which included reduced government spending and a freeze on wage increases. Capital flight reduced the supply of capital and resulted in higher interest rates. Additionally, the government's austerity program resulted in reduced demand for products and services, higher unemployment, and lower disposable income. Imports from the U.S. dropped dramatically in 1995. About one-third of this decline included the importation of capital goods, such as technology, materials, and updated machinery, which are critical to Mexico's industrialization program.

Another problem area has been Mexico's failure to reduce restrictions on U.S. and Canadian investment in Mexico in a timely fashion. While the reduction of trade barriers has resulted in greater U.S. exports to Mexico, U.S. firms have experienced problems getting the required approvals for new ventures in Mexico from the Mexican government. For example, under the NAFTA agreement, the United Parcel Service (UPS) was supposed to receive government approval to use large trucks for deliveries in Mexico. As of the end of 1995, UPS had still not received approval. As a result, UPS has been forced to use smaller trucks, which puts it at a competitive disadvantage vis-a-via Mexican companies, or to subcontract delivery work to Mexican companies that are allowed to use bigger, more cost-efficient trucks. Other U.S. companies such as Bell Atlantic and TRW have faced similar problems. TRW, which signed a joint venture agreement with a Mexican partner, had to wait 15 months longer than anticipated before the Mexican government released rules on how it could receive credit data from banks. TRW claims that the Mexican government slowed the approval process in order to placate several large Mexican banks.

A final area of concern for KFC has been the increased political turmoil in Mexico during the last several years. For example, on January 1, 1994, the day NAFTA went into effect, rebels (descendants of the Mayans) rebelled in the southern Mexican province of Chiapas on the Guatemalan border. After four days of fighting, Mexican troops had driven the rebels out of several towns earlier seized by the rebels. Around 150—mostly rebels—were killed. The uprising symbolized many of the fears of the poor in Mexico. While President Salinas' economic programs had increased economic growth and wealth in Mexico, many of Mexico's poorest felt that they have not benefited. Many of Mexico's farmers, faced with lower tariffs on imported agricultural goods from the United States, felt that they might be driven out of business by the NAFTA agreement. Therefore, social unrest among Mexico's Indians, farmers, and the poor could potentially unravel much of the economic success achieved in Mexico during the last five years.

Further, President Salinas' hand-picked successor for president, Luis Donaldo Colosio, was assassinated on March 23, 1994, while campaigning in Tijuana. The assassin—Mario Aburto Martinez, a 23-year-old mechanic and migrant worker—was affiliated with a dissident group upset with the PRI's economic reforms. The possible existence of a dissident group has raised fears of further political violence in the future. The PRI quickly named Ernesto Zedillo, a 42-year-old economist with little political experience or name recognition, as their new presidential candidate. Zedillo was elected president and replaced Salinas in December 1994. However, political unrest is not limited to Mexican officials and companies. In October 1994, between 30 and 40 masked men attacked a McDonald's restaurant in the tourist section of Mexico City to show their opposition to California's Proposition 187, which would have curtailed benefits to illegal aliens (primarily from Mexico). The men threw cash registers to the floor, cracked them open, smashed windows, overturned tables, and spray-painted slogans on the walls such as "No to Fascism" and "Yankee Go Home."

Despite these worries, the passage of NAFTA, the size of the Mexican market, and its proximity to the United States have resulted in a number of opportunities for KFC and other U.S. businesses. During the first five months of 1995, exports from Mexico to the United States jumped 33.5 percent from the previous year as lower tariffs lowered the price of Mexican goods to the American consumer. In fact, during this period, Mexico ran up its highest trade surplus with the U.S. in Mexico's history.

The peso devaluation has also made it less expensive for U.S. and Canadian businesses to buy assets in Mexico. This has enabled businesses to more easily fund expansion in Mexico through new capital at a lower cost. As well, for companies already operating in Mexico, raw materials can be imported from outside of Mexico by converting dollars into pesos at a more favorable rate.

For many U.S. companies, the protection of technology and patents is a major concern. In June 1991, a new patent law was passed which replaced the old 1976 law. Patents will now last for 20 years rather than 14. Chemicals, pharmaceuticals, and animal feed will benefit from product patent protection for the first time, opening up the Mexican market to U.S. firms in these fields. Trademarks are now valid for an initial 10 years and are renewable for 10 years, up from the previous five-year terms. Patents on industrial designs are now valid for 15 years, up from 7 years. Additionally, a new copyright law was passed in August 1991. The new law will protect sound recordings and computer software for the first time.

KFC's approach to investment in Mexico is to approach it conservatively, until greater economic and political stability is achieved. While resources could be directed at other investment areas with less risk, such as Japan, Australia, China, and Europe, the Mexican market is viewed as KFC's most important growth market outside of the U.S. and second largest international market behind Australia. Also, significant opportunities existed for KFC to expand its franchise base throughout the Caribbean and South America. However, PepsiCo's commitments to these other markets are unlikely to be severely affected by its investment decisions in Mexico, as PepsiCo's large internal cash flows could satisfy the investment needs of KFC's other international subsidiaries regardless of its investments in Mexico. The danger in taking a conservative approach in Mexico was the potential loss of market share in a large market where KFC enjoys enormous popularity.

First International Bank of California[1]

Julius S. Brown, Loyola Marymount University

Mary Mulligan, Loyola Marymount University

S taring out the window of his office, overlooking the city of Los Angeles after a long day, Manuel Cruz, President of First International Bank of California (Bancal), was contemplating the success that he had attained in life at such a young age. Born in Guadalajara,[2] the youngest of four children, Cruz spent the first eighteen years of his life in Mexico. Guided by the direction of his parents, who stressed the importance of education, Cruz was a diligent student, with an impressive academic record. His scholastic achievements earned him entrance into Harvard University in 1975, at the age of eighteen. There, he earned his bachelor's degree as well as his MBA.

Upon graduation, Cruz received an offer to work at the New York office of Bancal, a well-known United States commercial bank, headquartered in Los Angeles, with assets amounting to $45 billion. He began his career as a bank administrator, using his analytical skills to make decisions concerning the credit and investments of the bank and its customers. Having familiarized himself with the operations of Bancal, and having established a variety of contacts, it was decided that Cruz would travel to Los Angeles, where he would be groomed to assume the role of controller. It was in this capacity that Cruz served Bancal for seven years.

His ability to control the company's finances did not go unnoticed. Additionally, what set Cruz apart from his colleagues was the way in which he

---

[1] Note: This case is illustrative of financial analysis as of 1995.

[2] Guadalajara, with three million people, was the second largest city in Mexico and a strong commercial center.

interacted with other employees. Cruz seemed to gain the respect of his co-workers, strengthening relationships that he made with fellow employees as he climbed the corporate ladder. No doubt, it was his intellectual capabilities coupled with his excellent "people skills" that made Cruz the top contender for President of Bancal nearly three years ago. At the age of thirty-nine, Manuel Cruz, was one of the youngest Presidents that ever operated Bancal.

As the sun set over the city of Los Angeles, Cruz realized that his past successes would help him to face the new challenges ahead. Specifically, his main concern was addressing the Board of Directors' request that Bancal consider expansion into Mexico. Clearly, their interest was a result of the recent passage of the North American Free Trade Agreement. Additionally, it was a well-known fact that Cruz had a well-established contact in Guadalajara, Luis Ramirez, managing director of Grupo Turismo S.A. de C.V., one of the nation's leading tourist operator/developers. Ramirez, who was a longtime friend of Cruz's father, had expressed his interest in establishing a working relationship with Bancal, in the event that NAFTA was ratified. He explained that his company needed working capital in dollars, which was in short supply. Further-

Exhibit 1	Guadalbank Balance Sheet 12/31/94 ($1.00 U.S. = M. Pesos 4.925)	
	Assets (U.S. dollars)	
	Cash and Equivalents	87,384,333
	Securities	352,092,333
	Real Estate Loans	126,085,691
	Commercial & Individual Loans	629,191,642
	Farm Loans & Other	89,000,000
	Real Estate and Other Assets	12,328,333
	Total Assets	$1,296,082,332
	Liabilities and Capital	
	Demand Deposits	233,659,000
	Time Deposits	397,586,666
	Other Deposits	56,899,333
	Long-Term Liabilities	303,264,000
	Loss & Revaluation Reserves	168,103,333
	Equity Capital	136,570,000
	Total Liabilities and Capital	$1,296,082,332
	Outstanding Shares	150,000,000
	Book Value Per Share	$0.91 (M. Pesos 4.48)
	Market Price Per Share (?)	$1.00
	Return on Equity	20.6%

$100,000,000 would purchase more than the necessary controlling interest if the buy decision is implemented.

more, he pointed out that if Bancal developed a strong relationship with Grupo Turismo, there was a possibility that the other members of the conglomerate would make capital commitments with Bancal. He also noted that Bancal could potentially benefit from locating in Guadalajara, where a strong American presence had not yet been established in the banking sector, as U.S. banks typically looked to Mexico City. Cruz was also pleased to find out that there was a possibility that Bancal could buyout an existing Mexican bank, known as Guadalbank. Cruz was able to obtain a copy of the bank's balance sheet and earnings summary, as illustrated in Exhibits 1 and 2. Consequently, since the passage of the trade agreement, expansion into Mexico had been an area of interest for Bancal.

Although Cruz was excited about the possibility of entering into the Mexican banking market, he realized that he must proceed with caution. Bancal had not had any previous working relationships in Mexico. Moreover, the bank was not very familiar with the banking sector in Mexico, as well as the new laws that govern the industry, since NAFTA had passed. As a result, Cruz decided to turn to two of his subordinates, Sandra Mireles, Vice-President of Marketing for Bancal, and Steve Brown, Vice-President of Finance.

Cruz was pleased to find that Mireles, a California native and the offspring of Mexican parents, was fluent in Spanish. A graduate of Wellesley, with an MBA from Harvard, Mireles had just been promoted to her new position. Previously, she was employed as a manager of commercial lending. Her predecessor at Bancal was dismissed because he had a habit of not fully researching Cruz's proposals. Thus, since this was Mireles' first assignment as the new Vice-President of Marketing, she knew that she must assume the task of gathering *all* of the pertinent information on the banking industry in Mexico, the implications of NAFTA on banking, and Grupo Turismo—a promising, potential large-scale customer for Bancal.

Exhibit 2	**Guadalbank Earnings Summary 12/31/94** **(In U.S. Dollars; $1.00 U.S. = M. Pesos 4.925)**	
	Interest Income	$137,461,336
	Less Interest Expense	40,903,739
	Net Interest Income	96,557,597
	Miscellaneous Income	10,844,903
	Total Income	$107,402,500
	Provision For Loan Losses	35,893,000
	Personnel/Operating Expenses	21,053,000
	Total Expenses	$56,946,000
	Income Before Taxes	$50,456,500
	Taxes	22,273,900
	Net Earnings	$28,182,600
	Earnings Per Share	$0.1879

THE HISTORY OF THE BANKING INDUSTRY IN MEXICO

Mireles' research had turned up the following information: The banking sector in Mexico had experienced significant changes over the past decade. The history of the banking system could be broken down into three major phases, beginning in 1982 with the nationalization of banks in Mexico.

- *Phase 1:* During this time, the government took over ownership of the banks and appointed its own presidents to replace the existing officers. Additionally, control was exercised via regulations. Thus, the government imposed restrictions on the banks in such a way that its interests were satisfied. For instance, at the same time that the banks were nationalized, the government budget deficit was large, amounting to as much as 16% of the gross domestic product.[3] As a result, restrictions were put in place, in efforts to reduce the government's cost of financing. Included were interest rate controls, selective portfolios, and required reserve ratios.

  Eventually, however, as the deficit shrank, the borrowing needs of the government also diminished. As a result, the government was not benefiting, as it had in the past, by the restrictions, and thus sought to reduce them.

- *Phase 2:* The second phase was a transitional period, during which emphasis shifted from public sector to private sector interests. The government was willing to shift its emphasis to the private sector because it no longer experienced the benefits of the restrictions as it had when the government deficit was high. The idea was to allow banks to operate in an arena in which banks could effectively serve the needs of the private sector. In addition, in 1985, the government began to sell minority shares in commercial banks. Clearly, these actions laid the groundwork for the privatization of the Mexican banks.

- *Phase 3:* 1991 marked the end of the deficit that plagued Mexico. This was made possible by cuts in government spending coupled with the low cost of financing the deficit (made possible by the government imposed restrictions). At the same time, it signaled the beginning of a major privatization program. Thus, banks were returned to the private sector by means of government auctions. Interestingly, banks were sold for 2.5 to 5.3 times their book value, indicating the importance of commercial lending for the private sector. Obviously, these banks, having made sizable investments, were doing everything that they could to recover their initial investment and to make substantial profits.

Profits during the first eleven months of 1992 rose 64%. At the same time, however, the fall of the Mexican stock market, coupled with an economic slowdown, made it difficult for banks to raise capital. Consequently, only the strongest banks were emerging viable under the recent privatization program. The most notable players included: Banco Nacional de Mexico (more commonly referred to as Banamex), Bancomer, and Banca Serfin. In 1991, the three combined held approximately 62% of the total banking assets in Mexico. After the devaluation in 1994, this figure dropped to 50%. A breakdown of their markets is shown in Exhibit 3.

---

[3] Gross Domestic Product (GDP) is the total value of goods and services produced by a country in a year, less net income sent or received from abroad.

Exhibit 3   **Asset Distribution of Earnings**

	Commercial	Mortgages	Credit Cards	Other consumer loans
Banamex	60	26	11	3
Bancomer	58	28	8	6
Serfin	81	16	2	1
Others	83	11	5	1

MEXICAN BANKS ... WHERE THEY STAND IN TODAY'S COMPETITIVE ENVIRONMENT

Realizing that efficiency was the key to success, Mexican banks tried to identify areas in their operations in which they needed to make improvements. For instance, there were not enough skilled risk analysts in the Mexican banking sector. Furthermore, as the number of loans was expected to grow some 20%, the need for capable analysts became increasingly important. Also, Mexico lacked the state-of-the-art technology that provided many of its U.S. neighbors with a unique competitive advantage. Thus, Mexican banks had to address these key issues.

In addition to the aforementioned concerns, Mexican banks' primary focus had to be on the most recent developments surrounding the passage of the North American Free Trade Agreement—considering that this agreement would have profound effects on the Mexican banking sector.

THE NORTH AMERICAN FREE TRADE AGREEMENT ... WHAT IT MEANT TO THE BANKING SECTOR

The ratification of NAFTA was expected to have a direct effect on the banking sector in Mexico. Additionally, the financial services chapter of NAFTA establishes the rules that define the treatment by each NAFTA country, of the other's financial firms, investments in the financial sector, and cross-border services. Specifically, the agreement declares that "each country agrees to allow financial institutions of other countries to establish and operate in its market through subsidiaries." Consequently, U.S. banks will be able to set up subsidiaries in Mexico that can compete with Mexican banks. Previously, foreign banks were allowed to operate only representative offices, with the exception of the large New York bank, Citibank. Operating in Mexico since the early 1930's, Citibank was the only U.S. bank with branches in Mexico. Clearly, Citibank reaped the benefits of larger lending limits and lower funding costs, as it was allowed to open branches.

Although Mexico was opening up the banking sector to its U.S. neighbors, Mexico was making sure that U.S. banks proceeded slowly. There was a limit on the amount of market share that American subsidiaries could control. Initially, U.S. banks were restricted to an aggregate market share of 8%, and by the year 2000, this figure will increase to 15%. However, Mexico reserved the right to intervene if the market share of U.S. banks rose too quickly, until the year 2007, when restrictions end.

Specifically, individual U.S. banks will be limited to 1.5% of the total market share. In addition, during this transition period, U.S. banks can acquire Mexican banks, so long as they do not exceed the 1.5% limit. Following this period, in the year 2000, banks will be allowed to make acquisitions amounting to 4% of total market share. Subsequent expansion beyond this point will only be possible via internal growth, which includes capital received from the parent. Acquisition will no longer be an option.

Originally, eighteen foreign competitors had received charters to enter into the Mexican banking sector. It was estimated that these banks made $3.25 billion in new loans available in 1995. In addition, Mexico's financial sector was expected to grow 10% a year for the next three to five years. This figure is double the annual growth rate of Mexico's gross national product.[4] At the end of 1994, the banking industry was made up of institutions with assets amounting to $200 billion, compared to the $3.5 trillion industry in the U.S. While there was one bank for every 4,000 people in the United States, there was one bank per 18,000 people in Mexico. Given these figures, analysts claimed that Mexico was "underbanked" and that as the Mexican economy recovered, there would be a large demand for financial services provided by banks.

Although Mexico expected that competition from the U.S. was inevitable, it was extremely difficult for those who paid large sums of money to acquire the recently privatized banks to see U.S. banks receive permission to compete head-to-head with them. In addition, Mexican banks were feeling the impact of the sluggish economy, the lack of state-of-the-art technology, as well as the lack of adequate credit rating services. Not surprisingly, the profitability of most Mexican banks had decreased substantially. Even the three largest banks have suffered with a combined decrease in profits amounting to 44.5%.

GRUPO TURISMO . . . A POTENTIAL CUSTOMER

One of the *main* reasons for Manuel Cruz's interest in establishing a subsidiary in Mexico was the fact that he had a powerful and influential Mexican contact, Luis Ramirez. Having taken advantage of the petrodollars circulating in Mexico in the 1970's, Ramirez started his own company, Estrella, which built and marketed upscale condominiums. Then, in 1987, he sold his company to the well-known conglomerate Grupo Amarillo, which operates in the steel, tourism, and retail markets. Ramirez then became involved in the tourist division of Amarillo, known as Grupo Turismo, and held the position of managing director.

---

[4] Gross National Product (GNP) includes production by a country's facilities abroad.

In order to get a better sense of Turismo's interest and potential commitment in establishing a relationship with Bancal, Mireles booked a flight to Guadalajara to meet with Ramirez.

THE MEETING

Upon arriving in Guadalajara, Mireles met with Ramirez, who, like the typical Mexican businessperson, took the time to acquaint Mireles with the city, followed by lunch at the "Guadalajara Grill." The lunchtime conversation was spent recounting the stories about Ramirez's recollections of Manuel Cruz as a child growing up in Guadalajara, since Ramirez was a close friend of Cruz's father, Antonio. Fortunately, with Mireles' upbringing, she knew that business discussions would have to be postponed until a relationship was established between the two. The following day, the two began to discuss the idea of Bancal entering into Mexico. But first, Ramirez needed to tell Mireles more about Grupo Turismo.

Ramirez began, noting that tourism was Mexico's third largest single source of revenue, right behind maquiladoras[5] and oil. In addition, Grupo Turismo represented the tourism division of Grupo Amarillo. Basically, Turismo could be classified as a tourist operator/developer, although as Ramirez continued his explanation, it appeared as though Turismo was involved in a number of other industries. For instance, the primary area in which Turismo was involved was site development. Turismo developed land for what it called "megadevelopments." Other companies within the group operated hotels and built holiday homes. In fact, Grupo Turismo was the largest owner of hotels in Mexico. Thus, Turismo was a major real estate developer and tourism company with annual revenues of 1.7 billion new Mexican pesos (about $340 million at current exchange rates).

Additionally, as Turismo penetrated the Mexican market, it was beginning to look to other countries, such as Costa Rica. Specifically, the plan was to develop hotels, a marina, and a golf course, spanning 2,225 acres along the Costa Rican coast. No doubt, this would allow Grupo Turismo to diversify its business and to increase its profit margins.

After establishing the business in which Turismo operated, the discussion naturally shifted to finance. Specifically, Grupo Amarillo's assets totaled about $1 billion, with Turismo's assets amounting to roughly $600 million. (A consolidated balance sheet and income statement for Grupo Amarillo are provided in Exhibits 4a and 4b.) Ramirez continued, noting that Grupo Turismo had an $80 million initial public offering in December of 1992. Each share sold for 3,100 pesos (as of July 1993, the exchange rate was approximately 3,300 pesos/$), and each American Depository Share (ADS), representing ten shares, sold for $10.10. By mid-January, the share price increased to 3,300 pesos.

Growing at an annual rate of 15–20%, Turismo was investing heavily in new megadevelopments, and was in need of capital. Thus, the company was particularly interested in any new opportunities that NAFTA could provide, in the form of competitive commercial bank loans from new U.S. entrants.

---

[5] Maquiladoras enable manufacturers to ship machinery, raw materials, and components into Mexico for processing, assembly, and packaging. Products are then shipped back to the U.S.

Exhibit 4a	Grupo Amarillo—Consolidated Income Statement—Year Ended Dec. 31, 1994	
	(In 000's of Mexican New Pesos)	*(In 000's of U.S. Dollars)**
Net Sales	1,436,726	$291,721
Other oper. inc.	133,013	27,008
Total Revenues	1,569,739	318,729
Other oper. exp.	880,732	178,829
Sell., gen., & admin. costs	302,724	61,467
Tot. cost of financing	7,483	1,519
Costs & expenses	1,190,939	241,815
EBT & profit sharing	378,800	76,914
Income Taxes	29,075	5,904
Emp. Profit Sharing	2,349	477
Inc. Tax & empl. profit shar.	31,424	6,381
Net Consol. Earnings	347,376	70,533
Net earn. of minor stk	99,162	20,134
Net earn. of majority stk	248,214	50,399
Yr end shares oustg	402,193	81,664

*Note: Converted to U.S. dollars at Dec. 31, 1994, spot rate: P 4.9250/$1

COUNTRY RISK ANALYSIS

In addition to the considerations given to the potential customer in Guadalajara, it was necessary to conduct a comprehensive country risk analysis of Mexico, in efforts to determine the feasibility of establishing a subsidiary. To begin the process, Mireles decided that it was necessary to gather general background information on Mexico.

MEXICO AT A GLANCE

Mexico is a democratic, representative, and federal republic, comprised of 31 states and a federal district. Each state is free and sovereign in all internal affairs but is united in a federation established according to the principles of the Constitution.

In terms of its economic situation, Mexico's GDP increased by 6.5% annually between 1965 and 1980 but only 0.5% yearly by 1988. Weak oil prices, rising inflation, a foreign debt exceeding $100 billion, and worsening budget deficits added to the nation's economic problems in the mid-1980s, although the economy began to improve at the end of the decade. In the late 1980s the GDP was $176.7 billion (about $1,760 per capita). The World Bank estimated that

Exhibit 4b   **Grupo Amarillo—Consolidated Balance Sheet—Year Ended Dec. 31, 1994**

	(In 000's of Mexican New Pesos)	(In 000's of U.S. Dollars)*
Assets:		
Cash & equivalents	126,647	$ 25,715
Receivables	732,601	148,751
Inventories	393,433	79,885
Integrated Resort Complexes	400,356	81,290
Prepaid Expenses	17,908	3,636
Current Assets	1,670,945	339,278
Long-Term Receivables	336,186	68,261
Integrated Resort Complexes	430,063	87,322
Prop. Plant & Eq., net	2,494,216	506,440
Investments	38,314	7,779
Other Assets	42,457	8,621
Total Assets	5,012,181	1,017,702
Liabilities:		
Current Liabilities	1,109,448	225,269
Long-Term Debt	1,166,640	236,881
Other Liabilities	362,737	73,652
Minority Stockholders	193,814	39,353
Shareholder's Eq:		
Majority Stk. Eq.	1,373,987	278,982
Minority Stk. Eq.	805,555	163,564
Total Shareholders' eq.	2,179,542	442,547
Total Liabil & sh' eq.	5,012,181	1,017,702
Net current assets	561,497	114,010

*Note: Converted to U.S. dollars at Dec. 31, 1994, spot rate: P 4.9250/$1

Mexico's gross national product, measured at average 1989–1991 prices, was $252.4 billion U.S. dollars, equivalent to $2,870 per person. Over the period from 1980 to 1991, it was estimated that GNP increased in real terms at an average annual rate of 1.5%, although GNP per capita declined by .5% per year, due to population growth.

Generally speaking, the standard of living in Mexico is low compared to the U.S. In addition, recent political turmoil has severely hampered the country's economic progress. Specifically, in efforts to stimulate the economy, the Zedillo administration had developed a plan to remove many restrictions on foreign investment, and had continued an extensive privatization program started by the previous administration of Carlos Salinas de Gortari.[6] Moreover, important restrictions have been replaced with competitive tariffs to encourage foreign participation in the Mexican market.

In spite of the government's efforts, Mexico's economy has been stagnating, at times even posting negative growth. The situation prompted government officials to increase spending and to lower interest rates. This resulted in a substantial weakening of the peso against the dollar. In late 1994, the Zedillo administration made a bold move, allowing the peso to float. As a result, in just one day, the peso lost more than 20% of its value, the largest drop against the dollar in a decade. Clearly, the devaluation had a direct impact on investor confidence in Mexico. The U.S. government had initially guaranteed an $18 billion line of credit. However, the entire bailout package, which was arranged by the United States in conjunction with the Bank for International Settlements (BIS), the International Monetary Fund (IMF), and commercial banks, totaled $50 billion. Specifically, the monetary aid was used to stabilize the peso. In addition, it was necessary to use some of the funds to pay approximately $6.78 billion in tesebonos—short-term, dollar-denominated debt instruments.

As a result of the devaluation the Mexican economy plunged. Additionally, since December about 2,000 workers in the banking sector lost their jobs. Thus, domestic consumption fell drastically as the purchasing power of local citizens diminished. GDP is expected to shrink at least 2% in 1995. Consequently, the government is relying on exports to trigger growth, with exports accounting for one quarter of the total GDP. In addition, inflation, according to Finance Minister Guillermo Ortiz, is expected to drop dramatically. The peso is expected to float, and the finance ministry, in efforts to improve the economy, is looking to provide tax incentives to promote long-term investments.

POLITICAL AND FINANCIAL RISK

Mireles began her risk analysis (illustrated in Exhibit 5) with the identification of the political and financial variables that she believed posed a significant potential threat to Bancal as it contemplated entering into the Mexican market. Next, she assigned a risk rating to each of the variables, based on a scale of 1–10 (10 being the most risky). A weight, representing the importance of each variable, was also assigned, such that the sum of the weights totaled 100%. Finally, she considered the importance of each dimension, resulting in an overall country risk rating.

POLITICAL RISK ANALYSIS

Beginning with the political risk factors, Mireles cited political tensions as a notable risk. That is, recent events had clearly shown that the electoral process could be quite a destabilizing force. For example, tensions grew in the past election, as the leading Presidential candidate, Luis Donaldo Colosio, was

[6]Both Ernesto Zedillo and Carlos Salinas de Gortari obtained their Ph.Ds in Economics from American universities.

Exhibit 5	Country Risk Analysis For Mexico—Sandra Mireles*		
	Rating assigned by co to factor (Range is 1-10)	Wt assigned by co to factor based on importance	Wtd Value Factor
Political Risk Factors			
Political Tensions	7	40%	2.8
Turmoil	6	30%	1.8
Attitude of Host Gov't	2	30%	0.6
		100%	**5.2=political risk**
Financial Risk Factors			
Inflation	6	40%	2.4
Credit Risk	7	40%	2.8
Unfavorable Gov't Policies	4	20%	0.8
		100%	**6.0=political risk**

	Rating as Determined Above	Wt assigned by co to each risk category	Weighted Rating
Category			
Political Risk	5.2	60%	3.1
Financial Risk	6.0	40%	2.4
		100%	**5.5=overall country risk rating**

*Format adopted with permission from Jeff Madura, Florida Atlantic University. See: J. Madura, *International Financial Management* (St. Paul: West Publishing Company, 1992), p. 577.

assassinated. In addition, such political upheaval tends to have several ramifications for businesses, often resulting in capital flight. Specifically, in light of the aforementioned incident, the peso dropped in value. Translating this risk into a quantifiable figure, Mireles chose to rate political tensions a "7" and assigned a 40% weight.

In addition to political tensions, Mireles cited turmoil, or the threat of uprising, as yet another factor to consider. Once again, recent events had indicated the potential for insurrection. For instance, in 1994, conflict occurred in the state of Chiapas. The campesinos, the farmers of Southern Mexico, turned to armed conflict in protest against the government's decision to allow foreigners to purchase farmland. Thus, the threat of internal warfare was real and could seriously impact businesses that operate in the country. Mireles assigned a risk of "6" to this variable, and weighted it 30%.

Rounding out the political factors was the attitude of the host government. Although there are guidelines that the NAFTA countries must abide by, Mexico did reserve the right to intervene in the event that it felt that market share was rising too quickly. Clearly, this appeared to be a subjective judgment that is contingent upon the attitude of the host government. Moreover, the major banks in Mexico were already worried by the competition that they were facing from the U.S. Consequently, the U.S. banks that establish subsidiaries in Mexico must strive to maintain strong, positive relations with the Mexican government. Based on her calculations, Mireles assigned a risk of "2" and a weight of 30%.

FINANCIAL RISK ANALYSIS

After determining the political risks, Mireles assessed the financial risks of opening a subsidiary. First, she looked at inflation, exchange, and interest rates. In terms of the inflation rate, Mireles' findings showed that Mexico had the highest inflation rate of the three NAFTA countries, which affected the purchasing power of its people. Thus, the Zedillo government has had to intervene from time to time in attempts to keep the inflation rate down.

Along with the inflation rate, Mexico has experienced exchange-rate as well as interest-rate fluctuations, which often are clearly a function of the stability of the country. High interest rates can slow the growth of the economy and inevitably reduce consumers' purchasing power, just as changes in exchange rates can influence demand. Clearly, these fluctuations can lead to translation and transaction gains/losses for subsidiaries, which may present a formidable risk. Mireles assigned a risk of "6" and a weight of 40%.

The risk of default, or credit risk, must also be considered. This is already a problem for banks operating in Mexico, as approximately 4.5% of the total loans are overdue. The December 31, 1993, figures for Banamex and Bancomer's past-due loans as a percentage of total loans amounted to 7.35% to 7.42%, respectively.[7] Clearly, Bancal must seriously contemplate this risk. Mireles rated it a "7" with a 40% weight.

Finally, Mireles tried to analyze the threat of unfavorable government economic policies. There was the previous government's nationalization of the banks to consider. Additionally, the policies of the administration during the period of nationalization, imposing unfavorable requirements such as interest-rate controls, selective portfolios, and required reserve ratios, because it was in the self-interests of the government, needed to be considered. More recently, the new administration was accused of a double cross when it went on record that it would not change its policy regarding a fixed dollar exchange rate only to later float the peso, shocking both investors and the citizens of Mexico.

In addition, Mexico was tightening the rules for the financial sector, after the recent reports of alleged fraud at two Mexican banks. Nevertheless, under NAFTA, the Mexican government may be more likely to implement favorable policies as they seek to uphold the free trade agreement. In fact, there was even speculation that the Mexican government might consider easing market share restrictions, permitting U.S. banks to increase their presence in Mexico, given Mexico's economic woes resulting from the devaluation of the peso. Based on her findings, Mireles rated this a "4" with a weight of 20%.

After rating and weighing the various political and financial variables, Mireles assigned an overall weight of 60% to the political risk and 40% to the financial risk. Her results, displayed in the exhibit, show a political risk of 5.2, a financial risk of 6.0, and an overall country risk rating of 5.5, indicating moderate risk.

---

[7]The industry average for past-due loans for the first nine months of 1993 was 9%.

THE RETURN HOME

As the plane landed at LAX, Sandra Mireles began to think of the work that awaited her. Within the next week she would have to seriously analyze the collective data that she gathered on the banking industry, NAFTA, Grupo Turismo, and Mexico. She had to look at all aspects of Cruz's proposed idea of opening a subsidiary in Mexico. In addition, Mireles knew that the presentation she would make to Cruz would be a true test of whether she was the right person to replace her predecessor.

A SECOND OPINION

While Mireles was returning from her stay in Guadalajara, Steve Brown was making preparations for his departure to Mexico. Brown, Vice-President of Finance for Bancal, was asked to assess the risk of entering into Mexico. Cruz believed that it was essential to have a finance as well as a marketing person make independent analyses.

Brown, a native of Massachusetts and a graduate of Boston College, was beginning his twentieth year with Bancal. A member of the finance department since he started with the company, Brown knew little about the Mexican culture. He was chosen for the assignment based on his seniority and his strong financial background.

BROWN'S VISIT WITH OFFICIALS IN GUADALAJARA

Prior to his departure, Brown was quickly briefed by Mireles on the banking industry in Mexico, NAFTA, and Grupo Turismo, so as to prepare Brown for his analysis. Mireles also gave Brown a list of the political and financial risk factors that she evaluated, though she withheld her numbers.

Relying on the translation of an interpreter, Brown met with government officials the morning of his first day in Guadalajara to discuss the political ramifications of NAFTA, the financial policies of the new administration, in light of the recent devaluation of the Mexican peso, and to try to develop an idea of the government's sentiments regarding the entrance of foreign firms into Guadalajara. Also, he met with the Director of Finance for Grupo Turismo, Ricardo Silva, who discussed with Brown the desire of Grupo Turismo to start a working relationship with Bancal.

BROWN'S POLITICAL RISK ANALYSIS

Brown's findings are summarized in the country risk analysis provided in Exhibit 6. Using the same factors that Mireles evaluated, Brown began with his assessment of the political risk factors. Beginning with political tensions, he noted, much like his colleague Mireles, that political upheaval had been on the rise in Mexico. Assassinations and protests were not uncommon and these

Exhibit 6	Country Risk Analysis for Mexico—Steve Brown*		
	Rating assigned by co to factor (Range is 1-10)	Wt assigned by co to factor based on importance	Wtd Value Factor
Political Risk Factors			
Political Tensions	10	35%	3.5
Turmoil	9	35%	3.2
Attitude of Host Gov't	7	30%	2.1
		100%	**8.8=political risk**
Financial Risk Factors			
Inflation	10	40%	4.0
Credit Risk	10	30%	3.0
Unfavorable Gov't Policies	9	30%	2.7
		100%	**9.7=political risk**
	Rating as Determined Above	Wt assigned by co to each risk category	Weighted Rating
Category			
Political Risk	8.8	30%	2.6
Financial Risk	9.7	70%	6.8
		100%	**9.4=overall country risk rating**

*Format adopted with permission from Jeff Madura, Florida Atlantic University. See: J. Madura, *International Financial Management* (St. Paul: West Publishing Company, 1992), p. 577.

events tend to have a direct impact on businesses operating in Mexico. With this in mind, he assigned a risk of "10" and a weight of 35%.

The second factor—turmoil—was assessed by Brown and given a rating of "9" and a weight of 35%. He believed that the Chiapas incident was still a real threat that the Mexican government had to contend with, and that such events could shake investors' confidence. In addition, he was concerned with the role of drug traffickers, especially in light of the March 24, 1993, assassination of Cardinal Juan Jesus Posadas Ocampo outside of the Guadalajara airport. Posadas' death was said to have been the result of the outspoken position that he took in response to the drug problem in Mexico. According to officials, Joaquin Guzman and Hector Luis Palmer Salazar, known for their ties to drug cartels, were arrested in connection to the cardinal's death.

Finally, Brown analyzed the attitude of the host government. He noted that the government officials with whom he met appeared to be extremely supportive of Bancal. They tried to assure Brown that everything would go well for the bank, as long as the market share restrictions were not violated. Nevertheless, Brown knew that the Mexican banks were already feeling the pressure from

U.S. banks since the passage of the North American Free Trade Agreement and might eventually appeal to the government for assistance. Keeping this in mind, Brown assigned a risk of "7" and a weight of 30%.

FINANCIAL RISK ANALYSIS

Turning to the financial risk factors, Brown evaluated the risk of the inflation, exchange, and interest rates. He did so in light of the substantial devaluation of the peso. That is, he noted the effect of the fallen peso on the banking industry in Mexico. Specifically, the central bank might have to increase the amount of money in circulation, which could contribute to inflationary problems for the country. Also, banks that made dollar-denominated loans would have to account for a possible increase in bad debt expense, as the devalued peso would make it increasingly difficult for banks' customers to repay their loans.

Interest rates are likely to remain high if U.S. investors are skeptical, and move their investments out of Mexico. Additionally, rates are likely to increase further, as those investors who stay in the Mexican market and bear the risk will demand such an increase in the returns on their investments. Currently, consumer interest rates are quoted at 30%, and after the devaluation this figure is likely to increase as prices and wages rise. Thus, interest rates might continue to increase, hindering economic growth. Based on his findings, Brown rated the risk of the inflation, exchange, and interest rates a "10" and gave it a weight of 40%.

When evaluating the credit risk, Brown looked at the past-due loan figures for the banking industry, as Mireles had done in her analysis. Brown also took into account the fact that, given the current financial woes that plague Mexico, the risk of default is likely to increase. Brown assigned a risk of "10" and a weight of 30%.

Finally, Brown evaluated the risk of unfavorable government policies. Like Mireles, he noted the restrictions imposed by the government when the banks were nationalized, which were clearly unfavorable for banks operating in Mexico. Brown was also concerned by the government's reversal of the "peso policy," which would have an impact on all businesses operating in Mexico. Thus, Brown assigned a rating of "9" and a 30% weight. As Exhibit 6 illustrates, the overall political risk is "8.8" while the financial risk is "9.7." Brown weighted the political risk factor 30% and assigned the financial risk a weight of 70%. Brown's overall country risk rating is 9.4.

CRUZ PREPARES FOR THE RESULTS

While his subordinates were making their analyses in Guadalajara, Cruz gave serious thought to his plan to enter into Mexico. Cruz was determined to take a long-range view. His belief was that, given the current economic situation in Mexico, few ventures would appear to be attractive in the short run. Nevertheless, as the country recovered, foreign investment would be critical.

Cruz was particularly intrigued by the opportunity to obtain Grupo Turismo as its first customer. Ramirez and Cruz had a longstanding relationship. Over the years, Luis watched his friend's son grow up to be a successful businessman. Now, thirty years later, they had an opportunity to work together for the mutual benefit of Bancal and Grupo Turismo. Above all, Cruz knew that he could trust Ramirez, and the camaraderie that existed between the two was essential to the success of any deal that Bancal would make in Mexico.

The initial thought was to open one branch in Guadalajara, with an initial outlay of $100 million. Further expansion would be feasible only based upon the success of the first Bancal office. Additionally, it was anticipated that Bancal would be able to attract other large accounts, once word was out that Grupo Turismo was working with Bancal. This was the proposition that Cruz was thinking of presenting to the Board of Directors, but only after hearing from the direct reports of Mireles and Brown.

MIRELES AND BROWN PRESENT THEIR FINDINGS

Three weeks later, the day had finally come. Fraught with anxiety yet appearing to be in control, Mireles entered into the President's office and proceeded to submit her final recommendation. . . . Brown was scheduled to give his opinion that afternoon.

The Mejia Family Tire Company

Mark J. Kroll, University of Texas at Tyler

Leslie A. Toombs, University of Texas at Tyler

Jennifer Videtto, University of Texas at Tyler

I n the spring of 1995, Antonio and Mercedes Mejia were deep into one of their late-night discussions of the future of their family and their business. As their business was not only the family's only source of income, but absorbed both their lives and the lives of their children, in many ways their business's future was their family's future. The business had been growing and they so much wanted to expand it in order to provide a career for their children, but Mexico's economy was so unpredictable and there was the endless talk of more "devaluations."

HISTORY

In 1985 Antonio Mejia and his wife, Mercedes Lopez de Mejia, who lived in a suburb of Guadalajara, Mexico, got a call from a friend looking for some tire rim liners. His friend, who was in the trucking business, was looking for a favorable price and was not having any luck with his normal suppliers. Although Antonio had virtually no experience with truck tires, he decided to make some calls. He was able to find a supplier who quoted a price which allowed him to sell his friend the liners he needed at a fairly healthy profit. The Mejias decided to explore the opportunities in tires and related products a little more as a result of their experience.

Antonio Mejia, forty-seven years old, had previously worked as a professional basketball player, a basketball coach, a drawing professor, and an agronomy engineer. His wife, Mercedes Lopez, had been a telephone operator with

Telefonos de Mexico before they were married. They both readily admit that before going into the business they knew absolutely nothing about tires or related products. In addition, the Mexican economy was in bad shape, with rapidly rising prices and interest rates. However, the time they chose to begin their business was to a certain extent very fortuitous as well. The Mexican market was being opened up to foreign manufacturers who were looking for dealers in this new market. New brands from the U.S., Japan, and Korea entered the market. This put tremendous pressure on Mexico's domestic tire and rubber products producers. Many Mexican manufacturers of tires, tubes, and liners went bankrupt in the face of the new competition. The tire and related products industry was decidedly in turmoil when the Mejias entered it. There was uncertainty and volatility, but there were also opportunities.

The Mejias went to work building relationships with suppliers, and in time had relationships with a number of domestic and imported labels. They established relationships with such firms as Goodyear and Euzkady-Goodrich in tires, Robbins and Tornell in tubes, and Hulepack in tire liners. Initially the Mejias' business consisted of simply soliciting orders from trucking firms such as Southern Jalisco and Omnibus de Oriente, going to the wholesalers' or manufacturers' warehouses to pick up the products ordered, and delivering them to the customer. Such an arrangement was obviously advantageous due to the very low capital requirements needed to operate the business. However, over time it became necessary to carry inventory in order to respond more quickly to customer needs, which necessitated a warehouse and some office space. In order to accommodate the growing business, an office was located in the Mejias' house and a small warehouse was built on the lot.

The Mejias' business is located in Huentitan el Bajo, a suburb of Guadalajara, Jalisco, Mexico, Mexico's second largest city with a population of approximately 6 million people. The suburban community of Huentitan el Bajo is located on the rim of a canyon known in the area as Huentitan's Barranco. This keeps the community from expanding, but also makes it a popular location for homes of the wealthy seeking a great view and for weekend homes. It is also home to some very poor residents. As a result, the community is a mixture of both quite poor families with few resources and the very wealthy, which is not an unusual situation in Mexico. The Mejias' company is located at their residence. It has a large back yard which is used to store merchandise, a small warehouse, and an office in the house in which all of the company's functions are performed. Four high walls surround the house so no one can see it. A small sign hangs at the main entrance, but it is only 3 feet by 2.5 feet, so it is not easy to see. In fact, the only reason the sign is there is because it is required by Mexican law. Automobile traffic is light in the neighborhood, so the sign is rarely seen anyway; in effect, the only people who know there is a tire store in the area are the neighbors.

THE CURRENT SITUATION

The business has for the most part focused its attention in the area of larger sizes of tires and related products (sizes from 16 to 22 inches) for trucks and buses. As mentioned earlier, the business essentially sells three types of products: tires, tubes to be installed in tires, and tire liners, which are flat rubber

Exhibit 1

Summary of Mexico's Financial Situation

Year	Pesos Per Dollar	Inflation Rate (%)	Prime Lending Rate (%)
Jan. 1990	2682	26.65	37.06
Jan. 1991	2947	22.66	22.55
Jan. 1992	3076	15.51	18.77
Jan. 1993	3.12*	9.75	18.56
Jan. 1994	3.10	6.97	15.50
Jul. 1994	3.39	7.05	
Jan. 1995	5.40	35.00	45.12
Mar. 1995	6.03	26.70	†

*Mexico issued a new currency, which resulted in the conversion of 1,000 pesos into 1 "new peso."

†During 1995, owing to the currency crisis, interest rates became very volatile—so much so that lending virtually stopped. The loans that were made sometimes had interest rates in excess of 100%.

rings which are mounted on a truck tire rim prior to tube and tire installation. The purpose of the liner is to prevent contact and friction between the wheel rim and the tube. Excessive friction can lead to high temperatures inside the tire, an explosion of the tube, and a flat tire. The Mejias are the Guadalajara regional distributor for Linermex tire liners. This is the only exclusive distributorship they presently have. Over the past few years the Mejias have built their dealer relations and added brands. Today they represent the following brands by product category (the country of origin is in parentheses):

Tires: Goodyear (U.S.), Firestone (U.S./Japan), Euzkady-Goodrich (Mexico), Yokahama (Japan), Tornel (Mexico), Toyota (Japan), Michelin (France)

Tubes: Goodyear (U.S.), Hulepack (Mexico), various Korean brands distributed by Vermar Industries

Tire Liners: Tire-Linermex (Mexico), Hulepack (Mexico)

Car tires can range from N$120 to N$360 ("N$" indicates new Mexican pesos) at retail. However, large truck tires range between N$1,200 and N$1,800. Tubes retail for about N$60, while liners go for about N$15. Given that many of these products are imported from the U.S., and given the dramatic decline in the value of the peso versus the dollar (see Exhibit 1), it is expected these prices will rise significantly in the near term.

In some instances the Mejias purchase directly from the manufacturers, as in the case of tire liners, but most of their purchases are through wholesalers representing various imported and domestic brands. A list of their major suppliers can be found in Exhibit 2. This list is not exhaustive, but represents the bulk of their purchases.

■ Inventory Management

While the Mejias maintain some minimal levels of inventory, much of their sales are still done by first receiving an order from the customer and then picking up the merchandise from the manufacturer's or wholesaler's warehouse. It

Exhibit 2	**Major Suppliers**

Suppliers	*Brands*
Tires:	Tires:
Super Ruedas del Estado de Mexico	Euzkady-Goodrich
Centro Llantero Reyna	Firestone
Servicentro de la Zona Occidente	Goodyear
Implementos de la Llanta	Michelin
Servicio a las llantas Piedad	Tornel
Importadora de articulos Bedak	Toyota
Renovadora de articulos BAMM	Yokahama
Tubes:	Tubes:
Industrias del Vermar	Goodyear
Comercializadora Galgos	Hulepack
Tire Liners:	Tire Liners:
Hulepack	Hulepack
Tire-Linermex	Tire-Linermex

is crucial that inventory be kept as low as possible, as working capital is very expensive. Mexican interest rates are quite high in contrast with those in the U.S., with the current prime rate set at 50%. The Mejias keep most of the popular car tire sizes in stock and can fill orders out of inventory. However, truck tire orders usually come in large numbers (between 10 and 30 tires). Given the cost of carrying such quantities of expensive truck tires in inventory, the Mejias generally cannot fill the complete order, and usually ask the customer to accept a portion of the order immediately and receive the rest in a couple of days. These terms are generally acceptable to their customers. The Mejias' estimates of their sales volume percentages by customer category are presented in Exhibits 3, 4, and 5.

Even with a concerted effort to keep inventories lean, the Mejias have seen their asset base, which typically is 80 percent inventory, grow steadily over the years. In 1988 the business ended the year with assets of N$68,243, of which they estimate N$40,000 was in inventories. In August of 1994 the Mejias' accountant estimated assets totaling N$492,517, with inventories representing N$404,000 of that number. After adjusting assets for inflation, the August 1994 assets represent a 275% increase over the end of year 1988 assets. Exhibit 6 provides estimates of closing year total asset and inventory figures for each year the business has existed.

■ Operations and Financial Management

The Mejias do not regularly generate financial statements, and oftentimes their accountant simply "estimates" their financial position and performance. The accountant does not regularly produce a balance sheet and income statement. As a consequence, exact business performance is not possible to measure. They do know at the end of the month what their total sales were, and they know

Exhibit 3   **Mejias' Tire Sales by Category**

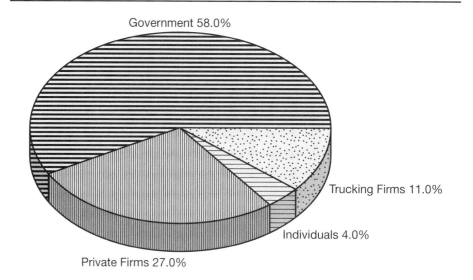

Government 58.0%

Trucking Firms 11.0%

Individuals 4.0%

Private Firms 27.0%

Exhibit 4   **Mejias' Tube Sales by Category**

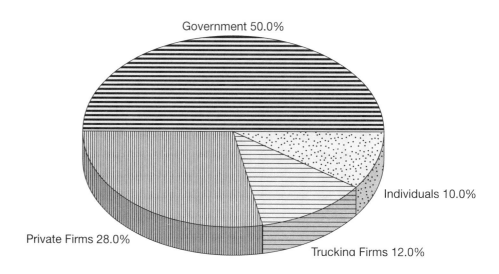

Government 50.0%

Individuals 10.0%

Private Firms 28.0%

Trucking Firms 12.0%

Exhibit 5

Mejias' Tire Liner Sales by Category

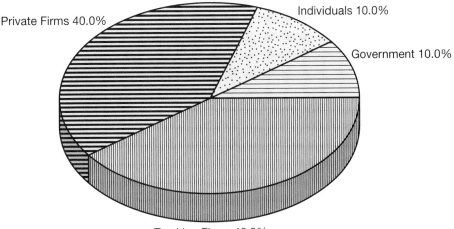

Private Firms 40.0%

Individuals 10.0%

Government 10.0%

Trucking Firms 40.0%

Exhibit 6

Total Assets and Inventories for years 1988 to 1994

	Total Assets	*Inventories*
December 31, 1988	N$68,243	N$56,000
December 31, 1989	N$122,977	N$100,841
December 31, 1990	N$296,423	N$238,734
December 31, 1991	N$318,709	N$254,967
December 31, 1992	N$363,511	N$290,809
December 31, 1993	N$406,426	N$325,141
August 31, 1994	N$492,517	N$404,014

what they paid in cost of goods sold. However, the family's living expenses and the business's operating expenses are often commingled. This kind of imprecision in financial reporting is common among Mexican sole proprietorships and partnerships. As the Mejias have no debt of any kind, they are not required by lenders to provide financial statements. However they are required to pay taxes. In Mexico small companies are taxed at approximately 20% on income and all companies are required to pay a 2% tax on their assets. The Mejias estimate that before any salaries or wages are paid to any members of the family, with no depreciation or rent being charged against the business for their building, and with no depreciation being charged for either of the business's two vehicles, the business earns a return of about 15 percent on sales. The sales for the most current month by category are presented in Exhibit 7.

Since this is a family-owned business, the family members perform much of the work involved in running the business. Various family members perform such responsibilities as selling, delivering the merchandise, collecting on

Exhibit 7	August Sales (orders)	

Customers:

Government Departments		
Sistecozome	13 sales = N$4,430
SIAPA	5 sales = N$9,500
SSBS	1 sale = N$101,512
Individuals	5 sales = N$7,927
Private Companies	
Tuberias Ind.	2 sales = N$2,134
Albarran	8 sales = N$9,880
Aga	5 sales = N$12,890
Others	2 sales = N$30,280
Trucking Business	
Centro Colonias	4 sales = N$2,899
Fletes Tapatios	1 sale = N$12,291

Total Sales for the Month = N$193,743

accounts, and acting as storekeeper. The distribution of responsibilities is generally as follows.

Antonio Mejia Medina calls on and meets new customers or does some prospecting for new customers by phone and fax. He plans and organizes new projects such as finding new foreign suppliers. He works with current suppliers, placing orders, trying to negotiate better prices, and paying accounts payable. He and his wife make decisions concerning changes in products and prices. He and his wife also decide what levels of inventory to maintain in anticipation of future sales. The Mejias rely primarily on judgment and intuition to prepare their sales forecasts. In an effort to facilitate inventory decisions, they often make calls to key customers inquiring about anticipated purchases. Finally, when the store is short-handed he helps with loading and unloading merchandise and takes customers phone or fax orders.

Mercedes Lopez de Mejia performs many of the same functions her husband does. As mentioned above, they are both involved in decisions concerning pricing and products offered. They are also both part of the decision-making process concerning inventory levels and judgmental sales forecasting. Like her husband, she also works with customers, trying to find new ones or filling orders for existing customers. She also works to negotiate better prices from suppliers, and is constantly phoning alternative sources to find a better deal.

Antonio Mejia Lopez, Jr., the Mejias' oldest son, is 19 years old. He is a full-time college student majoring in international marketing. When not attending college, he too gives price quotes to customers, takes orders, helps load, unload, and deliver merchandise. He also helps with office work, including paying invoices and light typing.

Saul Mejia Lopez, 18, and Juan Paulo Mejia Lopez, 16, are the Mejias' two teenage sons. They too help out around the store, picking up and delivering merchandise and loading and unloading inventory.

Mercedes Mejia, 12, is the Mejias' only daughter and their youngest child. Her responsibilities primarily involve helping her mother in the office and doing some typing, faxing, and other clerical work. The Mejia family members perform much of the pick-up and delivery of merchandise, and work in the warehouse. One employee they have recently hired has relieved the Mejias of some of the order taking, paperwork processing, and warehousing, thus freeing them to develop their customer base. They have also recently hired a salesperson to help build sales volume. He receives a commission of approximately 5% on the sales he makes, but no salary or expenses. At present, the salesperson covers only the Guadalajara area. They also hired an outside accountant to keep the firm's books. This was done so that balance sheets could be prepared to facilitate the computation of the required tax payments.

The business essentially operates via phone and fax machine. However, the fax is the only modern technology which is employed in the operations of the business. The company owns a computer and a printer, but they are both stored in the warehouse and are not being used. Antonio Mejia Medina is reluctant to use "new technology" and believes that invoices typed on a typewriter and sales recorded by hand are more accurate methods of billing and record keeping. His son, Antonio Mejia, Jr., is trying to convince him to use the computer and printer as a means to increase operational efficiency.

MISSION AND GOALS

In terms of a mission for the business, the Mejias have never really given it much thought. When the business began with only N$1,000 in capital, the emphasis was on lining up as many sales as possible and moving the products from supplier to customer as quickly as possible in order to minimize inventory carrying costs and maximize cash flows. Because working capital was virtually nonexistent, it was critical that accounts receivable be kept as low as possible as well. However, despite the Mejias' best efforts, oftentimes they could not meet their customers' needs due to inadequate inventories and their customers' unwillingness to wait for what they needed. Additionally, they often found themselves in the trap of having to meet their suppliers' payment schedules without having received payment from their customers. Before 1994 customers were extended credit ("net 30"). However, after the major peso devaluation in 1994, no more credit was extended because it was not financially feasible to do so. Within the family there is a keen understanding of the fact that each sale represents a direct benefit to every member of the family. They also have a well-developed awareness that the only way to be successful is to satisfy the customer's needs as completely as possible at a competitive price.

In terms of goals for the business, there are few if any formal objectives which have been articulated, other than the obvious need to increase sales. One clear goal which has emerged is the definition of a list of customers who will receive credit when the family decides to sell on a credit basis again. Early on the Mejias were concerned with generating sales and were not quite so concerned with their customers' credit history. More recently, however, due to the money tied up in accounts receivable, a few bad debt write-offs, and the peso

devaluation, they have ceased to extend credit. They are considering implementing a new credit policy where new customers are required to pay cash for
their first two purchases with the company. Thereafter the customers could
apply for credit terms of "net 15." Additionally, as the business has become
more heavily involved with large commercial and government accounts, the
Mejias have found it necessary to build their inventory levels in order to meet
these customers' needs in a timely way. Given the very high interest rates in
Mexico, this is a heavy burden for the family. Yet they were able to build their
inventory without incurring any debt.

RESPONDING TO THE MARKET OPPORTUNITIES

In terms of customers presently served, the Mejias attempt to cover the market,
from individual passenger car tire buyers to trucking companies and government departments with large truck fleets. Given their small size, the Mejias
account for a minuscule portion of the total tire and related products market in
the Guadalajara market. While they are not captive suppliers of any one customer or group of customers, they would not be difficult to replace as a supplier and government sales are an important market for them. The Mejias
estimate there are as many as 50 direct competitors in the greater metropolitan
area which represents their market. The Mejias do not have a service facility,
and therefore do not mount or service tires. This puts them at something of a
competitive disadvantage to those suppliers who offer a full complement of
services in the passenger car tire market. However, the Mejias have been able to
overcome this disadvantage to a certain extent by offering lower prices. In
addition, the retail automobile tire market is not a segment the Mejias are pursuing due to the capital requirements needed to build a facility and the relatively keen competition in the passenger car segment. As a result, car tires
account for less than 10% of the Mejias' total sales, while government and commercial sales account for the vast majority of sales.

In keeping with the Mejias' conservative approach to doing business, they
have done no advertising in the past, and plan none for the future. Other than
the small sign out front of the building, the only promotional materials are business cards the family passes out to potential customers. Sales growth has come
either through direct contacts made by the Mejias with potential new customers,
or through word-of-mouth from existing customers. As another reflection of
the Mejias' conservatism, all of the firm's growth has been financed internally.

Because tire, tube, and liner distribution is a relatively easy industry to
enter, competition is very intense. As most of the Mejias' competitors have
access to either the same brands they do, or very close substitutes, the Mejias
feel as though they must compete on a price basis. The Mejias achieve their
low-cost–low-price strategy by developing very strong relationships with suppliers who like doing business with them. While working hard to develop personal friendships has helped get good prices from suppliers, so has a policy of
paying at time of delivery for all merchandise. This cash-and-carry style has
endeared the Mejias to their major suppliers. Unfortunately, wholesalers will
also make sales directly to large commercial accounts willing to place large
orders. Such arrangements obviously undercut retail dealers, making them
unable to compete with distributors' prices.

This aggressive pricing strategy could be duplicated should the competition work to pursue a low-cost strategy. In addition, the Mejias really do not feel comfortable with their ability to develop a marketing plan or decide on an appropriate product mix. Thus far they have essentially reacted to the market by trying to respond to the individual customer inquiries they have received. The family anticipates that Antonio, Jr., will provide much needed marketing expertise when he completes his international marketing degree. Thus the development of a proactive marketing plan is one of their priorities.

In response to the competitive pressures, the Mejias have discovered it is very beneficial to have a few friends employed in either their major commercial or government accounts. The cultivation of these relationships is one of the primary marketing thrusts of the Mejias. These social relationships with corporate and government officials allow the Mejias to receive vital information concerning plans for major purchases and competitors' bids. This is especially true when large orders are up for grabs, as bidding for these orders is extremely competitive, and rivals tend to cut their margins to the bone. Sometimes it is necessary to provide kickbacks or gratuities in order to cement a relationship, especially with major buyers. Additionally, it has proven helpful to have friends inside their suppliers' organizations, as they can supply the Mejias with information concerning product availability and pricing. As Mr. Mejia says, "having a friend in the right place in a company can make a lot of difference." This practice is not unique to the Mejia family. Rather it is the customary, prevalent way of conducting business in Mexico.

THE SITUATION IN MEXICO

■ Before and After Carlos Salinas

On December 20, 1994, the Mexican government of Ernesto Zedillo did what it said it would never do—it allowed the Mexican peso to float against the U.S. dollar. This sent the peso into a free fall against the dollar and seriously undermined the confidence investors had in Mexico. Due to the dramatic peso decline, prices in Mexico shot up, along with interest rates (refer back to Exhibit 1). The crisis was a long time in its development, and will require a painful period of adjustment.

Both the economy and society of Mexico have been undergoing a significant transition in the past 8 to 10 years. Since the election in 1988 of President Carlos Salinas de Gortari, the country has embarked upon a major political and economic restructuring. This restructuring has fundamentally changed (or threatens to change) the way Mexican society functions, which had previously been the same since the end of the last revolution in 1920, which brought to power the Institutional Revolutionary Party (or the PRI, as it is known). The PRI has for the most part dominated Mexican political and economic processes since the 1920s. This led to a closed economy and a paternalistic, often corrupt government which controlled much of the economy. This control was often achieved through direct government ownership of many key industries (e.g., oil, railroads, steel, telecommunications, and banking) or very protective trade regulations.

Because of state ownership and protectionism, much of Mexican industry became inefficient and noncompetitive. This arrangement also led to corruption, and the distribution of wealth and economic opportunity became concentrated, with a large portion of the population deprived of educational and economic opportunities. The economic hardships have been exacerbated by Mexico's historically high birth rate, which has led to large numbers of young people without adequate education or employment prospects. Until the last few years, Mexico's economy had been tortured with rampant inflation. It was not uncommon for the annual inflation rate to top 100 percent. This led to extraordinarily high interest rates and a rapidly devaluing peso. One of the major accomplishments of the Salinas administration was the ratcheting down of inflation to single digits annually. This allowed interest rates to come down and stabilized the value of the peso versus the dollar for at least a while. However, the peso was kept artificially high in relation to the dollar in order to attract foreign capital. This led to significant trade deficits and a serious drawing down of Mexico's foreign reserves as the Central Bank of Mexico tried to defend the peso.

President Salinas, who was the 1988 PRI candidate for president, committed the country to fundamental political and economic reforms, though some would contend they were still not fundamental enough. He privatized most of the industries which had previously come under state control, though the government continues to control the oil industry. He liberalized trade laws and exposed numerous Mexican industries to foreign competition for the first time in many decades. He negotiated the North American Free Trade Agreement (NAFTA) with Canada and the U.S., which will dramatically change the economic structure on the North American continent. Specifically, it will allow firms such as the Mejias' to import duty free directly from foreign suppliers, leading to more intense competition. This intense competition may lead to a shrinking of the Mexican rubber industry due to direct competition with imported rubber products from the rest of North America. Salinas also worked to prosecute some of the most serious cases of government, labor union, and business corruption, though many would argue he did not go nearly far enough. Finally, he attempted to create the impression that elections in Mexico are fair, and that if the PRI loses, it will relinquish power in either national or local offices. In fact, during President Salinas' tenure he ordered some gubernatorial elections invalidated, and the opposing party candidates certified as the winners.

The 1994 election campaign was a very stormy one in which the original PRI candidate, Donaldo Colosio, was assassinated. His replacement as the PRI candidate, Ernesto Zedillo, was elected. He has committed his administration to greater economic growth, greater educational opportunities, and cleaner government. This has proven threatening to those who have been in power for decades or have benefited from the PRI's long reign. In recent years another political party, the National Action Party (known as PAN), has begun to emerge as a legitimate force in Mexican politics. PAN's orientation is one of more political conservatism (i.e., less government involvement in society and the economy) than the PRI and has shown itself to be fairly popular in northern and western Mexico, where it has won some governorships. In fact it is anticipated that the PAN candidate will win the governorship of Jalisco (the state in which Guadalajara is located) in the next election.

The opening up of Mexican markets to foreign competitors, the aggressive effort to bring inflation under control, the privatization of vast sectors of the

Mexican economy, along with significant deregulation of the economy has made for a great deal of turmoil in Mexico. While many have suffered due to the transition, many opportunities for creative entrepreneurs have also been created. Additionally, given the bold economic reform policies of President Salinas and the passage of NAFTA, a great deal of foreign capital has been attracted to Mexico. In fact, just prior to President Zedillo taking office, expectations were for materially higher levels of economic growth in the coming years.

■ Ernesto Zedillo Takes Over

Unfortunately, the optimism which greeted the new president was short-lived, as the peso came under intense pressure in late 1994 due to Mexico's growing trade and current accounts deficits. Simply put, the Central Bank could no longer keep the peso at an artificially high exchange rate versus the U.S. dollar. On December 20, 1994, within weeks of President Zedillo's inauguration, the government announced it was lowering the targeted trading range for the peso against the dollar. In effect, the Mexican government was saying the peso could no longer be supported at the previous exchange rate. This sent currency markets into a panic, causing massive selling of pesos for dollars. The Central Bank of Mexico, as a result of the tremendous pressure on the peso, could not even support the new lower value of the peso, and on the second day of the crisis was forced to float the currency. This action in effect allowed the currency markets to establish the value of the peso in relation to the dollar.

By early January 1995, the peso had lost almost 40 percent of its value in relation to the dollar. This meant foreign investors were taking huge losses on their investments in Mexican bonds and other financial securities, as the values of such securities in dollars fell with the peso. As a result, these investors also panicked, and began dumping stocks and bonds. This forced interest rates in Mexico to skyrocket. In January 1995, consumer loans in Mexico were quoted at interest rates in excess of 50 percent. At the time, the Mexican Stock Market was collapsing. For a review of the history of the value of the peso versus the U.S. dollar, inflation rates, and prime lending rates, refer back to Exhibit 1.

On January 8, 1995, in an effort to help, the U.S. Federal Reserve began buying pesos for dollars. This action caused the peso to stabilize, and bought the Mexican government time to develop an economic plan with the help of the U.S. and World Bank. In the same week, President Clinton pledged U.S. help in stabilizing the peso and restoring confidence in Mexican markets. While these actions caused a short-term strengthening of the peso and Mexican financial markets, the question remains whether investor confidence in the Mexican economy is so damaged as to force interest rates to stay very high, resulting in economic stagnation and even higher unemployment.

The potentially good news for the Mexican economy is that Mexican-made goods will be much cheaper in relation to foreign-made goods. This should lead to Mexican producers, including Mexican rubber products producers, taking market share away from foreign suppliers. It should also make Mexican-made products more attractive to foreign buyers. If this occurs, it would solve the problem which caused the crisis in the first place—Mexico's foreign trade imbalance. It may also lead to a resurgence in the Mexican rubber industry as domestically produced products fall in price versus foreign rubber products.

THE MEJIAS' FUTURE: ALTERNATIVES FOR GROWTH

While the past few years have been nothing if not challenging for the family, Mexico's future appears to be a mixed bag. The political and economic outlook seems fairly positive, and the economy could start growing again if the country can put the latest crisis behind it. The Mejias' sons would like to join the business and make a career of it after college. In order to provide the family with a comfortable living, Antonio Mejia Medina and his wife, Mercedes, know they will have to grow the business. Their present location represents a handicap because it is located in a residential area on the west side of Guadalajara rather than in a major commercial center, and they know there are other steps which need to be taken to achieve the sales volumes and profit levels which will allow the family the economic security they hope for. In order to achieve their ambitions, several issues must be addressed.

Given that their sons are presently in school, if the Mejias are to expand sales of their present operations in the near future they will have to hire more employees to generate and service sales. However, Mr. Mejia is concerned about the consequences of such a move. If he pays his new employees on commission he is fearful they will either generate sales which are not very profitable or make sales to customers who are not very creditworthy. He has been stung in the past with a few bad credit risks and is quite fearful of more such experiences should he put new employees on commission. He is equally concerned commissioned employees may promise terms which tie up a lot of working capital in order to make a sale. Even worse, Mr. Mejia has heard of sales reps collecting on accounts and then quitting. On the other hand, he is not eager to bring in new help on an hourly rate. He is concerned they will not generate enough new profitable business to justify their positions.

The family is examining the pros and cons of several alternatives which they could pursue to help achieve their family goal of economic security. The Mejias see an opportunity in becoming a supplier of the many "llanteras" or small neighborhood tire repair and sales shops scattered throughout the community. There are literally hundreds of these small neighborhood shops in Guadalajara. They generally sell used tires, new tubes, and tire liners. While the volumes are quite small in these little shops, cumulatively they represent a significant volume in terms of tubes and liners, but they rarely sell new tires. The Mejias have on occasion made sales to llanteras, and these sales have been profitable. However, because most such sales are in very small volumes of inexpensive items such as tubes and liners, Mr. Mejia has not been eager to pursue this market due to the time invested versus the volume generated.

There are several alternatives which would allow the Mejias to expand beyond their present niche. One alternative would be to add services such as tire mounting and balancing, brake repair, and alignment, which they presently do not provide. This would involve adding service bays to the present location, or opening an entirely new one in the area. The second alternative the Mejias are considering is opening a similar store in another location in order to capture a larger portion of the market in the Guadalajara area. Preferably the new location would be closer to some of their major customers in the center of the city.

Both of these alternatives would require major capital commitments on the part of the Mejias and interest rates are likely to be high for some time. This level of risk may be too high for some of the more conservative family members, especially Antonio. In addition, the alternative, involving adding services, would take the Mejias into a market with which they are not familiar. The second alternative would not represent a new field for the Mejias, but would require careful study in order to determine where they should locate a second store. Mr. Mejia assumes there are market research techniques which would help with this problem, but he personally has no such expertise. Additionally, he would again face the issue of how to compensate and manage his salespeople at the new location.

Given the intensity of the competition in the Guadalajara market, the Mejias have also thought about opening a business similar to their present store in another, smaller city in the region. Some very preliminary research suggests the markets may be fairly attractive in Colima (224 kilometers away), Tepic (227 kilometers away), Aguascalientes (254 kilometers away), or Guanajuato (301 kilometers away). All of these cities are fairly large, and the Mejias feel they could be very competitive in these markets. Exhibit 8 illustrates the locations of these cities as well as Guadalajara.

Finally, the Mejias know that they could achieve very significant growth if they could import products directly from the U.S. and free themselves of their dependence upon wholesalers in Mexico. This will be especially critical in light of the dramatic decline in the value of the peso, which will significantly increase the costs of U.S.-made goods. The Mejias estimate that even after they pay transportation costs, buying from distributors on the U.S. border will add 3 percentage points to gross profits because they will not have to pay the Mexican distributor markup.

Better yet, they could perhaps become a wholesale distributor for a tire brand. Unfortunately, most of the major tire brands already have exclusive wholesale distributors in the Guadalajara area. However, in order to import directly the business would have to be prepared to commit a great deal of working capital to inventory as manufacturers require that large orders be placed. Second, while the Mejias know importing represents a great opportunity, they do not have the slightest idea as to how to go about it.

The Mejias know they have acquired some valuable expertise in tire retailing, they know they have developed a fairly strong customer base, they know there are opportunities out there, and they know they need to grow, but how? Which way should they go in order to build their family business and secure their children's future as well as their own?

Exhibit 8   **Potential Markets**

City	Distance From Guadalajara	Population
Aguascalientes	254 km	872,000
Colima	224 km	459,000
Guanajuato	301 km	90,000
Tepic	227 km	872,000

Cemex: A Rock Solid Company

John Holm, University of Texas at Tyler

Mark Kroll, University of Texas at Tyler

Walter Greene, University of Texas Pan American

Internet site of interest: **www.cemex.com**

In late December 1994, the Mexican government decided to let the value of the peso float. As a result, its value in dollar terms immediately fell by more than fifty percent. This sudden and unexpected devaluation led to a financial crisis and a drastic downturn in the economy of a country that was also having political problems. The ensuing recession lasted through 1995 and the economy will probably not stabilize until 1996.

During these troubled financial times, it was expected that most Mexican businesses would suffer, as often happens during a recession. However, one company actually thrived and experienced continued success throughout 1995 and 1996—Cementos Mexicanos, or Cemex. Cemex is the fourth largest producer of cement in the world. It is based in Monterrey, Mexico, but owns cement plants in Spain, Venezuela, Panama, the Caribbean, and the United States. It is these international plants that are helping Cemex become a strong Mexican company that is not being pulled down by the Mexican recession. Currently, almost two-thirds of Cemex's sales come from its foreign operations (see Exhibit 1).

For the past ten years, the CEO of Cemex has been Lorenzo Zambrano, the grandson of the founder. He has embarked on an aggressive growth strategy which has made Cemex an industry leader with operations in 26 countries (Smith 1995). Zambrano has embarked on a policy of entering foreign markets "whose economic cycles are not linked to that of Mexico" (Cemex 1994).

What has made Cemex such a strong and growing company? Cement is pretty much the same no matter from where or from whom it is purchased, so cement manufacturers must differentiate themselves in ways other than the

Exhibit 1   **Cemex's 1995 Sales (breakdown by country)**

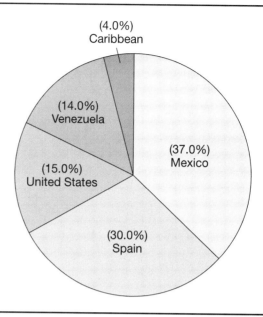

Source: Cemex 1995 Annual Report

physical product. For Cemex, one such way of achieving this kind of competitive advantage is through its foreign operations, which give it the ability to ship from low-cost manufacturing facilities to markets where demand is strong and prices are relatively high. The ability to produce and ship from and to various markets allows Cemex to compete with the other major cement producers in Europe such as Switzerland's Holderbank and France's Lafarge Coppée.

THE HISTORY OF CEMEX

Cemex began operations in 1906 with the founding of Cementos Hidalgo in Mexico. Growth and development were achieved by entering international markets and maintaining a product line that was primarily cement. In 1931 Cementos Hidalgo and Cementos Monterrey, a rival firm, merged, creating what is now known as Cementos Mexicanos, or Cemex. Throughout the 1960s and 1970s, Cemex built new plants and acquired other cement manufacturers in Mexico. It began exporting in the late 1970s, which helped keep the company going during the contraction of the Mexican economy at that time. Acquisitions continued to increase and more new plants were brought on line. In 1989, Cemex acquired Cementos Tolteca, with seven plants and an annual capacity of 6.8 million tons. A major period of international expansion began in 1992 when Cemex bought two large cement producers in Spain, Valenciana, and Sanson. Vencemos, a Venezuelan cement firm, and Cemento Bayano in Panama were acquired in 1994. In 1995, a plant in New Braunfels, Texas, was acquired and another plant in Mexico began operations. Total production capacity is now at 55.8 million metric tons per year.

INDUSTRY

Portland cement is the most common type of cement used in construction. It is made up of a combination of quarried limestone, clay (or shale or kaolin), and sand. These components are ground and mixed together by either a wet or dry process. The wet process involves mixing the limestone and clay with water to form slurry, which is then heated in a kiln to form a hard substance called clinker. In the dry process, which is more fuel-efficient, the original materials are not turned into slurry, but are directly heated to form clinker. After either process, the clinker is mixed with gypsum and ground into a fine powder called cement. When mixed with water, sand, and stone, the mixture forms concrete or mortar (*Lafarge 10K*).

The cement industry is growing rapidly, due in part to increased demand in the construction industries in both less-developed countries and industrialized nations. This has provided opportunities for many cement companies to establish plants in different regions around the world, resulting in global competition between the leading firms. Cement producers must now, more than ever, concentrate on their internal strengths to distinguish themselves from their competitors. Consumers no longer have to depend on one supplier but now can be selective and choose which cement producer can provide quality goods at the best prices.

Since cement is a commodity, the growth of the cement industry depends largely on construction and economic growth in the world economy. If someone wants to build factories or houses, they need cement. Third World and developing countries are where the most growth is projected and Cemex already has a head start.

From 1991 to 1994, cement consumption grew by more than nineteen percent ("Set" 1995). In 1994, global consumption of cement was 1.4 billion tons, or $80 billion, and was growing at an annual rate of 3.6% a year (Lenzler 1994). In Latin America and Asia, the consumption of cement is growing at twice the rate of the local economies (ibid). In many of these countries, European cement producers such as Switzerland's Holderbank and the United Kingdom's Blue Circle Industries have already entered the market. Even in the U.S., approximately two-thirds of cement production is from non-U.S. producers, including Cemex.

INTERNAL STRENGTHS

Cemex sees itself as having five core competencies which have allowed it to become successful: low-cost operations, use of technology, management competence, market positioning, and financial strength. Cemex prides itself on its low-cost operations. Its Spanish plants have some of the highest productivity levels of any cement plant worldwide. Technologically, Cemex is also very current, with a computer network system which "links all of Cemex's offices in Mexico and abroad via a network of satellite dishes, leased lines, and microwave communications" (Smith 1995). Zambrano uses this system to obtain information on any of Cemex's worldwide plants at any time and allows him to react quickly to rapidly changing market conditions.

For Cemex, going "global" was not just a matter of buying overseas plants and suppliers. They had to improve internally as well. Zambrano once said that Cemex had to "improve faster than any other cement company in the world" (*Chief Executive*). He wanted the employees of Cemex to learn new ways to be productive. To do this, he went straight to the employees and asked them what they thought the barriers to an improved Cemex were. He asked them to imagine what the Cemex of the future would be like. The employees were shown how their performance, even at the lowest level, influenced Cemex's overall profits. They identified effective and ineffective practices in the company. The top managers would set goals and let the employees, working in teams, figure out solutions. These teams have redesigned such areas in Cemex as maintenance management and inventory systems, as well as human resources. The result was an increase in productivity of 25 percent and they identified $40 million in savings that could go to the bottom line (ibid).

ACQUISITIONS

In the early 1990's, senior management at Cemex decided to develop an international presence and increase the company's share in markets that did not have economies linked to Mexico. This strategy would reduce dramatic fluctuations in cash flows since revenues would be obtained from countries with growing economies even when the Mexican economy is in recession. Prior to its global expansion, Cemex had made acquisitions primarily in the U.S. and Mexico. In the 1980's, it acquired Cementos Anahuac and Empresas Tolteca, its two largest competitors in Mexico, increasing its market share to approximately three times that of its closest competitor (Peagan 1995). Cemex's first major international acquisitions occurred in 1992 when it bought two Spanish cement plants, Valenciana and Sanson, for $1.84 billion. This acquisition surprised many investors who thought Cemex was just content to stay in Mexico where it had been performing quite well (Fink 1992). The stock price sank, as often happens to an acquiring company. However, the acquisition gave Cemex a foothold in Europe, where many of the world's other large cement producers are located. The two companies were combined to form Valenciana de Cementos, Spain's largest cement producer.

In April 1994, Cemex purchased a 60% stake in Vencemos, a Venezuelan cement producer, for $320 million. The results from this operation were consolidated in the 1995 financial statements. Also in 1994, Cemex purchased Cemento Bayano, a Panamanian plant giving Cemex a 50% market share in Panama. Cemex also bought its first production facility in the U.S., a cement plant in Texas purchased from one of Cemex's competitors, Lafarge Coppée of France. Previously, Cemex was involved in the U.S. market only through ready-mix concrete plants owned by its subsidiaries.

Cemex's international operations have contributed a great deal to the company's profits. Operating profits from the plant in Spain have risen from $37.7 million in 1993 to $95.5 million in 1994 and $200 million in 1995. Exports from the Venezuelan plant doubled to 2 million tons in 1995 and operating profits were $120 million. The operating margin at the Panamanian plant is 25 percent and all the revenues there are denominated in dollars.

MARKET POSITION

Cemex's policy on market positioning is to "achieve a leading market share in each geographical area in which [it] has production operations" (*Cemex 1994*). Currently, Cemex is the market leader in Mexico, Spain, Venezuela, and Panama and has a dominant position in the Caribbean. Cemex is a growing presence in the United States with one cement plant in Texas and several ready-mix concrete plants operated through Sunbelt Corporation, its subsidiary in California, Arizona, Texas, and Florida.

Cemex has achieved a leading share in most of the markets in which it operates through a continuous focus on the cement business and a selective yet ambitious international expansion plan. In Mexico, the company has capitalized on its market leadership position by becoming a low-cost vendor concentrating on productivity maximization and cost reduction. Long-term growth in the domestic markets for housing and public infrastructure in Mexico is expected to grow by an average of 7.0% per year for the next five years. In the Mexican cement market 78% of the cement is sold in bags to retailers for use in small-scale construction. Five percent of sales are to industrial customers and seventeen percent of sales are to ready-mix concrete producers. This is in contrast to the U.S., where 80% of cement sales are in the ready-mix concrete segment (Peagam 1995). Cemex has increased its ready-mix business in recent years with 167 ready-mix plants operating in 50 Mexican cities (ibid).

In the U.S., Cemex strengthened its position in the cement market by increasing productivity and reducing costs. Most of Cemex's plants in the U.S. are part of its subsidiary Sunbelt Corporation. Prior to 1994, Sunbelt was mainly involved in the ready-mix concrete business as well as the trading and distribution of building materials. However, it acquired a cement plant in Texas, making it Cemex's first cement plant in the U.S. The regional headquarters for U.S. operations were recently moved to Houston, Texas. Cemex is continuously evaluating its operations in America to keep them in line with the overall long-term objectives of the company.

Cemex has continued to keep up with local demand in the various countries in which it has made acquisitions and has some of the highest production levels per workers for cement plants in the world. In Spain, Cemex is the largest cement producer, with a 28% market share, and has 11 cement plants, 133 ready-mix concrete plants, and 7 marine terminals. Demand for domestic cement is increasing around 5.5%–7% per year. With its acquisition of Vencemos in 1995, Cemex was able to achieve a leading market share in Venezuela. Currently Cemex accounts for 50% of the domestic market share for cement and 30% of the ready-mix cement market. In Venezuela, it operates 4 cement plants, 4 marine terminals, and 22 ready-mix concrete plants. The company hopes to capitalize on the long-term growth prospects for the country's building industry. With its acquisition of Cemento Bayano, one of Panama's leading cement companies, in September of 1995, the company established a large presence in the Central American market. In Panama, Cemex is benefiting from being the country's lowest-cost cement producer. Finally, Cemex has been in the Caribbean since 1991, and recently has strengthened operations there through strategic alliances and joint ventures. These decisions have resulted in the company producing about 80% of the region's traded cement.

PRODUCTION CAPABILITIES

Cemex's production capability in Mexico was 27.8 million metric tons per year in 1995, an increase of 3.2 million metric tons over the previous year due in part to the building of its nineteenth plant in Mexico. In Spain, Cemex has a production capability of 11.8 million metric tons per year, which includes the joint capacity of the Valencia and Sanson plants. Cemex used to produce only concrete aggregates in the U.S., but with its recent acquisition of a cement plant in Texas, its U.S. production capabilities have increased from 2.9 million to 3.8 million combined tons of cement and aggregates per year. Production capabilities in Venezuela are at full capacity, producing 3.2 million tons per year. The Caribbean region is an area with high potential for growth. In 1994, Cemex acquired 100% ownership of a terminal in Freeport, Bahamas, with a 600,000 metric ton capacity, and 51% of another terminal in Nassau, Bahamas. Also in the same year, it acquired a 20% ownership in Trinidad Cement Limited, a company that has the capability of producing 500,000 metric tons of cement per year. Cemex's recent acquisition of Cemeto Bayano in Panama has increased Cemex's overall production capacity by 363,000 metric tons per year (*Cemex 1994*).

DISTRIBUTION

One of the reasons why Cemex is able to distribute more than 44 million metric tons per year worldwide is because it is able to produce at a lower cost. For example, Cemex can produce a metric ton for $25, well below the industry average of $35 per ton. Cemex's strategic locations in different countries and low production costs have enabled it to fully utilize its productive capacity and sell the excess production in other countries such as Guatemala, Brazil, Ecuador, and Peru. Currently Cemex has 19 cement plants, 167 ready-mix concrete plants, and 3 marine terminals in Mexico. Cemex operations in the U.S. include one cement plant, 16 marine terminals, and 65 ready-mix concrete plants. In the Caribbean, Cemex operates 2 cement plants and 9 marine terminals and it operates a commercial office in Hong Kong (*Cemex 1994*).

Five percent of the world's cement consumption is traded through imports. Cemex has an extensive trading system which accounted for 8 million tons of cement and clinker in 1995. It has trading relations with 54 countries. Cemex has direct operations in Mexico, the U.S., Venezuela, Hong Kong, Brazil, and several Caribbean nations. It has trading relations with Panama, Honduras, Costa Rica, El Salvador, Denmark, Greece, France, Holland, Ireland, Nigeria, Peru, Taiwan, and several islands in the Caribbean.

Cemex's exports have increased dramatically in recent years. Exports from Mexico increased 196% between 1994 and 1995 (see Exhibits 2 and 3). One of the reasons for this is the weak state of the Mexican economy. Cemex took this opportunity to establish new trading relationships with the Far East including Indonesia, Malaysia, and the Philippines.

MARKET POTENTIAL

The market potential for Cemex in each of its six major demographic locations is excellent, with the industry growing in each of the last few years. Mexico and Spain have averaged about 7 percent growth in demand per year in their cement

Exhibit 2   **Cemex's Mexican Exports in 1995 (percentage of total volume exported)**

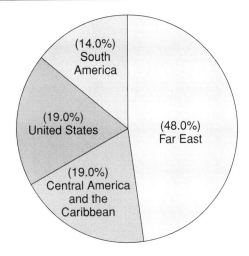

Source: Cemex 1995 Annual Report

Exhibit 3   **Cement Exports (million metric tons)**

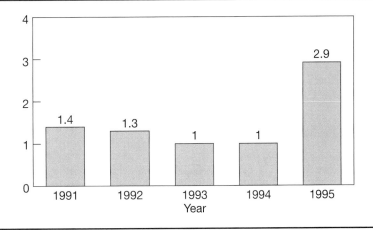

Source: Cemex 1995 Annual Report

industries. The southern regions of California, Texas, and Florida have averaged around 10 percent growth for the past three years. In 1995, Venezuelan officials introduced drastic plans to reverse falling economic activity, and Cemex is in a great position to reap the benefits of the inevitable industry upswing. The Panamanian government has committed itself to major public sector development projects which will extend past the year 2000, and this plan has already stimulated construction sector growth to over 20 percent of last year's level.

As Cemex continues to expand globally, its growth potential increases. Potential markets for the cement industry can be found throughout developing countries where there is a need to import concrete and cement products. Cemex has been aware of this for many years and continuously attempts to increase market share in these areas. Most recently, the company has been focusing on markets in Asia and the Pacific rim. Cemex's Hong Kong office is studying several ventures in China. Zambrano says, "We will be there one way or another in the next two years" (Smith 1995).

OTHER OPERATIONS

While Cemex is mainly in the cement and ready-mix business, it is also involved in the tourism industry. Cemex's Marriot CasaMagna hotels in Puerto Vallarta and Cancun are among the leading hotels in those areas, which, in 1994, ranked first and second in local occupancy rates respectively. With the peso devaluation in December, the purchasing power of foreign currency has increased, thus strengthening the prospects for an increased number of foreign visitors. Exhibit 4 features the structure of Cemex.

FINANCIAL INFORMATION

With the rapid pace of Cemex's acquisitions comes worries among investors about the amount of debt Cemex is taking on. The price of Cemex stock dropped from $9.40 in November 1994 to $3.33 in February 1995. Does this mean that the frenzied pace of acquisitions is adversely affecting Cemex in terms of its stock price? Many investors seem to think so. Recently, the stock price has gone up to around $7.50 but with all the recent acquisition activity that Cemex is promoting as being beneficial to the company, why hasn't the price gone up significantly? When Cemex recently announced the proposed acquisition of two Colombian cement companies for $600 million, its share price dropped 4 percent. Cemex's P/E ratio is also low at 6 compared to other Mexican cement firms which have P/E's of 15.

While the number and size of Cemex's acquisitions are impressive, the amount of debt it is taking on is even more impressive. Prior to making its Spanish acquisition, Cemex issued $1 billion in debt, the largest issue ever for a Latin American company. Investors were somewhat apprehensive, but the issue received an investment grade from Moody's and Standard and Poor's. Cemex remains confident in its ability to handle its debt (Smith 58). It had even made moves in anticipation of a peso devaluation. A $400 million convertible bond was issued at 4.25 % to "recycle short-term debt to a more manageable three-year maturity" (ibid). Cemex's CFO, Gustavo Caballero, has slowly extended the company's debt maturity time frame from two years to four and a half. He is also discussing a deal with Citibank and J.P. Morgan & Co. to roll over $350 million in swap loans backed by Cemex shares (Smith 59). Cemex has a total of $3.2 billion in dollar-denominated debt out of a total of $3.9 billion. Seventy-eight percent of Cemex's debt is long term. Exhibits 5 and 6 contain Cemex's 1995 income statement and balance sheet.

Exhibit 4

Cemex Structure

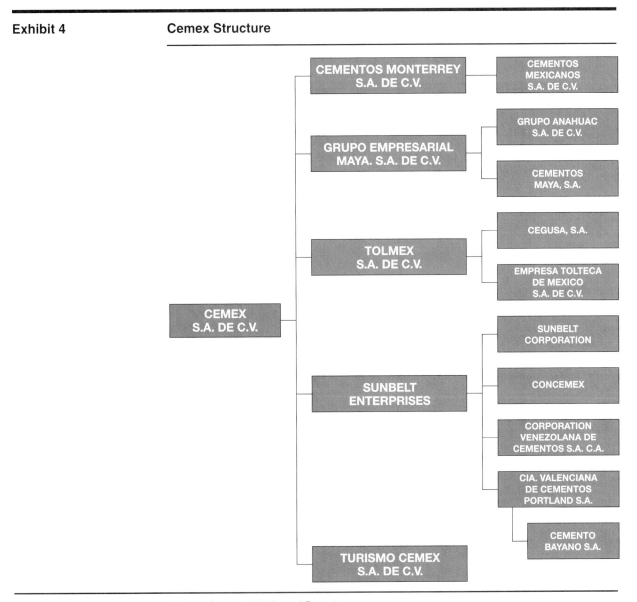

Source: Cemex 1995 Annual Report

EXTERNAL ENVIRONMENT

The external environment in each of the countries in which Cemex operates varies. In the U.S., fluctuating interest rates and the anti-dumping order concerning the imports of Mexican cement have hindered sales, but large demand in America for cement has kept private-sector spending strong and created an urgency to reach an agreement concerning laws which prevent cement importation.

Mexico's economic status is the principal reason why Cemex has engaged in its international diversification strategy. The Mexican economic outlook remains uncertain at present. Public and private sector spending have been severely reduced as a result of the peso devaluation, and the government's

Exhibit 5

CEMEX, S.A. DE C.V. and Subsidiaries—Consolidated Balance Sheets
(thousands of constant Mexican pesos as of December 31, 1995)

	December 31	
	1995	1994
Assets		
Current Assets		
Cash and temporary investments	$ 2,741,139	3,729,917
Trade accounts receivable, less allowance for doubtful accounts of $379,143 in 1995 and $353,713 in 1994	2,969,375	2,964,942
Other receivables	1,180,995	1,202,417
Inventories	2,614,667	2,129,217
Other current assets	847,513	977,872
Total current assets	10,353,689	11,004,365
Investments and Noncurrent Receivables		
Investments in affiliated companies	1,599,276	5,278,324
Other investments	265,954	423,276
Other accounts receivable	1,182,348	29,087
Total investments and noncurrent receivables	3,047,578	5,730,687
Property, Machinery, and Equipment		
Land and buildings	16,315,240	14,496,371
Machinery and equipment	55,015,31	41,204,087
Accumulated depreciation	(33,961,654)	(27,374,852)
Construction in progress	805,426	3,192,051
Total property, machinery, and equipment	38,174,323	31,517,657
Deferred Charges		
Excess of cost over book value of subsidiaries and affiliated companies acquired	12,641,905	11,270,083
Other deferred charges	2,347,136	2,885,050
Accumulated amortization	(1,863,224)	(1,627,263)
Total deferred charges	13,125,817	12,527,870
Total Assets	$ 64,701,407	60,780,579
Liabilities and Stockholders' Equity		
Current Liabilities		
Bank loans Notes payable	3,535,801	2,388,081
Current maturities of long-term debt	2,388,822	1,095,208
Trade accounts payable	1,203,010	1,031,305
Other accounts payable and accrued expenses	2,088,794	2,110,830
Total current liabilities	10,019,721	8,127,892
Long-Term Debt		
Bank loans	7,224,282	5,294,357
Debentures	48,750	222,256
Notes payable	18,566,015	19,569,355

Exhibit 5 (continued) **CEMEX, S.A. DE C.V. and Subsidiaries—Consolidated Balance Sheets (thousands of constant Mexican pesos as of December 31, 1995)**

	December 31	
	1995	*1994*
Current maturities of long-term debt	(2,388,822)	(1,095,208)
Total long-term debt	23,450,225	23,990,760
Other Noncurrent Liabilities		
Pension plan and seniority premium	528,011	453,656
Deferred income taxes	1,074,498	57,674
Other liabilities	379,678	276,182
Total other noncurrent liabilities	1,982,187	787,512
Total liabilities	35,452,133	32,906,164
Excess of book value over cost of subsidiaries acquired	129,771	132,284
Stockholders' Equity		
Majority interest:		
Common stock—historical cost basis	45,222	40,838
Common stock—accumulated inflation adjustments	1,367,526	1,367,526
Additional paid-in capital	6,374,826	3,318,849
Excess (deficit) in equity restatement	(7,756,821)	127,751
Retained earnings	16,349,515	14,058,611
Net income	5,868,907	2,893,114
Total majority interest	22,249,175	21,806,689
Minority interest	6,870,328	5,935,442
Total stockholders' equity	29,119,503	27,742,131
Total Liabilities and Stockholders' Equity	$ 64,701,407	60,780,579

budget reductions have hurt infrastructure spending. Overall construction activity dropped by 22% in 1995. Cement demand has also fallen. The economy of the U.S. is growing but not as fast as in the past. Construction activity is expected to increase by only 2% in 1996. Construction spending has also increased around 4% per year across southern regions. Increased residential and commercial property developments resulting from lower long-term interest rates in the U.S. will be beneficial to Cemex. In Spain, the development of residential units has remained strong because government subsidies have helped to increase levels of cement consumption.

The Venezuelan government began a new economic recovery plan in 1994 to reverse some of the hardships faced by that country. So far, their efforts have indirectly and dramatically improved the cement demand in Venezuela and benefited Cemex in 1995 and 1996. However, the economy is still very slow. Forty-six percent of Cemex's products made in Venezuela were exported. Even so, the market share increased from 47% to 49%. The Venezuelan government is currently trying to stimulate building industry growth with the "settlement

Exhibit 6
Income

Cemex, S.A. DE C.V. and Subsidiaries—Consolidated Statements of
(thousands of constant Mexican Pesos as of December 31, 1995)

	Years ended on December 31	
	1995	1994
Net sales	$ 19,821,210	16,176,647
Cost of sales	(12,088,257)	(9,329,364)
Gross profit	7,732,953	6,847,283
Operating expenses:		
Administrative	(1,987,702)	(1,410,202)
Selling	(1,012,548)	(1,094,394)
Total operating expenses	(3,000,250)	(2,504,596)
Operating income	4,732,703	4,342,687
Comprehensive financing income (cost):		
Financial expenses	(5,038,987)	(2,766,632)
Financial income	561,313	2,692,595
Foreign exchange loss, net	(2,823,440)	(1,105,527)
Monetary position gain	11,682,191	1,055,786
Net comprehensive financing income (cost)	4,381,077	(123,778)
Other expenses, net	(1,251,416)	(1,025,269)
Income before income tax, business assets tax, employees' statutory profit sharing and equity in income of affiliates	7,862,364	3,193,640
Income tax and business assets tax, net	(1,275,104)	(75,666)
Employees' statutory profit sharing	(13,349)	(65,323)
Total income tax, business assets tax, and employees' statutory profit sharing	(1,288,453)	(140,989)
Income before equity in income of affiliates	6,573,911	3,052,651
Equity in income of affiliates	136,609	187,122
Consolidated net income	6,710,520	3,239,773
Minority interest net income	841,613	346,659
Majority interest net income	$ 5,868,907	2,893,114

of public debt to contractors, the granting of easy-term housing loans, and the reactivation of infrastructure projects, including the building of railroads, dams, and a subway in Valencia. In addition, the creation of concessions under which the private sector would be allowed to participate in public infrastructure projects continues to be discussed" (*Cemex 1994*).

Panama has been an active market for Cemex for many years. Although its economy has slowed down somewhat, Cemex's plants have been performing very well. Cemex's market share increased to 51% and the company will be involved in a $336 million highway from Colon to Panama City to begin construction in 1996. Finally, the Caribbean region, with over 20 countries and 33 million people, is an area with high potential for growth in its economy and in the demand for cement. Because of fast development rates, there are many opportunities for construction and building material companies, particularly in Haiti and the Dominican Republic, with increased domestic and foreign spending. Cemex had a plant in Cuba as a joint venture between Mexico and Cuba, but recently pulled out after a request from the U.S. State Department that foreign companies not use confiscated American property.

THE ANTIDUMPING CONTROVERSY

Everything is not perfect at Cemex, though. Along with other Mexican producers of cement, it has been engaged in an ongoing battle with the United States for several years over claims by the U.S. that Mexico is dumping its cement on the U.S. market. Some U.S. cement producers claim that Mexican companies are selling their cement at a cheaper price in the U.S. than in Mexico.

The controversy began in May 1990, when the Department of Commerce (DOC) put antidumping duties on Mexican cement. Some U.S. cement producers had claimed that certain parts of the cement industry, in particular those in the South and Southwest, were being injured by the dumping of Mexican cement. They petitioned the DOC to impose duties on imported cement. This petition was unusual in that it claimed injury to only a certain segment of the U.S. cement industry. Antidumping petitions normally involve an entire industry because if an import duty is imposed, it goes into effect at all ports of entry, not just in the injured area (Lande 1994). The Mexican producers complained and appealed to GATT using this reasoning and in 1992, a GATT panel sided with the Mexican producers, giving the reason that the American claims were coming only from regional cement producers and were not industry wide ("Set" 1995). However, the U.S. chose not to abide by the GATT ruling. The import duty on Mexican cement was raised from 43% to 62% of its imported price in May 1995 (ibid). Some Americans think the duty is too low, since Cemex, they claim, had not been giving them enough information concerning its costs and prices. However, with its international operations, Cemex can get around the antidumping duty by exporting to the U.S. from its Spanish plant.

COMPETITORS

Cemex is the dominant producer of cement in Mexico and has high market shares in many of the other countries in which it has plants. However, it is not the biggest cement company in the world and must compete with other cement producers both on a global basis and within Mexico. The two largest competitors are Holderbank, located in Switzerland, and Lafarge Coppée, located in France. In addition, there are many cement producers in the United States and the Caribbean with which Cemex must compete for market share.

HOLDERBANK

The world's largest producer of cement is headquartered in Switzerland. Holderbank is a holding company which engages in the production and sale of cement, ready-mix concrete, and other concrete products. It first began to expand in the 1950's when it entered markets in Brazil, Chile, Colombia, Costa Rica, Mexico, Peru, Venezuela, and Argentina (Lenzler 1994). It also has plants in Vietnam, Australia, and New Zealand. Holnam, the largest cement company in the U.S., was formed by merging Holderbank's U.S. assets with those of Ideal Basic Industries (ibid).

Apasco, Mexico's second largest cement company, is a subsidiary of Holderbank and competes directly with Cemex. Apasco operates 6 cement and 84 ready-mixed concrete plants in 40 cities in Mexico (McDermott 1994). Like Cemex, Apasco has a satellite communications system which it uses to keep track of the various operations of its plants. As Holderbank already has companies in Canada and the U.S., Apasco competes with Cemex only in the Mexican cement market. Both companies are planning increases of production and capacity, but the Mexican recession could put their plans on hold for now. Apasco had sales of $650 million in 1993, an 18% increase over the previous year. Holderbank also competes with Cemex through its cement plant in Venezuela.

LAFARGE COPPÉE

This French corporation is the second largest producer of cement in the world. It owns cement plants all over the world. Sixty percent of its sales are in Europe. It must compete with Cemex in Spain through its subsidiary Asland S.A. Lafarge Coppée competes in the U.S. cement market through its subsidiary Lafarge Corporation, which operates plants mostly in the upper midwest. It controls approximately nine percent of the U.S. cement market (*Lafarge 10K*). Lafarge does not directly compete with Cemex in the U.S. since most of Lafarge's plants are in the northern half of the U.S. and Cemex competes primarily in the southern states. Lafarge used to have some plants in Texas as well as ready-mix terminals, but sold them to Cemex, which gave Cemex its first U.S. cement plant.

OTHERS

In the Caribbean market, Cemex competes with Devcon International, one of the largest manufacturers of cement and cement products in the region. The company makes ready-mix concrete, crushed stone, concrete block, and asphalt and distributes bulk and bagged cement (*Devcon 10K*). It distributes its products to the U.S. Virgin Islands, Antigua, Barbuda, St. Maarten/sSt. Martin, Dominica, and the British Virgin Islands. It is a well-established company and will be a challenge for Cemex with Cemex's new facilities in the Caribbean and Cuba.

CONCLUSION

While the future of Mexico's economy remains uncertain, Cemex's future appears bright. Almost one-third of their revenues are denominated in U.S. dollars which is helping to lessen the tremendous debt burden it is under.

Thanks to Zambrano's international expansion plans, Cemex has become one of the largest cement producers in the world and is continuing to grow. Having cement plants in many different parts of the world, from the Caribbean to Europe, has given Cemex an edge over its competition. However, Cemex must be careful in its acquisitions strategy. While the company's capacity has dramatically increased over the past five years, its stock price has not. Some investors are skeptical about the prices Cemex is paying for these acquisitions. Cemex also must look to other markets, primarily in Asia, and continue to work to decrease its debt.

BIBLIOGRAPHY

"Cementos Mexicanos (CEMEX)." *Euromoney (Emerging Issues Supplement)*, Sep. 1993, 34.

"CEMEX: A New Foundation." *Chief Executive (CEO Brief)*, Jul/Aug. 1995, 10-12.

Cemex 1994 Annual Report.

"Cemex Wows Market With $1bn Blockbuster." *Euroweek*, 28 May 1993, 1.

"The Children With the Magic Powder." *The Economist*, 21 May 1994, 76-77.

Devcon 10-K 1995.

Fink, Ronald. "Cemex: The Spanish Acquisition(s)." *Financial World*, 27 October 1992, 21-22.

Heaney, Kathleen, and Mark Stockdale. "Cement (domestic); Cement (international)." *Institutional Investor*, Jun. 1993, SS14-SS15.

Lafarge 10-K 1995.

Lande, Stephen. "Dumping on Cement Dispute." *Business Mexico*, Sep. 1994, 44-46.

Lenzler, Richard. "Set In Concrete." *Forbes*, 18 July 1994, 42-43.

Marray, Michael. "Cemex Confounds the Sceptics." *Euromoney (Worlds; Best Credits Supplement)*, Sep. 1993, 37.

McCarthy, Joseph L. "Lorenzo Zambrano." *Chief Executive*, Sep. 1993, 27.

McDermott, Terry. "Laying the Foundation." *Business Mexico*, Jul. 1994, 39-40.

Peagam, Norman, and Michael Marray. "Cemex: Foreign Ambitions." *Euromoney*, May 1993, 137-138.

"Set In Concrete." *The Economist*, 3 June 1995, 28-29.

Smith, Gail, and John Pearson. "Cemex: Solid As Mexico Sinks." *Business Week*, 27 February 1995, 58-59.

Vogel, Jr., Thomas T. "Mexico's Cemex, Hurt by Peso's Fall, Gets Financing From Citibank, J.P. Morgan." *Wall Street Journal*, 27 Jan. 1995, A3.

A League of His Own

Daniel O. Lybrook, Purdue University

Michael L. Menefee, Purdue University

As Mark Dimmich sat in his darkened office and rehashed the events that led to the current state of affairs, he wondered if owning a minor league baseball team was all it had been cracked up to be. The local media was on him, criticizing him for not being a better General Manager. The President of the Parks Board that had once given promises of help was criticizing him in the public media and undermining him behind his back. Local industry had not lived up to their promised support. The whole affair was simply a lot different than expected. What a mess! Should he just drop the whole thing? Or should he try again next year and go it alone, correcting his mistakes as he saw fit? Would a shared ownership design ease the burdens?

HISTORY

Jim Gonzales, the previous year's general manager, had started working toward a new beginning for the Lafayette Leopards independent baseball team before the dust had settled from the failed experiment of its participation in the Great Central League last year. Though he had not secured financial backing, he really felt that minor league baseball could make a go of it in Lafayette.

Jim felt like he had learned from last year's experiences. Current common knowledge said that it takes a few years for independent baseball to turn a profit. After only one year of being in existence, Jim felt about a minor league franchise like Ray Kinsella in the movie *Field of Dreams*—"Build it and they will come." So he was very upbeat about trying again in Lafayette. He would try to build and organize the league himself without Dick Jacobsen, the former league President.

THE ENVIRONMENT

The city of Lafayette, Indiana, is situated in the mid north region of Indiana, 60 miles northwest of Indianapolis and 120 miles southeast of Chicago. Tippecanoe County, of which Lafayette is the county seat, has a year round population of approximately 125,000 permanent residents. The major population centers in the county are Lafayette, with about 45,000 people, and West Lafayette, with about 25,000 people. These sister cities are self governed as is the surrounding county. During the fall to spring school year, an additional 30,000 students live in the area and attend Purdue University in West Lafayette. In the summer, the students at Purdue number about 8000.

The county is the business and industry center of this region of Indiana. The local Chamber of Commerce boasts a membership of close to 1000 businesses. Other than Purdue, which is the area's largest employer with over 12,000 employees, there are several large manufacturing concerns operating within the county. Wabash National (a truck trailer manufacturer), Eli Lilly (a drug manufacturer), Fairfield Manufacturing, Rostone Corp., Alcoa, Caterpillar, Subaru-Isuzu, TRW, and Landis Gyr all have facilities in the county.

To attend a professional baseball game, the closest major league teams are the Cubs and White Sox; 2 1/2 hours travel by car to Chicago. Recent surveys have stated that to attend a major league game costs a family of four around $100 not counting the transportation. With a driving time from Lafayette of seventy minutes, the closest minor league teams in the area were the Class AAA Indianapolis Indians and the Class A Danville, Illinois, club. Fort Wayne and South Bend also have minor league teams, but the drive from Lafayette is more than two and one half hours.

Indiana is legendary for basketball fanaticism and every boy at some time in his formative years dreams of playing for his favorite school, whether it be a secondary school or university. The area has also traditionally been very strong in youth baseball and youth baseball interest. There is a very strong summer youth program supported by the Parks and Recreation Department in Lafayette. Organized baseball starts with five year olds with T-ball leagues and continues up to American Legion ball for 17 and 18 year olds. This affords participation opportunities to a large percentage of those interested. This is carried over into the county through various township recreation boards. Of the five high schools in the county, three have played in an Indiana state baseball championship game in the last ten years, which speaks well of the interest and caliber of play in the area. Lafayette Jefferson has won the title twice and most recently played for the title just ten years ago. The county high schools, Harrison and McCutcheon, have each been in the title game in the last three years. Harrison won this year, and McCutcheon came in second two years ago. There is plenty of baseball competition and interest at the high school level.

Purdue is a member of The Big Ten athletic conference and plays a very competitive brand of baseball in the spring of each year. They will play approximately 25-30 home games each year and will draw crowds of 400-500 fans. This is close to the capacity of the Purdue baseball field. Their season ends in early June. An average of two to three players each year are drafted by major league organizations.

Lafayette also plays host to the international Colt World Series each summer. This tourney is played in the first two weeks of July. The format is a double elimination tournament for 14 and 15 year old players. There are eight teams that qualify from as far away as Puerto Rico and Hawaii. The tournament schedules two games per night over its two week venue and routinely draws over 1500 fans to Loeb Stadium Baseball Field for each session.

LOEB STADIUM

Loeb Stadium is a 2400 seat capacity ballpark operated by the Lafayette Parks and Recreation Department. It is located in a corner of the 600 acre facility called Columbian Park. Within this park are tennis courts, a large swimming pool, the city zoo, three meeting facilities, an outdoor amphitheater, a playground, various rides, and concessions. Parking for approximately 120 cars is available in a lot next to the ballpark. This lot also serves as parking for the zoo and for general park use and is free of charge.

The ballpark has recently been renovated with major alterations to update the restrooms, dressing rooms, and general appearance. It is as good a facility as you will find in a city the size of Lafayette. Bill German, the head of the Parks Department, was the linking pin between the city government and the baseball team. Bill agreed to give this year's edition of the Leopards the rate of $3000 for the rental of the ballpark for the season—30 games—with an option for the next season. This rate covers electricity for the lights and maintenance on the field. The Leopards were responsible for their own personal liability insurance.

PHOENIX FROM THE ASHES—A NEW START

Jim Gonzales felt that last season was a learning experience in what NOT to do. It was marked by a trail of unpaid bills and eventual lawsuits against the combination team and league owner, Dick Jacobsen. When the original general manager of the Leopards had gone unpaid for the initial two months of the season, he quit and Jim Gonzales—then the manager of the baseball team—took over to try to finish the season. The Leopards had won the title but the league, The Great Central League, had disintegrated at the conclusion of the season.

Jim was and is a baseball man and he felt that the problems had been primarily Jacobsen's. So he wanted to try again. Almost immediately upon the conclusion of the last season, Jim Gonzales and Bill German, Director of the Lafayette Parks Department, started to contact local businesses to try to garner financial support for the 1995 team. One potential investor, Brad Cohen, was quoted in the *Lafayette Journal and Courier*, the local newspaper: "We want to do everything we can to make sure that this team comes back. But baseball is like any business. You've got to impress your customers to bring them back. You've got to find a few people who can put in $1000 or $2000 and not expect to get it back. You can't expect someone to get a ten percent return on their money after the first year or two. It's an investment in the heart."

Jim felt that one of the important issues was to maintain the name of the team to build on the name recognition earned in the initial season and to establish continuity for the future. A potential problem was that if Jacobson had copyrighted the name, this year's version of the Leopards might have to pay for the name or—at the worst—not be able to use it. This would be a blow to his goal of continuity through identification. Upon checking, Jim found that

Jacobsen had overlooked this copyrighting detail. So the Leopards name was the new organization's for the taking.

Among Gonzales' objectives for the Leopards:

- an operating budget of $120,000
- season ticket sales of at least 700; these would be priced at $100 each
- a board of directors to include a team representative and community member from each city in a six team league, with teams based in Richmond, Anderson, Lafayette, and Terre Haute in Indiana, and two teams in the Chicago area. The Great Central League had four teams located in Minneapolis, Minnesota, Mason City, Iowa, Champaign, Illinois, and Lafayette, Indiana.

A FINANCIAL ANGEL COMES FORTH

Jim eventually was contacted by Mark Dimmich who owned a local paint and body shop. Mark was interested in supporting baseball in the community because he and his family had attended some games and had enjoyed the Leopards the previous season. Mark felt that a night at the ballpark was a quality family experience and contributed to positive personal values. He especially liked the alcohol free environment of the ballpark. In March, he agreed to provide the necessary financial support for 1995. Mark and Jim prepared a trial budget based on the previous year's expenses and revenues to try to minimize any surprises that Mark might encounter (see Exhibit 1). The Leopards were in business again. Jim became very involved in getting the new league operating. Mark felt that hiring a full time general manager was more of an expense than he wanted to incur. Plus it was an expense that had not been included in the trial budget. So Mark was left with the Leopards general manager's hat as well as his other personal business to run. Jim was more interested in the formation of the league now that Dimmich had agreed to support a team and he eventually abandoned the promotional aspect of the Leopards. In addition, Jim was not adept at promotion. He was a baseball man. It was left to Mark to do the best that he could. At this point, there were two months left before the start of the season. Richmond opted to join a different independent league—The Frontier League—and negotiations with potential owners in Terre Haute broke down. Jim had firm commitments from three teams, but had trouble lining up a fourth. Then East Chicago came in and the league started the season with four teams: the Merrillville Muddogs, East Chicago Conquistadors, Lafayette Leopards, and Anderson Lawmen.

The initial agreement called for each team to pay the league $15,000. This money would go toward three major objectives: contract a sports statistical service to keep league records, pay for game baseballs (which the fans were allowed to keep if a foul ball was caught, as a promotional plus), and to pay for umpires. A sixty game schedule was worked out, with each team having 20 single game home dates and 5 doubleheaders. The league scheduled the start of play on June 13. Because of the heavy demands on Loeb Stadium for the Colt World Series the first two weeks in August and the American Legion Sectional and Regional, the Leopards schedule was unbalanced. It was skewed, with the majority of home games scheduled early in the season. In August, the Leopards had five home dates with ten road dates. The season was scheduled to end in late August with two rounds of playoffs.

Exhibit 1   **Trial Budget for the Lafayette Leopards**

Revenues:	
Gate	—
Concessions (15% of Gross)	—
Souvenirs	—
Ballpark Advertising	—
Program Ads/Sales	—
Expenses:	
Ballpark Rent	$3,000
Administrative (1.5 Staff)	25,500
League Fees	15,000
Player Salaries	36,000
Liability Insurance	2,000
Travel Expenses	15,000
Laundry	2,000
Game Promotions	10,000
Marketing	15,000
Insurance for Promotions	500
Total	$124,000

The first round of the playoffs would be August 22–25. Mark felt that he did not get a very high priority when it came to scheduling these games. He said that if Lafayette really wanted professional baseball, the Park Board would have to give the team a higher spot in the pecking order. Instead of supporting the Leopards, the Park Board and the city administration gave either no support at all, or second class citizen status at best. It seemed the Colts came first, then American Legion baseball, and finally the Leopards. Mark was left on his own to try to make this experiment work.

THE PARK BOARD

The Park Board is made up of seven members. The primary responsibility is to administer the physical facilities and programs of Lafayette city parks. There are seven of these spread around the city, with Columbian Park being the largest. The yearly budget for the park system is seven figures. Bill German is the head of Lafayette Parks Department, an appointed position. He sits as a member of the board as well as being responsible for administration of year round recreation.

Jim Gonzales had a good relationship with Bill German and the board. But Jim's background was in baseball, not business. Mark Dimmich thought that the Leopards would have to be run more professionally. The Park Board was leery of the Leopards because the previous owner had bounced two months of rental checks for the ballpark and had left a trail of unpaid bills around town. The board was suing for the money, plus damages, from the previous owner. The board had taken some heat for this from local business, who also supported the summer programs with sponsorships and advertising.

Largely because of this, the relationship between Mark and the board was strained. They were afraid of getting burned again and Mark wanted the Leopards to succeed and needed a sweetheart deal to enable this to happen. Mark never received this.

Bill German became openly critical of Mark's marketing strategies, being quoted in the local newspaper saying that Mark should put more emphasis on getting people to the ballpark instead of emphasizing outfield fence advertising. Bill felt that the Leopards needed to sell tickets and then try to get the fans to come back to more games, accentuating the municipal park attractions and working more in tandem with the overall park system. But he also became critical in private conversations around town.

GETTING STARTED

The Leopards, by virtue of being the only one of these four teams to field a team last year, had a head start in filling their eighteen man roster. By early June, Jim had seventeen players signed for the season, six of whom had played for the Leopards the previous year. Jim Gonzales had been a college coach in Texas before coming to the Lafayette team and had numerous Texas connections. Many of the signees came from recommendations from college coaches in Texas, where the quality of college ball is excellent. On June 4, an open tryout camp was held locally at Loeb Stadium. A $10 registration fee was charged for each prospect. Twenty-three potentials showed for the tryout. One of the players said it best—"It would be a dream. There's nothing better than that. It's what every kid wants to do. There's nothing better than putting a baseball uniform on." Although that particular player was not signed for the team, the roster was filled with a recent Purdue grad who had not been drafted by the major league clubs. Each player signed for between $500 and $750 a month depending on experience and skill level. The season was scheduled to last two and a half months, including the playoffs. Jim started the season with ten position players and eight pitchers.

LEOPARDS REVENUES

Minor league baseball teams garner revenue from four primary sources—gate receipts, concessions, parking, and advertising. Gate receipts cannot be accurately predicted, but some preseason operating revenues could be garnered from season ticket sales. Season tickets were priced at $100 for adults and $70 for retirees and children under 12. Concessions and the sale of Leopards logo items would largely depend on the attendance at the games. Advertising would depend on the local market's perception of what the individual business would be getting for their advertising dollar. Parking revenues were nonexistent because of the location of the ballpark.

Single game tickets were priced at $5 per game for adults and $3 per game for retirees and children under 12. A change from the year before was the fact there were no reserved seats so the ticket buyer could sit anywhere he or she chose. Season ticket sales were actually sold as a block of twenty-five tickets for a $1 discount per ticket. The tickets were not dated for any specific game and could be used at any game. With the purchase of a season ticket, you could use one or five or ten, etc., at any game that you chose. Total season ticket sales before the season started numbered 40.

Mark contracted with a local caterer to provide concessions at the games. The menu featured Polish sausage for $2, hot dogs and popcorn for $1, chili dogs for $1.50, nachos for $2.50, Pepsi products for $1, and O'Douls nonalcoholic beverage for $3. To get concessions, a fan had to go to a stand under the bleachers. There were no vendors. Alcoholic beverages are not permitted to be sold at Loeb. This is a policy set by the Parks Board and there is some sentiment on the board to alter that policy in the future. Mark, a non-drinker, supported the non-alcoholic policy because he felt that alcohol would cause more problems than it would be worth and perhaps tarnish the reputation of the events, impacting attendance. The Leopards received fifteen percent of the gross concession sales from the caterer. The average fan spent about $4 a game on concessions at Loeb.

The three most readily available sources of advertising revenue for a baseball team are yearbooks, programs, and ballpark advertising. The game program, which retailed for $1 each, was a four page, 8 1/2 by 11, two color, traditionally laid out baseball program with a Leopards roster insert. It featured a score card on the inside pages with ads purchased by local businesses. There were ten 1/8 page ads, three 1/4 page ads and one full page ad, with the balance taken up by the Leopards and the scoresheet. Rates for the season were $300 for an eighth page, $500 for a quarter page, and $1500 for a full page. These rates were for the full season, but Mark would prorate them if that is what it took to sell out the program.

There were a number of promotions at the games tied to program purchases based on the program numbers. A fan had to buy a program to be included in these. The Leopards did not print a yearbook.

The other advertising revenue—ballpark billboards—became a very interesting scenario. On the outfield fence at Loeb were thirty-four advertising signs paid for by local businesses to the Parks Department with the money earmarked for the summer youth baseball program. If the Leopards were going to generate any revenue from these, Mark would have to resell the signs. He tried to resell them for $1000 each but found few takers. The common sentiment among the advertisers was that they had already paid for the ads and they would be visible at the park even if they did not ante up again. In order to generate advertising revenue, Mark spent $2000 for tarps. He hired a local fan to drape the tarps over the existing advertising on game days. Mark was then able to sell advertising on the tarps. He sold three ads and took one, for his business for a total of four. (Pepsi, the only soft drink sold at Leopard games, took one, the local TV cable company took one, a local bank took one, and Mark's business had one.) Mark felt that it was not ethical to give advertisers different rates. If Pepsi had paid X dollars for its ad then any prospective advertiser should also pay that rate, a yearly take it or leave it approach. Two thirds of the way through the season, he changed his tune and a local industry agreed to pay for a sign as part of a company night promotion.

The parking at Columbian Park was free to the public. The lot next to the ball-park holds about 120 cars. This lot is used by all visitors to the park and there is no mechanism to charge for parking. Therefore, his parking revenues were zero.

PROMOTIONS

The players appeared at a few youth baseball league outings but on the whole did not participate widely in community events. Jim seemed very reluctant, almost intimidated, to ask them to do much more than show up for practices and games.

Mark tried to get some help from local business and industry and knocked on doors all over town. He sold tickets to companies for the reduced rate of $3 in quantity. Fairfield Athletic Association bought a couple of hundred tickets that they distributed free to workers and their families. Staley bought some and sold them to their workers for $1. Cat bought some and resold them for $3 to employees. Cat had a night at Loeb and bought an outfield ad. Purdue, Lilly, and Wabash National stayed out of any promotion, though they were all approached.

THE SEASON

The Leopards started the season by winning at home in front of 800 fans. But the overall play was sloppy and two games into the season, a Leopard was released by Gonzales for attitude reasons. Another infielder was signed to take the spot. A pitcher was released because he lived two and a half hours away and could not make every game because of a conflict with his financial analyst job. Another pitcher was signed to replace him. This type of personnel activity is more the norm than the exception in these types of independent leagues.

At the end of the first week of play, the Leopards were last in the league in attendance, averaging 650 fans a game. Merrillville was first with an average of over 1300 a game.

BALL GAME PROMOTIONS

It is a promotional adage that you must turn minor league sports into a carnival atmosphere to draw fans. Some say the zanier the better. One famous story concerns dressing a person up as a taco and having the food item race a small child around the bases. When the child wins, the young fan gets a free ticket. The spectacle is intended to turn fans into repeat attenders.

The Leopards also featured a number of promotions during the games. Each game program was numbered. Between the top and bottom of the second and third innings a program number would be drawn. The first number would win an O'Doul's cap and T-shirt. The second winner received a coupon for a pizza from a well-known franchise.

In the middle of the fourth, two fans were selected by the Leopard mascot, Blooper. Both were given a bat which they stood up with the head of the bat touching the ground and the contestant's nose touching the handle. The first participant to complete ten rotations around a bat and run to first base won a pair of tickets to a future game. Blooper was a person dressed in a Leopard suit who walked around the park during the game, followed by an attendant to keep young children from pulling Blooper's tail.

Another program number was drawn in the middle of the fifth. This lucky fan stood at home plate and tried to throw a baseball into a trash can laying on its side on second base. If the ball went in the can AND stayed, the fan won $100. Sound simple? No one won the $100 during the entire season.

If your ticket number was selected in the seventh inning and a Leopard hit a grand slam home run OUT of the ballpark in the bottom of the seventh, that lucky recipient won $10,000. It would have been great publicity if someone had been able to collect this, but no Leopard connected for a grand slam and no fan was able to collect in this contest.

On the back of every ticket was a coupon which, when presented at the ice cream stand across from the park, got the holder a free extra scoop of ice cream with the purchase of a regular cone. There were fewer than five hundred of these redeemed.

The other promotion during games was a 50/50 drawing. Before the game, fans could purchase tickets, one for a dollar or three for two dollars. During the eighth inning, a number was drawn and the lucky person split the pot 50/50 with the ball club. On one memorable occasion late in the season, the lucky winner's split totaled ten dollars!

There were a number of promotions during the early part of the season. But as the season wore on and revenues started going south for Mark, these were stopped as a cost-cutting measure.

On June 24, an Elvis Presley impersonator performed before 550 fans for an hour after the game. After five games Lafayette still ranked last in the league in attendance with an average of 493 fans per game. Jim Gonzales said, "I won't say we have been disappointed in the crowds. We have played on a couple of nights where we had conflicts, like Harrison playing in the state finals."

On July 3, the Leopards swept a doubleheader and moved into first place for the first time all season. Three hundred and forty fans attended the games. After ten home games the Leopards were averaging 427 fans a game. The local newspaper polled fans in a highlighted box on the front sports page and asked "If you have gone to a game, what made you decide to attend? If you haven't seen them play, what has kept you away?"

Following are some of the comments that were received:

"You've got to get more local players. That would help ticket sales."

"The Leopards only have three other opponents. When there's so much local interest in youth baseball, that is a limiting factor."

"Paying $5 to watch them play another team 20 times is not appealing."

"I went because I want to support them. But they also had an Elvis impersonator and my eight year old son likes Elvis."

"We never know when the games are."

THE MEDIA

The local paper gave favorable coverage to the Leopards, covering all home games with a staff reporter. The paper ran a Leopard schedule nearly every day on page two of the sports section with starting times prominently displayed.

Away games were covered with line scores and phoned in stories. Updates of player statistics were printed weekly. All in all, the local paper provided a positive marketing opportunity. Sports columnists regularly wrote about the team and issues surrounding the team. The need for aggressive marketing was extolled in many of these. The paper also published letters from fans who supported the team.

The Leopards also received TV coverage with short clips shown on the 6:00 or 11:00 p.m. news along with the game results. Not much human interest was included in their coverage. The Leopards did not receive any radio coverage.

THE SECOND HALF

At the All Star break, the Leopards were still in first place by percentage points. They were still last in the league in attendance, averaging 372 fans. Just five games exceeded 400. The two home games prior to the All Star break drew 245 and 118 fans. Gonzales stated, "As far as an entire organization, I'm a little disappointed in the attendance. Mark Dimmich has put his neck on the line to keep the ball club here in town, and I thought more people would support that because he's a local person."

Mark said on July 22, "The amount of money I lose is going to depend on how the rest of the season goes. I probably need a lot more promotional stuff. But all that takes money. I knew I could never do as much as I wanted to. But as far as costs go, I have done this about as cheaply as I could to minimize my losses. A team in a town like this would have to draw 500 to 800 fans a game to make this worthwhile."

On August 13 a crowd of 58 fans showed for a day game between the league's top two teams, Lafayette and Anderson. It was played in the afternoon as a rain makeup but could not be played at night because of schedule conflicts with the Colt World Series.

The season was winding to a close. The playoff format had been changed twice in the previous two weeks. On August 15, the integrity of the league was jeopardized when the East Chicago team walked off the field during a game with the Leopards. The core of the team had been experiencing a series of personality conflicts that culminated in their decision to quit after an inning and a half. They forfeited the game and told the Leopards that they were through for the year. This team had been in turmoil because their management had been extremely unstable from the beginning. The Anderson owner assumed responsibility of the East Chicago team to try to finish the league's first year. The Conquistador players returned after two days and in fact did finish the season after the one game hiatus.

Dimmich was extremely concerned because he was the only owner to have paid the $15,000 league fee as of August 15. Mark was keeping the league office open by paying the rent himself. He had signed a one year lease for $975 a month. Of this the league was paying $450 a month, which was coming from his ante. Dimmich stated, "I would like to keep a team here next year, but I can't see myself being fully involved in it. It's certainly been a lesson."

The season further unraveled on August 18 when Jim Gonzales announced he was quitting at the end of the season. He cited lack of community support, as evidenced by the average attendance of 350 fans per game. He said, "I look at this, and I say, I've done everything I really think I could possibly do and nothing has changed in the two years. Maybe they need someone else in here to do something different. I think Mark Dimmich kind of looks at it the same way."

On August 20, the Leopards beat East Chicago 12-2 to clinch the league championship for the second year in a row. At the completion of the game, Jim Gonzales said the season was over and there would be no playoffs. Two of four teams had honored their $15,000 dues commitment, which was enough for the league to break even. If everyone had paid, the league would have had $30,000 to prepare for 1996. Gonzales said, "We just got to the point where we felt that we were being real honorable with the things we were doing, and a couple of teams weren't. We just said that we needed to stand up and make a decision." Dimmich said that playoffs would not enhance revenues or lessen his losses and could increase losses. Mark said, "I hated to quit without playing the league championship but I felt like I had to make a statement to the other team owners." Gonzales said, "There was talk about playoffs but I don't think any good would come out of it. They would be counterproductive. Our hearts were not in it. I don't know if we could play for another week. It got to the point where it was not any fun to come to the ballpark." And so the 1995 season was over. Mark estimated his 1995 losses at over $20,000.

Now Mark is sitting in his darkened office. He is left with $1500 worth of Leopards souvenir items, an option for the next year at Loeb Stadium, a copyrighted team name, a mascot suit, and a concept for a professional baseball team for Lafayette. What should he do?

Church's Chicken in "Navajoland"

Jon Ozmun, Northern Arizona University

Casey Donoho, Northern Arizona University

Mike Nelson watched from his table as a Navajo family stood at the counter and ordered fried chicken, mashed potatoes, gravy, and biscuits. As they moved away from the order taker, a young couple made their order and a line started to form behind them. It was the beginning of the lunch "rush" at the Church's Chicken Restaurant in Window Rock, Arizona. "It's going to be another good day selling drumsticks in 'Navajoland'," Mike thought to himself.

Nelson was the owner of the Church's Chicken Restaurant (CCR) in Window Rock. The business had been started in 1991 and had been a success almost from the first day. Fast food was as popular on the Navajo Reservation as it was in the rest of the country, and fried chicken seemed to be preferred over hamburgers, tacos, and pizzas by the Native American consumers.

The success of the Window Rock restaurant had prompted Nelson to consider expansion into other population centers of the Navajo Reservation. His first choice for the next Church's Chicken Restaurant was Tuba City, Arizona. Nelson preferred this location because it was one of the largest communities on the reservation and because he was already established in the community with other two retail businesses—a Tru-Value Hardware and a V&S Variety store. As Nelson watched the restaurant begin to fill with the lunch crowd, he wondered if Tuba City was the right location choice for his next "drumsticks" business.

BACKGROUND

Michael Nelson, a Navajo, was born and raised on the Navajo Indian Reservation. He attended Bureau of Indian Affairs (BIA) boarding schools from the first through the twelfth grades. Nelson attended the BIA high school in Ft. Wingate, New Mexico, where he played on the "Bears" football and basketball teams. After graduating from high school, Nelson enrolled at Fort Lewis College in Durango, Colorado, and graduated with a BS in Business Administration.

After graduation, Nelson worked three years for the Farmers Group Insurance Company. For the next six years, he worked at the Office of Navajo Economic Opportunity as budget and office manager and business research assistant. He left this position to become a Community Economic Industrial Planner for the Phoenix Regional Small Business Administration, working with representatives of manufacturers, distributors, franchisers, banking and investment institutions, and municipal and civic leaders on and off Indian reservations. Nelson held this position for three years. He then rejoined the Navajo Tribe as an Economic Planner in the Navajo Economic Planning Office developing feasibility studies and business plans for Tribal programs.

In 1971, Nelson formed Michael Nelson & Associates, Inc. (MNA). During the years which followed, he received numerous awards and honors for his contributions to the Navajo business community. Nelson received the Small Business Administration's Incentive Award in 1970. In 1984 he was named the "Outstanding Indian Business Person of the Year" by the U.S. Organization of Indian Businesses. In 1985 Nelson was named "Outstanding Businessman" by the Minority Business Enterprises in the USA.

MICHAEL NELSON & ASSOCIATES

MNA was incorporated in the State of Arizona in October 1971. Nelson's first business venture was a clothing store in Window Rock—Navajo Westerners Store. He later added the V&S Variety Store in Tuba City, convenience stores in Dilkon and Teesto, Arizona, and Tru-Value Hardware stores in Window Rock, Kayenta, and Tuba City. The most recent addition to Nelson's small retailing "empire" was the Church's Chicken Restaurant in Window Rock in 1991. All businesses of MNA are located on the Navajo Reservation.

MNA's retail stores have combined assets of over $2 million. In fiscal 1994, MNA profits exceeded $200,000 on sales revenues of over $6 million. MNA employs a work force of 70 Navajos in its operations. MNA annually contributes over $800,000 to the Navajo Reservation economy through salaries and wages alone.

CHURCH'S CHICKEN RESTAURANT—WINDOW ROCK

In 1990, Nelson obtained a franchise from Church's Chicken Restaurants, Inc., for the purpose of opening a restaurant in Window Rock, Arizona. In the process, he obtained exclusive rights to Church's Chicken Restaurants in the Arizona portion of the Navajo Indian Reservation. Window Rock is the capital of the Navajo Nation and, according to the 1990 U.S. Census, had a population of 6,187. The Window Rock market area population was 11,718 (1990 U.S. Census).

For his CCR location, Nelson leased space in the newly constructed Window Rock Plaza Shopping Center. For an annual payment of $36,000, the Navajo Tribe provided Nelson a new 3,000 square foot facility finished to his specifications. Nelson opened the restaurant in 1991 and it made a $23,000 profit the first year. Sales revenues and profits grew steadily each year and during 1994, Nelson realized a net profit of $78,000 on sales of $710,000 (see Exhibit 1).

From the onset in Window Rock, Nelson had faced strong competition for the customers' business. There were ten different restaurant choices available to the customer, including two popular franchises—Kentucky Fried Chicken (KFC) and Lotta Burger. Nelson chose to compete directly with KFC for three reasons. First, fried chicken was the "right" product. Nelson's experience convinced him that his target market had a strong preference for fried food. Second, he believed that the Church's franchise offered distinct advantages over KFC: CCR prices were about 10% lower and portions were larger (CCR cut a chicken into six pieces while KFC cut the chicken into seven pieces.). CCR also allowed the flexibility to add items to the regular franchise menu and this was not possible with KFC. Third, he believed that the Window Rock KFC had a few very good employees, but overall the franchise was poorly managed and the physical facility was over twenty years old and poorly maintained.

Nelson's analysis of the competitive situation in Window Rock proved to be correct. The KFC franchise was especially vulnerable to the newer, better managed CCR. Nelson later learned some specifics from Carla Yazzie, one of the day managers at the KFC whom he hired during CCR's third year of operation. Yazzie told Nelson that revenues at the KFC dropped dramatically as soon as the CCR opened for business. Yazzie indicated that by the end of the first year of direct competition, KFC's revenues were down substantially, from about $500,000 in 1990 to about $250,000 in 1991. In the next two years, KFC's revenues recovered slowly to approximately $450,000.

Exhibit 1   **Historical Financial Statements—Church's Chicken Restaurant—Window Rock, Arizona (in thousands of dollars)**

	1994	1993	1992	1991
Revenues	$712	$664	$594	$457
Cost of Sales	250	235	232	174
Gross Profit	462	429	362	283
Lease Expense	36	36	36	36
Other Operating Expense	306	286	274	201
Total Operating Expense	342	322	310	237
Depreciation	11	18	27	16
Interest	11	4	6	3
Before Tax Profit	98	85	19	27
Income Tax	20	17	3	4
Net Profit	$ 78	$ 68	$ 16	$ 23

THE TUBA CITY OPTION

Starting a new restaurant in Tuba City was a complex undertaking, but Nelson was convinced that it could be very successful. For a physical facility, a new building was to be constructed on land controlled by Nelson and adjacent to one of his existing businesses, the V&S Variety Store. The location was on the corner of two major traffic arteries, State Highway 264 and Navajo Boulevard. Nelson had employed an architect in Flagstaff, Arizona, to develop plans for the building and following this had obtained a firm bid for the cost to construct the building. After including the additional costs for equipment, fixtures, and installation, the total cost for the physical facility ready to do business was $700,000.

Tuba City had a larger retail trade sector than Window Rock. There were eleven restaurants, including a 7-year old, successful KFC (operating out of a clean, attractive facility), plus a McDonald's, a Taco Bell, and a Dairy Queen. The proposed location of the Church's Chicken Restaurant was between the KFC and McDonald's and across the street from Taco Bell and Dairy Queen. The restaurants were located within one-half mile of each other on Highway 264.

Nelson had already met with Jennifer Simpson, a Commercial Loan Officer at Norwest Bank in Prescott, Arizona, and indicated that he wanted to finance the new business with a combination of internal and external funds (see Exhibit 2). Nelson had an excellent record in his business relations with Norwest. They had provided the bulk of the financing for his CCR at Window Rock and he was current on his loan repayments. Simpson was receptive to the idea for providing funding to Nelson provided that the new business venture met their loan criteria.

Norwest's loan request package included five years of pro forma income and cash flow statements (see Exhibit 3—Letter from Norwest Bank). Based on his experience with Norwest Bank in obtaining financing for the CCR in Window Rock, Nelson knew that the Loan Officer would require detailed substantiation

Exhibit 2	**Capital Requirements and Sources Summary Church's Chicken Restaurant—Tuba City, Arizona**	

Requirements	
Design and Construct Facility	$500,000
Fixtures, Furniture & Equipment	200,000
Inventory	10,000
Beginning Cash	40,000
Total Requirements	$750,000
Sources	
Cash from Michael Nelson	$100,000
Norwest Bank - Loan	650,000
Total Sources	$750,000

Exhibit 3   **Letter from Norwest Bank**

Mr. Michael Nelson
Church's Chicken Restaurant
Window Rock, Arizona 86887

Dear Mr. Nelson,

It was a pleasure to meet with you last week and discuss the proposal to open a new Church's Chicken Restaurant in Tuba City. Norwest Bank would appreciate the opportunity to provide the financing for this business venture. We invite you to submit a loan application for this proposal at your earliest convenience.

The major categories to be addressed in your loan proposal are:

1. An assessment of the market to be served including demographics, economic factors, and present and anticipated competition.
2. A description of the marketing strategy to be employed.
3. A management plan including the identification of key personnel and their responsibilities.
4. A financial plan including pro forma annual income and cash flow statements for the first five (5) years of operations.

As I noted in our conversation, it is very important that you generate a sales forecast that is based on a reliable methodology and is not overly optimistic. The traffic count model you mentioned, using information from your Window Rock restaurant, together with sales estimates from the Kentucky Fried Chicken restaurant in Tuba City and justifiable growth projections should satisfy our requirements in this area. Our loan review committee will accept cost estimates that are based on your experience with the Window Rock operation.

The loan amortization schedule for your pro forma income and cash flow statements should be based on the following information:

Interest rate: 9.75%

Term of loan: Seven years (84 months)

Principal and interest payments would begin as soon as the restaurant opens for business and would be due monthly.

I hope to receive your loan application in the near future.

Sincerely,

Jennifer Simpson

Commercial Loan Officer

---

for his projected revenues and costs. The proposed business must also be able to show a positive net income by the third year and a cumulative positive net income for the five-year period. Finally, the proposed business must show positive pro forma cash flows over the period; that is, it must be able to meet its annual cash requirements without the need for additional cash infusions.

As he watched the customers come and go, Nelson went over in his mind the information required for the loan application. Firm, reliable estimates of the costs for the physical facilities at Tuba City had been made. Historical income statements were available from the Window Rock restaurant to use in estimating the costs for the new restaurant. The major tasks remaining were the development of a five year sales revenue forecast and subsequent pro forma financial statements.

THE SALES FORECAST

Prior to his meeting with Ms. Simpson at Norwest Bank, Nelson had met with a business consultant regarding several financial aspects of the proposed restaurant, including the sales forecast. The consultant had advised Nelson to build a base level (first year) sales forecast using his experience at the Window Rock restaurant together with traffic count information from Window Rock and Tuba City. This base level sales forecast could then be adjusted each year for expected growth in his target market. When this sales forecasting technique had been discussed with Simpson, she was willing to use it.

Traffic counts would be taken at both the CCR in Window Rock and the KFC in Tuba City. These counts would be obtained during an identical time frame on the same days. Based on his experience in Window Rock, Nelson knew that weekdays were busier than weekends, so he decided to collect hourly traffic counts on a Tuesday and Saturday of the same week. In addition, sales revenues would be collected on an hourly basis at the CCR in Window Rock. The traffic count data had two uses: first to compare the size of the markets in Window Rock and Tuba City, and second to estimate the revenues of the KFC in Tuba City. With this information and Nelson's experience in competing directly with KFC in Window Rock, a base level sales forecast could be made. The traffic counts and revenue data were completed on January 28, 1994, and the results are shown in Exhibit 4.

Once the base level sales forecast was developed, forecasts for the remaining four years could be made using a "growth model" approach. Using this approach, the second year's revenues would be based on the base year; the third year's based on the second year; and so forth. The adjustment for growth would be based on either Nelson's experience at CCR in Window Rock or the expected retail sales growth in the Tuba City market. To facilitate this step, Nelson had gathered information on income and population growth in Arizona, the Navajo Nation, and Tuba City. This data is summarized in Exhibit 5.

THE PRO FORMA FINANCIAL STATEMENTS

Nelson planned to complete the pro forma income statements by using the sales forecasts together with information from the historical income statements at the CCR in Window Rock. To generate the pro forma cash flow analysis, he intended to use a procedure he had learned while developing an earlier loan proposal. During the five-year period of analysis, he did not plan to vary inventory substantially from its beginning level of $10,000. Therefore, cash flow generated annually from operations could be estimated by the following calculation:

$$\text{Cash Flow} = \text{Net Income} + \text{Depreciation} - \text{Principal Payment}$$

If this calculation was positive, "cash flow" would be positive. Alternatively, if the calculation was negative, this indicated a negative "cash flow," requiring an infusion of additional capital to the business.

Exhibit 4   **Traffic Counts and Sales Data**

Location: Kentucky Fried Chicken—Tuba City, Arizona

Dates: Tuesday, January 24, and Saturday, January 28, 1995

	Traffic		Customers Walk-ins		Customers Drive-ins	
	1-24	1-28	1-24	1-28	1-24	1-28
Time Period						
10–11AM	975	192	13	3	5	2
11–Noon	1125	789	50	14	11	5
Noon–1PM	1386	878	74	36	32	7
1–2PM	758	803	62	18	12	8
2–3PM	615	492	38	21	13	8
3–4PM	819	643	19	21	11	7
4–5PM	691	511	36	5	8	4
5–6PM	1085	728	36	18	14	6
6–7PM	702	803	13	67	14	10
7–8PM	706	945	28	40	19	9
8–9PM	380	783	20	46	9	14
9–Close	—	363	—	24	—	7
Totals	9242	7930	389	313	134	87

Location: Church's Chicken Restaurant—Window Rock, Arizona

Dates: Tuesday, January 24, and Saturday, January 28, 1995

	Traffic		Customers Walk-ins		Customers Drive-ins		Sales	
	1-24	1-28	1-24	1-28	1-24	1-28	1-24	1-28
Time Period								
10–11AM	186	320	11	10	8	2	$ 93	$ 40
11–Noon	248	851	18	36	12	9	188	154
Noon–1PM	1311	813	62	21	10	2	399	107
1–2PM	608	404	34	16	9	10	162	123
2–3PM	1083	973	79	30	12	12	138	152
3–4PM	507	762	26	26	14	10	120	156
4–5PM	668	761	53	20	8	3	201	100
5–6PM	1071	836	31	28	16	14	174	182
6–7PM	801	615	35	30	24	16	248	206
7–8PM	768	468	34	24	20	14	189	148
8–9PM	1405	534	36	33	14	9	301	255
9–Close	523	620	—	6	—	10	—	125
Totals	9179	7957	419	283	147	111	$2213	$1748

Exhibit 5   **Demographic Data**

Market Area Populations - Current and Forecast

	Census 1990	Forecast 1995	Forecast 2000
Window Rock	6187	6806	7487
Window Rock Market Area	11718	12890	14179
Tuba City	7983	8901	9924
Tuba City Market Area	8983	10002	11141

Population and Personal Income Growth Rates (%)

	1990	1991	1992	1993	1994	1995	1996–2000
Arizona Population Growth	2.3	2.1	2.4	2.4	2.5	2.5	2.6
Personal Inc. Growth	5.6	4.5	6.6	7.0	8.1	8.3	8.0
Per Capita Inc. Growth	3.3	2.1	4.2	4.6	5.6	5.8	5.4
Navajo Nation Per Capita Income Growth	1.9	0.6	2.7	3.1	4.1	4.3	3.9
Tuba City Population Growth						2.2	2.2

Source: U.S. Census 1990 - Population and Housing Characteristics of the Navajo Nation

THE DECISION

Nelson was scheduled to meet with the Norwest Commercial Loan Officer in two weeks. The project would either move ahead or be aborted based on the pro forma financial statements.

Nelson refocused his attention to the activity at the restaurant. He noticed that the lunch "rush" was about over and most of the booths were now empty. Two employees, Navajo youths of high school age, were busy tidying up the facility. Glancing outside, he observed a slow but steady stream of drive-in customers arriving and departing with their "drumsticks." "I will sure be excited to get started on my next restaurant," Nelson thought to himself.

Distinctive Displays Deux

William S. Silver, University of Denver

C. Thomas Howard, University of Denver

Maclyn L. Clouse, University of Denver

"Jaime, this isn't working. I'm not telling you how to run your business, but the numbers show that we're not making any money on these accounts. You can't make chicken soup out of chicken poop."

With these parting words, Robert Hackett, the Vice President/ Controller of Distinctive Displays, stormed out of Jaime Sampson's office. For the second time in as many weeks, they had been arguing about the problems with the new people who came over from the acquisition of Environs. Was it only six months ago that everyone had been excited about the acquisition, and the opportunities for growth it represented? As Owner and President of Distinctive Displays, Jaime once again found himself thinking about his company—its past, present and future.

THE COMPANY

In 1969, Jaime Sampson was nearing the end of a professional ice hockey career. In preparation for the transition to a new career, he began to work part-time as an industrial designer. But the thought of going to work for someone else was not at all appealing to him and so he moved to Portland and formed Distinctive Displays, an exhibit design and production company. Over the years Distinctive Displays evolved into a "full service company" providing design, fabrication, graphics, shipping, set-ups, dismantling, and storage of exhibits.

Although exhibits are produced for a variety of applications (e.g., for sales offices, meeting rooms, store displays), Distinctive Displays had specialized in custom exhibits for national trade shows. Most of Distinctive Displays' clients were organizations that needed exhibits developed for trade shows sponsored by their industry associations. For example, the Ski Industries of America had a trade show every year in March to show products that were to be available for the following year (winter ski season). People who attended these shows were buying their inventory for the following year or they were trying to find out what type of advertising and marketing support the companies would provide to them. Distinctive Displays helped exhibitors determine ways to impact the attendee at different levels, so that they were drawn to an exhibit, and so that they remembered it.

The Account Executives at Distinctive Displays were the primary contacts with the clients. In order to provide the best service, Account Executives sat down with clients and determined the type of shows they wanted to go to, the size of the exhibits, the products they wanted to promote, and the marketing objectives for the exhibit. A good Account Executive tried to nurture the relationship so that the client returned for new exhibits each year. Upon determining the client's needs, the Account Executive passed on the information to an Exhibit Designer, who created a representation of the exhibit for presentation to the client. Originally these presentations consisted of three-dimensional models and two-dimensional drawings. In the past few years, the Designers at Distinctive Displays had been using CAD to make three-dimensional graphic presentations to clients. The CAD technology enabled them to create a number of different views of the exhibit, and to more easily incorporate changes into the design.

Once the client approved the design, it went to the Production department, where professional builders constructed the exhibit. These builders came from a wide variety of backgrounds including furniture, crafts, home building, general construction, and stage production for theater. Distinctive Displays was a small non-union shop. Occasionally some people came by and talked about setting up a union, but none of the workers were interested because of the benefits they already received. A lot of the problems that could have existed in a larger shop did not occur at Distinctive Displays, which prided itself on having a "professional" environment at work. Distinctive Displays traditionally had a very low turnover rate, and most employees had worked more than five years for the company.

COMPANY MISSION AND GOALS (FROM THE COMPANY MISSION STATEMENT)

Although the primary product to its clientele was service, Distinctive Displays was a creative resource whose basic market area included the design, fabrication, and installation of Industrial Trade Show Exhibits, Interiors, and Visual Merchandising Components. The objective of this creative organization was to sell its products and services through imaginative design, component craftsmanship, coordinated integral skills, and orderly management in both detail and system, in order to produce a tangible profit for self-investment and future growth.

Distinctive Displays was a highly action-oriented and result-motivated firm. It prided itself in its ability to analyze needs, solve problems, and select forms and materials expressive of the dynamics of visual and structural communication. Skills, tools, and environment; men and women, attitudes, and creative challenges epitomized the resources directed in the service of on-time, on-price delivery of powerful selling devices to the client.

COMPANY STRATEGY AND PERFORMANCE

Distinctive Displays' fundamental strategy was to work with major regional corporations to meet their needs with respect to exhibits at trade shows throughout the United States. Accounts ranged in size from $10,000 annually to as high as $200,000. Exhibits, once constructed, were reused as often as six times at various trade shows. Consequently, dismantling, shipping, storage, and set up represented a significant portion of total revenues. Distinctive Displays was able to meet a customer's needs from the very first contact all the way through to the final disposal of the exhibit, a period extending as long as two years.

Compared to its chief regional competitors, Distinctive Displays was a very efficient operation. Among other things, it had the highest sales per employee, the second highest sales per square foot of space, the highest net worth, the highest current ratio, and the highest Dun and Bradstreet (DB) credit rating.

However, in the 1990s, the business situation had changed. The market was more competitive and the company had not performed well financially. For example, sales declined an average of 2.2% from 1990 through 1994, and return on sales declined from 8.6% to 4.4%, compared to a national average of 8.8% (in the $1.3 to $2 million sales category). By late 1994 Sampson felt that Distinctive Displays could no longer continue to operate as it had in the past. "I had the gut feeling that we weren't going to be able to do it anymore. The numbers made it obvious. The look of Distinctive Displays was going to change; and, personally, I was getting tired. I was having to work more hours, and I was getting less in return."

POSSIBLE NEW DIRECTIONS

Sampson considered a number of alternatives. The easiest option was to sell the company to one of his larger competitors. Giltspur had offered him a sweetened deal, including the presidency of the company in 3 to 5 years, if he would sell to them. Although this alternative probably represented the most personal financial gain, Sampson didn't really want to work for someone else. Nor was he ready to cash out and spend all his time golfing.

A second option was to attempt to penetrate the national trade show market by opening satellite offices in other cities. While the national market seemed a good opportunity for growth, opening new offices seemed inefficient since Sampson felt that Distinctive Displays had been underutilizing both human and facilities resources. Sampson estimated that Distinctive Displays could have handled about $3.5 million in sales, about $1.5 million dollars more business than it had in 1994.

A final option was to acquire one of the competitors and move up to a significantly higher level of sales. Sampson felt that this alternative was attractive because Portland was building a new convention center. He thought this might have opened a new market for Distinctive Displays: companies outside the region with trade show exhibits in the new convention center. This new opportunity combined with a strengthening regional economy might have allowed Distinctive Displays to take advantage of its excess capacity. Also, an increase in size might have forestalled the entry of a national firm, such as Exhibitgroup or Giltspur, which could have been attracted to the Portland market as a result of the new convention center.

ACQUISITION OF ENVIRONS

The best prospect for an acquisition involved Environs, Inc., a company formed by Lee Hanson in 1983. Environs was widely recognized as the most creative company in Portland's permanent exhibit and display market. Permanent exhibits were used by home builders, manufacturers, retailers, and many other businesses, primarily in sales offices, store displays, and conference rooms.

Hanson's skills were mainly in the areas of sales and marketing. Because of her creative talents and a strong local economy, Environs' company sales doubled every year between 1985 and 1989. With regard to other aspects of the business, Hanson knew little about the cost of producing displays and, in her own words, Environs' production process was "organized chaos." She found it exhilarating to create "monuments" but had little patience for the many details of running a business. She loved to compete and win; until 1992 she was winning.

In 1992 Hanson made what proved to be two fateful decisions. With help from strong sales and profit growth, she convinced a local savings and loan to extend Environs an unsecured $215,000 line of credit. In addition, she purchased a 40,000-square-foot building with a mortgage from another local savings and loan and moved Environs to the new location. Consistent with Hanson's style, Environs' new facility included an elaborate display and sales area and a smaller production area. When the Portland economy turned soft in 1993, Environs lost two of its major customers, accounting for more than 50% of sales. By 1995 sales had dropped by 30% relative to 1992 and losses were exceeding $100,000 per year.

Throughout 1994 and early 1995 it seemed that the "big" deals came just in time to keep the doors open. However, in the fall of 1995, Sampson heard that Hanson was having difficulty making tax payments, and had begun the process of closing down her company. At this time Hanson contacted Sampson and the possibility of an acquisition was raised.

Sampson entered into negotiations with Hanson feeling as if he held all the trump cards. "That was a wonderful way to enter a negotiation because all I had to do was listen. And I could have said no. I knew Lee was going to go bankrupt. She realized that she had no alternative for the near future. However, I felt that it was important to negotiate in good faith. I wanted to determine what would best serve both of our interests so we both could make the company grow. I wanted her to show up here with bells and whistles on, and saying, 'I have got a real good opportunity here. I can bring what I do best, to a company I respect and a guy I can work with, and maybe we can turn it into something bigger than the sum of its parts.' So she was quite pleased in that the agreement far exceeded anything she expected to receive. I gave her more incentive than was really required."

The deal with Hanson had three main components. The first part had to do with the former employees of Environs. Distinctive Displays agreed to hire six production workers and two Account Executives. Sampson felt he was generous in that he agreed to match their former wages. All of the new personnel were placed on a 90-day probationary employment status, as specified by company policy. The second part of the agreement contained provisions specific to Hanson, who was given the title of Executive Vice-President. Her compensation package included a 10% commission on sales, $50,000 annual salary, $9,000 annual car allowance, and $9,000 annual expense allowance.

The third section of the agreement concerned special provisions involving the long-term position of Lee Hanson. Fifty percent of the net profit percentage reported on Distinctive Displays' year-end income statement of sales credited to Lee Hanson (and the two former Environs Account Executives) was to be paid to Hanson at an agreed-upon time after the first year. If Hanson were to continue her employment with Distinctive Displays after the end of the first year: 1. Upon the first day of the second year of employment, she would receive 10% of the sale price of Distinctive Displays in the event of such sale; 2. Upon the discontinuance of employment for any reason after the end of the first year, provision 1. above would be void and Hanson would receive 10% of the equity of Distinctive Displays.

THE VISION OF THE FUTURE

Sampson was pleased with the agreement for a number of reasons.

I thought she would bring $1 million worth of diversification work. I knew she had a direct conduit into the developers market in Portland, which is primarily interior designs, and good national contacts. I didn't expect her to bring over any trade show exhibit work, but I thought the permanent display work would enable Distinctive Displays to capture incremental revenues with the same shop. Lee liked the fact that she could have autonomy with her same client base, but that the burden of production and finance would be off her shoulders.

I was also excited on a more personal level. I had first become aware of Lee in the early 1980s as our respective companies grew to prominence in Portland's regional market. In 1985, while I was president of the Exhibit Designers and Production Association, I invited Hanson to join the association. From that time on we had stayed in close contact with one another. I had always been impressed with Hanson's creative and marketing abilities and the speed with which Environs became a major player in the industry. Through the years, mutual respect helped to build our relationship.

I liked the situation in that Hanson would work for me as my Executive VP for Marketing. I was concerned that Hanson tended to be too reckless in business decisions, and too unorganized in the way she managed her work. I thought Hanson and her sales force would infuse a new burst of energy into Distinctive Displays, but I would be able to monitor and control her activities. With time, I hoped that Hanson would develop a broader business perspective that would have enabled her to take over the leadership of the company. I wanted to mentor her through this process.

There was a new sense of expectation throughout the company. Everyone was excited. People were very receptive and friendly to their new colleagues. I had to make adjustments upward to level the salary of my people with the salary her people were making. My people were happy they got paid more. (In some cases too much as far as I was concerned. I felt that Lee was over-paying her people.) We were getting shop people that knew how to do permanent exhibits. Before they started we had a meeting. I told them that I wanted to be sensitive to the fact that this was a new culture for them. I said "I want to learn from you. Teach us. We'll both learn from each other."

■ Culture Clashes

However, Sampson soon discovered that this arrangement was not going to proceed as smoothly as he hoped. Reports from the shop floor suggested that many of the former Environs employees were having difficulty accepting Distinctive Displays' way of doing business. They believed that the ways in which they did their job were adequate, since these methods used to work for them when they worked at Environs. A good example was the issue of touch-up kits.

When a Distinctive Displays exhibit went out, it included a touch-up kit of everything necessary to set it up, clean it, and repair it. The touch-up kits were a unique aspect of the service that Distinctive Displays offered its clients. Sampson had a great deal of pride in his exhibits. More than once he stated that his booths were prepared better than anybody else's in the industry. The former Environs employees had a great deal of trouble understanding the importance of putting together the touch-up kits. If they bothered to put together the touch-up kits at all they were haphazard and incomplete.

Another example was in the preparation of existing exhibits that clients wanted to re-use. At Distinctive Displays these exhibits were taken from storage and given a complete overhaul. They were cleaned, checked for all the parts, and then fixed up and made to look as good as possible for shipment to the show. The approach of the former Environs employees was to just send out the old exhibit, and then send out spare parts later if the client called and complained. The attitude was one of "Oh well, it's just a mistake. No big deal. We'll just fix it."

The dress code at Distinctive Displays also created friction with the former Environs employees. The company policy was that employees couldn't wear cut-off shirts or shorts. Current and prospective clients often visited the building and wandered through the production area and Jaime wanted to maintain an atmosphere of professionalism. However, the former Environs employees felt it was unfair for them to have to wear their nice clothes when they would only get ruined on the job.

In short, Jaime was told by some of his production staff that the work ethic of the former Environs employees was different from that of the Distinctive Displays people. They lacked pride in their work, and didn't have a sense of professionalism. They tended to take a short-cut anytime they could. If they could be late to work and get away with it, they would do it all the time. When the production department was given a project with many specifications, the Distinctive Displays people tended to view it as a challenge. The Environs people tended to complain about how rigid things were and how the Designers did not allow them enough creativity.

However, not all the reports from the shop floor were negative. The shop foreman, John Mattia, painted a more promising picture. He felt that the people from Environs had some unique production and design talents, and that many of the comments that Jaime had heard were more a matter of professional jealousy than actual work problems. He attributed much of the trouble to the fact that any time you have two cultures coming together, there is bound to be some friction. According to Mattia, "The Environs culture was more carefree. Their people didn't sweat the little details, and were more than willing to work with the client to make any changes or correct any problems. By contrast, the Distinctive Displays approach was more formalized. We got all the project specifications straight up front, and charged the client for any changes."

Based on his conversations with Mattia, Jaime maintained a sense of optimism that the problems would work themselves out. He let go a few of the people that either didn't have the necessary skills to be productive at Distinctive Displays, or that couldn't work under the Distinctive Displays system. He looked forward to the annual meeting, which he saw as a great opportunity to get everyone working together as a high-performance team.

ANNUAL MEETING

Every year in March, Distinctive Displays had its annual meeting. People left work early, went home, got dressed up, and came back to the shop, where the catered event was held. The employees had 30 days prior to the meeting to submit anything they wanted to have discussed at the meeting.

In March of 1996, the atmosphere at the annual meeting was very positive. The general sentiment among all employees was, "Let us get it together and make it work!" For many employees, the meeting was a learning experience. Jaime put on an elaborate presentation with graphs comparing Distinctive Displays to the rest of the industry. He explained the general business strategy and discussed specifics regarding client base, location, volume, profits, and losses.

It was at this meeting that Jaime first felt some doubts about the commitment and capability of Lee Hanson. He had asked Lee to prepare a sales and marketing presentation for the meeting.

> During the meeting she bombed. She was not prepared, had no notes, talked in generalities and in cliches. She basically shot from the hip and did what she does best—sweet-talk people. I said to myself that we had a problem here. It was evident to other Distinctive Displays employees that it was an embarrassment to me personally, since I had brought her in, and she was not the same caliber of leader they were used to. I began to suspect that the reason there were problems with some of the other Environs employees was due to their having the same carefree and nonchalant attitude that I had seen in Lee.

PERFORMANCE OF LEE HANSON AND THE FORMER ENVIRONS ACCOUNT EXECUTIVES

> After the meeting I raised my antenna and more closely observed Lee's performance. However, I always felt that I should not be my brother's keeper. I wanted to be an agent for her success and provide her with whatever she needed, whether it was marketing, or expenses, or accounting.

Despite some of these misgivings, Jaime was still strongly committed to making the acquisition work.

> I really had only some superficial observations that things could be wrong. I went into this whole thing knowing that there was a potential for loss. I thought I could turn it around. If someone told me that I couldn't turn it around I would not have agreed with them. The revenue numbers looked good.

In late June of 1996, Robert Hackett, the Controller of Distinctive Displays, requested a meeting with Sampson to discuss the company's recent performance.

He brought up three concerns involving Lee Hanson and the former Environs employees. The first issue had to do with the margins on the permanent display exhibits. They had projected the million dollars of new volume on a cost and margin basis as trade show exhibits. As it turned out, the structures of the permanent display market and the trade show market were very different.

Robert Hackett described these differences.

> The market demanded low prices. We thought that because of our efficiency, management team, better facilities, technology, and accounting that we could make a profit in this market. However, clients were critical of any price increase. Previously, permanent displays were constructed piece-meal, where components for the overall exhibit came from many different sources. Lee was able to put the whole thing together by herself and for 17% more than what the client could do himself without the headache. When we tried to raise the margin to 60% the client decided it was worth it to do it by himself. They tended to view the exhibit as a conglomerate of pieces of wood, and thus had a commodity mentality. We saw ourselves as providing successful sales results for the client.

A second problem Robert raised had to do with collecting from the permanent display clients after the exhibits had been built.

> The accounts receivables for Lee and her Account Executives averaged 102 days, compared to 36 days for everyone else. We couldn't work with fifty-three days of float. Clients liked to keep the Account Executives hanging on a string. They would say "We have a $50,000 project next month—make sure you help me out on this one." Our policy was that the Account Executives should not take a carrot like that. Every project needed to be its own profit center.

A third concern Robert discussed involved the way in which Lee and her people managed their projects.

> They gave away too much. We knew how much a project would cost before we would build it. We priced along a matrix and the client signed off according to this price. If there were any changes or problems then costs went up. Instead of telling their clients it would cost them for not making the decision today, or for not getting the camera-ready artwork done in time, Lee and her Account Executives gave these services away after the fact because they were so willing to please the clients. In addition to a "please-the-client-at-all-costs" mentality, Lee and her people were running the costs up on their projects because of sloppy work. In our business, the Account Executive was the only one who knew everything about the project. If he could not pass on the information correctly to production, then problems could occur in colors, pricing, time frames, etc. If the Account Executive came back and said that this is not what he told the client, then we would need to go back and do it again.

■ Decisions

Sampson wondered what would be the best course of action for himself, and for his company.

> It's not that I wasn't concerned about the points that Robert was raising, it's just that Robert has a typical CFO mentality. He sees everything in terms of black and white—what do the numbers show? But this type of thinking leads to short-term management. I had to be concerned with the strategic implications. We had in part accomplished our goal. Our business volume went up and we were using up our excess capacity. The one down side was that we weren't making enough profits on this new business.

But I wasn't sure whether the fault lay in Lee and her people, or in the permanent display market. Lee had done very well up until the past year, and was well-respected in the permanent display industry. I wondered if I had done a good job of harnessing her talents. And I wasn't sure that it was her fault if her clients were late on payments. Furthermore, I was still trying to be sensitive to the fact that we were new to the permanent display market. Our pricing may have been wrong, and our systems might have needed some adjustment.

I was thinking at the time that if the permanent display market turned out to be unprofitable, I could move Lee into trade shows. In the back of my mind I was looking for help. I was hoping that just by osmosis she would see trade shows and would learn to do them. My CFO, Robert, kept pressing me to cut my losses and move on. He insisted that Lee and her people did not want to learn new ways of doing things. But I kept thinking back to my reasons for taking Lee on. They still seemed to be valid. If I got rid of Lee, I would be right back where I started from.

Mac's Model Toys

Horace O. Kelly, Jr.,
Wake Forest University

Thomas S. Goho, Wake Forest University

John S. Dunkelberg,
Wake Forest University

INTRODUCTION

Mac Jones had just finished the busiest Christmas season he had ever enjoyed in his part-time business of supplying model toys to model railroad enthusiasts. As he sat by the fire in his parents' home in Indiana before returning to school, he realized he had a major decision to make about his career. At age 21, Mac was four and a half months away from graduating from a major southeastern university with a degree in Business Administration and he could not get excited about going through the process of interviewing for a job with a large corporation. His part-time business of the past four years had been a rewarding experience and, in fact, had paid for a large percentage of his college education. The more he reflected on how much he enjoyed this business, the more he realized that what he really wanted to do was pursue the business full time and see if he could grow it to the point where he could enjoy a comfortable living from it.

After dinner that evening, Mac was sitting by the fire as his father came into the room. "What's up?" his father asked. "You seem like you are very deep in thought." Mac replied, "I was just thinking about what I want to do when I graduate. The more I think about it, I believe I would like to try to take our part-time business to a full-time basis. What do you think, Dad?" "Gosh, I don't know Mac," replied Larry, Mac's father. "It is one thing to run a business like this part-time where there is nothing on the line, but trying to do it on a full-time basis and pay yourself a full-time salary, hire people to help you run it, and, of course, we could not run it from the basement anymore—this is a big decision, Mac. Have you really thought through all the things you would have to do to go full time?"

Mac basically ran the business during the summer months when he was not in school and relied on his father to handle the details of the orders and billings during the school year. So, his father's opinions were valuable to Mac because both had seen the business grow over the years and they were both familiar with how it had been operated.

The more they talked that evening, the more enthusiastic his father became. "You know, Mac, if you do this right, I mean consider all the factors involved, I do not see why it could not be done. After all, we have been pretty successful just on the part-time basis, and you have done most of the work yourself. If it is really what you want to do, I think you should give it a try!"

His father's enthusiasm was infectious and before the evening was over, Mac had made his decision to explore the possibility. He decided that upon returning to school, one of his primary objectives would be to work on and complete a business plan for his venture and see what steps he needed to do to transform this profitable part-time activity into a successful full-time business.

■ Company Background

Mac's Model Toys began in 1988 as a mail order business targeting the model train enthusiasts segment of the "die-cast metal" replica market (miniature models of actual cars, trucks, construction equipment, made to scale with high quality finishes). The enthusiasts use these models to accessorize their model train layouts to give them a more realistic appearance.

Even from its beginning, Mac's Model Toys had a niche in this market place. It became the first distributor to offer a large selection of affordable, high quality die-cast metal replicas targeted specifically to the model train segment of the market. While there were several competitors in the die-cast metal replica market (at least other companies that manufactured and sold these models in toy stores), none were targeting this particular segment of the market.

The company grew slowly in the early years because advertising funds were limited (see Exhibits 1 and 2 for customer and sales growth figures). Most of its early sales were generated through selling at model train enthusiasts trade shows and shipping orders by mail and UPS that resulted from placing an occasional inexpensive ad in publications that catered to this market, such as *O Gauge Railroading Magazine* and *O Scale News.*

Exhibit 1	History of the Number of Customers

Year	Number of Customers
1988	97
1989	206
1990	410
1991	826
1992	2,189
1993	3,167

Exhibit 2   **Historical Sales and Net Income**

Year	Total Sales	Net Income
1988	$ 2,550	$ 505
1989	$ 5,281	$ 1,113
1990	$ 10,985	$ 2,345
1991	$ 21,066	$ 4,198
1992	$ 91,786	$18,675
1993	$204,465	$25,213

Currently, Mac attends about twelve trade shows a year with a fairly sophisticated display. He passes out brochures to everyone who comes by his booth and sells over the counter to these customers.

THE INDUSTRY

The die-cast replica market is fairly large. It consists of mass-produced regular toys from well-known producers such as Matchbox and Tonka; limited selections from standard toy makers such as Mattel and Hasbro; and, handmade detailed collectibles from a large assortment of small makers and manufacturers.

Mac's research from industry publications and a recent survey completed for *O Gauge Railroading Magazine* indicates that this total market exceeds $80,000,000 in annual revenues. Of this, an estimated 12.5% is spent on die-cast metal replicas and accessories. Consequently, the total potential market for the segment Mac is pursuing is estimated to generate total annual sales of approximately $10,000,000. Based on Mac's sales figures, he currently estimates his share of this segment of the market to be about 2%; but, he believes he can achieve about 3.5% after his first full year of full-time operations, resulting in total sales of about $350,000.

Based on the *O Gauge Railroading* survey, Mac estimates that the market will grow at approximately 2.5% per year in terms of revenues for the next 20 to 25 years. He sees this as his "window of opportunity" because there is evidence that the number of enthusiasts in model railroading is steadily declining but the existing customers, as they move into retirement, will have more time and disposable income to pursue their hobby and the figures indicate they will be around in significant numbers for about 25 years. The data presented in Exhibits 3 and 4 are from the *O Gauge Railroading* survey, including responses from over 3,000 readers representing approximately 10% of the magazine's total circulation of 30,000 subscribers. The typical model train enthusiast is between 40 and 60 years of age (67%), and most make their purchases equally between mail order and model train shows (49.2 and 48.2%, respectively).

Mac interprets these figures as a positive indication of the future of this industry. The typical enthusiast is a person who is most likely at the peak of his earning power. Further, as they approach retirement, the hobby will likely take on an even greater significance as they will likely have the disposable income

Exhibit 3

Model Train Enthusiasts Age Groupings

Age	Percentage
Under 30	3
30 – 39	11
40 – 49	34
50 – 59	33
60 – 69	13
70 and Over	6

Exhibit 4

Method of Purchasing Model Toys

Method	Percentage*
Mail Order	49.2
Train Shows	48.2
Hobby Stores	36.5

*These figures represent the percentage of the survey respondents who said they made purchases from each outlet. A single respondent may have made purchases from more than one outlet.

Exhibit 5

Target Market Summary and Highlights

- 67% between 40 and 60 years of age
- 64% have been in the hobby for over 20 years
- 49% use mail order for purchasing
- 48% use train shows for purchasing

and the time to pursue the hobby even more vigorously. Mac believes that although the target market may decrease only marginally in numbers of enthusiasts, the amount of money spent by the existing members will likely increase. In any event, even if the sheer numbers of customers increase only marginally, based on an analysis of their ages, there is still a window of opportunity of about 20 to 25 years where sales should continue to increase.

Further evidence that was encouraging to Mac was a survey he conducted on his own. From a copy of the Lionel Collector's Club of America's annual membership roster, Mac randomly selected 175 names from the 12,000 members and mailed a questionnaire and one of his catalogs to each potential respondent. The sample was skewed to the northeastern states since that is where a substantial source of his revenue is generated. Seventy-eight completed questionnaires were returned. Further, Mac and a friend each personally interviewed 11 respondents at two model train shows in Atlanta and

Philadelphia to bring his total number of interviews to 100. The findings, although not based on scientific sampling, were encouraging.

- 69% of the respondents were between 40 and 60 years of age
- 70% had incomes over $40,000
- 25% had incomes over $80,000
- 57% had been involved with the hobby for 20 years or more
- 60% spent over $750.00 annually on the hobby
- 58% indicated that mail order was the primary mode of purchase (42% indicated train shows as primary source)
- Over two thirds attend at least 1 trade show per year (30% attend between 4 and 6 shows per year)
- Over 66% indicate this is a "year-long hobby"
- 76% of those still employed are in "professional" positions (Managerial/ Engineering/Sales/Marketing)—22% are retired

THE DIRECT COMPETITION

As mentioned previously, the standard toy makers such as Mattel, Hasbro, Matchbox, and Tonka represent some competition but are not considered direct competitors.

In fact, no one retailer or supplier dominates this very dynamic market. The industry for the die-cast metal replicas, and more specifically the targeted segment of the model railroad enthusiasts, is even further segmented because of its size and the nature of the products offered. Since no one retailer is capable of carrying all the products in the die-cast industry, retailers are forced into segmenting themselves according to the types of products they sell (e.g., trucks, trains, automobiles, construction equipment, to name a few). They are also segmented on the size (scale) of the products they carry and the pricing strategy used (markups in this industry range from 85% to over 150% on most products).

Since the segmentation is so varied, it is difficult to isolate direct competitors to Mac's Model Toys. Judgmentally, this is why Mac's has been successful in increasing its market share annually. In fact, only one direct competitor can be identified who focuses on the same primary market where Mac's has positioned itself.

Eastwood Automobilia is a very serious competitor. Eastwood sells many of the same or similar products as Mac's. The only differentiating advantages that Mac's enjoys over Eastwood is inventory, and to some degree, price. Mac's has a much more comprehensive inventory and selection than does Eastwood and sells the products for less than Eastwood. Eastwood uses a high quality color catalog; they have an 800 number for placing orders; and it is estimated that Eastwood currently has about a 10% share of the $10,000,000 model train enthusiast market. Eastwood spends heavily on advertising and they have a strong name recognition in the market place.

Despite the competition from Eastwood, one fact that favors Mac's is that Eastwood targets multiple segments of the toy replica market so it does not concentrate specifically on the model train segment. Mac sees this as an advantage to him because it dilutes Eastwood's marketing and advertising efforts.

Mac feels his concentration, his more competitive pricing and the fact that he carries a much larger selection than Eastwood (for this market segment) give him some unique advantages over his primary direct competitor.

Mac realizes that if he is to compete with Eastwood and all the other direct and non-direct competitors, and if he is to grow this business so that it can support him on a full-time basis, much needs to be done.

ORGANIZATION OF THE BUSINESS

Presently, the company is organized as a sole proprietorship. This was easier for Mac to keep up with when the business was just a part-time operation, run primarily by Mac and his father, Larry.

Mac believes that, in the future, he will need to reorganize in order to protect himself and his father from possible liability issues as well as take advantage of some of the tax benefits afforded by other types of organization. Realizing the need for professional advice, Mac made appointments with an attorney and an accountant to discuss the alternatives.

BOARD OF DIRECTORS OR ADVISORS

Since the undertaking of going from a part-time business to a full-time career brings with it many challenges, Mac realized that some "organized" advice would be invaluable. Regardless of the type of corporation Mac chooses, he feels that he will need either an advisory board or a regular board of directors to aid him in his decisions.

Mac's father, Larry, has been involved in the business since its inception and loaned the business $15,000 to help get it started. He plans to continue his involvement in the business and has been a strong ally. It seemed very logical to Mac to invite his father to be one of his advisors or board members.

Mac has been doing business at a local bank for years and had a long conversation over the Christmas break with his banker, Sam Torrance, about the feasibility of going full time with this business. Mr. Torrance was very encouraging concerning the idea and even suggested that a loan for increasing Mac's inventory could easily be granted if Mac felt he needed it. Mr. Torrance had watched the business grow over the past 5 years and his positive attitude convinced Mac that Mr. Torrance would be a valuable member of the board.

After some encouraging conversations with Mr. Robert Broadwell, an attorney, and Mr. Lemuel Jackson, a CPA, Mac felt very comfortable asking them to assist him. Mac's reasoning was that having these professionals as advisors would afford him quite valuable advice from time to time and might save him some fees for soliciting the same advice.

Mac also felt it was important to have continuous feedback from both the supply and retail sides of his business. He asked his largest wholesale supplier, Fred Womble, and his largest retail customer, Orval Beck, if they would be interested in serving as advisors and they both agreed enthusiastically.

Now that the proposed seven-member board had been thought out, Mac asked each if he would be willing to serve during the formative years without compensation and they had all agreed if Mac decided to go into business fulltime. Mac's next step was to get the group together to present his business plan and solicit their suggestions.

FUNDING

Since this was an ongoing business, there was no need for large amounts of start-up capital. Mac realized, however, that to take this business full time, a significant increase in inventory would be necessary. He also realized that he could no longer run the business out of his father's house and he further realized that it would require additional employees to make the business run smoothly. Mac and his father could simply not do all that was necessary to run this business on a full-time basis by themselves.

He did not want to ask his father for any more loans. In fact, he wanted to find a way to pay off the $15,000 loan from his father so he could own the business outright. Knowing that the business had a pretty good cash flow situation and that his banker was amenable to a loan, Mac put together the following list of financial requirements that would be necessary for him to take the big step to a full-time business.

1. *Staffing.* Mac realized that with the responsibilities of growing and managing the business, he would need a full-time secretary to handle the everyday job of processing orders, keeping his customer database up to date, and handling payroll and tax records. He felt that he could find a competent person for a beginning salary of $15,000 per year with gradual increases built in as the business grew.

He also realized that he would need some help in filling orders from inventory, packaging those orders, and supervising the shipping requirements. He felt that he could save some money and overhead by hiring high school or college students on a part-time basis. As the business grew he would probably have to have full-time people as assistants so he built that projection into his financial statements. For the first year or two, he felt that he could find someone for $5.00 per hour/20 hours a week and probably expand that to two people in the second year. He knew that his father was still willing to put in some time on the business so between himself, his father, the new secretary, and the part-time student, he felt comfortable with his staffing plans for the first year or two.

Mac proposed a salary of $25,000 for himself in the first year with a $5,000 increase each year to achieve a salary of $50,000 in year five.

2. *Selling Expenses.* Trying to account for all of his expenses in selling his products, Mac listed the following:

- *Credit Card Discount.* Mac estimated that about 50% of his total sales will be through credit card purchases. This has been true historically and he further estimated that this will likely increase over the years to around 60%. The effective credit card discount is 2%; therefore, for year one, based on total sales projections of $350,000, the credit card expense would be about $3,500.

- *Sales Tax Expense.* The state from which Mac will operate charges 2% sales tax. Since most of Mac's orders come from out of his home state, sales tax is not usually charged. Therefore, he has not built in an expense for this since it will be minuscule.
- *Advertising Expense.* Mac realizes that his advertising budget will have to significantly increase if he is to grow the business. Therefore, he has built in an advertising budget of 4% of total sales. He plans to aggressively increase his advertising budget over the next five years from $14,000 in year one to $40,000 in year five.
- *Automobile Expense.* Traveling to shows is a large part of this business. Exposure at these shows generates name recognition for the business, builds new customers, and generates some sales. It is something that Mac realizes he will have to do on a consistent basis. Since he already has the displays built, his budget reflects only travel expenses of $6,000 the first year, increasing to $9,500 by year five.
- *Hotel Expense.* Mac anticipates hotel expenses to these trade shows to be about $1,200 for year one. This averages $80.00 per show for 15 shows, with gradual increases through year five.
- *Rental Expense.* A major expense will be rental space for the business. Mac feels that he will need a minimum of 2,000 square feet of warehouse space increasing to around 4,000 square feet by year five. Since he will not be operating a walk-in business where nice surroundings will be necessary, he can find suitable warehouse space in his hometown for about $5.00 per square foot.

CASH FLOW

After studying past cash flow statements, Mac recognized that, historically, the ending cash flow balance of the business had been between $7,500 and $15,000; this had always been reinvested in inventory. However, taking this business to a full-time basis would require a much larger inventory and his estimated cash infusion was going to have to be around $20,000. Based on his conversations with his banker, Mac knew that there would be no problem with obtaining the loan so he built this into his thinking. (See Exhibits 6, 7 and 8 for Pro Forma statements for the first five years.)

LOAN FROM LARRY JONES

As mentioned earlier, there exists a $15,000 loan from Mac's father that needs to be resolved. Mac could simply arrange a payback schedule for his father but he also wants to compensate his father's involvement in the business. Slightly complicating the issue is the fact that Mac wants ultimate control of the business (at least as much as practical) but does not want to alienate his father since his father has contributed so much to the business.

Mac's plan is to convert this existing personal loan into privately held shares in the company. This conversion of the Larry Jones debt to private stock will

Exhibit 6	Pro Forma Income Statement				
	Year 1	*Year 2*	*Year 3*	*Year 4*	*Year 5*
Sales					
Retail Sales	$280,000	$393,750	$503,750	$610,000	$ 750,000
Wholesale Sales	$ 70,000	$106,250	$146,250	$190,000	$ 250,000
Total Sales	**$350,000**	**$500,000**	**$650,000**	**$800,000**	**$1,000,000**
Less: Sales Refunds	($700)	($984)	($1,259)	($1,525)	($1,875)
Net Sales	$349,300	$499,016	$648,741	$798,475	$ 998,125
Cost of Goods Sold (COGS)					
Beginning Inventory	$ 50,000	$ 70,000	$ 80,000	$100,000	$ 125,000
Plus Purchases	$230,000	$316,250	$426,250	$535,000	$ 680,000
COG Available for Sale	$280,000	$386,250	$506,250	$635,000	$ 805,000
Less Ending Inventory	$ 70,000	$ 80,000	$100,000	$125,000	$ 155,000
Net Cost of Goods Sold	$210,000	$306,250	$406,250	$510,000	$ 650,000
Gross Margin	**$139,300**	**$192,766**	**$242,491**	**$288,475**	**$ 348,125**
	40%	39%	37%	36%	35%
Operating Expenses					
Selling Expenses					
Salary Expense	$ 25,000	$ 30,000	$ 35,000	$ 40,000	$ 45,000
Secretary Wages	$ 15,000	$ 15,500	$ 16,000	$ 16,500	$ 17,000
Employee Wages	$ 17,500	$ 25,000	$ 32,500	$ 40,000	$ 50,000
Credit Card Discount	$ 3,500	$ 5,168	$ 6,927	$ 8,769	$ 11,250
Sales Tax Expense	$ 336	$ 473	$ 605	$ 732	$ 900
Advertising Expense	$ 14,000	$ 20,000	$ 26,000	$ 32,000	$ 40,000
Automobile Expense	$ 3,000	$ 3,375	$ 3,750	$ 4,125	$ 4,500
Gasoline Expense	$ 3,000	$ 3,375	$ 3,750	$ 4,125	$ 4,500
Hotel/Travel Expense	$ 1,200	$ 1,400	$ 1,600	$ 1,800	$ 2,000
Shipping Expense	$ 10,500	$ 15,000	$ 19,500	$ 24,000	$ 30,000
Supplies Expense	$ 1,750	$ 2,500	$ 3,250	$ 4,000	$ 5,000
Total Selling Expenses	**$ 94,786**	**$121,791**	**$148,882**	**$176,051**	**$ 210,150**

Exhibit 6 (continued)   **Pro Forma Income Statement**

	Year 1	Year 2	Year 3	Year 4	Year 5
General Expenses					
Rent Expense	$ 10,000	$ 10,000	$ 15,000	$ 15,000	$ 20,000
FICA	$ 4,399	$ 5,393	$ 6,388	$ 7,382	$ 8,568
Unemployment Tax	$ 1,869	$ 1,939	$ 1,879	$ 1,689	$ 1,400
Workers' Compensation	$ 1,050	$ 1,200	$ 1,500	$ 1,500	$ 1,800
Accounting Fees	$ 1,000	$ 1,050	$ 1,100	$ 1,150	$ 1,200
Inventory Insurance	$ 1,400	$ 1,600	$ 2,000	$ 2,500	$ 3,100
Inventory Property Tax	$ 350	$ 400	$ 500	$ 625	$ 775
Legal Fees	$ 1,500	$ 750	$ 1,000	$ 1,250	$ 1,500
Office Furniture Lease	$ 500	$ 550	$ 600	$ 650	$ 700
Postage Expense	$ 3,500	$ 5,000	$ 6,500	$ 8,000	$ 10,000
Printing Expense	$ 10,500	$ 15,000	$ 19,500	$ 24,000	$ 30,000
Telephone Expense	$ 3,500	$ 5,000	$ 6,500	$ 8,000	$ 10,000
Utilities Expense	$ 1,800	$ 1,800	$ 2,700	$ 2,700	$ 3,600
Miscellaneous Expense	$ 350	$ 500	$ 650	$ 800	$ 1,000
Total General Expenses	**$ 41,718**	**$ 50,182**	**$ 65,817**	**$75,246**	**$ 93,643**
Total Operating Expenses	**$136,504**	**$171,973**	**$214,699**	**$251,297**	**$303,793**
Operating Profit	**$2,796**	**$ 20,793**	**$ 27,795**	**$37,178**	**$ 44,332**
Other Income/Expenses					
Interest Income	$ 88	$ 125	$ 163	$ 200	$ 250
Interest Expense	($1,478)	($1,196)	($892)	($562)	($204)
Total Other Income/Expenses	($1,391)	($1,071)	(729)	($362)	$ 46
Profit Before Income Taxes	**$ 1,406**	**$ 19,722**	**$ 27,066**	**$ 36,816**	**$ 44,378**
	0.4%	3.9%	4.2%	4.6%	4.4%
Federal Income Tax (15%)	$ 211	$ 2,958	$ 4,060	$ 5,522	$ 6,657
State Income Tax (4%)	$ 56	$ 789	$ 1,083	$ 1,473	$ 1,775
Profit After Income Taxes	**$ 1,139**	**$ 15,975**	**$ 21,923**	**$ 29,821**	**$ 35,946**
	0.3%	3.2%	3.4%	3.7%	3.6%

Exhibit 7   **Pro Forma Cash Flow Statement**

	Year 1	Year 2	Year 3	Year 4	Year 5
Receipts					
Total Sales	$350,000	$ 500,000	$650,000	$800,000	$1,000,000
Interest Income	$ 88	$ 125	$ 163	$ 200	$ 250
Bank Loan	$ 20,000	$ 0	$ 0	$ 0	$ 0
Total Receipts	**$370,088**	**$500,125**	**$650,163**	**$800,200**	**$1,000,250**
Cash Disbursements					
Purchases	$230,000	$316,250	$426,250	$535,000	$ 680,000
Salary Expense	$ 25,000	$ 30,000	$ 35,000	$ 40,000	$ 45,000
Secretary Wages	$ 15,000	$ 15,500	$ 16,000	$ 16,500	$ 17,000
Employee Wages	$ 17,500	$ 25,000	$ 32,500	$ 40,000	$ 50,000
Accounting Fees	$ 1,000	$ 1,050	$ 1,100	$ 1,150	$ 1,200
Advertising Expense	$ 14,000	$ 20,000	$ 26,000	$ 32,000	$ 40,000
Automobile Expense	$ 3,000	$ 3,375	$ 3,750	$ 4,125	$ 4,500
Credit Card Discount	$ 3,500	$ 5,168	$ 6,927	$ 8,769	$ 11,250
FICA	$ 4,399	$ 5,393	$ 6,388	$ 7,382	$ 8,568
Gasoline Expense	$ 3,000	$ 3,375	$ 3,750	$ 4,125	$ 4,500
Hotel/Travel Expense	$ 1,200	$ 1,400	$ 1,600	$ 1,800	$ 2,000
Inventory Insurance	$ 1,400	$ 1,600	$ 2,000	$ 2,500	$ 3,100
Inventory Property Tax	$ 350	$ 400	$ 500	$ 625	$ 775
Legal Fees	$ 1,500	$ 750	$ 1,000	$ 1,250	$ 1,500
Miscellaneous Expense	$ 350	$ 500	$ 650	$ 800	$ 1,000
Office Furniture Lease	$ 500	$ 550	$ 600	$ 650	$ 700
Postage Expense	$ 3,500	$ 5,000	$ 6,500	$ 8,000	$ 10,000
Printing Expense	$ 10,500	$ 15,000	$ 19,500	$ 24,000	$ 30,000
Rent Expense	$ 10,000	$ 10,000	$ 15,000	$ 15,000	$ 20,000
Sales Refunds	$ 700	$ 984	$ 1,259	$ 1,525	$ 1,875
Sales Tax Expense	$ 336	$ 473	$ 605	$ 732	$ 900
Shipping Expense	$ 10,500	$ 15,000	$ 19,500	$ 24,000	$ 30,000
Supplies Expense	$ 1,750	$ 2,500	$ 3,250	$ 4,000	$ 5,000
Telephone Expense	$ 3,500	$ 5,000	$ 6,500	$ 8,000	$ 10,000
Utilities Expense	$ 1,800	$ 1,800	$ 2,700	$ 2,700	$ 3,600
Unemployment Tax	$ 1,869	$ 1,939	$ 1,879	$ 1,689	$ 1,400
Workers Compensation	$ 1,050	$ 1,200	$ 1,500	$ 1,500	$ 1,800
Bank Loan Principal Payments	$ 3,389	$ 3,670	$ 3,975	$ 4,305	$ 4,661
Bank Loan Interest Expense	$ 1,478	$ 1,196	$ 892	$ 562	$ 204
Federal Income Tax	$ 211	$ 2,958	$ 4,060	$ 5,522	$ 6,657
State Income Tax	$ 56	$ 789	$ 1,083	$ 1,473	$ 1,775
Total Cash Disbursements	**$372,338**	**$497,820**	**$652,218**	**$799,684**	**$ 998,965**
Net Cash Flow	($2,250)	$ 2,305	($2,055)	$ 516	$ 1,285
Beginning Cash Balance	$ 10,000	$ 7,750	$ 10,055	$ 8,000	$ 8,516
Ending Cash Balance	$ 7,750	$ 10,055	$ 8,000	$ 8,516	$ 9,801

Exhibit 8   **Pro Forma Balance Sheet**

	Year 1	Year 2	Year 3	Year 4	Year 5
Assets					
Cash on Hand	$ 7,750	$10,055	$ 8,000	$ 8,516	$ 9,801
Accounts Receivable	$ 5,000	$ 6,500	$ 8,000	$ 10,000	$ 12,000
Inventory	$70,000	$80,000	$100,000	$125,000	$155,000
Prepaid Expenses	$ 100	$ 100	$ 100	$ 100	$ 100
Total Assets	**$82,850**	**$96,655**	**$116,100**	**$143,616**	**$176,901**
Liabilities					
Current Liabilities:					
Account Payable	$ 6,000	$ 7,000	$ 8,000	$ 10,000	$ 12,000
Total Current Liabilities:	$ 6,000	$ 7,000	$ 8,000	$ 10,000	$ 12,000
Long-Term Liabilities:					
Bank Loan	$15,339	$11,034	$ 7,060	$ 3,339	$ 0
Total Long-Term Liabilities:	$15,339	$11,034	$ 7,060	$ 3,339	$ 0
Total Liabilities	**$21,339**	**$18,034**	**$ 15,060**	**$ 13,339**	**$ 12,000**
Owner's Equity					
Common Stock (10,000 @ $5)	$50,000	$50,000	$ 50,000	$ 50,000	$ 50,000
Retained Earnings	$11,511	$28,621	$ 51,040	$ 80,277	$114,901
Total Owner's Equity	**$61,511**	**$78,621**	**$101,040**	**$130,277**	**$164,901**
Total Liabilities & Owner's Equity	**$82,850**	**$96,655**	**$116,100**	**$143,616**	**$176,901**

serve as a formalized investment for Larry equalling 30% ownership. Mac will retain the majority ownership of 70%. In order to adequately compensate his father, Mac decided, in addition to the value of the shares, to pay Larry 8% interest on the original principal. In addition to interest, one-third of the retained earnings value will be added to the stock repurchase price (allowing Mac to ultimately own 100% of the business). Between the proposed conversion of Larry Jones' debt and the $20,000 loan from the bank, sufficient operating capital for the proposed expansion is secured. Mac believes that his father will accept this proposal and should any additional capital be required in the coming years, it can always be accomplished through the sale of additional stock in Mac's Model Toys. Mac had not cleared this plan with his attorney, but in his mind it was workable—it compensates his father; it allows Mac to retain controlling interest in the company, and ultimately control it 100%; it allows for the needed expansion of inventory; and, it allows for growth through the sale of additional shares of stock, if necessary.

THE MARKETING PLAN

One of the key ingredients in this expansion is Mac's aggressive marketing plan. Mac's preliminary thinking is as follows: Mac wants his company to be positioned as the "die-cast connection" by offering the largest selection of affordable, high quality die-cast metal replicas.

This positioning strategy is well suited to the current competitive environment as it both satisfies the needs of the target market (in the survey Mac conducted, Price and Quality were the two driving forces sought by customers) and fills a void on the perceptual map of price versus quality in this market. For example, Mac's Model Toys' principal competitor, Eastwood Automobilia, offers some of the same products, but at much higher prices.

From the distribution perspective, Mac's is primarily a mail order business and utilizes UPS almost exclusively. The cost of shipping has always been borne by the customer and that has not posed a problem in the past. The other method of distribution is through the trade shows. Here the products are simply sold over the counter. Mac sees no reason to deviate from these two methods of distribution. They have worked well in the past and he plans to continue these as his primary methods of distribution.

Mac's primary marketing tool is its catalog. It is presently 16 pages, including pictures, and lists a full array of products offered. It is mailed out quarterly to a mailing list of over 3,000 customers. In the future, Mac intends to improve the catalog to a 4 color one and add additional products. Mac estimates that the costs will be $10,500 in the first year and up to $30,000 by year five. In between these quarterly mailings, one-page flyers are used to highlight closeouts, restocks, new items, and specials. Historically, these flyers have been very effective in moving items quickly and they serve to keep Mac's name constantly before his target audience.

Advertising in the past has been limited to occasional small ads in leading magazines that serve this market. Mac plans an aggressive increase in expenditures in this area. Beginning in 1994, Mac plans to devote a minimum of 4% of total sales to advertising in the form of full-page ads in trade and consumer magazines in the model train enthusiast market, specifically in *O Gauge Model Railroading* and *O Scale News.* These ads reach an audience of approximately 30,000 to 45,000 subscribers. Historically, each ad generates between $4,000 and $5,000 in gross sales with an average cost of between $500 and $1,000 per ad. In addition, these ads are encoded in order to track the individual ads so there is a built-in mechanism for measuring the success (or lack of it) for each ad. Mac also plans to install an 800 number for his business and this will appear in all ads after January 1995.

The importance of train shows cannot be overestimated. These serve to cater directly to the target market and are a small source of revenue from direct sales, but more importantly, a significant source for adding names to Mac's mailing list. This will be one of Mac's primary promotional techniques as he grows his business. He plans to attend between 12 and 15 shows per year; historically, a show typically generates about $2,000 to $3,000 in gross sales with an average cost to Mac of about $300.

Another form of promotion planned by Mac is new product reviews. Whenever Mac's Model Toys stocks a new product, there is an opportunity to submit a picture and description of the item to the magazine editors, who typically run the piece; this results in free advertising for Mac. Mac intends to take full advantage of this publicity form of promotion.

DEVELOPMENTAL PLANS FOR THE NEW BUSINESS

With the business already up and running, most of the typical developmental work of starting a new business has already been completed. Some of the key issues that still need to be resolved are:

- Finding a suitable and affordable warehousing and office location.
- Reorganizing the company.
- Finalizing the $20,000 loan for increasing inventory.
- Installing a sophisticated computer system for keeping up with the inventory, mailing lists, customer orders, and billing.
- Setting up the 800 number for orders from customers.
- Hiring the full-time secretary and part-time help outlined for year one.
- Exploration of additional target markets for the future. Mac has determined that for the time being, he will focus on the model train enthusiast target market. It is what he knows best and he has been quite successful supplying that market.

However, there are two additional market segments that he feels are worth exploring. First is the manufacturer/service company market. Mac has been involved in this market to a limited degree thus far, dealing with the BP Oil truck and the John Deere tractor. In this market, manufacturers or service companies contract with Mac to produce replicas of their products or machines for their own promotional purposes. Mac already has a contractual arrangement with a company in Iowa City, Iowa, for mass production of these "logo oriented" replicas and has completed a few projects over the years. It is a highly profitable market with mark-ups in the range of 125%. Mac feels with a little promotional effort on his part, primarily brochures, he can gain a substantial portion of this rather lucrative market. Admittedly, this is in the future since he wants to first concentrate on the "model train enthusiast" market, but it is something he is contemplating.

The second target market for the future is the "specialty toy collector" market. It is more fragmented and generates much less volume than the other two markets, but can command high profits—up to 200% in mark-ups. Because of the lack of volume in this segment, Mac does not plan to actively pursue this market except to satisfy existing customers' requests.

As Mac ponders the possibilities for building Mac's Model Toys into a full-time business, he also thinks about the job opportunities that several of his classmates have been offered. He feels that he would much prefer to work for himself, but does Mac's Model Toys have the potential to become a full-time business? He wonders if he has thought of everything and knows that he must make a decision soon or quickly start the interviewing game at school.

Kovacs Farms: The Flue-Cured Tobacco Business in Ontario

David R. Frew, Gannon University

S teve Kovacs arrived at Vanderbilt University as a freshman in the tumultuous 1960's. The culture of the middle south, the music, and the intellectual climate were new and exciting, wildly different from his home in Southern Ontario. Steve had grown up on a tobacco farm and learned an incredible work ethic. Tobacco farming was (and still is) backbreaking manual labor, and Steve, eldest of three sons, had been an exemplary son. He responded to his family's needs by learning to rise early, often working for several hours before the school bus came.

Steve's family was proud when their son won an academic scholarship to the prestigious American university. Even though it was hard to say goodbye in 1964, they wished him the best, hoping that pre-med studies would propel him toward a better life than he could have had "on the farm."

Steve excelled academically. What he lacked in scholastic preparation was more than compensated for by discipline, energy, and a farm-born work ethic. During his four undergraduate years he managed to graduate cum laude in microbiology and impress the faculty with his hands-on growing skills. He was a favorite in the university horticultural labs, learning to graft plants with success that the best faculty could only envy.

Vanderbilt also taught Steve two other important lessons. The first was that he did not want to be a physician. He became cynical about medical practice as a pre-med student and began to think that he would be happier in business or dealing with people (he had talent in both areas). Second, and more important, Steve met his soul mate and wife-to-be Connie. She was the most beautiful girl in freshman biology and it wasn't long until they were an item.

After graduation Steve and Connie moved to Toronto where he went to work for a public accounting firm as an auditor. His farming background had taught him a lot about business and Steve's work ethic and people skills made him a natural with clients. Steve's boss encouraged him to enroll in the University of Toronto's MBA program as a part time student and by 1975 he had earned his MBA, completed the tests to become a Registered Public Accountant (Canadian CPA), and settled into professional life in the city. By this time he and Connie were married and had two children.

THE CALL OF THE FARM

But something was nagging inside Steve, telling him that he was in the wrong line of work. He was a success and had made lots of money. He and Connie had purchased a house in the suburbs for $80,000 which was appreciating rapidly, and they had managed to save almost another $100,000 through a self-designed investment plan. In the fall of 1975 Steve and Connie's oldest child began school and Steve began to develop an appreciation for the lack of teachers in the public school systems. As he worked with the Parents' Association and spent time in school he struck up a relationship with the principal. One day at an accidental meeting, his son's principal said, "Steve, if I had a faculty of persons like you, with a variety of experiences and enthusiasm, this would be a truly great school!"

That evening Steve and Connie talked about their life. They had plenty of money and security but Steve was growing frustrated with his job. The accounting firm had taken advantage of his enthusiasm, using him on the most challenging assignments. Meanwhile as Steve's career progressed he spent less time with his family. More importantly his work was becoming stale. After several year-end audits and tax preparations, there was not much to learn.

At Christmas time Steve asked his son's principal if he was serious about the teaching offer. Shortly after the first of the year, he had become a middle school teacher instructing 7th through 9th grade Business, Biology, and Geography. The principal loved him almost as much as the kids since he could teach almost any subject: bookkeeping, math, biology, chemistry, history and more. And at first Steve loved it too. He had more time with his family. He drove his kids to school each day and had an opportunity to see them at lunch. He enrolled in evening graduate classes in a program which was paid for by the Toronto Regional School System, earning a Master's Degree in Education in 18 months.

By 1980 external circumstances would have suggested that Steve's career transition was a success. His family was happy, he and Connie had adjusted to their lower income, their cash savings still allowed them to live well (especially for a teacher), and his teaching was regarded as exceptional. But the sleepless nights returned. This time, however, Steve and Connie were talking about the work ethic (or lack thereof) of his students. Steve was deeply troubled by his observation that most students were sleepwalking through high school. He wondered if any of them would be able to work hard and become a success as he had at Vanderbilt. He also worried about his own children. What was he teaching them by bringing them up in this urban environment? Would they have the advantages of understanding practical things and being able to work hard (as he had on the farm in Walsingham, Ontario)? The tobacco farm was beginning to look better and better.

In December, Steve took his family to Walsingham after Christmas to celebrate the holidays with his family. His parents, now in their mid 60's, were still running two of the family farms, and his brothers had never left the area. This year, however, things were not as festive as usual. After dinner, Steve's brothers asked him to go for a walk. Once they passed the barn their discussion grew serious.

Tobacco farming is intense work and the elder Kovacs had grown tired of the day-to-day demands. Earlier that year he had announced to Steve's brothers that he was selling out of the tobacco business and going into a new line of work on the farm. A Hungarian immigrant, Mr. Kovacs was an avid hunter and had always dreamed of owning a wild boar hunting farm. Northern Europeans value boar as a holiday treat (as North Americans love turkey) and he decided to build a boar raising business. His plan was to fence in a farm with its uncleared woods and use the barn as the epicenter of a guided hunting operation. He would purchase breeding stock, raise it in the barn where he had once raised chickens and cows, and then allow the boar to roam the fenced-in woods.

Hunters would come to the farm to hunt boar for a fee, or if they preferred, Mr. Kovacs would slaughter and ship the meat on demand. Steve's brothers were concerned that the idea was foolish and would risk family finances. "He has finally lost it Steve," exclaimed Joe Kovacs. "He thinks that all of his old Hungarian and Dutch cronies are going to come here and pay big bucks to shoot wild pigs!" "Most of Dad's friends are living in old people's homes and eating canned Christmas turkey with dentures," added Steve's youngest brother Mat. "You have to talk him out of this!"

Pondering the dilemma, Steve gave his brothers the answer that his father had given him years earlier about going to Vanderbilt. "Dad is a smart successful businessman and he has worked all of his life. He deserves to follow his dreams. And after all he made a success out of a crazier venture, like tobacco, hasn't he!" That evening, as Steve's dad outlined his plans, Steve nodded approval, offering a toast. Connie added that it was time for the parents to take it a little easier and have some fun. On the drive back to Toronto, however, Steve shared his concerns with Connie. He was secretly worried about his dad and about the boar farm venture.

THE ONTARIO TOBACCO INDUSTRY

Most people are shocked to learn of the tobacco business in Southern Ontario. The tobacco belt there is a 1000 square mile area just north of Central Lake Erie extending 15 to 20 miles south of the lake shore. The retreat of the Wisconsin glacier from Central Lake Erie (just west of Long Point) deposited a sandy soil mixture which, in combination with the high rainfall and moderate temperatures caused by proximity to the lake, created perfect tobacco growing conditions.

The first growers were the local Indians. The tobacco grown in the region was an important source of trade and commerce among Native Americans prior to the arrival of the Europeans. When settlers migrated to the north shore of Lake Erie (today's Ontario), the crop was growing in the wild.

The primary thrust in the growth of the business was an expansionist move by a North Carolina based tobacco company (The American Tobacco Company) which decided to experiment with farming and processing near Leamington, Ontario (80 miles west of today's tobacco belt). The first experiments with burley (cigar) type tobacco were a success. In a few short years a steady stream of southerners was emigrating north to Canada to join the new tobacco business.

By the 1920's cigarettes began to replace cigars in the North American market. But the transition from burley to the flu-cured (cigarette) tobacco did not work well in Leamington. Gradually farmers shifted east toward the central portion of Lake Erie until they came to the "Norfolk Sand Plain" (today's tobacco belt) where soil conditions were perfect. By the 1940's they had developed agricultural strategies which differed slightly from those of the Carolinas but were quite efficient, resulting in plant quality equal to that of the south.

Farmers in Ontario begin production by planting seeds in sterilized soil inside greenhouses. As sprouts develop they are carefully cultivated in heated conditions and climatized by systematically removing glass from the greenhouses. By mid May the greenhouses are open to the elements and the heartiest of the plants are culled out for transplantation to the fields. By early June all of the young tobacco shoots are planted in neat rows in the fields. The crop is then tended just as it would be in the south. In the fall plants are individually picked, tied on stakes, and hung in out-buildings (called kilns) for drying. The kilning (drying) process is an art. Doors and windows are alternately opened and closed, heat is added, and the stakes of plants themselves are rotated in order to achieve optimum drying.

Drying success is so critical to the ultimate quality (and market value) of the product that most farmers hire a Carolina-based professional kilner to orchestrate the process. The kilner makes strategic decisions relative to how long to leave the crop in the drying building, when to move it up and down (within the kiln) for best effects, and when and for how long to open windows or add artificial heat. Once dry, plants are moved to the main barn for sorting, bailing, and storage but during the critical kilning process the tobacco is in the absolute control of the kilner, who is to tobacco approximately what the old German brew master was to beer.

In 1957 a tobacco cooperative called the "Ontario Flue-Cured Tobacco Marketing Board" was formed in the tobacco belt and settled in Tillsonburg. The organization, which was drawn together to help give Ontario's industry a competitive advantage on the world market, soon evolved into an economic force. Today's "Marketing Board" includes a headquarters building, a tobacco museum, and three organized annual tobacco auction sites (Aylmer, Delhi, and Tillsonburg) which operate in the Dutch style (beginning at a high price and bidding down). The Dutch system results in fast transactions (900 metric tons per day). The tobacco board meets each year to establish market price minimums which insure each farmer a reasonable economic reward for the year's crop. They also broker relationships between buyers and the eight registered Canadian processors who in turn process, package, and ship the crop either domestically or overseas. Perhaps their most important annual duty, however, is the estimation of the following year's market size. This figure, in combination with each farmer's quota, governs the amount of tobacco which can (legally) be sold.

The system works like this: The Marketing Board annually announces to the tobacco farmers the percentage of the total Ontario quota which will be grown and sold the next year. The Marketing Board controls 323 million pounds of tobacco quota. Thus if, during a particular year, the potential import and export market is estimated to be 60% of that (323 million pound) total, farmers are instructed to grow 60% of their individual quotas. As might be expected, the farmers wait with anticipation to hear this figure each year. This has been even more true recently since growing efficiencies have created excess farm capacity.

TOBACCO, SIN TAX, AND HEALTH CARE

The tobacco industry in Southern Ontario grew steadily during the post-war period. When demand for cigarettes began to falter in the late 1970's as a result of negative publicity regarding smoking, European and Asian demand picked up dramatically. For tobacco farmers the only discernable change was in the country of origin of the purchasers at the auctions. Since 50.1% (1992) of Canadian tobacco is exported, domestic demand for cigarettes has not been an issue. Within Canada itself, the number of new smokers is declining in Ontario, but increasing in Quebec.

The biggest changes in the industry came about as a result of political processes. In the late 1970's pressures grew in Canada to develop a national health plan. While each province was left to the design details, the final programs which were presented to the Canadian public were all similar. Best known of these is the Ontario Health Insurance Program (OHIP) which has been cited by many Americans as a model plan (OHIP was the basis for much of the Clinton initiative).

Even though OHIP managed to eliminate insurance and litigation as component parts of the health care costs, the Ontario plan promised to be quite expensive. The plan promised "womb to tomb" coverage and it extended health care benefits to every member of society. Politicians were pleased with the potential benefits of OHIP and the elimination of private insurance and litigation costs, but worried about program funding. Just as they were entering discussions, the media was beginning to exclaim the terrible health hazards of smoking. There was a social concern that somehow the tobacco industry should be made to pay the health care bill since so many diseases were linked to smoking.

It did not take long for Ontario (and other provincial) legislators to conclude that the way out of the funding dilemma was to tax tobacco. In a round of what now looks to have been "magical thinking," the architects of OHIP projected that a schedule of slowly increasing taxes on cigarettes, levied both at the farm and consumer levels, could be used to fund health care. It was reasoned that tax revenues could be specifically targeted at health care costs associated with smoking as well as public health programming aimed at convincing Canadians to stop using tobacco products. Legislators reasoned that the decreasing stream of cash resulting from reduced smoking (and subsequent tax revenues) would coincide with the end of smoking by the general public. This would be accompanied by an eventual decrease in health care costs associated with the cessation of the treatment of smoking-related health problems.

The economics of the situation, however, proved to be quite different. Cigarette advertising (especially in U.S. based media) increasingly seemed to attract new (young) smokers, and the demand for cigarettes proved to be inelastic. As prices went up, the quantity of cigarettes smoked per consumer did not change. To exacerbate the situation the systematic linkage between cigarette taxes and the cost of health care (which rose dramatically during the 1980's) continued to drive up the cost of a package of Canadian cigarettes relative to U.S. prices. By 1990 a Canadian pack cost $6.00 as compared to the US. price of $1.50. The tax differential created a natural opening for smuggling, offering an immediate advantage of $4.50 per pack (or $40.00 per carton). Given the fact that the Canadian/U.S. border is some 4000 miles long and mostly unpatrolled, the opportunities were too good to be ignored.

Visionaries among the early architects of OHIP had recognized the potential for cigarette smuggling and other tobacco tax avoidance manipulations and decided to design a new grower control system. Prior to 1975, each individual tobacco farm was restricted to 50 acres of crop. Farmers generally produce 2200 to 3000 pounds per acre. A bale of tobacco weighs approximately 48 pounds and results in roughly 125 cartons of cigarettes (at 200 cigarettes per carton).

In 1976 a new quota system was introduced in which tobacco farmers owned "shares," granting the right to sell tobacco. At the onset of this system the number of shares granted to each existing farmer was based statistically upon the number of farms that were operated and the amount of tobacco that had been produced in the recent past. The original share system was based upon a per share par value which was established for each share. To grow and market a pound of crop legally, a farmer had to own a share of quota. Tobacco shares were valued at $1.00 and placed on the commodity market. The shares soon developed a financial life of their own, however, and values rocketed from their original ($1.00) designated value to $2.20 by 1980. Private investors were selling and buying tobacco shares in anticipation of shifts in the world market. A number of farmers noticed that the market value of their quota (shares) was far in excess of potential crop profits. A farmer who had been cultivating 100 acres of crop, for example, might have 250,000 shares which could be converted instantaneously to $550,000.00

Farmers began to cash out and retire, leaving vacant 100 acre tobacco farms for sale. The problem for potential entrants into the business was that the market value of the shares had risen to the point where it was impossible to get started in the business. The uncertainties in the financial market along with general turbulence in the industry sent tobacco growing into a tail spin, with total Ontario sales falling from 209 million pounds in 1975 to a low of 110 million pounds in 1987. In response to this trend share values fell to $1.00 in 1986, $.65 in 1987, and a record low of $.25 in 1989 (by 1994 the share value had risen to $1.05).

THE NEW PROHIBITION

As the 1980's wore on more and more Canadians began to "dabble" in contraband cigarettes. There had been plenty of impetus for this kind if activity in the 1930's when the U.S. enacted its prohibition against liquor. Canadians from along the borders (especially in the Lake Erie and St. Lawrence River areas) had made millions during those adventuresome years running alcoholic beverages to welcoming American "gangsters." For Canadians, who were legally allowed to manufacture and sell booze, rum running was almost considered an honorable profession. Consequently the folk lore of smuggling (which was still alive and well as cigarette problems began to emerge) made Canadians more inclined to dabble in shady enterprises.

Tax avoidance mechanisms took a number of different turns during the 1980's. Natives, for example, purchased cigarettes on a tax-free basis acting from treaty rights. They then sold them at slightly less than market values, enjoying huge profits. Organized smugglers used more extreme measures. These ranged from secreting thousands of cartons of cigarettes (purchased in the U.S.) in trucks and sneaking them across Buffalo's Peace Bridge or the Ambassador Bridge in Detroit. In general, customs officials are too busy handling traffic to catch anyone. In 1993 a lumber truck carrying plywood was found to have all but the top layers of wooden panels hollowed out and containing thousands of cartons of cigarettes. In 1992 a series of tanker trucks were found to have false panels installed in the tanks and loads which proved to contain thousands of cartons of cigarettes instead of fuel oil. Customs officials estimate that they are catching only 10 to 15 percent of this kind of traffic.

Store owners or their suppliers are known to drive across the bridges in passenger cars, purchase hundreds of cartons of cigarettes, and recross the borders into Canada claiming that they have nothing to declare. The chance of getting caught this way has been estimated to be well below 5%.

The most "romantic" smuggling goes on in the spirit of the old rum runners with American boats transferring huge loads of cigarettes (purchased in the U.S.) to Canadian vessels which simply do not report to customs. During the summer of 1993 this kind of activity was so rampant in the St. Lawrence River that the U.S. Coast Guard announced it would no longer perform night time rescues. There was so much smuggling activity in the river after dark that they were afraid of being fired upon by cigarette smugglers who were overzealous about protecting their stock. In the early winter of 1994, the RCMP reported a gunfight in which police officers set off in pursuit of smugglers in snowmobiles running loads of cigarettes across the frozen St. Lawrence.

For tobacco growers there is another more pressing avenue for contraband sales, the "illegal" sale of non-quota crop. Most of the farmers who have purchased the rights to sell quota actually produce more than their allowable quota. This is because they don't want to take the risk of having too little to bring to market. For the average farmer this overage is usually in the neighborhood of 8 percent of quota. When the selling season is over it is not unusual to have 100 or more bales of tobacco left in the barn. It is not legal to sell that tobacco, but since Canada enacted its GST (a value added tax), many citizens have complained that their income, sales, and other taxes (compared to those of the U.S.) are unreasonable. Many Canadians feel that the existing quotas and taxation systems are obstacles to be avoided, and have reacted by developing an increasingly troublesome "black market economy."

In this environment it is not surprising that small entrepreneurs travel the tobacco belt stopping at farms to inquire about "extra" bales of tobacco. They are willing to pay well over the fixed market price for a bale on a "cash basis." These black market entrepreneurs take tobacco home, dry it in homemade equipment, and process it into cigarettes (using commercially available rolling machines). These are packaged in innocuous "generic type packages" given counterfeit tax stamps and sold to retail outlets. There is growing concern among farmers that a large amount of product is being sold that way and if they do not take advantage of this opportunity, they are simply missing the "boat."

In February 1994 the Premier of Quebec announced that he was going to take steps against the growth of cigarette smuggling by lowering taxes. Bob Rae, Premier of Ontario, objected, stating that this action would put his province in a terrible predicament. Ontario was increasingly dependent upon revenue from cigarette taxation and he was unable to lower taxes, but there was no way (legal or otherwise) to stop cigarettes from moving between provinces. The Quebec policy change would both stimulate existing tax avoidance schemes in Ontario and begin an inflow of the product from Quebec. To put the taxation problem in perspective, in 1993 an average bale of tobacco netted the farmer $80 and the government $3700. As the farmers complained that they were being squeezed out of business by taxes, smuggling, and government mishandling, Canada was becoming increasingly dependent upon tobacco tax revenues.

THE 1980 BOAR FARM

To escape the craziness of the turbulent tobacco business elder Kovacs cashed in some of his tobacco quota in 1980, purchased a vacant farm, and began his boar shooting farm. His timing in cashing out shares was exquisite. The paper transaction generated cash which allowed for the purchase of a new (fourth) farm with buildings, restoration of the house on that farm into a lodge for the hunters, and the conversion of a number of outbuildings into bed and breakfast accommodations. In addition, breeding stock was purchased and a number of vehicles were added to transport hunters around the area. The farm was fenced in, a barn was converted for boar raising with a butchering facility, and the necessary licenses were obtained.

The first hunting season was reasonably successful. Everyone had heard of the venture and their long-time allegiance with the Kovacs family inspired them to at least visit if not take a stab at boar hunting. At year end Mr. Kovacs was happy to tell his family that he had come within $20,000 of breaking even. Steve and his brothers were growing concerned.

The second year, Mr. Kovacs grew discouraged when business worsened. Steve's brothers' fears seemed to be coming true. Modern Canadians were simply not interested in eating boar meat. To make matters worse elder Kovacs fell in late December and broke a leg. During his recovery in early January, Steve's mother had a heart attack.

In February Steve and his brothers had a conference with the family physician. "You have to talk him into retiring, Steve," suggested Doc Peterson. "They're just too old to be starting such a wild new business venture. People their age should be living in condominiums and going to Florida for the winter." "You're the only one who can do it," added his brothers. "He listens to you!"

In early March, Steve visited his father's banker to ask for financial details. The elder Kovacs' farm holdings now included 4 farms (600 total acres) with a total of 11 houses. Three of the farm houses were used by Mr. Kovacs and Steve's two brothers. One was rented and the others were either vacant or dedicated to the bed and breakfast operation at the Boar Farm. The estimated market value of all of this property (with buildings) was only $387,000 because of the current high cost of tobacco quota and the fact that there were many vacant farms in the region.

Steve's youngest brother Mat had lost interest in farming. He lived in one of the houses but commuted to a job in Simcoe. His interest in the situation was simply concern for his father and mother. The next older brother, Joe, was actively farming. He had not, however, been able to save much money since he had never really done anything but work for his father on the farm.

After speaking to his brothers and mother Steve developed a plan and went back to Toronto to discuss it with Connie. His old accounting firm helped with the legal problems, and Steve's principal granted him a leave as of March break to go home to square things away on the farm. In late March, Steve approached his father with the following proposal.

Two separate corporations would be drawn up. The first would be a land holding corporation which would own all of the farm lands and buildings except those lived in by the family. This corporation (consisting of Mr. and Mrs. Kovacs (one share), Steve, and his two brothers) would lease the farmland to a second corporation consisting of Steve and Connie. Steve's farming brother would be a salaried employee of the farming corporation. The farming corporation would buy the main farmhouse, barn, kilns, tobacco quota (of 150,000 shares) and surrounding 10 acres from elder Kovacs for $300,000. This would include all of the supplies, stock in process, and farming equipment, as well as the equipment purchased for the Boar Farm.

The three brothers (including Steve) would keep the houses where they were currently living and each would own 10 acres of land immediately surrounding their houses. Steve's two brothers were to pay an agreed upon market value for their individual farm houses in the form of a monthly payment (annuity) to their parents. Steve agreed to pay his brother an annual salary of $35,000 (approximately what his parents had been paying him).

The land-holding corporation agreed to lease the land to Steve for the nominal fee of $1000 per year for five years and then for 10% of farm operation profits over the next 8 years. It was agreed that the question of land rental fees would be reevaluated after that time. Under Canadian tax law the Land Holding Corporation is independent from the Farm Corporation.

STEVE AND CONNIE'S TOBACCO FARM

At first, elder Kovacs objected. But after family persuasion, and his growing sense of Steve's enthusiasm for the new venture, he agreed, signing the official papers in April of 1982. Steve and Connie told the kids that they would be moving to Walsingham. Steve was looking forward to a life style where he and Connie could work together, and involve their children in their dream.

Back in Toronto, Connie sold their home and a car. Coupled with the most liquid parts of Steve's investment portfolio and his teacher's pension, they were able to raise $307,000. Steve paid his parents $150,000 and placed the remaining cash in the farm bank, receiving a $250,000 line of credit. Steve's parents purchased a condominium in Port Rowan, some 20 miles away, for $90,000 and vacated the main farm house making space for Connie and the kids when school ended that spring.

As Steve and his brother worked the farm that first year, his accountant's mind began to think in terms of diversification. Even with his considerable growing skill, and his ability to digest and learn the latest scientific support information from the Marketing Board and its research station in Delhi, he recognized the inherent risk in having all of his "financial eggs" in one basket. He had a healthy line of credit and felt confident of his relationship with the bank but still a few bad years could cripple him. Tobacco farmers generally use Mexican Mennonites to do much of the manual labor and the wages paid to them are not great, but could he withstand a crop failure? Long-term statistics suggested that the average farmer would lose a crop once in 12 years. Steve hoped that if this eventuality came to be, it would be in the 10th or 11th year, if at all.

As the last of 1982's tobacco plants were being transplanted to the fields and the rush of spring planting was ending, Steve developed his first diversification strategy. He was lying in bed with Connie one night talking about his ideas when she reminded him of his Vanderbilt days. "It's too bad you're through with the greenhouses, Steve," she remarked. "That was your favorite part of college." "Wow," he replied, "I should think of something to do with those greenhouses between May and March, shouldn't I?" The next week a truck backed up to the barn and dropped off several thousand ornamental tree cuttings, mostly evergreen types. By the end of the month the cuttings were growing happily in the main greenhouses, being jump-started in the rich tobacco soil.

The landscape tree business represented Steve and Connie's first major diversification. The plan was to accelerate the normal growth of these trees by greenhousing them for the first summer. In early spring, before tobacco planting, the trees are moved to the fields where they are cultivated into commercial landscape type plants selling for $100 or more, depending upon type. As Steve concentrated on growing, Connie studied decorating and landscaping trends, in an attempt to predict the kinds of trees which would be in demand in 6 to 10 years. By the third year they identified a lucrative substrategy. In late November, Steve would walk the fields looking for stunted trees which did not seem to have optimum growing potential. These would be marked, cut, and sold as Christmas trees.

At the first annual meeting of the landholding corporation, Steve's dad suggested that the various outbuildings, the lodge from the boar farm, and two unused farmhouses be actively rented or offered as bed and breakfasts. Steve's mom, who was feeling quite well by now, offered her services in the reclamation, redecorating, and management. There were 11 buildings in total plus the lodge, which could accommodate up to four families. In the second year of operation, the lodge and five of the smaller outbuildings were listed as a part of Ontario's "Farm Vacation" program and business grew. By the third year Steve and his brother had renovated three of the other buildings and converted the remaining three to permanent housing. The rental income as well as the bed and breakfast business provided a flow of cash for the land-holding corporation.

The first three crop years were successful beyond Steve's expectation. The marketing board established average percentage bases of over 50% and Steve's growing skills resulted in production excesses of 18%. The fourth year, 1986, was a disaster. Steve's crop was infected with blue mold and he lost almost 70% of the total. That fall was a depressing time for Steve and Connie. They spent a lot of time riding the back acres (land not used for tobacco) in their truck talking and worrying, wondering if they could withstand another bad crop.

As they rode one sunny November afternoon, Connie commented on the beauty of the back acres and the fact that no matter what, they could always depend on their rental incomes. "I have an idea!" Steve blurted out. "Let's develop some residential lots. We're already in the business. We own the land, and we have most of the equipment. What do we have to lose?" That afternoon Steve and Connie used their tractor to mark the proposed locations of several roads leading to the first of 30 lots which they marked off on a map of the farms. They selected non-tillable wooded land, within sight of streams and close to roads. They quickly realized that this idea would create a second major diversification. And with changes in the housing market and suburban sprawl, Walsingham (considered rural in the 1970's) was fast becoming the outreaches of suburbia for residents of Simcoe, Port Dover, and Delhi.

Following a good crop year in 1987, Steve observed that the value of his tobacco quota had fallen to $.32 (from a high of $2.20). In a move motivated as much by land acquisition for his real estate venture as it was by the potential to buy more quota or to price average, he purchased another 120 acres with a house, barn, and 100,000 shares of quota. The $74,000 farm was owned by the land holding corporation, while the quota ($32,000) was purchased by Steve and Connie.

In 1988 he planted tobacco on the new farmlands, adding to his old crop totals (his enlarged quota was 250,000). Providentially 1987 was a good market year, with total Ontario sales rising from 110 to 130 million pounds and the grower's quota percentage increasing from 28.6% to 37.3%. The quota rose again in 1989 but fell in 1990, sending a wave of discouragement through the grower's community. By the end of 1992 (even though quota percentages had risen again to about 47%), Steve and many of his fellow tobacco farmers were increasingly concerned with the politicization of the tobacco business and the role of tobacco in the Free Trade Agreement. In the U.S., content restriction legislation was passed which threatened exports ($20 million in 1992) to America. The farmers complained that they were not being protected under Free Trade and that the federal government was underrepresenting their export needs as they worried about NAFTA.

In 1991 Steve launched a new (financially based) diversification which was associated with his real estate development project. He had begun to recognize that a large number of persons were having a difficult time securing financing for purchasing the homes that he was building. In his view many "good risks" were turned down for mortgage loans. After two exceptionally good crop years, Steve had accumulated a relatively large reserve of cash which was languishing in low-interest bank accounts. Steve organized a consortium of five fellow farmers in similar situations and convinced them to begin a business of loaning mortgage funds to individuals who were having difficulty securing loans to buy his houses. He reasoned that even if a few defaulted, he would be in control of their property and able to resell it. In the first year they each invested $200,000 and incorporated in an organization which is financially independent from the farm operations. They are loaning funds at 11 to 14% to home buyers and have had no defaults to date.

GINSENG AND THE FUTURE

But this diversification was not the total answer to insecurities in the tobacco market. By this time the Marketing Board had gathered powerful statistics to indicate the extent and seriousness of the contraband tobacco market. Their data suggested that the entire industry could be heading toward a financial crisis.

As tobacco farmers throughout the region watched the wild gyrations of the market they increasingly turned to the Marketing Board for advice. The laboratories at Delhi had preached diversification (as a risk minimization strategy) but had found little success with raising other crops in the sandy tobacco soil. In the late 1980's, however, the marketing board began to suggest the production of ginseng. There was (and still is) a surplus world demand for ginseng root and the crop is easily adapted to the conditions of Southern Ontario's tobacco belt.

The difficulty with growing ginseng lies in the extreme cost of production (estimated at 45 to 50 thousand dollars per acre) in combination with the relative lack of information about growing technologies and disease prevention. Ginseng is harvested as a root. It is grown under a cheesecloth canopy (simulating its natural habitat at the floor of mature forests) which is supported by a network of stakes placed at three foot intervals. It takes three to four years to bring a crop to harvest, and tobacco farmers worry that several kinds of unpredictable calamities could occur during that time. A 10-acre diversification into ginseng, for example, would cost approximately $500,000, creating the potential for financial disaster. There is also a concern that if a large number of farmers begin production, there could be an oversupply.

On the positive side, Ontario's earliest ginseng farmers report that they are harvesting between 2200 and 2600 pounds per acre and selling at prices ranging from $55 to $70 per pound. Top-end production could result in potential profits of $132,000 per acre per three year growing cycle. This would mean $1.3 million for a ten acre crop. There is an added concern, however, that the profit potential could stimulate interest in British Columbia and other provinces, thus further risking an oversupply.

As the 1994 crop season approaches Steve and Connie are puzzling over the dilemma of how to plan the next several years for their business. Tobacco is still highly profitable and one simple solution to the future might be to hold steady on existing diversifications and try to ride out the decade by maximizing attention to the tobacco crop. As they approach 50 years of age, however, they wonder how much longer they can keep up the work pace demanded by the tobacco business. Their two children are in high school now, and if the crop holds out until the year 2000 they will both have graduated from college, allowing Steve and Connie to ease their work pace and go into semi-retirement. The increased politicization and changes in the externals of the tobacco business, however, are more than troubling to Steve and Connie, and they are concerned that the industry could self-destruct.

As they consider the strategy of working hard for 5 to 10 more years and then retiring, however, they are concerned about their family. The land holding partnership has thrived since Steve developed it, but it has done so through the shepherding and success of Steve and Connie's initiatives. If they were to withdraw, the elder Kovacs (now in their 70's) and Steve's two brothers could be left in a tenuous position with regard to making a living. Steve and Connie also wonder if their own children might not be interested in returning to the farm after college. Given employment prospects these days, it might be useful for them to keep things going at the farm until such time as their two sons can return to take over the farm.

If they were to diversify, Steve and Connie wonder how much emphasis they should place in each of the individually incorporated ventures. Should they reduce their risk by adding ginseng production to tobacco, and continuing with real estate development? Lately they have been wondering about the construction of multi-unit dwellings in either condominium or apartment formats. Given the economy in North America, these kinds of units might be the easiest to sell over the next decade, and maintaining ownership or managership of them would insure a continuous cash flow. A diversification strategy of some sort would help insure against the potential financial problems of another crop failure, such as the blue mold experienced across Southern Ontario 1986.

Steve and Connie are also concerned about the fate of the land holding corporation with respect to its agreement to lease farm lands at 10% of the tobacco crop profits (before corporate taxes). In recent years, Steve's brothers, who have been surprised at the profit which Steve has been able to make, have expressed some concern that the land holder's share of profits has been too low. If the family votes to take a significantly higher percentage of pre-tax profits, the relative value of profits from other diversifications may increase. There is also some concern that the family land holding corporation will vote to take a percentage of the landscape tree profits. At first this venture seemed an innocuous sideline, but as Steve's brothers noted his success they have been questioning why these profits (from a crop also grown on the leased land) should not also be shared.

When Steve began to develop real estate, he was sensitive to this issue. Consequently he negotiated a deal to buy real estate development lands outright from the land holding corporation at the rate of $1000 per half acre lot. This price will be up for discussion in 1995, as well, and Steve and Connie wonder how the conclusion of that issue will affect their real estate activities. Another impending family matter relates to Steve's youngest brother, Mat. Things have not gone well for him in his job, and he has been discussing either "buying into" the business or joining his other brother as a salaried employee of the farm operations. Over the years Steve has increased Joe's salary by an average of 5% per year and paid Mat on a per diem basis for work which needed to be done. Mat's interests and skills lie more in the area of construction and repair than farming. One possible use for Mat would be to have him take over operations of the bed and breakfast business now that Steve's parents are reaching their mid 70's.

In any event, Steve and Connie are looking to slow down their frenetic pace. During the early years they often found themselves working 80- to 100-hour weeks. They feel that this has often been at the expense of their family as well as the overall quality of their life together. There are lull times in the business, and they have been able to take winter vacations to places like Florida, the Bahamas, and Europe, but they are soon hoping to slow their "everyday" pace so that they can enjoy life and their beautifully remodeled farmhouse a bit more.

TECHNICAL NOTES ON THE TOBACCO INDUSTRY

The following data represent recent developments, industry statistics, and the position of the industry in the provincial and national economy.

1. Contraband cigarettes represent the most visible problem in the industry, from both grower and government perspectives. It is projected that

by 1996, contraband consumption will exceed legal consumption. Black market shoppers save as much as $35 per carton. Criminals can earn as much as $25 per carton.

2. There are two general sources of contraband, domestic and foreign. Current trends indicate that the foreign sources are growing more rapidly than domestic, thus hurting both the farmer and the government. In 1992, the domestic totals were 8,640,000 pounds while foreign contraband totalled 15,744,000 pounds. In 1993, these totals grew to 20,213,000 pounds (domestic) and 13,475,000 pounds (foreign).

3. The revenue loss in taxes to the federal government is estimated to be between $1.3 and $2.0 billion. Without consideration of the (spinoff effect) multiplier this is estimated to have cost the Canadian economy $5.6 billion in 1993.

4. It was originally argued that increased taxation would reduce smoking. With consideration of the contraband totals this is clearly not the case. Some economists have argued that the availability of reduced price contraband product has, in fact, stimulated smoking behavior.

5. In 1992 an export tax was initiated which made sales to nondomestic sources (a growing component of the Canadian Tobacco Industry) far less profitable. In addition this export tax opened doors to black market source tobacco.

6. Enforcement agencies have had little success at either catching smugglers or deterring the use of counterfeit tax-paid labels.

7. Ontario tobacco constitutes 93% of Canadian crop totals. There are 1,642 individual owners of production quota who are organized into 1,483 production units. There are an estimated 58,400 acres planted.

8. The average domestic price of a pound of tobacco is $1.70. Exported product averaged $1.50. The 1992 minimum price was $1.40.

9. The four major importers of Canadian tobacco include United Kingdom, United Stares, Germany, and Hong Kong. The minor importers (but growing) include Zimbabwe, Holland, Czechoslovakia, Hungary, Poland, Yugoslavia, Romania, Turkey, Ukraine, Russia, and Bulgaria.

10. In March 1984 the retail price of Ontario cigarettes fell by almost $2.00 per pack as a result of federal and provincial tax roll-backs. The tax adjustment was said to be a temporary measure to allow in-depth study of taxation versus contraband.

The Hue-Man Experience Bookstore

Joan Winn, University of Denver

I began telling everyone who came in the store that this was the largest African American bookstore in the country. I really didn't know if that was true, but it was the largest one I had ever seen in my travels and everyplace I go I'm always looking for bookstores. Maybe eventually I'll uncover one that's larger and I'll have to acknowledge it, but until then I won't say anything different. So I began to create that image in people's minds, nationally as well as locally.

CLARA VILLAROSA, OWNER

What began in 1984 as an attempt to set up an independent business targeted to affluent African-Americans, was by 1992 a 3,000-square-foot retailing establishment and north Denver community landmark. The Hue-Man Experience Bookstore specialized in books, cards, jewelry, and artwork by and for people of color (hence the "Hue" in "Human"). While most patrons lived within five miles of the bookstore, the Hue-Man Experience Bookstore had gained a national reputation, attracting frequent out-of-town visitors. By 1994, Clara Villarosa was looking at expansion. The availability of the building next door kindled her dream of creating an Afrocentric retail and cultural center.

HISTORY

The Hue-Man Experience Bookstore grew out of the dream of a woman who had already made it in corporate America. Clara Villarosa started out professionally as a psychiatric social worker, working in an outpatient (non-residential) clinic in Chicago, after she received her Masters Degree in Social Work in 1954. Like many women of her generation, she dropped out of the workforce when her children were born. In 1968, when her daughters were five and nine years old, Clara and her husband moved the family to Denver. Clara soon took a position in the Department of Behavioral Sciences at Denver's Children's Hospital. By the time she left the hospital in 1980, she had become the Director of the Department of Behavioral Sciences, and, eventually, the Assistant Hospital Administrator. After entering a doctoral program in social work and law, she started a consulting business.

I wanted to help African Americans move up the corporate ladder and I thought I could sell that idea to large corporations. As a social worker I had some skills, but I didn't know how to knock on doors, to get a business off the ground. When I ran out of money I took a temporary job at United Bank. I started out in employee relations and moved quickly up the corporate ladder, becoming the Vice President of Human Resources within two years. Again I found myself in the position of being the highest African American on the payroll. But, as often happened in those times, I hit the glass ceiling. People were extremely resentful and angry about African Americans and Affirmative Action and I received a significant backlash. So I left the bank. But left the bank with some money. I think they *wanted* me to quit.

Her consulting business had taught her that she wanted to sell something tangible, and at the same time, something that would relate in a positive way to the African-American community.

And I came up with books, because I've always been a reader. My father was a reader and I grew up immersed in books. We [the African-American community] had had a bookstore in Denver, but there wasn't one now, so my dream was to create the largest African-American bookstore in Denver.

This time, Clara researched her market and wrote a business plan, outlining the financial and marketing requirements of her ethnic bookstore concept. With the help of two friends, and her severance from the bank, she got together $35,000 and secured a lease on a two-story row house in a run-down residential/commercial area north of downtown Denver in a predominantly African-American area. The Hue-Man Experience Bookstore opened in 1984. In 1986, realizing that business and friendship don't always mix well, Clara arranged to buy out her partners' shares over a two-year period by selling shares of the business to interested friends and customers. In 1993, the Hue-Man Experience Bookstore was governed by a 9-member board of directors, elected annually by Clara, who owned 58%, and 31 shareholders. Financial performance for the Hue-Man Experience Bookstore for 1990-1993 is given in Exhibits 1 and 2.

THE BOOKSELLING INDUSTRY

In 1992, book sales in the United States exceeded $16.1 billion, according to the Association of American Publishers. The American Book Trade Directory estimated that there were about 27,000 retailers of books in the United States, 15,700 of which were privately-owned independent bookstores. The largest book retailers were general bookstore chains, which had sales of $2.9 billion in 1992 from a total of 2768 outlets. Exhibit 3 contains sales information for the largest bookstore chains in 1991-1992.

Major chain expansion began in the late 1970s to mid-1980s, with 1,000–20,000-title mall outlets proliferating toward the end of the 1980s. As mall growth slowed, the focus changed to superstores, huge discounters which averaged 200,000 titles, five to ten times the number offered by specialty or mall stores. Barnes & Noble opened its first superstore in September 1990, in a Minneapolis suburb. The 15,000-square-foot store was patterned after such well-known independent booksellers as Oxford Books in Atlanta, Powell's Books in Portland, the Tattered Cover in Denver, and Waterstone's in Boston.

Exhibit 1　　　　　**Financial Information: Income Statements for 1990-1993**
Statement of Income for the period ending 12/31

Income	1990	1991	1992	1993
Revenue				
Books	$181,134	$216,922	$272,542	$269,751
Cards	$ 26,024	$ 26,517	$ 25,811	$ 23,106
Prints	$ 13,503	$ 15,579	$ 13,994	$ 9,616
Jewelry	$ 3,903	$ 2,152	$ 1,759	$ 1,438
Miscellaneous	$ 17,274	$ 16,967	$ 14,712	$ 7,154
Catalogue	$ 13,098	$ 18,268	$ 21,338	$ 6,828
Tapes and Magazines	$ 3,924	$ 2,724	$ 4,342	$ 5,310
Reimbursed postage	$ 1,428	$ 3,070	$ 3,345	$ 2,433
Total Revenue	$260,288	$302,199	$357,843	$325,636
Cost of Sales				
Books	$121,719	$143,793	$196,666	$152,104
Cards	$ 14,613	$ 12,769	$ 17,603	$ 14,583
Prints	$ 6,146	$ 11,100	$ 8,487	$ 3,453
Jewelry	$ 956	$ 612	$ 1,435	$ 325
Miscellaneous	$ 8,942	$ 6,396	$ 2,665	$ 5,946
Tapes and Magazines	$ 3,568	$ 2,437	$ 8,319	$ 4,044
Catalogue	$ 3,336	$ 5,661	$ 779	$ 120
Freight and postage	$ 1,733	$ 2,770	$ 6,663	$ 740
Framing supplies	$ 1,815	$ 590	$ 1,379	$ 538
Inventory(increase)/decrease	($1,094)	$ 5,617	($4,047)	$ 8,034
Total Cost of Sales	$161,734	$191,745	$239,949	$189,887
Gross Margin	$ 98,554	$110,454	$117,894	$135,749
Administrative Expenses				
Officer Salary	$ 26,000	$ 26,814	$ 29,599	$ 24,973
Salaries	$ 20,874	$ 27,193	$ 27,647	$ 26,706
Employee Benefits		$ 160	$ 169	$ 3,454*
Advertising	$ 3,848	$ 4,406	$ 4,740	$ 3,309
Promotional	$ 2,677	$ 1,364	$ 758	$ 13
Accounting and legal	$ 4,008	$ 4,101	$ 3,389	$ 4,256
Vehicle expense	$ 2,822	$ 3,010	$ 3,433	$ 4,517
Bank and credit card service charges	$ 3,791	$ 2,208	$ 6,407	$ 1,175
Janitorial/cleaning expenses	$ 276	$ 164	$ 240	
Consulting/contract labor	$ 2,568	$ 2,510	$ 328	$ 676
Contributions	$ 864	$ 900	$ 229	$ 293
Dues and subscriptions	$ 907	$ 1,242	$ 933	$ 1,977
License and fees		$ 10	$ 26	$ 95
Depreciation	$ 3,015	$ 4,453	$ 4,027	$ 3,997
Entertainment	$ 971	$ 257	$ 1,409	$ 3,299

Exhibit 1 (continued)   **Financial Information: Income Statements for 1990-1993**
Statement of Income for the period ending 12/31

Income	1990	1991	1992	1993
Travel/conferences	$ 4,011	$ 1,530	$ 1,576	$ 2,082
Rent	$ 9,078	$ 7,677	$ 7,350	$ 12,495
Repairs and maintenance	$ 869	$ 662	$ 2,008	$ 2,609
Security	$ 322	$ 520	$ 458	$ 556
Telephone**	$ 5,147	$ 7,689	$ 9,995	$ 7,577
Utilities	$ 2,445	$ 2,722	$ 2,636	$ 3,055
Insurance		$ 1,462	$ 1,164	$ 173
Office supplies and equipment	$ 4,082	$ 3,345	$ 4,259	$ 4,667
Printing			$ 598	$ 2,194
Store supplies	$ 1,686	$ 3,681	$ 2,722	$ 3,264
Taxes—personal property	$ 148	$ 284		$ 486
Taxes—payroll	$ 4,156	$ 4,826	$ 4,970	$ 4,409
Freight & postage	$ 4,242	$ 357	$ 1,254	$ 5,280
Miscellaneous	$ 1,284	$ 319	$ 1,254	$ 436
Total Expenses	$110,091	$113,866	$123,578	$128,023
Other income (expense)				
Interest earned	$ 348	$ 283	$ 168	$ 105
Other income	$ 5,000	$ 325	$ 779	$ 7
Interest expense	($566)	($297)	($2,146)	($155)
Bookstore Net Income (loss)	($6,755)	($3,101)	($6,883)	$ 7,683
Total Building Income (Expense)		($639)	$ 5,674	$ 390
Net Income/ (Loss)	($6,755)	($3,740)	($1,209)	$ 8,073

*In 1993, Clara added health-care coverage for the employees. Due to the prohibitive costs, this was discontinued by the end of the year, in favor of increased wages.

**Includes Yellow Pages advertising and 1-800 phone lines.

Exhibit 2A　　　　**Financial Information: Balance Sheets for 1990-1993**
Balance Sheet as of 12/31 for the year ending:

Assets	1990	1991	1992	1993
Current assets:				
Cash and cash equivalents	$ 6,401	$ 14,675	$ 11,891	$ 13,787
Accounts Receivable—Trade			$ 681	$ 1,998
Prepaid employee benefits			$ 1,134	
Inventory—merchandise	$61,153	$ 55,536	$ 59,583	$ 65,579
Total current assets	$67,554	$ 70,211	$ 73,289	$ 81,364
Property and equipment				
Building		$ 79,260	$ 79,260	$ 79,260
Construction in progress			$ 8,900	$ 8,900
Leasehold improvements	$ 6,701	$ 6,701	$ 6,701	$ 6,701
Furniture and fixtures	$ 3,323	$ 3,323	$ 3,323	$ 3,323
Machines and equipment	$16,889	$ 21,888	$ 23,944	$ 25,917
Less accumulated depreciation	($13,994)	($18,887)	($25,557)	($33,977)
Other assets				
Organizational expense	$ 5,056	$ 5,056	$ 5,056	$ 5,056
Less accumulated amortization	($5,056)	($5,056)	($5,056)	($5,056)
Total fixed assets	$12,919	$ 92,285	$ 96,571	$ 90,124
Total Assets	$80,473	$162,496	$169,860	$171,488
Liabilities and Stockholders' Equity				
Current liabilities:				
Accounts payable	$11,847	$ 12,060	$ 19,686	$ 14,219
Security deposits		$ 870	$ 870	$ 370
Payroll taxes payable	$ 3,429	$ 2,960	$ 2,606	$ 107
Sales tax payable	$ 2,618	$ 3,357	$ 4,596	$ 3,886
Property Taxes Payable		$ 806	$ 792	$ 2,413
Deferred revenue	$ 100	$ 100	$ 2,209	$ 100
Interest Payable—SBA Loan		$ 1,140	$ 1,140	$ 498
Officer Loans	$ 4,400	$ 4,400	$ 4,400	$ 4,400
Accrued Interest—Shareholder			$ 2,097	$ 2,383
Total current liabilities	$22,394	$ 25,693	$ 38,396	$ 28,376
Noncurrent portion—SBA Loan		$ 72,000	$ 66,948	$ 70,255
Total Liabilities	$22,394	$ 97,693	$105,344	$ 98,631
Stockholders' equity:				
Common stock	$46,102	$ 56,282	$ 56,282	$ 56,282
Paid in capital	$47,902	$ 47,902	$ 47,902	$ 47,902
Retained earnings	($23,201)	($35,925)	($39,381)	($39,669)
Dividends	($4,502)			
Net profit (loss)	($8,222)	($3,456)	($287)	$ 8,342
Total Equity	$58,079	$ 64,803	$ 64,516	$ 72,857
Total Liabilities & Equity	$80,473	$162,496	$169,860	$171,488

Hue-Man Experience Bookstore Income Statement Comparisons
1993-1994 Statement of Income for the period ending 12/31

Income	1993	1994	% Change
Revenue			
Books	$269,751	$271,374	1%
Cards	$ 23,106	$ 29,932	30%
Prints	$ 9,616	$ 1,785	–81%
Jewelry	$ 1,438	$ 1,664	16%
Miscellaneous	$ 7,154	$ 7,195	1%
Catalogue	$ 6,828	$ 7,536	10%
Tapes and Magazines	$ 5,310	$ 6,153	16%
Reimbursed postage	$ 2,433	$ 2,373	–2%
Total Revenue	$325,636	$328,012	1%
Cost of Sales			
Books	$152,104	$186,181	22%
Cards	$ 14,583	$ 17,471	20%
Prints	$ 3,453	$ 437	–87%
Jewelry	$ 325	$ 790	143%
Miscellaneous	$ 5,946	$ 4,433	–25%
Tapes and Magazines	$ 4,044	$ 4,727	17%
Catalogue	$ 120	$ 9,132	7519%
Freight and postage	$ 740	$ 233	–69%
Framing supplies	$ 538	$ 325	–40%
Inventory (increase)/decrease	$ 6,034	($21,964)	–464%
Total Cost of Sales	$187,887	$201,765	7%
Gross Margin	$137,749	$126,247	–8%
Administrative Expenses			
Officer Salary	$ 24,973	$ 26,166	5%
Salaries	$ 26,706	$ 29,477	10%
Employee Benefits	$ 3,454	$ 3,548	3%
Advertising	$ 3,309	$ 2,575	–22%
Promotional	$ 13	$ 2,127	16299%
Accounting and legal	$ 6,256	$ 5,807	–7%
Vehicle expense	$ 4,517	$ 3,000	–34%
Bank and credit card service charges	$ 1,175	$ 1,983	69%
Consulting and contract labor	$ 676	$ 449	–34%
Contributions	$ 293	$ 1,190	307%
Dues and subscriptions	$ 1,977	$ 1,465	–26%
Depreciation	$ 3,997	$ 3,997	0%
Entertainment	$ 3,299	$ 3,928	19%
Travel/conferences	$ 2,082	$ 1,866	–10%

Exhibit 2B (continued)   **Hue-Man Experience Bookstore Income Statement Comparisons**
1993-1994 Statement of Income for the period ending 12/31

Income	1993	1994	% Change
Rent	$ 12,495	$ 8,820	−29%
Repairs and maintenance	$ 2,609	$ 2,706	4%
Security	$ 556	$ 448	−19%
Telephone	$ 7,577	$ 7,975	5%
Utilities	$ 3,055	$ 2,694	−12%
Office supplies and equipment	$ 4,667	$ 2,078	−55%
Printing	$ 2,194	$ 569	−74%
Store supplies	$ 3,264	$ 3,788	16%
Taxes—personal property	$ 486	$ 215	−56%
Taxes—payroll	$ 4,409	$ 4,548	3%
Freight & postage	$ 5,280	$ 3,800	−28%
Miscellaneous	$ 436	$ 447	0%
Total Expenses	$129,755	$125,666	−3%
Other income (expense)	($43)	$ 6	
Bookstore Net Income (loss)	$ 7,951	$ 587	−93%
Total Building Income (Expense)	$ 390	($2,535)	−750%
Net Income/(loss)	$ 8,341	($1,948)	−123%

Exhibit 3 U.S. Bookstore Chain Sales
Sales of 11 Largest Trade Bookstore Chains, 1992-91

Chain	Ownership	92 Sales[a]	91 Sales	% Change	Total Stores at Year-end
Waldenbooks	K-Mart	$1146.0	$1139.0	.06	1260
Barnes & Noble	public (in 1993)	1086.7	920.9	18.0	916
Crown Books	Dart Group	240.7	232.5	3.5	247
Borders Books	K-Mart	116.0	82.5	40.6	22[d]
Books-A-Million	public	95.1	72.8	30.6	107
Encore Books	Rite-Aid Corp.	65.2	52.3	24.7	103
Lauriat's[b]	Chadwick-Miller	49.0	46.0	7.0	56
Tower Books[b]	MTS Inc	33.0	29.0	13.8	15
Kroch's & Brentano's[b]	Waldenbooks	30.0[c]	33.0	−9.0	20
Rizzoli Bookstores[b]	private	24.0	21.0	14.3	11
Taylor's Inc.[b]	private	20.0	17.5	14.3	11
Totals		$2905.7	$2646.5	9.8%	2768

[a]Sales in millions. Figures are for calendar 1992 or most current fiscal year.
[b]Estimated sales.
[c]Store totals do not include nine Basset Books transferred to Borders at year-end.
[d]Sales estimate is a projection for year ending June 30, 1993.
Source: *Publishers Weekly,* June 14, 1993.

The hallmark of the chain superstores was discounting, selling mainly fiction, celebrity biographies, and other books that appeal to the general public. Increasing competition was coming from mail-order catalogues, warehouse clubs, discount retailers, non-book specialty stores (such as the Nature Company, Sutton Place Gourmet, and Toys Я' Us), and university bookstores (which have expanded their textbook holdings to include popular books and sidelines such as cards and clothing, and, more recently, books targeted to young adults known as "Generation X" or "13th Gen"). Both chain and independent bookstores have been increasing their use of book catalogues and newsletters, which promote best-sellers or discount specials and also serve as promotional tools to get more people in the stores.

Profit margins among the large chains were estimated at less than 1%, which made volume critical to this business. The American Booksellers Association surveys independent booksellers annually for financial operating performance information. Exhibit 4 shows estimates of financial performance based on *Publishers Weekly* data compiled from Barnes & Noble, Books-A-Million, and Crown Books; and ABA's ABACUS results, based on reports from 199 bookstore operations.

Fiscal 1993 reports from the large chains showed revenue increases of 19%. Profit margins and operating income were similar to 1992 levels, resulting in operating margins for each of the two years of 3%, nearly twice the independents' 1.62%.

Exhibit 4　　　　**Comparison of Independent and Chain Bookstore Profitability Estimates of Bookstore Expenses (as % of Total Sales)[a]**

	Chains Composite Dollars (millions)[c]	Chains %	Sample Independents Composite Dollars[c]	Indep %
Net Sales	$1197.8	100%	$170.5	100%
Receipts from Books[b]	1078.1	90	136.4	80
Receipts from Sidelines[b]	119.7	10	34.1	20
Cost of Goods Sold	816.3	68.2	106.4	62.4
Gross Profit	381.5	31.8	64.1	37.6
Operating, selling, and administrative expense	317.8	26.5	61.4	36.0
Occupancy Costs			12.3	7.2
Advertising			4.9	2.9
Depreciation and amortization	27.6	2.3		
Operating profit	36.1	3.0	2.8	1.6
Interest expense	29.9	2.5	.34	0.2
Income before tax	6.2	0.5	2.42	1.4
Income tax	5.5	0.4	.68	0.4[b]
Net Income	0.7	0.1	1.7	1.0

[a]Calendar year 1991 or fiscal year ending 1992. (Most independents operate on a calendar year; chains report earnings on a fiscal year basis.)

[b]Estimate from anecdotal reports.

[c]All dollars are millions.

Source: *Publishers Weekly*, October 18, 1993.

Barnes & Noble attributed a 144% increase in sales in 1992 to its new superstores. In 1993, 30% of Barnes & Noble sales were from its 135 superstores, 77 of which were added in 1993. Another 75 stores were planned for 1994 and for 1995. Encore Books, which operated only one superstore in 1993, planned to open four more by mid-1994. Waldenbooks' superstore operations were under the name of Borders, a previously-independent 19-store chain purchased by Kmart in the fall of 1992. Borders (which also includes Walden's Basset Book Shops) had 30 superstores in 1992 and planned to open 20 more by the end of 1993. Crown planned to increase its 22 superstores to 40 by the end of 1993. Books-a-Million, with 10 superstores in 1992, expected to open five more in 1993. Tower books had 15 stores by the end of 1992; Lauriat's was positioning its new Royal Discount Bookstores as superstores.

Many independent bookstore owners were concerned that the industry was going the way of hardware stores and neighborhood pharmacies. According to John Mutter of *Publishers Weekly*, there was fear that superstores were creating "a concentration of power that threatens the diversity of what gets published and what is available for the public to read.[1]" The American Booksellers Association was cooperating with the Federal Trade Commission in investigating business practices and pricing policies which appeared to threaten the small independent book retailers.

While chains offered cheap prices, few could offer the personal service of independents who knew their customers. This was particularly true in the growing breed of specialty book stores. Some specialty booksellers focused on a particular subject, such as Armchair Sailor in New York, which specialized in nautical books; Victor Kamlin, Inc., in Rockville, Md., which specialized in Russian literature; Books of Wonder in New York, which specialized in children's books; Sports Central: The Ultimate Sports Bookstore in Palo Alto; or Books for Cooks in Baltimore. Others, like Salt of the Earth Bookstore in Albuquerque, Midnight Special in Santa Monica, California, and Odyssey Bookshop in South Hadley, Massachusetts, prided themselves on community involvement by promoting multicultural authors. Some stores focused on one particular market group, such as Charis Bookstore in Atlanta, which positioned itself as a feminist bookstore; OutBooks in Fort Lauderdale and A Different Light in San Francisco, which targeted lesbians and gays; and Shrine of the Black Madonna in Detroit and Hue-Man Experience Bookstore in Denver, which catered to African-American clientele.

Bookselling and publishing by and for African-Americans had surged since 1988. An increasing interest in African-American culture, aided by school curriculum reforms, fueled a growth in bookstores catering to African-Americans. According to Wade Hudson, who ran Just Us Books in New Jersey, "African-Americans are hungry for knowledge and understanding about their experience, so they are looking for books that provide it."[2] Until recently, these books had been published by small independent publishing operations or by the authors themselves, and sold out of car trunks at book conventions. More recently, the major publishers and national distributors entered this market, providing easier access to booksellers through mainstream distribution channels.

"Bookstores used to assume there was no market because blacks didn't come in asking for titles like these, but that's because they assumed the stores wouldn't stock them," commented Mr. Hudson. Kassahun Checole, president of the Red Sea Press, the largest distributor of African-American titles, started out in the publishing business. "The Red Sea Press now distributes titles from about 60 publishers, approximately half of them African-American."[3]

Bookseller and publisher Haki Madhubuti believed that "A good 30%-35% of the people who buy our books aren't black."[4] He began the African-American Publishers and Booksellers Association in 1989, which held trade meetings and special sessions at the American Booksellers Association convention. This group became the first "specialty" segment within the ABA. As of 1992, there were several segments, such as a travel group and mystery group, which held roundtable discussions at national and regional meetings and put together newsletters, catering to specialty bookstore owners.

THE DENVER MARKET

According to the 1990 census, Colorado had almost 3.3 million residents, nearly 2 million of whom lived in the greater metropolitan Denver area. While only 4% of Colorado's population was black, the city of Denver was nearly 13% black, 60% of whom lived north of downtown. The Denver metropolitan area had a total African-American population of nearly 100,000, 60,000 of whom lived within the Denver city limits.

According to Scarborough Research Corporation, Denver ranked 10% above the national average in the popularity of reading in 1993, ranking 22nd out of 209 surveyed metropolitan areas. Forty-three percent of metropolitan Denver households were considered "avid readers." Both Denver and Boulder, 35 miles away, boasted independent superstores which had been in existence for over twenty years.

The Tattered Cover was a Denver landmark, located in a former department store in Cherry Creek North, an established shopping area with nearly a million square feet of retail and service businesses. The Tattered Cover had 40,000 square feet of selling space on four floors, and boasted over 220,000 titles. Across the street was the prestigious Cherry Creek Shopping Center, which opened in August 1990, a one million-square-foot mall comprised of luxury and specialty stores (including Doubleday Book Shop and Travelday's Book Shop, both owned by B. Dalton, and Brentano's, owned by Waldenbooks). Recent competitors, located in suburban areas, included five Barnes & Noble superstores, each with approximately 10,000 feet of selling space. A sixth Barnes & Noble superstore was planned in a renovated theater building about two miles east of the Tattered Cover.

There was a wide variation in retail lease rates in Denver, depending upon the location. Rents in Cherry Creek North averaged between $17-$28 per square foot (calculated on a yearly basis). Rates for the Cherry Creek Shopping Center, immediately south of Cherry Creek North, were estimated to be about twice that rate.

The Denver area had over one hundred independent retailers of new and used books. Specialty bookstores included Murder by the Book, which specialized in mystery fiction; Astoria Books and Prints, which specialized in rare books and artwork; Hermitage Antiquarian Bookshop, which specialized in collectibles and first editions; Isis Metaphysical Bookstore, which specialized in books on metaphysics, crystals and jewelry, and new-age music; Category Six Books, specializing in gay and lesbian literature; Cultural Legacy, which specialized in books in Spanish; and numerous children's bookstores and religious specialty stores.

The Hue-Man Experience bookstore was located on Park Avenue West, a well-traveled thoroughfare about a mile north of downtown, bordering the area known as Five Points, named for the five tramway lines that once intersected there. Five Points is one of Denver's largest residential areas, encompassing over 1,000 acres. With its close proximity to the downtown area, Five Points used to be a cultural center for African-Americans, with more African-American–owned businesses than any other place in the U.S. except for Harlem. This began to change in 1959 with the passage of Colorado's Fair Housing Act. During the 1960s and 1970s, many of the more affluent African-Americans moved to other, more integrated, neighborhoods. In 1993, the area was populated with small service and retail establishments and run-down houses. According to 1990 census data, the average household income in Colorado was $36,015 (U.S. average was $29,199). Half of the residents in the vicinity of Five Points had an annual household income under $35,000; nearly 30% of the households reported an annual income under $15,000.

Walking in the vicinity Five Points was probably not advisable, especially after dark. In 1993, this area had the third highest crime rate in Denver: 315.2 crimes reported per 1,000 population. In 1992, Five Points ranked second. The highest crime area (consistently since 1989) was North Capital Hill, which bordered Five Points to the south, with 413.2 crimes reported per 1,000 population in 1993. While these numbers include car thefts and petty robbery as well as gang violence and homicides, Five Points was generally viewed as a undesirable part of town.

THE HUE-MAN EXPERIENCE BOOKSTORE OPERATIONS/LAYOUT

The Hue-Man Experience Bookstore began operations out of a two-story row house, one of four attached residential apartments. Within two years, Clara expanded her store into one of the adjacent row houses, convincing the landlord to do renovations to connect the two houses. With 4,200 titles occupying 3,000 square feet, Hue-Man Experience was, very likely, the nation's largest African-American bookstore.

Two cash registers, or Point of Sale computer terminals, were located just inside the door. Afrocentric greeting cards and note cards were located in a separate room adjacent to the checkout area. Afrocentric art created a backdrop for the checkout area, which was surrounded by a glass case displaying ethnic jewelry. An employee was always on hand to greet people and offer assistance. Each room was arranged around a particular theme or subject. Popular titles and classics were on the main floor, in what was once a living room. Upstairs, there were rooms devoted to sports, religion, music, and children's books.

Specialty cards, calendars, and jewelry comprised approximately 20% of sales. Fine art prints and ethnic artwork by local artists were displayed on the walls throughout the store and in two browsing racks. Calendars featuring African-American history and African-American art were also prominently displayed. During the holiday season, two rooms upstairs were full of distinctive boxed Christmas and Kwanzaa cards. People who bought books as gifts could also purchase gift wrapping and gift bags with African designs. Like most specialty stores, these sidelines were an integral part of the store's identity, geared specifically to the African-American market. Cards and jewelry typically have a bigger markup than books, and bring added traffic into the store.

Industry insiders recognized that books were often an impulse purchase, bought on a whim for self-fulfillment or to be given as a gift. Both small mall boutiques and large chain stores understood the importance of lighting and displays to get people in the door to browse. Location and name-recognition were important here too, especially for independent booksellers.

Because of the fixed maximum price of most items, inventory control was critical to profitability. Computerized inventory control systems attached to Point of Sale (POS) terminals were considered essential for large store success. These computer programs ranged in price from around $400 (for software which runs on most PCs) to over $5000 (for systems that include POS, cash registers, and scanners). Some of the more expensive computer systems available could be connected to on-line electronic ordering systems with wholesalers or major distributors to expedite reorders and returns. Others could tie into banking networks for credit card authorization and check scanning. Hue-Man Experience used a program called "Booklog," a menu-driven system which was easy to use, even for "non-computer" people. This program kept track of purchases and sales, keeping sales histories to track fast- or slow-moving items. A customer file was kept that was used for identifying frequent buyers and sending out announcements or newsletters.

Employees were critical to the success of independent booksellers, whose customers relied on service. Many booksellers had difficulty finding competent employees, people who read and who were knowledgeable about books, people who were personable, people who were willing to work hard. Wages in most bookstores ranged from $4.50–$5.50 per hour, far less than most full-time employment. Even in Denver's strong economy, booksellers such as the Tattered Cover and Hue-Man Experience Bookstore have had no trouble finding competent, well-educated employees. Employees at both stores would readily tell you how much they enjoyed their jobs.

There were four full-time employees at the Hue-Man Experience Bookstore. Turnover was low, with employees typically staying over a year, a rarity in minimum-wage positions. The employees at the Hue-Man Experience Bookstore conveyed a sense of ownership, not only to the bookstore, but also to the cultural community. One employee at Hue-Man Experience Bookstore, a college graduate who majored in African-American Studies, had stayed at the store for over a year because she enjoyed learning more about her culture and interacting with African-Americans in her community.

MARKETING

I started out with a marketing plan but there were many flaws because it was based on Anglo book purchasing behavior. We were unable to anticipate the difficulty in getting African-American people to buy books. I had to go back and reevaluate my marketing strategies. We thought people would come because the idea was unique. It was an upscale store with ambiance, patterned similar to Tattered Cover, which really has a national presence. And we thought that people would come—particularly middle-class people with disposable incomes and a higher education level, because that was the population that I was close to. But it took a lot more marketing to get people in. The variable we didn't count on is that the store sold not just books, but culture. The customers we attract have to be culturally connected.

Clara originally put out fliers and took out ads to publicize her store, but quickly realized that she wasn't reaching her market. And she soon understood that the people who came into the store were not the well-to-do clientele that she had envisioned.

We found out that our market was the working class. So we had to direct our advertising to these people. Unfortunately, they don't belong to a lot of groups. They belong to churches but marketing from churches is very difficult because pastors do not want you to come into their congregation to sell something—other than what they sell. So we've tried to determine what our people buy and why they buy what they buy. We've studied the psycho-demographics of our population and tried to create a presence in the community. And we also were trying to create a national presence because people make purchases based on prestige so the bookstore had to develop the prestige.

So Clara Villarosa began telling everyone who came in the store that this was the largest African-American bookstore in the country. And she became an influential figure in the African-American community. She did book reviews on the radio. She was active in community and civic affairs. She was appointed to the governor's council for business development and serves on the Board of Directors of the Small Business Development Center and the Metro Denver Visitors and Conventions Bureau. She was a "friend of the library," she worked with the Denver Center for Performing Arts (DCPA), the Cleo Parker Robinson Dance Company, and Eulipions Cultural Center. She was willing to be involved in

> . . . anything that's culturally related, because I enjoy ethnic events. I like the theater and the ballet and all of that, so I get involved. DCPA currently performs one black play a year, maybe someday they'll do two. I host the director and cast for a reception here in the store and I invite my customers in so that they can touch and feel the cast and it advertises the show and helps sell tickets. Cleo Parker Robinson—her dance troupe is an African-American dance troupe, and I work with her and find out what she's doing. Eulipions is an African-American theater company. I was a founding member of their Board of Directors and served for 8 years. If an author—an African-American author—is coming to town to make a speech or presentation, I ask if they want their book sold at the events or if they want to come to the store for a signing. Of course they will! I'm not stupid! But I really have to hustle and seek out opportunities. And so I've been nominated for a zillion awards and won most of them. I'm a small business, I'm retail, I'm a minority-owned business.

In the ten years since the store had been opened, Clara had become much better at marketing. By the end of 1993, the only paid advertising was in the form of "courtesy ads," ads placed in local programs or newsletters. These ads generated good will, but she did not believe that she reached new customers with those ads. Word of mouth was the main source of advertising. But word of mouth was cultivated through sophisticated public relations. She has been featured in *Ms. Magazine, Executive Female,* and *Publishers Weekly.* She was on the board of directors of the American Booksellers Association and a member of the Mountains and Plains Booksellers Association. She was instrumental in putting together a feature exhibit entitled "Black and Read: Books by African-American Authors and Illustrators" at the ABA convention, which met in Denver in 1990.

> African-Americans come to Denver for many conventions but how do I locate them? So by serving on the board [of the Denver Metropolitan Visitors and Conventions Bureau] I will be instrumental in putting together a fact sheet of things to do and places to go in Denver for Africa-American visitors. I'm also learning about other industries—the hotel industry—all of those are what I call my marketing strategy. I'm hosting a group of African-American educators here on Friday.

In 1989, at the suggestion of many out-of-town customers, Clara put together a 64-page mail order catalog. "They said, 'Send me the booklist.' They like to read it but they don't order. It's a different motivation to pick up the phone and order a book." But the catalog appears to create a feeling of connectedness and brings them back to the store. The book catalog was financed largely through "co-op" advertising, whereby publishers pay for most of the printing cost of ads for their books.

By 1992, Clara's book catalog was a more efficient 16 pages. The catalog was professionally produced, in a format similar to those found in upscale bookstores such as the Tattered Cover. In 1993, she began negotiating with Ingram's, a major book distributor, to jointly produce a catalog that would be distributed to other bookstores. This would be a glossy version of her newsprint catalog that other bookstore owners could use for their customers.

> My name would appear as a byline and Ingram's would do the layout and pick up the printing costs. Individual bookstores will put their name and address on it

for their own customers, which helps them publicize current titles. I know it's a lot of work to design this, but I'm already doing it for my own store. This way Hue-Man Experience will get national publicity.

She also published a quarterly newsletter, highlighting author signings and community events. A reduced copy of the newsletter appears in Exhibit 5. This newsletter was typically one page, printed on both sides, which could be mailed easily when folded and stapled. Regular customers were on the mailing list. Customers who spent at least $10 were added to this list. Clara found out the hard way that sending out unsolicited newsletters was not bringing in new customers. Regular customers were "the ones most likely to come back and most likely to come to store-sponsored events. They pay for the newsletter."

> PR is critical in this business—community connections. It's interesting, because that's what we built this store on—a community presence. Local people say that we have something of value and this creates pride and ownership. And we perpetuate that image by showing them that we care about them as individual customers and that we care about their community . . . We find that our customers expect to be treated well, everyone is greeted, everyone is treated warmly, nurtured. We have to recognize our history, based on segregation, discrimination. You still hear of sales people demanding IDs and avoiding eye contact with African-American customers. It happens every place. Not as often as before, but people are still uncomfortable around African-Americans. Even in Denver, which is a city that's pretty well mixed, an integrated city . . . There's no central African-American community because Denver was developed as an integrated city and people have dispersed to all areas of the city. People have moved to the suburbs, outlying areas, Aurora, Littleton. These people aren't inclined to drive the distance to the store very often. We have to create a destination place. There's no other traffic around here.

PLANS FOR THE FUTURE

In November 1992, Clara Villarosa bought the four houses that comprised the building which contained the bookstore, with financing backed by the U.S. Small Business Administration. She was able to buy the building for $79,000. With her track record as a successful retailer, she was able to secure a $72,000 24-year loan on the building, which appraised for $120,000. Her store occupied two units; the other two were rented to an art gallery and an ethnic apparel retailer.

Clara viewed her business as more than a bookstore. To her, it was a cultural center. She observed, "People who come here are culturally connected." She feared that, in 1993, Denver's African-American population was too dispersed to support a cultural center. She also recognized that there was strength in numbers: a larger concentration of attractive African-American businesses could serve as a catalyst for cultural connections.

> I'd like to create an Afrocentric Marketplace and position it as a mini-mall. So I bought this building two years ago. The other rented spaces in this building are complementary product lines. One . . . sells African clothing and cloth and accessories and the other is [an] . . . Art Gallery. I'd eventually like to work with them to make it a coffee shop also. The rent is fixed, it's stable, so they aren't going to deal with escalating rent costs. I offer limited services, I maintain the property, but we work cooperatively. I know the bookstore is the anchor. They each have their

Exhibit 5   **Promoting and Nurturing African-American Thought**

THE HUE-MAN READER

September, 19—

Author Signings

Maya Angelou

In Ms. Angelou's brand new book she is gracefully sharing her wisdom in a series of thought provoking personal essays. We all know her as one who can "sure turn a phrase." All that can be said about this book is my! my! my!

Wouldn't Take Nothing for My Journey Now
Friday, September 17
4:30 p.m. – 6:00 p.m.

Bebe Moore Campbell

Ms. Campbell's best selling novel about murder, love, passion and racism in the Mississippi Delta is being released in paperback. *Sweet Summer*, an autobiographical work is also being re-released. Some of you may have heard her provocative commentary on National Public Radio for Morning Edition.

Your Blues Ain't Like Mine (now in paperback)
Sweet Summer (re-released)
Saturday, October 2
4:30 p.m. – 6:30 p.m.

Ralph Wiley

Mr. Wiley will discuss his views from his latest book covering such diverse topics as racism as America's favorite pastime, relationships between Black men and women, Magic Johnson and AIDS, multiculturalism taught in schools, Clarence and Anita, and "The Silence of the Lambs." He shares a penetrating vision to challenge our often comfortable way of life. His previous best selling book was *"Why Black People Tend to Shout."*

What Black People Should Do Now
Friday, October 29
5:00 p.m. – 7:00 p.m.

EVENTS

THEATRE
The Eulipions Culture Center presents
"Spunk"
by George C. Wolfe
Sept. 9th thru Oct. 2
Thurs., Fri., Sat. 7:00 p.m.
This play is a collection of short stories by Zora Neal Hurston adapted for theatre.
For tickets call 295-6814
$2.00 off with this flyer!

DOLLAR DAYS
IRS
(Inventory Reduction Sale)
Great savings on select books priced at $1.00 each!
Sept. 21, 22, 23, 24, 25

STORY HOUR
Story Telling!
Bring the children one and all every third Saturday
1:00 p.m. – 2:30 p.m.
Next one September 18th

READINGS
Sandra Gould Ford, publisher of the *"Shooting Star"* literary magazine will discuss **How to Get Your Book Published** and read from her award winning works
Friday, September 24th
5:30 p.m. – 7:00 p.m.

Barbara Avent will read and sign copies of her new poetry book
"The Leopard Speaks About Changes in Life"
Saturday, October 30
2:00 p.m. – 4:00 p.m.

own customer base but we feed off of each other. We want to create a synergy that will create more traffic for everyone. I'm working on joint PR [with the clothing store and the art gallery].

Around the corner from the Hue-Man Experience Bookstore was another row-house building, which faced the side street. The first floor of this building housed an artist co-op, a store that sold blues tapes, a custom hat shop, and a caterer. Rents were about $4 per square foot (per year), or $400 per month for each tenant. Three of the leases were month-to-month contracts. The second floor was boarded up and uninhabitable due to fire damage several years before.

In September 1993, this building went up for sale. By December 1993, the asking price was reduced from $150,000 to $95,000. The roof had recently been repaired, but needed replacement. The building would need extensive renovation, estimated as high as $200,000, for the upstairs to be used for retail space. One prospective buyer estimated that a new floor could be put in for about $50,000 so that the upstairs could be used as storage.

The Mayor's Office of Economic Redevelopment had targeted the Five Points area for low-interest redevelopment loans. Clara believed that "There's potential for lots of retail activity in this area, but it will be slow in coming." A light rail transit system, connecting Five Points to downtown, was scheduled to open in October 1994.

> . . . . I had hoped that the catering operation [around the corner] would also serve food, but she just wants to cater; and my suspicion is that they're not stable tenants. The top floor of the building . . . needs to be renovated for retail or office space. I think the purchase is still an option.

Clara Villarosa was confident that she could get financing for expansion without diluting her ownership in the business. Business loan rates were going for as low as 10%. But, even if she could obtain the building at less than the current asking price, she was not sure that this would be a prudent investment at this time. At this point in her life, Clara was particularly concerned about the income potential of any expansion effort. "I'm getting older," she observed candidly. "Right now it takes all of my energy and all of my effort just to keep [the bookstore] afloat." At the same time, she still had a vision of creating an Afrocentric Marketplace with national recognition.

ENDNOTES

1. Mutter, J. (January 4, 1993). Heated competition gets Hotter. *Publishers Weekly*, p. 43.
2. Goddard, C. (January 20, 1992). Aiming for the mainstream. *Publishers Weekly*, p. 29.
3. Ibid, p. 30.
4. Ibid.

Presque Isle State Park (Is This Place for the Birds?)

David R. Frew, Gannon University

C. Louise Sellaro, Youngstown State University

Harry Leslie was a legendary windsor knot tier, but tonight he was not having much luck. As he struggled in front of the bedroom mirror his wife called from the kitchen to remind him of his 7:00 p.m. meeting. "Better hurry it up Harry, it's almost 6:15 and you said that you were going to get there early!" "OK, OK," he muttered, "I'm almost ready." As she kissed him on his way out, neither acknowledged the tension that Harry felt. He hadn't mentioned it often as the fateful evening approached, but tonight's community information meeting had the unsettling potential to threaten his job. And this was, indeed, Harry's dream job: Chief Superintendent of Presque Isle State Park.

Harry closed the door carefully as he stepped out of the lighthouse that was home to his family (see Exhibit 1). The structure was old (1892) and a gust of November wind could easily rip the massive door from its hinges. It was a cold, clear night and the surf was pounding the beach near the lighthouse. As he bent his 220-pound frame into his car, Harry savored his family's living quarters. They lived in a working lighthouse on the north beach of a beautiful state park. His children had a magical existence with a beach at the back door and woods near the front entrance.

While he was driving the seven miles of deserted beach road toward the park gates and the city, a park police cruiser pulled next to him, waved, and motioned to the two-way radio. "Good luck boss, you're going to need it," chuckled officer Brandon. "Thanks, but I don't think it will be all that bad," replied Harry. "People are basically reasonable when it counts!"

As he left the park and headed toward the university where the public forum was to be held, Harry hoped that these had not been empty words. His

Exhibit 1

Presque Isle State Park

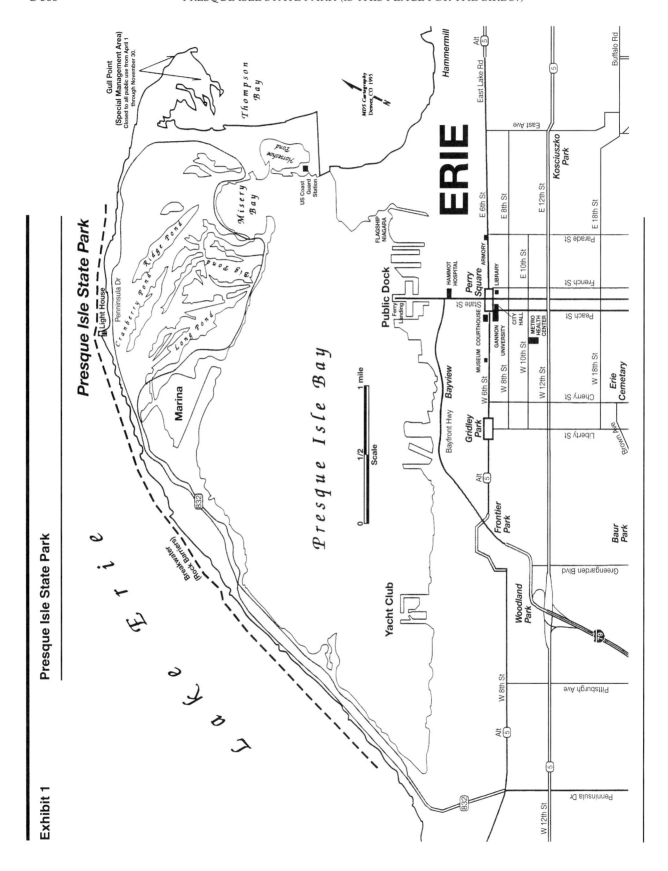

predecessor had caused himself political difficulties by making what he had considered "reasonable" changes at the park. Ultimately, however, community turmoil over those changes had helped to initiate his transfer to the political offices of Pennsylvania's Department of Environmental Resources (DER) in Harrisburg, a fate which didn't interest Harry. He was an outdoor person, not a bureaucrat or politician, and loved living in the park, being involved in day-to-day problems and using a hands-on approach. If a tree fell in a windstorm, Harry might be first at the scene, setting up warning signs and cutting away branches with his chain saw. He was less political and more practical than the previous park chief, and the park staff loved that about him.

The public meeting had been announced four weeks ago and was to be an information session. Harry and his staff had worked hard to develop a park management plan, an attempt to balance the diverse interests of the park and its constituency groups. The dilemma concerned how to juggle the various needs of the community and fit them into a strategic plan that would be acceptable to the various stakeholders who had concerns about how the park was to be used "for the public good."[1] He was also aware of the political "noise" that any of these factions could make if they didn't get their own way. But his plan was a reasonable one. It split the difference between commercial interests in the park and the concerns of the environmentally-oriented groups.[2]

Harry's hope for the meeting was that there would be a group of understanding individuals in attendance and that he could orchestrate a compromise. He believed that somehow all of the involved individuals and groups would have an important common interest: the well-being of Presque Isle.

It was 6:35 as Harry steered his car onto university grounds and threaded his way between people walking along the narrow campus road. He was amazed at the congestion. There were hundreds of people walking the narrow road to the parking lot, and cars were illegally parked on the lawn. Approaching the parking area, Harry's heart almost stopped as he realized what was actually happening. The parking lot was full and the crowd was streaming toward the lecture hall and *his* meeting!

Suddenly someone in the crowd recognized Harry's state vehicle, and a voice from the crowd yelled, "There's Leslie, the guy who's trying to ruin our park!" "Great," he thought to himself, "my career is ruined and I get a parking ticket all in the same evening."

PRESQUE ISLE STATE PARK[3]

Presque Isle State Park (see Exhibit 1) is a sand spit peninsula which extends seven miles into Lake Erie. The peninsula joins the mainland just west of Erie, Pennsylvania, creating a sheltering arm that forms a beautiful natural harbor. The city of Erie is located near the center of Lake Erie's southern shore, and the peninsula has historically been critical to the development of the area. The population of Erie itself has stabilized at approximately 115,000, but the surrounding suburbs have been growing steadily. Combined, the areas have reached a population of 250,000.

The peninsula is one of central Lake Erie's two major sand spits, and is a unique geological and biological preserve. Presque Isle, along with its mirror image twin Long Point across the lake on the north shore, create a hydrodynamic lake effect which is said to be critical to the health of the entire lake. The eastward flowing waters pass between the points over a relatively deep water trench and increase in depth and velocity as they flow into Lake Erie's eastern basin. At the line which connects the tips of the two peninsulas, the average width of Lake Erie changes from forty-five to twenty-seven miles.

Presque Isle is a biologist's dream, and a classic example of secession forestation. The secession process, which is essential to the continued health and structural integrity of the peninsula, is activated at its eastern tip, an area called Gull Point. Secession is driven by a combination of natural forces. In late summer, water levels drop and winds calm. Sand, carried by westerly winds, comes to rest along the peninsula's north beaches just east of Gull Point, causing a series of sculpted sand bars. In the fall there are always several strong storms from the northeast (nor'easters). The winds tend to push the sandbars back (southwesterly) toward Gull Point creating parallel beach lines some thirty or forty feet east of the original beach.

Over the winter, water levels fall again. The effect on the beach looks as though nature is creating a double water's edge (two beaches). In the spring, cottonwood trees, common along freshwater beaches and the quintessential species on Presque Isle, pollinate by releasing fluffy air-driven seed balls. As spring winds freshen and water levels rise, these cottonwood balls are blown into the water. The cottonwood seeds float back onto Gull Point, and become lodged on the previous year's newly formed sand ridge. Over the summer the seeds root along the outer sand bar, forming a structure covered with scrub brush near the newly developing beach.

Assuming that this new ridge survives the next year's storms and water level shifts (which it does approximately thirty percent of the time), Presque Isle will have grown to the east by the width of the new parallel beach line. This (secession) is the process which has systematically driven Presque Isle eastward. A helicopter view of Presque Isle's eastern tip shows a series of arch-shaped rows of cottonwood trees. From the water's edge moving westward, rows grow further apart and the trees get taller. As the cottonwoods mature, organic materials build up near their bases and the curved rows of trees develop ridge lines to go with them. The older the secession line, the higher the ridge. Between the easternmost ridges, which are tiny compared to their westerly cousins, there are ponds formed by the water which is trapped between the parallel ridges.

As the ridge lines mature and grow taller (moving east to west), the pond structures between them also change. The eastern ponds are bottom-water fed, clearwater repositories with fish (trapped by secession) and limited plant growth. The second tier of ponds (to the west) usually develops a variety of marine algae and other plant life. As the ponds along Gull Point age, they change to marshy areas and finally rich soil which separates and nourishes the organic materials between the mature ridge lines.

From an ecological perspective, Presque Isle represents a rare environment where climax forest secession can be studied in a compact area. As a further bonus, the variety of structures provided by the secession environment makes a productive home for a vast array of birds and mammals. Presque Isle and Long Point create an important bird flyway. The area is registered as a National Natural Landmark, and the process of plant and animal succession is a source of both research and educational interest. Researchers, college professors, and students from across the U.S. and Canada have been engaged in the study of birds at both Presque Isle and Long Point for decades.

BUSINESS AND LOCAL INTERESTS

To the local recreational and business communities, the easterly growth of the peninsula and the scientific interests of academics are more of a threat than a benefit. The regional economy has always been fueled by tourism rather than science.[4] Since the park was established in 1921 and a roadway built to its popular bathing beaches and picnic groves, millions of people have flocked to Erie and Presque Isle.

Since the demise of the local industrial base in the 1970's, tourism has taken on even more importance to the regional economy.[5] By 1990, economic data suggested that tourism, anchored by visits to Presque Isle, was the number two component of the regional economy. Attendance at Presque Isle has consistently been greater than that of Yellowstone National Park. By 1990, a wall of motels, restaurants, fishing tackle shops, bike rental centers, and other amusements had built up near the park entrance. Regional chambers of commerce estimate that the summer population of the Erie area is 160% of its winter totals.

For the tourist-based economy, any threat to the use of the peninsula is a potential business crisis, and there have been many threats over the years. In the 1950's, there was concern that the narrow western arm of the peninsula might wash away due to erosion. The continuous eastward motion of wind and water tends to wash sand from the western beaches toward Gull Point. Thus the natural process which causes secession threatens the peninsula's narrow western arm, beaches, and park entrance.

Since before the 1950's it was common for storm waters to break through the western arm, making the peninsula into an island. As a result, it was not unusual for visitors to be unable to exit the park. This problem was tackled by the U.S. Army Corps of Engineers which launched a rebuilding program in the late 1950's, adding dredged beach sand to the western arm of the peninsula. At the same time, an improved roadway system was built, solving the problem of weekend traffic congestion.

The Corps of Engineers has long suggested that, if left to its own devices, Presque Isle would ultimately separate from the mainland, becoming an island and continuing its relentless eastward migration away from Erie. Since the major rebuilding of the western arm, the Corps has continuously trucked sand to the peninsula to protect the bathing beaches.

This ongoing renewal plan had a multimillion-dollar price tag, so to save money, the Corps made a decision in the early 1980's to replenish the beaches with sand from quarrys south of Erie. Quarry sand is much coarser and less aesthetically pleasing than the dredged sand used in the early days of beach nourishment. But the coarser sand is less expensive, and it has been therefore argued that its heavier consistency will help hold the beaches in place.

During the middle 1980's, high water levels in combination with several severe fall storms did significant damage to the beaches. As in the 1950's, lake waters overflowed the peninsula, closing roads and reminding the public of the fragile nature of Presque Isle. Therefore, in a "final" move to stabilize the peninsula, the Army Corps announced a new program using parallel rock mound barrier reefs which were to run parallel to the north beach at a distance of approximately 500 yards from shore.

Theoretically the rock mound reefs would attenuate wave action from either prevailing southwesterlies or the fall/spring nor'easters. The movement of sand from west to east would be slowed to a manageable rate and only a small amount of material would have to be added to beach fronts to ensure stabilization. The final project was completed at a cost of more than twenty-three million dollars over a three and one half-year period.

As the last of an immense flow of federal and state tax dollars was spent for this project, a low water cycle began on the lake and it was beginning to appear that the threat of the loss of Presque Isle, or its roadways, had subsided and that the Army Corps had overreacted. Investment in tourism at the entrance to the park accelerated once more with two new bars, a restaurant, a windsurfing/rollerblading center, condominiums, and a scuba diving shop.

PARK ADMINISTRATION

Erie's first settlers were attracted to the natural harbor formed by Presque Isle. They generally came via water, arriving by schooner or bateaux in the late 1700's. They settled on the creek inlets which emptied into the sheltered bay. As the town developed in the 1800's, the peninsula became a harbor barrier and a wilderness area utilized by citizens for hunting, fishing, and recreation. The federal government (whose needs decreased after hostilities with Canada and the War of 1812 ended) and the City of Erie both saw the land mass as an important strategic acquisition.

In 1921, while city and federal governments quibbled over ownership, the state of Pennsylvania negotiated a complex political deal in which the federal government could use an area for a Coast Guard station, but the State owned the peninsula. Meanwhile, the city was assured that a park would be developed for the well-being of the local population, and the city's water supply infrastructure (on the peninsula) would remain under the jurisdiction of the city of Erie.

Thus began a long history of state administration and the controversies which were to arise in later years. In the first and possibly most significant of all developments, it was determined that a roadway system would span the length of the park. In prior years a crude road ran from the mainland for the first few miles along the north beaches. Governor Fisher's proposed roadway was to loop around the eastern end of Presque Isle and encourage "motoring." Citizens could tour with automobiles to view flora, fauna, and wildlife.

Between 1938 and 1994, however, the volume of traffic grew at rates beyond the imagination of early park architects. Weekend totals reached astronomical numbers and the extension of park driving hours during summer months resulted in a constant stream of automobiles circling Presque Isle's fourteen-mile roadway system.

Over the first decades of development several personnel additions were needed in park administration, which now reports to Pennsylvania's Department of Environmental Resources. By 1982, the staff consisted of the superintendent, administrative staff, maintenance, a police department, the marina staff, and a lifeguard organization. (Later review of the Park personnel revealed the lack of a full-time naturalist position. An on-site individual was needed to continuously assess and monitor park preservation activities.) A number of superintendents were involved in the development of Presque Isle, but the greatest growth occurred between 1956 and 1986 under the direction of long-time Superintendent Michael Wargo. During the Wargo regime the park matured, a 473-boat marina was constructed, tourism grew, and the Corps of Engineers initiated and completed major renovations.

Upon Wargo's retirement, the state, which was beginning to sense the potential for both growth and political controversy, appointed Eugene Giza to the post. Giza was young and ambitious and understood the park's growth potential. He was also politically astute and sensed that there might be a linkage between park use and funding. The budget had undergone cuts in the early 1980's, and Giza developed activities which would encourage visitation and rationalize more funding. Unfortunately, budget cuts continued.[6]

Under the Giza administration the following developments occurred:

1. Old-fashioned "hole in the ground" outhouses were replaced with modern lavatory facilities. These featured an above-ground sand mound leach bed (similar to a septic system) and did not have to be emptied on a regular basis.
2. An all-purpose black top trail was built along the south (bayside) edge of the park. This encouraged hiking, running, biking, and rollerblading.
3. Winter activities such as festivals and carnivals were initiated.
4. A cross-country ski trail system was developed and an entrepreneur was given concession rights.
5. Running and bike races were encouraged in the park.
6. A Citizen's Advisory Committee was formed to shepherd the park.

THE ENVIRONMENTAL BACKLASH

As early as the Wargo administration, an environmentalist reaction against peninsula policies began to build. Local groups such as the Audubon Society and the Birdwatchers began raising objections to park projects. The most significant blow to the continuity of tourist-related developments came when Presque Isle's own Citizen's Advisory Group began to lean toward environmental issues.

In summary, the environmental position was that too many park decisions were designed simply to increase use. This subsequently threatened the delicate environment, plants, animals, and water quality. An example was the early decision to place a roadway around the park and encourage motoring. Environmentalists argued that the delicate sand spit could not tolerate this volume of carbon-spewing gasoline engines. From an environmental posture it would have been preferable to make park visitors leave their automobiles at the park gates and hike or bicycle to the eastern portions of the park, or to operate an electric tram service to the eastern beaches and picnic areas.

Using this early decision as an example, business and tourist interests argued that the accessibility of park roads kept a constant stream of people (sightseers, swimmers, picnickers, hikers, and fishermen) traveling to the park. Any constraint to free access represented a threat to business. The increasingly vocal environmentalists cited examples of abuses of the park by motorists who crowded the roads. They polluted the air, parked cars in unauthorized areas, and disturbed plant life. This posed a threat to animals such as deer and foxes by changing their natural patterns of behavior, frightening them during late evening drives, and even hitting them with automobiles.

Some more reasonable environmental voices understood that old practices, like allowing automobile access, were not likely to be reversed. These ongoing threats to the park's environment, it was argued, created a special responsibility for park administration to be careful of the environmental implications of new decisions. As the Giza administration began its efforts to increase usage (and hopefully the budget allocation from Harrisburg), seeds of the final conflict were firmly sown.

Superintendent Giza explained to the environmental groups that his usage-driven decisions would ultimately be in the best interests of the park. Increased funding, he argued, could be used to safeguard the park's fragile geology and ecology. With more funding he could hire a full-time naturalist and initiate programs of public environmental awareness. And many of his ideas—for example, 10K races and biking—would be easy on the environment. But as defects in decisions began to emerge, various groups began to lose patience and take public stands against new programs.

While a number of these new plans which were perceived as a threat to the park were not actually the inventions of Giza, he began to take the administrative heat for them. During the final years of his administration the following issues came to the attention of the public:

1. **The Presque Isle Marina** opened in 1962, grew to 473 slips, and added underground fuel tanks as well as sewage treatment facilities.
2. **The Lagoon System** was connected to the marina lake, and a continuous navigable loop was created. This action joined two previously separate wetland and pond areas, and allowed plant life from the two areas to invade each other.
3. **Parking Lot and Pavilion Construction** continued through the 1980's, taking a toll on mature trees.
4. **The All-Purpose Trail** was built in 1984 to allow hikers and bikers access to the south waterfront, but wetlands had been violated and endangered plant species were compromised.
5. **Lyme Disease** was reported in the park and linked to mismanagement (oversupply) of the whitetail deer herd.
6. **Sand Mound Toilets,** constructed along the entire length of the park, had replaced the older pit toilet outhouses. The new design, viable in other (primarily mountainous) regions, proved to be inappropriate for a sand spit peninsula.
7. **Beach Replenishment** shifted from the use of dredged Lake Erie sand to quarry sand in order to save money.
8. **Rock Mound Barrier Reefs** were constructed between 1989 and 1992 to solve the problem of sand replenishment by slowing erosion. It was argued that these structures were not aesthetic and would lead to water pollution in the stagnant areas behind them.
9. **Beach Closings** occurred due to fecal coliform and other contaminants. Closings were beginning to occur at the same general time the sand mound toilets and the barrier reefs were installed.

While most of the environmental issues fell on deaf ears with respect to the business community and the general public, the beach closings were another matter. What would a closed beach, or even the rumor of a closed beach, do to tourism, business, and the public view of the park? This dilemma quickly raised a previously altruistic issue to the level of a real problem.

THE GULL POINT CONTROVERSY

The "mother of all controversies" however, was the Gull Point issue. Gull Point, the 319-acre eastern tip of the peninsula had become a popular summer congregating point for local boaters. The natural curves of the point provide protection from prevailing southwesterly winds. The pristine beach, located miles away from public beaches and roadways, creates a sanctuary for boaters. Generations of persons had grown accustomed to anchoring, picnicking, and swimming at the tip of the point.

Boating season in Erie begins in early May and lasts through October, although there are a few hearty souls who push both extremes of the season. As the summer months progress, an increasing number of boaters is attracted to the Gull Point anchorage. The waters to the east of Gull Point and its sand spits offers protection from all but easterly winds. The many odd-shaped inlets of the developing sand spit tip, as well as the secession sand ponds, serve as an additional attraction, especially to boaters in shallow draft vessels. By early July a typical weekend finds hundreds of sail and power boats anchored at Gull Point. Sooner or later, boaters would find their way onto the fragile tip of the point where they participate in a variety of seemingly innocent activities: picnicking, sunbathing, hiking, exploring, and Frisbee.

Boaters knew that this area of Presque Isle was officially declared a bird sanctuary in 1957, and most Gull Point visitors perceived themselves as being careful about their usage of the area. They would yell at their children for throwing rocks at birds and go out of their way not to put a beach blanket on a nest. They thought they were being good citizens.

In the early days of the bird sanctuary, park police were unlikely to enforce the issue of the bird sanctuary. After all, many boaters reasoned, Gull Point is 319 acres and we are simply using the edge of the beach! What harm could that possibly do?

By the end of the 1980's, however, a storm of protests arose from environmental groups. They pointed to the huge list of endangered bird species which needed to make use of the peninsula. They further noted the critical nature of the water's edge to many of these migratory birds. A number of species reach the safe haven of Gull Point in a weakened condition, desperately needing respite at the water's edge to gather food and regain strength so they can continue their migration. Even episodic (weekend) disturbances by boaters could spell doom for these birds.[7] Other species used Gull Point for the express purpose of raising young, and episodic boat traffic could threaten the breeding process. The environmental groups were demanding that boaters, as well as hikers, stay away from Gull Point.

In and around Erie, the piping plover became the symbolic "poster child" of the Gull Point movement. This diminutive shore bird had become rare on Gull Point, almost in synchrony with the increase in the recreational boating industry. By the early 1990's, environmental groups were pointing to the fact that the endangered creature was no longer able to nest on Gull Point and asked if this might be the first of a long series of birds that would cease to exist as a result of lenience granted to suit the whims of boaters.

GUNFIGHT AT THE OK CORRAL

As Harry stepped through the doorway of the lecture hall, the crowd grew quiet in anticipation. This was clearly a revisitation of Wyatt Earp, badge and all, trying to settle things between the forces of good and the forces of evil. "Folks," he began, "my name is Harry Leslie and the important thing is that we do what is right for future generations and for Presque Isle!" As he presented the main points of the park's new management plan, Harry began to realize that the question period might not go as smoothly as he had hoped. His plan included a variety of objectives: increasing park visitor capacity, limiting the number of approved duck blind locations, and prohibiting access to Gull Point from April 1 to November 30. It also included an additional 200 pages of meticulous detail: history, definitions, lists, and more. This was clearly the finest piece of systematic work ever produced in the name of planning for Presque Isle.

But the members of the audience wanted specific assurances. "Do you mean to tell me that I can't take my family to Gull Point in my boat any more?" "Who appointed you the king of the peninsula?" commented a second. "Are you going to refund the money that I spent for my boat?" asked a third. "What do you mean increased visitor capacity?" questioned a birdwatcher. "There are already too many people in the park!" "How come boaters can't disturb seagulls, but hunters can shoot ducks?" asked an irate sailor. "Typical liberal commie type," retorted a row of duck hunters who owned grandfathered rights to duck blinds within the Gull Point bird sanctuary.

As the session with the overflow crowd grew more agitated and ugly, Harry's stomach began to hurt. Many of these folks were the wealthy, the influential and elite forces of the community, and they acted like the fans at a professional wrestling match. As he struggled to answer questions, maintain order, and explain his environmental management plan, his thoughts turned to his children, sleeping in their lighthouse home. Would he really be able to maintain the lifestyle that had become such an important part of their family life? Or was his dream rapidly disintegrating into a nightmare?

END NOTES

1. Presque Isle State Park operates under the Pennsylvania Bureau of State Parks. This division of the Department of Environmental Resources sets forth strategic management direction for all the Commonwealth's park areas. Management at Presque Isle incorporated this framework into its 1993 Strategic Management Publication. Agency goals must be developed within the context of these planning documents.

2. The mission of Presque Isle State Park is to conserve the park's natural and historic resources for current and future generations and to provide educational and recreational activities. Presque Isle's goals are set up to achieve the overall mission of the park. These goals are to manage park attendance while maintaining the fragile ecosystem and preserving the natural historical resources.

   The *Resource Management Plan* compiled and published by park management details key activities and strategically critical tasks that provide a foundation for the organization's structure and direction.

3. The Pennsylvania Legislature formed the Pennsylvania State Park and Harbor Commission in 1921 under Act 436. This Commission was given authority to acquire, develop, and operate Presque Isle State Park, which was formerly known as the Pennsylvania State Park at Erie.

4. Tourism now brings in approximately $80 million per year to the Erie area; this is mainly a function of visitor attraction to Presque Isle State Park. This industry has historically been viewed as a renewable, resource-based industry, and under this perspective tourists are perceived to *view* area attractions, but do not *consume* them. However, an increased recognition of the fragility surrounding the environment and its natural resources has now begun to change this perception, and for Presque Isle, tourism is perceived as competing for scarce resources and capital. The perception is based on an increasing awareness that a different type of tourist-consumption is occurring in the form of deleterious effects on the ecosystem.

5. The demise of Erie's industrial base during the late 1970's and early 1980's had a great impact on Presque Isle and the tourist economy. Massive layoffs and plant closings had resulted from revolutionary changes in the steelmaking and shipping industries which were the area's primary economic base. In a short time, tourism was a strong component of the local economy.

   An analysis of Presque Isle State Park attendance records suggests that during periods of economic downturn, people are more inclined to take comparatively inexpensive trips to a local state park. Travel is dependent on the course of the U.S. economy and visits to the park may be viewed as an alternative to longer, more expensive trips. Since competition for discretionary spending becomes intense in a sluggish economy, park visitation and tourism take on additional importance for the financial health of the local community.

6. Presque Isle's status as a state-controlled entity makes if vulnerable to threats not shared with the private sector. Its operating budget is solely funded by the Department of Environmental Resources, which must allocate a shrinking budget to over 100 parks. Presque Isle is not permitted to spend all the revenue it generates, as those funds are turned over to the state for allocation among all the state parks.

7. In 1937 the Park and Harbor Commission was supported by special legislation which gave the Commission jurisdiction over the waters up to 500 feet off the shores of Presque Isle, including the waters of Misery Bay. This was done to prevent encroachment by moored houseboats; today this code enables the park to prohibit water-skiing within the 500 feet of coastal waters surrounding the Park.

The Case of the Mystery Trawler

David R Frew, Gannon University

C. Louise Sellaro, Youngstown State University

The normally jovial mood at the winter meeting of Erie Pennsylvania's SONS (Support Our Native Species) OF LAKE ERIE fishing organization was tense and reserved. Most of the regular attendees were aware of the growing tension that was about to come to a head that evening. There had been persistent rumors that one of their most vocal members, Ed Concilla, was scheduled to make another of his "blockbuster" announcements. SONS is a local sports fishing group which has been focusing on two concerns with respect to the management of Lake Erie's fish population (biomass). (1) The introduction of non-native species, dating to the earliest days of fish management, has thrown the delicate balance of the lake's ecosystem into a series of crises over the years threatening the highly desirable native species, and the long term viability of fishing. (2) Commercial fishing, trawling in particular, can not be sustained in Lake Erie because the inherent profit motive and the inability of government enforcement (four U.S. states and one Canadian province are involved) to control such a vast water territory continues to lead to over fishing.

As an organization, SONS has devoted its energies to the development of legislation which has made commercial fishing on the American side of Lake Erie next to impossible. Their political activities have accelerated and become more effective over the years. And they have been a "thorn" in the side of Erie's dwindling commercial fishing fleet. Most members, however, are more interested in fish than politics. They prefer dedicating energies to the improvement of the lake's stocks of the two most prized Lake Erie fish, the Yellow Perch and the Walleye (also called Yellow Pike or Yellow Pickerel). SONS has used private funds to develop a hatchery system for these species as well as a program for creating better fish habitat in the waters surrounding Erie.

Ed Concilla, long time member of SONS, had just completed his leadership of a political battle with the local commercial fishing fleet. Commercial fishing had seen its best days on Lake Erie's south (American) shore with the number of licenses plummeting after the demise of the Blue Pike in the late 1950s. As of 1995, there were only nine licensed commercial fishermen in Erie's harbor. Three of these were under suspension for license offenses such as improper net sizes or understated catch totals. These kinds of infractions had helped to fuel Concilla's argument that commercial forces were apt to overfish in an effort to maximize profits. Ed was quite proud that the interdiction which had helped to shut down these fishermen was motivated by pressure from SONS.

He was even more excited by prospects of the end of gill netting (the primary fishing technology used by American fishermen). As of 1996, thanks to legislation motivated by his long fight, fishermen would be allowed only the use of trap nets. Trap netting is a method which allows commercial fishermen to target desired species and sizes thus avoiding what SONS claims to be a tremendous resource waste, the killing of incidental species. In gill netting, commercial fishermen inadvertantly capture fish which are too small, too large and of the wrong species. These extra fish usually die from being trapped in the nets. In trap netting (the approved new technology), unwanted or inappropriate sized fish are returned unharmed.

Commercial fishermen argued vehemently that they could not make a living trap netting. They claimed that equipment transition costs would force them out of business. They also suggested that profits from commercial fishing were marginal, even in light of an existing well-understood technology and fully amortized nets. SONS rationalized their actions, which seemed about to throw these fishermen out of work, suggesting that the ultimate demise of commercial fishing was simply a matter of time! In a complex political settlement, the Pennsylvania Fish Commission passed legislation requiring sport fisherman to purchase a special "Lake Erie Stamp" to be affixed to the PA fishing license of anyone wishing to fish in Lake Erie. Revenue from this extra fee would be given to commercial fishermen to either retrofit their tugs or to help ease them out of business.

There was plenty of grumbling around the commercial fishing community in Erie's downtown harbor. Word on the docks was that the sports fishermen had won again due to their superior political influence. SONS had all but achieved its goal of ending commercial fishing in Erie. Commercial fishermen argued that there was no possibility of retrofitting with trap nets given the small stipend which was to be offered. Even if it were feasible, they did not know enough about trap netting to take such a risk. In their view, this deal was a one time buy out opportunity. Almost to a man, the fishermen said that they would take the money and run.

"It seems a shame" said one local fisherman. "My grandfather and father fished for a living in Erie since 1933. This is what I have wanted to do since I was a boy helping my Dad! Now what will I hand down to my son?" Another fisherman added his concern. "Where will local restaurants and markets get fresh fish to sell to the public? What will happen to the tradition of a Friday night perch dinner? And who will Ed Concilla and his SONS group go after next?" "Mark my words", he continues, "as soon as the Erie fishermen are gone he'll be after the Canadians from Port Dover!"

THE HISTORY OF CENTRAL LAKE ERIE'S FISHING INDUSTRY

During the 1800s Lake Erie was a virtual highway from Europe and the East Coast to the expanding frontier. Before railroads emerged, the only way for settlers or supplies to move to the frontier was via Lake Erie. Europeans and their goods arrived on the eastern seaboard in Montreal or New York, traveled to Buffalo on either the St. Lawrence River or the Erie Barge Canal (New York City to Buffalo), then traversed the Lake by schooner or steamboat. Erie was a particularly important port due to its downtown entrance to the Erie Extension Canal linking Lake Erie with Pittsburgh, the Ohio/Mississippi River system, and points south to New Orleans.

As the port town of Erie was settled, its inhabitants noticed the tremendous proliferation of fresh fish in the lake. In the earliest days it was possible to go to the lake shore and gather fish with a basket. The primary reason for the abundance of fish was the natural harbor and structure created by the peninsula which protected the city. On the Canadian side of the lake (due north) there was (and continues to be) a mirror image peninsula called Long Point. Long Point creates a similar productive environment for fish. In fact Long Point, which is roughly three times larger than Erie's peninsula (now designated as Presque Isle State Park), provides an even better fish habitat because of its larger size. Although Lake Erie is roughly 50 miles wide, the tips of the two peninsulas are only 27 miles from each other with the international boundary running between them. Taken together the underwater structure from these two great peninsulas made Central Lake Erie the fresh water fishing capital of the world.

In the spirit of the industrial revolution, commercial fishing industries emerged on both sides of the lake. It was created by entrepreneurs who used a variety of methods to capture and sell the plentiful fish from shore. In the earliest days the common technology was pound netting, a system which employed long runs of nets sent perpindicular from shore and attached to poles. Fish, migrating along the beaches, would be herded into the ends of these net systems and unable to escape. To harvest the catch, the shore-bound pound netters used a variety of techniques to remove fish. All of the fish which were caught via this method were lost to the lake and it's fish biomass. Attractive species were marketed to locals while undesirable fish were ground up for fertilizer.

Ultimately, pound netters found that the seasonality of near shore fish runs, in combination with overfishing, limited their catch. This, in turn, led to a shift in technology in which boats were used to get out into deeper waters and follow the fish to their changing locations. The most important innovation in offshore commercial fishing was the gill net which was introduced in 1852 (in Erie) by Captain John Nash. A gill net resembles a huge tennis net. It is anchored to the lake bottom and has small weights along its lower extremity. It is suspended under the water's surface by floats along its the top edge. From the fishes' perspective a gill net looks like a huge tennis net stretched across its path. The net's internal openings (squares) are of a size which allows the fish to swim into, but not pass through, the individual holes. As the fish struggles to back up and free itself, it is caught by the gills and unable to move. Theoretically, the net's opening size allows fishermen to target preferred species and sizes. Smaller fish pass through the openings and larger fish bounce off and then swim around the net. In reality, net hole sizes are difficult to control and many unwanted fish are lost to drowning as they become enmeshed in the netting and struggle to free themselves.

The next major innovation in commercial fishing was the development of processing plants. Rather than each commercial fisherman struggling to market his own catch, specialty businesses called processing plants began to appear. The fishermen would bring their day's catch to the processor to do the cleaning, storage and marketing. This encouraged fishermen to focus their attention on finding and catching fish. By the early 1900s there were active processors on both sides of the lake. Still uncontrolled, in the sense of fishing regulations (catch limits), the fishermen focused their attention upon catching fish and delivering to the processors.

The first boat fishermen used sail and row boats. To increase range and efficiency, however, they soon shifted to engine driven boats. The early vessels were modeled after the tug boats which were in common use in Lake Erie towing sailing ships up the Detroit River or towing large floating masses of lumber. As such they were called "fish tugs", a name which has persisted through the years. The first tugs were powered by coal. By the 1950s most had been repowered with diesel engines. The typical fish tug ranges in size from 40 to 60 feet (overall).

The development of fish processing plants and the increasing fishing capabilities of the tugs soon encouraged the growth of the fresh fish market on both sides of the lake. On the Canadian side, the construction of railroad spur lines linked Port Dover with the large cities of Ontario and encouraged the shipment of fresh fish to Toronto and Windsor. In Erie, processors had instant access to the bigger city markets such as New York and Chicago, since railroad lines were built along the south shore by the 1870s.

From the mid 1800s until late 1920s there was no sign that the productivity of the lake could be challenged. There seemed to be an infinite supply of fish. Lake Erie fish were mild and sweet tasting. They grew rapidly in popularity as transportation to larger markets became increasingly possible. Throughout the early 1900s there was a steady increase in the number of fishermen and a corresponding improvement in the efficiency with which the fish tugs could find and capture their prey.

THE FIRST SIGNS OF TROUBLE

By the middle 1920s there were tell-tale signs that the lake's capacity to supply fish was being challenged. The two favored species of the early days were the Herring (Ciscoe) and the Whitefish. Herring was a firm, sweet fish which could be transported long distances without spoiling. Whitefish, while more subject to transportation spoilage, had grown to be a regional delicacy. A single smoked or baked whitefish would provide Sunday dinner for a large family.

In 1925, Herring suddenly vanished from Lake Erie causing a shock wave in the commercial fishing community. Fortunately for many fishermen, the demise of the Herring coincided with the beginning of prohibition. From an international perspective, this period of history presented fishermen on both sides of Lake Erie with an incredible business opportunity. In Canada, it was legal to manufacture and sell alcohol, but not to drink it. On the US shore, it was legal to drink personally owned liquor but not to manufacture, buy or sell it. For much of the early period of prohibition, commercial fishermen who had traveled freely across the relatively narrow lake selling their catch to the processing plants (U.S. or Canadian), were easily able to switch their cargo to booze. On the Canadian shore a cargo of liquor headed for Erie, PA, was euphemistically called "Midnight Herring".

The prohibition experience highlights the interrelatedness of the American and Canadian fishing industries. For the fishermen in tugs, who often encountered each other in mid-lake, contacts and technological cross fertilization had occurred on a regular basis since the mid 1800s. Fishermen copied each other's innovations and techniques, sold to processing plants on either shore, purchased fish tugs and equipment from each other and generally became an integrated community. It would not be until the fishing shortages of the 1950s began to plague the central lake that they would grow protective of their international territories. During prohibition these contacts increased, as Canadians passed their illicit cargo to Americans in mid-lake.

Shortly after prohibition, there was a mysterious return of the prized Herring. Commercial fishermen began to bring in big catches again in the late 1930s. But just when things were looking good, the Herring disappeared for a second and final time (as a commercial species). Soon after World War Two, the commercial community began to actively fish for Blue Pike (also called Blues or Blue Pickerel). This species was much like the Herring in taste and texture, only larger and easier to clean. By the early 1950s business was booming once more. The market had accepted the substitution of Blues for Herring, Whitefish were still plentiful, and the number of fishermen was growing. Veterans on both sides of the lake used G.I. benefits to finance their way into the fishing business.

In the late 1950s, however, the Blue Pike (now officially listed as extinct) disappeared more suddenly than the Herring. The loss of this species brought public attention to Lake Erie and its management. Some pointed to the increasing pollution of the lake as a cause for the demise of the Blues. This view called into question the health risks of consumption of Lake Erie fish, regardless of availability. Others began to question the management of fisheries and ask if commercial fishing could have, in fact, caused the demise of the fish population.

Conflicts began to rage on both sides of the lake. The sports angling communities began to demand governmental control of what was perceived to be commercial overfishing. Working class people were finding it increasingly difficult to catch dinner at the local pier. They blamed the commercial fishermen, whom they had seen unloading tons of fish from their tugs. And as government control increased there was a new concern for the international boundary and the age old incursions by commercial fishermen seeking to maximize their catch by chasing fish into the waters of the "wrong" country. There were incidents throughout the 1960s of U.S. or Canadian Coast Guard authorities impounding and fining tugs for fishing out of their own waters.

PUBLIC POLICY AND NEW TECHNOLOGY

As their businesses collapsed around them, fishermen on both shores asked their respective governments for assistance. In the United States, the Republican administration let the commercial fishermen know that they were "on their own". If they couldn't make a living fishing, they were advised to look for other work. Given the sheer number of (voting) sports fishermen, as compared to commercial tug owners, this was an easy political decision. The more social-istic Canadian government, however, responded quite differently. To save jobs in fishing, the federal government provided grant money for commercial fish-ermen to learn a new fishing technology called trawling. In addition, govern-ment funds were provided for acquiring equipment needed to convert fish tugs from gill netters to trawlers.

Atlantic seacoast fishermen were brought to the Canadian shores of Lake Erie in the late 1950s and early 1960s to retrain Port Dover's commercial fisher-men. By the early 1960s, most of the north coast fleet was equipped for both gill netting (as in the past) and trawling. In trawling, a huge parachute-shaped net is dragged along the bottom of the lake in deep water. The net bottom slides along the floor of the lake guided by two sleds (or doors) which are heavy slid-ing weights designed to hold the net down. The top of the trawl net (like a gill net) is suspended in the water by floats.

The target species of the trawl is the Smelt, a small but sweet tasting fish which seemed to enter the lake from northern lakes at about the time that the Blue Pike disappeared. The trawling technology, however, captures any fish unfortunate enough to find itself in the path of the trawl net. To make matters worse, as nets are raised from the typical trawling depths of 100 feet or more, fish captured within the net die as their swim bladders burst from the pressure differential.

The U.S. commercial fishing community immediately cried foul, complain-ing that Canadian trawlers would soon fish the lake dry. Sports anglers were similarly suspicious of this new technology. Canadian officials, however, argued that trawlers would only target Smelt (a generally undesired species) allowing an insignificant incidental species catch overage of less than 10 per-cent. This would result in fishermen being extremely careful to trawl only in places where they were assured that Smelt and no other species were running. Another aspect of the pro-trawling argument was that the licensing fees paid by the fishermen would be used to set quotas, enforce regulations, and conduct lake management studies. By the mid 1960s, annual commercial quotas for each species had been set on both sides of the lake. As trawling evolved on the north shore the fishermen were pleased to learn that they could export most of their catch to the Japanese market which paid top dollar for this tasty, fresh water delicacy. It seemed that Smelt trawling was an economic gift to the Cana-dians, shoring up their numbers as the fishing community dwindled on the U.S. shore.

By the 1960s, the fishing industry on both sides of the lake had reoriented the consuming public. Slowly but surely, both Erie and Port Dover consumers developed a taste for Yellow Perch and Walleye. And while the Whitefish declined to almost nothing, the Blue Pike remained extinct, and the Herring became a rare and minor catch, the tradition of the Perch dinner (especially on Friday evenings) became an institution on both lake shores. Perch had at one time been thought of as a nuisance fish. In the 1920s there had been several serious proposals to try to eliminate the fish from the lake. But it had always been a favorite catch for sports fishermen. During the 1940s and 1950s, when commercial fishermen were going through transitions of species and technol-ogy the local piers and off shore shallows were increasingly populated by enthusiastic anglers. These citizens with fishing poles were searching for both fun and a free meal. This sector of the population had always realized the value of Perch as a dinner time staple.

In Erie, a number of restaurants and several fish markets developed reputations by using fresh Perch as a business staple. Erieites grew to regard a Perch dinner as an inexpensive but delicious tradition. In Port Dover, the connection was even stronger Entire businesses such as the lakeside Erie Beach Hotel (fine dining) and Knechtels (casual) built reputations in an increasing tourist economy on the basis of the Perch dinner. Unlike Erie, with its 225,000 resident population base and diversified economy, Port Dover was fundamentally a fishing and tourist town. Its population base of only 2000 permanent residents was dependent upon the interacting tourist and fishing businesses.

Tourism had originally developed in Port Dover as a result of the railroad spur lines built to haul fish north from the processing factories to Ontario's big city markets. Tourists of the 1800s began riding these railways to Port Dover's summer time beaches and restaurants. As the years wore on, the town became a summertime tourist Mecca. Much of its charm grew out of the fishing industry as well as the traditional Perch dinner.

Commercial fishing thrived on the North Shore through the 1970s and 1980s. Most licensed fishermen utilized two technologies. They obtained trawling licenses for Smelt and gill netting licenses for Perch and Walleye. The Smelt were primarily exported to Japan through Port Dover's processing plants. Perch and Walleye were sold to both the regional and international restaurant/retail markets. On the U.S., side the commercial fishing business was in a virtual state of collapse. By the 1980s there were only a few licensed tugs in the town harbor, and the processing plants had disappeared. Erie's commercial business had been replaced by a new breed of sports fisherman. Instead of fishing for Perch from the local piers and break walls, the modern fishermen used their affluence to purchase large fishing boats which could be used for deep water trolling and down rigging. This industry (including charter boats) emerged both as a result of the introduction of Salmon and renewed efforts toward a Lake Trout nourishment program. These kinds of programs were developed by various state fish commissions along the U.S. shore. By the mid 1980s Michigan, Ohio, and Pennsylvania were all stocking Lake Erie with these large, exciting to catch, sports fish. In response to deep water fishing possibilities, a huge new sports fishing industry emerged which appealed to an entirely different type of person from the old fashioned bucket (Perch) fisherman.

THE MISSING PERCH

In the early 1990s Perch catches began to dwindle. The demise of this popular species was noted by both the commercial and sports fishing communities. And as the Perch disappeared, fingers of blame began to point in all directions. Some believed the introduction of Zebra Mussels to Lake Erie as the primary cause. This little pest was introduced to the great lakes in the mid 1980s when it was released with ballast water by an ocean going freighter. In a few short years the Zebra Mussel, a voracious biological filtering device with no natural predators, had become a major blight. Beaches were littered with millions of the small snail-like creatures. Under water, the Zebras stuck to everything that didn't move. Each tiny individual mussel has the capacity to filter two liters of water per day clarifying a murky lake into crystal clear water.

At first glance, it seemed that the little creatures were doing the lake a great service. Subsequent analysis by biologists, however, suggested that the mussels were destroying the lake's natural ecosystems and would ultimately threaten the viability of the entire food chain. Biological speculation on the developing Perch problem was that Zebra Mussels had ruined the conditions needed for the fish species to thrive and were at fault for dwindling stocks.

The sports fishing community had an entirely different view. They blamed commercial fishermen, and in particular, Canadian trawlers. After so much publicity about the trawling techniques utilized by the Japanese in the Pacific, who dragged huge parachute shaped nets (square miles in area), U.S. sports fishermen were convinced that trawling had eliminated most of theYellow Perch from the lake. Having all but put an end to commercial fishing on the U.S. side, anglers began to set their sights on Canadian trawling.

The Canadian commercial industry was quick to defend itself against these charges. They made the point that high license fees and catch taxes supported a monitoring infrastructure which engaged in lake study and management, and provided strict control over fishing. In Port Dover, for example, there were specific license restrictions placed upon each fisherman. Licensees are only allowed to fish in specified zones, during certain times of the day, and with carefully inspected equipment. As each tug returns from a day's fishing, the boat and its catch is inspected and the contents weighed so that each fisherman stays within his species quota. Species quotas are set each year based upon the prior year's catch totals, size averages and biological studies of the lake. The fishing business is controlled in the same way as other Canadian agricultural commodities, through a system of marketing boards and supply management. Each year, biologists from Ontario meet with Ohio, Pennsylvania, New York and Michigan representitives to study the lake and establish the next year's fisheries limits for each political area.

But the commercial fishermen from Canada made an even more damning criticism of sports anglers and their assertions. Biological studies of Lake Erie, which were sponsored by funds from the commercial industry, suggested strongly that it was sports fishing manipulations over the years which had most damaged the lake and its fish biomass. American attempts to stock non-native as well as native sports fish (usually species near the top of the food chain) had led to the very real possibility that the entire lake could (as biologists put it) "crash". Scientists were quick to note that the basic problem with the U.S. approach has always been top-down-species-management (attention to the species at the top end of the food chain with little regard for the food chain, itself). In the U.S., for example, Salmon were introduced in Michigan, Ohio, and Pennsylvania as a stimulus to the sport fishing industry. But no attempt was made to evaluate the lower end of the food chain; to ask what the Salmon would eat. Commercial fishermen have consistantly noted that a favorite food of the salmon is the Yellow Perch.

The extinction of Lake Erie's Blue Pike may have been be the single most disturbing example of dysfunctional top-down-species-management. During the 1950s the state of Michigan was attempting to develop a stocking program for Lake Trout, but soon found that the fish they placed in Lake Michigan did not reproduce. They reasoned that this was due to a lack of forage fish and subsequently experimented with the introduction of Smelt from inland northern lakes to Lake Michigan. As it turned out, Smelt did extremely well in the great lakes system traveling from Lake Michigan to Lake Huron and down the Detroit River to Lake Erie.

In hindsight, the best scientific explanation for the demise of the Blue Pike is as follows: After Smelt arrived in Lake Erie, the Blue Pike began to increase significantly in size (historical catch records are available). Biologists have repeatedly demonstrated that species procreation is possible only within a narrow range of normal (statistically average) weight and that the Blues fell prey to this problem in the late 1950s. The overfed Blue Pike (feeding voraciously on the new Smelt) simply lost interest in procreation as a result of this sudden abundance of food.

Canadian commercial fisherman, accused of overfishing quickly counter with this and other examples of mismanagement by U.S. sports angling interests; often by such well meaning government agencies as the Pennsylvania Fish Commission. These mismanagement stories begin with the Smelt, and continue through other non-native species like the Salmon. Even the stocking programs of native species, which often result in fry which fail to thrive in the natural lake environment, are criticized by commercial interests. They charge that this genetic manipulation destroys the species' natural ability to procreate.

MEANWHILE BACK AT THE MYSTERY TRAWLER MEETING

Ed Concilla stepped to the podium and adjusted the microphone. As he fidgeted, the crowd sensed that something important was about to happen. As harbingers of this intuition, the normally absent news media (Just what is newsworthy about fishing?) was present in full force, including newspaper and television reporters with film crews. The media had obviously heard the same rumors which were circulating among SONS members; that Ed was about to drop a bombshell.

"Gentlemen," began Ed, "I want to begin by saying that I have always had a good relationship with the Commercial Fishing Industry in Port Dover. But what I am about to tell you will probably make that group quite mad at me. Just as we are beginning to win our long term war against U.S. commercial overfishing, we are experiencing a new kind of international piracy. There are one or more trawlers from Port Dover making night time fishing raids of the American Perch grounds."

After a dramatic pause, Concilla continued. "I have seen these trawlers personally, and so have at least four or five other Erie fishermen. The mystery trawler(s) is gray and has no name, markings or numbers. It is working the U.S. shore in the middle of the night and trawling without lights. The trawler appears to have radar. When the crew spots an American ship approaching, they instantly lift their nets and run for the international border at speeds in excess of 40 knots."

During the question period, Concilla explained that he had been unable to get a picture of the Mystery Trawler because it was too fast for his 28 foot (charter fishing) power boat. He did note, however, that the Mystery Trawler always "escapes" into Canadian waters. Ed introduced a number of other fishermen who concurred with his observations noting that they had also seen the mysterious unmarked trawler. Ed concluded by noting that the bulk of Port

Dover's fishermen were honest, hard working and followed the rules. "But", he added, "they are under increasing pressure to catch Perch and this economic problem has apparently caused one or more of them to cheat by making illegal runs into U.S. waters".

As the question period continued the television people rushed away, anxious to make deadlines for the 11:00 news. Ed Concilla had no way of knowing that he was about to incite an international incident!

BED TIME IN PORT DOVER

Les Murphy literally crawled into his bed in Port Dover. His back hurt, and as usual, his wife admonished him for working too hard. Since Les had taken over The Port Dover Fish Company the year before, he had been working like a Trojan to make his dream work. Les always looked forward to a few moments of mindless television watching each evening before falling asleep. Glancing at his watch, he grabbed his remote and dialed up an Erie station for the nightly news. Like generations of Port Dover residents who grew up before cable Television, Les had gotten used to watching Erie TV stations. Unlike the London or Toronto channels, Erie's stations were clear and static free, coming as they did, straight across the lake.

As his old television set warmed up, Les thought one more time about his new job and the challenge that it presented. A third generation member of a traditional Port Dover commercial fishing family, Les had been distraught to see the developments of the late 1980s. In quick succession between the late 80s and the early 90s a number of negative events occurred. First, the Perch catch began to diminish. Soon after, there were rumblings of change in the local processing plant businesses. Olmstead Fisheries sold out to Heinz Foods (an American firm) and announced that henceforth, Olmstead would not process fish. Instead, they would be a transfer station, accepting fish from local fishermen, packing them in ice and sending them by truck to their headquarters near Windsor. The final blow to the local industry was an announcement the next year that Misner's, the town's largest and oldest plant, was going out of business.

As a depression set into the town over these events, the local fishermen began to question the viability of their industry. Was this the end of freshwater fishing as a commercial venture? Port Dover locals had watched the demise of the fishing business in Erie and were not blind to the possibility that such a fate could befall them, as well. But Erie had fall-back industries. The death of the fishing business had not crippled that city as it threatened to do in Port Dover. Even the tourist business was clearly at risk. Would visitors come to Port Dover in the absence of the romance of the fishing business?

What would Port Dover be like without the fishermen, the fish tugs, the perennial nets, and other paraphernalia lining the docks? And what about the annual fisherman's festival, or the quaint art work depicting fishing? And most important, could Port Dover and its restaurants survive without its fresh fish dinners; the tasty Perch, Walleye, and Whitefish which had drawn generations of visitors to the town's harbor center?

Feeling the spirit of his fishermen grandfather and father, Les Murphy took it upon himself to save the town. Using his own resources, he resurrected an old processing plant on the waterfront, christening it, Port Dover Fish Company Ltd. His company would buy from the fishermen, and process fish. Using his contacts with the Misner family (who were going out of business) he was able to buy all the equipment needed (scalers, refrigerators, sizers, cleaning benches, etc.) at a very reasonable price. Soon there was hope among the members of the fishing and tourist business community. Les would provide a secure source of fish for the local restaurants and hotel. In addition, individual fishermen would have a choice about where to sell their catch. Port Dover Fish Company would provide an alternative, in effect forcing Olmstead to remain competitive with respect to the price paid to fishermen.

Naturally there were risks associated with this altruism. Many called Murphy crazy for his business idea. But Les remained optimistic about the lake and its supply of fresh fish. As his business limped through its first years he quietly noted biologist's reports that while the Perch catch was dwindling, Whitefish and Walleye stocks were increasing dramatically. In fact the Whitefish, which had been nearly forgotten as a commercial catch, seemed to be making a dramatic comeback. Some credited the Zebra Mussel and water clarification for the return of the Whitefish.

THE BOMB HITS

As Les Murphy's old RCA crackled to life, an Erie newsman was just switching to taped coverage of the Mystery Trawler. "Yes folks", a voice contended, "a Mystery Trawler from Port Dover has been plying the waters near Erie stealing American Perch. No wonder you fishermen out there have not been catching much lately", continued the reporter! "Not only do these Canadians invade U.S. waters, but according to local fishermen who have seen them, they use Japanese trawling technologies which trap all the living fish and simultaneously destroy the lake's bottom structure, making it impossible for any fish to breed in the future".

This was not the kind of mindless television tonic that Les had been looking for to help him fall asleep! Instead, it rocketed him off his bed directly toward the phone. By the time that he got there, however, it was already ringing. At the other end was fisheries biologist, and Port Dover resident, Rob Varey. Rob wanted to know if Les had seen the 11:00 news from Erie.

The next morning Les Murphy held a war council with Rob Varey and Frank Prothero (a regional historian with an interest in fishing) at his fish company office. Together they placed a conference call to a university professor friend in Erie to ask for assistance. As they spoke, they developed a strategy for damage control. They asked their U.S. contact to take the real facts surrounding the situation to both the local media and the SONS organization to ask for some balanced coverage. To assist with this mission the following Fax message summary was sent to Erie:

To the citizens of Erie, PA:

1. The Commercial Fishermen of Port Dover are upset and angry over recent media accusations leveled by SONS of Erie. We believe that this media coverage could hurt our industry, the town of Port Dover and, ultimately, the overall health of Lake Erie

2. Port Dover Fish Company Ltd. is making a gallant effort to sustain itself and the commercial business in Port Dover. Your publicity can not help us, either in the market place or politically.

3. It has been license fees from Canadian commercial fishing over the last two decades which have sponsored the only scientific and systematic studies of Lake Erie and its fish biomass. Without commercial fishing and its management programs the lake would be left to the whims of uncontrolled groups such as SONS whose stocking programs proceed without scientific verification and may do more harm than good.

4. Over the years, there has been more harm done to the fish in Lake Erie by management attempts of sports fishing interests than by commercial fishing. Witness the introduction of Smelt, the demise of the Blue Pike, and the introduction of Salmon.

5. Port Dover's fishermen work under the close scrutiny of their own controlling group. Our catch limits are regulated on an annual basis, after careful study of the lake and its fish populations, and an annual discussion with authorities from your American states.

6. Individual fishermen are inspected on an almost 100% basis so that there can be no cheating on catch limits as there has been in recent years on the U.S. side of the lake.

7. Fishing at night is strictly prohibited. It is impossible to imagine that a tug could sneak out of Port Dover's harbor on a regular basis and go undetected.

8. The commercial fishing license fees are so high that fishermen would not risk being caught breaking international laws in such a flagrant manner.

9. Fish tugs trawl at speeds of 4 to 5 knots and have maximum speeds of only 10 or 12 knots. There is no tug which could evade a 30 foot charter fishing boat by running toward Canadian waters at 40 knots as stated in your media coverage.

10. If you are seeing a commercial sized vessel move at those speeds it must be a gas well maintenance boat rather than a fish tug.

11. If the vessel that you see is actually trawling you should consider the possibility that it is a rogue American fisherman rather than a Canadian.

12. The fishing community in Port Dover has had a long and friendly relationship with Erie and its people. Over the years, we have shown up in force with our tugs for your harbor festivals. We have done business in your city and rescued American boaters in distress. We are more than insulted by this response to our friendship!

Armed with the Port Dover Fax and personally convinced that allegations of a Mystery Trawler were either preposterous or in error, the American friend went both to SONS and the media to see if he could initiate a discussion, retraction or apology for the offensive media coverage. He was told by the media that a story in which the Mystery Trawler was explained away was simply not newsworthy. SONS members noted that Ed Concilla sometimes exaggerates his claims but that he probably saw "something".

Upon hearing the disappointing news that there would be no retraction, or romantic story sanctifying the Port Dover fishing community, Les Murphy was more than disappointed. And as he crawled into his bed the next night, he tuned in a television station from Toronto. To his chagrin, the Toronto reporter led off the evening news with two stories about fishing, the Lake Erie story followed by a vigorous discussion of the Canadian seizure of a Spanish trawler which had been fishing the Atlantic, off the Grand Banks. The reporter noted that the entire fishing industry was in serious trouble in Canada and hypothesized that most fishermen would soon join Newfoundlanders in being out of business.

Growing more depressed, Les began to mentally obsess about his business, worrying about next year's bottom line, how the Ontario Ministry of Fishing would react in their development of next years fish quota, and why he had ever begun this stupid business venture in the first place. Would he be able to pay off his bank loans? Would he fail in his attempt to save commercial fishing and the town? And why had his altruism forced him out of a comfortable retirement to take such a silly business risk?

Suddenly he was on his grandfather's fish tug. He was steaming through Lake Erie's waters off Port Dover with his friends Rob Varey and Frank Prothero. Rob handed Les a pair of binoculars and pointed to the horizon. There, not a mile away and shrouded by fog, was an aluminum canoe with letters on its side. It's occupant was waving a paddle in an obvious distress signal. Closing on the canoe, Les was able to make out the letters on the side . . . . SONS of LAKE ERIE. And sitting in the canoe was, none other than Ed Concilla. Pulling the throttle of the big fish tug back to all-ahead-full Les took careful aim at the center of the canoe. But from the front of the tug an excited voice screamed . . . No! No!. You can't do it! Les was about to ask Rob Varey, "Why the hell not?", when the fog cleared and the person yelling turned out to be Geraldo Rivera on the television set admonishing a guest to change his ways.

"For God's sake Les", implored his wife, "why are you watching stupid American talk shows in the middle of the night and getting all excited? You have been yelling and thrashing around in bed for the last 30 minutes. Please turn the set off and try to get some sleep!"

The University of Texas Health Center at Tyler

Mark Kroll, University of Texas at Tyler

Godwin Osuagwu, Texas College

The health care industry in the United States is in transition, and as a result, so is the University of Texas Health Center at Tyler. Evidence of this transition can be seen in the unwillingness of both public and private payers of health care costs to accept rising prices. This focus on cost has led to rural hospital closings, rapid growth in Health Maintenance Organizations, strategic alliances and realignments of medical institutions, governmental reimbursement funding reductions, and rising levels of indigent care loads. Compounding the complexity of the transition are such forces as rapidly advancing and costly technology and the increasing competition among health care providers. Ironically, in an era of cost-consciousness, the rapidly advancing costs of technology has led to investments in gigantic infrastructures at both local and regional levels.

Against this backdrop, the University of Texas Health Center at Tyler (UTHCT) attempts to fulfill its three-part mission of providing patient care, conducting research, and providing education related to cardiopulmonary diseases and training physicians for a career in family practice. Since the Health Center receives a percentage of its operating resources from the State of Texas, it must provide certain levels of indigent health care to the poor in its region. It must also provide care to indigents with tuberculosis from anywhere in the state. However, the Center has not refused services to any Texas indigent regardless of the nature of their illness. As health insurance premiums rise, more and more people have lost their coverage. As a result, private hospitals frequently refuse treatment and refer patients to state-supported institutions. This trend, in conjunction with the closings of many of the region's rural hospitals, as well as federal reimbursement reductions, compels many individuals to seek care at the Health Center under indigency or charity status. In fact, most indigent patients erroneously believe that the UTHCT is a "free" hospital.

Unfortunately, state funding levels for this type of care have not kept pace with demand, which has seriously undermined the financial base of the institution. However, the Health Center must provide competitive wages in order to attract nursing and select allied health care personnel who are in short supply. While other private health care providers can get by with minimum staffing, UTHCT must strive to meet state standards pertaining to staffing-to-patient ratios. Additionally, the Health Center must operate in the competitive local hospital market for a paying patient base while using costly technology and instrumentation. Most of the major strategic issues confronting the Health Center are ultimately related to the dilemmas faced by the health care industry. Compounding the Health Center's problems however have been reductions in State general revenue appropriations as a percentage of the total operating budget for research, operations and maintenance.

The Health Center is, as are most health care providers, undergoing a transition from providing most of its services on an inpatient basis to providing more outpatient care. And local competition for specific patient groups has increased, as health care organizations form Health Maintenance Organizations (HMO's). A typical example of this is the Health Center's major competitors recently launching a major push into geriatric ambulatory care for senior citizens in order to position themselves for Medicare HMO's.

In addition to the issues just mentioned, there is the unique issue of the hospital's research mandate. The Health Center had been successfully increasing its levels of grant-funded research, but recently its grant-funded research revenues have flattened out.

HISTORY

The Health Center was established in 1947 as a state tuberculosis sanitarium. It operated under the State Board of Control by act of the 50th Texas Legislature. Over the years, the institution changed in a number of ways. Its role and scope was expanded to adapt to new medical technology and to the changing health care needs of the state and region.

The institution was established at the site of a deactivated World War II army infantry training base, Camp Fannin, and is located eight miles northeast of Tyler, Texas. The State acquired 614 acres and the existing facilities of the base hospital from the federal government. Most of the base's 1,000 beds were in rows of wooden barracks, with each barrack accommodating 25 beds in an open ward. The first patients were accepted in 1949.

Supervision of the East Texas Tuberculosis Sanatorium was later transferred to a newly formed Board of Texas State Hospitals and Special Schools. In 1951, the Texas Legislature changed the hospital's name to the East Texas Tuberculosis Hospital. Its role and scope were changed from simple custodial care to treatment using newly developed drugs.

Although there were several legislative bills enacted during the 1940s and 1950s changing the institution's governing authority, it was not until 1969 that its scope was expanded beyond the care and treatment of tuberculosis patients. In that year the legislature authorized the institution to develop pilot programs aimed at treating other respiratory diseases such as asthma, lung cancer, chronic bronchitis, emphysema and occupational diseases related to asbestos. In 1971 the Texas Legislature gave the institution a broader mission of education and research as well as patient care. The name was changed to the East Texas Chest Hospital to be operated under the Texas Board of Health. This program expansion into education and research reflected the increasing stature of the facility and its scientific capabilities.

In 1977, Tyler State Senator, Peyton McKnight, introduced legislation transferring control of the hospital to the Board of Regents of the University of Texas System. This legislation authorized the Regents to use the institution as a teaching hospital and to change its name to the University of Texas Health Center at Tyler. The UT System controls six medical schools and research/teaching hospitals around the state. It also reaffirmed the institution's role and scope as a primary state referral center for patient care, education and research in the diseases of the chest.

The physical face of the institution has also changed dramatically over the years. In 1957, the State completed a 320 bed, six-story brick and masonry structure which allowed for removal of most of the wooden barracks. A few of these structures still remain and have over the years been renovated for use as research laboratories. Other major building programs were initiated in the late 1960s and early 1970s. An outpatient clinic was added to the hospital in 1970. In 1976, the State appropriated $17 million for construction of a completely modern hospital facility. A six-story, 320 bed hospital was built adjacent to the original structure, doubling the size of the complex. At the same time, the lower three floors of the old hospital building were renovated for support services. In 1984, the top three floors of the old hospital were also renovated to house additional offices and allow for expansion of programs in cardiac and pulmonary rehabilitation and cancer treatment.

The Watson W. Wise Medical Research Library was dedicated in 1984 which gave support to an expanded research faculty and the addition of new departments such as biochemistry, microbiology and physiology. In 1987, the Health Center's Biomedical Research Building was completed. Currently, construction is underway on an $11 million expansion of its ambulatory care facilities which will house and expand the outpatient clinic, clinical laboratory, radiology and surgical facilities. This addition will facilitate delivery and handling of ambulatory patient services. The facility will also provide space for the Family Practice Residency Program and other clinics, as well as space for clinical research. Many of these activities are presently carried out in converted hospital inpatient space as the center has reduced its bed count and increased its ambulatory care volume.

In terms of medical staff, the Health Center currently has sixty primary care and specialty physicians. Ninety-five percent of the Center's physicians are board-certified, and many are certified in two or three areas.

In carrying out the mission and purpose of the institution, UTHCT has gone from custodial care only to a three-fold purpose of patient care, education and research. Open heart surgery became available in 1983, and the Health Center's Pediatric Pulmonary Service was also designated as one of the State's regional Cystic Fibrosis Centers. In 1985, the Health Center was designated as a national Cystic Fibrosis Satellite Center. The first post-graduate medical education program in East Texas, residency training in family practice was launched in 1985 in cooperation with two Tyler hospitals. In 1995, the Health Center had 18 residents in the three year program, and was graduating six a year. That same

Exhibit 1   **The University of Texas Health Center at Tyler Operative Procedures**

	Fiscal Year 1993	Fiscal Year 1994	Fiscal Year 1995
Coronary Bypass	77	64	92
Angioplasty	48	60	58
Thoracic	135	133	115
Vascular	126	204	354
Abdominal Procedures	175	283	274
All Other Procedures	1,134	1,009	1,347*
Total Procedures Performed	**1,695**	**1,753**	**2,240**
Inpatient	894	810	909
Outpatient	368	457	589
Total Patients	**1,262**	**1,267**	**1,498**
Amputation		33	
Bone Marrow Biopsy		74	
Breast		112	
Bronchoscopy		218	
Hernia		110	
Mediastinoscopy		13	
Pacemaker/Defibrillator		19	
Rectal		44	
Thyroid/Parathyroid		19	
Tracheostomy		9	
Vital Port		83	
Lesion		105	
Cyst		35	
Temporal Artery		11	
Carpal Tunnel		16	
Gynecological		110	
Orthopedic		18	
Podiatry		29	
Ear, Nose, & Throat		82	
Misc.		239	
Total		**1,347**	

*The following is a list of "all other procedures" performed in the operating room.

year, the Health Center was performing a host of surgical procedures. The number and types of procedures performed in recent years is provided in Exhibit 1. In 1995, the Health Center was given a $1 million grant by the Texas Legislature to establish a Center for Pulmonary Infectious Disease Control.

Exhibit 2   **Extramural and State Research Grant Support**

	FY 1993	FY 1994	FY 1995
Federal	$1,335,711	$1,295,579	$1,245,144
Private	384,774	173,391	496,712
Other	665,786	602,745	374,927
Total	$2,386,271	$2,071,715	$2,116,783
Number of Grants	22	16	21
Extramural Funds/Investigator	$ 82,285	$ 64,741	$ 72,992
State Funding	$3,522,051	$4,151,697	$4,271,067

Grant research funding increased rapidly in the 1980's, but that growth has tapered off in recent years. In 1983, research funding was $78,347 and by 1985, funding reached $808,836. Completion of the biomedical research building in 1987 and recruitment of research scientists resulted in more external funding. In 1988, $2,896,061 in external research grant dollars were received. For the last three years the number and amounts of grants has held steady (see Table 2 for details). This external research funding comes from such external sources such as the National Institutes of Health, the Texas Affiliate of the American Heart Association, the American Lung Association of Texas, the Muscular Dystrophy Foundation, private medical-research foundations, and several industrial and pharmaceutical firms. In 1992, the Health Center was awarded its first two biomedical research patents. The following year it was awarded two more biomedical research patents. In addition to external grant funds, as noted in Exhibit 2, the State has maintained its support for research at about $4 million annually.

THE COMPETITION

Competition for paying customers between the two local general hospitals, Trinity-Mother Frances Health System and East Texas Medical Center, is intense. While UTHCT has historically been a specialized, state-supported center for the treatment of cardiopulmonary diseases, more recently the Center has entered the fray for paying customers. This has been in response to rising costs, lower state appropriations, and indigent care demands. However, its two major competitors are very formidable.

The Trinity-Mother Frances Health System is one of UTHCT's two major competitors in the area. It was founded in 1937 by the Sisters of the Holy Family of Nazareth. What started as a 60 bed facility with a handful of attending physicians has grown to a 350 bed hospital which is the hub of a medical complex with over 350 affiliated physicians, 10 satellite rural health clinics, a huge outpatient clinic on the hospital's campus, a large OB/GYN unit, a home health care center, a 13,000 square foot wellness center, an emergency medical services system which can provide level II trauma care, an acclaimed heart and lung institute, spine and joint institute, cancer care institute, and eye institute.

The most significant recent development for Mother Frances has been its affiliation with Trinity Clinic, the region's largest group practice, to form the Trinity-Mother Frances Health System. The joining together of Mother Frances and Trinity integrated the practices of over 75 specialist physicians into the hospital's network. This has made Mother Frances a very formidable regional competitor, capable of offering a very comprehensive list of medical services.

Trinity-Mother Frances has also aggressively moved to strengthen its position in other ways. It has negotiated health maintenance organization (HMO) and preferred provider organization (PPO) agreements with several of the area's largest employers. Developing HMO and PPO relationships with employers was made much easier with the affiliation of Mother Frances with Trinity Clinic, as the combined organization can provide virtually any inpatient or outpatient service needed. Additionally, Trinity-Mother Frances has negotiated referral relationships with smaller and less comprehensive hospitals in the region which are not part of the East Texas Medical Center organization (discussed below). These referral relationships feed patients into the various specialized care units such as the heart and lung institute which has performed over 30,000 heart procedures in the last 12 years.

The largest health care organization in the East Texas region is East Texas Medical Center (ETMC) which was first opened in 1951 with 110 beds. Today ETMC is the primary referral facility for a network of five rural community hospitals, three affiliated rural hospitals, 14 rural clinics, and 14 home health care locations. ETMC's emergency medical services unit is responsible for providing emergency medical services for Smith County (in which Tyler is located) and 10 surrounding counties. This network has a radius of over 100 miles from Tyler and essentially overlaps the service region of UTHCT. The parent organization of ETMC is East Texas Medical Center Regional Health Care System, a non-profit corporation founded in 1949.

ETMC has undergone a number of expansions since it was first opened, with numerous specialized service units being added. Today, in addition to the primary 410-bed hospital, ETMC also operates a level II trauma center which treats over 36,000 patients a year. It houses a recognized cancer institute and cardiac care center which is equipped with state-of-the-art technology. The Center is also home to the East Texas Neurological Institute and the ETMC Behavioral Health Center which provides comprehensive mental health services. The emergency medical services unit operates the largest non-profit ambulance program in Texas. ETMC is supported by over 300 staff physicians.

FUNDING AND THE QUEST FOR PAYING PATIENTS

It is important to recognize that the Center's operating budget is comprised of general revenue appropriations from the State, research grant funding, and locally generated revenues from services rendered to patients who are able to pay. Over the years, the percentage composition of the operating budget coming from appropriated versus locally generated funds has changed significantly. General revenue appropriations have decreased from 66% of the operating budget for fiscal year 1982 to 36% of the operating budget for fiscal year 1995. Consequently, the Health Center has been forced, like its competitors, to generate local funds through the paying patient base (see Exhibit 3).

Exhibit 3

The University of Texas Health Center at Tyler
Comparative Statement of Revenues and Expenditures
Current Funds For Fiscal Years ending August 31, 1993, 1994, and 1995

	Fiscal Year 1993	Fiscal Year 1994	Fiscal Year 1995
Current Revenues			
State Appropriations	$19,057,480	$27,211,218	$26,163,857
Federal Grants and Contracts	1,543,153	1,379,879	1,238,273
State Grants and Contracts	609,322	672,446	756,335
Private Gifts, Grants, and Contracts	1,287,677	1,433,463	2,282,365
Endowment Income	17,869	19,566	30,029
Sales and Services of Hospitals	35,051,548	27,675,077	28,285,473
Sales and Services of Auxilliary Enterprises	179,180	184,764	188,289
Professional Fees	7,200,056	7,279,864	7,580,420
Other Interest Income	331,054	205,189	237,167
Other Sources	539,412	670,741	705,497
Medicare Cost Recover	2,957,397	3,478,158	5,016,828
Gains/Losses on Investments		(23,914)	(9,723)
Total Current Revenues	**$68,774,148**	**$70,186,451**	**$72,474,810**
Current Expenditures			
Education and General			
Instruction	$ 2,646,937	$ 2,937,540	$ 3,206,049
Research	$ 5,500,613	$ 5,974,905	$ 6,142,470
Hospital	$43,229,374	$46,978,306	$48,992,977
Institutional Support	$ 8,919,614	$10,709,241	$11,104,922
Operation and Maintenance of Plant	$ 3,843,867	$ 4,381,307	$ 3,729,309
Total Educational and General Expenditures	**$64,140,405**	**$70,981,299**	**$73,175,727**
Auxiliary Enterprises	**$ 149,706**	**$ 171,112**	**$ 174,330**
Total Current Expenditures	**$64,290,111**	**$71,152,411**	**$73,350,057**
Excess of Revenue Over Expenditures	**$ 4,484,037**	**($965,960)**	**($875,247)**

Complicating matters is the fact that the Health Center's operating budget must support educational programs as well as some of the research activities. State appropriations for indigent patient care, in actual dollars, have remained relatively constant over the past 10 years. However, indigent care levels provided have dramatically increased over the same period. In 1983, indigent care and bad debt write-off were about $12 million. Since 1988 that number has been running about $16 million. For an analysis of state funding and medical care losses for fiscal year 1993 see Exhibit 4.

As a result of the growing gap between funds received from the State to provide indigent care and the amount actually provided by the Health Center, the institution must compete for paying patients with other local hospitals. Due to the fact

Exhibit 4   **Sources and Uses of State Funds and Indigent Care and Bad Debt Losses**

State Funds Received:	**$17,019,533**
Use of State Funds:	
Instruction	$ 2,740,452
Library	
Primary Care Residency	
Continuing Education	
Other	
Research (total general revenue cost)	$ 4,116,158
*Indigent Care (hospital and physician pure charity)	$12,254,665
Actual Indigent Care Delivered:	$14,346,407
Deficit of State Funds to Cover Above Costs:	**($2,091,742)**
Contractual Allowance & Other Adjustments	$14,093,409
Bad Debt Write-Off	3,535,805
Subtotal	$17,629,214
Indigent Care (total from above)	$14,346,407
Total Write Off	**$31,975,621**

* In addition to the pure charity cost which is classified as Indigent care, the Health Center also has the following adjustments to hospital and physician revenue:

that the Health Center, Trinity-Mother Frances Hospital, and ETMC offer similar health care services such as cardiology and cardiovascular surgery, competition for market share is intense. Both ETMC and Trinity-Mother Frances aggressively advertise and promote their institutional images, services and facilities.

While the Health Center does not advertise in a competitive or comparative manner with the local hospitals, it has in recent years begun using both print and television to build customer awareness and institutional image. Its advertising stresses that it is both a health care provider and a research facility, and therefore provides state-of-the-art medicine. In its recent ads, it has used the tag line "UTHCT—bringing you tomorrow's medicine today." Unfortunately, the Health Center has a somewhat higher ratio of patients are disproportionality older, or have advanced tuberculosis or other serious pulmonary diseases. High risk status generally accompanies indigency status because patients have not received basic health care and wait longer before seeking medical attention, at which point, the disease process is advanced. The higher risk ratio puts the Health Center at something of a competitive disadvantage as such patients require longer hospital stays and are more costly to treat.

In addition, given the Health Center's mission of patient care, education and research, the focus of the institution is not on direct competition with local hospitals. In effect, while the Health Center is a hospital in the traditional sense, it is also much more. In order to achieve all three dimensions of its mission, the hospital's financial and managerial resources must be divided, as it is the combination of the three elements which compose the Health Center's "product." For example, in the treatment of asbestos related diseases, the patient benefits significantly through specialized treatment that is unavailable at the local hos-

Exhibit 5   **Texas Population by Age, 1990 and 2030**

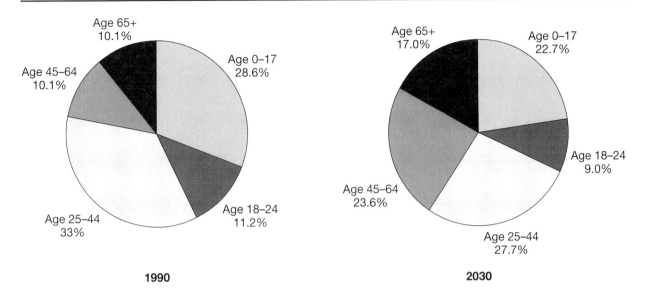

1990

2030

pitals. Grant funded research provides the combined efforts of a clinical researcher, who works at the molecular level of the disease, with an experienced pulmonary disease physician specialist. The patient can participate in clinical trials, such as a new drug therapy, which most likely lead to improvements in treatment of the disease. Further, the Health Center's advanced technology instrumentation base, which includes three electron microscopes, improves diagnostic capabilities. These microscopes provide ultra-high magnification for enhanced research studies and patient care. Therefore, the Health Center provides specialized products for research and patient care.

CUSTOMERS (MARKET)

The Health Center is located in the middle of Smith County, Texas in an area known as East Texas. The hospital's primary patient base is derived from the surrounding population of its twenty-four county service area. It bases its forecasts for future patient loads and program implementation on the demographics of this region. East Texas, like the rest of the state, is increasing in population. The Health Center service area had a population of approximately 1,108,938 in 1994. Analysts project a 1.4% to 2.1% annual population increase through the year 2000. Age is another important factor in the analysis of the Health Center service area demographics. Percentages of the State population by age group is provided in Exhibit 5.

For the years 1980-2030, the 0-17 year old age group of the Texas population will decline from 28.6% of the population to 22.7% while the 45-64 group will increase from 10.1% to 22.2% of the population. The 65 and older group of the

Texas population will increase from 10.1% to 17%. Therefore, the population in Texas is both aging and growing. These trends will obviously have an impact on the direction of patient care for the elderly at the Health Center as well as Texas and the nation.

Many hospitals and physicians statewide refer patients to the Health Center for diagnosis and treatment, especially when pulmonary problems are suspected. However, the bulk of patients come from the surrounding 24 county East Texas service area.

Patient referrals are from group practices, physicians, hospitals, governmental agencies, and self-referrals. Most patients admitted for diagnosis and treatment are referred because their clinical problems require specialized diagnosis and treatment provided by the Health Center. Many times, referrals are made for acutely ill pulmonary patients requiring longer than average intensive care. This is especially true for advanced tuberculosis and asbestosis cases.

Exhibit 6A   **The University of Texas Health Center at Tyler Population of Service Area by County 1994 and 2030**

	1994	*2030*
Anderson	50,029	56,620
Angelina	73,701	99,762
Bowie	83,435	85,547
Camp	10,566	11,117
Cass	30,574	36,129
Cherokee	42,457	56,459
Gregg	109,502	127,451
Harrison	59,348	85,475
Henderson	62,288	88,240
Hopkins	30,636	39,036
Houston	21,722	22,450
Hunt	67,114	83,131
Kaufman	57,692	133,968
Marion	10,069	11,506
Morris	13,215	13,256
Panola	22,543	25,089
Rains	7,198	9,982
Rusk	44,496	56,260
Shelby	22,538	26,131
Smith	159,434	204.633
Titus	25,495	36,386
Upshur	33,280	44,814
Van Zandt	40,062	52,337
Wood	31,544	55,522
Total	**1,108,938**	**1,461,301**

It is important to recognize that the Health Center has an unusual patient population because of its specialties in pulmonary care which attracts older patients, commitment to indigent care, and aging population. These factors and especially its pulmonary referral status, have resulted in greater demands being placed on the Center for medical services. In recent years, a great deal of indigent care has been provided not only to people in counties within the service area, but also to a large number of Texans outside the east Texas area. Tuberculosis tends to be concentrated in indigent populations. At present, approximately 28% of the indigent care the Health Center provides is to patients residing outside the immediate east Texas service area. This accounts

Exhibit 6B   **The University of Texas Health Center at Tyler Service Area by County**

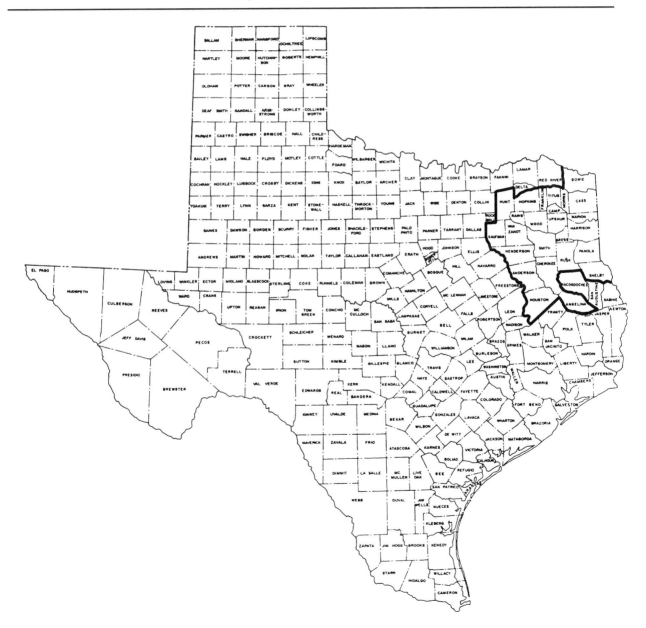

for about 30% of the total cost of indigent care services provided. In one attempt to rein in indigent care costs the Center has recently started limiting the prescription drugs they will provide free of charge and has placed limits on the amount of indigent care provided by the general medicine clinic and the family practice clinic.

In an attempt to capture more of the insured patient market UTHCT began seeking to establish itself as an HMO service provider for some of the region's larger employers. After negotiating with several providers, the Health Center signed a contract with one of the area's largest employers. On January 1, 1993 UTHCT became the primary care provider for the company's 2000 employees. The Health Center also began providing contracted medical care to Smith County's jail inmates in October 1994. Also in September 1995, the Center adopted an HMO plan for its 1100 employees and those of the University of Texas at Tyler, an academic unit of the UT System also located in Tyler. The Health Center has also negotiated preferred provider (PPO) contracts with a number of large insurance companies. The Health Center has also been aggressively marketing its occupational health services. These services are primarily aimed at helping employers reduce the risks of their workers suffering work-related injury or illness, thus reducing medical and disability costs over the long run.

As is true for many health care organizations, UTHCT has seen a major shift in its patient volume away from inpatient toward outpatient services. As Exhibits 7, 8, and 9 indicate, the Health Center has reduced its number of beds available and converted the space to outpatient services. While the number of beds has declined, the occupancy rate has essentially remained flat. In contrast, the number of outpatient or ambulatory visits has increased about 25 percent in the last two years. It is in anticipation of a continuation of this trend that the Health Center has almost completed a new $11 million outpatient treatment center and family practice clinic. This facility will be occupied by October of 1996.

Exhibit 7

The University of Texas Health Center at Tyler Hospital Financial Analysis Fiscal Years 1993, 1994, and 1995

Financial	*Fiscal Year 1993*	*Fiscal Year 1994*	*Fiscal Year 1995*
Impatient	$36,293,171	$32,637,506	$33,389,305
Outpatient	$13,524,552	$13,892,494	$14,786,423
Gross Revenue	$49,817,723	$46,530,000	$48,175,728
Impatient	$18,906,664	$18,403,385	$17,285,969
Outpatient	$ 9,469,428	$ 9,903,129	$10,572,309
Cash Collections	$28,376,092	$28,309,514	$27,858,309
Misc. Patient Care Revenue	$ 323,103	$ 345,484	$ 289,292
Revenue/Bed	$ 218,634	$ 225,086	$ 271,458
Collections/Bed	$ 113,896	$ 126,920	$ 140,536
Days in Accounts Receivable	72.18	72.11	66.58

Exhibit 8

The University of Texas Health Center at Tyler Hospital Statistical Analysis Fiscal Years 1993, 1994, and 1995

Statistical	Fiscal Year 1993	Fiscal Year 1994	Fiscal Year 1995
Operating - Staff Beds	166	145	123
Revenue / Bed	$218,634	$225,086	$271,458
Collections / Bed	$113,896	$126,920	$140,536
Staff / Bed Ratio (Adjusted)	3.69	4.07	4.80
Cost / Bed Ratio	$ 994	$ 1,090	$ 1,140
Admissions	3,520	3,134	3,280
Inpatient Days	36,530	29,937	29,292
Average Daily Census	100.1	82.0	80.3
*Average LOS - TB/ATB	61.7	42.6	40.9
Average LOS without TB	7.5	7.1	6.6
Total Average LOS	10.7	9.1	9.3
Occupancy Rate	62.3%	56.6%	65.4%
Observation Occupancy	3.3%	2.8%	3.5%
Total Occupancy Rate	65.6%	59.5%	68.9%

*LOS: Length of Stay; TB: Tuberculosis Cases; ATB: Atypical Tuberculosis Cases

Exhibit 9

The University of Texas Health Center at Tyler Annual Clinic (Ambulatory) Summary Fiscal Years 1993, 1994, and 1995

Statistical	Fiscal Year 1993	Fiscal Year 1994	Fiscal Year 1995
Total Visits	80,178	91,097	100,245
Visits / Day	265.5	293.8	326.3
*Visits / PCP (NON FP)	2,482.4	2,982.4 2,607.9	
**Visits / FP	2,151.1	1,999.0 2,275.2	
Clinic Rooms	77	97	96
Staff / Rooms	1.2	1.1	1.6
Staff / MD	2.39	2.48	2.61

*Primary Care Physicians (PCP), which include Internal Medicine, Managed Care, General Pediatrics
**Family Practice Clinic Physicians (FP)

REGULATION AND ECONOMICS

In the health care field, regulations are an integral part of the economics which drive the industry. Regulations are promulgated by numerous government and industry agencies. These include the Health Care Financing Administration (HCFA), Department of Health and Human Services, the American Hospital Association, Food and Drug Administration (FDA), Texas Department of Health and Joint Commission on Accreditation of Hospitals Organization (JCAHO).

Operational regulations for the Health Center are imposed by the State of Texas and the University of Texas System. While these entities prescribe the operational parameters, the Prospective Payment System for Federal Medicare/Medicaid reimbursement has had the most significant impact on the health care industry and the Health Center in recent years. Enacted in October, 1984, the system established "Diagnosis Related Groups" (DRG), whereby Medicare/Medicaid reimbursement payments to health care providers are based entirely on the diagnosis of the patient. This system does not reimburse for actual costs incurred for patient care if the required treatment varies from the average costs of the "normal" treatment routine. It only pays the health care provider the average costs associated with a particular course of treatment. For example, a given rate and length of hospital stay is established for reimbursement for open heart surgery. If complications arise and the patient care costs exceed the given rate and length of stay (a common occurrence when dealing with the poor), the provider does not receive federal reimbursement payment for the additional costs over the pre-determined rate. In addition, many treatments are only reimbursable as an outpatient charge. A material portion of the hospital's losses on care provided comes from the mismatch between reimbursement rates and actual costs. See "contractual allowances and other adjustments" in Exhibit 4.

The initial intent of the system was to standardize rates, force efficiency, reduce utilization rates among Medicare/Medicaid patients, and shift some of the health care cost burden from the federal to the state level. Cost control became a real objective for the health care industry. The Health Center has monitored the progress of the new system and tried to anticipate its impact on the institution. As a result, inpatient hospital rooms were converted to outpatient clinics, and the construction of the ambulatory care clinic became a priority.

In addition, the industry will be impacted by another reduction in federal reimbursements which appears to be on the way. The Federal Budget Agreement of 1990 has targeted approximately $2.0 billion in Medicare spending. These reductions specifically affect reimbursement adjustment factors for indirect medical education, such as the residency program at the Health Center. As a teaching facility which receives this factor benefit, the Health Center would obviously be negatively impacted, though the magnitude has not yet been assessed. The economic implications of all the factors mentioned are enormous for the Health Center. Currently, 40% of the institution's paying patients are covered by Medicare. This percentage is projected to increase significantly, based on the industry projection that the Medicare patient base will double by the year 2025.

GOVERNANCE

The UT System is presided over by a board of regents, made up of members from diverse professions and backgrounds which include business people, educators and physicians. Each is considered to be knowledgeable and successful in a given field. They are external to the University of Texas System, and typically have significant positions of power and influence in their chosen career fields. In addition, the members usually have political and persuasive powers with the Texas Legislature in order to secure funding and associated legislation for the system.

The board of regents sets the financial and operating guidelines of the University of Texas System through operating budgets, capital expenditure approvals, program implementation and related activities confirmations. The board essentially supports or rejects recommendations from the administrators of the universities and medical centers in the system. The board of regents implements its decisions through the chancellor of the University of Texas system. The Health Center's education mission has also been impacted by state funding reductions as well. It receives funding from the University of Texas System for salaries for physician residents, but these funds have been reduced over the last several years.

The management of UTHCT is organized along functional lines according to business, research and medical classifications. The organizational chart for the Health Center is illustrated in Exhibit 10. The clinical division is directed by an Executive Associate Director who is a physician and who also holds an MBA.

He possesses a very keen business mind geared towards quality, cost-effectiveness, efficiency, and productivity. He is supported by assistant administrators and physician leaders along functional lines. A search is in progress for the replacement of the deceased Associate Director for Research. The business division is directed by the Executive Associate Director for Administration and Business Affairs who holds a masters degree in health care administration. He is supported by assistant administrators along functional lines.

This group of directors, administrators and assistant administrators comprises the administrative staff. They meet weekly to develop policy and to implement strategic plans and to perform various administrative functions.

The strategic plans developed by the directors are distributed to administrators and to the next management level, department heads. Based on input from these groups, the plan is revised by a committee which includes representation from the medical, research and education divisions. The Strategic Plan which emerges forms part of the basis for budget requests for special programs, operating funds, equipment and personnel.

Strategic decision-making authority is vested in the administrative staff. Both the department heads and administrative staff are responsible for making operational decisions. Most routine operations are managed by department heads who control departmental budgets. Accountability at each management level is maintained through a criteria based job performance evaluation system.

Standing committees form another important part of the Health Center's management structure. These committees utilize several techniques to communicate with employees at various levels of the organization. Formal meetings, hearings, interviews, questionnaires, and review of documentation enable the

Exhibit 10　　**Organization Chart: The University of Texas Health Center at Tyler**

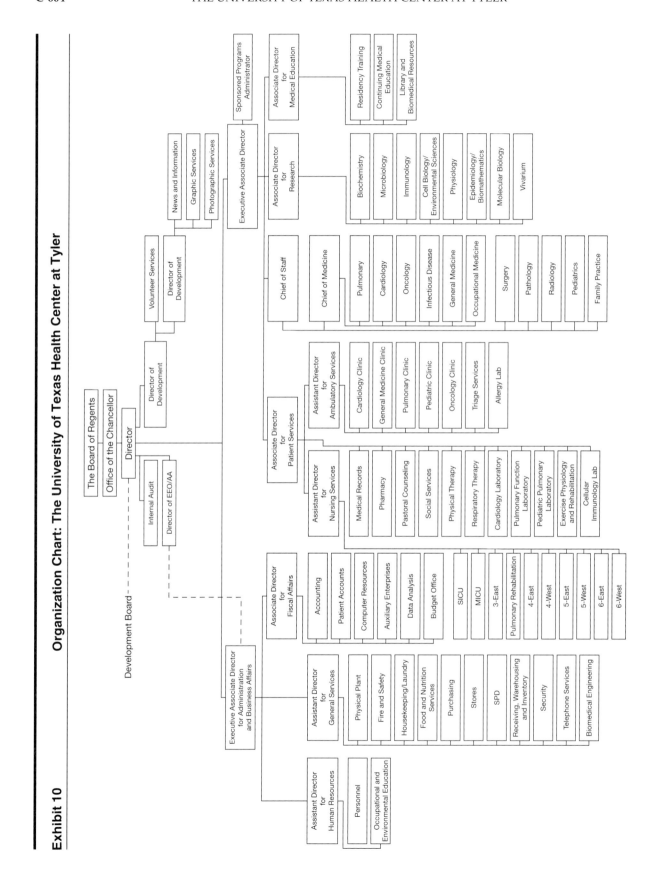

committees to perform their assigned functions. Most of the committees are required by health care accrediting and governmental agencies as well as the University of Texas System.

The communication network between management levels varies among the divisions. Medical management divisions generally communicate through formal meetings and memos. Weekly medical staff meetings are conducted by the Chief of Staff to discuss medical concerns, to distribute policy changes, and to solicit feedback from the staff.

Monthly department head meetings provide an avenue for communication among the medical, educational, business, and research groups. This is a critical communication link because of the complex and unique nature of a university health center. In addition, routine informal information exchange occurs at all levels in managing operations. A recently created public affairs department also produces three separate Health Center internal newsletters, as well as a number of patient information and education brochures.

Given the Health Center's threefold mission, faculty members are appointed to positions in either research or clinical areas. Members may be appointed as an instructor, assistant professor, associate professor, or professor. Positions are also defined by a specialty field of practice. All new faculty members initially receive one-year appointments, which are reviewed annually for renewal.

To join the Health Center's clinical faculty, a candidate must have at least a medical doctorate degree from an accredited school and be licensed to practice medicine in Texas. To be considered for promotion, the clinical faculty member must demonstrate competence in four areas: clinical practice, service to the institution, research, and teaching. A physician who recently has completed a residency program or fellowship initially is appointed as an instructor and usually serves in that position for two years before being considered for promotion to assistant professor. Promotion from assistant to associate professor requires five years of experience and evidence of performance in the four areas just mentioned. Promotion to professor also usually requires five years of service. Elements that go into the promotion decision include peer evaluation and recognition as an authority in a specialty through lecturing and publication in medical journals. Additionally, for promotion from instructor to a professorial rank, board certification in a specialty is desirable but not mandatory.

Physician faculty are in effect employed by the Health Center full time, therefore, they do not have private medical practices. To fulfill the clinical practice dimension of their positions, physicians are provided with private offices, an outpatient clinic area, laboratory, radiology, and ancillary services; they are also provided nursing, clerical, and support staff personnel. In addition, the Health Center provides medical malpractice liability insurance and legal assistance, along with retirement plans and other benefits. All physicians are salaried, compensation for increases in patient visits and resultant income for the Health Center may lead to additions to a physician's base salary.

LOOKING AHEAD

The UT Health Center at Tyler has made significant progress in the implementation of its threefold mission to provide patient care, conduct research and provide education. Patient volumes have grown over the years, especially out-patient (ambulatory care) services, and these services are provided by nation-ally recruited, highly qualified and published clinical physicians andconsulting staff. The Health Center has acquired additional medical and surgical intensive care suites, a heart catheterization laboratory and an open heart operating suite. The Health Center now provides a full range of services for cardiovascu-lar diagnosis, treatment and rehabilitation, including coronary angioplasty and coronary bypass. When the new ambulatory care center is opened, the center should have more than adequate space and state-of-the-art facilities. Nationally known for its pulmonary disease capabilities, the Health Center has the most highly developed program for comprehensive evaluation and treatment of occupational lung diseases in Texas. In addition, it is now conducting some of the most advanced research in the world in such areas as pneumonia and asbestosis.

In fiscal year 1995, hospital admissions were 3,280 inpatients who spent a total of 29,292 days at the Health Center (see Table 8). In 1995, the Health Cen-ter saw over 100,000 outpatients. The Health Center also graduates new family practitioners from its Family Practice Residency Program. The Health Center has also become a significant player in the region's HMO competition.

However, changing economic conditions, reductions in both state and fed-eral funding, and the increasing costs of providing health care programs present both opportunities and challenges. Being partially state funded requires the Health Center to provide indigent health care. In fact the Health Center has had to absorb large losses in indigent care since many private hospi-tals in the region refuse to treat the indigent and refer them to state institutions. State and federal funding, however, have not kept pace with the increases in recent years nor does it appear adequate funding for future indigent care will be forthcoming. Additionally, adequate future funding of Medicare and Med-icaid appears suspect. Improving its services to paying patients and increasing that portion of the Center's business has become a key element of the Health Center's strategic plan to offset indigent care losses.

In the future UTHCT plans to continue its tripartite mission of providing health care services to the east Texas region, conducting research focused pri-marily on pulmonary diseases, and providing education and training. How-ever, in order to respond to the new realities of the health care environment, the Health Center has adopted several key strategies it intends to pursue in the near course: First, it wants to maintain the current HMO relationships it has with its two HMO clients. Second, the Health Center will attempt to use its occupational medicine program (which grew out of its asbestosis treatment work) as a means for marketing additional health care services to the region's employers and attract more industry-related pulmonary cases from across the state covered by insurance. Third, the Health Center will attempt to develop a regional Medicaid managed care network with UTHCT playing a central role. Fourth, UTHCT will attempt to develop and market a Medicare HMO as well as one for its own employees. Fifth, the Health Center wants to elevate its stat-ure in the region as the premier provider of outpatient services. It wants to become the region's provider of choice of such services, and not be thought of as "the state chest hospital." Finally, the Health Center plans to develop rela-tionships with health care providers (physician groups and clinics) who are not directly employed by the Health Center so it may become a more comprehen-sive marketing conduit for managed care services.

With regard to its research component, the Health Center will have to more aggressively pursue external research grants if it is to build its status as a research institution. Given the stagnation in state support for research, attracting alternative funds will become more and more critical. So while UTHCT has come a long way from its days as a tuberculosis hospital housed in converted army barracks, the challenges are as great as ever. The Health Center must simultaneously become a more aggressive competitor in the health care services marketplace and grow in its role as a center of research and learning.

Lord Nelson at Trafalgar

Mark Kroll, University of Texas at Tyler

On August 15, 1815, Napoleon Bonaparte sailed into permanent exile on board the Royal Navy ship the *H.M.S. Bellerophon*. Two months earlier he had been defeated by England and its allies at the Battle of Waterloo. That battle represented the last chapter in a tumultuous and bloody period in European history, the end of the Napoleonic Wars which had bled Europe for 15 years. Though no one knew it at the time, it also represented the last battle fought between England and France. Previously, from the time of the Norman conquest of the British Isles in 1066 until Waterloo, the English and French had been periodically at war.

The victory at Waterloo of course represented the culmination of the brilliant military career of Sir Arthur Wellesley, the Duke of Wellington. However, as is true for most great successes in warfare as well as commerce, the precursors which allowed Wellington to achieve his great victories over Napoleon were essential to its attainment. One, if not the most important, precursor to Wellington's success took place ten years before Napoleon's defeats in a great sea battle which was just as tumultuous and strategically important. That was the Battle of Trafalgar. The results of Trafalgar provided England undisputed supremacy of the seas for over 100 years, insured that Napoleon could never threaten an invasion of England, and made it possible for Britain to send its armies, such as the one led by Wellington, abroad without fear of those armies being destroyed in route in naval action.

At Trafalgar the Royal Navy was commanded by England's most celebrated naval officer, Vice Admiral Lord Viscount Nelson K.B. Lord Nelson's role at Trafalgar was very eloquently assessed by U.S. Navy Rear Admiral A.T. Mahan, who commented: "Rarely has a man been more favored in the hour of his appearing; never one so fortunate in the moment of his death."

THE GEOPOLITICAL AND MILITARY SITUATION IN 1805

England and France had been at peace from 1783 to the rise to power of Napoleon Bonaparte. As Napoleon's intentions for conquest both in Europe and abroad became clear, England once again found itself at odds with its old nemesis. Given his quick success at being able to dominate the European Continent, he began to contemplate conquests off the continent. His first major expedition was his successful invasion of Egypt. However, Napoleon's success in Egypt was quickly rendered pointless when the British under Lord Nelson destroyed the French fleet supporting the invasion in 1798. This victory effectively marooned the French expeditionary force and Napoleon in Egypt. This British victory followed one off Portugal known as the Battle of St. Vincent, which was just as devastating to the French and materially weakened the French Navy.

On the heels of these naval defeats, the possibility of invading England and ridding himself of a constant source of frustration must have periodically entered Napoleon's mind. It does not appear to have ever become so important as to prevent him from planning other conquests, but by 1804 he was seriously entertaining invasion plans. However, once again the major constraint was sea power, or the lack thereof. To invade England successfully the invader must be able to get its army across the English Channel without its being destroyed in the process. This required in 1804 at least temporary naval control of the Channel. The problem for Napoleon was that throughout this period the English maintained a very powerful fleet off the northwest coast of France, guarding the entrance to the English Channel.

Napoleon began assembling an invasion force in the northern French coastal city of Boulogne in 1803. By 1805 he was ready to invade, but was still no closer to gaining naval supremacy in the English Channel. So in that same year he decided upon a plan to at least temporarily gain control of the Channel and mount an invasion. Having brought Spain into the war on his side, he had at his disposal both the French and Spanish fleets. The problem for Napoleon was that his navy was spread among various squadrons which were either bottled up in ports by British blockade, or in remote locations. If he was to clear the Channel he would have to concentrate all of his naval forces into a single fleet, and then attack the British fleet guarding the Channel. In 1805 he devised a plan which seemed very workable for a soldier, but proved very ineffective when applied to naval forces.

On the face of it the plan was simple, and seemed doable to Napoleon. He would order all of his admirals and their squadrons to break out of the various ports in which they were located, and sail to Martinique in the West Indies. Martinique was France's strongest outpost in the Caribbean. After the various squadrons rendezvoused in the West Indies, they would sail under the combined command of French Vice Admiral Pierre Villeneuve for the English Channel. Once in the Channel they would either do battle with the British fleet, or alternatively, draw them away from the Channel so the crossing could be accomplished (see Exhibits 1 and 2).

While the plan made great sense to a general, the admirals had their doubts. Fleets at sea in those days had no way of communicating with each other. It was quite possible for one fleet to sail within a relatively small distance of another and never meet, especially when sailing at night. Second, when forced

Exhibit 1   **European Theater 1805**

to rely on wind for propulsion, the chances of fleets being able to keep schedules were impossible. Finally, Napoleon did not count on Admiral Nelson's dogged pursuit of the largest of the fleets under the command of Admiral Villeneuve to the West Indies, which forced him back to Spain before the plan could be hatched. As a result, by the time the Battle of Trafalgar was fought Napoleon had given up on his navy and his invasion plans, and was marching his army south. The British had no way of knowing this and saw the destruction of the greater portion of the French-Spanish fleet as the only means of insuring the safety of England from invasion. Such a destruction was the British Admiralty's primary goal in 1805, and they saw Lord Nelson as the commander who could achieve it.

The combined French-Spanish fleet, having failed to link up with other French squadrons, sailed back to the west coast of Spain, having heard Nelson's fleet was closing on them. This was in spite of the fact Nelson's fleet at that time was only half the size of the combined fleet. When they reached the Spanish coast the combined fleet was attacked by a British squadron and suffered the loss of two ships. From there they made their way to the Spanish port of Cadiz, where they were to resupply and rethink their plans. Upon entering Cadiz, the British Mediterranean fleet quickly took up blockade positions. Not long after, Nelson's fleet arrived to join the blockade. It was readily apparent to the officers and men of the combined French-Spanish fleet that in all likelihood they could not leave Cadiz without a fight with the Royal Navy.

Exhibit 2

Fleet Movements Before Trafalgar

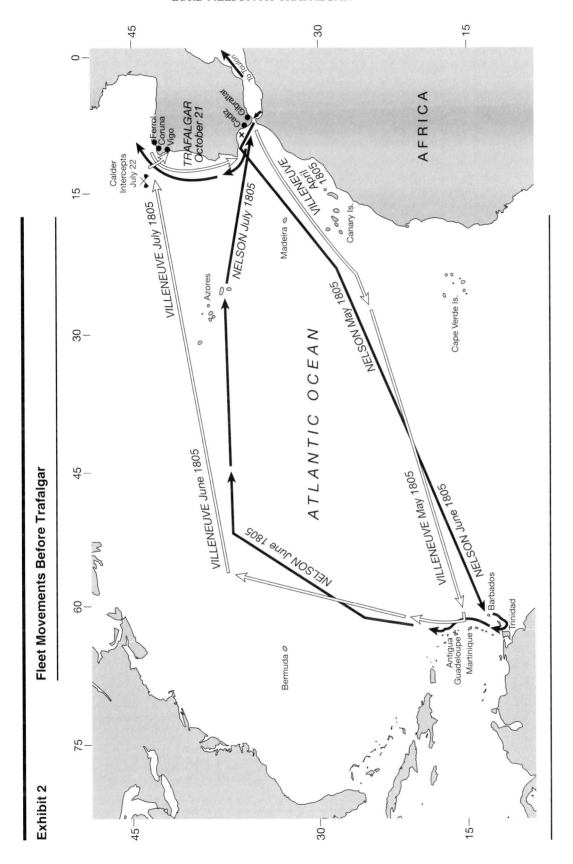

THE COMMANDERS: NELSON VERSUS VILLENEUVE

Horatio Nelson was born in 1758, one of eight children and the third of five sons, to the Reverend Edmund Nelson and his wife Catherine Nelson. His father was pastor of the Anglican parish at Burnham Thorpe, a small village on the east coast of England. The day after Christmas in 1767 Catherine Nelson died, leaving her husband and their eight children. The family was not destitute, but was far from wealthy. The family had, through Catherine Nelson's family, some connections to the landed aristocracy which had secured Edmund his present position. More important to Horatio's future was Catherine's older brother Captain Maurice Suckling, who had distinguished himself in battle against the French in the Caribbean.

As a boy Horatio became fascinated by the sea and sailing. As Burnham Thorpe lay among the estuaries and ports on England's North Sea coast, Horatio was exposed early to sailing and maritime life. He was also formally schooled in his early years at the Royal Grammar School in Norwich and the Paston School in North Walsham. As the son of a parson who, though formally educated at Cambridge, had neither position nor wealth, there were two primary avenues for Horatio to pursue. He could, as did his father and elder brother, attend Cambridge and hope to secure a comfortable assignment after ordination, or pursue a military career. Given Horatio's fascination with the sea and the exploits of his uncle Maurice, he longed for a career in the Royal Navy.

In 1770 the Spanish captured the Falkland Islands from the British. Most considered them not worth a fight, but British honor was at stake, so the Navy was mustered. Horatio's uncle Maurice was recalled to command the 64-gun *Raisonnable*. Horatio saw this as his opportunity and beseeched his father to request his uncle Maurice take him to sea as a midshipman. With that the small, thin 12 year old began his naval career. From 1771 to 1777 Nelson served on both merchant and Royal Navy ships. During these years he participated in voyages to the West Indies, the East Indies, and the Arctic.

In 1777, at the age of 19, he passed the examination to become a lieutenant and was immediately assigned to the frigate *Loweswift*, which was ordered to Jamaica. As is unfortunately often the case, military careers flourish best during war. Such was the case with Nelson's. At the time of his first posting England was at war with its American colonies, which required significant naval support. In 1778, when the French and later the Spanish entered the war as American allies, the potential for advancement in the Royal Navy became all the better. So, by 1779, at the age of 21, Horatio Nelson was made post-captain and given command of the frigate *Hinchinbroke*. Attaining such rank made his eventual promotion to flag officer a matter of seniority.

From 1779 through the end of the American Revolution he was given various assignments in Central America, the Baltic Sea, and the West Indies. The end of the war found him in command of the frigate *Boreas* in the West Indies. While in the Caribbean he met Fanny Nisbet, whom he married two years later. In 1787 he sailed with his bride to England. Shortly thereafter he entered perhaps the most difficult period of his career, for in 1788 he was sent back to Burnham Thorpe on half pay. It is also unfortunately the case that peace is perhaps the worst thing that can happen to a military career.

The years 1788 to 1793 were difficult for Nelson as he did not see himself in any other role than that of a naval officer. Other officers often turned to other professions which they enjoyed, or came out of the war with enough prize money from captured enemy ships to live comfortably. Neither was the case with Nelson. He spent these years using whatever connections and sources of influence that were available to him to secure a command. However, as had previously been the case, it took the threat of war to return him to service. England began to muster its naval forces following the French Revolution and the ascent to power of Napoleon Bonaparte. On January 6, 1793, Nelson returned to active duty and was away at sea almost continuously until his death at Trafalgar in October 1805.

In terms of who Lord Nelson was as a person, as with any bright and capable person, it is a difficult question to answer with complete satisfaction. However, there are some consistent themes in his personality and view of the world and his place in it. First of all, he was utterly fearless. By all accounts of those who served with him, Nelson consistently exposed himself to every bit as much danger if not more than he asked any subordinate to face. In evidence of this fact one need only know that by the time the Battle of Trafalgar occurred he had lost his right arm and virtually all the use of an eye, and then lost his life at Trafalgar at age 47.

His courage might have come from another theme which seems consistent—Nelson was a very fatalistic man. He appears to have believed in providence and that he had a fate which he must see through. This belief in divine intervention in the lives of men was common in the 19th century. He likely believed that his fate, a fate ordained by God, was to accomplish for his nation great victories at sea, only to be killed in the process. Just prior to the beginning of action at Trafalgar he was bidding farewell to one of his captains, Henry Blackwood, who reported their last conversation as follows:

> He [Lord Nelson] then again desired me go away [to Blackwood's ship]; and as we were standing on the front of the poop, I took his hand, and said, 'I trust, my Lord, that on my return to the *Victory* [Nelson's flagship], which will be as soon as possible, I shall find your Lordship well, and in possession of twenty prizes.' On which he made this reply: 'God bless you, Blackwood, I shall never speak to you again.'

It has been suggested Nelson had a death wish at Trafalgar, on account of the tremendous danger to which he exposed himself and his flagship. It is just as likely he believed that it was his destiny to die in such a battle and there was little he could do to prevent it.

As was also characteristic of many in the Royal Navy, Lord Nelson's allegiances were very clear to him—to king and country. He appears to have had an unshakable belief in England's destiny to be a great power and that the rightful head of state was King George III, who was not even English, but German. However, Nelson also believed that the ultimate power to govern did and should reside in Parliament. In fact he had contemplated a political career. He was an active participant in the House of Lords upon his being given title. While the divine right of kings had been rejected in America and France, it still lived in the mind of Lord Nelson.

Another curious feature of Nelson's was his vanity. How much of his success was owing to a need to be admired and exalted cannot be measured, but it is clear glory, and the position and status it brought, were very important to Nelson. In his reports and written correspondence he rarely shies from making clear his own contributions to whatever successes he had to report. Those who met him report his inclination to make it known to all involved who he was and what he was. It is of course possible such displays of vanity were a reflection of an insecure man of humble birth attempting to create an identity for himself when immersed in the English aristocracy.

Regardless of Nelson's concern for his own prestige, it is also true that he was most generous with praise of his colleagues and subordinates. He consistently took pains to make sure those who had earned credit got their full measure. In addition, he worked to see that those who had served him well were looked after to the extent it was in his power to do so. His fellow officers and subordinates, as a result, seem to have been able to see past Nelson's vanity and find a faithful friend and superior who they knew they could count on.

In terms of leadership style, one would have to conclude he was not the martinet many British officers of his era were. An incident occurred in the hours just before battle was joined at Trafalgar which illustrates Nelson's style. A common seaman was wetting down some stowed canvas hammocks with a bucket so they would not catch fire. A Royal Marine officer was splashed with some of the water the sailor had thrown, and began cursing the sailor. Nelson saw the incident, came over, and told the officer the sailor was doing his job and that he was in the way, and that he should have gotten the whole bucket full for not being more careful. On the other hand, he did enforce Royal Navy regulations fully. For instance, he had two crew members hanged when it was determined they were homosexuals. He had high expectations for his officers and crews, but they all knew he held himself to a standard every bit as high as the one he held them to. A common theme throughout his career as an admiral was a willingness to trust subordinate officers and rely on their individual initiative in executing his plans. This undoubtedly grew out of his own willingness as both an admiral and a captain to deviate from orders when he perceived greater advantage could be gained by following another course of action.

In terms of tactics, Lord Nelson was perhaps the most innovative commander the Royal Navy had at the time. Most European naval officers of the era were schooled in a very regimented approach, normally involving engaging the enemy in a parallel fashion in line of battle. In fact, the large warships which were built to engage in major sea actions were referred to as "sail-of-the-line." In his two most important victories prior to Trafalgar Nelson had improvised tactics quite different from this traditional approach. This willingness to innovate was something both his superiors in the Admiralty and his subordinates admired in him and counted upon. The French, including Admiral Villeneuve, anticipated Nelson would, in the coming battle, depart from traditional tactics. What Nelson would do they had no idea. Villeneuve often dismissed Nelson's methods as rash and impulsive in discussions with subordinates, but there is no question the fact that they were facing Nelson weighed heavily on Villeneuve and his men.

Additionally, Nelson was not above playing mind games with his opponents. For instance, prior to the battle at Trafalgar the Royal Navy had been blockading the port of Cadiz, in which the combined fleet was anchored. Admiral Collingwood, who was Nelson's second in command, had taken up blockade positions within clear view of the port, as was customary in such situations. This was done while Nelson made a quick trip to London to clarify with the Admiralty what he had done and why, and what his plans were for facing the combined fleet. Upon Lord Nelson's return, he ordered his fleet to back off over the horizon and out of view of the enemy. He left only one or two fast-sailing frigates on watch. In this way his enemy knew only that the Royal Navy was present, but in what strength and how close they were left to guess.

Trafalgar was not the first occasion in which Admiral Pierre Villeneuve faced Lord Admiral Nelson. In 1798 Villeneuve had been involved in what became known as the Battle of the Nile, fought in Aboukir Bay off the coast of Egypt. The battle had been Nelson's first major success as a flag officer, resulting in the Royal Navy capturing or destroying all but two of the 13 French sail-of-the-line in the battle. One British sailor recounted it as being an awful sight, with the bay filled with the burned, naked bodies of the enemy. Admiral Villeneuve managed to escape the British with his flag ship and one other sail-of-the-line. As one would imagine, it left an indelible impression on Admiral Villeneuve.

Pierre Charles Jean Silvestre de Villeneuve was born in 1763 in Valensole, France, to an aristocratic family. He graduated from the French Royal Naval Academy, and from there entered the French Royal Navy. France was not long after plunged into revolution and the resulting political upheaval. During the administration of the National Convention which organized France's first Republic, Villeneuve achieved the rank of captain in 1793. Because of political purges and turnover in French naval leadership, Villeneuve advanced rapidly and by 1796, at the age of 33, was a rear admiral.

His first major action as a flag officer was the Battle of the Nile, which, as mentioned earlier, was a devastating defeat for the French Navy. The defeat also resulted in Napoleon's Middle Eastern campaign being frustrated and his expeditionary army being marooned in Egypt. While Villeneuve survived the battle and managed to save the only ships to escape British capture, upon his return to France Napoleon erroneously accused him of being largely responsible for the defeat. The charge was without foundation, and later Napoleon not only promoted Villeneuve to Vice Admiral, but made him commander-in-chief of the combined French-Spanish fleet. To his credit, Villeneuve had opposed the Egyptian campaign. Even so, Napoleon appears to have never had a great deal of confidence in Villeneuve or any of his naval commanders. So at age 41, with little combat experience and having never successfully led a naval attack against the British, Admiral Villeneuve was sent out by Napoleon to face Lord Nelson.

Whether or not Villeneuve had confidence in his own ability to command is an interesting question. Given he had not been able to successfully engage the British prior to Trafalgar, and did everything he could to avoid a fight with Nelson on previous occasions, it might be concluded he lacked confidence in his own tactical skills. What is quite clear is he had little confidence in either his French subordinates or his Spanish allies. His assessment was that accuracy in timing of maneuvers was very important, and French admirals were not always efficient at it and Spaniards were worse. In fairness to Villeneuve, his lack of confidence in his subordinates was at least to some extent justified and shared by Lord Nelson, who essentially counted on poor leadership and seamanship in his planning for Trafalgar. No doubt owing to this lack of confidence, Villeneuve did not think much of Napoleon's plan to have the French and Spanish fleets rendezvous in the West Indies and then attack the British fleet in the English Channel. It was only Napoleon's insistence that he sail that sent Villeneuve to the West Indies. After the attempt to combine various French and Spanish fleets failed to work, Villeneuve saw his role primarily as preserving the combined fleet.

Villeneuve's lack of experience in tactical skills showed at Trafalgar as Nelson's experience paid off. One area in which he showed his lack of skill was in his use of his frigates for reconnaissance. Frigates at that point in naval warfare were the eyes of a fleet. They, being smaller and much faster than capital ships, were used by Nelson as forward observers, messengers, and scouts. As mentioned earlier, during his vigil outside of the port of Cadiz waiting for the French, he kept his sail-of-the-line over the horizon and out of site of Villeneuve. Even so, he always knew what the combined fleet was doing as he used his frigates as forward observers. When there was news to report, the frigates would signal the main fleet. This allowed Nelson to stay far enough out to sea to keep the enemy guessing as to his strength, position, and maneuvers. When the combined fleet did sail out of Cadiz, Nelson's frigates were able to tell him their course, disposition, and position. With such intelligence, Nelson was able to stage the battle to his design.

In contrast, Villeneuve kept his frigates in port with his fleet. When he left Cadiz and sailed to meet Nelson, his frigates were to the land side of his fleet, rather than being deployed as forward observers in a position to ascertain Nelson's intentions. Villeneuve only knew what Nelson's intentions were when the British fleet was within clear view, and it was too late to respond with any kind of countertactics.

THE COMPARATIVE ADVANTAGES OF THE ROYAL NAVY

It was reported that during his conveyance by the Royal Navy into exile on St. Helena, Napoleon commented to the captain of the *Bellerophon* that "In all my plans I have always been thwarted by the British Fleet." While his remark was a bit of an exaggeration, made by a man who was the captive of others, it did reflect the deep respect the former emperor had for the Royal Navy. It was also true that during his imperial reign Napoleon kept a bust of Lord Nelson in his official chambers. He is said to have sat carefully studying it from time to time. On his trip to St. Helena, his captors later reported he was very quizzical about what it was that made the Royal Navy such a formidable force.

While Napoleon was indisputably the master of Europe from 1800 to 1814, he was indeed frustrated on many occasions by England, and especially the Royal Navy. The struggle between England and France in fact has been likened to that of a fight between an elephant and a whale. Both are very large and powerful animals, but are very dissimilar in terms of preferred circumstance in which to operate. The elephant threatened more than once but could never master the narrow strip of sea between France and England. On the other hand, the whale eventually came on land, and, with some help, defeated its nemesis (Warner, 1971: 150).

By the time the Battle of Trafalgar was fought, the Royal Navy had achieved a decided superiority over its opponents. This superiority was not so much in numbers of ships, though in numbers the Royal Navy was somewhat larger than the combined French-Spanish Navy allied against it. Rather the Royal Navy enjoyed advantages which were largely intangible, such as seamanship, leadership, morale, cohesiveness, and determination to decide the issue regardless of the costs.

England had not been one of the early nations to send forth its ships on voyages of discovery, as had the Portuguese and Spanish in the 15th century. However, from the time of the English privateers during the reign of Elizabeth I, the sea had been one of the few avenues for advancement in what was otherwise a very class-conscious society. A young man willing to endure the hardships and perils of sea could improve his lot in either the merchant fleet or in the Royal Navy. This became even more the case as England became a colonial power with possessions spread around the globe. Good sailors who could bring home trade goods successfully, or capture enemy prize ships in actions with the Royal Navy, were essential to England's economic vitality. Not surprisingly, therefore, while most European nations worshipped their generals, England worshipped its famous sailors. England possessed, by the time Nelson was a boy, a maritime culture which prized seamanship. Napoleon himself might have summed it up best when reflecting on his ultimate defeat while in exile on St. Helena when he observed "there is a specialization in this profession [seamanship] which blocked all my ideas. They always returned to the point that one could not be a good seaman unless one was brought up to it from the cradle." Lord Nelson, his officers, and sailors had in fact been raised to go to sea.

For largely the same reasons as the quality of its general seamanship, the Royal Navy enjoyed an officer corps which was accomplished, confident, and determined. From childhood future English navy officers had legends which they idolized and sought to emulate. In Lord Nelson's case, his heroes when he joined the Royal Navy as a midshipman at age 12 were Admiral Lord Rodney and Admiral Lord Hood, who had made their own fame against the French. The Royal Navy had in its midshipmen corps an apprenticeship system which insured a continuous flow of young men who had practical experience to induct into its officer corps as lieutenants. While achieving entry into the officer corps and advancing to the rank of post-captain was certainly subject to political influence, it was also influenced by individual merit. An adolescent of modest background, such as Nelson, could, with the help of an uncle who was a navy captain, enter the service as a midshipman and achieve rapid advancement through skill, daring, and determination. In fact, the Navy was one of the few avenues for upward mobility open to a child of a rural parson, such as Nelson; a route to high position if he was prepared to take the risks.

Promotion above the rank of captain in the Royal Navy in the 18th and early 19th centuries was strictly by seniority. However, the realities were that those who had demonstrated initiative and ability were given important commands, while those less accomplished stayed home on inactive status, even if they were senior in rank. This was the result of a curious arrangement whereby officers both with and without command were still considered serving officers. However, if an officer did not have an assignment he was sent home on half pay. He could remain on that status the rest of his life if he did not receive another command. He would continue to rise in rank as his seniority lengthened, but if the admiralty had decided he was not worthy of command, he might stay on half pay at home for the rest of his career. On the other hand, an officer who was valued would be given major commands even though there might be a number of officers of higher rank growing old at home. Such was the case with Lord Nelson, who at Trafalgar held the rank of Vice Admiral, about half way up in the ranks of admirals, though he was commander of an entire theater of operations. So while political connections and influence might put an officer on the track to the rank of flag officer, it was performance that got him commands with full pay and the opportunity to win prizes in battle.

The reason the Royal Navy had an arrangement by which it furloughed active officers on half pay for extended periods of time was that, as with any nation, during peace time the need for officers declined. However, by retaining officers in the service rather than retiring them, the Royal Navy could quickly staff its ships with experienced officers when war broke out. Nelson himself was "dry docked" this way from 1787 to early 1793. Quite often officers had two professions, one which they pursued in peacetime and the other during war. Such an arrangement provided the Royal Navy with a certain measure of continuity; as the ranks of its seamen would change from conflict to conflict, the officer corps remained intact. For example, Vice Admiral Cuthbert Collingwood, Nelson's second in command at Trafalgar, first met Nelson in the West Indies when they were both young officers, and they remained friends for life.

In contrast the French Navy and its officer corps had experienced a great deal of turmoil in the late 18th and early 19th centuries, owing to the political upheavals which had plagued the country from the time of the French Revolution to the final exile of Napoleon. Those officers with long naval careers which predated the Revolution fell from favor while young officers who had been appropriately groomed by the Revolutionary Government rose through the ranks quickly. Admiral Villeneuve, the combined fleet commander at Trafalgar, achieved flag rank at 33, and was considerably younger than Nelson at the time of the battle. His second in command, Rear-Admiral Dumanoir le Pelley, was 35 at the time of the battle. Both men had seen limited action during the course of their careers.

The English also had a considerable advantage over the combined fleets of France and Spain in the cohesion and esprit de corps of its officers and sailors. The English shared a common culture, both in terms of the society in which they had been brought up and in the Navy they served. In contrast, the French and Spanish officers who commanded at Trafalgar were at best somewhat suspicious of each other. Spain, to a certain extent, was a reluctant ally pulled into the war by the French. Don Federico Gravina, the senior Spanish flag officer at Trafalgar, had requested he be relieved of his command when he was placed under the French Admiral Villeneuve. He was convinced to stay on by the Spanish government, but he was not enthusiastic about doing so. In an action with another British fleet just prior to the combined fleet's arrival at Cadiz, two Spanish ships were lost while no French ships were lost. This fact engendered a feeling among the Spaniards, likely unfounded, that their ships had been sacrificed to protect the French.

Further evidence of the disaffection which existed between the two sides can be found in the reception the French received upon arriving in Cadiz, Spain. The city's authorities were initially unwilling to provide any supplies or stores for the combined fleet. Only after being specifically ordered by the Spanish government in Madrid to cooperate was help forthcoming. This is in contrast to the reception the British received following the Battle of Trafalgar. Following the battle it was necessary for a British party to visit Cadiz, from which the combined French-Spanish fleet had sailed, in order to deal with prisoner exchanges. The British reported that during their visit they could not have been treated more hospitably nor could their reception have been warmer. In fact, within a few years the Spanish were engaged in a civil war in which much of the population sought to overthrow a Spanish monarchy being supported by Napoleon. In this effort they were aided by the British Army under Sir Arthur Wellesley, later Duke of Wellington.

As a result of the less than complete confidence the two parties in the French-Spanish alliance had in each other, and owing to what can only be described as a lack of confidence in themselves, the combined fleet approached the battle at Trafalgar with great trepidation. The Spanish in fact felt that in the coming battle they would be sacrificed by the French who commanded the combined fleet.

Perhaps just as debilitating for the combined fleet crews was a general sense of unease and pessimism about the coming engagement with the Royal Navy. This pessimism started at the top with Napoleon, who had little confidence in his Navy's chances against the Royal Navy, and filtered down through the ranks. And there was good reason for morale being low. Neither the Spanish nor the French had been able to win major engagements with the British throughout the careers of those involved at Trafalgar. The British had many heroes who had won many great victories, but those victories had come mostly at the expense of the French. This apprehension was heightened by the fact the combined fleet knew they were facing Lord Nelson, a commander who had badly beaten the French before and was spoiling for a final showdown now. In fact the French admiralty's anxieties were so great about fighting the Royal Navy that it was their fondest hope that they could somehow lure the British fleet guarding the English Channel away from its station and allow Napoleon to cross his army, without ever actually having to fight the British. The anxiety that pervaded the combined fleet existed despite their outnumbering the British fleet at Trafalgar 33 sail-of-the-line to the Royal Navy's 27.

The fact that a sense of foreboding existed in the combined fleet should not be confused with cowardice. There is plenty of evidence of bravery and gallantry on the part of both French and Spanish crews. One French ship, the *Aigle*, lost two-thirds of its ship's company at Trafalgar. French Admiral Lucas' ship sustained 490 deaths and 81 wounded. The *Algeciras*, French Admiral Magon's flagship, had 77 killed and 142 wounded in the battle, and Admiral Magon was himself killed while directing action. Spanish forces likewise fought gallantly, but paid heavily in lives lost. On the *Santissima Trinidada*, flagship of Admiral Cisneros, 200 men were killed in the battle. Nor was the pre-battle anxiety owing to any doubts about the worthiness of their ships. Both French and Spanish ship construction was in fact much admired by members of the Royal Navy, and if anything, considered superior to their own.

In terms of tactics, both navies (save for Lord Nelson) followed a time-honored doctrine in terms of how a naval battle was to be fought. That doctrine called for the warring fleets to each form a line of battle as though both were strands of beads laid side-by-side. The two lines of ships would then determine the issue in such an array. One of Nelson's major contributions to naval warfare was his willingness to depart from traditional tactics. The French likewise recognized the limitations of conventional tactics. Admiral Villeneuve in fact expressed dismay at how uninspired French fleet tactics were. However, he also viewed Nelson's tactics as reckless, though there was no denying the successes Nelson had achieved in earlier engagements. Nelson's stunning victory over the French in the Bay of Aboukir off the Egyptian coast in 1798, which stranded Napoleon and the French Army in Egypt, was the result of Nelson flying in the face of naval convention. All his superiors, subordinates, and opponents came to expect the unexpected from Nelson. "The Nelson touch," as it was referred to, appears to have inspired members of the Royal Navy and created a sense of dread in his opponents.

One final intangible which undoubtedly influenced events at Trafalgar was the eagerness of the British for a fight with the combined French-Spanish fleet, which would decide the issue of naval supremacy once and for all. From Nelson down to the ordinary seaman, worn out by years of blockading French and Spanish ports or chasing the French and Spanish fleets throughout the Mediterranean, the Atlantic, and the Caribbean, a decisive battle was much desired. Prior to Trafalgar, Nelson had spent over two years chasing the French fleet through the Mediterranean, across the Atlantic to the West Indies, and back across the Atlantic for the purpose of engaging it. This was in spite of the fact that throughout his pursuit, as was the case at Trafalgar, the French fleet held numerical superiority over the British. An officer on one of the British sail-of-the-line commented in his diary how members of his crew had chalked "victory or death" on their guns just prior to Trafalgar. Lord Nelson himself perhaps summed up the British attitude in an entry in his diary during the pursuit of the enemy before Trafalgar when he wrote:

> The business of an English Commander-in-Chief being first to bring the Enemy's fleet to battle on the most advantageous terms to himself (I mean that of laying his ships well on board the Enemy's as expeditiously as possible), and secondly to continue them there without separating until the business is decided . . . if the two fleets are both willing to fight, but little maneuvering is necessary; the less the better: a day is soon lost in that business. . . .

THE BATTLE OF TRAFALGAR

Having failed to combine the various elements of the French and Spanish Navies into a single force in the West Indies with which to attack the British in the English Channel, having been chased out of the West Indies by Lord Nelson, and then having been on the losing end of an engagement with an English fleet under Sir Robert Calder off the Spanish coast, Villeneuve and the combined fleet retired to Cadiz, Spain, on August 20, 1805. There, the British Mediterranean fleet under Vice Admiral Cuthbert Collingwood took up blockade station outside the port of Cadiz and waited. Nelson, having spent the previous years blockading and then chasing the combined fleet across the Atlantic, returned to England to report to the admiralty. His fleet joined Collingwood's off Cadiz.

By the time Villeneuve had taken refuge at Cadiz, Napoleon had, for all practical purposes, given up on crossing the English Channel, as he realized his navy would never gain him any kind of window during which to cross the channel in force. He then decided to turn his attentions to his Austrian and Russian adversaries, and relegate his navy to playing whatever supporting role it might in the Mediterranean, or making life miserable for the British in the West Indies.

On September 28, 1805, Lord Nelson rejoined the British fleet off Cadiz. His fleet consisted of 27 sail-of-the-line, 4 frigates, a schooner, and a cutter. The British faced a combined fleet of 33 sail-of-the-line. For perhaps the first time in three or four years, both Nelson and the British Admiralty were on the same page as to what his purpose was—to blockade the combined fleet at Cadiz until such time as the French commander-in-chief chose to do battle or attempt an escape. They believed, correctly, that in Nelson they had the leader who could destroy the French fleet. For his part, Nelson was determined that battle would be joined and the combined fleet destroyed. Such a victory would make an invasion of England virtually impossible and give the British free reign in terms of sending its armies overseas. Neither Nelson nor the Admiralty had yet discovered Napoleon had given up on his plans for invasion.

■ Lord Nelson's Battle Plan

As mentioned earlier, conventional wisdom called for an attacking fleet to approach its opponent in a single line of sail which would be brought alongside the enemy's line and battle be joined. Nelson rejected this strategy for several reasons. First, he was very concerned that given all the time it would take to maneuver his fleet into such a formation and then alongside the combined fleet, the enemy might escape or manage to get back into the port at Cadiz. Second, given his confidence in his officers and men, he was sure that the quicker he could get his individual ships joined in battle with the enemy, the more damage would be incurred and the greater the victory. Finally, he wanted to confound the enemy and confuse them as to his intent. As a result, Nelson resolved to attack the enemy's fleet in two separate columns, attacking in a perpendicular direction, as two wedges going through the single line of enemy ships (see Exhibit 3). One column would attack the enemy's line about a third of its length from the front, while the second column would attack the line about a third of a way from its rear. What was Nelson's intended result? To quote him, "I think it will surprise and confound the enemy. They won't know what I am about. It will bring forward a pell-mell battle, and that is what I want." He wanted a "pell-mell battle" because he was convinced that in a scrambled set of one-on-one engagements, superior English seamanship, gunnery, and leadership would carry the day.

In keeping with Nelson's inclination to expose himself to hazardous situations, his own flagship, *H.M.S. Victory*, would spearhead the column attacking the front of the enemy line, with his career-long friend Collingwood leading the other column aboard the *H.M.S. Royal Sovereign*. The one major problem with Nelson's plan was that it exposed the ships at the heads of the columns to tremendous enemy fire for a significant period of time before they could bring their own guns to bear. In addition, the first ships to reach the enemy line would likely find themselves initially engaged with multiple enemy ships. As a result, it was anticipated the damage and casualties sustained by the lead ships would be the worst suffered by any Royal Navy ships in the battle. In contrast, by the time the ships at the rear of the columns joined the battle the issue could very well be decided. Subordinate officers suggested Nelson's ship at least fall back to the second position in the column, but Nelson would have none of that.

While Nelson's plan was simple, it was reported to have sent an "electric shock" through the fleet owing to its departure from orthodoxy and its boldness. Likewise, simply having Nelson in command seems to have added to the fleet's confidence level and eagerness for the coming battle.

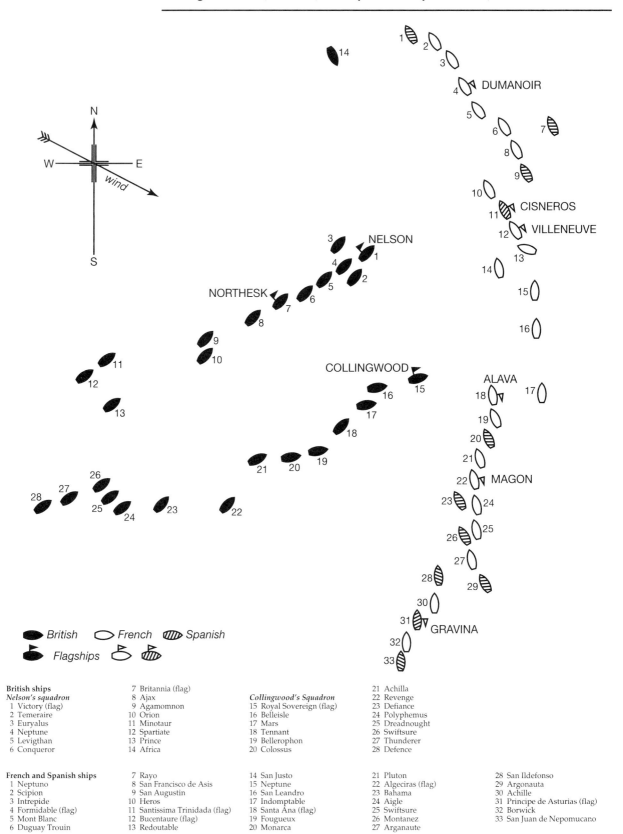

British ships

Nelson's squadron
1 Victory (flag)
2 Temeraire
3 Euryalus
4 Neptune
5 Levigthan
6 Conqueror

7 Britannia (flag)
8 Ajax
9 Agamomnon
10 Orion
11 Minotaur
12 Spartiate
13 Prince
14 Africa

Collingwood's Squadron
15 Royal Sovereign (flag)
16 Belleisle
17 Mars
18 Tennant
19 Bellerophon
20 Colossus

21 Achilla
22 Revenge
23 Defiance
24 Polyphemus
25 Dreadnought
26 Swiftsure
27 Thunderer
28 Defence

French and Spanish ships
1 Neptuno
2 Scipion
3 Intrepide
4 Formidable (flag)
5 Mont Blanc
6 Duguay Trouin

7 Rayo
8 San Francisco de Asis
9 San Augustin
10 Heros
11 Santissima Trinidada (flag)
12 Bucentaure (flag)
13 Redoutable

14 San Justo
15 Neptune
16 San Leandro
17 Indomptable
18 Santa Ana (flag)
19 Fougueux
20 Monarca

21 Pluton
22 Algeciras (flag)
23 Bahama
24 Aigle
25 Swiftsure
26 Montanez
27 Arganaute

28 San Ildefonso
29 Argonauta
30 Achille
31 Principe de Asturias (flag)
32 Borwick
33 San Juan de Nepomucano

■ Admiral Villeneuve's Plans

Admiral Villeneuve's strategy upon leaving the port at Cadiz was to sail westward toward the Cape of Trafalgar, and then south, and then eastward into the Mediterranean. In this way he hoped to elude the British fleet which he assumed was positioned just over the horizon out of Cadiz. However, he and his officers recognized the chances of getting away without a fight were not great. In light of that fact, there was strong reluctance on the part of some French and virtually all the Spaniards to leave Cadiz. They felt their men needed additional training, the weather appeared threatening, and the British could only grow weaker the longer they had to remain at sea in blockade.

Villeneuve likely recognized these very good reasons for staying in port. However, despite all the misgivings, Villeneuve ordered the fleet would put to sea on October 18th. This was likely in response to news he had received from friends at the French Ministry of Marine that Napoleon had appointed a new commander for the combined fleet, and he was on his way to take over. Villeneuve, in what might have been a vain attempt to salvage his career, decided to put to sea and perhaps at some point in the future achieve a victory which might restore his career.

■ The Battle

The battle unfolded more or less as Lord Nelson had envisioned it. The one feature of such engagements which may seem odd to the 20th century reader is the snail's pace at which events unfolded. While Villeneuve ordered his fleet out of Cadiz on October 18, it was not until the 21st that the battle was joined. Huge, lumbering sail-of-the-line moved very slowly and maneuvered very clumsily. As a result of this fact, once an admiral had committed his fleet to a particular strategy, his ability to make major alterations in terms of deployment of his fleet was very limited. In addition, given these ships were propelled by sail, things rarely went completely according to plan due to wind speed and direction. Once committed, an admiral had to rely upon the initiative of his individual captains and ships, something Nelson felt very good about doing.

One of the most notable actions Nelson took just prior to the engagement was to send a signal to the British fleet which subsequently became famous: "ENGLAND EXPECTS EVERY MAN WILL DO HIS DUTY." Though it sounds very patriotic and inspiring, it did not necessarily have that effect on the fleet. Many responded with comments such as "Have we not always done our duty?" His second in command, Admiral Collingwood, reacted to his old friend's signal with the response that everyone in the fleet knew what was expected of them that day. Nevertheless, cheers went up from the fleet, and the signal became the stuff of legend. The next signal was the last Nelson ever sent his fleet, and remained atop the *Victory* until it was shot away: "CLOSE ACTION AND KEEP IT UP."

A little before noon on October 21st, 1805, Collingwood's flagship *Royal Sovereign* came under fire about half an hour before the *Royal Sovereign* could open up. However, when it did the results were devastating. One of Collingwood's trademarks was being able to deliver three well-placed broadsides in less than five minutes. It was something Collingwood drilled hard at, as did other commanders in the Royal Navy. At Trafalgar this gunnery skill proved very effective. At 12:24 Lord Nelson's flagship *H.M.S. Victory*, at the head of the other column, came under fire, and 15 minutes later it too was in position to open up with broadsides from its starboard guns. From that point on the lead ships of both columns were engulfed in a vortex of cannon fire, smoke, and flame as they closed with the ships of the combined fleet.

Nelson's own behavior is worth a comment. When he came to his position on the quarter deck just prior to the action he was joined by Captain Hardy, his flagship commander, Captain Blackwood, the frigate commander, John Scott, his secretary, Alexander Scott, the ship's chaplain, and Dr. William Beatty, the ship's surgeon. Captain Blackwood encouraged his Lordship to accompany him to his frigate, which would be safer and would offer a better view. Nelson declined. Both Dr. Beatty and Captain Hardy suggested that perhaps his Lordship might not wear his customary uniform, which had four very distinctive stars of orders embroidered on the left breast, as it would make him a marked man for French snipers stationed high up in the riggings. Nelson agreed it was probably not the best idea to be wearing such a coat, but said it was too late to change it.

The battle became more or less the pell-mell, close-action, ship-to-ship fight Nelson had sought. Though, as mentioned earlier, the French and Spanish did not want for courage, after a couple of hours of fighting it became clear who was going to carry the day. By four o'clock the combined fleet had been for the most part either captured, destroyed, or forced to flee. Of the 33 sail-of-the-line which had left Cadiz, 11 made it back to Cadiz, four made for the Straits of Gibraltar, and 17 were demasted, of which 13 were in the hands of the British and one was ablaze. It had been the most successful afternoon in the history of the Royal Navy.

Shortly after the *Victory* engaged the enemy Nelson's secretary, who was standing near him, was decapitated by cannon fire, then Hardy was wounded in the foot. At about 1:15 in the afternoon, during the most severe fighting the *Victory* saw in the battle, Lord Nelson was still pacing the quarter deck with Captain Hardy. At that time a French sniper's bullet entered the upper left breast of Lord Nelson, traveling downward through his lung and breaking his spine. He was taken below where it was determined his wounds were mortal. The *Victory's* log book contained the following entry by its commander: "Partial firing continued until 4:30. When a victory having been reported to the Right Honourable Lord Viscount Nelson, K.B. and Commander-in-Chief, he then died of his wounds."

THE BATTLE'S CONSEQUENCES

In the days following October 21st additional British fleet action led to additional enemy ships being captured, and the totality of the Royal Navy's success was made all the greater. The results gave Britain undisputed supremacy at sea, which lasted into the 20th Century, when it was supplanted by the U.S. Navy. England and France never again fought a major sea battle, and Napoleon's range of operations was thereafter confined to the continent of Europe. In 1808, three years after Trafalgar, Spain became embroiled in a popular uprising against its monarchy which was installed by Napoleon. The British sent troops to Spain under the command of Sir Arthur Wellesley, later Duke of Wellington, to support the rebels. The French also sent in troops. Napoleon, having given up on any conquests off the European continent, went on to defeat the Russian-Austrian alliance and then invaded Russia in 1812. He was forced to retreat from Russia and, after several years of fighting, Wellesley evicted the French from Spain and launched an attack on France. In 1814 Britain, along with its allies Austria, Russia, Prussia, Sweden, and Portugal, defeated Napoleon under Sir Arthur Wellesley. Napoleon escaped from exile on the island of Elba and returned to France to attempt a comeback. Wellesley, then Duke of Wellington, and his allies again defeated Napoleon at Waterloo, and he was once again sent into exile.

For the commanders at Trafalgar, the battle represented closure of both men's lives. Lord Nelson's remains returned to London for one of the most elaborate state funerals in England's history. The body was taken from the *Victory* and transported up the Thames River by a column of barges. When it reached the Admiralty, the body lay in state overnight. On January 9, 1806, Nelson's coffin, made from the wood of the mast of a captured French ship, was borne in a processional so long that its head reached St. Paul's Cathedral before its end departed the Admiralty. Over 10,000 soldiers marched along with over 30 flag officers and 100 captains of the Royal Navy. At the end of the four-hour service, as the coffin was being lowered into its crypt in St. Paul's, Sir Isaac Heard recited the various titles held by Lord Nelson, and then concluded "the hero who in the moment of victory fell, covered with immortal glory."

For Admiral Villeneuve, the results were quite different. He and his flagship were captured at Trafalgar. He was taken to England as a prisoner of war, but was allowed to attend Nelson's funeral. In the spring of 1806 he was paroled and returned to France. On April 22, 1806, anticipating court martial, he committed suicide in Rennes, France.

As might be expected, in the decades following Trafalgar tacticians of various navies have studied the battle for lessons which might have general application. However, the lesson which emerges is that Lord Nelson knew his ships and men, knew his enemy, and designed a strategy which was likely to work in only that one moment in history. His genius in all his battles was recognizing the uniqueness of the circumstances and acting accordingly. Perhaps Nelson's only lasting contribution to naval warfare was to recognize there were no strategies which were always appropriate.

REFERENCES

Aldington, Richard. *The Duke: Being an Account of the Life and Achievements of Arthur Wellesley, First Duke of Wellington*. New York: Viking Press, 1943.

Aubry, Octave. *Napoleon: Soldier and Emperor*. New York: J. B. Lippincott Company, 1938.

Ballard, Colin R. *Napoleon, An Outline*. New York: Books for Libraries Press, 1971.

Carr, Albert. *Napoleon Speaks*. New York: Viking Press, 1941.

Castelot, Andre. *Napoleon*. New York: Harper and Row Publishing, 1968.

Corbett, Julian Stafford, Sir. *The Campaign of Trafalgar*. New York: Longmans, Green, 1910.

Fournier, August. *Napoleon I, Volume I*. New York: Henry Holt and Company, 1913.

Pocock, Tom. *Horatio Nelson*. London: Pimlico, 1994.

Walder, David. *Nelson*. New York: The Dial Press, 1978.

General Electric Fires Ed Russell

Joseph Wolfe, University of Tulsa

Joann Babiak, University of Tulsa

Internet site of interest: **www.ge.com**

L ooking back Ed Russell remembers how quickly and quietly it was done. He was summoned from his headquarters in Worthington, Ohio by his boss and GE Plastics Senior Vice President Glen Hiner on November 11, 1991 to ostensibly attend a budget revision meeting at division headquarters in Pittsfield, Massachusetts. After being ushered into Hiner's office and exchanging a few obligatory pleasantries Hiner handed over a letter telling Ed he was being discharged immediately as Vice President and General Manager of General Electric Superabrasives (GES). To soften the blow and extend executive courtesies his $190,000 salary, an $85,000 incentive compensation award, the company's life insurance policy worth more than $750,000, and company health benefits and privileges, which included a 1990 XJS Jaguar costing GE $1,168.57 per month, would continue for one year unless he found another job beforehand. He was then put on a company jet and told to return immediately to Worthington and clear out his office. As Ed Russell recalled, "The whole thing took 15 minutes."

Thus ended a once-brilliant 18-year career at General Electric built on many successes as well as the eye and approval of Jack Welch, GE's often-feared but greatly respected CEO. Although in a state of shock Ed did not believe he was fired for the reasons given by Glen Hiner which were poor performance, incompetence, and possessing the "wrong values". Instead he felt he was fired for not going along with an industrial diamond price-fixing scheme hatched between his boss and the giant diamond firm of DeBeers or helping to cover-up fraudulent behavior and malfeasance by executives forced into his division by Hiner. In an attempt to get back his job and to salvage his reputation he filed a civil action suit on April 21, 1992 claiming wrongful termination in violation of Ohio's whistleblower statute, Ohio Rev. Ann. Code §4113.52 as well as contacting the Federal Bureau of Investigation and aiding in a Justice Department investigation of price-fixing and collusion between GE and DeBeers.

Russell's lawsuit opened a Pandora's box of alleged corporate wrongdoing. These wrongs were brought to light through his use of the media and included reports of a long line of unsavory, illegal, and sensational activities conducted in the industrial diamond industry. One activity was a "stock parking" scheme conducted between General Electric and the Mitsui Company to falsely inflate the earnings of GE Plastics (GEP). Another included Operation Tailhook-like activities perpetrated by various executives at sales conventions and business trips. One final revelation was collusion between GE and DeBeers to destroy a South Korean entrant in the industrial diamond industry. In this effort Henry Kissinger's political influence was also brought to bear.

For its part General Electric felt Russell's charges were "pure nonsense." John Beatty, a lawyer representing GE said Ed Russell "never blew any whistles at all, and we think we can prove it. Even if he did, that's not why he was fired. He was fired for very, very poor performance. We look forward to the trial and are confident it will show that Mr. Russell was discharged due to significant performance issues." Even though GE felt it was blameless in the matters revealed by Russell it began to spend about $1 million a month to defend itself and its executives. GE responded to his allegations by claiming that Russell himself, through various actions during and after his employment, was guilty of a number of transgressions. These were identified as:

1. Breach of fiduciary duty
2. Breach of employee duty of loyalty
3. Breach of an Employee Innovation and Proprietary Information Agreement
4. Violation of Ohio Revised Code §133.51(c) and §1333.81 and misappropriation of confidential information
5. Unjust enrichment

As Russell's February 21, 1994 trial date neared GE faced an on-going Justice Department investigation, three shareholder suits and three class action suits related to his disclosures. GE also had to absorb the ill-will created by the large volume of stories appearing in both the popular and business press as well as an hour-long PBS "Frontline" documentary on collusion in the diamond industry featuring a segment on Russell himself. Additionally the "turnaround" skills and management methods of Jack Welch as GE's CEO, as well as the morals and honesty of many of Russell's former business associates, have been questioned. To many people it is a David and Goliath story with Russell being a lone and courageous individual who was treated unfairly and has taken his story public. Others believe, however, this lawsuit is merely a ploy to improve his severance package. Because Ed's final termination is effective a few months before his 55th birthday he does not receive those superior pension and insurance benefits attached to that retirement age. GE's Cincinnati-based lawyers are even more direct by stating Russell was using his lawsuit "to leak selected documents to the press or others in an effort to extort a settle-ment."

NATURAL AND MAN-MADE DIAMONDS

Natural diamonds are lumps of carbon transformed by intense heat and pressure into the world's hardest (10 on the Mohs hardness scale) and oldest material, formed as long as 3.3 million years ago. These diamonds, sometimes known as "boart" or black diamonds, are forged from carbon deep in the earth's magma. At that depth, which can reach 300 miles, the heat is extreme. The material's heat causes it to expand and the resulting pressure drives it through fissures and cracks to the earth's surface. In the process it produces a very long volcanic shaft often called a pipe. On its travels the shaft's diameter is relatively narrow and varies in its thickness from less than one mile to as little as a few yards. This varying diameter creates an additional pressure source on the carbon material as it rises.

While the public's perception is that diamonds are rare and difficult to find more than 3,000 pipes, of which only 50 or 60 have ever been worked, exist in South Africa, the world's greatest diamond-producing area. Moreover diamonds are found throughout the world. Most recently they have been discovered in Canada's Northwest Territories south of the Arctic Circle. Exhibit 1 summarizes various estimates of the world's supply of diamonds for the year 2000 by country.

Since the early 1980s the world's natural diamond output has doubled and is now about 100 million carats (one carat equals 1/142 ounce avoirdupois or 200mg) a year. Of this production more than half are not gem quality. Gemstones have few flaws or inclusions such as tiny bubbles, hairline cracks, feathers, clouds or specks of uncrystallized carbon. They possess a clear, white or near-white color on a 23 grade color scale of D (colorless) to Z (yellow) and are large enough in their boart state to yield a product that can be sold profitably after grinding and polishing. A stone with many inclusions, or one that possesses a yellowish color or a size that is too small to profitably cut and polish, is termed "industrial grade". While this diamond grade is inferior as an ornament or object of beauty it possesses great utilitarian value as a grinding, sanding or boring material. In this application industrial diamonds minimize tool wear, allow precision cutting and reduce production down-time needed for tool replacement. These diamonds are also used in machine tools as boring bits, grinding wheels and cutting tools as well as for stone cutting and in cement construction for cutting and finishing poured concrete. Current applications of industrial diamond material include toolstones, die stones, drilling bits, grinding wheels, saw blades, electronics, chemical processings, medical technology, and military technology. Approximately 90% of all industrial diamond material are used for grinding wheels and saw blades.

The importance of industrial diamonds has increased dramatically over the years as manufacturing processes have become faster and more precise. In the 1930s about 25,000 carats of industrial diamonds were consumed while by the late-1960s this consumption had increased one thousand fold. With this rapid increase the demand for industrial diamonds outstripped nature's supply which accelerated research into the production of man-made diamonds. In the 1800s scientists had tried to produce synthetic diamonds and these efforts were intensified after World War II as advanced technologies were brought into play. In 1951 GE began its research into the development of synthetic diamonds but several problems had to be solved.

Exhibit 1   **Estimated Natural Diamond Production in Carats by Major Producing Nations for the Year 2000**

Country	Low	Best	High
Angola	700	2,500	5,000
Australia	35,000	37,000	41,000
Botswana	11,000	17,000	20,000
Brazil	300	700	2,500
Central African Republic	400	500	600
Commonwealth of Independent States	11,000	16,000	19,000
Ghana	300	350	600
Guinea	250	450	700
Indonesia	100	400	500
Ivory Coast	200	250	500
Liberia	100	200	400
Nimibia	500	900	1,200
Peoples Republic of China	500	1,000	2,000
Tanzania	50	125	200
Sierra Leone	250	400	650
South Africa	6,550	9,750	12,000
Venezuela	350	500	600
Zaire	16,000	24,000	27,000
Other and Illicit Sources	450	575	1,550
Total	84,000	112,600	136,000

Source: Cited in Peter Harben and Richard Nötstaller, "Diamonds- Scintillating Performance in Growth and Prices," *Industrial Minerals* (March 1991), p. 43.

The process G.E. ultimately developed in 1954 was able to create 60 to 70 tons of industrial diamonds per year. GE began to market its synthetic diamonds shortly thereafter and by 1957 large quantities were available. They were also superior to natural diamonds as they were easily cut and shaped due to their uniform size, quality and friability.

In the late 1970s GE's patents for its high temperature-high pressure technology expired but this fact did not open the industry to new competitors. Beginning in the late-1950s GE and DeBeers had entered into a series of patent cross-licensing agreements that made it extremely difficult for other companies to enter the synthetic diamond business. During this time GE had also made DeBeers the sole licensee of its patented technology. Today the industrial diamond market consumes about 250 million carats a year of which over 80% of these carats are synthetic or man-made and in 1992 worldwide sales were about $600 million with GE and DeBeers sharing about 80% of those sales.

DEBEERS, ANGLO AMERICAN AND THE DIAMOND CARTEL

The DeBeers diamond cartel and the myriad operations and cross-ownerships which support the combine, has a rich and varied history. In 1871 a South African farmer named DeBeers sold his rich diamond mine, the Kimberly claim, to Cecil John Rhodes and the Rhodes family. Nine years later the Rhodes amalgamated their numerous mine claims to form DeBeers Consolidated Mines with financial backing by the English Rothschilds. This new entity soon formed a trust to control the supply of diamonds and ultimately their prices. This was done by acquiring each and every start-up mining company upon its formation. At that time these companies were constantly forming because of the great availability of diamond lodes in South Africa, the site of the world's most numerous kimberlite pipes and alluvial diamond fields.

Cecil John Rhodes died in 1901 and was eventually succeeded by Ernest Oppenheimer of Friedberg, Germany who had a major interest in the Premier Diamond Mining Company of South Africa. Oppenheimer then bought control of Consolidated Mines Selection and used Consolidated to purchase some of the country's richest gold fields and to persuade other German landowners to merge with him. In 1917 the Oppenheimers formed the Anglo American Company to obtain money from J.P. Morgan and other American bankers and mining companies. Because of the rampant anti-German sentiment found in the United States during World War I the name Anglo American was chosen to disguise the company's true German background.

Ernest Oppenheimer, through the Anglo American company, acquired highly productive diamond fields in German Southwest Africa (now Namibia) in 1920. This new supply of diamonds allowed Anglo American to break the monopoly over the supply of diamonds held by DeBeers. Anglo American subsequently took control of DeBeers and restored monopoly conditions in 1929.

When World War II ended in 1945 Anglo American and DeBeers extended its controls to gold mining and by 1958 it became South Africa's largest producer. The company is also one of the world's largest producers of coal, uranium and copper and it expanded its interests into industrial diamonds and finance in the 1960s and 1970s. Anglo American's holdings have also been shifted as it adjusts to new sources in the world's supply of diamonds and other mineral wealth. When knowledge of diamond discoveries in the USSR arrived in the west in the 1950s DeBeers approached its government officials. DeBeers now has exclusive sales rights to all uncut gems found in Russia's Siberian mines.

Botswana is also a major producer of diamonds in terms of value. Diamond production in this country is in the hands of the DeBeers Botswana Mining Co. (Debswana) which is a 50/50 partnership between DeBeers Consolidated Mines Ltd. and the Botswana government. Debswana also owns 5% of DeBeers and accordingly is represented on its board of directors. In Tanzania diamonds are obtained from the Williamson mine which has received a capital infusion of $6.3 million by its joint owners, the Tanzanian State Mining Corporation and DeBeers. A listing of the vast Anglo-American DeBeers holdings is provided in Exhibit 2.

While these entities mainly control the supply of diamonds Anglo American also controls their demand through various marketing and distribution operations. The sale of gemstones is directed through various selling organizations and those who are dependent upon them—the Central Selling Organization,

Exhibit 2   **Selected Anglo American Affiliates and Operations**

Affiliate/Operation	Activity
Amic	Holding company for Anglo American's manufacturing, forestry and timber products interests
Amquip Ltd.	Manufacturer of construction mining and material handling equipment
Anglo American Coal Corp. Ltd.	Coal mining and export
Anglo American Farms Ltd.	Grain, produce, meat and wine production
Anglo American Industrial Corp. Ltd.	Steel, automobiles, paper and chemicals
Anglo American Gold Investment Co. Ltd.	Investments in diamond and metals mining
Anglo American Property Services Ltd.	Real estate property management
Anamint	Diamond trading
Boart International Ltd.	Suppliers of drilling equipment and services
DeBeers Centenary AG	Gem and diamond brokers
DeBeers Central Selling Organization	Marketing of gem and industrial diamonds
DeBeers Consolidated Mines Ltd.	Diamond mining and marketing
Johannesburg Consolidated Investment Co. Ltd.	Holding company for mining finances
Minorco	A Luxembourg-based holding company which owns 100% of Minorco U.S.A.
Rustenburg Platinum Holdings Ltd.	Platinum mining
South American Investments Ltd.	Mining and other investments in S. America
Vaal Reefs Exploration and Mining Co. Ltd.	Gold and uranium mining in South Africa
Western Deep Levels Ltd.	Gold and uranium mining in South Africa

Sources: A. Chai, A. Campbell and P. Spain (Eds.), *Hoover's Handbook of World Business. Austin, TX: Reference Press*, 1993, pp. 132-133 and 1994 *Directory of Corporate Affiliations*, Vol. VI. New Providence, NJ: Reed Reference Publishing Co., 1994, pp. 72-73.

The Diamond Corporation, The Diamond Purchasing and Trading Company (Purtra) and the Diamond Trading Company, its three "sights" found in London, Kimberley and Lucerne, Switzerland and about 150 "sightholders" who place their orders for diamonds through the brokers I. Hennig & Co. Ltd., W. Nagel, Bonas & Company Ltd., H. Goldie & Co. and J.P. Morgan. Industrial grade diamonds are sold by the Central Selling Organization through either Industrial Distributors (Sales) Ltd. or Diamond Product (Sales) Ltd. Industrial stones are sold directly to tool manufacturers but grits and powders are sold via authorized distributors with The Industrial Diamond Division handling the sales of DeBeers' natural and synthetic industrial diamonds. The supply share of industrial diamonds held by DeBeers was 57% in 1970, 61% in 1980, and is estimated to be 63% in 2000 (Harben & Nötstaller, 1991).

JACK WELCH, GENERAL ELECTRIC AND GENERAL ELECTRIC SUPERABRASIVES

General Electric ws America's fifth largest company with 1993 sales of $60.6 billion and profits of $4.3 billion and 274 manufacturing plants in 26 countries. Although it operates as a vast conglomerate dealing in the businesses of aircraft engines, household appliances, turbines and turbine generator sets, electric lamps, search and navigation equipment, electromedical equipment, plastics materials and resins and finance, its roots lie in Thomas Edison's invention of the light bulb in 1879. GE was established as a New York State corporation in 1892 from the merger of the Edison General Electric Company and the Thomson-Houston Company. Even though Edison left the company in 1894 his emphasis on research remained. By combining its strength with J.P. Morgan's backing, GE created one of the nation's first corporate research laboratories in 1900. A series of successful inventions and applications in the elevator, trolley car and home appliance industries followed and sales grew to $456 million in 1940, $2.6 billion in 1952 and $25 billion in 1980. Despite this phenomenal sales growth, however, GE's earnings had flattened and the company was considered an unwieldy and underachieving giant.

Into the picture stepped John (Jack) F. Welch, Jr. who had worked his way through GE via chemicals, components and consumer products. Given a need for change Welch acted quickly and was soon labelled "Neutron Jack" for the speed, impatience and abrasive methods he used to change the company. He jettisoned GE's air conditioning business in 1982, housewares and mining in 1984 and semiconductors in 1988 while concentrating on medical equipment, financial services and high-performance plastics and ceramics.In shedding these operations he had two guiding principles: fix, close, or sell all poorly performing operations and make the remaining ones first or second in their industries. Additionally Welch felt GE's culture had to change. In a letter to GE's stockholders in 1990 Welch stated the 1990s-style leader must learn to delegate, facilitate, listen and trust. This leader must also cast aside those personal insecurities that support the walls of parochialism, status-seeking and the "functionalitis" found in rigid bureaucracies. To impress these ideas on GE's management team and to insure flexible, creative responses to business opportunities and to create a boundaryless organization, the company created the management values statement found in Exhibit 3 after conducting many "think sessions" throughout all management levels.

Although Welch sold off many of GE's operations he also acquired a number of high-performance ventures. In 1986 the Employers Reinsurance Company was acquired for $1.1 billion and the National Broadcasting Company (NBC) was obtained for $6.4 billion. One year later GE swapped its consumer electronics division for Thomson of France's CGR Medical Equipment unit. GE's most recent acquisition, the investment banking firm of Kidder, Peabody, was completed in 1990.

Today's GE is a much different company from the one Jack Welch came to head in 1981. Since becoming CEO he has sold $12 billion in GE businesses and bought $26 billion more. At the beginning of his tenure GE's only market leaders were lighting, motors and power systems and only aircraft engines and plastics were truly global. Today 11 of its 12 business groups are first or second in their markets with the 12th one, NBC, the 16 subject of much divestment

Exhibit 3   **General Electric's Management Values**

G.E. MANAGEMENT VALUES

G.E. leaders, always
with unyielding integrity:

Create a clear, simple, reality-based, customer-focused vision and
are able to communicate it straightforwardly to all constituencies.

Set aggressive targets, understanding accountability and
commitment, and are decisive.

Have a passion for excellence, hating bureaucracy and all the
nonsense that comes with it.

Have the self-confidence to empower others and behave in a
boundaryless fashion. They believe in and are committed to Work-Out
as a means of empowerment and are open to ideas from anywhere.

Have, or have the capacity to develop, global brains and global
sensitivity and are comfortable building diverse global teams.

Stimulate and relish change and are not frightened or
paralyzed by it, seeing change as opportunity, not threat.

Have enormous energy and the ability to energize and invigorate
others. They understand speed as a competitive
advantage and see the total organizational benefits
that can be derived from a focus on speed.

Source: Reprint from "Turning Soft Values Into Hard Results," *Leaders Magazine,* Vol. 16, No. 4 (October, November, December 1993), p. 4.

discussion. When Welch took over business units, they typically had 9 to 11 management levels between the CEO and the line worker. Now there are 4 to 6 levels and it has 229,000 employees, of which about 45.0% came aboard since 1981, compared to 412,000 in 1981.

Because of GE's dramatic changes and the energy and creativity Jack Welch brought to the situation he has often drawn great admiration from the business press and fellow executives. Jack Welch was *Chief Executive* magazine's CEO of the year in 1993. This was a dramatic turnaround from his role as the most infamous SOB of the 1980s and the person *Fortune* magazine once labelled America's toughest boss. Now that some of GE's major changes have been accomplished Welch talks of "soft" values such as nurturing, openness and caring. He also believes, however, the only appropriate answer to bad leadership is to "take them out [and] clear the forest" so the company's real team players can excel.

Jack Welch started his GE career in plastics and he naturally takes a special interest in this business and the people it employs. Its current top executives include Gary Rogers, President and CEO of GE Plastics, Maura J. Abeln-Touhey, V.P. and General Counsel, Robert H. Brust, V.P. of Finance, and John Blystone, V.P. for GE Superabrasives. GE Plastics currently manufactures high-performance engineered plastics used in automobiles, computer housings and other business equipment, ABS resins, silicones, man-made diamonds and laminates. Its 1992 sales were $4.9 billion and its 1993 sales were $5 billion with respective operating profits of $740 and $834 million. Future expansions are

Exhibit 4

**GE Plastics and Superabrasives Income and Operating Profits
(In millions of dollars)**

	1990	*1991*
Revenue:		
GE Superabrasives	$ 268.8	$ 281.4
Other materials	4,871.2	4,662.6
Total revenue	5,140.0	4,944.0
Cost of Goods Sold:		
GE Superabrasives	211.8	213.6
Other materials	3,918.2	3,675.4
Total COGS	4,130.0	3,889.0
Operating Profit:		
GE Superabrasives	57.0	67.8
Other materials	953.0	987.2
Total profit	$1,010.0	$1,055.0

Sources: General Electric 1993 *Annual Report,* p. 35 and court depositions.

planned as it recently bought a commercial resin business in Mexico as well as conducting a joint venture in that country. It is also completing the construction of a compounding facility in India and will shortly begin constructing another compounding facility in Singapore. Exhibits 4 and 5 respectively present simplified income statements for GE Plastics and the General Electric Corporation.

While obtaining these financial results GE has been a leader as a corporate citizen and it has received many awards for its accomplishments as a socially responsible company. Amongst its many recognition awards GE earned Harvard University's George S. Dively Award for Corporate Public Initiative in 1990 for the involvement of GE volunteers in nationwide education programs. The National Science Foundation presented its first National Corporate Achievement Award to the GE Foundation in 1992 for its support of minority students, faculty and professionals in science, engineering and mathematics. In 1993, GE, the GE Foundations and GE employees contributed almost $68 million to support education, the arts, the environment and human services organizations worldwide. Additional support for many other community projects came from volunteer help given by GE employees. These efforts entailed hundreds of thousands of labor hours. Last, based on the "College Bound" program GE created in 1989, the company was awarded the President's Volunteer Action Award in 1994. This is a program that has doubled the number of college students coming from selected poor and inner-city schools in 12 cities where GE has major facilities.

Exhibit 5   **General Electric Financial Highlights**
                       (In millions of dollars)

	1993	1994	1995
Revenues	$60,562.0	$57,073.0	$54,629.0
Earnings before accounting changes	5,177.0	4,725.0	4,435.0
Net earnings	$ 4,315.0	$ 4,725.0	$ 2,636.0
Dividends declared	$ 2,229.0	$ 1,985.0	$ 1,808.0

Source: *General Electric 1993 Annual Report*, p. i.

ED RUSSELL'S FALL FROM GRACE

Ed Russell joined GE in April 1974 after graduating at the top of his MBA class at Columbia University's Business School. Earlier he had received a Bachelor of Science degree in Chemical Engineering from Worchester Polytechnic Institute. His first GE assignment was as manager of its Group Strategic Planning and Review Operation at corporate headquarters in Fairfield, Connecticut. In this capacity he managed the strategic planning process for the company's $1.4 billion Consumer Products Group. Two years later Russell became Vice President and General Manager of GE's Gesamex Lamp division and was responsible for the manufacture and sale of lighting products in Mexico. In 1978 he became manager of GE International Lighting. In this position Ed headed a 5,000 person operation with manufacturing sites in Brazil, Chile, Philippines, Turkey, Venezuela and Canada. GE International Lighting was also in charge of exporting all lighting products produced by GE's American factories. Under Russell's supervision the division's sales increased 47.4% while earnings rebounded from a $3 million loss to a $20 million profit.

On April 1, 1986 Ed became General Manager of GE Superabrasives and was later made a Vice President and corporate officer of the same unit in early-1990, one of only 127 such officers in GE. In addition to the promotion he also received a personal note from Jack Welch saying "Congratulations on the wonderful job you are doing. I am so pleased for and proud of you. This is a hard-earned, well-deserved promotion." When Russell joined GES it had 2,000 employees with manufacturing facilities in Worthington, Ohio and Dublin, Ireland. Under his command sales rose to $70 million in 1989 from only $16.5 million in 1986 and its actual return-on-sales consistently exceeded budgeted returns as shown in Exhibit 6.

Unfortunately for Russell's long-term career aspirations GES was placed within the GE Plastics Group under the direction of Glen H. Hiner in September, 1986. Over time Hiner proceeded to place his own people in key GES positions and a culture and value clash erupted almost immediately. Russell would later write a memo stating Hiner's people lacked "mid-America values and

Exhibit 6   **GE's Actual vs. Budgeted Return-on-Sales**

	Return on Sales	
Year	Budgeted	Actual
1986	$10.0	$16.5
1987	20.0	30.5
1988	30.0	50.0
1989	50.0	70.0
1990*	54.0	57.0
1991	43.0	n.a.

*In this year the GE Plastics Group switched from annual budgets to periodically revised operating plans. This planning system was later discarded.

Source: Civil Case filing C-1-92-343, April 21, 1992, Vol. 1, pp. 9–10.

work ethics and for the most part are heavy drinking womanizers, expense-account cheats [and are] the pond scum of American industry." Those individuals included Pieter Rens, GES International Sales Manager; Jay Ferguson, GES Finance Manager; Peter Foss, GES Marketing Manager; Steve Palovchik, GES International Sales Manager.

Hiner also made a number of decisions with which Russell disagreed. Some decisions adversely affected the costs and profitability of Russell's operation, other decisions frustrated Ed's product development ambitions and other decisions and actions supported Ed's feelings that Hiner possessed an improper tolerance for moral improprieties or condoned and rewarded outright illegal activities.

In 1988 Glen Hiner installed a new overhead allocation system in GEP. Under this system the entire division's costs became intermingled. Russell quickly found the system favored those with high costs by shifting some of their expenses to the more profitable divisions, such as GES, which had either controlled or cut their costs. Especially irksome to Ed as a cost item was a $3 million annual charge allocated to GES to pay "maintenance" fees for a questionable "stock parking" scheme created by Hiner to inflate GEP's profits. In this plan, which was not approved by GE's accountants, GE Plastics sold the stock it had acquired in the Asahi Diamond Industrial Co. to Mitsui & Company, one of Japan's largest trading houses, for $80 million and an approximate $41 million paper profit in 1989. By doing this GEP's earnings were artificially inflated to offset a $115 million third quarter deficit. As part of the arrangement GE agreed to repurchase the stock at its original price while paying Mitsui an annual carrying charge fee of $3 million. Mitsui's letter of agreement acknowledged GE's corporate accountants opposed putting the buy-back arrangement in writing:

> Mitsui's basic stance is to keep shares of Asahi Diamond on our side at your strong request until when you will be in a position to buy back shares from us. . . . Under any circumstances, our extra costs for this transaction should be fully borne by GE.

In defending its actions GE contended Russell never objected to parking stock until his operation's results started to deteriorate. Jack Welch said he did not know of the affair until meeting with Ed to discuss Superabrasive's performance. "The way it came up as I recall, is that Mr. Russell was describing why he was having these numbers problems and one of the elements of his numbers problems was a charge to carry this stock." Supposedly surprised by this revelation Welch got mad but denies he was mad at Russell himself or sought revenge. "I was angry with our naivete, in my view, in being hooked into the 'courtesy' with the Japanese." Russell also alleged that Welch offered Mitsui a China distributorship rather than having to buy back the Asahi stock which had fallen in value over the interim period. GE corporate spokesperson Joyce Hergenhan says the charge about Welch's offer was "absolutely, categorically untrue. During the course of a general business meeting in Fall 1991 Jack Welch told Mitsui that they owned the Asahi stock and would have to live with its market fluctuations."

In another matter Russell claimed Hiner suppressed his plan to get GE into the gemstone business for fear of upsetting DeBeers and endangering other agreements made between them. This indicated to Ed that collusive activities or agreements existed between Hiner and DeBeers executives.

Since May 1970 GE had possessed the technology for making gemstone quality artificial diamonds. The technology, however, was too expensive to operate and produced gemstones that were not price-competitive with DeBeers' natural diamonds. Throughout 1988 and 1989 General Electric R&D teams under Russell's management worked on process improvements. These efforts were successful in mid-1990 and produced uniform artificial gemstones which could be cut and polished easily and cheaply. This process improvement, as stated by Russell, produced diamonds for "several hundred dollars per carat as opposed to current prices of several thousands of dollars per carat for natural gemstone diamonds." To merchandise these diamonds Ed met with the Swarovski family, owners of a number of Austrian jewelry stores, to sell 2-3 carat-sized blue-colored man-made diamonds. Hiner vetoed Russell's plan in January 1991 and all negotiations ceased with the Swarovskis. When asked for confirmation about Russell's story the Swarovski family refused to comment.

Hiner's actions on another occasion further indicated to Russell that collusion existed between GE and DeBeers. In the early-1990s the Iljin Corporation of South Korea was attempting to enter the industrial diamond industry. To accelerate its entry it hired-away from GE Chien-Min Sung, one of its key laboratory scientists who had deep knowledge of the artificial diamond growing process. While GE was suing Iljin in Boston's federal court for unfair trade practices, Russell contended it was also working with DeBeers to undermine Iljin's efforts by other methods. He says he warned Glen Hiner in August 1990 to not ask for DeBeers' cooperation "in restricting supplies of critical diamond equipment", namely tungsten carbide dies and anvils, to the Iljin Corporation. It appears GE took Iljin very seriously. Patricia A. Sherman, a top GE lawyer, said it was imperative the Iljin problem be solved as it had received "news this week that Iljin [had] captured three of GE's major customers in Korea, with estimated lost sales of up to $100,000 per month." GE's general counsel, Benjamin W. Heineman, characterized the company's battles with Iljin as "trench warfare". For additional troops in his war Heineman allegedly asked Henry Kissinger, who had been a GE consultant for many years and was about to visit

South Korea, to "sound very threatening about how this use of stolen information threatens" Seoul's relations with the United States and General Electric. Henry Kissinger through his consulting firm denied he pressured the Korean government and that he (1) merely advised GE on strategy with Iljin and (2) met with only a mid-level Korean official in GE's behalf.

Ed Russell also felt he was constantly stymied in his attempts to correct the illegal or questionable activities perpetrated by Hiner or various executives installed by him. In November 1987 he brought knowledge of a kickback scheme to Hiner's attention. This scheme involved European customers, GE's Pieter Rens and Sergio Sinigaglia, GES's Swiss distributor. Sinigaglia first added a "processing charge" to the price of the industrial diamonds. The European customer then payed the inflated price to Sinigaglia with half the processing charge going to him and the other half deposited in the customer's secret Swiss bank account. Under this scheme the customer's industrial diamond expenses were greater thereby reducing the firm's tax liability. The customer would also have a tax free source of personal income. A GE internal investigation of the scheme concluded it violated company policy No. 20.4 but Hiner did not take disciplinary action and instead promoted the sales manager and continued using the GE distributor. Hiner denies he promoted him and said he had "absolutely no knowledge" of a Swiss bank account scheme.

According to Russell, he discovered in November 1987 that Pieter Rens had met with the managing director of Diamant Boart, S.A., a Luxembourg industrial diamond company controlled by DeBeers, in an action which he believed was to fix industrial diamond prices. He reported this meeting to Hiner and the matter was investigated internally as a violation of Section 20.5 of GE's policies regarding antitrust activities as well as violating GE's antiapartheid policy No. 20.12 which prohibited all business with South African companies. In April 1988 Russell believed Rens again attempted to fix industrial diamond prices in the United States through European companies and reported the activity to Hiner for disciplinary action. Instead of disciplining him Hiner promoted him away from Russell's supervision and made him Managing Director of GE Plastics for France.

Russell was also extremely troubled by the immoral or wasteful and expensive behavior exhibited by various GE executives within GE Plastics. Although he did not complain about these activities he noted the following episodes perpetrated by various GE executives:

1. The violation of German Currency laws and company policy 20.4. This entailed the creation of a Swiss bank scheme through a GE Swiss Distributor.

2. The sexual harassment of a female secretary. This harassment ceased only when Glen Hiner transferred the male offender to Europe and only after it was feared the secretary's husband might get involved.

3. An executive with an on the job alcohol problem who drank continuously during his trip in Japan. When the executive returned from Japan he was drunk in the office and accused Russell and his wife of a 20.4 violation for trying to help the son of a Chinese employee. The charges against them were proven false but Russell considered this "the worst type of personal harassment." At the company's 1990 Florida sales meeting the same executive punched holes in the hotel's walls, threw beer bottles and sexually harassed female associates. $5,000 worth of damage caused by him was covered-up by falsifying company expense records. When this executive was in Russia he was drunk again and vomited

outside a government ministry while on a business call. Later, while sitting in a Russian hotel, he smashed a beer bottle as he threw it across its lobby.

4. An executive who on his trips to the Orient always stopped off in Bangkok to spend extended weekends with prostitutes at the best hotels. When he later left GE he handed over an expense bill that was almost $70,000. Other executives laughed it off as a good experience for him.

5. One executive took a $20,000 transfer allowance to move to Worthington but never moved and never payed back the allowance. This same executive was out all night and arrived at the office so drunk he was unable to prepare the exhibits for Russell's September 4, 1991 presentation to Jack Welch.

6. A salesman charged several hundred dollars worth of golf balls to his expense account. This person also obtained a temporary $20,000 loan from GE to join a local country club and only repaid $6,000 of the loan. This subordinate rolled over his expense account for amounts ranging $6000-$7000 to pay the mortgage on his house. By doing so he avoided the IRS rule that prohibited keeping loans out for more than six months.

7. A subordinate who uses the company's station wagon for personal use and has the company pay for its gasoline.

8. A senior vice president whose "lifestyle is one of incredible disgust. He conducts restructuring meetings at resorts such as Troutbeck. He keeps on the payroll a valet and 'companion'." While attending GES's 1989 sales meeting in Hawaii $200,000 was spent on various amenities. A "daily delivery of Tulips were flown in from Holland for his room, along with a specific type of pillow for his bed."

Ed's problems increased in late-1990 when his unit's profits dropped to $57.0 million and he was sometimes chided for his puritanical views and failure to recognize the importance of male bonding. The unit's climate seemed to deteriorate and in early 1991 Steve Palovchik went over Russell's head to complain about problems in GES. Hiner recalls "We had a private meeting in Pittsfield at which time Mr. Palovchik described to me a business in disarray and in what I would describe as a palace revolt that was under way in GE Superabrasives." Hiner immediately telephoned Jack O. Peiffer, GE Senior Vice President for Human Resources who enlisted Dr. Bradford D. Smart's aid. Smart is a well-known Chicago industrial psychologist and President of Smart & Associates, Inc. Peiffer told Dr. Smart that Russell was "in deep trouble job-wise. Some of his subordinates have gone above his head and have complained about his leadership style."

Brad Smart met with Russell in Chicago and provided him a report on April 29, 1991 listing a number of his strengths. Russell was characterized by such phrases as "very conscientious," "responsible," "very hard worker," "excellent analytic abilities," "accessible," "warm, supportive and caring," "takes responsibility for problems" and that he had "greatly improved the organization climate," had "particularly good relationships with hourly work force," and had "successfully implemented" GE programs. Smart, however, had previously issued a preliminary report on April 16, 1991 showing Russell in a different light based on interviews conducted with various GES staff members. Pieter Rens, Peter Foss, Jay Ferguson and Steve Palovchik told him Russell was "totally lacking in strategic vision or leadership capabilities". They "also expressed deep concern about Mr. Russell's sometimes violent temper, viewing him as a 'loaded cannon'." On a leadership scale of 1 to 10 with "10" being the highest rating, Russell's subordinates rated him a "3." Based on his assessment of the situation Smart thought Russell "could be fired at any moment".

While problems within GES were slowly leaking out two unimpressive and troublesome strategy analysis briefings Russell made to Jack Welch and his group of senior executives appeared to seal his fate. Ed's first damaging presentation was in early-April 1991 at GE's Pittsfield headquarters attended by Welch, Dennis Dammerman, GE's Senior Vice President for Finance and other GE officials.

During the meeting Dammerman questioned Russell at length about problems with MBS diamonds. Ed tried to reassure them by saying everything was "fine" and that events were "under control". However, after Ed left the meeting Dammerman told Welch "That son of a gun lied to us. He sat here and lied about what's happening out there." Dammerman told Welch things were not fine at all. Uncertain about Russell or GES's situation Welch sent Robert Nelson, GE Vice President for Financial Analysis, to Worthington to make an on-site evaluation. Nelson remembers Welch saying his investigation should be "along the lines of, 'Can we get a handle on what the numbers look like out there? What's happening in inventories? Sniff around and see what's going on.'" He also had the impression Welch believed Russell had been untruthful during his strategy session.

Ed's second and final top management presentation was held on September 4, 1991. After that meeting during his helicopter ride back to headquarters Jack Welch Faxed a note to Hiner saying he had until the end of the year to fire Ed. In a follow-up memo written to Glen Hiner Welch said in part ". . . Russell has to go. He made a fool of himself in July (sic), and yesterday, he appeared totally out of it. Imagine a presentation to you and I, and [Russell] had no numbers and more importantly knew none." Russell also appeared unable to answer Welch's questions. "I was probing him, questioning him, and he wasn't giving me anything but air." Welch also said Russell's responses were vague "50,000 feet, high altitude" answers and that he brushed over the problems in MBS diamonds. In total Russell "didn't get to the heart of the problem, which was DeBeers, DeBeers' quality, DeBeers' yields [of MBS diamonds] . . . He didn't understand the seriousness and the magnitude of the issues we were trying to deal with."

By October 1991 rumors where swirling through GES's offices that Ed was going to be fired. The rumors obtained greater credence for Ed when his secretary, Denise Maurer, told him Peter Foss was telling people that Russell would be replaced by Gene Nesbeda, a GE Plastics man. Nesbeda had accompanied Hiner on his last trip to London to meet with DeBeers representatives and was known to be house-hunting in near-by Columbus, Ohio. With this news on his mind Ed dictated a "Fellow GE Associates" letter on his Lanier dictating machine in the late afternoon of October 30, 1991. In that letter Ed outlined his feelings about the situation while cataloging some of the problems he saw with the personnel he had to work with in recent years. After summarizing GES's accomplishments Ed cited events involving sexual harassment, expense account fraud, price-fixing schemes with DeBeers and anti-competitive actions. Of his relations with Glen Hiner Ed wrote:

> The problem has been, is, and will always be fundamental cultural differences with Glen Hiner and GE Plastics. In Glen's own words, we have always had a "chemistry" problem. GE Plastics' management team lacks the mid-America

values and work ethics, and for the most part, are heavy drinking womanizers; expense account cheats, who disregard property, etc. They are the pond scum of American industry. They are not honest. Integrity at GE Plastics is a oxymoron, and Jack Welch has looked the other way.

Later when Mrs. Maurer transcribed the Lanier cassette she was shocked over its contents and discussed them off the record with Christopher Kearney, a GES lawyer and personal friend. "I told him that Ed had written a document that was very damaging and that he was just in a state of mind that I was afraid that he was going to do something with it and I was very concerned about the people that were being attacked in this letter." Although Kearney asked to see the letter Maurer said "No" but instead discussed "Ed's state of mind at the time and just how he had been acting and just the chaos that was going on in our office." The letter was never circulated although Russell sent a copy of it for safekeeping to his brother-in-law in Seattle.

On November 11, 1991 Ed Russell was fired by GE and Glen Hiner thus beginning Ed's next battle. He was not replaced by Gene Nesbeda, however, but instead by John Blystone, another GE Plastics man.

THE WHISTLEBLOWER LAWSUIT

After considering his situation and how he was treated Ed contacted James B. Helmer Jr., a Cincinnati lawyer who had previously represented a number of other GE whistleblowers. One of his better-known plaintiffs was Chester Walsh, whose fraud allegations in the sale of jet engines to Israel led GE to admit to four criminal charges and the payment of $69.0 million in fines and penalties in 1992. Russell's trial was scheduled for February 21, 1994 in Cincinnati before U.S. District Judge Herman Weber. GE's lead attorney was Chicago lawyer Daniel Webb who, when he was a Justice Department lawyer, prosecuted Lt. Col. Oliver North. In his lawsuit, which sought either reinstatement in his job or reimbursement for lost pay and undetermined damages, Ed alleged that a conspiracy existed between Glen Hiner, various GE executives and DeBeers officials to fix high-grade industrial diamond prices and that he was wrongfully terminated for protesting these illegal activities.

To substantiate his allegations Russell disclosed that on July 23, 1991 Glen Hiner asked him to prepare a briefing paper for an upcoming London meeting, only one of a series of meetings Hiner had already had with DeBeers since 1989. Although Hiner instructed Ed to prepare a paper dealing with possible technological exchanges, Russell believed the meeting's real purpose was to discuss fixing prices on industrial diamonds. Hiner also told Russell to make only one copy of the paper and to have as few people as possible involved in its creation.

Although the document went through a number of drafts written by a team headed by Dr. Mark Sneeringer, GE Superabrasives Manager of Research and Development, Russell delivered it on September 3, 1991 to Glen Hiner as a one-page paper. In that briefing paper Russell claimed he had written a strong warning about the meeting's anti-trust implications and recommended the meeting not be held. Despite Russell's admonition Hiner and others from GE met with DeBeers officials on September 19, 1991. As proof that a price-fixing scheme emerged from the meeting Ed observed that after he was fired GES announced list-price increases of 12-15% on January 20, 1992. DeBeers followed with similar increases in February.

Many in the industry found the price hikes inexplicable and unjustified. Industrial diamond prices had fallen steadily since the mid-1950s and the demand for them was weak due to low demand for mining, automobile manufacturing and road cutting and oil drilling equipment. Elsewhere it was noted by Peter Bell, Vice President for Technology at Norton Inc., that industrial diamond prices should be falling, not rising. "Generally industrial prices follow gem prices, although not in a one-to-one manner. Gem prices are fairly low [now] because of the recession and the low inflation rate." In response to Russell's allegations and the industry's observations Brian Cullingworth, Director of Public Affairs at DeBeers' Industrial Diamond Division Pty said "Fierce competition characterizes the relationship between GE and DeBeers and any suggestion of price-fixing or other violations is absurd."

Under the requirements of the Ohio whistleblower statutes require an employee who claims he was wrongfully terminated because of his whistleblowing activity file "a written report that provides sufficient detail to identify and describe" a violation of a state or federal criminal statutes. See Appendix A for the relevant text of Ohio's whistleblower statutes. This requirement was created so the employer can respond to the employee's complaint by either (1) explaining why the employer feels its actions did not violate any relevant laws, or (2) rectifying the situation if the employee was correct and a crime had been committed or was about to be committed. The statute was also written this way to protect the employer from retaliatory lawsuits initiated by hostile ex-employees, or from fabricated claims of corporate wrongdoing for the litigant's personal gain and to guard against the plaintiff's selective recall. Accordingly the existence and contents of Ed Russell's briefing paper was a cornerstone to his whistleblower suit although he said the action warned against in the paper was only one of a long series of illegal actions perpetrated by GE executives.

Because Russell complied with Hiner's request to produce only one copy of the briefing paper, this document could not be appended to his brief as evidence of prior notification. Therefore as part of the lawsuit's discovery process he supoened the paper from GE. In a sworn deposition Hiner confirmed a copy of the paper existed and that it was in his trip folder at GE Plastics' headquarters. Unfortunately it could not be found by either Hiner, his secretary Louise E. Koval, or GE Executive Audit Manager Robert H. Swan who conducted a company-wide search from April-July 1992. In this search more than 20 GE auditors and lawyers were involved and more than 10,000 labor hours were expended. The search also covered several locations in the United States as well as foreign offices in Europe, the Far East and Saudia Arabia. As had been the case from the litigation's very beginning, GE pledged complete cooperation. Other evidence of its cooperative attitude can be seen from the following excerpt of an April 22, 1992 letter addressed to all GE employees from Maura Abeln-Touhey, GE Plastics General Counsel.

> The United States Department of Justice, in conjunction with the Federal Bureau of Investigation, is currently conducting an investigation into the Company's pricing practices in the superabrasives business and its sale of securities of the Asahi Diamond Industrial Company Ltd.
>
> The Company intends to cooperate fully with the government in this investigation by providing information requested by the government. Yesterday, the Company received a subpoena for documents from a Federal grand jury investigating

this matter. The subpoena calls for, among other things, documents relating to the production and sale of industrial diamonds in the United States and abroad, travel and expense records of Company executives, correspondence and memoranda relating to contacts with competitors and internal electronic mail dealing with these and related topics. Accordingly, it is essential that all documents, including electronic files, bearing on this matter be preserved, whether or not called for by the subpoena. Nothing that is conceivably relevant to this investigation should be destroyed, altered or removed.

The judge hearing the case was very concerned about this important paper's disappearance although the state's whistleblower law does not require the parties to preserve evidence of a written report describing the alleged violations.

When asked whether the briefing paper contained any warnings about antitrust implications Hiner could not recall whether the warning did or did not exist. He did recall that when Russell delivered the final briefing paper he did not mention any antitrust concerns he had about the DeBeers meeting.

In late-May 1992 a preliminary, a three page draft version of the briefing paper was discovered in Steve Palovchik's files. In commenting on the similarities between this draft and its final version Russell said "we took [the] first two pages, and we made them the last two pages of the memo . . . because page 1 and 2 are really just an appendix. The final briefing paper was three pages. It had a main page, which I called—was the one-page mail. It had these two things attached to it, which were perceived assets and DeBeers and GE." Because Mark Sneeringer was the person most involved in writing both versions of the paper his opinions and ideas about its creation and contents were solicited. As for why so few people should be involved in its drafting Sneeringer said "The knowledge that DeBeers and GE were considering this meeting was thought to be potentially harmful from the standpoint that customers, if they heard about it, may have a misperception as to the meaning of the meeting." Sneeringer also felt Russell "did not like the idea of the meeting as laid out [and was] planning to annunciate some of those risks in the briefing paper." Sneer-inger acknowledged, however, that Russell did not tell him to state warnings or cautions in the briefing paper about antitrust risks or concerns or of GE's violation of its policy regarding apartheid in South Africa.

In pre-trial proceedings Russell's lawyers suggested this document could also constitute a complaint and therefore fulfilled the Ohio whistleblower statute's requirements of prior notice. GE's lawyers immediately challenged the value of the draft paper on a number of grounds. Russell first said the final paper was three pages in length but later stated it contained one page with a two-page appendix to bring it into line with the only proof he had that he had warned GE in advance. Additionally, Mark Sneeringer swore the early draft's antitrust language was deleted from the final version delivered to Hiner. According to him the last version did not use the term antitrust and did not suggest a violation of the law. Given these ambiguities about the briefing paper's form and content and its importance to the whistleblowing case GE contended Russell "surely would either produce this mysterious briefing paper or be more specific about its contents if he could. His failure to do so amply demonstrates that he cannot honestly allege that he ever provided GE with a written report describing a violation of law before he was given a notice of termination."

GE DEFENDS ED'S FIRING

Despite the plaintiff's allegations about price-fixing and corporate wrong-doing GE steadfastly maintained it fired Russell for poor performance. As Jack Welch said in summarizing why he was fired, "In two words, poor performance." Welch became concerned about GES' operations and particularly Ed's management style. The CEO saw that inventory levels were rising although the end-user market was in a recession, the division's products were losing their technological edge to DeBeers and reports of a "palace revolt" had come to his attention through Jack Peiffer. Earlier in April 1991 Peter Foss reported that a technology gap existed in metal-bonding saw diamonds (MBS), the highest quality and most profitable synthetic diamond application with net profits of about 30% in 1989. "That's where DeBeers had taken the leadership position away from us. Our customers told us when I joined in 1990 that we had not been listening to them when they told us in the '80s that we needed to get our technology in shape and to improve our product line." In the high-quality MBS market segment Foss stated DeBeers had obtained more than 50% of the market while GE's share had fallen to less than one-third.

Word also came to Jack Welch that Russell's new wife Shirley Costantino, a former GES marketing executive whom he married in 1988, was masterminding the office and influencing business decisions. The situation was discussed by Welch and others during a performance review and Welch made a note to himself "Make sure his wife is out of the business equation." Commenting on this particular notation Welch commented "That's a pretty strong statement. I don't recall ever seeing this in an evaluation of any GE officer, to keep a family member out of the running of the business, in my 25 years in the business." Denise Maurer said the office staff called Russell's wife "Nancy Reagan" although Ed says statements about his wife's role are "gross exaggerations."

Even though Ed had been a rising star for many years at GE the company contended his performance began to fall shortly after his promotion to vice-president. It also maintained his firing should not have been a surprise as he had received many warnings his performance was below expectations. His incentive pay was reduced for 1990 and Russell recognized that a deficiency existed when he wrote to Hiner "I fully realize the bad miss we had in 1990." Hiner said he warned Ed as early as February 1991 that his performance was becoming even more unsatisfactory although he received a $15,000 raise five months later. In a meeting held on October, 23, 1991 Hiner told Russell he was "evaluating whether [he] could continue being [GES'] leader" and would soon let him know whether he was going to be replaced. Ed was also told at this time he had no support from his staff, his peers, or his customers. The interviews by Brad Smart were also cited as evidence of failures on Ed's part. Jack Peiffer said those interviews found "Mr. Russell was viewed by his subordinates as being untrustworthy, insecure, paranoid, indecisive, inconsistent, a poor communicator, and unproductive." Russell claimed, however, the negative comments came from three individuals forced on him by Hiner. These were also the people whose activities had troubled Russell regarding improper business practices.

Ed's credibility as a whistleblower was challenged by GE's contention that it had received no prior warning from Russell that its meeting with DeBeers was perceived by him to be unlawful. No copy of Russell's briefing memo was available to support his contention that he had emphatically warned Hiner about illegal activities. Russell also did not mention his anti-trust concerns to Hiner after the memo had been delivered and its draft version made only a passing mention of problems associated with theLondon meeting. Moreover, Russell certified in February 1990 he was unaware of any violations of GE's policy requiring compliance with antitrust laws. Jack Peiffer, who conducted Russell's exit interview, also noted he did not mention any unethical or illegal practices or violations of company policies at that time other than a complaint over expense reports. Ed claims, however, he reported violations of GE's policies Nos. 20.4, 20.5 and 20.12, as well as those of No. 30.3 during this interview. Additionally, on the evening Russell was fired Brad Smart spoke to him when he was back at his Worthington office. Although Smart did most of the talking and offered Russell his condolences, at no time during this call, or in any of his counseling sessions or other telephone conversations with Smart, did Russell express the fear he might be fired for protesting or reporting criminal misconduct by GE employees.

GE'S LEGAL BATTLES AND COURT EXPERIENCES

General Electric is no stranger to the world's courts. In this regard it is well-armed to defend itself. The corporation has a 435-lawyer in-house law department and also has at its disposal the lawyers from such law firms as Weil, Gotshal & Manges (500 lawyers in New York), Sidley & Austin (637 lawyers in Chicago), Davis, Polk & Wardwell (397 lawyers in New York) and Mayer, Brown & Platt (496 lawyers in Chicago). The law firms of Arnold & Porter (310 lawyers in Washington, DC) and Dinsmore & Shohl (125 lawyers in Cincinnati) work exclusively on the Edward Russell case. GE's legal department, under the guidance of Benjamin W. Heineman, Jr. has developed over the past six years the reputation for being one of the most formidable legal teams available. To obtain this repute he has hired lawyers away from some of the country's most prestigious law firms and they have been paid law-firm market rates or better. Heineman, whose vita includes a Rhodes scholarship, a Supreme Court clerkship, government posts and a private law partnership, earns $1.2 million a year from GE which makes him America's second highest paid corporate general counsel.

This legal team has had to defend GE quite often. In a case directly related to industrial diamond price-fixing the Kidder Concrete Cutting Co. and Kidder Building & Wrecking Co. filed a class action suit against both GE and DeBeers charging they have established artificially high prices for their industrial diamond products. Other cases have been international in scope. Herbert Steindler, a GE international sales manager, pleaded guilty to four felony counts involving a scheme to divert funds from defense contracts between GE and the Israeli government. The parties received seven-year prison terms and a $1.7 million forfeiture judgment. GE itself pleaded guilty and paid $69 million in fines and penalties to settle charges of conspiracy, money laundering and failing to make and keep accurate books and records. Through its own internal investigation GE fired a top executive and disciplined about 20 of the unit's high-level managers.

In another international military-related matter, a shareholder suit filed in January 1994 before the New York State Supreme Court is pending. This action entails charges of fraud and violations of the Foreign Corrupt Practices Act in connection with U.S. government-funded sales of military equipment to Egypt by GE's Aerospace unit. GE had sold the unit to the Martin Marietta Corporation in 1993 and the plaintiffs charge the sale's proceeds to GE were depressed due to the ongoing criminal investigation.

JUDGEMENT DAY ARRIVES

Amidst the vast number of claims and counterclaims and the assertions and denials made by all parties, truth must be determined and injustices rectified. To some great degree Russell has tried his case in the popular and business press but now the legal system must decide the legitimacy of his claims. Was Ed treated unfairly by GE and is he being punished by this huge conglomerate for standing up to criminal behavior? Does guilt lie within other parties at GE and the industrial diamond industry and what forces led to the collapse of Ed Russell's career?

APPENDIX A: ABSTRACT OF THE STATE OF OHIO WHISTLEBLOWER LAW

4113.52 Employees to report violations of state or federal law; retaliatory conduct prohibited

(A)(1)(a) If an employee becomes aware in the course of his employment of a violation of any state or federal statue or any ordinance or regulation of a political subdivision that his employer has authority to correct, and the employee reasonable believes that the violation either is a criminal offense that is likely to cause an imminent risk of physical harm to persons or a hazard to public health or safety or is a felony, the employee orally shall notify his supervisor or other responsible officer of his employer of the violation and subsequently shall file with that supervisor or officer a written report that provides sufficient detail to identify and describe the violation. If the employer does not correct the violation or make a reasonable and good faith effort to correct the violation within twenty-four hours after the oral notification or the receipt of the report, whichever is earlier, the employee may file a written report that provides sufficient detail to identify and describe the violation with the prosecuting authority of the county or municipal corporation where the violation occurred, with a peace office, with the inspector general if the violation is within his jurisdiction, or with any other appropriate public official or agency that has regulatory authority over the employer and the industry, trade, or business in which he is engaged.

(b) If an employee makes a report under division (A)(1)(a) of this section, the employer, within twenty-four hours after the oral notification was made or the report was received or by the close of business on the next regular business day following the day on which the oral notification was made or the report was received, whichever is later, shall notify the employee, in writing, of any effort of the employer to correct the alleged violation or hazard or of the absence of the alleged violation or hazard.

(3) If an employee becomes aware in the course of his employment of a violation by a fellow employee of any state or federal statute, any ordinance or regulation of a political subdivision, or any work rule or company policy of his employer and the employee reasonably believes that the violation either is a criminal offense that is likely to cause an imminent risk of physical harm to persons or a hazard to public health or safety or is a felony, the employee orally shall notify his supervisor or other responsible officer of his employer of the violation and subsequently shall file with that supervisor of officer a written report that provides sufficient detail to identify and describe the violation.

(D) If any employer takes any disciplinary or retaliatory action against an employee as a result of the employee's having filed a report under division (A) of this section, the employee may bring a civil action or appropriate injunctive relief or for the remedies set forth in division (D) of this section, or both, within one hundred eighty days after the date the disciplinary or retaliatory action was taken, in a court of common please in accordance with the Rules of Civil Procedure.

(E) The court, in rendering a judgment for the employee in an action brought pursuant to division (D) of this section, may order, as it determines appropriate, reinstatement of the employee to the same position he held at the time of the disciplinary or retaliatory action and at the same site of employment or to a comparable position at that site, the payment of back wages, full reinstatement of fringe benefits and seniority rights, or any combination of these remedies. The court also may award the prevailing party all or a portion of the costs of litigation, and if the employee who brought the action prevails in the action, may award the prevailing employee reasonable attorney's fees, witness fees, and fees for experts who testify at trial, in an amount the court determines appropriate.

Source: Ohio Rev. Code Ann. §4113.52 (Baldwin 1990). Title 41, Labor and Industry, Ohio Revised Code Annotated Complete to November 1, 1990, USA: Banks-Baldwin Law Publishing Co., 1990, pp. 163-164.

APPENDIX B: WHISTLEBLOWING LAW AND THE WHISTLEBLOWER

Traditional American employment relationships stipulate that either party may terminate the relationship at any time or "at will". This at will relationship, however, exposes both the employee and the employer to risk regarding the terms and conditions of ongoing employment. It is easy to see that the large corporation, with its vast economic resources, could use the at will doctrine maliciously or to stifle dissent when employees complain about such matters as fairness, favoritism, workplace safety, undue performance pressure, sexual harassment, and rights and discrimination. Through collective bargaining unions have been able to protect their members from many of these abuses but this protection is afforded only to those who are unionized. More than two-thirds of the American labor force is not unionized and accordinngly collective bargaining does not help them. Many industries are not unionized and those in the professions or executive ranks can be subjected to employer reprisals.

More recently a special group of laws have been created to protect workers from an employer's abuse of the at will doctrine when those workers seek to expose unsafe or illegal activities engaged in by the employer. These so-called whistleblower laws have been created at both the state and federal levels and basically protect the employee from retaliatory acts by the employer for blowing the whistle on them.

Three broad types of whistleblowing cases are commonly seen in court.

1. The employee refuses to participate in an illegal act which the company says must be performed. If the firm threatens to fire the employee under these conditions the courts have found in most cases the company's behavior to be wrongful and damages must be paid to the wronged employee.

2. The employee reports the employer's illegal acts to internal or external sources and is subsequently terminated, harassed or otherwise wronged by the company. Some courts have upheld the whistleblower's rights in these circumstances but in some states the whistleblower's rights have been protected only when the employee must choose between breaking the lawor losing his/her job.

3. The most difficult problem for the courts occurs when an employee criticizes company acts that are legal but that can also cause public harm. In most instances employees cannot complain about legitimate activities and no legal duty exists to support the whistleblower's claims.

Based on the observations of whistleblowers by Billie Garde and Bruce Fisher four basic types can be drawn—the Visionary, Deep Throats, Nitpickers, and Bad Faith whistleblowers. The Visionary is an idealistic individual who sees a bigger picture and attempts to correct perceived injustices. In this struggle he seems to be a heroic figure embarking on a solitary crusade to correct corporate wrongs. Deep Throats are pragmatists who are torn between the fear of personal reprisals if they report company wrongs while simultaneously fearing injuries to the public good if they maintain their silence. This type tends to operate behind the scenes and sends or telephones anonymous clues and tips to corporate executives and the media. The Nitpicker holds all people accountable for even the smallest infraction. This type abhors waste in any form as well as the abuse of corporate resources. In the public's eye the Nitpicker often seems petty and is unflatteringly portrayed as a childish "tattle tale". The fourth type is the Bad Faith whistleblower. This person's intentions are to make a pre-emptive strike prior to experiencing adverse action by the employer. This type uses as ammunition information about alleged corporate improprieties to counter justifiable attempts by the employer to terminate, demote, or transfer the employee. Bad Faith whistleblowers use their claims of company wrongdoing as bargaining chips to secure desired personal outcomes.

Source: Billie Pirner Garde, "Representing the Whistleblower—A Case or a Cause?" *Trial* (July 1992), pp. 32-36 and Bruce D. Fisher, "The Whistleblower Protection Act of 1989: A False Hope for Whistleblowers," *Rutgers Law Review* (Winter 1991), pp. 355-416.

Dow Corning Corporation: Marketing Breast Implant Devices

Todd E. Himstead, Georgetown University

N. Craig Smith, Georgetown University

Andrew D. Dyer, Georgetown University

In December 1991, a federal court jury in California awarded a $7.3 million payment against Dow Corning to Mariann Hopkins, a silicone gel breast implant wearer who claimed injury to her autoimmune system.[1] The recipient was just one of thousands of women who had undergone breast implant surgery over the past twenty-five years. Throughout the 1980's there had been considerable questioning of the safety of these implants. The federal court judgment was seen as a landmark victory by the plaintiff's lawyers. Dow Corning and other breast implant manufacturers now were facing the possibility of substantial litigation from women claiming to be harmed by silicone gel implants. With perhaps as many as two million breast implant operations completed, the potential existed for thousands of lawsuits to be filed against the manufacturers.[2]

As it entered 1992, Dow Corning's exposure to product safety issues with silicone gel implants became more apparent. On January 6, 1992, the Food and Drug Administration (FDA) requested that breast implant producers and medical practitioners halt the sale and use of silicone gel breast implants, pending further review of the safety and effectiveness of the devices.[3] As a precautionary measure, Dow Corning retained former attorney general Griffin Bell on January 10, 1992, to conduct a complete investigation of the company's development, production, and marketing of silicone gel breast implants. On February 3, 1992, Dow Corning took a pretax charge of $25 million to earnings in 1991 to cover costs associated with frozen inventories, dedicated equipment, and other related costs.[4]

On February 10, 1992, Dow Corning's board elected Keith R. McKennon chairman and CEO. McKennon was a career Dow Chemical employee. His previous role was president of Dow Chemical USA. Having managed two previous product crises for Dow Chemical (including Dow's Agent Orange pesticide crisis) now he was charged with the decisions of what to do with the silicone gel implant product line and how to manage the legal, regulatory, and public relations challenges facing Dow Corning. Since breast implants represented less than 1% of total 1991 revenues,[5] McKennon might have been tempted to question whether Dow Corning should even continue with the implant products, despite the benefits to women resulting from their use in reconstructive and cosmetic surgery.

DOW CORNING

Dow Corning Corporation was founded in 1943 with a mission to develop the potential of silicones. Silicones were new materials, unlike anything found in nature or previously manufactured. They were based on silicon, which was an element refined from quartz rock, a form of silica. The resulting chemical compounds were the basis for an infinite range of versatile, flexible materials that ranged from fluids thinner than water to rigid plastics, each with unique properties.

Dow Corning was established as a 50/50 joint venture by The Dow Chemical Company of Midland, Michigan, and Corning Glass Works (now Corning Inc.) of Corning, New York. Corning provided the basic silicone technology while Dow Chemical supplied the chemical processing and manufacturing know-how. Both companies provided initial key employees and maintained their ownership of Dow Corning from the outset.

The Dow Corning venture became successful in developing, manufacturing, and marketing silicone-based products. It grew steadily from 1943 in revenues, profits and employees and by 1991 generated revenues of $1.85 billion and income of $152.9 million, with some 8,300 employees.[6] In 1991, it was ranked 241 in the Fortune 500.[7] (For a five-year summary of Dow Corning's financial statements, see Exhibit 1.) In addition to developing silicone products, it had expanded development to related specialty chemical materials, poly-crystalline silicon, and specialty health care products. With some 5000 products, Dow Corning served a wide range of industries including aerospace, automotive, petrochemicals, construction, electronics, medical products, pharmaceuticals, plastics, and textiles. It had become a global enterprise with 33 major manufacturing locations worldwide, R&D facilities in the U.S., Japan, France, Germany, Belgium, and the U.K., and over 45,000 customers from countries including the U.S., Europe, Canada, Latin America, Japan, Australia, Taiwan, and Korea.

In the early 1990s, Dow Corning was seen as a model corporate citizen. It was a pioneer in corporate ethics, renowned for its Business Conduct Committee. The committee comprised six managers, who performed an ethics audit of every business every third year and reported results to the Audit & Social Responsibility Committee of the Dow Corning board. In October 1990 the committee audited Dow Corning's implant operation. It found no substantial ethical problems related to implants.

Exhibit 1

Dow Corning Corporation: Five-Year Summary of Selected Financial Data

Consolidated Balance Sheets (in millions of dollars)

Year ended:	12/31/91	12/31/90	12/31/89	12/31/88	12/31/87
Assets					
Current Assets					
Cash and cash equivalents	$7.9	$9.1	$4.1	$36.9	$10.8
Short-term investments	0.4	1.9	3.3	5.1	3.0
Accounts and notes rec.	334.1	336.3	293.4	289.6	258.8
Inventories	358.7	281.2	251.8	242.2	242.1
Other current assets	110.0	84.7	64.5	53.5	57.2
Total current assets	811.1	713.2	617.1	627.3	571.9
Property, plant, equipment					
Land and land improvements	107.4	95.8	92.5	88.6	80.1
Buildings	391.3	354.3	276.1	241.0	214.6
Machinery and equipment	1,533.9	1,272.3	1,109.7	1,066.3	1,000.5
Construction-in-progress	179.4	235.9	242.6	140.3	56.7
	2,212.0	1,958.3	1,720.9	1,536.2	1,351.0
Less accumulated depr.	(1,000.1)	(846.6)	(740.3)	(705.2)	(630.2)
	1,211.9	1,111.7	980.6	831.0	721.7
Other Assets	96.9	97.5	80.4	70.5	67.6
	$2,119.9	$1,922.4	$1,678.1	$1,528.8	$1,361.2
Liabilities & Shareholders' Equity					
Current liabilities					
Commercial paper payable	41.4	—	—	—	$39.7
Notes payable	$59.3	$104.0	$23.6	$13.0	7.3
Current portion of long-term debt	4.0	13.2	0.5	5.4	30.9
Trade accounts payable	135.3	121.0	107.3	114.2	90.3
Income taxes payable	28.2	26.0	36.8	29.2	42.7
Accrued payrolls and employee benefits	52.4	43.3	31.2	33.2	30.9
Accrued taxes, other than income taxes	15.8	16.3	18.9	19.7	12.3
Other current liabilities	113.6	70.3	68.2	79.4	71.5
	450.0	394.1	286.5	294.1	325.6
Long-term debt	286.8	267.7	274.3	200.4	95.7
Other Liabilities	198.5	196.9	190.4	183.9	183.7
Minority interest in consolidated subsidiaries	77.1	65.3	54.8	54.1	48.7
Stockholders' equity					
Common stock, $5 par value—2,500,000 shares authorized and outstanding	12.5	12.5	12.5	12.5	12.5
Retained earnings	1,028.8	953.4	853.8	758.0	668.5
Cumulative translation adjustment	66.2	32.5	5.8	25.8	26.5
Stockholders' equity	1,107.5	998.4	872.1	796.3	707.5
	$2,119.9	1,922.4	$1,678.1	$1,528.8	$1,361.2

Exhibit 1 (continued)   Dow Corning Corporation: Five-Year Summary of Selected Financial Data

Consolidated Statements of Operations and Retained Earnings (in millions of dollars except per share amounts)

Year ended:	12/31/91	12/31/90	12/31/89	12/30/88	12/31/87
Net Sales	$1,845.4	$1,718.3	$1,574.5	$1,476.8	$1,303.0
Operating costs and expenses:					
Manufacturing cost of sales	1,195.5	1,105.2	1,000.8	954.4	842.1
Marketing and administrative expenses	380.8	351.6	314.2	293.3	263.8
Implant costs	25.0	–	–	–	–
Special Items	29.0	–	–	–	–
	1,630.3	1,456.8	1,315.0	1,247.7	1,105.9
Operating income	215.1	261.5	259.5	299.1	197.1
Other income (expense)	10.4	(0.5)	6.9	5.8	15.4
Income before income taxes	225.5	261.0	266.4	234.9	212.5
Income taxes	58.3	80.1	94.6	75.3	74.1
Minority interests' share in income	14.1	9.8	9.2	9.1	3.4
Net income	153.1	171.1	162.6	150.5	135.0
Retained earnings at beginning of year	953.2	853.8	758.0	668.5	587.5
Cash dividends	(77.5)	(71.5)	(67.0)	(61.0)	(54.0)
Retained earnings at end of year	$1,028.8	$953.2	$853.6	$758.0	$668.5

Source: Dow Corning 10K Filings.

In 1991, Dow Corning was headed by John Ludington as chairman and Larry Reed as president and CEO. The organization was divided into two primary line organizations, Area Operations and Business Organization. Area Operations was responsible for sales and service of Dow Corning products around the world and was grouped into the U.S., Inter-America (Canada & Latin America), Europe, and Asia. The Business Organization was responsible for the development and manufacturing of Dow Corning's products and was organized on a product line-of-business approach.

Dow Corning's product line in 1991 included gasket sealants and windshields for the aerospace industry; silicone rubbers for the automotive industry; adhesives and sealants for the building trade and for consumer home improvement; and fluids, emulsions, and transdermal patches for the pharmaceutical industry, as well as a variety of medical products, such as tubing, adhesives, and surgical implants.

■ Dow Corning Wright

In 1991, Dow Corning Wright Corporation, a wholly owned subsidiary, manufactured and sold silicone gel breast implants for Dow Corning. It also manufactured and marketed metal orthopedic implants for Dow Corning. Dow

Corning Wright was headquartered in Arlington, Tennessee, and was headed up by chairman Bob Rylee and president and CEO Dan M. Hayes, Jr. It reported to Dow Corning's Business Organization and was considered a stand-alone line of business. Dow Corning Wright was established in 1978 when Dow Corning acquired Wright Medical, a small manufacturer of orthopedic hips and knees. Dow Corning then transferred all of its medical devices manufacturing and sales to this new subsidiary, including the breast implants. Dow Corning Wright 1991 revenues were approximately $80 million.[8]

■ Breast Implant Devices

Various options to achieve breast augmentation had been tried since the sixteenth century. Materials such as ivory, glass, and paraffin had been used for contour enhancement (by applying these materials to the breast externally). The first augmentation mammaplasty was accomplished in the late nineteenth century. Following this operation, a variety of non-silicone materials were injected or implanted to cosmetically alter or reconstruct breasts. The most successful implant device, developed during the 1950s, was a product with an outer sack made of polyurethane foam or silicone and filled with saline.

The next breakthrough came in 1962, when Dow Corning was approached by two plastic surgeons who wanted help in further developing breast implants for mastectomy and congenital deformity victims. The surgeons had designed an implant and had begun limited production, but looked to Dow Corning to apply its silicone gel and manufacturing expertise. In 1964, as a result of this request, Dow Corning developed a product based on an envelope of silicone elastomer (a rubber-like elastic substance) filled with silicone gel. The product was touted to be superior in terms of its look and feel for the recipients and was less likely to migrate over time through body and muscle tissue that surrounded the breast, compared with saline fluid-filled implants. Silicone gel breast implants became the market leader from that time on.

The advantage of silicone gel implants was that the silicone could hold its shape. This was particularly important for reconstructive patients, where there was little or no foundation to build on. Saline implants (made with salt water contained in a silicone envelope) were "water-like" and were unable to hold any shape by themselves. As a result, they were much less effective in providing either an enhanced figure or a complete reconstruction.

From 1965, when Dow Corning launched the first silicone gel breast implants, demand for the product was consistently high. Other manufacturers entered the market and the company became one of seven manufacturers in the U.S. producing the silicone gel product. Dow Corning introduced new models over time, with improvements in gel texture and envelope characteristics. The implants were available in a variety of sizes and contours. During the period 1965 to 1992, Dow Corning sold approximately 600,000 implants, 45% of them outside the U.S.[9] Dow Corning's market share of breast implants never exceeded 25% (once the industry had become established). In 1991, chairman Bob Rylee admitted that the breast implant line had sustained five consecutive years of financial losses, but the company continued selling them because millions of women were "counting on them."[10] Dow Corning also supplied silicone to the other implant manufacturers. During the 1980s, Dow

Corning's focus on medical devices moved to knee implants, and breast implants were not viewed as a strategic product. In 1991, Dow Corning's market share of breast implant sales was approximately 18%. It was the third largest supplier behind McGhan and Mentor.

■ Sales Agents

Dow Corning Wright's medical devices were sold by independent agents who had contracts to sell the products in specified geographic areas. They were paid a commission on sales and were reimbursed for expenses. In 1991, Dow Corning had some 70 medical device agents across the United States who were managed by a Dow Corning national sales manager, supported by two marketing staff. Some of the more senior agents also coordinated or supervised other agents regionally.

Some independent agents also sold non-Dow Corning products, though typically these products did not compete with Dow Corning's line. The agents relied on their strong relationship with the surgeons to make sales and maintained that relationship by providing quality products and good service. Of the 70 independent agents operating in 1991, two relied heavily on Dow Corning's breast implants, with some 50% of their sales derived from Dow Corning implants. For the remaining agents, their primary focus was hip and knee implants, with between 5% to 25% (an average of 10%) of their sales coming from breast implants.[11]

Geography was the major contributor to variations in volume, with certain regions having a higher demand for implants than others. The Pacific region was the site of the most (approximately 25%) breast augmentation procedures in the early 1990s, followed by the South Atlantic region with 21%, according to the American Society of Plastic and Reconstructive Surgeons (ASPRS). New England had the fewest procedures, with only 1.5%. California represented 19% of the total, Florida 12%, Texas 10%, and New York 4%.[12]

MEDICAL DEVICES INDUSTRY

Breast implant products were considered part of the medical devices industry, an industry that was generally fragmented, with 97% of manufacturers employing 500 employees or less and 70% of manufacturers employing 50 employees or less.[13] Medical devices (also known as surgical appliances and supplies) included crutches, wheelchairs, orthopedic devices and materials, surgical implants, bandages, hearing aids, and protective clothing. In 1991, the U.S. manufactured and shipped some $10.7 billion worth of medical devices, growing 6.4% from 1990. The industry employed an estimated 89,500 people in 1991, up 3% from 1990; 58,300 of these employees were engaged as production workers. U.S. exports of medical devices also grew in 1991 by 18% to $1.4 billion, the fourth consecutive year of double digit growth.[14] The principal export items included respiratory products, orthopedic equipment and supplies, as well as artificial joints and internal fixation devices.

The principal manufacturers of breast implants in 1991 were: Baxter Healthcare Corporation (Deerfield, IL), Bioplasty Inc. (St. Paul, MN), Cox-

Uphoff (Carpinteria, CA), Dow Corning Corporation (Midland, MI), McGhan Medical Inc. (Santa Barbara, CA), Mentor (Santa Barbara, CA), Porex Technologies (Fairburn, GA), and Surgitek (Racine, WI).

■ Regulation

When Dow Corning first sold implants in 1965, the medical devices industry was not subject to specific government regulation. The Food and Drug Administration unit of the U.S. Department of Health and Human Services was given the responsibility to regulate all medical devices and device establishments on May 28, 1976, following the Medical Device Amendments to the Federal Food, Drug, and Cosmetic Act of 1938. Its goal was to ensure that the medical devices consumed by the public were safe and effective by regulating the industry, by analyzing product samples, and by researching the risks and benefits of those products. The 1976 amendments directed the FDA to issue regulations to set up an approval process for new devices and classify existing ones into Class I, II, or III, depending on the degree of testing necessary to provide reasonable assurance of the safety of the device.

At that time, the FDA classified breast implants as "Class II" devices, a rating that did not demand testing as a condition for remaining on the market. While an advisory panel was formed in 1977 to look at cosmetic implants, the lack of conclusive studies and the panel members' own positive experience with breast implants allowed the implants to be classified as "safe" with no more research necessary. Some FDA scientists disputed this finding, based on feedback from doctors who claimed that the implants could break or leak. A new panel in 1982 voted that there was insufficient evidence to establish the product's safety and efficacy. It went on to recommend that silicone gel–filled breast implants be placed at the top of the FDA's list for review. But the lack of consumer complaints lowered the priority on implants, as the FDA screened its huge backlog of other devices. John Vilforth, the FDA's medical devices division manager during the 1980's, commented during a later interview that few of the million or more women with implants had complained to the FDA and that the longer term effects allegedly occurring in 1991 had not been observed in the previous decade. The FDA took no action on implants between 1982 and 1988.

In January 1989 the FDA reclassified breast implants as "Class III," and on April 10, 1991, required all manufacturers (including Dow Corning) to submit, within 90 days, implant safety and effectiveness data in pre-market approval applications (PMAAs) for the FDA's evaluation. According to its 10-K filing, on July 8, 1991, Dow Corning submitted 30,000 pages of documentation along with its PMAA, detailing silicone gel breast implant manufacturing processes, product design and labeling, and 30 years of safety studies. After previewing the PMAAs, on September 25, the FDA ordered manufacturers to provide more implant risk data to the physicians who inserted them, while the FDA continued its review. In November 1991 the FDA's Advisory Panel, after hearing testimony, recommended keeping implants on the market, noting that the psychological benefits outweighed the health risks. It was up to FDA Commissioner David Kessler to make the final decision, however, and on January 6, 1992, Kessler requested that producers and physicians halt the sale and use of breast implants for 45 days. Dow Corning voluntarily suspended shipments on that day.

PLASTIC SURGERY

■ Background

The plastic surgery profession began to formalize in the 1930's, although it had been practiced for centuries. Plastic surgeons were qualified surgeons who specialized in surgery either to reconstruct a human deformity or to enhance or modify a human feature. In 1992, there were over 5,000 certified plastic surgeons in the U.S. In the early 1990's, these plastic surgeons performed over 1.5 million procedures a year, with average fees ranging from $100 to over $6,000 per procedure.[15]

Plastic surgeons typically specialized in certain procedures and/or parts of the anatomy. For example, they would specialize in procedures such as skin grafts or nose surgery (rhinoplasty) or could specialize in a certain body part such as the hands or face. Plastic surgeons performing breast implant surgery typically became specialized in that procedure, and would average one implant operation per week. For these plastic surgeons, breast implant procedures represented from 20 to 40% of their income.[16]

■ Types of Plastic Surgery

The two main categories of plastic surgery were general reconstructive and cosmetic:

General Reconstructive Plastic Surgery.

Over one million reconstructive procedures were performed yearly by plastic surgeons in the early 1990's in the U.S. Reconstructive surgery was performed on abnormal structures of the body caused by birth defects, developmental abnormalities, trauma or injury, infection, tumors, or disease. It was generally performed to improve the patient's function, but may also have been done to approximate a normal appearance. Reconstructive surgery met the needs of two different categories of patients: those who had congenital deformities (known as birth defects) and those with developmental deformities (resulting from an accident, infection, disease, or aging). In the early 1990's, tumor removal was the leading procedure, constituting almost half of all reconstructive plastic surgery. Breast reconstruction was one of the top ten procedures. In 1990, 30,000 women received breast implants for reconstruction. Approximately 20% of all implant operations between 1965 and 1991 were for reconstructive surgery after undergoing a mastectomy operation.[17] In 1992, according to ASPRS statistics, 1% of reconstructive patients were under 19, 11% were between 19 and 34, 54% were between 35 and 50, 29% were between 51 and 64, and 5% were over 64. The average surgeon's fees for a breast reconstruction procedure using implants was $2,340 in 1992.[18]

Cosmetic Plastic Surgery.

Cosmetic surgery was performed to reshape normal structures of the body to improve the patient's appearance and self esteem. In 1990, 120,000 women received breast implants for cosmetic reasons. It was the leading cosmetic plastic surgery procedure. Other popular procedures included eyelid surgery, nose reshaping, liposuction, collagen injections, and facelifts. Approximately 80% of all breast implant operations between 1965 and 1991 were cosmetic augmentations.[19] In 1992, according to the ASPRS, 3% of the breast augmentation (cosmetic) patients were under the age of 19, 60% were between 19 and 34, 34% were between 35 and 50, 3% were between 51 and 64, while none were over 64.[20] ASPRS estimated that its members billed $330 million a year for breast implant procedures in the early 1990's.[21] In 1992, the average surgeon's fees for a breast augmentation procedure using implants was $2,754.[22]

■ Surgeon Selection of Medical Devices

In buying medical devices such as breast implants, plastic surgeons looked primarily at four criteria in making their selection:

Quality.

The quality of the products had to be uniform and consistent. The surgeon could only inspect the product at the time of the operation, when the product was removed from its packaging. A faulty product would cause the operation to be delayed or postponed while backup supplies were sought.

Service.

Product availability was mandatory at the time of surgery, and had to meet the schedule of the surgeon. Successful suppliers therefore had to ensure very high service levels and were subject to high inventory carrying costs as a result.

Price.

Price, while not the dominant factor in the purchase decision, needed to be consistent with alternatives and enable the procedure to be affordable for the patient.

Relationship.

The relationship between the sales agent and the surgeon was critical. The surgeon relied on and trusted the agent to provide the best and latest products together with quality service. Without such a relationship, it was unlikely that a medical device manufacturer could sell its products to a surgeon regardless of how well it scored in the other three criteria above.

Dow Corning felt that its strongest attributes were quality and relationships. Dow Corning generally had very strong credibility with the plastic surgeons, based on its leadership and innovation of new products. Dow Corning's scientists and physicians were highly regarded by the plastic surgeons and were constantly researching and publishing on key areas of interest. The independent agents were well connected to the plastic surgeons and provided an effective channel for Dow Corning's products.

■ Patient Selection of a Plastic Surgeon

Patients requiring or requesting plastic surgery were either referred by their physician to a plastic surgeon or selected their plastic surgeon directly. The latter was especially the case for cosmetic surgery, where the costs were not covered by health insurance. In selecting a plastic surgeon, patients used a number of steps to decide which surgeon would be best:

- Gathering names of plastic surgeons from friends, family doctor, nurses, hospitals, advertisements, and directories (e.g., the Plastic Surgery Information Service, state and city directories of certified plastic surgeons).
- Checking the credentials of the surgeons, such as their training, board certification (i.e., certified by the American Board of Plastic Surgery), hospital privileges (i.e., approved to perform the specific procedure at an accredited hospital), and experience and membership of professional societies (e.g., ASPRS, which required certification by the American Board of Plastic Surgery together with a peer review, adherence to a strict code of ethics, and continuing education to maintain membership).
- Consulting and interviewing the surgeon to compare personalities and obtaining opinions on the type of surgery and approach. Typically, the interview also included discussion of the surgeon's fees and an assessment of the way the surgeon answered questions and described the risks involved. Generally, patients would pay a fee for this consultation and thus would have narrowed down the list of potential surgeons to two or three by this stage.

According to a pamphlet prepared by the ASPRS and distributed in plastic surgeons' offices, a good plastic surgeon should exhibit some or all of the following qualities:[23]

- Has been recommended by a friend who has had a similar procedure
- Has been recommended by a family doctor or operating room nurse
- Is listed by the American Society of Plastic and Reconstructive Surgeons
- Is board-certified by the American Board of Plastic Surgery
- Has completed a residency in a specialty related to (your) procedure
- Has answered all (your) questions thoroughly
- Has asked about the patient's motivations and expectations of the surgery
- Has offered alternatives, where appropriate
- Has welcomed questions about professional qualifications, experience, cost, and payment policies
- Has clarified the risks of surgery and the variations in outcome
- Has made sure that the final decision to undergo surgery is the patient's decision.

CONSUMER NEED FOR IMPLANTS

Reconstructive breast surgery patients had usually contracted a form of breast cancer, but also could be accident victims, or women with a congenital deformity. The most common reconstructive surgery took place after a patient had undergone a mastectomy (surgical removal of one or both breasts). Augmentation surgery patients desired an increase in breast size to enhance their appearance (known as augmentation mammaplasty).

▪ Reconstructive Surgery

Without plastic surgery, reconstructive surgery consumers faced spending the rest of their lives with one or both breasts removed. The silicone gel breast implant operation provided them with a solution to regain their original physical appearance. Hence, the availability of breast implants was a major breakthrough for women suffering from breast cancer. In the early 1990's, about one woman in nine developed breast cancer in the U.S. It was the most commonly occurring cancer in women, accounting for more deaths than cancer of any other part of the body except the lungs. It was the leading cause of death among U.S. women aged 40-55.[24]

Before implants were available, some women refused to undergo a mastectomy, opting for lumpectomy (surgical removal of the breast tumor) or radiation or no action at all. While a lumpectomy or radiation abated the cancer's growth, neither treatment necessarily eliminated the breast cancer and, if unsuccessful, the patient could face a painful and premature death. Women refusing mastectomies were either afraid of the operation or were concerned with the permanent disfiguration and their perceived inability to be accepted back into society.

But with breast implants available, women were more accepting of the mastectomy operation. During the February 1992 FDA Advisory Panel hearing into breast implant safety, breast implant recipient Elaine Sansom testified:

> My mother's fear of losing her breast kept her from an early diagnosis, which allowed her cancer to spread before her mastectomy. She lived horribly from that point on, going through the rounds of chemo [therapy] and radiation; having a tumor eat through her first vertebra, ending up in a halo vest with bolts in her head . . . Being diagnosed with breast cancer [myself] was devastating . . . The choice to have implants was life-saving for me. Because I'm a diabetic, I wasn't a candidate for other types of reconstruction. If silicone gel breast implants had not been available at that time, my decision would have been a different one.[25]

In a letter to the *Washington Times* on January 31, 1992, another silicone breast implant recipient wrote:

> Since the FDA's moratorium on silicone breast implants has occurred, I would like you to hear the other side (the majority)—from satisfied recipients. I am one of nearly 2 million . . . These lifelike implants have helped the majority of women to recover faster physically and psychologically by restoring their femininity. I would rather die than be denied the option of having to go through life horribly disfigured. The alternative saline implants are a poor substitute, and they, too, are surrounded by silicone . . . Just give us the facts—we will decide, along with our doctors. Don't legislate my life anymore.[26]

▪ Breast Augmentation Surgery

Breast augmentation surgery consumers were women who wished to enlarge their breasts for appearance reasons. The images portrayed by fashion models and "sex symbols" had created certain perceptions regarding the size of women's breasts. As a result, clothing sizes and designs, as well as male expectations, centered around the "appropriate" size for a woman's breasts. However, normal variations in humans resulted in a wide variation in breast sizes and some women developed smaller breasts than others. Breast augmentation surgery offered an approach for these women to artificially enlarge their breasts permanently to a size that they felt was perceived as being more suitable for their figure and lifestyle.

Given the breast implant controversy, many examples were reported of women who had undergone augmentation surgery and their reasons why. Carol Lachnit, journalist with the *Los Angeles Times*, wrote:

> Back in 1991, Patricia Fodor was a newlywed with "a cute little figure" and the belief that silicone gel breast implants would enhance it. It was "a self esteem issue," she said. Because she worked in a doctor's office, Fodor even got a discount on the procedure.
>
> . . . Catherine, a 64-year-old Orange County woman . . . [received] her implants in 1987, when she was 58. "I was one of those women who didn't get everything some women have," she said. "I have poor hair, fine, thin hair. I can't do much about my hair, but for my bust, I thought this would be great. I was so thrilled." Catherine immersed herself in the world of ballroom dancing. She had gowns made to show off her new figure. She made friends and "everyone commented on how good I looked," she said.[27]

Other comments from breast augmentation surgery patients were included in an article in the *Washington Times*, January 29, 1992:

> "I just wanted to be average," sighs Janet, 34, of Alexandria, Virginia. Having her breasts enlarged from a "boyish" 32 A to a "beautiful" 36 C has improved Janet's self-image and outlook. She says she can shop in half the time, buy clingy clothing on sale and doesn't feel at all self-conscious. "You wouldn't look at me on the street and say, 'There goes a busty woman,'" says the 5-foot-4-inch, full-time mother. "I look just right."
>
> "Look, there's a pressure on women for physical beauty," says Janet, who does aerobics regularly. "Models can get three times their salary when they get implants, and if that doesn't tell you something about our society. . . . " She calls it an "unfair, idealized image of beauty," but Janet subscribes to it.
>
> . . . . And Jacki Buckler, 26, credits her new 36 C breasts—"very round, very full"—with giving her the confidence to go back to the University of Maryland to finish her degree in oceanography. "I'm pushing myself now," the part-time Giant cashier and waitress says . . . "I did this [the surgery] for myself, for no one else," Miss Buckler says. She paid for the $3,500 procedure in monthly $600 installments and says she hasn't regretted the expense or the pain of surgery for a minute.[28]

CONSUMER PROBLEMS WITH THE PRODUCT

By 1985, some 1.3 million implant operations had been completed.[29] Already, though, complaints were being received by the manufacturers and the FDA from customers citing painful hardening lumps and seepage of the silicone gel into the body after the implant bag had ruptured. Concerns began to arise about the potential of implants to rupture, the tightening of scar tissue that often formed around implants, causing the breast to harden, and the possible seepage of silicone, which was alleged to be responsible for generating a host of immune-system disorders that were painful, debilitating, and untreatable.

Over the next seven years, consumer activists in Washington, D.C., began to challenge the product's safety, while plastic surgeons and some women's groups lobbied to defend implants.

A variety of documents began to be released by Dow Corning and other manufacturers revealing that medical studies performed as early as the 1970's had warned of possible problems with implants.[30] Consumer activists criticized the manufacturers for "hiding" the information, the plastic surgeons for not questioning the safety of the implants, and the government for being negligent and not acting on the studies earlier. Leading the charge was Public Citizen's Health Research Group (Public Citizen), an organization founded by Ralph Nader and Dr. Sidney Wolfe to represent consumer interests in health-related matters. Public Citizen became actively involved in the implant controversy in 1988 after it obtained internal Dow Corning and FDA documents that suggested silicone gel implants were not safe for human use. It continued to lobby Congress and the FDA and also provided information packets to consumers and acted as a clearinghouse for plaintiff attorneys.

With growing legal activity and media attention, implants eventually assumed a higher priority on the FDA's agenda. FDA action increased by the end of the 1980's, when the FDA forced several implant products off the market after it was discovered that the foam covering the silicone slowly disintegrated at body temperature. This disintegration allowed a chemical known as TDA to be released, which in very high doses developed cancer in rats. By 1991 and the FDA's request that manufacturers provide evidence of research on the safety of implants, Public Citizen had begun selling $750 kits of evidence to trial lawyers interested in filing suits on behalf of disgruntled customers. The Command Trust Network, a nationwide educational network of 8,000 "implant victims," raised $30,000 and gave interviews to hundreds of reporters.[31]

The ASPRS, meanwhile, dedicated $1.3 million to lobby for the continued use of implants. In October 1991 it orchestrated a Washington "fly in," during which it paid for 400 women to travel to Capitol Hill and lobby congress to keep implants a viable choice for women. Simultaneously, it placed newspaper ads and organized a letter-writing campaign of 20,000 letters to the FDA.[32] In November 1991, the FDA hearings were given the report by its Advisory Panel, which concluded that the psychological importance of the implants outweighed the medical risks.

In December 1991 the verdict in the case of *Mariann Hopkins vs. Dow Corning* was announced, awarding Ms. Hopkins $7.3 million in damages, based on claims of damage to her autoimmune system.[33] Following the court's decision, Mariann Hopkins' lawyer, Dan C. Bolton, wrote to FDA Commissioner Dr. David A. Kessler about concerns with silicone breast implants. An extract from this letter appears as Exhibit 2.

The verdict was followed by the FDA moratorium on the sale of all silicone gel breast implant devices until such time as the agency received evidence to allay fears of any links to disease. Canada followed the U.S. by placing a similar ban, however the U.K. and France allowed implants to remain on the market. The moratorium, which prevented the sale of silicone gel implants unless their installation was clinically supervised (i.e., a study sponsored by the manufacturer and the FDA), sparked strong reaction from plastic surgeons and feminist groups. The plastic surgeons stood by the product and their surgical procedures, while the feminist groups claimed that women were being deprived of the right to make their own medical decisions.

Exhibit 2   **Excerpt of Letter from Mariann Hopkins' Attorney Dan C. Bolton
                            to FDA Commissioner David Kessler, December 30, 1991**

I am writing to express my serious concerns relating to the dangers of silicone breast implants and the conduct of a principal manufacturer of breast implants, Dow Corning Corporation, in engaging in a consistent pattern of corporate deceit and dishonesty relating to the safety of implants . . .

Mariann Hopkins . . . underwent breast reconstruction with silicone gel–filled breast implants manufactured by Dow following a bilateral mastectomy for fibrocystic disease in 1976. A bilateral rupture of the implants was discovered in February 1986. Mrs. Hopkins suffers from mixed connective tissue disease, an immune disorder, caused by her exposure to silicone gel.

On December 13, 1991, the jury unanimously rendered a verdict in the amount of $840,000 for compensatory damages, and $6,500,000 for punitive damages . . . the jury found that Dow's silicone breast implants were not properly designed and manufactured, that Dow had failed to warn of risks associated with implants, that Dow had breached implied and expressed warranties relating to its product and that Dow had committed fraud. The jury also found by "clear and convincing evidence" that Dow's fraud, in addition to its "malice" and "oppression," warranted the imposition of punitive damages. Under California law, "malice" means conduct that is "intended by the defendant to cause injury to the plaintiff or despicable conduct which is carried on by the defendant with a willful and conscious disregard of the rights and safety of others." "Oppression" requires a finding by the jury that the defendant has engaged in "despicable conduct that subjects a person to cruel and unjust hardship in conscious disregard of that person's rights."

Considerable evidence was presented at trial that Dow was aware of the risks of silicone as early as the 1960's, and continued to market a medical device intended for long-term use despite the absence of any studies demonstrating the long-term safety of silicone in the human body. Dow's conduct is especially unconscionable in light of the fact that Dow's own product literature represented that breast implants were safe for long-term use by women.

. . . the time has come to hold implant manufacturers, such as Dow, accountable for the safety of their product. I urge you to take appropriate steps to ensure that women do not continue to be victimized by irresponsible companies that are more concerned with their financial well-being than the health and safety of consumers . . . Dow's corporate response to the increasing numbers of women injured by its dangerous and defective implants was to issue a warranty program in the mid-1980's. This program provides partial reimbursement for the medical expenses incurred in removing implants because of rupture or immune sensitization so long as the physician extracts a release from the patient extinguishing all of her legal rights against Dow. This conduct is not only legally questionable but morally indefensible.

A lawsuit filed after this moratorium by an augmentation surgery patient was reported in the *San Diego Union-Tribune*, January 30, 1992:

A woman who was given Dow Corning Corp.'s silicone gel breast implants to improve her figure has sued the company, claiming they made her ill and accusing the company of ignoring safety warnings about the devices, her attorney said . . . Stanley Rosenblatt said yesterday the Dade County woman, identified only as "Jane Doe," is in her 30's and received the breast implants in 1985 to enhance her figure. She is seeking $100 million in damages. The lawsuit, filed in Dade County Circuit Court, claims the woman was in perfect health before the operation but has since suffered "recurrent flu, recurrent strep throat, infections, excessive hair loss, constant fatigue, excruciating joint pain, rashes across her face and a constant low-grade fever." The woman has been bedridden "for months at a time" because of systemic lupus erythematosus, a disorder of the immune system, the suit claims . . . Dow Corning ignored warnings from its own employees about implant defects and concealed the information from doctors, patients, and federal regulators, the lawsuit alleges. "Plaintiff is a victim of an incredible 'con' perpetrated upon the public at large and women in particular," the lawsuit said. It accused Dow Chemical of constructing a "vast experiment" on 2 million women that should have been performed on laboratory animals instead . . . The surgeon is not being sued because Dow Corning convinced him the implants were safe, Rosenblatt said. The woman still has the implants but is deciding whether to have them removed, he said. The lawsuit alleges an internal company memo shows Dow Corning salespeople misled surgeons by washing "the often greasy gel implants before showing them to physicians, with full knowledge that the product was dangerous to women."[34]

Pamela Johnson filed a lawsuit against another implant manufacturer. The following extract from the *Houston Chronicle* explains her complaint:

> Johnson's first set of breast implants, manufactured by MEC, [were] surgically implanted in 1976. O'Quinn [her attorney] said the company led Johnson's doctor to believe the implants had been tested and engineered so that the outer shell would contain the silicone gel, that the gel was cohesive and would not run if the shell ruptured, and that, if the gel did escape the shell, it would not harm human tissue. The doctor was told [that] the product would last a lifetime, O'Quinn said . . . In 1989, Johnson's implants ruptured. Her doctor, believing the product's problems had been solved, then inserted a new set of silicone gel implants . . . The second set was removed that same year, and another implant done, with a product made by a different manufacturer. Those implants were removed [in early 1992].[35]

Despite these suits, Dow Corning defended its product. Bob Rylee, Dow Corning Wright's chairman, stated that implants represented less than 1 percent of Dow Corning's $1.8 billion in revenues and the true risk with implants was less than 1 percent.[36]

■ Ongoing Investigations

The FDA Advisory Panel was scheduled to reconvene on February 18, 1992, to reconsider implant PMAA's. In addition to the FDA studies, another probe into Dow Corning's breast implants was launched on January 30, 1992, by the Los Angeles County district attorney's office, under its Corporate Criminal Liability Act.[37] The investigation was to determine whether Dow Corning sold the breast implants without fully disclosing health risk information required by law. District attorney Ira Reiner had requested that Dow Corning provide substantial information about the product, including laboratory data, internal memoranda, and copies of informational and promotional material about the implants (Exhibit 3 provides Dow Corning's implant package insert). L.A. County's Corporate Criminal Liability Act makes it a felony for corporate managers to fail to provide regulatory agencies with written notification of a "serious concealed danger" associated with a product and penalties included up to three years' imprisonment and fines up to $1 million.

At the same time, Dow Corning had hired Griffin Bell, a former U.S. attorney general and a circuit court judge, to investigate the company's development and marketing of the implants. He planned to select independent scientific and medical experts to assist his investigation, with free access to all of Dow Corning's records, resources, and employees. Bell's final recommendations would be made available to the FDA and the public. Dow also announced on January 29, 1992, that it would make public internal memoranda and other information by the week of February 10.

Lawyers and Public Citizen criticized the delays in having the documents released, claiming that the documents had been locked up for years and that, if the FDA had been given earlier access to the information, breast implants would have been off the market a long time ago.[38] Dow Corning disputed this view, stating that the FDA had possession of the relevant documents for many

---

Exhibit 3   **Outline of Package Insert for Dow Corning's 1985 SILASTIC II Brand Mammary Implant H.P. Package Insert (with excerpts)**

Description

Specific Advantages

"Envelopes have greater tear propagation resistance."
"A special silicone layer within the envelope provides a barrier to significantly reduce gel bleed."
"Generally recognized as having acceptable level of reactivity."

Indications

"Criteria for patient selection must be the responsibility of the surgeon."

Contraindications

"A mammary implant may not be well tolerated in any patient who exhibits certain types of psychological instability, e.g., does not want implants, displays a lack of understanding, or inappropriate motivation or attitude."
"These are general, relative contraindications and each individual patient must be evaluated by her surgeon to determine the specific risk/benefit ratio."

Precautions and Warnings

"SILASTIC brand medical-grade silicone elastomers made exclusively by Dow Corning are among the most non-reactive implant materials available."

Possible Adverse Reactions and Complications

"Thousands of women per year have had cosmetic or reconstructive surgery with implantation of mammary prostheses. A number of patients are reported to have significant complications or adverse reactions. Typically, a patient undergoing a surgical procedure is subject to unforeseen intra-operative and post-operative complications. Each patient's tolerance to surgery, medication, and implantation of a foreign object may be different. Possible risks, adverse reactions, and complications associated with surgery and the use of the mammary prosthesis should be discussed with and understood by the patient prior to surgery. The adverse reactions and complications most likely to occur with the use of this product are listed below. IT IS THE RESPONSIBILITY OF THE SURGEON TO PROVIDE THE PATIENT WITH APPROPRIATE INFORMATION PRIOR TO SURGERY."

1. *Capsule Formation and Contracture*

2. *Sensitization*

"There have been reports of suspected immunological sensitization or hyperimmune system response to silicone mammary implants. Symptoms claimed by the patients included localized inflammation and irritation at the implant area, fluid accumulation, rash, general malaise, severe joint pain, swelling of joints, weight loss, arthralgia, lymphadenopathy, alopecia, and rejection of the mammary prosthesis. Such claims suggest there may be a relationship between the silicone mammary implant and the reported symptoms. Materials from which this prosthesis is fabricated have been shown in animal laboratory tests to have minimal sensitization potential. However, claims from clinical use of the silicone prosthesis in humans suggest that immunological responses or sensitization to a mammary prosthesis can occur. If sensitization is suspected and the response persists, removal of the prosthesis is recommended along with removal of the surrounding capsule tissue. This procedure is recommended to minimize the amount of residual silicone that may be left at the implant site."

3. *Implant Rupture Gel Extravasation*

"Dow Corning is not responsible for the integrity of the implant should such techniques as closed capsulotomies (manual compression) be used."
"As reported in the literature, when an implant ruptures gel may be released from the implant envelope despite the cohesive properties of the gel. If left in place, complications such as enlarged lymph nodes, scar formation, inflammation, silicone granulomas, and nodule formation may result."
"These potential consequences should be understood by the surgeon and explained to the patient prior to implantation."
"In the event of a rupture, Dow Corning recommends prompt removal of the envelope and gel. The long-term physiological effects of uncontained silicone gel are currently unknown."
"The patient should be informed that the life expectancy of any implant is unpredictable."

Exhibit 3 (continued)   **Outline of Package Insert for Dow Corning's 1985 SILASTIC II Brand Mammary Implant H.P. Package Insert (with excerpts)**

4. *Infection*

5. *Hematoma*

6. *Serous Fluid Accumulation*

7. *Interruption in Wound Healing*

8. *Skin Sloughing/Necrosis*

9. *Incorrect Size, Inappropriate Location of Scars, and Misplacement or Migration of Implants, etc.*

10. *Palpability of Implant*

11. *Asymmetry*

12. *Ptotic (Drooping) Breast*
    "It is important that this possibility be discussed with the patient."

13. *Nipple Sensation*
    "This should be discussed in detail with the patient."

14. *Microwave Diathermy*

15. *Implant Gel Bleed*

16. *X-ray Pre-Operative & Post-Operative*
    "Post—Some physicians state an implant may pose difficulties in detecting tumors in certain locations in the breast via xeromammography."

17. *Calcification*

18. *Absorption of Biologicals By Implants*
    References to Carcinogenesis
    "During the past twenty years of clinical use, the medical literature indicates that the silicone mammary prosthesis is not carcinogenic."

Instructions for Use

1. *The surgeon should discuss possible risks, consequences, complications, and adverse reactions associated with the surgical procedure and implantation of the mammary prosthesis with the patient prior to surgery.*

2. *Surgical Procedures*
   "Prior to use, the prosthesis should be carefully examined for structural integrity."

3. *Packaging*

4. *Recommended Procedure for Opening Package—Sterile Product*

5. *To Clean and (Re)Sterilize Mammary Implants*

References

Warranty

"Dow Corning warrants that reasonable care in selection of materials and methods of manufacture were used in fabrication of this product. Dow Corning shall not be liable for an incidental or consequential loss, damage, or expense, directly or indirectly arising from the use of this product."
"Dow Corning neither assumes nor authorizes any other person to assume for it any other or additional liability or responsibility in connection with this product. Dow Corning intends that this mammary implant product should be used only by physicians having received appropriate training in plastic surgery techniques."

years. Dow Corning also claimed to have performed some 900 studies into the safety of the implants, none of which concluded that implants would cause harm to the recipient.[39] Plaintiff lawyers, keen to obtain any new information surrounding implants, estimated that there were as many as 1,000 suits filed or about to be filed alleging that the implants had caused cancer, immune system disorders, or connective tissue disease.[40]

NEW APPROACH REQUIRED

The seriousness of the implant issue had now escalated. On February 10, 1992, the same day Keith McKennon was appointed to chairman and CEO of Dow Corning, the company yielded to public pressure and disclosed 100 potentially embarrassing company documents that came to light in the Hopkins trial and more recently had been leaked to the press.[41] McKennon had been asked by the board to personally assemble Dow Corning's strategy and action plan to resolve conclusively the implant situation.

With many stakeholders to satisfy and ethical issues to deal with, the problem was going to be complex to solve. His first step was to understand what caused the implant controversy in the first place and to decide whether Dow Corning should continue to market this sensitive product. McKennon also had to assess the validity of the customer complaints, estimate the financial and legal exposure from future customer litigation, respond to the FDA's moratorium announcement, and determine the potential damage to Dow Corning's brand name and reputation.

REFERENCES

1. Marcotty, Josephine, "Implant Lawsuits: Floods of Litigation Possible Because of Health Problems with Silicone Gel," *Star Tribune*, 30 January 1992, p. D1.

2. Appleson, Gail, "Court Orders Kept Breast Implant Data Secret for Years," *Reuters*, AM cycle, 30 January, 1992.

3. Ressberger, Boyce, "Silicone Gel Data Faked, Firm Says," *Houston Chronicle*, 3 November, 1992, p. A7.

4. Dow Corning Corporation, Form 10-K, 31 December, 1991.

5. Marcotty, op. cit., p. D1.

6. Dow Corning Corporation, Form 10-K, December 31, 1991.

7. *Fortune*, 20 April, 1992.

8. *Ward Business Directory of U.S. Private and Public Companies*, 1992.

9. McMurray, Scott, and Thomas M. Burton, "Dow Corning Plans to Quit Implant Line," *Wall Street Journal*, 19 March, 1992, p. A3.

10. Burton, Ghomas M., Bruce Ingersoll, and Joan E. Rigdon, "Dow Corning Makes Changes in Top Posts," *Wall Street Journal*, February 11, 1992, p. A3.

11. Gary E. Anderson, Executive Vice President, Dow Corning Corporation, interview, January 7, 1994.

12. American Society of Plastic Reconstructive Surgeons (ASPRS), *1992 Statistics*, Arlington Heights, IL, 1992.

13. According to the U.S. Food and Drug Administration.

14. U.S. Department of Commerce, *U.S. Industrial Outlook 1993* (Lanham, MD: Bernan Press).

15. ASPRS, op. cit.

16. Pisik, Betsy, "Dangerous Curves; For Many Women, Rewards of Breast Implants Worth Risks," *Washington Times*, 29 January, 1992, p. E1.

17. Lachit, Carroll, "Controversy That Won't Go Away," *Los Angeles Times*, 7 October, 1993, p. E1.

18. ASPRS, op. cit.

19. Lachit, op. cit.

20. Ibid.

21. Ibid.

22. ASPRS, op. cit.

23. ASPRS, "How To Choose a Qualified Plastic Surgeon" (Arlington Heights, IL: ASPRS, 1992).

24. U.S. Department of Commerce, *Statistical Abstract of the United States*. Bureau of the Census, Washington, D.C., 113th edition, 1993.

25. Samson, Elaine, National Organization for Women with Implants, FDA Panel Hearing, February 1992.

26. *Washington Times*, "FDA Chief David Kessler Joins the Hysteria Over Silicone," 31 January, 1992, p. F2.

27. Lachit, op. cit.

28. Pisik, op. cit.

29. Drew, Christopher, and Michael Tackett, "Access Equals Clout: The Blitzing of FDA," *Chicago Tribune*, 8 December, 1992, p. C1.

30. Byrne, John A., "The Best Laid Ethics Programs," *BusinessWeek*, 9 March, 1992, p. 69.

31. Ingersoll, Bruce, "Industry Mounts Big Lobbying Drive Supporting Implants," *Wall Street Journal*, 14 February, 1992, p. A5.

32. Drew, op. cit.

33. Cooper, Clair, "Thousands Await Decision as Implant Suit Hits Appeals Court," *Sacramento Bee*, 19 June, 1993, p. A6.

34. United Press International, "Dow Sued Over Breast Implants," *San Diego Union-Tribune*, 30 January, 1992, p. A9.

35. Piller, Ruth, "Trial Starts in Lawsuit Against Maker of Silicone Gel Implants," *Houston Chronicle*, 11 December, 1992, p. A33.

36. Marcotty, op. cit.

37. Steinbrook, Robert, and Henry Weinstein, "County Will Investigate Maker of Breast Implants," *Los Angeles Times*, 31 January, 1992, p. zB1.

38. Appleson, op. cit.

39. Anderson, op. cit.

40. Appleson, op. cit.

41. Burton et al., op. cit.